New Forces in the World Economy

A *WASHINGTON QUARTERLY* READER

New Forces in the World Economy

edited by

BRAD ROBERTS

The MIT Press
Cambridge, Massachusetts
London, England

The contents of this book were first published in *The Washington Quarterly* (ISSN 0163–660X), a publication of The MIT Press under the sponsorship of The Center for Strategic and International Studies (CSIS). Except as otherwise noted, copyright in each article is owned jointly by the Massachusetts Institute of Technology and CSIS. No article may be reproduced in whole or in part except with the express written permission of The MIT Press.

Erik R. Peterson, "Looming Collision of Capitalisms?" *TWQ* 17, no. 2 (Spring 1994); James R. Golden, "Economics and National Strategy: Convergence, Global Networks, and Cooperative Competition," *TWQ* 16, no. 3 (Summer 1993); Richard E. Feinberg and Delia M. Boylan, "Modular Multilateralism: North–South Economic Relations in the 1990s," *TWQ* 15, no. 1 (Winter 1992); Murray Weidenbaum, "Greater China: A New Economic Colossus?" *TWQ* 16, no. 4 (Autumn 1993); John D. Sullivan, "Democracy and Global Economic Growth," *TWQ* 15, no. 2 (Spring 1992); Ernest H. Preeg, "The Post–Uruguay Round Free Trade Debate," *TWQ* 19, no. 1 (Winter 1996); Daniel F. Burton, Jr., "Competitiveness: Here to Stay," *TWQ* 17, no. 4 (Autumn 1994); Ernest H. Preeg, "Krugmanian Competitiveness: A Dangerous Obfuscation," *TWQ* 17, no. 4 (Autumn 1994); Thomas J. Duesterberg, "Trade, Investment, and Engagement in the U.S.–East Asian Relationship," *TWQ* 17, no. 1 (Winter 1994); Ernest H. Preeg, "Who's Benefiting Whom? A Trade Agenda for High-Technology Industries," *TWQ* 16, no. 4 (Autumn 1993); Kenneth Berlin and Jeffrey M. Lang, "Trade and the Environment," *TWQ* 16, no. 4 (Autumn 1993); Richard E. Bissell, "The Natural Resource Wars: Let Them Eat Trees," *TWQ* 17, no. 1 (Winter 1994); Jeri Jensen-Moran, "Trade Battles as Investment Wars: The Coming Rules of Origin Debate," *TWQ* 19, no. 1 (Winter 1996); Paula Stern and Raymond Paretzky, "Engineering Regional Trade Pacts to Keep Trade and U.S. Prosperity on a Fast Track," *TWQ* 19, no. 1 (Winter 1996); Gary Hufbauer and Jeffrey J. Schott, "Toward Free Trade and Investment in the Asia–Pacific," *TWQ* 18, no. 3 (Summer 1995); Sidney Weintraub, "The Depth of Economic Integration between Mexico and the United States," *TWQ* 18, no. 4 (Autumn 1995); Georges Fauriol and Sidney Weintraub, "U.S. Policy, Brazil, and the Southern Cone," *TWQ* 18, no. 3 (Summer 1995); Thomas J. Duesterberg, "Prospects for an EU–NAFTA Free Trade Agreement," *TWQ* 18, no. 2 (Spring 1995); Erik R. Peterson, "Surrendering to Markets," *TWQ* 18, no. 4 (Autumn 1995); Roy C. Smith, "Risk and Volatility," *TWQ* 18, no. 4 (Autumn 1995); David D. Hale, "Is It a Yen or a Dollar Crisis in the Currency Market?" *TWQ* 18, no. 4 (Autumn 1995); W. R. Smyser, "Goodbye, G–7," *TWQ* 16, no. 1 (Winter 1993); Raymond Vernon, "The Japan–U.S. Bilateral Relationship: Its Role in the Global Economy," *TWQ* 13, no. 3 (Summer 1990); Ethan B. Kapstein, "Governing Global Finance," *TWQ* 17, no. 2 (Spring 1994); J. Carter Beese, Jr., "Reengineering Regulation: Maintaining the Competitiveness of U.S. Capital Markets," *TWQ* 18, no. 4 (Autumn 1995); W. R. Smyser, "The Bundesbank: America's German Central Bank," *TWQ* 17, no. 2 (Spring 1994); Donald R. Sherk, "U.S. Policy Toward the Multilateral Development Banks," *TWQ* 16, no. 3 (Summer 1993); Steve Charnovitz, "Promoting Higher Labor Standards," *TWQ* 18, no. 3 (Summer 1995); Joseph LaPalombara, "International Firms and National Governments: Some Dilemmas," *TWQ* 17, no. 2 (Spring 1994).

Selection and introduction, copyright © 1996 by The Center for Strategic and International Studies and the Massachusetts Institute of Technology.

All rights reserved. No part of this book may be reproduced in any form or by any means, electronic or mechanical, including photocopying, recording, or by any information storage and retrieval system, without permission in writing from The MIT Press. For information please address the Subsidiary Rights Manager, The MIT Press, Journals Department, 55 Hayward Street, Cambridge MA 02142; e-mail: journals-rights@mit.edu.

Library of Congress Cataloguing-in-Publication Data

New forces in the world economy / edited by Brad Roberts.
    p.   cm. — (A Washington quarterly reader)
Articles previously published between 1990 and 1996 in The Washington quarterly.
Includes bibliographical references.
ISBN 0-262-68089-0 (pbk. : alk. paper)
1. Economic history—1990–. 2. International economic integration. 3. International finance.
4. International economic relations.
I. Roberts, Brad. II. Series.
HC59.15.N49 1996
337—dc20
                                                                                                                      95-26404
                                                                                                                           CIP

Contents

vii Introduction
     Brad Roberts

I. The Global Economy of the 1990s

3   Looming Collision of Capitalisms?
     Erik R. Peterson

15   Economics and National Strategy: Convergence, Global Networks, and Cooperative Competition
     James R. Golden

39   Modular Multilateralism: North–South Economic Relations in the 1990s
     Richard E. Feinberg and Delia M. Boylan

53   Greater China: A New Economic Colossus?
     Murray Weidenbaum

67   Democracy and Global Economic Growth
     John D. Sullivan

79   The Post–Uruguay Round Free Trade Debate
     Ernest H. Preeg

II. The U.S. Competitiveness Debate

95   Competitiveness: Here to Stay
     Daniel F. Burton, Jr.

107 Krugmanian Competitiveness: A Dangerous Obfuscation
     Ernest H. Preeg

III. New Directions of Trade and Investment

121 Trade, Investment, and Engagement in the U.S.–East Asian Relationship
     Thomas J. Duesterberg

139 Who's Benefiting Whom? A Trade Agenda for High-Technology Industries
     Ernest H. Preeg

157 Trade and the Environment
     Kenneth Berlin and Jeffrey M. Lang

175 The Natural Resource Wars: Let Them Eat Trees
     Richard E. Bissell

193 Trade Battles as Investment Wars: The Coming Rules of Origin Debate
     Jeri Jensen-Moran

IV. The New Regional Dimension

207 Engineering Regional Trade Pacts to Keep Trade and U.S. Prosperity on a Fast Track
Paula Stern and Raymond Paretzky

217 Toward Free Trade and Investment in the Asia–Pacific
Gary Hufbauer and Jeffrey J. Schott

227 The Depth of Economic Integration between Mexico and the United States
Sidney Weintraub

239 U.S. Policy, Brazil, and the Southern Cone
Georges Fauriol and Sidney Weintraub

251 Prospects for an EU–NAFTA Free Trade Agreement
Thomas J. Duesterberg

V. The Global Power of Financial Markets

265 Surrendering to Markets
Erik R. Peterson

279 Risk and Volatility
Roy C. Smith

295 Is It a Yen or a Dollar Crisis in the Currency Market?
David D. Hale

VI. The Governance Agenda

325 Goodbye, G–7
W. R. Smyser

339 The Japan–U.S. Bilateral Relationship: Its Role in the Global Economy
Raymond Vernon

351 Governing Global Finance
Ethan B. Kapstein

363 Reengineering Regulation: Maintaining the Competitiveness of U.S. Capital Markets
J. Carter Beese, Jr.

375 The Bundesbank: America's German Central Bank
W. R. Smyser

393 U.S. Policy Toward the Multilateral Development Banks
Donald R. Sherk

403 Promoting Higher Labor Standards
Steve Charnovitz

427 International Firms and National Governments: Some Dilemmas
Joseph LaPalombara

Introduction

THE WORLD ECONOMY has moved to the center of the international political stage in the mid-1990s. With the end of the Cold War, economic factors have assumed increasing importance relative to strategic factors in the foreign policies of the major powers. Moreover, a genuinely global economy is rapidly emerging, one that is defined not just by trade but also by investment and the diffusion of advanced technologies and expertise. This volume examines the features of the emerging world economic order. It surveys the new forces in the world economy with an eye toward their political and policy implications. It is conceived not just as a tool for economists seeking to understand a changing economy but also for political scientists and policymakers, who must increasingly understand the way in which economic realities impinge on the sources of order and disorder in the post–cold war era.

In sketching out the post–Uruguay Round trade policy debate in this volume, Ernest Preeg writes that the debate about free trade in the new era "is not fully engaged and remains conceptually ill-defined. . . . a full-scale debate on short- and longer-term objectives for the international trading system—writ large to include investment, competition, and technology-oriented policies—should begin." Thus he neatly defines the purpose of this volume—to bring into focus key trends in a rapidly changing world economy, to explore critical substantive issues, and to help stimulate a debate in the academic and policy communities not just about the trading system but also about the evolving policy agenda of the United States as it confronts new economic realities.

This volume draws on materials published in *The Washington Quarterly* between 1990 and 1996. *TWQ* is a journal of international public policy issues published by The MIT Press for the Center for Strategic and International Studies of Washington, D.C. It has a broad intellectual purview. Economic issues are but one set of themes given sustained attention by the journal as part of a broader effort to think afresh about statecraft, international security, and, more broadly, the international engagement of the United States. Two other compendiums of articles from the journal were published by MIT Press in 1995: *Weapons Proliferation in the 1990s* and *Order and Disorder after the Cold War.*

As a compilation of articles, this volume includes materials published at different times for different purposes. Their organization here into chapters suggests an orderliness to the original editorial plan where none existed. We have simply set out to capture some of the best new thinking on the subject and we present a selection of it here in cumulative form. Please note that authors have not been given the opportunity to update their articles prior to their republication here. Although parts of some essays have necessarily been overtaken by events, each contri-

Introduction

bution makes arguments that remain relevant in any assessment of the new global economic agenda. Please note further that all biographies are current to the time of original publication. The views expressed are those of the authors and should not be attributed to any institutions with which they are or were affiliated or to the publishers, CSIS and MIT Press.

Chapter I offers a survey of new forces in the global economy. One is the changing political context wrought by the end of the Cold War and the greater economic competition emerging among the industrialized democracies that heretofore had to submerge competing interests in the name of cold war solidarity. These competitive forces are weighed against those compelling greater cooperation economically. This chapter also reviews the changing nature of North–South economic relations, the growing prominence of Asia in the global economy, the link between democratization and liberalization, and the new demands on trade policy after the conclusion of the Uruguay Round. These articles reveal a world economy undergoing rapid and profound changes in the post–cold war era and subject to a large set of new political demands.

Chapter II reviews the debate about the competitiveness of the U.S. economy vis-à-vis other economically advanced states. The articles included here assess the strengths and weaknesses of the U.S. economy and predict the likely evolution of the competitiveness debate. They reveal a United States well positioned to prosper and lead in the new world economy, but also a country reluctant to undertake the burdens of adjustment and the responsibilities of leadership.

Chapter III sketches out the emerging patterns of trade and investment and their connection to other political concerns. What impact will protectionist pressures in the United States and elsewhere have? Can free trade cope with the new demands of high-technology industries and environmental politics? How will the trading system respond to new environmental concerns? The articles included here reveal a rapidly changing world economy. They also underscore the importance of an international economic policy agenda that does more than simply and mechanically extend the past into the future.

Chapter IV explores the growing prominence of regional free trade groupings in the overall trading system. Free trade organizations and movements in Asia, the Americas, and in the transatlantic community are described and evaluated. Authors offer a generally optimistic assessment of the prospects for these groupings. They also explore the critical policy question related to the linkage between regional and global efforts: Are they complementary or conflictual?

Chapter V focuses on the new global power of financial markets. These markets have changed fundamentally over the last decade, with consequences for the autonomy of states and the authority of national policymakers little contemplated or understood. The articles included here describe the new prominence of these markets, evaluate the risks and uncertainties they present in this new era, and speculate about their future roles.

The final chapter, VI, focuses on issues of public policy and the governance of the emerging global economy. Articles included here evaluate the continuing and future roles of institutions like the G–7, the multilateral development banks, the Bundesbank, and the International Labour Organization, as well as important bilateral relationships. They also explore questions related to the capacity of national governments to govern an economy characterized increasingly by the interaction of nongovernmental actors, whether transnational firms or global markets. Authors home in on the continued roles and authority of governments in a context of waning capacity.

The picture that emerges from these articles is of a world economy that is both extremely dynamic and facing an uncertain future. The positive forces leading to greater prosperity are numerous and compelling. But the sources of friction are many. So too are the instances in which economic forces appear to have outstripped both our understanding of them and our capacity to manage them. Moreover, it is essential that this picture become familiar to those in international politics accustomed to consigning economic questions to near irrelevance. The emerging global economy is creating fundamental new political realities that will touch directly on the nature of relations of power among states and thus on their foreign policies and security perceptions. A comprehensive worldview is essential if policymakers are to shape constructively the opportunities inherent in this period of global political and economic transition.

This editor owes a debt of gratitude to the many authors whose work is included here. Their energy in helping to shape the public debate and their skill in crafting new ideas and cogent arguments have made my work a pleasure. I also owe a very large debt to my colleague Ernest Preeg, who has carried the title of associate editor for economic policy on the *TWQ* masthead, a title that little conveys his role as tutor, critic, and catalyst in the process of generating these materials. Useful advice, assistance, and support has come from many other quarters, not least from Erik Peterson and Michael Mazarr, who succeeded me in summer 1995 in the leadership role in the journal as I relinquished the tasks of journal management and returned to full-time research and writing as an analyst at the Institute for Defense Analyses. Lastly, this volume also reflects the editorial skill and commitment to quality of those members of the *TWQ* editorial staff who, over the years, have made such a great difference: Yoma Ullman, Nicholas Koukopoulos, James Rutherford, and Denise Miller, in particular.

Brad Roberts
Washington, D.C.
October 1, 1995

I. The Global Economy of the 1990s

Looming Collision of Capitalisms?

Erik R. Peterson

ACCELERATING GLOBAL economic integration is bringing national economic policies into sharper competition, especially among the advanced capitalist economies. How these competing domestic policies are managed through the turn of the century and beyond will have profound implications not only for the international economy but also for broader international security and political relations. The risk is that increasingly nationalist economic policies, fanned by deteriorating economic conditions and social pressures, will propel the preeminent economic powers—and the rest of the world with them—into an era of "*realeconomik*" in which parochial economic interests drive governments to pursue marginal advantage in an international system marked by growing interdependencies.

The conclusion in December 1993 of the General Agreement on Tariffs and Trade (GATT) Uruguay Round, the culmination of seven years of tortuous negotiation by governments to strip away more of their own policy prerogatives, refuted the proposition that the major economic powers—the United States, the European Union (EU), and Japan—were leading the collective effort to break down traditional trade barriers and trade-distorting domestic policies globally. Although it culminated in agreement, the process revealed the extent to which those powers were disinclined to do the "heavy lifting" in liberalizing their policies that many of the less prominent economies had already done to advance the round. In effect, the protracted negotiations highlighted the thresholds of national tolerance among the predominant economies beyond which the political costs for the respective governments were unacceptably high.

There is little doubt that the current economic troubles confronting Washington, Brussels, and Tokyo were a major factor in limiting the scope of the final GATT agreement. Those troubles have also elevated the levels of economic nationalism and unilateralism, both of which can be expected to intensify further as longer-term structural problems in all three economies generate additional political and economic dislocations in the years ahead.

Because of the increasingly binding constraints placed on national economic policy-making by the process of global economic integration, the temptation for the major economies to engage in defensive strategies by supporting national "strategic" industries—especially high-technology in-

---

Erik R. Peterson is director of studies at CSIS.

dustries—could bring the major capitalisms into collision. The operative question is whether the governments concerned will succumb to the growing tendency to "pursue relative gains at the expense of mutual gains [and] political power at the expense of economic welfare,"[1] or whether they will be able to devise a system of rules and an appropriate institutional vehicle to defuse the potential for escalating economic clashes between respective "national champions."

Accelerating Economic Globalization

It has long been recognized that the traditional line of demarcation between domestic and international economic policy-making is fading. Economic shocks ranging from the oil embargo by the Organization of Petroleum Exporting Countries to the "Black Monday" international stock market crash in October 1987 have underlined the susceptibility of national markets to developments abroad. For governments worldwide, the internationalization of the world economy has also meant the progressive deterioration of their capacity to manage their economies. Macroeconomic policies have been increasingly undermined by the offsetting effects of international responses; an increase in interest rates to decelerate economic growth, for example, is more likely than ever before to be countered by an increase in interest-sensitive capital flows from abroad.[2]

But international trade and investment linkages have expanded to such an extent that sensitivities of economies to decision making in other economies are now substantially more pronounced. Advances in communication and information technologies, the pursuit by multinational enterprises (MNEs) of complex cross-border strategies, the formation and development of regional trading blocs, the GATT process, economic liberalization undertaken in a host of developing economies, and ongoing efforts at marketization in former command economies are metamorphosing the international economic and financial system. As these elements bring about higher levels of global integration, constraints on national economic policy-making will continue to grow—and with them the potential for wider conflict over national policies.

The real-time capabilities offered by new communication and information technologies have already had a tremendous impact on international capital flows. Daily global capital movements have increased to well over $1 trillion in 1992. The implications of these movements for national macroeconomic policy-making are profound. Alan Greenspan, chairman of the Federal Reserve, noted in August 1993 that the internationalization of finance and the reduction in constraints on international capital flows "expose national economies to shocks from new and unexpected sources, with little if any lag."[3] As a result, he stressed the importance central banks should attach to developing new ways of assessing and limiting risk. But those ways remain to be identified.

Nowhere has the impact on policy-making of these cross-border capital flows been more obvious recently than in the EU, where international speculative pressures played a significant role in the partial collapse in the European Monetary System in 1992. Those forces contributed to the circumstances that led London and Rome to withdraw from the semifixed exchange rates under the Exchange Rate Mechanism (ERM); since the British and Italian withdrawal, they have also forced the Spanish to devalue the peseta and brought the Belgian franc under extreme stress. As the *Economist* noted in October 1993, "[t]he financial markets have discovered, in a way they are unlikely to forget for years, their power to crack the system."[4] In short, we have entered a new stage in the development of international finance in which financial markets—and even some individuals—can dramatically influence the outcome of policy decisions by states.

MNEs are another major driver of global economic integration. By virtue of increasingly complex strategies involving multitier networks of firms that are geographically dispersed and through strategic alliances with other firms, MNEs are establishing unprecedented linkages among economies worldwide. According to the United Nations Conference on Trade and Development (UNCTAD), the strategies of MNEs have generally moved beyond a "simple integration" approach involving strengthened links with their foreign affiliates and with independent firms serving as subcontractors or licensees; the new strategy, which UNCTAD characterizes as "complex integration," provides for heightened geographical distribution of the value-added chain.[5] That MNEs account for a staggering one-third of world private productive assets suggests how important the ramifications of such a shift of strategy are.[6]

According to UNCTAD, sales by MNEs outside their countries of origin were $5.5 trillion in 1992—as opposed to total world exports for the same year of about $4.0 trillion; furthermore, the stock of foreign direct investment (FDI) worldwide reached $2 trillion in 1992, as opposed to one-half that amount in 1987.[7] These data reflect the substantial role that MNEs are playing in integrating the world economy and suggest the extent to which private-sector forces have become a factor in national economic decision making. As discussed in greater detail below, a number of countries with policies that were previously anathema to MNEs have refashioned their approaches so that attraction of foreign investment is a key component of their economic development strategies.

The development of regional trading blocs has also generated higher levels of economic interdependence and by definition represents the voluntary acceptance by the respective member states of constraints on national policy prerogatives. Because the EU, the North American Free Trade Agreement (NAFTA), and the emerging trading framework in Asia are based on political as well as economic considerations, the trend toward regionalism transcends the surrender of policy prerogatives for purely economic reasons.[8] Nevertheless, the impact is to advance economic integration between member states. In the case of the EU, where the impact of German monetary policy clearly transcends the national economic challenges inherent in reunification, the linkages may be more pronounced than some member states would want.

The GATT process, of course, has also steadily broken down barriers between international and domestic policy-making. The GATT is no longer the vehicle through which only tariff barriers are broken down; the non-tariff barriers that were the focus of the Tokyo Round and the issues at the fore of the Uruguay Round—trade in services, trade-related investment measures, intellectual property protection, price supports and subsidies, countervailing duties, dumping, and dispute settlement—have exposed the nerves of national economic interests as never before. The demonstrations from Brussels to Tokyo attested to the degree to which GATT negotiations have become (and should be) a major domestic political issue. By definition, the GATT process and the Uruguay Round—in the event it is ratified—represent "another stake in the heart of the idea that governments can direct economies."[9]

Economic and financial liberalization in developing economies represents another stimulus to growing integration. A select number of developing countries with liberalized investment environments are now primary targets of portfolio and foreign direct investment flows.[10] Over the past 10 years, international portfolio investment in developing countries has mushroomed. Market capitalization has grown by a factor of 11, from $67 billion in 1982 to $770 billion in 1992. As a percentage of world equity market capitalization, developing countries increased their share over this period from 2.5 percent to 7 percent. The trend can be expected to continue as secondary markets in developing countries widen and deepen. Simply put, the key reason for this rapid growth in developing-country capital markets is profitability. According to the International Finance Corporation, emerging stock markets took 8 of the top 10 positions as best performing markets last year.[11] Gains of over 20 percent were registered in markets stretching from Mexico City to Amman to Bangkok. In addition, over the past eight years emerging markets as a group have significantly outperformed their counterparts in developed countries.[12]

The pattern of FDI to developing countries has been no less extraordinary. According to UNCTAD, FDI flows to developing countries increased from $25 billion in 1991 to $40 billion in 1992; if high growth is sustained in Asia and Latin America, annual flows could double in real terms to $80 billion by the end of the century.[13] What is behind this trend? Simply put, economic liberalization has replaced statism, trade liberalization has followed protectionism, and privatization has replaced nationalization. For these countries, the necessity of conforming their national economic decision making to the realities of the international system is now a matter of record. In many cases, those adjustments have extended beyond actions to attract FDI inflows to include fundamental policy shifts such as imposing discipline on fiscal deficits, developing clear legal and commercial systems, streamlining bureaucracies, simplifying taxation systems, and liberalizing trade policies.[14]

Although they are not yet as fully integrated into the world economic system, the former command economies that are seeking to marketize their systems are another driver of international integration. For the first time since the beginning of the century, they are opening their economies to the world economic system and enacting national policies designed to encourage the development of market forces.

Integrating Markets Versus Integrating Policies

It should be stressed that there are fundamental differences among these forces driving international economic integration. Some can be referred to as "organic" integration—the private cross-border flows of capital, goods and services, technology, and information driven in large part by MNEs. Others promote "inorganic" integration—the formal and politically oriented trade agreements forged among countries to reduce tariff and non-tariff barriers and harmonize trade-relevant domestic economic policies.

Organic integration is the result of strategies enacted by international private-sector actors to maximize the efficiency of their operations in the light of increasing global competition. As noted above, to an ever greater extent MNEs are distributing their operations internationally regardless of political institutions and frameworks to seek innovation or to achieve cost savings at various stages in the value-added chain. Although the pattern of this distribution of economic activity may be (and often is) influenced by regional economic blocs such as the EU and the NAFTA, it will be influenced only to the extent that such frameworks can be incorporated into prevailing global strategies. Increasingly, however, that activity is falling outside the regional blocs and generating higher levels of more global economic integration in the process.

These kinds of private-sector-driven economic dependencies must be differentiated from the "inorganic" or formalized efforts at economic cooperation undertaken among and between states. Such arrangements are based by definition on perceived mutual gains from economic cooperation, but generally they also represent a mixture of economic and political concern. The EU is clearly grounded in political and security objectives advanced in the period immediately after World War II; for its part, the NAFTA also has a strong political character. As a result, the inorganic integration fostered by regional blocs may not necessarily reflect the market fundamentals that are driving the interdependence now created by the private sector. Furthermore, the political nature of regional blocs suggests the possibility that they might be tempted to engage in aggressive trade policies that could generate a protectionist equivalent of an arms race.[15] They could ultimately become the means by which organic integration is resisted.

Together, these organic and inorganic forces driving economies into heightened interdependence can be compared to a set of tightening constraints in a linear programming model that serve to progressively limit the area in which national economic policy-making is feasible. It follows that governments are likely to resist the restrictions this kind of global convergence places on their policy prerogatives, especially when they are facing acute short-term economic challenges or when the adjustments forced by growing integration entail profound economic or social change. In short, integration of policies is lagging behind integration of markets.

Capitalisms in Collision?

The salient question is how governments can protect their national economic interests in an increasingly integrated global economic and financial framework. More and more, the preeminent economic powers in particular are finding the answer in drawing lines beyond which they will resort to defensive strategies grounded in parochial interests. The result is the development of political conditions that encourage the outbreak of economic nationalism.

The current political and economic environments in the United States, Europe, and Japan do not augur well for the level of cooperation necessary to avoid the neomercantilist confrontation that could flow from competing national policies. The overarching security concerns generated by the common threat from the erstwhile Soviet

Union are a thing of the past, and immediate economic concerns now overshadow residual security ties. It is a time of fundamental redefinition of security, political, and economic relations—but the process of redefinition is proceeding in the absence of the international leadership and corresponding institutions necessary to meet the challenges of escalating economic rivalry.

The trauma that Washington experienced in fall 1993 in deciding on whether to adopt a free-trade agreement with Mexico—an economy only 4 percent of the U.S. gross national product and with a $5.5 billion trade deficit—amounted to a highly visible demonstration of U.S. attitudes about trade. Although of course the NAFTA was adopted, the emotional and sometimes vacuous debate served to highlight the extent to which economic nationalism threatens the historic role of the United States as leader of the global economic system. But apart from the NAFTA debate, there are other symptoms of this uncertainty. Regular calls in the U.S. Congress and elsewhere for unilateralist approaches to trade and foreign investment issues suggest that the concepts of "fair" rather than "free" trade and "reciprocal treatment" rather than "national treatment" in international capital flows are steadily gaining ground.

These warning signs are the result of the growing perception in the United States that new approaches are necessary to ensure fair access for trade and investment by U.S. firms. The perception is grounded in the view that what was recently referred to as "unilateralist national treatment"[16]—namely, the position on international investment that Washington has maintained for decades—is not being reciprocated by many of its investment partners. Of course, the recent domestic economic difficulties have thrown fuel on the fire.

In Europe, where the economic problems at present are even more pronounced,[17] where the partial collapse of the ERM has generated profound doubts about the outlook for a single European currency, and where the tenuous ratification process of the Maastricht agreement has left leaders searching for ways to advance the integration agenda, attention is predominantly inward. The seriousness of the challenge was underlined in October 1993 when the president of the European Commission, Jacques Delors, warned that the then European Community was drifting toward becoming a free-trade zone that could break up in as little as 15 years.[18] The EU is clearly in a period of intense consolidation and restructuring.

Japan is also engaged in political and economic soul-searching. The Hosokawa coalition has embarked on a program of political reform with potentially important longer-term implications for Tokyo's position in the international economic system. The outcome, however, is by no means assured. To sustain the reform process that it initiated immediately prior to the November 1993 meeting of the members of APEC (the Asia–Pacific Economic Cooperation), the government must continue to pass through the political thicket of its own eight-party coalition before contesting with the opposition Liberal Democratic Party to push through its initiatives. It must also do so against the backdrop of stagnating or declining growth, severe volatility in the financial markets, less than promising longer-term growth projections, and a highly resistant bureaucracy.

When considered together, these

developments in the United States, Europe, and Japan have led some analysts to revisit arguments advanced in the 1970s about the ungovernability of democracies.[19] But there is also reason to question whether relations between the capitalist countries themselves will be governable. It is no exaggeration to suggest that the political agendas in all three major economic powers are predominantly inward-looking and focus primarily on reviving national economic growth and employment. All three are engaged in economic triage. Evidence of economic parochialism in the pursuit of those objectives appears to be growing on a day-by-day basis. In short, they could be on a course that suggests the potential for the rise of neomercantilism.

"Strategic" Trade at Issue

In particular, there is the possibility of an escalation of industrial policies that would bring "national champions" and "strategic" industries—especially those in high technology—into sharper conflict. The magnitude of the threat has been set out by the Organization for Economic Cooperation and Development (OECD):

> Government support for economically strategic industries could become a major source of international dispute in the 1990s. The move over the last decade towards subsidies and other forms of state assistance for important technologically advanced sectors is set to accelerate. The proliferation of such policies, which affect a relatively narrow band of often identical sectors, could well develop into a keenly competitive "subsidy race," with harmful and far-reaching implications for the international system of trade, investment and technology.[20]

Despite the predominately unfavorable—or, at best, mixed—experience with allocating government resources in support of strategic industries,[21] the temptation for governments is to engage in "picking winners" because of the political benefits they engender and the rationale under "strategic trade" theory that "technology trajectories" have a clustering effect of positive externalities extending throughout a wider part of the economy.[22] Some advocates of this theory suggest that such interventionist national policies can be advanced without undermining the pursuit of an open, integrated world economy.[23] Others point to the impending competition for "national futures."[24] That this new genre of thought on competition theory is predicated on results with pronounced sensitivities to changes in assumptions has not prevented it from assuming rising political currency.[25] Nor have the new political advocates of strategic trade been deterred by steadily mounting empirical evidence suggesting that protection and subsidization of industries can actually weaken their competitive position.[26]

Whatever the underlying explanations, from the standpoint of competing national policies the advancement of strategic trade objectives can be achieved through a wide array of policy measures—including but not limited to trade-related policies such as "orderly marketing agreements," industrial and technology policies that provide subsidy, research and development support and other "cover," discriminatory procurement practices, and exemption of relevant sectors from antitrust law.

Assuming such strategic trade policies are adopted more fully by all three major world economic powers, it follows that competition between the respective "beggar-thy-neighbor" approaches could mount quickly because they are based on zero-sum thinking. As Michael Porter has noted,

> [i]f the rate of innovation slows because an "us versus them" attitude leads to subsidy, protection, and consolidation that blunts incentives, the consequences for advanced and less advanced nations alike are severe.[27]

Government intervention in a host of sectors has been a long-established practice in the EU. From ESPRIT to EUREKA, from Concorde to Airbus, from the TGV rail initiative in France to aircraft production in the Netherlands, industrial policy is already a part of the European economic topography. In Japan, where the connection between the government and the private sector is also well established, decision makers have a less visible but nevertheless significant role in promoting industries through a variety of policies. And in the United States, where sector support has been less prevalent, momentum is mounting for a shift to a higher profile for the government in selected strategic industries. The shift is in response to the perception that "our competitors close off their markets to American firms while looking for ways to tap into our rich market . . . and we let them."[28] A senior Clinton administration official recently put it this way: "If no one else wants to play the game [our way], we'd look pretty silly [doing nothing] while they clean our clock."[29]

These divergent positions on industrial policy serve to highlight the more general differences between the capitalisms of the United States, the EU, and Japan. At issue is the differing relationship between government and business in each of the major economic powers and how those relations translate into national policies that have international repercussions. At one end of the spectrum is the consumer-oriented system of capitalism in the United States, where linkages between government and business have been loose and sometimes at odds as a result of the tradition of limiting the extent to which market concentrations occur; at the other end is Japan, which by fostering a producers-oriented form of capitalism is marked by substantially closer ties between the public and private sectors; and in the middle is the EU, where government intervention—traditionally based on social welfare criteria—is more pronounced than in the United States.[30]

A Multilateral Response?

A common approach by the three preeminent economies to defining acceptable limits to industrial policy is necessary if spiraling competition for marginal advantage is to be averted. The prospect for the negotiation of multilateral rules governing industrial policy is, however, remote at best. No international framework is in sight that could represent a release valve for the emerging pressures associated with these competing policies. The Group of Seven (G–7) falls substantially short of representing a forum through which a detailed agreement could be reached. Despite its past attention to the issue, the OECD is not likely to become the forum for the United States, the EU, and Japan to seek to reconcile their differences because of the large membership involved, although the OECD could take an active role in defining more specifically how the highly industrialized economies might proceed more generally in fashioning an approach to the issue. The experience of the Uruguay Round suggests that the next stage of negotiations under the Multilateral Trade Organization will be equally if not more arduous as differences in competition and investment policies come to the fore.

Furthermore, no single economic power seems predisposed to spearhead an effort to defuse the potential of conflicting industrial policies. In the meantime, "competition between governments [is progressively replacing] competition between companies as industrial activities become more and more global."[31]

It is an irony that at this critical historical juncture—when many of the former command economies are embarking on transitions to market systems and a number of developing countries have substantially liberalized their economies after decades of failed statist policies—the highly industrialized powers are in economic distress and embroiled in efforts to reinvigorate their domestic economies. If, as expected, the macroeconomic difficulties in the United States, Europe, and Japan persist or intensify, the attempt at integration into the world economy by significant parts of the second and third worlds—a historically unprecedented development that for decades has been the lodestar of the highly industrialized states themselves—will have been unassisted by the major global economic players and in some ways impeded by their paralysis.

Another fundamental irony of the immediate post–cold war period is that with the decline of the threat from Moscow, the emphasis is shifting from the clash between capitalism and communism to the differences between the "capitalisms" of the highly industrialized economies. The threat is that traditional political and security linkages will be recast as subordinate features of a competition for industrial advantage—or supremacy.[32]

In the face of rising domestic economic problems and accelerating global economic integration, the manner in which the major economic powers manage their relations through the turn of the century and beyond will have an enormous impact on the world economy. A descent into a period of *realeconomik*, pitting government against government in a global competition for markets, would have a deleterious effect on the capacity of those same governments to meet future national and international economic challenges. Such a descent would also threaten the integrity of political and security relations in a highly uncertain period. To avoid this outcome, policymakers need to heed the advice of Akio Morita, who in an open letter to the G–7 heads of state in June 1993 argued:

> You, as political leaders, have the power to take the steps necessary to make the increasing de facto globalization of business the most creative, positive, and beneficial force it can be, rather than the source of new international conflict.[33]

The author gratefully acknowledges the research assistance of Marcus Castain in the preparation of this article.

Notes

1. Theodore H. Moran, "An Economics Agenda for Neorealists," *International Security* 18 (Fall 1993), p. 211.

2. See, for example, Marina von Neumann Whitman, "The State of Business: Global Competitiveness and Economic Nationalism," *Harvard International Review* 15 (Summer 1993), pp. 5–6.

3. Speech presented at meeting on "Changing Capital Markets: Implications for Mon-

etary Policy," Jackson Hole, Wyoming, August 19, 1993.
4. "Europe's Monetary Future: From here to EMU," *Economist,* October 23, 1993, p. 25.
5. UNCTAD, *World Investment Report 1993: Transnational Corporations and Integrated International Production* (New York, N.Y.: United Nations, 1993), pp. 4–5, 115–133.
6. *Ibid.,* p. 13.
7. *Ibid.,* pp. 13–14.
8. See Paul Krugman, "Regional Blocs: The Good, the Bad and the Ugly," *International Economy* 6 (November/December 1992), pp. 54–56.
9. "The World Wins One," *Wall Street Journal,* December 15, 1993, p. A–16.
10. Argentina, Brazil, the People's Republic of China, Egypt, Hong Kong, Mexico, Nigeria, Singapore, Taiwan, and Thailand. See UNCTAD, *World Investment Report.*
11. International Finance Corporation, *IFC Emerging Stock Markets Factbook 1993* (Washington, D.C.: IFC, 1993), p. 3.
12. *Ibid.,* p. 3. The report notes that from the end of 1988 to the end of 1992, markets in Argentina, Chile, Colombia, Mexico, Pakistan, Thailand, and Venezuela rose more than 100 percent in dollar terms as compared with 51 percent in the United States.
13. UNCTAD, *World Investment Report.*
14. DeAnne Julius, "Liberalisation, Foreign Investment, and Economic Growth," *Shell Selected Papers,* March 1993, pp. 4–5.
15. Krugman, "Regional Blocs: The Good, the Bad and the Ugly," p. 55.
16. See Office for Technology Assessment, *Multinationals and the National Interest: Playing by Different Rules* (Washington, D.C.: OTA, 1993).
17. See, for example, Arnaud de Borchgrave, "Eurogloom Foreshadows Social Upheaval," *Washington Times,* October 4, 1993, p. A–12.
18. Despite ratification of the Maastricht treaty, Delors states that "What I see is European construction drifting towards a free-trade zone, that is to say an English-style Europe, which I reject." See "Delors Fears EC Drifting towards Break-up," *Financial Times,* October 18, 1993, p. 2. See also "Delors Bloodied but Unbowed," *Financial Times,* October 23, 1993, p. 3.
19. See, for example, the articles on ungovernability by Michel Crozier, Samuel P. Huntington, and Joji Watanuki in *American Enterprise* 4 (November/December 1993), pp. 28–41. The three authors originally addressed the issue in a research effort in the early 1970s sponsored by the Trilateral Commission, chaired by Zbigniew Brzezinski, which culminated in the book entitled *The Crisis of Democracy* (New York, N.Y.: New York University Press, 1975).
20. OECD, *Strategic Industries in a Global Economy: Policy Issues for the 1990s* (Paris: OECD Publications, 1991).
21. See inter alia "When the State Picks Winners," *Economist,* January 9, 1993, pp. 13–14; "Europe's Technology Policy: How Not to Catch Up," *Economist,* January 9, 1993, pp. 19–21; Daniel Malkin, "Industrial Policy in OECD Countries," *International Economic Insights* 4 (March/April 1993), pp. 22–23; Barrie Stevens, "Strategic Industries: What Policies for the 1990s?" *OECD Observer,* no. 172 (October/November 1991), pp. 4–7; and Candice Stevens, "Industrial Internationalisation and Trade Friction," *OECD Observer,* no. 173 (December 1991/January 1992), pp. 27–30.
22. See Wayne Sandholtz et al., *The Highest Stakes: The Economic Foundations of the Next Security System* (New York, N.Y.: Oxford University Press, 1992).
23. See Peter F. Cowhey and Jonathan D. Aronson, *Managing the World Economy: The Consequences of Corporate Alliances* (New York, N.Y.: Council on Foreign Relations Press, 1993).
24. Sandholtz, *Highest Stakes,* p. 182.
25. Michael E. Porter, *The Competitive Advantage of Nations* (New York, N.Y.: The Free Press, 1990), p. 812, n. 46.
26. For a recent comparison of selected manufacturing industries in the United States, Germany, and Japan, see McKinsey Global Institute, "Manufacturing Productivity" (Washington, D.C., October 1993). See also Paul Betts, "Penalties for Excess Baggage," *Financial Times,* December 1, 1993, p. 13.
27. Porter, *The Competitive Advantage,* p. 682.

28. Scott Gibson and Saul Goldstein, "The Plane Truth: How European Deals Are Killing U.S. Jobs," *Washington Post*, October 10, 1993.

29. Hobart Rowen, "A Little Boost from Washington," *Washington Post*, October 7, 1993, p. A–23. Rowen was quoting President Bill Clinton's science adviser, John H. Gibbons.

30. Whitman, "The State of Business," p. 7.

31. Stevens, "Industrial Internationalisation," p. 30.

32. For a provocative account of the role of the United States in the emerging international economic system, see Edward N. Luttwak, *The Endangered American Dream: How to Stop the United States from Becoming a Third-World Country and How to Win the Geo-Economic Struggle for Industrial Supremacy* (New York, N.Y.: Simon & Schuster, 1993). See also Luttwak's related article, "From Geopolitics to Geo-Economics: Logic of Conflict, Grammar of Commerce," *National Interest*, no. 20 (Summer 1990), pp. 17–23.

33. Akio Morita, "Toward a New World Economic Order," *Atlantic Monthly*, June 1993, pp. 88–89.

Economics and National Strategy: Convergence, Global Networks, and Cooperative Competition

James R. Golden

THE UNITED STATES needs a national strategy that responds to the central post–cold war political, economic, and military realities: the end of East–West confrontation, economic parity across the developed regions of the West, the information technology revolution, the proliferation of weapons with enormous lethality, and the growing importance of intrastate war. In the emerging environment the threats to national security are real, but they are more diffuse and less likely to provide a clear focus for standing alliances or to justify the subordination of economic issues to security concerns. Instead, national strategy will have to balance economic and security interests and support approaches that develop international consensus: cooperation will be essential in providing institutions that promote international economic stability and effective crisis management. At the same time the United States must meet the economic challenge of sustaining high and rising levels of national income in the face of intense regional competition. The national strategy, in short, must blend cooperation and competition in ways that respond to the new environment.

The world's new political structure centers on a triangle of competing regions that have achieved economic parity—Europe, North America, and Japan[1]—loosely tied to developing regions on their peripheries. The three developed regions are integrated by the globalization of production and finance and by the network structures of the information technology revolution, but they are separated by differences in culture and by regional markets and institutions that tie various industries to their respective home bases. The combination of convergence in economic performance and the new structure of global networks has altered the nature of regional competition in ways that have profound strategic implications.

If the first industrial revolution can be characterized by a focus on steam, iron, and railways in national firms, and the second by electricity, chemistry, automobiles, and consumer durables in increasingly multinational

---

James R. Golden, Colonel, U.S. Army, was a senior staff economist on the President's Council of Economic Advisers and now serves as professor and head of the Department of Social Sciences at the U.S. Military Academy.

firms, the third centers on microelectronics, biological engineering, and new materials in internationally networked firms. The transforming power of the third revolution lies in the impact of information technology in integrating related technologies, reducing transactions and processing costs, and changing industrial structures.

The information technology revolution is having repercussions for strategy at many levels. One of the most significant has been in the changing structure of industrial organizations and corporate networks. The growing access to and importance of information flows is transforming traditional hierarchical firms into more horizontal organizations that emphasize flexibility, coordination, on-time production, and long-term relationships with suppliers and customers. In the information technology industry in particular, research and development (R&D) relationships extend across firms through horizontal information networks that have redefined traditional corporate boundaries. Perhaps ironically, the same firms that cooperate in R&D activities then compete aggressively in product markets. Corporate strategy now requires *cooperative competition*, a framework that simultaneously enhances mutual performance and shapes the form of competition. In this sense cooperation and competition are not alternative approaches to relationships; both elements are always present to some extent. The cooperative component enhances the competition by making both parties more effective, and at the same time the structure of cooperation limits the scope of acceptable competition.

That insight—that competitors must also cooperate in research networks in order to compete effectively in product markets—captures the essential impact of the information revolution for other levels of strategy as well. The new network relationships are redefining regional power balances, altering patterns of economic growth, and shifting the structure of potential alliances that will come into play in dealing with the proliferation of sophisticated threats. In this setting, national strategy must balance cooperation and competition to achieve national objectives. I use the term cooperative competition in a strategic sense to stress the importance of building cooperative networks that will permit the United States to pursue objectives in concert with other nations while still competing with them for the location of high-value economic activities. The cooperative element of the strategy recognizes the need to create the public goods, or infrastructure, needed to provide the stability essential for efficient interaction.[2] The competitive component recognizes that national objectives still differ, that the distribution of wealth, income, and power will continue to be a national concern, and that, sadly, political and economic competition may occasionally spill over into armed conflict.[3] National strategy must recognize both components by working to create a network of infrastructure relationships to keep the international competition within acceptable limits and by developing the capacity to respond effectively when the competition exceeds those limits.

A National Strategy

Before we examine the new economic environment and the components of a strategy of cooperative competition in more detail, we need to address the possibility of sustaining *any* U.S. national strategy. By a national strategy, I mean a vision of the process through which national resources will be used to achieve national objectives. National strategies may be distinguished by the relative roles given to the private and public sectors, the emphasis given to different policy instruments, and the importance assigned to various possible outcomes. National strategies are seldom explicit, and the implementation of strategy rarely flows from objectives to resource allocation. Objectives, concepts, and means normally evolve together.

In modern mixed-market economies national strategy starts from the premise that a wide range of national objectives will be pursued through decentralized economic markets in which firms and consumers are relatively free to make informed decisions that influence their own welfare. The rationale for government action results from market failures, in the sense that some distortion in information or incentive structures is producing the "wrong" signals for private actions, or from a desire to alter the distribution of income that results from private decisions. Judgments on what constitutes a market failure or an unacceptable distribution of income are obviously intensely political decisions, and those judgments and the extent and form of intervention to correct perceived failures differ substantially from country to country. Japan and France intervene in that process with a structure of indicative planning to coordinate public and private actions in selected industries. The U.S. government has traditionally rejected such explicit industrial planning, although its regulatory framework and its large intervention through defense research, development, and procurement have large sectoral impacts.

In theory U.S. national strategy would begin with a structure of private activities based on the operation of free markets and then provide a framework for modifying the use of the nation's resources to achieve national objectives derived from enduring national interests. In practice national objectives conflict, and consensus on how to achieve them is limited. The actual allocation of public resources is settled in an often heated political process that is constitutionally designed to balance competing interests. Policy formulation is rarely driven by overarching strategy: instead there is an overlapping web of public policies fashioned by a broad array of agencies that compete for resources in the political arena, urged on by many private interest groups with divergent concerns. Effective coordination of those policies in ways that preserve the vitality of the private sector and eliminate the most egregious inconsistencies in public programs is difficult because the costs of identifying and obtaining the right information and overcoming the frictional problems of defining and implementing policies are enormous. The government's energy and resources are limited, so at best the nation might be able to coordinate the use of a subset of national resources in pursuit of its most important national interests.

As a result the central role of strategy is to elevate a narrow set of policies to prominence for more careful coordination. In the post–World War II period the analytical device for narrowing national strategy to a manageable scale has been to focus on "security" strategy, based on an assessment of national interests that are at risk in the international arena. Economic policy rarely entered explicitly into this framework, aside from the economic constraints imposed in the budget process. The National Security Act of 1947 institutionalized the security strategy framework in a system centered on the integrating functions of the National Security Council and its staff. Since 1986 the staff has drafted the president's *National Security Strategy of the United States* each year, typically beginning with lists of national interests such as national survival, economic strength, cooperative relations with allies and friendly nations, and a stable world in which democratic institutions can flourish.[4] National security policy attempts to integrate economic, diplomatic, and military policies to deal with threats to those national interests.[5] This post–World War II emphasis on the peacetime coordination of national power to achieve security objectives applies the basic ideas of wartime "grand" strategy to the cold war setting.[6]

The "security" framework for strategy is ultimately based on a system of threat and coercion justified by the importance of preserving vital national interests. Thus security strategy is distinct from other government policy because of the vital importance of the issues involved and the sensitivity of the policy instruments. In the security framework, elements of national "power" become instruments for achieving security objectives. From this perspective economic "power," a term used by security analysts but rarely by economists, can be used directly to influence states and other international actors or indirectly as a foundation for generating other elements of power, such as military forces.

The advantages of focusing on national security strategy rather than broader national strategy are manifest. Threats to national security interests provide a clear focus for coordination across relevant agencies, particularly the Departments of State and Defense, in the realm of "high policy," which is less susceptible to partisan bickering. At least to some extent, the security strategy helps to identify capabilities needed to meet the threats, informs analysis of trade-offs across alternative military force structures and weapon systems, and ultimately influences strategic plans and budget decisions. The security focus also emphasizes the distinction between long-term planning and what many analysts feel is the sine qua non of strategy—the presence of an adversary—and reinforces the concept of "strategic thinking" with its web of moves and countermoves.

The disadvantages of the emphasis on security strategy are also clear, and they have become more obvious in the post–cold war era. When external threats become ambiguous and more remote, the logic and cohesion of the security strategy formulation is less compelling. The "threat" no longer provides a clear orientation for budget and force structure decisions, and the distinctions between security and other policies break down. Moreover, as economic issues become relatively more important, casting them in a security framework could actually be harmful. In practice, economic policy is not formulated by the actors in the national security system and it is not driven by national security strategy in any meaningful sense. By focusing on the narrow range of economic policy issues that are influenced by security strategy, the system deemphasizes such key issues as productivity and competitiveness that are handled in other agencies. Moreover, by focusing on threats to national interests in the international arena, an emphasis on economic security could incorrectly stress coercion against economic competitors rather than domestic policies to enhance competitiveness.

Although economics and security are clearly linked, the idea that economic policy is or should be driven by security interests is inconsistent with the post–cold war environment. More precisely, the security framework places economic relationships in a power balance perspective that may seriously distort the economic agenda by emphasizing zero-sum relationships, in which one actor gains at the other's expense, over the normal non-zero-sum relationships of economic exchange, in which both actors gain. The security framework is inappropriate for dealing with relationships when vital national interests are not directly challenged and the primary policy instruments do not involve threats and coercion. As the relative scope of issues involving military confrontation declines, the security framework provides a less compelling approach for organizing national strategy. Indeed, by making clear threats to national interests, or future capabilities to mount such threats, the organizing principle for strategy, the security framework may lead decision makers to miss the key point that U.S. national interests are increasingly defined in terms of managing competition within the context of cooperative processes.

In the evolving environment we need a new orientation on economics and security issues. Although the security framework and machinery will remain essential for dealing with direct threats to vital U.S. interests, that framework can no longer provide the sole organizing principle for national strategy. Samuel Huntington argues that the United States needs to move beyond the "national security state" of the postwar period to what he calls the "competitive state," whose goal would be "to enhance American economic competitiveness and economic strength in relation to other countries."[7] He notes that economic strength is needed to sustain defense outlays and that interaction in international markets is becoming a relatively more important means of achieving security goals. As he correctly argues, strong growth, productivity, and technological innovation generate international influence through world product, capital, and currency markets. Those markets provide the major forms of interaction among world powers and with the declining importance of military power in great power relationships they are increasingly important means for influencing international behavior.

Huntington correctly identifies the required shift away from a purely security framework for organizing national strategy, but his emphasis on the "relative" economic performance of the United States casts national strategy in a primarily competitive context. In the highly integrated global economy, however, too narrow an emphasis on competition might lead to policies that reduce efficiency and lower national welfare. An analysis of economic convergence and global industrial networks suggests that cooperation must also be a key element of national strategy. Indeed competitive steps that serve to isolate the U.S. economy from those networks would actually weaken relative U.S. economic performance.

The Economic Environment

The two dominant trends in the international economic environment are convergence in levels of income, growth, and productivity among North America, Europe, and Japan, and the evolution of global industrial networks with highly integrated, but remarkably stable, regional nodes. Although convergence in economic performance will not mean equality in economic power because of the differences in scale of national economies, it will mean that U.S. strategy must increasingly involve other major economic powers. That is not to say that the United States has lost its position among world economic leaders, or that it is destined to fall behind other industrial powers in the coming century. It will still be a hegemon in terms of its overall share of world markets, but it will not and should not be expected to dominate every industrial area.

The evolution of global industrial networks, in which firms in related industries develop long-term R&D as well as trade relationships, means that the three major industrial regions will be tied more and more closely together, enhancing convergence. That does not mean that regional policies will become less effective in the future. On the contrary, regional factors that determine the concentration of niches of particular industries may well become more, not less, important. The combination of convergence and global networks suggests new patterns of specialization that will alter the nature of regional cooperation and competition.

Convergence

Over the past decade a growth industry has developed around studies of the decline of the U.S. economy. Paul Kennedy's *The Rise and Fall of the Great Powers* published in 1987—with its thesis that "imperial overstretch" leads to excessive defense spending that crowds out private investment, lowers economic growth, and brings down great powers—came at the crest of a wave of writing on the decline in U.S. productivity growth, the apparent triumph of Japanese corporatism, and the emergence of twin U.S. budget and trade deficits.[8] Improved U.S. economic performance in the mid-1980s muted some of this criticism, but low-growth concerns returned in force with the recession of 1991 and its impact on the 1992 presidential campaign. The facts do not support the thesis of U.S. economic collapse, but they do show that convergence in economic standards and growth rates across Europe, Japan, and the United States is proceeding. That convergence does not imply a sharp reversal in the central position of the U.S. economy, but it does suggest that the extent of U.S. hegemony will decline and that the brief period of U.S. dominance in most key technologies has ended.

The record of U.S. output per hour worked, or labor productivity, presented in table 1 shows that U.S. workers became the most efficient in the world around the turn of the century. After World War II the United States briefly held a dominant position, but by 1984 the gap had closed considerably. The precise size of the gap is subject to a number of problems in computing and comparing international productivity figures, but a range of comparisons using different exchange rate benchmarks and labor input concepts suggest that by 1990 France and Germany had moved even with the United States, while Japan and the United Kingdom had reached roughly 70 to 75 percent of the U.S. level, respectively.[9] The surprisingly weak showing of Japanese workers reflects a wide range of productivity across industries, with levels in some industrial sectors equal to the best in the world, but with other sectors trailing far behind.

There has been enormous confusion over interpreting the economic record, primarily because of a lack of precision in differentiating among the concepts of slowing rates of growth, falling behind, deindustrialization, industrial

Table 1
Comparisons of Productivity Levels Across Countries, 1870–1984

(in each year the leader's productivity is set to 100)

Country	1870	1913	1950	1984
France	49	49	42	98
Germany	53	56	34	90
Japan	17	18	14	56
United Kingdom	100	80	59	81
United States	90	100	100	100

Source: Computed from Angus Maddison, "Growth and Slowdown in Advanced Capitalist Economies: Techniques of Quantitative Assessment," *Journal of Economic Literature* 25 (June 1987), p. 683.

Note: Maddison estimates gross domestic product per hour worked and converts to dollars using purchasing power parity exchange rates. This table divides the estimates for each year by the figure for the leader, the United Kingdom in 1870 and the United States in other years, and multiplies by 100 to estimate each country's percentage of the leader's productivity.

leadership, and convergence.[10] Productivity growth rates in table 2 show that output per worker rose faster in other developed economies than in the United States after 1950, and the pace of productivity improvement fell off sharply in each of the countries listed after 1973. The slower productivity growth in the United States does mean that others are catching up to U.S. levels, but it does not mean that the United States will inevitably fall behind. Growth rates in gross domestic product (GDP) in table 3 show that while each country but the United Kingdom was catching up to the United States in the period from 1950 to 1973, the United States has held its own since then, with France growing at about the same rate and only Japan, the country furthest behind in productivity, growing more rapidly. The de-

Table 2
Comparisons of Average Annual Growth Rates in Productivity Across Countries in Selected Periods, 1870–1990

(percent per year)

Country	1870–1913	1913–1950	1950–1973	1973–1984	1984–1990
France	1.7	2.0	5.1	3.4	2.4
Germany	1.9	1.0	6.0	3.0	1.9
Japan	1.8	1.7	7.7	3.2	3.4
United Kingdom	1.2	1.6	3.2	2.4	1.4
United States	2.0	2.4	2.5	1.0	1.0

Sources: 1870–1984: Maddison, "Growth and Slowdown," table 2, p. 650. 1984–1990: computed from Organization for Economic Cooperation and Development, *Economic Outlook Statistics on Microcomputer Diskettes* (Paris, June 1992).

Table 3
Comparisons of Average Annual Growth Rates in Gross Domestic Product Across Countries in Selected Periods, 1870–1990

(percent per year)

Country	1870–1913	1913–1950	1950–1973	1973–1984	1984–1990
France	1.7	1.1	5.1	2.2	3.8
Germany	2.8	1.3	5.9	1.7	3.0
Japan	2.5	2.2	9.4	3.8	4.7
United Kingdom	1.9	1.3	3.0	1.1	3.0
United States	4.2	2.8	3.7	2.3	3.5

Sources: 1870–1984: Maddison, "Growth and Slowdown," table 1, p. 650. 1984–1990: United Nations, Department of International Economic and Social Affairs, *World Economic Survey, 1991* (New York: United Nations, 1991), p. 210.

cline in productivity growth in all of the countries after 1973 suggests that the root cause is not unique to the U.S. economy. Moreover, the growth rates fall together from earlier levels in the period from 1973 to 1984, and they rise together in the subsequent period, suggesting a convergence in growth patterns.

Kennedy's thesis concerns the proposition of moving ahead and falling behind and argues from historical example that great empires lose economic steam from trying to sustain military hegemony too long. Growth rates in the United States and elsewhere, however, have little to do with military outlays. GDP growth rates in table 3 show that the slowdown after 1973 was quite uniform across the major economic powers, and indeed the slowdown in the 1970s occurred at a time of declining, not rising, defense shares of total GDP. As Huntington has argued so effectively, there is little evidence to support Kennedy's view as a description of current U.S. experience. Defense outlays in the United States never reached the share of GDP in Kennedy's other examples, and his other hegemons never reached the level of economic dominance achieved by the U.S. economy. Although savings and investment are lower in the United States as a share of GDP than in Europe and especially Japan, that is because of the much higher share of GDP that goes to consumption, not to the share that goes to defense. In Huntington's words:

> Consumerism, not militarism, is the threat to American strength. The declinists have it wrong; Montesquieu got it right: "Republics end with luxury; monarchies with poverty."[11]

Another version of the United States in decline emphasizes the loss of U.S. economic leadership, the idea that the nation is losing its position among the leaders in industrial technology. It is certainly true that the United States has lost the dominant technology position it held after World War II, but it still ranks first in most technology areas. In spite of a popular misconception that the decline in overall U.S. productivity growth has resulted from a loss of competitiveness in manufacturing, the growth rate in manufacturing productivity has not declined. Productivity growth in manufacturing per year averaged 3 percent from 1950 to 1973, fell to just over 1 percent for 1974 to 1982, and then soared to 5 percent from 1983 to 1989.[12] The United States still leads the world in output per worker, whether output is measured by GDP, as in table 1, by industrial products in general, or by manufacturing in particular. By one estimate, in 1989 manufacturing productivity in Japan and Germany stood at 80 percent of the U.S. level.[13] It is certainly true that Japan now leads the United States in productivity in some key manufacturing categories including transport equipment, machinery, and electrical equipment, but the overall record would still make the U.S. economy the world's industrial leader by any reasonable standard.

Another related misconception is that the United States is becoming deindustrialized by low manufacturing productivity growth, which is reducing the U.S. share of world manufacturing markets and driving workers to the lower-wage, slow productivity-growth services sector. But from 1965 to 1980 service sectors grew more rapidly as a share of total employment overseas than they did in the United States. In fact the service sector share of real national output in the United States has not been increasing, nor has the industrial sector share been declining. The apparent shift has been caused by the increase in the relative prices of services, and in fact the relative wage of service workers has been rising, not falling. In other words, workers are not being forced out of manufacturing by declining market share, they are being pulled into services by higher wages there. Deindustrialization is not a real phenomenon in terms of output; it is an illusion created by shifting prices and wages.[14] It is certainly true that while the shares of real output remained constant, the portion of the labor force employed in industry and manufacturing declined from 1980 to 1990, but that decline coincided with higher rates of productivity growth in those sectors than in other sectors of the economy. In short, U.S. productivity problems do not originate in the manufacturing and high-technology areas. In fact, the United States maintains its lead in the share of high-technology exports in world markets, and the major shift in the last two decades has been the improved position of Japan relative to Europe.[15]

A more persuasive interpretation of the data is that while the United States is not falling behind or deindustrializing, the economics of Japan and Europe have converged on U.S. productivity levels. We would expect growth rates to converge over time because followers have advantages in being able to borrow best industrial practices, often embodied in new capital, while the leader must absorb the costs and risks of developing new technologies.[16] Tables 1 and 2 suggest that other economies have in fact been converging on levels of U.S. productivity. The puzzle is not why convergence is occurring, but why the United States held out so long as a distant front-runner.

Before we race to implement policies to reverse the decline in U.S. productivity growth, we need to understand the sources of the productivity leadership the United States displayed earlier. It has been suggested that the U.S. surge to industrial supremacy after 1900 was based on an integrated internal market, the growth of transportation infrastructure, and the simultaneous development of resource extraction and specialization in industrial technologies that complemented those natural resources. Although the U.S. cost advantage in world mineral markets subsequently faded, the accumulated base of an educated work force and science-based technologies gave the United States a dominant position in a wide range of industries after World War II.[17] From that perspective, the unique advantages that sustained relatively high productivity growth in the immediate postwar period may now have faded. In particular, integration of world markets permitted other countries to gain the advantages of mass production, and large Japanese and European investments in education and R&D created the social conditions required for convergence.[18]

The point is not that the United States is destined to remain the world's productivity leader forever. It would be naive to assume that would be the case, but it is equally naive to expect that the United States will fall behind as other industrialized countries surge past it. Others will encounter problems in sustaining high productivity growth as they lose the advantages of technological followers and are forced to deal with lagging agricultural and services sectors.

Certainly large U.S. budget deficits constrain U.S. public and private investment, and policies to reduce the size of those deficits are clearly in order. U.S. trade imbalances and the loss of competitiveness in some key industries also pose serious challenges for economic policy. But while these are important issues that require attention, they have often been linked with broader arguments about U.S. decline. Convergence in economic performance across regions, however, has far different implications than a systematic process of falling further and further behind. Proponents of reform must, of course, show that U.S. problems are serious in order to stimulate action, and that may lead well-meaning analysts to exaggerate U.S. decline. There is also a danger, however, that excessive alarm could trigger unwarranted and counterproductive intervention in national and international markets. Indeed, the continuing growth of the U.S. economy depends on access to dynamic global networks.

Global Networks

Convergence in economic performance among the major economic powers has been reinforced by the emergence of global industrial networks that, driven by the revolution in information technologies, are transforming international markets, shifting traditional patterns of industrial organization, changing the specialization of labor, altering patterns of research, development, and innovation, and accelerating the integration of global capital and product markets. The competition that will determine future U.S. economic performance, living standards at home, and the ability to influence events abroad, will be waged in those global networks. Although the competition begins with the United States still in an economic leadership position, sustaining that lead will require an understanding of how globalization is proceeding and how regions can influence the process.

Global networks spring from regional home bases that provide competitive advantages to industries, or niches within industries, based on economies of scale and scope and the unique characteristics of local markets. Some standardized activities are footloose, shifting from one region to another in response to fluctuations in the costs of labor and capital or tax incentives. Other high-value, specialized activities concentrate in network nodes, or regions that contain firms linked to several intersecting networks. As a result, regions still matter, but they matter in ways that differ from the classical model of trade based on resource endowments. The key in the new competition is the ability to create the specialized resources that develop nodes in the global network. Economic strategy must therefore come directly to grips with the dynamic nature of "factor creation" and its impact on the location of high-value activities in global networks. Before proceeding to the full implications of convergence and global networks for national strategy, we need to examine how global networks are evolving and how the location of network nodes might be influenced by public policy.

Networks. Network concepts are transforming the global workplace and creating new forms of interaction across traditional enterprises. The key aspects of the new network structures include shifts from hierarchical to more horizontal relationships and a growing emphasis on long-term cooperation, both driven by the need and possibilities for more complete and timely communication. As Anthony Carnevale, reporting on the work of the Hudson Institute's Workforce 2000 project, argues, the workplace is being transformed by networks that build from individual work teams through links across organizations:

> Network structures grow from within and eventually extend beyond the boundaries of traditional organizational structures. . . . The whole organization becomes a network of working teams. In turn, the organization is a member of a network made up of other organizations that are its suppliers, customers, regulators, and financial backers.[19]

As a result, jobs are being redefined by the requirements for greater coordination, both within and outside the enterprise. The core corporation is itself a network linking strategic insight at the center to more autonomous points on the periphery that are in turn connected to other networks.[20] The critical tasks of the network involve the exchange and processing of information, creating a new set of critical skills and increasing the services component of total output. Robert Reich makes this point:

> In such global webs, products are international composites. What is traded between nations is less often finished products than specialized problem-solving (research, product design, fabrication), problem-identifying (marketing, advertising, customer consulting), and brokerage (financing, searching, contracting) services, as well as certain routine components and services, all of which are combined to create value.[21]

The new networks extend beyond the traditional exchange of goods and services across enterprises to include expanding cooperation in R&D.[22] The number of interlocking research agreements among corporations in the information technology industry has been exploding over the last decade. Separate clusters of arrangements across information technology firms are dominated by regional groups of Japanese, European, and U.S. companies, although the linkages also extend across regions.[23] This same transfer of technology across horizontally linked Japanese firms goes beyond the traditional *keiretsu*, or business group structure. Ken-ichi Imai calls the new configurations "network industrial organizations" to emphasize the central role given to creating and exchanging information in such enterprises.[24]

Although the use of the term *network* is widespread, its precise meaning varies in applications across fields from electronics to sociology. In a sense, everything is "networked" to everything else: more precision is needed to make the concept useful. Shumpei Kumon has provided the most precise formulation to date by classifying social systems according to the dominant form of interaction among actors in the system, which he divides into three categories: threat-coercion, exchange-exploitation, and consensus-inducement. In this framework the nation-state is an organization dominated by a threat-coercion orientation based on international law; the modern industrial organization based on property rights would be in the exchange-exploitation category; and organizations featuring consensus-inducement relationships based on information rights would be "modern network organizations." The new organizations evolve from the growing importance of shared information:

> The sharing of information and knowledge—about recognition and evaluation of facts, the setting of goals, and action to achieve those goals—is the prime concern of networks in general and network organizations in particular.[25]

Kumon has identified the key aspect of the new network relationships: the critical importance of communications flows. Of course, multinational firms have existed for a long time, but the essential difference is that the new network arrangements are not based on the ownership of subsidiaries in a hierarchical structure, nor on the arms-length impersonal interaction of the market, but on shifting patterns of personal interaction across firms based on information exchange. As a result the key players in the new system are the strategic brokers who are constantly creating and editing global networks. Vertically structured, hierarchical firms, with clear divisions of responsibility across different corporate levels and a top-down centralized information flow, are being overwhelmed by new organizations structured around a more horizontal flow of information within and across traditional corporate boundaries. These network industrial firms are winning the information technology competition.

Individual firms cannot afford the enormous costs nor bear the high risks of remaining at the cutting edge of all the technologies that are integrated in new products, but they also cannot miss a breakthrough that could create whole new product lines. Sharing proprietary information has enormous risks, but the risks of isolation from new technologies may be even greater. Network structures permit the development of trust needed for balancing exchanges over an extended period without the inflexibility that creeps into hierarchical organizations.

The emergence of global networks provides a clear challenge to traditional ways of thinking about national strategy. If firms are no longer national champions whose profits are closely tied to national markets but brokers linked in global networks, the pursuit of national economic interests through the support of "national" firms becomes problematic. If the exchange of value occurs by electronic transmission rather than the transfer of products, traditional commercial policies may be less important than policies that influence the location of network nodes. The new network structures are changing the organizing principles for the analysis of power. Albert Bressand makes this point:

> In such an environment, power will tend to reside in the capacity to influence interconnection and access rather than in the capacity

to enforce borders, a change that obviously is not confined to the economy but has deep repercussions for the national and international society.[26]

From this network perspective, national strategy will depend less on confrontation with opponents and more on the art of cooperation with competitors. National neomercantilist policies that attempt to shield "national" firms from "international" competition might simply isolate domestic workers from the high-value jobs available through global networks.

Network Nodes. How can public policy influence patterns of network "interconnection and access"? Global networks are transforming politics and economics by altering the national identity of products, technologies, corporations, and industries.[27] As a result, international competition will increasingly depend on the relative competence of the one resource that does not flow freely across borders in international markets—people. In Reich's terminology "high-value" businesses, based on specialized problem-solving skills provided by "symbolic analysts," are needed to ensure competitive advantage against "high-volume" foreign firms, because it is not products but skills that are traded in the global webs.[28] One dimension of national strategy must address the education of a labor force with the skills needed in the global economy. From a network perspective, labor with the appropriate skills will create network nodes of high-income activities.

Other factors are also important in capturing high-value network activities, and a substantial literature emphasizes the multiple sources of stability of regional network nodes.[29] For example, Michael Porter shows that data on 10 nations and over 100 industries indicate that leading industrial firms have stable ties to specialized regions. Porter argues persuasively that successful firms become masters of their "value systems," which include the firm's suppliers, distributors, and customers. Operating from a "home base" where the firm defines its strategy, develops its core products and process technologies, and maintains its most sophisticated production, the global firm reaches out through a "global network" of activities. The location of the home base is determined by a "national diamond" composed of factor conditions, demand conditions, related and supporting industries, and firm strategy, structure, and rivalry.[30] Porter's analysis correctly focuses on the new reality that competitive advantage lies not in the nation's endowment of resources, but in the pressure the environment places on the firm to invest and innovate. Sustainable competitive advantage in high-value products and technologies comes from the creation of "advanced" factors—such as communications infrastructure, graduate engineers, and research institutes—and "specialized" factors that are tailored for use in particular industries. The private sector creates those factors in response to constantly shifting international standards.[31]

Network nodes, then, depend on labor skills that evolve in a broader context of factor creation driven by education and training systems, public and private R&D, adaptation of innovations into commercially successful processes and products, and an environment of supporting services. National characteristics such as social and political stability, the definition of property rights, the structure of factor, product, and financial markets, labor-management relationships, the science and technical infrastructure, the education system, and attitudes toward innovation, all constrain a nation's approaches to factor creation and thus limit the industries in which the nation can successfully compete. Within that national environment, the complex processes of innovation and factor creation help to determine the structure of industry competitive advantage and hence the rate of productivity growth.

The synergies among the determinants of competitive advantage produce advantages to industrial concentration that cause the structure of competitive advantage, and hence the location of network nodes, to persist over time. The processes of concentration are "path-dependent" in the sense that early events change costs of future production, so network nodes tend to endure. A textile mill, for example, might be located on any of several different rivers in a region, but after the first mill is established, others might gain significant cost advantages from locating on the same river. Transitory advantages become locked into particular regions through the development of a pool of specialized labor, supporting trade and services, and the sharing of technological ideas.[32] The most spectacular current examples of concentration are in the industries that trade services, such as Hartford's insurance, Chicago's futures trading, entertainment in Los Angeles, and even Silicon Valley and Route 128, which are more centers for technological services than of production.[33] Improved communications and the reduction in transportation costs and trade barriers that have facilitated global markets have arguably increased the importance of these regional concentrations, because firms can leverage their local competitive advantages into wider and wider markets.[34]

The persistence of network nodes, or home bases, suggests a potential for strategy to influence the location of economic activity despite the prevalence of globalization. Regional distinctions persist in part because global firms must operate from and sustain large positions in their home markets. Moreover, despite the globalization of wholesale finance, regional differences in capital costs persist, perhaps because retail banking practices differ and exchange rate risks vary across regions. As a result, trade and technology policy differences sustain separable regions centered on the United States, Europe, and Japan, in which the rate of intraregional trade is growing faster than interregional trade.[35]

This analysis of the factors that influence the location of network nodes suggests a potential role for national or regional "strategic trade" policies to gain market share, lower production costs, and alter competitive advantage.[36] Japanese encouragement of the semiconductor industry might provide an example of success with such a policy. European subsidies have allowed Airbus to achieve a growing share of the commercial aircraft market, although it is not yet clear that Airbus will ever be profitable without the subsidies. At this point the evidence suggests that the short-term gains from government intervention in noncompetitive markets remain small.[37] Nonetheless, the strategic trade arguments make the superiority of free markets, particularly in high-technology areas, an empirical rather than a purely theoretical issue. Moreover, when the strategic trade arguments are linked with technology policies the dynamic impacts could be significant.

Competing technological policies across regions provide a potential realm for strategic efforts to capture network nodes, particularly in industries with broad impacts on other industrial sectors. If innovation and the creation of advanced and specialized factors are the keys to competitive advantage, many analysts argue that government assistance to promote innovation and factor creation might be in order. The central problem with such assistance is that market competition provides the driving force for innovation and creativity geared to commercial applications, and without that market test it is difficult to assess the future returns to government programs. Government intervention might, however, be useful if it is geared to correcting market failures, such as the private sector's reluctance to pursue projects not all of whose benefits can be appropriated by the firm. For example, if the project benefits all companies in an industry equally, no single company may have sufficient incentive to pursue the investment. In addition, the scale of some forms of R&D and the risks of failure to produce productive innovations may be so high that the private sector cannot pursue projects for which public benefits may outweigh public costs. Although there are clear theoretical justifications for some government support of innovation and factor creation, the precise level and form of that intervention remain controversial, and differing policies across various nations remain a source of friction. Writing on "national systems of innovation" has emphasized the justifications for alternative approaches to innovation across regions, although there is controversy over whether or not national borders are still important given the structure of internationally networked technology markets.[38]

The strategic trade and technology arguments become more persuasive when they are combined, because it is conceivable that a strategy for capturing critical technologies through strategic trade policies could have large dynamic effects. Some argue that there are strategic industries with large, long-term impacts on other sectors; that capturing them requires domestic production of components as well as products (semiconductors as well as computers); that technological development is path-dependent so you cannot just jump in at the next technological level; and that while the short-run gains from strategic trade policies are small, their long-term impact by capturing strategic technologies may be very large.[39] Those arguments provide a foundation for the use of government policy to attract and defend regional network nodes containing high-value activities with the potential for influencing long-term technological patterns. John Zysman correctly identifies technology policy and the regional competition for strategic industries as central issues for national strategy:

> Individually the components of a policy of technological development are already difficult international issues—intellectual property and anti-dumping or subsidy policies are examples—but when taken together as a matter of how to generate and retain advantage in technologies and industries on which future development will rest they are the basis of real conflict amongst the three regions of the Western economy.[40]

In sum, convergence in economic performance among the major economic powers does not mean that the United States is destined to fall behind new industrial leaders, but it does mean that future competition will occur on a more equal footing. That competition will center on efforts to capture the nodes of global networks that have resulted from the revolution in information technology. Earlier

U.S. advantages from an abundance of natural resources, a large integrated national economy that permitted mass production, and then a large lead in science-based R&D, have faded. In the new competition for network nodes, the United States will have to rely on other sources of competitive advantage by promoting the creation of the advanced and specialized factors valued in emerging global networks. The tactics to be used in the competition remain controversial, but the evidence is that the competition is already well under way and that it will focus on attempts to capture nodes of high-value activities in the context of global networks. As a result national strategy must reconcile cooperation in building global networks with the competition for network nodes.

Cooperative Competition

Theodore Moran argues that the United States is in decline but that the process is reversible, and that there are two competing grand strategies for achieving this: "sophisticated neomercantilism" and "transnational integration." Sophisticated neomercantilism would include managed trade to ensure market share for "national" firms in critical industries and swift reprisals against unilaterally defined unfair practices in U.S. markets, such as dumping goods below the cost of production or foreign subsidies for exports. Foreign investment in the United States would be carefully reviewed, public investment funds would be targeted on "national" champions, and transborder corporate alliances would be scrutinized to ensure U.S. firms could sustain favorable market positions.

The cluster of policies aimed at transnational integration, on the other hand, would feature trade liberalization along multilateral lines, generally open investment policies with performance requirements to enmesh foreign firms in the U.S. industrial base, the use of R&D credits for both domestic and foreign firms to promote the development of critical technologies, and a general presumption in favor of global alliances. In Moran's view the ultimate choice of a grand strategy depends not only on technical assessments of the effectiveness of the different policy components but also on an evaluation of the international repercussions of the regional confrontation implicit in the sophisticated neomercantilist approach and of the burdens of international leadership implicit in the transnational integration approach. He correctly notes that the appeal of the transnational integration strategy would be enhanced if U.S. budget deficits were reduced and the macroeconomic house were in better order.[41]

Although Moran overstates the extent of U.S. decline, his presentation of the two alternatives for grand strategy is compelling. The cluster of policies he calls "transnational integration" comes very close to what I have defined as "cooperative competition." Cooperative competition is superior to sophisticated neomercantilism on many counts. In the context of global networks that are increasingly the source of dynamic technological change, the economic risks of isolation implicit in sophisticated neomercantilism are enormous. Moreover, the sophisticated neomercantilist approach is inconsistent with the nature of the broader political and military challenges national strategy must also address, including arms proliferation, internal wars, the AIDS epidemic, environmental decay, drug traffic, and humanitarian relief efforts. The complexity of those challenges, and the limitations of national resources and approaches for dealing with them, mean that cooperation in political and security networks will be essential. The idea of networks is relevant here because of the increasing importance of the coordination of information flows in dealing with those sophisticated problems and because the precise set of countries willing to cooperate on a given issue will vary over time. As a result, international organizations will require greater flexibility in organizing themselves for specific tasks. Global political and security networks will perform the same kinds of functions as economic networks, providing an infrastructure that will enhance cooperation and constrain the nature of competition. From that perspective neomercantilism, sophisticated or otherwise, would constitute a set of economic policies that are inconsistent with the broader requirements of grand strategy.

Convergence in the economic performance of the three leading economic regions and the emergence of global networks underscore the importance of cooperative competition. Cooperation across those regions will be essential to avoid confrontations over the location of network nodes that could undermine the advantages of global networks. A narrow focus on "relative" U.S. economic performance might well miss the point that the level of economic well-being increasingly depends on the ability to operate in integrated world networks. Although it may well be possible to influence the location of network nodes, the form of the competition must be consistent with the need to cooperate in constructing and sustaining global political, security, and economic networks. In contrast to the zero-sum nature of cold war military confrontation with clear winners and losers, the creation of cooperative global networks is a non-zero-sum exercise in which all competitors can gain, albeit to differing degrees. In short, in the new environment the "competitive state" must promote cooperative competition.

The essence of the cold war strategy was economic and political isolation of the Soviet Union, bilateral nuclear deterrence, forward deployment of U.S. forces in standing alliances based on containment, economic and technological leadership by U.S.-dominated multinational firms, and catch-up growth in Europe and Japan. The new strategy of cooperative competition would be defined more in terms of networks of information flows among equals that provide for enhanced cooperation on technological developments and potential responses to international crises in a framework of shifting ad hoc coalitions and intense economic competition.

More broadly, the strategy of cooperative competition recognizes the key role of technological innovation and economic growth in meeting broad national goals, including internal well-being as well as external security. The economic dimension of the strategy stresses the reality that while the United States and its allies are building an international infrastructure that will improve the well-being of all the participants, they will still be competing with each other for markets. Although the United States needs to cooperate in providing the essential public goods that make international markets operate effectively and permit the mobilization of resources in response to common interests, it also needs to ensure that domestic firms are not disadvantaged in those markets.

Implications of Cooperative Competition

Cooperation. In the post–cold war era, the legitimacy for international action will increasingly derive less from narrowly defined security interests and more from international consensus on common approaches to key global problems such as the environment, the AIDS epidemic, drugs, the proliferation of weapons of mass destruction, the destabilizing consequences of internal wars, and humanitarian relief efforts. The complex problems of economic restructuring and defense conversion in the states of the former Soviet Union, "ethnic cleansing" in Yugoslavia, and starvation in Somalia suggest the scope of problems that will clearly be beyond the resources of any great power, including the United States. Cooperative international networks that can develop consensus and coordinate responses will be essential in dealing with those challenges. Local and regional political factors will inevitably change the coalition of potential actors in any given instance, so the international networks must be flexible enough to accommodate a changing cast of players in each instance. International burden sharing will then be measured in national contributions not to any one effort, but to the longer-term record of cooperation and commitment of resources in those instances permitted by unique national conditions.

The strategy of the United States, then, would be to play the role of strategic broker, forming, sustaining, and adjusting international networks to meet a sophisticated array of challenges. Charles Kindleberger stresses the importance of U.S. leadership in providing the essential public goods of what might be defined as network creation and maintenance.[42] Others lament the passing of U.S hegemony and the absence of a new hegemon that could take on these burdens, although coordination among a small group of states might provide those public goods as the relative U.S. position declines.[43] U.S. leadership should be focused on creating networks that will allow coalitions to act in concert because in the new global environment unilateral actions will be increasingly ineffective. Although the relative U.S. economic position has declined, it remains the only superpower and it still brings a unique array of advantages to the task of strategic broker, including economic influence, strategic military mobility, advanced communications, ethnic diversity, political stability, a strong democratic tradition, diplomatic alliances, and an established record of assuming an impressive share of the burdens of international responsibility. In short, U.S. strategy would be to help forge an array of international networks that would permit the international community to act in concert without the United States itself being forced to commit a disproportionate share of resources.

Ironically, from this perspective organizations such as the North Atlantic Treaty Organization (NATO) that now appear to some analysts as cold war relics are actually invaluable international networks for coordinating common responses in a host of situations. NATO provides precisely the kind of command, control, communications, intelligence, and logistics networks required for cooperative security or humanitarian efforts. Whether that particular organization will be the instrument for intervention is less important than the network relationships that will make cooperative efforts more feasible and efficient. Although NATO played a relatively minor direct role in Desert Shield and Desert Storm as an organization, the political and military networks it helped create were invaluable. Cooperative regimes on nonproliferation, the United Nations, the General Agreement on Tariffs and Trade (GATT), the World Bank, the International Monetary Fund, and other similar organizations provide established networks in which the United States has enormous influence and through which it can pursue cooperative competition. This does not suggest a surrender of U.S. sovereignty to international organizations: regional competition will remain intense and the United States has important regional interests. It does, however, imply that U.S. strategy should seek to extend leverage through cooperation in international organizations to shape and restrain the form of regional competition.

Competitiveness. Cooperative competition underscores the importance of economic strength as the foundation of national strategy, and economic strength depends on sustaining high and growing levels of productivity among U.S workers in the face of intense international competition. Despite the short-term dislocations of international integration, the United States should welcome the competition because it will induce the creation of the specialized and advanced factors of production needed for competitive advantage. Indeed, international networks will channel information, technology, and resources to those economies that provide the best home bases for each industrial sector. The key issue then is how each region is positioned for success in the home base competition, and what ground rules will be followed in competitive trade, industrial, and technology policies.

Virtually all analysts begin with the need for reform of education as a first step in improving U.S. competitiveness.[44] Next comes lowering the cost of capital through increased national savings, deficit reduction, and tax incentives for productive investment. The solutions here seem clear, although the short-run political problems will be enormous.

The next tier of potential reforms deals with coordination of strategic trade, industrial, and technology policies that are more controversial, particularly when they involve replacing market forces in picking the winners of the future. Policies toward particular industries can easily be distorted by special interests, and the record of industrial policies in other countries has been mixed at best.[45] The global network framework also makes it difficult to define national firms or to anticipate the full ramifications of any purely domestic policy. The approaches with the most promise, like education reform, deal with the processes of innovation and factor creation at a level above individual industries, focusing on compensation for market failures and emphasizing the need for competition within global networks. Instead of attempting to block the operation of global networks, effective strategy should center on steps to enhance efficiency within the new global structures.

Consensus is growing on two points that can enhance U.S. competitiveness in this new environment. First, government policies in a wide variety of areas—from health care, to the environment, to product safety, to antitrust, and a host of others—do affect productivity and hence competitiveness, but these policies are not centrally coordinated so as to assess those consequences. The role of national strategy is precisely to highlight the impact of policies on issues with the highest national interest and to force coordination and an assessment of trade-offs within that strategic context. That function should now be performed by the newly organized National Economic Council.[46]

Second, looking across the continuum of trade, industrial, and technology policies, the latter appear to offer the most fruitful areas for strategic review. The international trade framework is established in the GATT process, and although progress on the tough issues of agriculture and international property rights has been slow and painful, there is at least consensus on what constitutes "sin" in the trade area even if states have not yet agreed to sin no more. Regional progress and pressure through the North American Free Trade Agreement (NAFTA) should provide additional pressure within GATT to help open regional markets.[47] Similarly, industrial policies targeted on specific industries do not look any more promising now than they have for the last decade. In the contest between bureaucrats and the market in picking the winners of the future, the market appears to be the clear winner.[48]

Technology policies, however, at least warrant careful review as strategic instruments for several reasons. First, the reduction in defense research, development, and procurement means that the de facto technology policy of the United States is changing in important ways, and its government will need to decide if technology programs should be supported more explicitly.[49] Second, the interaction between government laboratories, research universities, and the private sector can have important synergies if it is tied to reaction to market forces, particularly at the level of "pre-competitive research" where there are applications in several industries.[50] New steps to integrate government laboratories with the private sector may suggest future patterns of cooperation. Third, focus on the innovation climate in general, rather than the promotion of specific technologies, provides the potential for enhancing productivity growth with the least downside risk. Policies such as tax incentives to encourage factor creation most closely match the results of research on the development of home bases for competitive advantage, and they are somewhat less susceptible than commercial or industrial policies to political pressure from particular interests.

Conclusion

Cooperative competition is a strategic framework for examining options, not a list of specific policy proposals. It does not propose a new world order in the sense of a desired set of outcomes or a fixed set of institutional relationships. Instead, it recognizes that international networks are an integral part of the new economic and political environment and that their structure will be modified by the strategic brokers of the future. The network perspective provides a flexible format for viewing emerging global regions that have less to do with geographic distinctions than with shifting patterns of interconnection.

Convergence and global networks have changed the economic landscape just as the end of the Cold War has changed the political and military environment. Regional competition for the home bases of global networks poses a challenge for U.S. strategy, and there is a real risk that the competition may erode the international institutions needed to deal with pressing global problems. Without those institutions, the United States will be severely constrained in pursuing its national interests, but the nation is also in an excellent position to influence events through those organizations. Cooperative competition recognizes that cooperation in building international networks and intense competition in the marketplace are not alternatives, they are two sides of the same strategy.

I am indebted to several of my colleagues in the Department of Social Sciences at West Point, particularly Joseph Collins, Michael Meese, Thomas Lynch, and Asa Clark, for their comments on drafts of this manuscript, although they have no responsibility for the remaining errors, which are mine alone. The ideas expressed here are solely those of the author and do not purport to represent the official position of the U.S. Military Academy, the Department of the Army, or the Department of Defense.

Notes

1. I am not defining these regions by geographical borders but as integrated economic networks. In particular, "Japan" as used here does not refer to the nation-state but to the broader network of investment, production, and technological standards that is anchored in Japan but extends into other parts of Asia.

2. William W. Kaufman and John D. Steinbruner argue in *Decisions for Defense: Prospects for a New Order* (Washington, D.C.: The Brookings Institution, 1991) for "cooperative" security, based on collective arrangements and arms-control agreements, as a replacement for the strategy of deterrence and containment. I do not favor rigid collective security arrangements with automatic triggers, but I propose a cooperative framework for reaching agreement on specific interventions. The framework would include a prior coordination of plans, capabilities, and interoperability that I would describe as a network. I would stress an architecture that provides for flexible coalitions, and I would emphasize the competitive aspects of the strategy as well as the cooperative elements.

3. Samuel P. Huntington calls for an integration of Franklin Roosevelt's welfare state with Harry Truman's national security state in the form of a new competitive state ("Advice for a Democratic President: The Economic Renewal of America," *National Interest*, no. 26 [Spring 1992], p. 17). As discussed later in this paper, I generally agree with that formulation, but I would stress the broader cooperative framework for that competition.

4. U.S. National Security Council Staff, *National Security Strategy of the United States* (Washington, D.C.: GPO, August 1991), p. 3.

5. Daniel J. Kaufman, David S. Clark, and Kevin P. Sheehan, *U.S. National Security Strategy for the 1990s* (Baltimore, Md.: The Johns Hopkins University Press, 1991), p. 5.

6. National strategy at this level is sometimes called "grand strategy." For example, see Edward Mead Earle, "Introduction," in Earle, ed., *Makers of Modern Strategy* (Princeton, N.J.: Princeton University Press, 1971). Earle argues on p. viii that "strategy is the art of controlling and utilizing the resources of a nation—or a coalition of nations—including its armed forces, to the end that its vital interests shall be effectively promoted and secured against enemies, actual, potential, or merely presumed," and he goes on to identify this highest form of strategy as "grand strategy." The term "grand strategy" is often associated with the level of wartime mobilization during World War II.

7. Huntington, "Advice for a Democratic President," p. 17.

8. Paul Kennedy, *The Rise and Fall of the Great Powers* (New York: Random House, 1987).

9. McKinsey Global Institute et al., *Service Sector Productivity* (Washington, D.C., October 1992), chap. 1, exhibit 1–4, between pp. 2 and 3.

10. Jeffrey G. Williamson, "Productivity and American Leadership: A Review Article," *Journal of Economic Literature* 29 (March 1991), pp. 51–68.

11. Samuel P. Huntington, "The U.S.—Decline or Renewal?" *Foreign Affairs* 67 (Winter 1988/89), p. 88.

12. Charles Steindel, "Manufacturing Productivity and High Tech Investment," *Federal Reserve Bank of New York Quarterly Review* 17 (Summer 1992), pp. 38–40.

13. McKinsey Global Institute, *Service Sector Productivity*, chap. 1, exhibit 1–3, between pp. 2 and 3.

14. Williamson, "Productivity and American Leadership," pp. 59–60.

15. Richard R. Nelson and Gavin Wright, "The Rise and Fall of American Technological Leadership: The Post-War Era in Historical Perspective," *Journal of Economic Literature* 30 (December 1992), p. 1955.

16. Alexander Gerschenkron, *Economic Backwardness in Historical Perspective* (Cambridge, Mass.: Harvard University Press, 1962).

17. Gavin Wright, "The Origins of America's Industrial Success, 1879–1940," *American Economic Review* 80 (September 1990), p. 665.

18. Nelson and Wright, "The Rise and Fall of American Technological Leadership," p. 1955.

19. Anthony Patrick Carnevale, *America and the New Economy: How Competitive Standards Are Radically Changing American Workplaces* (San Francisco, Calif.: Jossey-Bass Publishers, 1991), p. 86.

20. Robert B. Reich, *The Work of Nations: Preparing Ourselves for 21st Century Capitalism* (New York: Alfred A. Knopf, 1991), pp. 95–96.

21. *Ibid.*, p. 113.

22. Albert Bressand, "European Integration: From the System Paradigm to Network Analysis," *International Spectator* 24 (January–March 1989), p. 24.

23. John Hagedoorn and Jos Schakenraad, "Leading Companies and Networks of Strategic Alliances in Information Technologies," *Research Policy* 21, no. 2 (1992), pp. 163–190.

24. Ken-ichi Imai, "Japan's Corporate Networks," in Shumpei Kumon and Henry Rosovsky, eds., *The Political Economy of Japan*, vol. 3, *Cultural and Social Dynamics* (Stanford, Calif.: Stanford University Press, 1992), p. 220.

25. Shumpei Kumon, "Japan as a Network Society," in Kumon and Rosovsky, *Political Economy of Japan*, p. 128.

26. Bressand, "European Integration," p. 26.

27. Reich, *Work of Nations*, p. 3.

28. *Ibid.*, pp. 83, 113.

29. For more details on particular network nodes, see AnnaLee Saxenian, "The Origins and Dynamics of Production Networks in Silicon Valley," *Research Policy* 20, no. 5 (1991), pp. 423–437; A. J. Scott, "The Aerospace-Electronics Industrial Complex of Southern California: The Formative Years, 1940–1960," *Research Policy* 20, no. 5 (1991), pp. 439–456; N. Dorfman, "Route 128: The Development of a Regional High Technology Economy," *Research Policy* 12, no. 4 (1983), pp. 299–316; and Patrizio Bianchi and Nicola Bellini, "Public Policies for Local Networks of Innovators," *Research Policy* 20, no. 5 (1991), pp. 487–497.

30. Michael E. Porter, *The Competitive Advantage of Nations* (New York: Free Press, 1990), pp. 42, 54–55, 71–72.

31. *Ibid.*, pp. 77–80.

32. Paul Krugman, *Geography and Trade* (Cambridge, Mass.: MIT Press, 1991), pp. 36–38.

33. *Ibid.*, p. 66.

34. Michael J. Enright, "The Geographic Scope of Competitive Advantage" (Paper presented at the Association of Students of Geography of Utrecht [VUGS] Conference, Utrecht, Netherlands, October 1992), p. 25. This paper will appear in *Netherlands Geographic Studies* (forthcoming).

35. John Zysman with Laura Tyson, Giovanni Dosi, and Stephen Cohen, "Trade, Technology, and National Competition," in Enrico Deiaco, Erik Hornell, and Graham Vickery, eds., *Technology and Investment: Crucial Issues for the 1990s* (London: Pinter Publishers, 1990), pp. 198–199.

36. See, for example, Paul Krugman, *Rethinking International Trade* (Cambridge, Mass.: MIT Press, 1990); Elhanan Helpman and Razin Assaf, *International Trade and Trade Policy* (Cambridge, Mass.: MIT Press, 1991); and Elhanan Helpman and Paul Krugman, *Trade Policy and Market Structure* (Cambridge, Mass.: MIT Press, 1989).

37. Helpman and Krugman, *Trade Policy and Market Structure*, p. 178.

38. For a more complete development of the idea of a national system of innovation, see Christopher Freeman, "Japan: A New National System of Innovation?" in Giovanni Dosi et al., eds., *Technical Change and Economic Theory* (London: Francis Pinter, 1988), pp. 330–348, and David Mowery, "The U.S. National Innovation System: Origins and Prospects for Change," *Research Policy* 21, no. 2 (1992), pp. 125–144.

39. Zysman, "Trade, Technology, and National Competition," pp. 185–211. For a similar line of argument, see Organization for Economic Cooperation and Development, *Technology in a Changing World*, The Technology/Economy Programme (Paris: OECD, 1991), pp. 86–93.

40. Zysman, "Trade, Technology, and National Competition," p. 185.

41. Theodore H. Moran, *American Economic Policy and National Security* (New York: Council on Foreign Relations Press, 1993), pp. 74–81.

42. Charles Kindleberger, "Dominance and Leadership in the International Economy," *International Studies Quarterly* 25 (June 1981), pp. 242–254.

43. Duncan Snidal, "The Limits of Hegemonic Stability Theory," *International Organization* 39 (Autumn 1985), pp. 579–614.

44. Although the nature of that educational reform lies well beyond the scope of this analysis, I might note in passing that the structure of modern network organizations suggests a new framework for horizontally organized educational networks linked by information technologies.

45. For an excellent analysis of the limitations of targeted industrial policies in Japan and the Ministry of International Trade and Industry's new limited role, which is restricted primarily to the research level, see Yasusuke Murakami and Thomas P. Rohlen, "Social Exchange Aspects of Japanese Political Economy," in Kumon and Rosovsky, *Political Economy of Japan*, pp. 91–100.

46. Several authors have recognized the need for a new council to perform this function. See, for example, Huntington, "Advice for a Democratic President," p. 17.

47. For an excellent short summary of the relationship between NAFTA and GATT see Anne O. Krueger, "Government, Trade, and Economic Integration," *American Economic Review* 82, *Papers and Proceedings* (May 1992), pp. 109–114.

48. For a similar assessment see Michael L. Dertouzos, Richard K. Lester, Robert N. Solow, and the MIT Commission on Productivity Growth, *Made in America: Regaining the Productivity Edge* (Cambridge, Mass.: MIT Press, 1989), p. 109.

49. For an argument that greater horizontal coordination across public and private organizations is needed in R&D, standardization, education, and training, see *ibid.*, p. 105. That coordination has been improving. For a summary of recent policies in this area, see Carnegie Commission on Science, Technology, and Government, *Science and Technology in US International Affairs* (New York, January 1992), and U.S. Federal Coordinating Council for Science, Engineering, and Technology, Office of Science and Technology Policy, *Grand Challenges 1993: High Performance Computing and Communications, The FY 1993 U.S. Research and Development Program*, A Report by the Committee on Physical, Mathematical, and Engineering Sciences (Washington, D.C.: Office of Science and Technology Policy, 1992).

50. See, for example, Lewis M. Branscomb, "Does America Need a Technology Policy?" *Harvard Business Review* 70 (March–April 1992), pp. 25, 30.

Modular Multilateralism: North–South Economic Relations in the 1990s

Richard E. Feinberg and Delia M. Boylan

THE DISINTEGRATION OF the former socialist bloc has sparked a burst of optimism regarding East–West relations. But as politicians, businesspeople, and travelers alike rush to decode the East European mystique, few have pondered the future of the ties between industrialized nations and the South. When the subject is treated at all, predictions forecast benign neglect at best. In the absence of a Soviet threat, many doubt that Northern nations—particularly the United States—will take an active interest in developing countries. This paper argues differently: bipolarity's demise will allow the long-dormant seed of North–South cooperation to germinate as previously stymied North–South alliances emerge to forge solutions to common problems. But germination requires that the North *cultivate* such cooperative arrangements. The alternative is the risk of commercial, environmental, and security setbacks.

Clearly, the North and South are strongly linked through a variety of economic, cultural, and philanthropic connections. At the same time, as market forces in the South shake off their statist past, developing nations will increasingly seek, and be granted, seats at the international bargaining table. Moreover, the declining economic position of the United States makes multilateralism both a necessary and a feasible objective—necessary because often the United States will be unable to impose solutions unilaterally and feasible because such a backdrop of structural and ideological convergence will enable leaders in countries of both North and South to identify and act on areas of joint concern.

But even in the wake of such centripetal forces, smooth interaction will continue to be checked by the complexities and differences both between and within the two poles. An increasingly varied set of issues governs North–South relations, ranging from the core of trade, finance, and development strategies to the more uncharted areas such as ecology and human rights. Moreover, the tremendous upsurge and variety of non-state actors—nongovernmental organiza-

---

Richard E. Feinberg is executive vice president and director of studies at the Overseas Development Council (ODC). Among his books is *The Intemperate Zone: The Third World Challenge to U.S. Foreign Policy* (New York: Norton, 1983). Delia M. Boylan, former staff associate at the ODC, is currently pursuing her doctorate in political science at Stanford University.

tions (NGOs), international banks, transnational corporations, and think tanks—render the international arena a veritable mélange of assorted players.

At the same time, the developing world is far from uniform (witness the enormous disparity between the economic success of the rapidly developing states of East Asia and the dire straits of some countries in Sub-Saharan Africa). Despite trends toward liberalizing reforms, some of the countries in the South that are less well off will inevitably remain spectators, looking on as their neighbors progress.

Modular Multilateralism

What is needed, then, is a framework, both theoretical and applied, through which to view North–South relations, one that capitalizes on cooperation where common ground can be achieved but that does not ignore the complexities. The approach presented here—modular multilateralism—is a pattern of decision making among groups of nations, North and South, that share a common problem and seek a coordinated agreement. It is *multilateral* in that it involves many players coming to the table at the same time, and *modular* in that the particular actors at the table at any one time will shift according to the issue at hand.

Modular multilateralism is offered as an elastic framework for understanding and shaping North–South cooperation in the sphere of economics. It assumes diversity among participants as well as variety among issues. These factors underscore the need for highly specific modules with regard to substance, scope, and time horizon. Although this approach recognizes differences in power as indeed central to such an analysis, it also suggests strategies to redress disparities in power. In particular, the argument underscores the role of multilateral institutions in fostering and maintaining cooperation among nations.

An increasing array of issues already exists within the North–South economic sphere to which the modular approach has been successfully applied. This suggests that the approach might prove useful in other circumstances as well. Modular multilateralism is, therefore, at once an *analytical* framework for looking at the structure of North–South relations, a *predictive* tool for projecting economic interaction between the United States and the developing world in the 1990s, and a *prescriptive* model for collective decision making. Most emphatically, this article will illustrate the prescriptive utility of modular multilateralism by employing it as a policy tool to organize a strategic approach to concrete issue areas.

This framework could well be applied to some aspects of North–North, North–East, or even South–South relations, but it is posited here as a particularly useful, and indeed proven, mode of interaction between those countries loosely defined as "industrialized" and as "developing," that is, between the North and the South. Among those nations, the modular concept limits the number of actors in active play and allows for variation among components within these multilateral clusters according to the issue and over time.

Indeed, issue specificity is at the heart of the working logic of modular multilateralism, because the nature of the issue under discussion will determine who—and how many—will be the key players in the modules. Modular scope may vary from a simple three-actor interaction to a more extended North–South regional pact. Issues will also influence the appropriate time frame, dictating whether the module should be a one-shot, ad hoc arrangement to solve a time-sensitive matter, or an ongoing, long-term regime that might bear institutional formation. As a prescriptive model, modular multilateralism emphasizes the importance of the latter—evident in the discussions below highlighting the shortfalls of the Brady Plan and the potentials of Bush's Enterprise for the Americas Initiative—because modular multilateralism as a policy tool provides a framework for renovating policymakers' perceptions and behavior in tackling common problems with farsighted, coordinated solutions.

Regarding the players invited to join the negotiating game, modular multilateralism expands conventional thinking beyond the traditional nation-state. Modular components may be drawn from the kaleidoscope of different departments and agencies that handle different issues in the U.S. government or from federated government bodies such as states, provinces, and even municipalities. A South–South example of such cross-national, interdepartmental cooperation is offered by the relationship between the finance ministers of Chile and Mexico. The suspicion that these two high-level technocrats are confidants is borne out by their countries' closely coordinated international economic policies (which in turn seek tighter ties with the United States). Moreover, the entire montage of non-state actors—corporations and banks, citizens' nongovernmental agencies, and even think tanks—can form transnational alliances with like-minded counterparts in other countries. There are numerous instances of industrial country donor agencies or labor federations working cooperatively with local service providers or unions in pursuit of common goals. It is premature, however, to organize policy around a post-nation-state paradigm, for the nation-state remains the single most important aggregator of interests and definer of policies.

Within the Southern Hemisphere itself, increasing differentiation among nations makes it nearly impossible to talk about "the South" as a unitary concept. Modular multilateralism not only recognizes such differences but indeed reflects them in its issue-specific orientation to problem solving: only those Southern countries relevant to a particular negotiating module will form part of it.

To address some issues, a clear-cut leader will need to be identified. This leader will often be the United States, given its residual hegemony in the international system, but this need not always be the case. At times, other industrialized countries such as Japan or members of the European Community may also assume this role. Indeed, it is possible that even developing countries may play a shaping role. In other instances, effective policy will require the concurrence of nearly all states to deal with issues of universal relevance. The modular multilateralist approach thus not only embraces multilateral institutions as helpful in holding together cooperative modules of Northern and Southern players, but also prescribes their vital role in coping with the complexities of U.S. relations with the developing world in the 1990s.

To compensate for the disparities in power relations that are a reality of the international system, the modular multilateralist framework also suggests a variety of strategies that developing countries can pursue to at least partially offset such inequalities. For example, the "collective bargainer" strategy unites clusters of nations behind a single position, voiced by one spokesperson for a given issue.

Moreover, in light of the fact that all Southern nations are not equally well positioned to take part in all modules, the creation of a global safety net is recommended to catch those least-fortunate actors who inevitably slip between the cracks. Compensatory financial and trade initiatives designed to help such countries participate profitably in the international economic regime will encourage their continued cooperative posture.

We need to look toward a new era in which countries of the North and South can form cooperative coalitions that regulate competition, restrain conflict, and often arrive at mutually advantageous outcomes. Modular multilateralism attempts to take us beyond bipolarity to establish a new framework, not only so that we may understand how things already are, but so that policymakers might adjust their thinking to capitalize on how they will be. If astutely handled, such an approach could come to govern the way in which countries of the North and South—specifically the United States and the developing world—interact in the years to come.

A World in Conflict

Not surprisingly, most analyses of North–South economic relations tend to focus on conflict. Poor states, the argument goes, will seek a set of arrangements from the international system by which to redress their resource deficiencies, whereas rich states will pursue a more competitive, market-oriented agenda. Certainly, if income levels are the determinant variable, then the disparities between industrial countries and the rest of the world are great enough to provoke tension. The average per capita annual income of industrialized countries exceeds $17,000. The 17 better-off (upper-middle-income) developing countries, comprised primarily of South and East European and oil-exporting nations, have a per capita gross national product (GNP) of $3,240. The 42 lowest-income countries have a per capita GNP of $320.[1] None of the 74 low-income developing countries has a per capita GNP exceeding $2,000.[2]

Such objective differences in standards of living will naturally translate into conflicting interests. Nations will, therefore, continue to butt heads over tariff structures, product standards, and access to commodity markets. Debtors will seek to reduce interest payments to commercial banks. Equatorial nations will ask temperate states to pay the costs of conserving rain forests. And, although the debate has narrowed somewhat, nations will still disagree on the appropriate functions of the state, especially regarding its role in industrial production, export promotion, and income redistribution. Indeed, the list of disagreements is almost as long as the number of interactions between North and South.

A case in point would be global warming and climate control, which illustrate the potential of modular multilateralism to organize a flexible policy approach to a thorny problem. At present, no international regime exists to address global climate change. Currently, greenhouse gases in the atmosphere are mainly due to past and present activities of the developed nations. The projected population and economic growth in the developing world, however, will cause the source of the greenhouse problem to shift rapidly. In light of this, if the developed world alone enters agreements and takes concrete steps toward halting global warming, these efforts could be offset over time by inaction in developing countries. By the year 2050, projected global warming without the latter's cooperation would be 40 percent higher than with it.

Global warming is thus a very real, if not yet mature, potential North–South divide; it is not the only one. On environmental as well as many other issues, however, disagreement on the whole need not preclude progress on the parts. Some issues may take more time to work through, and others—like global warming—will mandate creating new rules for the world community. Yet today more than at any time in recent history, there are both feasible solutions and powerful incentives to compromise on many of those issues that separate—and at the same time bind—North and South.

Development Strategies

The modular multilateral approach applies in each of three basic issue areas: development strategies, finance, and trade. In each of these areas, this essay will examine the nature of the modular formation, its relative benefits, and how policy could better be organized to take advantage of its workings, concluding with an example of modular multilateralism in action drawn from a recent policy initiative toward Latin America taken by the Bush administration.

As the developing world casts off its statist past, a de facto convergence has emerged among countries of the North and South on the measures necessary to attain an orderly economy. This convergence on policy objectives may be as wide-ranging as fiscal balance, monetary restraint, exchange rate competitiveness, trade openness, and governmental efficiency, as well as the positioning of social safety nets. It paves the way for like-minded countries of both North and South to work more harmoniously toward economic development. The formation of effective modules requires that Northern nations be particularly attuned to region- and country-specific needs, while also remaining open and willing to enter into productive multilateral partnerships.

Market Reforms. Throughout the South, governments are working to restructure their public sectors in order to gain financial solvency. These nations are slashing budget deficits, often by raising taxes, cutting capital expenditures, and reducing subsidies to state-owned enterprises. In some cases, governments are shedding functions more appropriate to the private sector. To better husband scarce public resources, many essential programs are being targeted to benefit only carefully defined social groups.

At the same time, public- and private-sector relations are being revamped in many nations. Although few Southern intellectuals advocate absolutely unfettered markets, and most reject the extreme social costs of Pinochet-style liberalization, most also recognize the efficiency of price mechanisms. Increasingly the private sector is seen as a dynamic engine of growth, and governments view private business as a partner rather than a threat.

To increase exports, many governments have devalued their currencies and offered other incentives to the export sector. Although the exact formula varies across cultures, most Southern governments pursue some variant of industrial policy in which export promotion plays a major role. Governments often seek to lure foreign investors—with their access to technology, capital, and markets—into targeted export industries.

... But No "End to History." We have not, however, reached the end of history: debates persist—both between and within North and South—over matters such as the exact role of the state, the optimal fiscal policy mix, and the speed and pacing of liberalization. Moreover, many remain skeptical about the central government's ability to promote growth and equity simultaneously and are concerned about the human consequences of some of the structural adjustment measures.[3]

Clearly, a convergence in thinking on what makes sound economic policy is an encouraging development; it does not, however, give the North free rein to advocate blanket free-market solutions without sufficient attention to detail. The developing countries have become increasingly differentiated. Some (notably in East Asia) forge ahead with rapid industrialization, competitive agriculture, and explosive export growth, while others (notably in Africa and in zones of prolonged regional conflict) have actually lost ground in the last two decades. Policy must take into account this variegated Southern landscape. The North's basic neoclassical growth paradigm may not always fit, and less ambitious "survival" strategies—emphasizing food security and other basic needs—may in some cases be more realistic.

Moreover, although the United States implements most policy on development strategies primarily through the multilateral lending agencies—the International Monetary Fund (IMF), the World Bank, and the regional development banks—it does not always work with them in policy formulation. The assertive style of some U.S. officials raises hackles among staff and representatives of other governments in the multilateral agencies. Particularly annoying have been U.S. threats to withhold funding if its preferences are not accommodated. The United States displayed much ambivalence toward genuine multilateralism in its policy toward lending to Eastern Europe and the Soviet Union. When reform began to gain momentum in Eastern Europe, the U.S. government initially restrained the World Bank from devoting more staff to studying the problems of socialist transition. In the resulting vacuum, the more forthcoming Europeans forged ahead on their own to establish a new European-dominated bank to lend to Eastern Europe, the European Bank for Reconstruction and Development (EBRD).

In sum, convergence between policymakers North and South has laid the groundwork for effective cooperative relationships. Most visible in the budding partnership between the United States and Mexico, these trends prepare fertile ground for various modular multilateral arrangements. Nonetheless, for such modules to coalesce, Northern players must take note of regional idiosyncracies in their dealings with the patchwork of Southern players. Above all, they must prove themselves not only able but willing to act within the multilateral agencies with a strategic perspective that reaches beyond short-term power maximization toward long-term institutional fortification.

Finance

Paradoxically, just at the moment when the South is knocking at the North's door to signal its willingness to participate in the global economy, its capacity to do so is being undermined by unstable commodity and international capital markets. Nonetheless, recent attempts by the U.S. government in conjunction with Japan and various Southern governments to enact a partial solution to this crisis demonstrate a creative modular multilateral approach to problem solving, one that attempts to overcome perhaps the most crippling of the North–South economic divides.

The Brady Plan: A Missed Opportunity. The bottom line in North–South economic relations is the net transfer of financial resources—new loans minus amortization and interest payments. As a result of the sharp rise in real interest rates in the 1980s, the decline in commercial bank lending, and the creditor-led debt strategy, the developing countries have had to pay considerably more in interest and amortization than they have been receiving in new loans. The net transfer of financial resources to the developing world, which amounted to a *positive* $29 billion as recently as 1982, had become a *negative* $34 billion by 1987; the 17 highly indebted nations suffered a debilitating $28 billion swing—from a positive $11 billion to a negative $17 billion.[4]

At the end of the 1980s, the United States government crafted a new strategy for dealing with debt in the developing countries commonly known as the Brady Plan. This plan essentially removed the weight of U.S. government power from the creditor cartel and instead encouraged debtors to cut back on debt service. The Brady Plan proposed that banks write off portions of their stock of debt and accept reductions in interest payments in return for official guarantees on portions of the remaining assets. The intention was to reduce the negative resource transfer and thereby improve prospects for successful economic reform and growth within the debtor nations.

While conceptually bold and politically daring, the Brady Plan suffers from several defects.[5] First, it is insufficiently multilateral in design and implementation. Prior to announcing the plan, the U.S. Treasury consulted closely with the Japanese Ministry of Finance but not with the Europeans. A second defect is inadequate differentiation among developing countries. Although the creditors always claim to employ flexible, case-by-case strategies, and the composition of the financial packages has varied among countries, most of the deals tend to resemble each other in critical respects.[6] Finally, the strategy lacks an adequate set of incentives and sanctions to assure timely participation by the commercial banks, especially in poorer countries where bank exposure and therefore interest is small. The U.S. Treasury has reportedly argued for tougher measures to gain compliance, but the Federal Reserve Board has balked at undue government intervention in private markets.

Yet despite these weaknesses, the Brady Plan offers more than a symbolic attempt to promote integration of the South into the global economic system. Its very implementation involved hammering out specific agreements among a variety of countries, developed and developing alike (in this case the United States, Japan, Mexico, Venezuela, the Philippines, Costa Rica, Uruguay, and Morocco, with the assistance of multilateral agencies and some limited support from Western Europe). Ultimately, the United States failed to bring these disparate elements together in a long-term coordinating committee made up of international financial institutions, key creditors, and representative debtors. If successful, such a coalition would have legitimized the process, speeded and broadened its implementation, and facilitated cooperation from commercial banks to raise additional collateral as necessary. In theory, therefore, the Brady Plan had the potential to reach a working compromise through the modular multilateral framework, but in practice it became a missed opportunity.

Trade Policy

Trade policy offers dynamic illustrations of the modular multilateral system. Whether subsumed within the "globalist" General Agreement on Tariffs and Trade (GATT) framework, incorporated into bilateral policy, or contained within emerging modular arrangements, U.S. trade interests increasingly result in a differentiated policy that encourages the formation of North–South coalitions. But if the United States continues to pursue multiple-level trade relationships with developing countries, it may need to consider appropriate institutional channels to ensure smooth and coordinated implementation.

Inside GATT. Even as some industrial nations grow skeptical of the GATT system, developing nations have belatedly embraced it as the best protector of the weak in an age of incessant protectionist pressures. GATT is a rules-based system operating on principles of nondiscrimination and most-favored-nation treatment. In bargains struck among the powerful industrial nations, developing countries automatically gain from the concessions made by all parties. Moreover, GATT impedes powerful nations from selectively adopting tariff or other trade policies to the disadvantage of weaker parties.

Within GATT, negotiations are characterized by shifting coalitions among industrial and developing nations, depending on the issue at hand. For example, 14 nations formed the Cairns Group to foster more market-oriented policies on agriculture, with membership including such disparate developing country players as Argentina, Brazil, the Philippines, and Thailand, as well as industrial nations with strong agricultural exports such as Canada and Australia.[7] In the area of services, developing countries are split: some perceive an effort by industrial countries to overwhelm their infant financial markets and to extort monopoly rents on new product lines through patent enforcement; others judge that freer movement of services would enhance the competitiveness of their domestic industries, for which services are an input. Textiles drove additional cleavages between the developing nations because some enjoyed the secure quotas carved out by the Multifiber Arrangement (MFA), whereas other low-cost producers felt they could do better in a more open, competitive system. Finally, in the 1979 Tokyo Round of negotiations, the United States struck a more decisive "modular multilateral" bargain with a subset of developing nations in the area of subsidies. In exchange for a firm commitment to phase out export subsidies gradually, the United States agreed to extend an "injury test" in countervailing duty cases to participating developing countries.[8]

The Differentiation Principle. Recognizing that sensitivity to country and regional idiosyncracies is vital to sound trade policy, the United States has emulated GATT's "differentiation" principle in its own dealings with developing nations. The generalized system of preferences (GSP) of U.S. trade law, under which industrial nations grant preferential tariff treatment to eligible developing countries, is one extension of the special and differential principle.

The United States continues to apply this principle in other areas of its trade relations as well. For example, in presenting its agricultural reform proposals in the Uruguay Round, the United States allowed middle-income developing countries 12 years to phase in reforms, countries with per capita incomes below $500 15 years, and for industrial nations only 10. At the same time, the United States insists upon graduating countries, like the Asian tigers, that no longer warrant concessionary treatment due to their levels of income and international competitiveness and therefore can be expected to participate more fully in the framework of GATT rights and obligations. This graduation principle is designed to safeguard U.S. producers as well as to enhance the comparative positions of the poorer developing nations.

But the United States differentiates among developing countries not only by income and competitiveness but also by patterns of production. The alliance with agricultural exporters within the Cairns Group is an outstanding case. In the future, there should be more opportunities for such coalitions, be they based on output or on complementarity of production factors. For example, the emerging trade partnership between the United States and Mexico, which seeks to marry U.S. capital with Mexican labor, will forge a North American alliance that on some issues (investment and finance, energy, rules of origin, environment, and labor rights) may set precedents for agreements with other nations.

Emerging Modular Arrangements. As part of its strategic design to stem revolutionary impulses on the U.S. periphery, the Reagan administration extended special trade preferences to Central America and the Caribbean. The Bush administration, in addition to ongoing negotiations for a Free Trade Agreement with Mexico, is also pursuing such a special relationship with other countries in the hemisphere, among them Chile. Finally, the United States has also joined the Asian Pacific Economic Cooperation (APEC), a consultative mechanism to promote regional economic liberalization in ways that reinforce GATT; other members include Australia, Brunei, Canada, Indonesia, Japan, Korea, Malaysia, New Zealand, the Philippines, Singapore, and Thailand.

As the United States continues to pursue such modular arrangements with different groupings of countries in the future, it will need to give increasing attention to the institutional parameters involved. In 1990, President George Bush announced his willingness to enter into free trade agreements not only with Mexico but also with the whole of Latin America. Although enthusiasm for the concept was resounding throughout the hemisphere, the modalities, sequencing, and timetable for these negotiations remain unclear. The Bush initiative lacks an institutional framework to catalyze and coordinate the negotiating process, to assure that agreements are mutually consistent, and to ascertain their conformity with GATT. Clarification of such a mechanism is precisely the sort of operational detail that will need more attention if the modular multilateralist system is to take hold. The trick will be for the United States to take the lead in forging institutional arrangements supported by norms and regulations around which actors of different stripes can converge. Only by such purposeful leadership toward a modular multilateral approach, tempered by a sensitivity to the diverse interests and capacities of participating nations, can the United States hope to steer trade agreements in a mutually profitable direction.

A Recent Case Study: Hemispheric Economics

In response to a series of meetings with Latin American presidents, President Bush asked his Treasury Department to design a proposal that would give greater priority to economic development in the bolstering of U.S.–Latin American relations. Launched in a presidential address on June 27, 1990, this proposal called for significant write-downs of the $12 billion in debts owed to U.S. government agencies by Latin American governments; the authorization of $500 million to promote private investment; the creation of environmental funds in each country; and the establishment of the above-mentioned free trade area stretching from Alaska to Argentina. This Enterprise for the Americas Initiative (EAI) is thus not only indicative of the greater importance Latin America will have for the United States in the 1990s, but it is also functionally and organizationally illustrative of the opportunities and challenges in the emergent modular multilateral world.

As modular multilateralism predicts, like-minded countries will begin to form modular alliances to solve common economic problems as issues of dollars and cents become concerns of high policy. Thus, while participation in the EAI is broad, it is not universal. Rather, it is limited to the Western Hemisphere, and furthermore to those nations that agree with the Bush administration and the multilateral lending agencies in supporting free trade and private investment.

Moreover, collaboration will take place through multilateral institutions across discrete issue areas—trade, debt, investment, and the environment. Debt reduction is generally contingent upon countries working with the IMF and World Bank, and the money for private investment will be managed by the Inter-American Development Bank, with matching funds sought from Japan and Western Europe. It is also not yet clear whether the creation of a hemispheric free trade area will be coordinated by an existing or newly created multilateral body or remain fragmented.

Reflecting the world of decentralized power, the EAI seeks to engage not only governments and multilateral agencies but also the private sector and grass-roots organizations. Firms will help design bargaining agendas and affect outcomes by lobbying the U.S. trade negotiators, who have become exceedingly responsive to private-sector preferences. Most innovatively, the boards of the national "environmental trust funds" are to be largely composed of local environmental, community development, and scientific groups.

But this is not to say that the EAI is without organizational and administrative flaws. For example, it has suffered from the failure of the U.S. government to consult sufficiently. The United States announced the private investment initiative without adequate prior consultations with its prospective donor partners, and then publicly asked Japan and Western Europe to contribute. The administration may have erred further in announcing the U.S. intention to grant deep debt reductions unilaterally, thus breaking with the usual practice of each donor conditioning the granting of concessions upon other donors following suit. Finally, as noted above, the administration has failed to establish an institutional mechanism to coordinate the negotiations for the free trade area. In the case of the EAI, such institutions could help to coordinate and implement a program that, if successful, could considerably sharpen the Western Hemisphere's competitive edge.

Modular Multilateralism: A Case for Equity and Efficiency

As the examples in this paper suggest, modular multilateralism is an appropriate framework for understanding North–South interaction and builds upon fundamental changes in the international order. As a policy tool, it attempts to offer an organizational framework for solving economic problems across the North–South divide; in doing so it recognizes the importance of a decentralized state, issue- and region-specific idiosyncrasies, the role of empathy in dealing with poorer nations, and the emergence of nonstate actors. Finally, it recognizes the importance of institutions that provide rules, norms, and forums for tackling common problems.

Modular multilateralism is useful on grounds of both equity and efficiency, but it demands new behavior patterns to ensure its success. As the examples cited suggest, certain vestigial attitudes presently impede its effectiveness. Ill-timed or impatient unilateralism, reluctance to establish new mechanisms for multilateral coordination, and inadequate policy differentiation can generate unnecessary conflict and suboptimal policy outcomes.

And although NGO, private-sector, or bureaucratic interests will sometimes work with modular formations, they will also sometimes oppose cooperative solutions. Governments must therefore devise new approaches for forging winning coalitions that include both public and private actors.

Above all, as the Cold War's bipolarity recedes, the U.S. government's approach to crafting economic policy toward the developing countries must change if the modular multilateralist system is to develop and indeed, to flourish in those issue areas where it can be useful. Such a change in outlook will necessitate readiness, not resistance, to forming ad hoc secretariats where they are adequate and international coordinating mechanisms where they are necessary to give interested parties institutional recourse for confronting problems.

This change in outlook should also be reflected in the creation of a system of appropriate institutions to respond to this new economic order. In some cases, these mechanisms might already exist (such as the World Bank or the United Nations Development Programme), or they would need to be created to respond to new exigencies. One such example is offered in a recent study by the Overseas Development Council entitled *After the Wars*, in which editor Anthony Lake champions the need for the creation of an international fund to promote reconstruction of war-torn areas in the developing world. Such a fund would allow both the United States and Japan to work with other leading donor countries to promote innovative answers to problems confronting developing countries. Vehicles for such assistance could include technical training, management training, and private entrepreneurs, as well as bringing together international experts from various regions to share information and ideas on reconstruction and planning.[9]

Clearly, certain developing nations, like Mexico, will get more attention than others. Similarly, others will be too inconsequential to gain seats in the multilateral modules. In such cases, the United States will need to take the lead in actively working to construct mechanisms to address their needs. Here, a social safety net could be formulated precisely to attend to those countries that do not qualify for module participation. Although the compensatory financial and trade programs implied in such a concept would not halt the inevitable process of uneven development, they would at least offer recipients a better opportunity to join the mainstream of global economic integration.

In the end, the modular multilateral framework seems well suited both to the present state of the international system as well as to the ways in which it will most likely evolve over the next decade. Above all, by focusing on avenues for productive exchange, it offers the opportunity to reverse, or at least diminish, the historic antagonism characterizing North–South relations. For this reason, modular multilateralism can be seen not only as a practical response to cooperative problem solving in the 1990s but also as a step forward in the spirit of a more harmonious global order.

Notes

1. These upper-middle-income developing nations include South Africa, Algeria, Hungary, Uruguay, Argentina, Yugoslavia, Gabon, Venezuela, Trinidad and Tobago, South Korea, Portugal, Greece, Oman, Libya, Iran, Iraq, and Romania.

2. World Bank, *World Development Report 1990* (New York: Oxford University Press, 1990), pp. 78–79. Using a purchasing power parity index does not alter this conclusion. The differential between industrial countries and developing countries is narrower than that traditionally produced by using exchange rates, but it still stands at 7:1. See United Nations Development Programme, *Human Development Report 1990* (New York: Oxford University Press, 1990), table 16, pp. 158–159.

3. A thorough examination of the trade-offs and challenges in making adjustment compatible with the demands of political stability may be found in Joan Nelson, *Fragile Coalitions: The Politics of Economic Adjustment* (New Brunswick, N.J.: Transaction Books in cooperation with the Overseas Development Council, 1989).

4. World Bank, *World Debt Tables 1988–89* (Washington, D.C.: World Bank, 1989), p. 37.

5. A good analysis of recent U.S. debt strategy can be found in Peter Hakim, "The Brady Plan: An Interim Assessment," *Policy Focus* (Overseas Development Council), no. 5 (1990).

6. This point is amply demonstrated in Robert Devlin, *Debt and Crisis in Latin America: The Supply Side of the Story* (Princeton, N.J.: Princeton University Press, 1989).

7. The other members of the Cairns Group are Chile, Colombia, Fiji, Hungary, Indonesia, Malaysia, New Zealand, and Uruguay.

8. To date, signatories to the Subsidies' Code include the United States, Japan, Canada, and the European Community (together with many other Northern nations), as well as Brazil, Chile, Colombia, India, Indonesia, Korea, Pakistan, and Uruguay from the South.

An earlier version of this essay was delivered at the Aspen Institute conference on "The U.S. and the World Economy," Aspen, Colorado, August 17–22, 1991. It draws heavily on a longer paper with the same title recently published by the Overseas Development Council and on the authors' contribution to Kenneth A. Oye, Robert J. Lieber, and Donald Rothchild, eds., Eagle in a New World (New York: Harper Collins, 1991).

9. See Anthony Lake, ed., *After the Wars: Reconstruction in Afghanistan, Indochina, Central America, Southern Africa, and the Horn of Africa* (New Brunswick, N.J.: Transaction Books in cooperation with the Overseas Development Council, 1990).

Greater China: A New Economic Colossus?

Murray Weidenbaum

U.S. POLICYMAKERS AND business executives alike are ignoring a powerful long-term trend in Southeast Asia: the rise of the greater China economy. Paced by a rapid rate of investment and endowed with an abundance of trained human capital, the Asian rim has become the fastest growing part of the world, averaging over 5 percent a year in real economic growth. Many observers expect this trend to continue for at least the rest of this decade and perhaps well into the twenty-first century.[1]

Meanwhile, the United States remains preoccupied with political challenges in Europe and the Middle East and with economic competition from Japan. Maintaining the status quo in U.S. policies and attitudes could well result in American business firms losing the opportunity to participate fully in the major growth area of the next decades—greater China.

The strategic role of the Japanese economy in the Asian rim must not be underestimated, but another focus on economic developments in this region is also important. Over the years, scholars in the United States have referred to the Chinas as a multiple—two Chinas, three Chinas, and more. They have in mind the fact that several of the major economies of this region have a predominantly Chinese population and an unusual degree of interaction. In addition to the industrialized portions of mainland China, the overall Chinese economy includes such other rapidly growing areas as Taiwan, Hong Kong, Macao, and Singapore. This "bamboo network," which transcends national boundaries, also includes other key locations where business executives, traders, and financiers of Chinese background make important economic contributions. According to some estimates, Chinese companies in Malaysia, Thailand, Indonesia, and the Philippines make up about 70 percent of the private sector in those countries.[2]

The "Chinese-based economy" has resisted the global recession that in recent years has plagued virtually every advanced industrial nation. This informal economy is currently the world leader in terms of economic growth, industrial expansion, and exports (see figures 1 and 2). It contains an array of potential consumers that far exceeds the markets in Europe or the Western Hemisphere. Yet not all of the vast Chinese mainland can be viewed realistically as a potential for early modernization. The major economic development is occurring in the coastal provinces of Guangdong and

---

Murray Weidenbaum is Mallinckrodt Distinguished University Professor and director of the Center for the Study of American Business at Washington University in St. Louis, Missouri.

Copyright © 1993 by The Center for Strategic and International Studies and the Massachusetts Institute of Technology

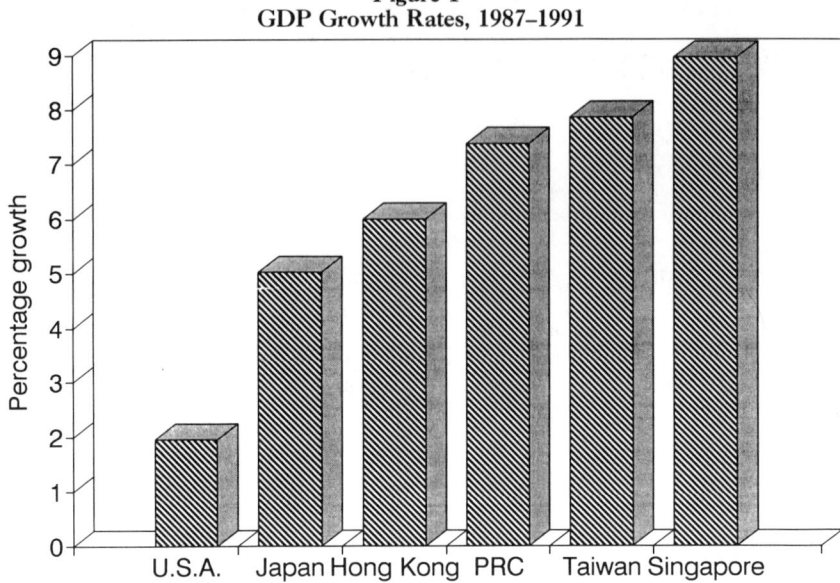

Figure 1
GDP Growth Rates, 1987–1991

Source: International Monetary Fund, *International Financial Statistics*; United Nations, *Handbook for International Trade and Development.*

Fujian, the special economic zones in Shenzhen and Xiamen, and the city of Shanghai. Although these areas are a modest fraction of the entire country, in the aggregate they constitute a very substantial economy.

Within the Asian rim, the dynamic pattern of "the Chinas" contrasts with the recent slowdown in the pace of Japanese economic and financial activity. Japan's foreign direct investment flows reached a peak of $67 billion in 1989 and have been declining since. The 1991 total came to a modest $41 billion, lower than the 1988 rate. Japanese direct investment in Asia declined simultaneously, from a peak of a little over $8 billion in 1989 to less than $6 billion in 1991. Moreover, Japanese banks have tended to reduce their participation in the international banking market. The $53 billion reduction in their foreign banking assets in the second quarter of 1992 was the largest recorded to date.[3] In absolute terms, of course, Japan continues to be the dominant economy in Asia and will continue to hold that position for many years.

The Chinese-Based Economy

Despite the current Japanese dominance of the region, the Chinese-based economy of Asia is rapidly emerging as a new epicenter for industry, commerce, and finance. This strategic area contains substantial amounts of technology and manufacturing capability (Taiwan), outstanding entrepreneurial, marketing, and services acumen (Hong Kong), a fine communications network (Singapore), a tremendous pool of financial capital

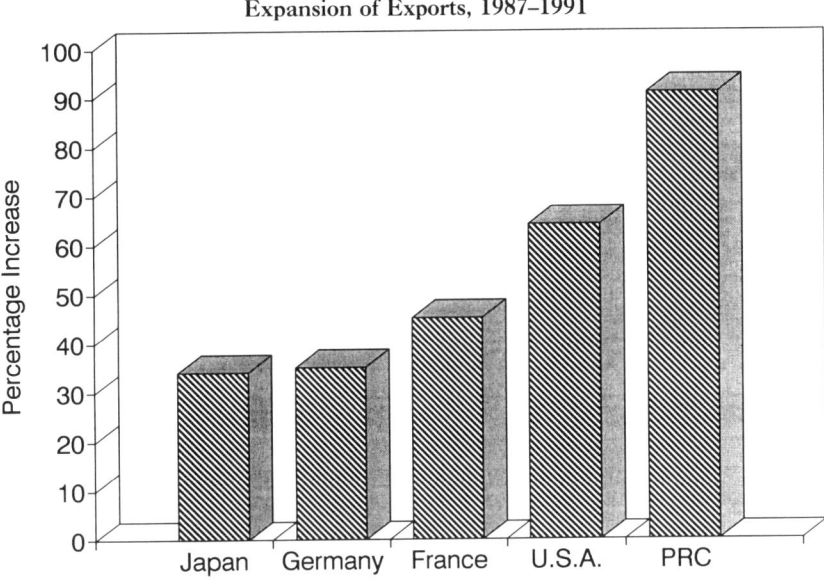

Figure 2
Expansion of Exports, 1987–1991

Source: International Monetary Fund, *International Financial Statistics.*

(all three), and very large endowments of land, resources, and labor (mainland China). A talking doll, to take a modest example, may be designed in Hong Kong, contain a computer chip made in Taiwan, and be assembled in the People's Republic of China (PRC). The Grande Group provides a more general example of this interrelationship. The bulk of its production is in Guangdong, its research and development is located in Taiwan, and its corporate headquarters is situated in Hong Kong.[4]

The informal Chinese economy differs from the more official economies, which are usually dominated by large multinational firms. Of the world's 500 leading industrial companies in 1991, only one, Chinese Petroleum, was part of the greater China economy (it is Taiwanese and is in 166th place). In comparison, 13 Korean companies make the list; the largest, Samsung, is the 18th largest industrial firm listed in the *Fortune* tabulation.

The Chinese-based economy consists in large measure of midsize, family-run firms, rather than the huge corporations characteristic of Japan, Western Europe, and the United States. Transnational networks seem to be the natural accompaniment of the Chinese trading tradition. These enterprises tend to be mostly engaged in light manufacturing and services such as shipping and retailing. These channels for the movement of information, finance, goods, and capital help to explain the relative flexibility and efficiency of the numerous ongoing informal agreements and transactions that bind together the various parts of the Chinese-based trading area.

From Guangzhou to Singapore,

from Kuala Lumpur to Manila, this influential network—often based on extensions of the traditional clans—is the backbone of the East Asian economy. A substantial amount of cross-investment and trade takes place, often on a family basis. Frequently, these business ties involve dealings by "overseas" Chinese with people in the province of the PRC from which they or their ancestors migrated. Thus, Hong Kong has provided about 90 percent of the investment in adjacent Guangdong, the most rapidly growing economic area of the PRC. Similarly, Taiwanese investors have been largely responsible for the expansion of the nearby Xiamen Special Economic Zone.[5]

To be sure, government is often heavily involved in the ownership if not the operation of many specific enterprises. In Taiwan, the KMT (the Nationalist party or Kuomintang) is the largest property owner, with widespread business interests. In the PRC, where there are numerous private ventures (often in collaboration with foreign investors), the government still owns a great variety of enterprises. These range from the central government's giant steel mills to local government factories. The trading companies, which engage in a variety of commercial, banking, and manufacturing activities, are owned by governmental units, ranging from the army to local counties.[6]

Enterprises owned by the PRC government often engage in overseas business ventures. A prominent example is the China International Trust and Investment Corporation (Citic), which has subsidiaries in Mexico, Australia, Canada, the United States, and Europe. Citic's Hong Kong subsidiary—considered its overseas crown jewel—owns 12 percent of Hong Kong telecommunications, 12.5 percent of Cathay Pacific, 46.2 percent of Dragonair, and 20 percent of a Hong Kong chemical waste plant.[7]

The close connection between public and private sectors and the several parts of the greater China economy is illustrated by the operations of the Shanghai Far East Container Company. This joint venture between Shanghai, Hong Kong, and Taiwan involves enterprises in all three areas to produce steel containers in Shanghai. An even greater extension of capitalism occurred in June 1992, when the city of Wuhan allowed Hongtex Development Company, a Hong Kong firm, to buy a 51 percent share of Wuhan No. 2 Printing and Dyeing Company. This transaction marked the first time a "foreign" company was allowed to acquire a majority stake in a state-owned enterprise in the PRC, albeit an ailing one. This development also illustrates the movement of industrialization from the coastal zone to the neighboring provinces of Guangxi, Sichuan, and Hunan.

In contrast, the city of Qiaotori, in Zhejiang province, has no state-owned enterprises. This metropolitan area has recently become the PRC's button-making capital. Seven Hong Kong and Taiwan companies have set up joint ventures there to produce buttons for the PRC's growing textile industry.[8]

Interrelationships

Several economic indicators, ranging from modest to basic, illustrate the close connections being developed among the "Chinas" despite their serious political differences. Eight years ago, the special economic zone of Xiamen in the PRC booked 10 telephone calls a month to Taiwan. Currently, such calls are averaging 60,000 a month, and the number continues to rise. In 1987, fewer than 7,000 Taiwanese visited the mainland. The present rate is approximately 1 million a year. Bilateral trade, which can legally be conducted only through third countries, was $1.5 billion in 1987. The current figure is about $6 billion, a fourfold increase.

Over 5,000 Taiwan enterprises have set up factories in the PRC, mainly in the South, or otherwise invested an aggregate of $5 billion in the Chinese mainland. In some instances, business firms in Taiwan are relocating entire factories in remote areas of the PRC in order to take advantage of cheaper labor and more readily available natural resources.[9]

The state of interdependence between the PRC (especially the coastal region of Guangdong) and Hong Kong is even more striking. Each is the other's largest trading partner and largest source of external investment. Three-fifths of all foreign investment in the PRC has been made by Hong Kong's Chinese entrepreneurs and is spread out over 17,000 enterprises.[10] A network of highways, ferries, hydrofoils, and air routes links Hong Kong and the coastal region.

A recent example of the joint development efforts is the $60 million project on the part of Hong Kong–based Tian An China Group to construct a large commercial and office building in the heart of Changzhou, an industrial city in Jiangsu province. Similar is the teaming up of Hong Kong's K Wah International Holdings with a variety of partners in the PRC to develop a commercial office tower in Shanghai. The partners include the Hwang Pu District Resettlement unit, the People's Bank of China, the Shanghai Land Development Company, and the Hwang Pu district government.[11]

The PRC has reportedly invested approximately $11 billion in Hong Kong trade, real estate, transport, and financial enterprises. One result is that the Bank of China is now the second biggest bank in the colony, as measured by volume of deposits. In the other direction, 80 percent of Hong Kong's manufacturing companies have branches in the PRC, employing more than 3 million workers. Apparently there are far more people working in the PRC for businesses owned by Hong Kong or on orders received from them than the entire manufacturing work force of Hong Kong itself (in a reported ratio of 4 to 1).[12] Thus, Hong Kong entrepreneurs, as well as Taiwan-based business firms, have helped smooth the transition from central planning. This cooperative endeavor is in contrast to the difficulties experienced in Eastern Europe and the former Soviet republics.[13]

Approximately 50,000 managers and professionals commute daily from Hong Kong to the nearby Guangdong province. About 60 percent of the PRC's exports go through Hong Kong. These reexports, in turn, account for the greater part of Hong Kong's exports. The data support the conclusion of William Purves, chairman of the Hong Kong Bank Group, that "investment and expertise channeled from Hong Kong have turned southern China into one of the industrial powerhouses of Asia."[14] In fact, what some observers call the greater "Hong Kong enclave" is likely soon to enjoy a gross domestic product as large as that of France.

Figures 3 and 4 illustrate the flows of trade between Hong Kong and Taiwan. The data hide the fact, however, that many of the PRC's exports to the West are shipped through Hong Kong, as is a large part of Taiwan's trade with the mainland.

The cross-border relationships in

Figure 3
Source of Imports to Hong Kong, 1991

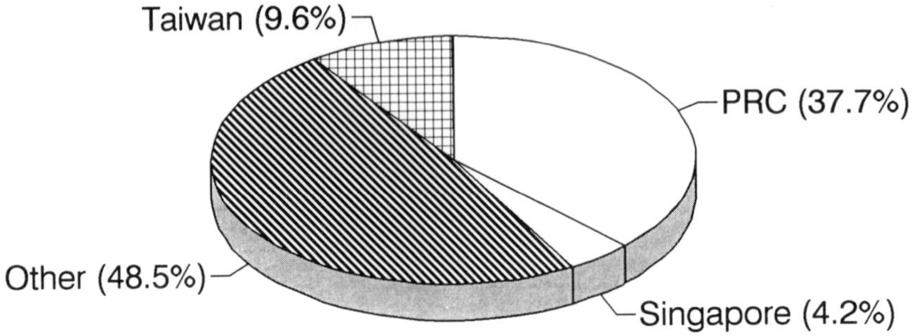

- Taiwan (9.6%)
- PRC (37.7%)
- Other (48.5%)
- Singapore (4.2%)

Source: International Monetary Fund, *International Financial Statistics.*

Figure 4
Destination of Exports from Hong Kong, 1991

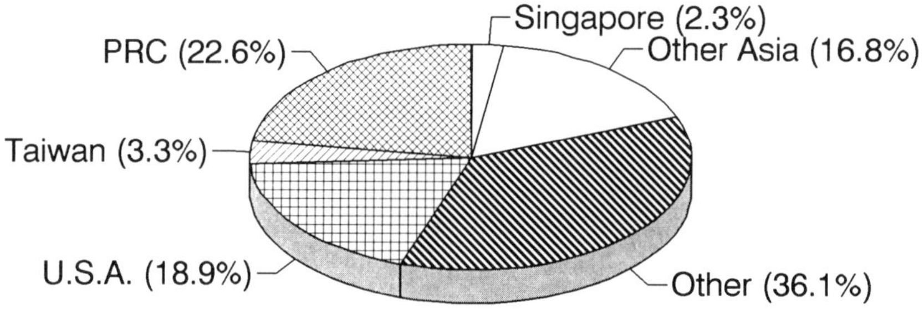

- Singapore (2.3%)
- Other Asia (16.8%)
- PRC (22.6%)
- Taiwan (3.3%)
- U.S.A. (18.9%)
- Other (36.1%)

Source: International Monetary Fund, *International Financial Statistics.*

the Chinese-based economy are not limited to the PRC, Hong Kong, and Taiwan. A Malaysian entrepreneur has teamed up with a counterpart in Hong Kong in a $130 million project to develop shops, offices, and housing in Shanghai. The Charoen Pokphand group, a Thai conglomerate owned by ethnic Chinese, has built more than 50 projects in the PRC, including a motorcycle factory, a brewery, and animal feed mills.[15]

Ethnic Chinese account for about 10 percent of the population of Thailand and 9 of the 10 largest business groups. In Indonesia, about 4 percent of the population is Chinese and all of the 10 largest business groups are owned by local Chinese entrepreneurs. Malaysia has mandated affirmative action programs for the Malay majority in view of the economic influence of local Chinese.

Macao, a neighbor of Hong Kong, is also undergoing a period of rapid growth. Although under nominal Portuguese sovereignty until 1999, this island economy is developing its ties with the rest of the greater China economy. The new airport being built on the island has the strong support of the PRC (thereby differing from the controversial new airport being planned for Hong Kong). The PRC's Chung Luen consortium holds an 8.67 percent interest in the company that is building and is also scheduled to operate the facility.[16]

At the more macroeconomic level, some private analysts, adding up the foreign exchange reserves of the various Chinas, come to a present total of $200 billion. That amount is far in excess of the foreign exchange holdings of any other economic power. It surely is an impressive financial aggregation with considerable potential for influencing the direction of future economic developments.

Indeed, in 1991 Taiwan alone was the largest single foreign investor in Malaysia and also in Vietnam. Cumulative foreign direct investment from the newly industrialized economies of Taiwan, Hong Kong, and Singapore is beginning to surpass that of both Japan and the United States in Indonesia, Malaysia, and Thailand. Not too surprisingly, the rapidly developing Asian rim countries are turning to new suppliers within their own region for their imports (see figure 5). These newly developing countries now buy 33 percent of their imports from other nations within the region compared to less than 24 percent as recently as 1985.[17]

The trend toward the internationalization of production within the greater Chinese area is not generally viewed, however, as motivated by the desire to integrate trade. Rather, the end objective is often to export final products to third countries in Western Europe and North America. Thus, trade data for Southeast Asia must be interpreted with this tendency in mind.

Forecasts of the Future

Zbigniew Brzezinski notes that, if the current 10 percent economic growth rate of the PRC is maintained, and assuming the successful assimilation of Hong Kong, the PRC could become the fourth global economic power by the year 2010, after the United States, Europe, and Japan. He notes that the industrialized province of Guangdong, with a population of more than 60 million, is the size of a large European nation.[18]

Robert S. McNamara, former president of the World Bank, has provided a longer-term appraisal of the economic prospects of the PRC. He states that if the PRC achieves its economic goals for the year 2000 and then moves forward at satisfactory but not spectacular growth rates, that nation's per capita income in 2050 may be roughly equal to that of the United Kingdom in 1965. The total size of its economy would approximate that of the United States or Western Europe.[19] One U.S. economist estimates that the economy of the PRC alone will exceed that of Japan by the year 2000. Another analyst forecasts that, if current growth trends continue, the PRC could be the world's largest economy by 2012.[20]

When we add to these forecasts the other parts of the greater China economy, the economic implications of the extension of current trends into the twenty-first century become awe-inspiring. We must take note, however, of the severe strains in the PRC that are arising as an economically backward, Communist-led nation attempts to move to an advanced capitalist regime. Almost by definition, adoption of a private enterprise system, however halting and incomplete, means the broadening of the society's power base and considerable decen-

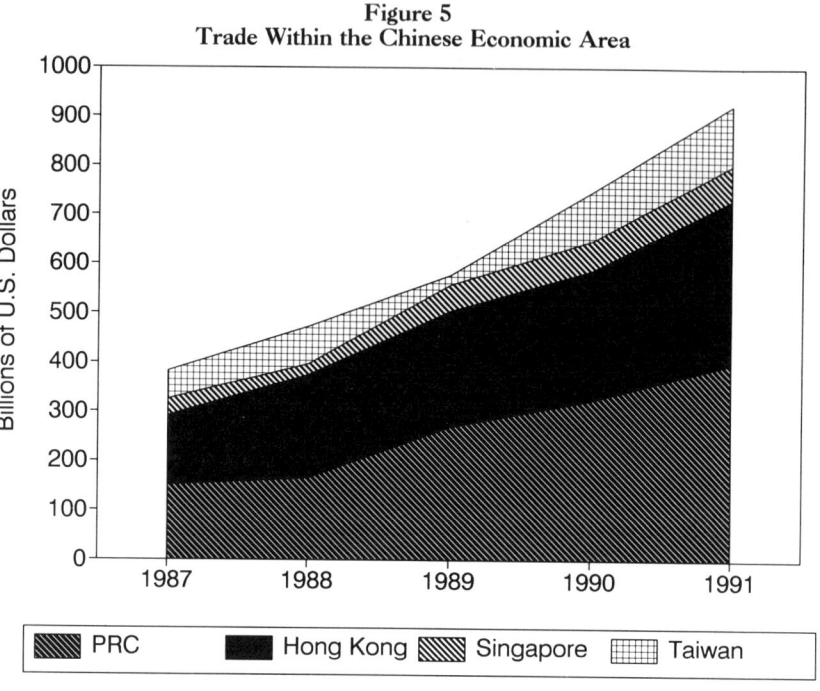

Figure 5
Trade Within the Chinese Economic Area

Source: International Monetary Fund, *International Financial Statistics*.

tralization of decision making. The existing power structure is not likely to respond to these changes passively.

Moreover, recent purchases of military aircraft by Taiwan have raised levels of tension in the area. This, in turn, increases the risk involved in making business investments in the greater China economy. On balance, it seems likely that the pervasive attractions of rapid economic development will, at least in the long run, overcome both political animosities and the cyclical tendency of the PRC's economic and political progress. The tragic events in Lebanon, however, show the limitations of this optimistic assumption.

Surely the more complete industrialization of Southeast Asia is a prospect that Western analysts and business leaders have not fully examined. Nevertheless, a few are already referring to a forthcoming "Chinese century." The "Chinese Productivity Triangle" and the South China Economic Community are other, and more modest, descriptions in use.[21] With the opening of the PRC and capital flows to it, greater China is rapidly becoming one of the world's most vibrant economies. It is no exaggeration to state that greater China is a potential economic superpower. Its 1.2 billion people now produce a combined gross domestic product approaching $1 trillion a year.

A historical parallel comes to mind: the key role in international commerce of the Hanseatic League. For many centuries during the late Middle Ages, the League tied together first the merchants and then many of the cities of northern Germany and the Baltic area. Historians stress the fact that the Hanse cities did not set up a joint or unified government. Rather, the business and government leaders cooperated on matters of mutual economic and financial interest. A shifting array of participants can be identified over the centuries. Some of the large German cities in the qualifying area did not participate at all, and many entered into the cooperative arrangements for only limited periods of time.[22]

Unlike the European Community or the North American Free Trade Agreement, the Hanseatic League was not a compact among sovereign powers, nor did it constitute a supergovernment. Individual members continued to owe their traditional allegiance to the specific political power that controlled the part of the region in which they resided. Technically, the League was an amorphous organization, lacking legal status and possessing neither finances of its own nor an independent army or navy.

Nevertheless, the Hanse merchants cooperated in many important ways, providing mutual support in times of danger. They constituted an identifiable economic grouping that competed with businesses in Holland, Italy, and on different occasions, many of the nations facing the Baltic Sea. Despite the obvious limitations of a nongovernmental organization spread over considerable distances—Bergen in Norway was an important Hanse location as was Novgorod in Russia—for almost five centuries the Hanseatic League was an economic power to be reckoned with.

No analyst can forecast with any degree of assurance the future nature of economic relationships in Eastern Asia. Will a modern version of the Hanseatic League be created? Will a counterpart to the European Community arise? Will the more modest arrangements being developed in North America be the precedent that will be followed? Or will the present informal relationships be relied on in view of their substantial success?

Whatever the answer, trends rarely move in a straight line for an extended period. In the recent past, setbacks have occurred in the economic and political development of Southeast Asia and future detours are likely. Some experts offer a more pessimistic assessment than is presented here. Ross Terrill of the East Asian Research Center of Harvard University believes that the PRC can never truly prosper while the Communist party retains its monopoly of power. Any gains resulting from piecemeal economic reforms, in this view, will merely benefit the Communists by pacifying the citizenry.

Other visitors to the PRC report that their dominant impression of the new economic zones, such as Guangdong, is one of official favoritism, inside deals, and outright bribery.[23] Consultant Steven Schlossstein believes that, under such circumstances, it will take at least 30 years for the PRC to lay the groundwork for durable growth. He notes the absence of a commercial code in the PRC as an example of how far the Chinese have to go to modernize.[24]

Great uncertainty surely attaches to the future of the greater Chinese economy. The PRC is making it clear that it wants to participate actively in determining the future direction of the economy of Hong Kong. But there is little clarity as to the nature of that participation and the desired direction of change. Likewise, the relations between Beijing and Taipei can at best be described as ambiguous. The political ties between the PRC and the rest of the Chinese trading area, notably Singapore, range from loose to nonexistent. The notion of political integration does not now appear as a realistic short-term prospect. What does seem likely, however, is continuing informal integration, perhaps leading to a de facto Chinese Common Market.

Forces of economic and business development seem likely to dominate, especially in the long run. As in Eastern Europe, communism did not lose popular support primarily because the people rejected the ideology of Marx (if they ever understood it). Rather, they saw the vastly greater benefits of democracy and private enterprise. Whichever specific course is followed in Southeast Asia, it is reasonable to expect that some type of positive response will occur to the economic unification that is now occurring in the two other major competitive areas, Western Europe and North America.

The Outlook

The rise of the greater China economy must be viewed in the context of the increasing globalization of business. Despite the many efforts of government to restrain or at least redirect trade and investment, individual businesses are succeeding in overcoming these obstacles to private decision making. The mobility of enterprises—of their people, capital, and information—is reducing the power of government. Public sector decision makers are increasingly being forced to understand that they now have to become internationally competitive in the economic policies they devise. In this era of computers, telephones, and fax machines, enterprises are extremely mobile.[25] The most striking examples of that mobility are the recent experiences of Chinese entrepreneurs.

Even in the face of official hostility, many Taiwanese firms and a great number of Taiwanese individuals are succeeding in establishing their business presence in the PRC. As we have seen in the case of Hong Kong and the mainland, the mutual economic interpenetration is even more striking. The formal power of government is not to be discounted—and its destructive ability has been vividly demonstrated in innumerable wars. Nevertheless, the continuing ability of entrepreneurs to respond to the power of economic incentives and technological advance surely is impressive.

Seasoned observers of the Asian rim warn U.S. executives against attempting to enter the Chinese market without appropriate strategic alliances. Smaller investors, in particular, are urged to obtain a corporate partner in the form of a Chinese firm from Hong Kong, Singapore, or Taiwan, preferably one with family connections in the mainland.

The PRC may well come to be seen by some of the developing nations in other regions of the world as an attractive alternative to both the West's market-oriented democracy and the unsuccessful Communist experiment. In its current phase of development, the PRC is combining key elements of the free market system (especially its competitive entrepreneurship) with a residually guiding governmental role, including substantial amounts of state ownership of industry.[26]

Looking ahead to the twenty-first century, the Chinese economic and trading area might well reach across the Pacific (some early manifestations are already evident in the Silicon Valley in California). Such a development would form a major part of the economic and Pacific equivalent of the North Atlantic Treaty Organization (NATO). But, unlike NATO and like the Hanseatic League of old, that area would not be dominated by a single government unit or depend on a military or political pact. On the contrary, it would be both contributor to and beneficiary of the world's largest and most open commercial region. Barring a major political setback in the intervening period, the Chinese economic area has the potential of providing a principal engine of world growth in the early twenty-first century.

Policy Implications

The expansion of the greater China economy, like any other major change, generates both threats and opportunities to those outside the area. U.S. business enterprises have participated in that growth in only a limited way. The reasons are many, ranging from the modest amount of new investment funds generated in the American economy to the attractions of Europe. The cultural, language, and ethnic background of Western Europe is shared to a large extent by the dominant population of the United States. Moreover, many U.S. firms are wary of making long-term commitments until the Clinton administration clarifies its policy on tariffs on PRC goods and services.

Nevertheless, an impressive array of U.S. firms are active in the Chinese economic area. The PRC is Motorola's largest market for cellular phones outside the United States and Boeing's second largest overseas market. More Coca Cola is sold to the PRC than to the rest of Asia combined. AT&T has concluded a landmark arrangement to make switches, advanced integrated circuits, and wireless phones in the PRC.

The future state of political relations between the United States and the PRC will help to determine the extent to which American business firms will participate in that rapidly growing market. Currently, much attention focuses on the continuation of most-favored-nation (MFN) treatment of Chinese exports to the United States. Strong arguments exist on both sides of that contentious issue. Those in favor of terminating that special treatment consider such action essential to show opposition to human rights abuses. The memories of the 1989 Tiananmen Square episode remain both painful and vivid.

On the other hand, many argue that extending U.S. economic ties with the PRC will enable that nation to see in the American experience the close connection between economic freedom and personal liberty. Students and scholars who come to the United States from greater China are serving as a human bridge between the two regions.

A related argument in favor of continuing MFN treatment of the PRC is more practical—to ensure that U.S. firms are able to participate more fully in the rising economic opportunities in that area.[27]

A similar array of pros and cons relates to supporting the PRC's entry into the General Agreement on Tariffs and Trade and to easing curbs on transfers of high technology. The irony in all this is that, proportionately, the major victim of reducing U.S. trade relations with the PRC is likely not to be the PRC itself, but Hong Kong. As noted earlier, that territory has become the key economic middleman between the mainland and the West.

Southeast Asia furnishes a striking

example of private enterprise taking the lead and government becoming the lagging influence. It is the frequently vilified multinational corporations that have paced the economic development of the greater China trading area. Particularly in the case of the United States, it is government policy that often generates the obstacles to cross-border undertakings. To be sure, great risks are involved in doing business in an area undergoing fundamental economic, political, and social change. But it is private enterprise that is especially suited to taking such risks.

The research for this paper was supported by the William H. Donner Foundation. The author is indebted to Janice Kinghorn for helpful research assistance, especially in the preparation of the charts.

Notes

1. This paper draws from Murray Weidenbaum, *Greater China: The Next Economic Superpower?* (St. Louis, Mo.: Center for the Study of American Business, Washington University, 1993). An earlier version was presented as the Wei-Lun Lecture at Chinese University of Hong Kong in December 1992.
2. "The Chinese Diaspora: The Fifth 'Dragon,'" *Conjoncture*, November 1992, pp. 155–160.
3. Richard Waters, "Japanese Banks Step Up Pace of International Withdrawal," *Financial Times*, November 13, 1992, p. 23.
4. Lena H. Sun, "South China Drives Boom Region," *Washington Post*, December 2, 1992, p. A–1.
5. "The Overseas Chinese," *Economist*, July 18, 1992, pp. 21–24; Joel Kotkin, *Global Tribes: Understanding the New Economic Paradigm* (Denver, Colo.: Center for the New West, 1992); Sally Stewart, Michael Tow Cheung, and David W. K. Yeung, "The Latest Asian Newly Industrialized Economy Emerges: The South China Economic Community," *Columbia Journal of World Business* 27 (Summer 1992), p. 30.
6. I am indebted to Professor William C. Jones of the Washington University School of Law for this point.
7. Tai Ming Cheung, "Middle of the Kingdom," *Far Eastern Economic Review*, January 21, 1993, pp. 48–52.
8. "Shanghai Joint Venture," *China Morning Post*, December 11, 1992, p. HS 1; Paul Mooney, "At China's Crossroads," *Far Eastern Economic Review*, November 19, 1992, p. 66; Nicholas D. Kristof, "Poor Chinese Town Bets Its Shirt on Making Buttons," *New York Times*, January 18, 1993, p. A–6.
9. Angus Foster, "Bitter Enemies Become Grudging Partners," *Financial Times*, November 13, 1992, p. 17; Sheila Tefft, "Taiwan Vote Signals Growing Support for Independence," *Christian Science Monitor*, December 22, 1992, p. 6; Sheila Tefft, "Taiwan Investors Exploit Growing Ties to Mainland," *Christian Science Monitor*, February 2, 1993, p. 8.
10. David H. T. Lan, "Hong Kong in the Year 2000," *Nikkei Weekly*, October 26, 1992, p. 14.
11. Eric Chan, "Tian An Signs Deal for Changzhou Project," *Hong Kong Standard*, December 10, 1992, p. 20; Sandy Li, "K Wah Links for $980 million Mainland Development," *Hong Kong Standard*, December 10, 1992, p. 19.
12. Lan, "Hong Kong," p. 6; Kevin Rafferty, "A Serious Case of Mainland Fever," *Emerging Markets*, September 23, 1992, p. 50.
13. Randall Jones et al., *The Chinese Economic Area: Economic Integration Without a Free Trade Agreement* (Paris: Organization for Economic Cooperation and Development, 1992), p. 5.
14. Quoted in Louis Kraar, "A New China Without Borders," *Fortune*, October 5, 1992, pp. 124–125.
15. Paul Blustein, "Forging 'Greater China': Emigres Help Build an Economic Power," *Washington Post*, December 1, 1992, p. A–1.
16. Harold Bruning, "Macau to Hold 51 pc Stake in Airport," *Hong Kong Standard*, December 10, 1992, p. 19.
17. Olin L. Wethington, "Capital Flows, Investment, and Growth" (Presentation to the Pacific Economic Cooperation Coun-

cil, San Francisco, Calif., September 24, 1992), p. 2.

18. Zbigniew Brzezinski, *Out of Control: Global Turmoil on the Eve of the Twenty-First Century* (New York, N.Y.: Charles Scribner's Sons, 1993), p. 194.

19. Robert S. McNamara, "A New International Order and Its Implications" (Paper presented to the Tokyo Conference on "Arms Reduction and Economic Development in the Post–Cold War Era," United Nations University, Tokyo, November 4, 1992), p. 4.

20. Charles Wolf, "Why Asia-Pacific Holds the Cards," *New York Times*, January 17, 1993, p. F-13. Wolf is director of economic research at the Rand National Defense Research Institute.

21. Stewart et al., "The Latest Asian Economy," p. 31.

22. This section draws heavily from Philippe Dollinger, *The German Hansa* (Stanford, Calif: Stanford University Press, 1970).

23. Dan Cordtz and Richard Meyer, "Inside China Today," *Financial World*, December 8, 1992, pp. 36–51.

24. Steven Schlossstein, "Kung-Fu Con Job: Ten Reasons Why China's Economic Potential is Grossly Exaggerated," *International Economy*, January/February 1993, pp. 36, 39.

25. Richard McKenzie and Dwight Lee, *Capital Mobility: Challenges for Business and Government* (St. Louis, Mo.: Center for the Study of American Business, Washington University, 1991); Murray Weidenbaum, "The Business Response to the Global Marketplace," *The Washington Quarterly* 15 (Winter 1992), pp. 173–185.

26. Brzezinski, *Out of Control*, pp. 194–195.

27. Barber B. Conable, Jr., and David M. Lampton, "China: The Coming Power," *Foreign Affairs* 72 (Winter 1992/93), p. 134.

Democracy and Global Economic Growth

John D. Sullivan

DEMOCRACY'S WORLDWIDE ADVANCE has been truly remarkable. Scarcely 15 years ago, a lonely band of countries held to democratic government and, even in the industrialized world, democratic values were under great pressure. Today, the remaining authoritarian regimes struggle to rationalize the basis of their legitimacy. Statist values, especially the Marxist varieties, which were once seen as the great alternative to democracy, are widely discredited by the simple phrase, "it doesn't work."

At the same time, a fundamental shift has occurred away from centralized economic policy toward market-oriented economic systems. The economic disintegration of the Soviet empire exposed the myth of scientific communism to all. Other types of centralized control, ranging from Latin America's state capitalism to African versions of socialism, have been widely discredited in the wake of the debt crisis. Today, the major challenges in economic policy are structural adjustment, privatization, and entrepreneurial development—all of which result in a drastic reduction in governmental control over the economy.

If the 1980s was the decade of political and economic transition, the 1990s must become the decade of consolidation and fundamental change. Although democratic systems have proved to be more durable than previously believed, the transitions in many countries are threatened by poor economic performance, lack of experience with market-based institutions, and the challenge of building participatory systems of governance. Indeed, it was economic failure, combined with political repression, that discredited statist and Marxist alternatives in many parts of the world. Although democracy offers the promise of a better life, democratic governments must prove themselves able to manage the economy in a way that fulfills that promise.

World Trends

Democracy is one of the few systems of government that is based on the idea of limits to governmental authority, especially in the economic arena. It should not be surprising, therefore, that the global wave of democratic transitions has been bound up with the upheaval affecting economic systems throughout the world. However tempting it may be to attribute the revival of democracy to general economic causes, the situation is far more

---

John D. Sullivan is executive director of the Center for International Private Enterprise (CIPE), an affiliate of the U.S. Chamber of Commerce, which has supported over 200 programs worldwide and is one of the principal participants in the National Endowment for Democracy.

complex. A brief review of recent changes in various regions of the world shows the inseparable nature of political and economic change as well as the politics of economics.

The politics of large-scale change combines a multitude of factors such as deeply felt human needs for political rights, economic freedoms, and civil liberties. Further, transitions to democracy are not simply the result of basic issues playing out in some automatic fashion. Their success or failure also turns on the qualities of leadership among those courageous individuals pressing for change and the wisdom of those holding power. Although the following review of recent changes in various regions of the world concentrates on the relation between fundamental political and economic structures, it must be kept in mind that the basic human needs for dignity and freedom as well as countless other factors influence the outcomes as well.

The first transitions to democracy in recent years took place in the mid-1970s in Spain and Portugal. A common element in each case was the desire of the elites to rejoin Europe and specifically to participate in the European Economic Community. The transitions differed greatly in other respects, however. The Spanish transition was managed carefully from the top over a long period while the Portuguese resulted from a military overthrow of a dictator.

In Latin America, the majority of the transitions from military domination to democracy occurred in the context of the general economic crisis of the 1980s. Simply put, the alliance of top military officers and the professional bureaucracy lost credibility both with their own peoples and with the international donor community. Conditions differed greatly, however, from country to country. For example, Argentina's military leaders were disgraced by their own folly in the brief war with Great Britain while Paraguay's rulers were thrown out by the military. International pressure played a very important role in the transitions in Central America, especially in Nicaragua, which held out against change as long as possible. Brazil's opening and the ongoing, although only partial, political reform in Mexico more closely resemble the Spanish case. Yet in each instance, the regime's economic failures were a key triggering condition.

The transition in Chile stands out as the great exception in the Latin American context because it was fueled by rising affluence, not economic decline. The economic strategy crafted by Chile's technocrats was exceptional. During the 1980s, Chile successfully diversified its exports, renegotiated its external debt, liberalized its market structures, and, as a result, turned in a very impressive economic growth rate. Yet, demands for political and civil liberties increased continually. The diversification of Chile's economy helped break the dominance of the old elites and set the stage for a growing middle class with a strong entrepreneurial orientation. By the time of the plebiscite in October 1988, a majority favored ending General Augusto Pinochet Ugarte's rule. It is vital to recall, however, that the opposition parties came together to pledge to continue the technocrats' economic policy.

Chile is the exception in Latin America, but the general pattern fits the East Asian reality very closely. During the 1980s, pressure for political liberalization continued to rise in South Korea, Singapore, Hong Kong, and Taiwan. Economic diversification, a rising middle class, and comparative affluence all fueled demands for elections and popular control over the government. In effect, economic liberalization preceded and helped create the conditions for political change.

For some years, it appeared that Thailand was well along in the same process. Despite a record of coups and attempted coups, the power of the legislative branch and increasing demands for free elections grew along with the economy. The success of the coup in February 1991 may be only a way station or it may point to a more fundamental flaw in the Thai political culture. Although the private sector is expanding, especially the small entrepreneurial sector, it appears that corruption and favoritism are expanding as well. Happily, although most of the country, including the business community, greeted the coup with favor, they also quickly began demanding political and legal reforms and a return to democracy.

It was in the Philippines, though, that political corruption gave rise to an apt phrase that accurately describes one of the central issues in development, namely, "crony capitalism." In the waning years of the Marcos regime, the economic system of the Philippines was a private enterprise economy for the most part but not a market economy. A pervasive pattern of licenses, quotas, and favoritism enabled a small group of traditional landowners and politicians to amass great fortunes. At the same time, these special privileges effectively undermined several essential conditions of an open market economy: competition, free prices, and market access. The general business community, along with a host of civic and social groups, formed the core of the rising opposition to the Marcos regime and the restoration of democracy.

Most recently, the collapse of communism in Central and Eastern Europe was clearly bound up with fundamental economic issues. Throughout the 1970s and 1980s, most of these countries borrowed heavily from Western banks in order to maintain a system in which significant numbers of state firms existed only due to massive subsidies. It was the economic turmoil in the Soviet Union, however, that precipitated the decision to allow each country to find its own way. Once Soviet domination had ended, events began to unfold quickly. The strong and vital Solidarity opposition movement in Poland pressed the limits to oust the former Communists from control of the executive branch and, more recently, to complete the process in the legislature. In Hungary, reformist elements of the Communist party led the process of change that finally turned and overwhelmed them. Some countries, such as Czechoslovakia, were able to succeed through peaceful protest, although violence erupted in others, reaching a peak in Romania. Whatever the path, the myth of communism collapsed in less than two years.

Events continue to unfold in the socialist world. The fate of the successor states to the Soviet Union will be unclear for some time to come. China and Vietnam continue to balance the contradictions of market-oriented economic reform with political centralism, while North Korea remains an enigma. Other socialist countries, such as Angola, Mozambique, and Mongolia, are all fairly far along in the process of economic and political reform. Only Cuba holds fast to the defunct orthodoxy, although it is an open question as to how long this will last now that massive subsidies from its former allies are coming to an end.

Even those countries that practiced a softer or more humane version of state socialism, such as India, have felt the impact of the changes in Central and Eastern Europe. India and Sri Lanka are among the few developing countries that have maintained a more or less continuous democratic political system, but both have faced severe political unrest, in part due to their poverty and lack of economic growth. At one point during the mid-1970s, India suspended the constitution and, even today, several state governments are ruled nondemocratically because of pressure from separatist movements.

India's milder version of Fabian socialism, drawn from British theorists, concentrated on the commanding heights of industry as did other countries in the region. For the last several years, successive Indian governments have been attempting to liberalize the economy, reduce the pervasive levels of corruption, and encourage new entrepreneurship. The government of Prime Minister P. V. Narasimha Rao, elected in July 1991, plans to hold off on any large-scale privatization, probably due to the potential for political unrest and ethnic conflict, always a danger in the South Asian region.

The African transitions, on the other hand, are only now beginning for the most part. The leaders and elites of the independence generation are fading from the scene. Some, like Zambia's Kenneth Kaunda, are leaving gracefully while others, such as Zaire's Mobutu Sese Seko, attempt to cling to power. In recent months, mounting domestic and international pressure, combined with very poor economic performance, have forced political change in countries as diverse as Kenya, Zimbabwe, Angola, and Mali. Nigeria and South Africa, the two giants of Africa, are now in the midst of transitions, both political and economic. Although South Africa's process of change is probably unique unto itself, Nigeria's experience is relevant throughout the region.

Economic failure combined with massive corruption spelled the end of Nigeria's second democratic republic at the hands of a military regime. Structural adjustment of the economy was inescapable, however, and has made some significant progress. At the same time, President Ibrahim Babangida is attempting to create new democratic institutions from the top down. His plan to overcome persistent ethnic, religious, and regional rivalries by mandating a two-party structure is novel and remains to be tested. The law prohibiting former office holders from taking part in the political process, seen as a means of ending corruption, is likely, however, to prove futile. Already the strings of power are being manipulated from behind the scenes by traditional politicians. As long as the political system exerts such great influence over day-to-day economic decisions, corruption is likely to follow and the poorer the country, the greater the degree of corruption. Unfortunately, these are issues that nearly all African countries face.

Only the Middle East and, to a lesser extent, the Islamic world in general seem to be exempt from the global drive toward greater political and economic liberty. In most cases, the core Middle Eastern countries are also protected by their oil revenues or by transfers from other oil-rich countries. The effects of culture and religion no doubt play a major role as well. Equally important is the relative lack of a civil society made up of autonomous associations and movements unconnected to government. In such cases, it is much more difficult to challenge the right of a single group to rule.

Still, in a world where few foresaw the collapse of communism while others maintained for years that the Confucian cultures of Asia could not develop economically, it would be risky in the extreme to predict the outcome. Countries such as Algeria, Egypt, Tunisia, Bangladesh, and Indonesia are undergoing fundamental economic reforms that have included, to some degree, pressures for political reform as well. Pakistan's renewed democratic institutions, while under great pressure, appear to be holding even in the midst of severe economic adjustment. In sum, it is too early to assess the degree to which Middle Eastern or Islamic countries can remain isolated from the surge of democratic reforms.

Core Issues

No one pattern emerges from this brief overview of events in the last decade. At a minimum, four broad groups of countries in transition can be found, at least at a general level. First, in countries such as South Korea, Singapore, or Chile, the rising affluence of the society liberates people to demand greater civil and political liberty. Conversely, in those countries facing economic collapse, especially in Latin America and parts of Africa, the revival of democratic institutions owes much to the failure of military or authoritarian governments to deliver on their promises of national development. Third, Central and Eastern Europe's experience is a unique combination of economic collapse, failure of Soviet power, rejection of an alien ideology, and intense desire for freedom. The fourth group, the successor states of the former Soviet Union, should be treated differently from Central Europe because they experienced a far longer period of communism and are undergoing a far greater degree of economic chaos.

What of the future? The four broad groupings suggested by recent history offer a starting point to look at the core issues each faces in sustaining or developing democracy and economic growth. Because of their history and the realities of the global economy, these four broad groups face vastly different levels of difficulty in accomplishing the goal they have chosen of building market-oriented, democratic societies.

The fortunate few whose democracies are being built in the midst of a healthy and relatively prosperous economy have the simplest task. As shown in Chile and South Korea, their newly elected leaders must strive to construct new patterns of decision making and build participatory political institutions. At the same time, they must maintain their sound economic policies and market-oriented economic institutions in the face of new political pressures for redistribution and social spending. Here the issue is to create a political culture that sustains their highly successful economic openings.

Most developing countries, however, face the dual challenges of building democratic political institutions while carrying out fundamental structural adjustment in their economies. In these countries, the politics of economic reform is complicated by demands for austerity in governmental spending versus the real hardships facing substantial portions of their populations. The new democratic leaders have to avoid the perils of populist appeals if they are to succeed economically. Yet they must also sustain enough immediate economic growth to build solid foundations for a democratic political culture. Recent progress in countries like Argentina and, to a lesser extent, the Philippines demonstrates that skillful leadership can perform the delicate balancing act of fostering a democratic political culture that supports painful economic adjustment.

The third group, the new Central and East European democracies, must not only completely transform their political and economic institutions, they must also deal with the legacy of more than 40 years of communism. Unlike the new democracies in the developing countries, the issue is not reform of economies based on private enterprise that included some elements of a modern market economy. Rather, all of the key institutions have to be built anew even while the rapid expansion of very small entrepreneurial sectors and the privatization of most industries is being promoted. The magnitude of the challenges differs from country to country with Hungary and Poland having the inherited advantage of relatively larger private sectors. The historical traditions of each society differ as well, with the Czech and Slovak Federal Republic joining Hungary, Poland, and the Baltics in having some democratic experiences in recent memory. These traditions, however removed in time and limited in scope, are vital to efforts in these countries to instill the moral and ethical values that are essential to a democratic society and that encourage the entrepreneurial spirit of initiative, creativity, responsibility, and freedom.

By far the greatest challenges, however, face the successor republics of the former Soviet Union. There are vast differences between the European republics and those of Asia, but each must cope with a set of grave issues in addition to those facing Central and Eastern Europe. The first is the simple fact that basic national identities are in a state of flux between some form of loose confederation and complete political independence. Indeed, the issues of ethnicity and shifting borders cast some continuing doubt on the unity of the Russian Federation as a national state. Basic economic issues are directly bound up with the question of national identity with regard to, for instance, the fate of the ruble as a common monetary unit, the portioning out of the center's assets and liabilities, ownership of natural resources, and the all-important issues of national defense. While Russia, Ukraine, Byelorussia, and a few other republics may become viable economic units in time, others are unlikely to attain economic independence.

In addition to questions of economic and political structures, all of the republics face the issues of value systems to a much greater degree than Central Europe. Having experienced a near isolation from the international arena for some 70 years, both the general public and the elites are having great difficulty in grasping the basic concepts of the modern world. Words like democracy and private enterprise have become so distorted in the Soviet environment that many of the basic building blocks contained in everyday language are simply not available. Further, in many of the Asian republics, Islam is a dominant factor that further complicates the evolution of national identity and the establishment of democratic societies for the same reasons described above.

The core issues that each of these four broad groups of countries must solve in the interest of political and economic progress are in some senses cumulative. The fortunate few face only the issues of creating democratic political institutions while most others must also cope with the structural adjustment essential to creating a market-oriented economy. Central and East European countries must begin at a more fundamental level by transforming their societies and value systems. The former Soviet Union faces all of this plus the most basic of questions, the size and shape of the nation itself.

The prospects for success are obviously greater for those countries that have fewer core issues to solve. The peoples of all of the nations described above, however, are striving to build democratic, market-oriented economic systems. Their individual conceptions of the ideal set of political institutions differ as do their ideas of the proper role of the government in the economy. Nevertheless, they have taken the decision to begin, affirming the global appeal of democracy.

What of other countries? The Chinese leadership continues to grapple with the contradictions of centralized political control and economic liberalization, which began almost a decade ago. To all appearances, the economic success experienced in the southern provinces continues to undermine Beijing's ability to impose political control. Despite the tragedy of Tiananmen Square, the signs point to the eventual emergence of political democracy. Conversely, Fidel Castro's Cuba continues to attempt to maintain both a command economy and the Communist political system. This is clearly untenable because Cuba cannot survive without massive external subsidies. Whether change will come is not the question, only when and how.

Within the developing world, the majority of the African countries are now experiencing increased pressure for political change. Given their economic plight, resolution of the issues they face will be difficult and prolonged. Democracy, however, is not an all or nothing condition. Free elections and basic political liberties are essential but not sufficient. Nor are elections necessarily the first step in building a democratic society. Many of the African countries are already creating participatory institutions in both the public and private sectors. As essential economic reforms proceed, the emerging private business community, a free press, trade unions, and other civic groups will continue to grow in stature and in their ability to affect governmental decisions, thus laying the basis for future democratic societies. Although such institutions take time to create, they can develop fairly quickly with assistance from developed nations.

The far smaller group of countries with more or less stable democratic institutions, such as India, Sri Lanka, Colombia, Venezuela, and Costa Rica, also requires assistance. Despite their democratic tradition, often well established, many of these countries suffer from internal violence and separatist movements that are typically sparked by ethnic issues, inequitable income distribution, and overall poor economic performance. Although Costa Rica handles these issues fairly well, most others do not. In circumstances such as those found in Colombia or Sri Lanka, the survival of democratic institutions cannot be assured without fundamental change in economic structures and policies.

The most difficult question remains the future of the Middle Eastern countries and the overall Islamic world, including some of the former Soviet republics. Progress in countries such as Indonesia and Pakistan argues in favor of the eventual development of democratic values compatible with Islamic cultures. Historically, Christian and Confucian values adapted to the requirements of market economics and democracy within a secular state. Seen from a distance, Islam may seem to be a single value or cultural system. In reality, it is very diverse and continually changing. One hope for the Islamic world is that the desire of people for basic human dignity, political freedoms, and civil liberties will help shape the culture of Islam just as it has other cultures over history. Courageous Arab democrats, like their counterparts in, for instance, Central Europe, are creating the civil society groups that provide the moral and ethical leadership essential for progress. Given the tendencies of those in power to maintain the existing systems, the most probable outcome is that change will occur first in those countries whose lack of oil resources forces more engagement with the international system. In short, authoritarian leaders in non-oil countries have fewer resources to prevent change.

Obstacles and Solutions

The great war of ideas that defines the twentieth century is finally over. The central ideals of democracy and market-based economic systems are now accepted in most of the world. At the most fundamental level, the idea that a self-appointed group of individuals can run a country is seen as folly. The transitions to democracy during the 1970s and 1980s, as well as those yet to come, are due to a variety of political and economic factors and to the quest for a higher quality of life by people everywhere.

Although the brief review of recent trends highlights various ways that changes in political systems affect and are affected by economic factors, it also rebuts any simple notion that economic change alone causes the development of democracy. The current situation in China is one of the clearest examples of the complex interactions of politics, economics, culture, and the demands for dignity and freedom by students, workers, and the emerging entrepreneurial groups. Today, China's leadership faces the dilemma faced to one degree or another by all those seeking to maintain centralized control after having lost their claims to legitimacy. Conversely, the situation is far better in those countries that are in the process of building democratic systems and market-based economies. Democratic values can provide the basis of legitimacy needed to surmount the challenges of fundamental economic and political reform.

Several common factors lie behind each of the specific situations faced by nations in transition, ranging from the easier tasks of constructing political democracy in conditions of relative wealth to facing the fundamental challenges of complete social transformation. At the most basic level the major obstacle to developing democracy is simply one of experience with democratic and market institutions. In short, how do market-based democratic societies work?

Few people realize how complex it is to establish and run the institutional infrastructure essential to a modern society. As the post-Communist countries continue to transform their structures, both they and the developed countries are gaining a new perspective on this issue. One of the frequent comments overheard during the last year has been, "The market hasn't emerged." The implicit thought is that a free enterprise system somehow establishes itself spontaneously. The same remarks are made, but less frequently, about political institutions, especially with respect to the day-to-day aspects of governmental decision making. In fact, the two areas are directly linked, for it is through the constitutional, political, and governmental processes that the basic rules and structures that form market mechanisms are established.

Hernan Buchi, the architect of Chile's economic transformation, has written that he needed over 500 trained people to introduce the essential reforms in the governmental bureaucracy.[1] Competent business managers, experienced entrepreneurs, accountants, bankers, and other professionals are also essential to a market economy. On the political side, well-trained and experienced legislators, political operatives, and elected officials at all levels, especially local government, are indispensable.

A second obstacle that must be overcome is the lack of educational opportunities and systems in most of the newly democratizing states. The institutional structures described above combined with sound economic policy are only part of the picture. Recent studies by the World Bank have confirmed what many have long thought. The highest levels of economic growth in the developing world over the period from 1965 to 1987 are for those countries that have both high levels of basic education and essentially sound economic policies.[2]

In addition to basic education essential to economic development, education in citizenship and values is also vital. Democracy requires tolerance, willingness to compromise, and respect for democratic procedures on the part of the overall population. Some of these values can be taught in the formal educational systems; others require national leadership such as the exemplary, selfless role played by Václav Havel, the president of the Czech and Slovak Federal Republic.

Communications and exposure form another area that is closely related to education. The information and communications revolutions of the last 30 years have produced societies in the developed countries that are far more informed than ever before. Most other parts of the world lag behind to a greater or lesser degree. The communications obstacle has several dimensions. First, of course, is the need for a free press and mass media to be responsible and effective in critically reporting and analyzing the claims of politicians and elected officials, especially regarding economic issues. The role of the media in establishing political freedom is well understood but their role in sustaining economic growth receives far less attention. Business and commerce require sound information on domestic and global economic conditions in order to devise business plans, market products, and attract investment. Building up a sound financial press with the freedom to circulate accurate information and the freedom to critique economic policy is essential.

A second dimension within the exposure and communications area is telecommunications. Few countries outside of the developed world have an adequate telephone system, much less access to international telecommunications networks. Most often this is simply due to the fact that most governments run the telecommunications industry as a state monopoly, and run it very badly. Such conditions make it nearly impossible to conduct business internationally and, very often, even between cities within the same country. Even a mild rain storm can knock the phone system out completely for hours if not days. All of these factors undermine economic growth and business performance.

Developing the institutional experience, educational systems, and communications infrastructure needed to run the institutions of a modern economy or political system is obviously a costly undertaking. In fact, nearly every specific obstacle that must be overcome in the quest for democratic development usually comes back to the question of resources. Not all countries face the same level of challenge of course. The group of newly industrializing countries, mainly in East Asia, and a few others such as Chile have far more freedom of action. Not only are their peoples already more educated and exposed, but they have access to the international capital markets and enjoy considerable economic growth internally. Nearly every other country in the world, however, faces severe resource constraints ranging on a scale from countries like Argentina or Hungary at one end to those like Ethiopia or Bangladesh at the other.

Even in the poorest countries, however, far more could be done than is being done. Financial resources are always limited, which means that priority has to be given to expenditures that build wealth. In this respect, the developing world provides a very poor track record, as do the countries of Central and Eastern Europe. Military expenditures nearly always outrank spending on education, as has been frequently noted. This pattern must change and, if need be, should be a condition for access to assistance from the International Monetary Fund, World Bank, or donors. Enormous funds could be freed up with the right measures.

It is here that the development of democratic values and institutions can play an especially important role. For the most part, the goal of military expenditures is the control of the domestic population, not the deterrence of external aggression. The further broadening of democracy may, in time, begin to rein in excessive military spending, freeing scarce capital for productive investments in education, communications, and business services.

U.S. Foreign Policy

In these changing times, U.S. foreign policy faces the most complex set of challenges and expectations since the end of World War II. In some ways the challenges are even greater. Alone among the great powers, a victorious and economically powerful United States both designed and underwrote global reconstruction in the 1950s. In the 1990s, it will be much more difficult to cope with the wreckage left behind by communism and the failure of statist development policy, particularly in Africa. Yet, the United States and the other industrialized countries now live in a world where global economic and political forces cannot be escaped. From the oil fields of the Middle East to the emerging markets of Asia and Africa, events affect the international flow of capital and trade as well as U.S. values to an unprecedented degree.

Fortunately, meeting the challenges of democratic development demands relatively less in the way of funds but much more in sophistication and creativity than the earlier challenges of controlling disease or building physical infrastructure. Of the many aspects of the foreign policy agenda two warrant special attention: leadership and assistance.

In the area of leadership the United States has made great strides during the last 15 years. Although the transitions to democracy were essentially the work of national patriots, essential support from the United States played a vital role at important moments. The most visible examples were in the Philippines and Chile, where U.S. policy eased the transition process. In a less visible area, U.S. policymakers played a vital role in working with the Soviet decision makers of the time during the critical two-year period leading up to free elections throughout Central and Eastern Europe.

Today, continuing leadership is vital to sustain the new democracies and encourage liberalization in other countries. U.S. diplomats working in Africa can play a vital role in countries like Kenya and Nigeria where progress is now a real possibility. China, of course, is one of those cases where quiet diplomacy can persuade or, if necessary, pressure the gradual easing of political restrictions.

Leadership is not limited to the purely political aspects of diplomacy. U.S. policy toward the World Bank helped create a new sensitivity toward the private sector and democratic development. Because the Bank is an intergovernmental institution, outside pressure from the major donor countries is one of the few ways to generate fundamental rethinking of its policies and, more important, of the Bank's technical assistance to developing and transitional countries.

Leadership, however, is not simply a matter of quiet diplomacy or discussion of technical and policy issues within international institutions like the World Bank or the North Atlantic Treaty Organization (NATO) structure, important as these are. Leadership demands a larger framework to integrate the domestic and international policies of the United States and its allies. At the end of World War II, the United States publicly committed itself to two simultaneous processes. First, the creation of the postwar Bretton Woods system provided the structures needed to build an effective international economic system within which specific policies like the Marshall Plan could be carried out. Second, the policy of containment and the creation of the NATO alliance provided an international security system capable of defending Europe and the United States. In both cases, the core issues were then, as they are today, the preservation of freedom in democratic societies and market-based economic systems.

Today, the demands on leadership are far greater because fewer resources are available from the United States. On the one hand, leadership will require the coordination of the United States and the other industrialized countries to face the magnitude of the collapse within the former Soviet empire. At the height of the Great Depression, the U.S. economy contracted by some 8 percent per year, leading to a cumulative contraction of 30 to 35 percent. Within the former Soviet Union, the impact could be several times as much. The economies of Central and Eastern Europe will be hit again by the loss of their markets in Russia as will a number of other countries ranging from Cuba to India. The collapse will have profound consequences for the entire international system.

On the other hand, leadership will require a framework that integrates the elements of domestic and international policy into a seamless web to sustain domestic support for U.S. policy. Some of the elements are in place, although not articulated as such. For example, the resurgence of democracy in the Americas combined with economic recovery can go a long way to addressing the need for new markets for U.S. goods. The Enterprise for the Americas Initiative and the free trade agreement with Mexico could become part of the framework for integrating U.S. domestic and international interests in a clear and compelling way. More than technical, legal, and economic explanations are required, however. Presidential leadership can and must join the global trend toward democracy with the fulfillment of the United States's own interests.

Simultaneously, the area of U.S. assistance policy must be addressed if existing U.S. capabilities are to sustain presidential leadership. Here the record is more mixed. For the most part, the U.S. foreign aid programs including the Peace Corps, the U.S. Agency for International Development (AID), and the U.S. Information Agency (USIA) are not seen as a "serious" part of basic foreign policy. This is tragically shortsighted, particularly because similar agencies play a much greater role in Japanese and European foreign policy. One indication of this lack of attention is that the basic authorization legislation for AID frequently fails to pass in Congress, while the executive branch has often left the agency to run on its own.

A deliberate upgrading of the status of the foreign assistance programs, probably entailing a complete reorganization, would be in the long-run best interest of the United States. Alone among the great powers of the modern age, the United States fails to balance fundamental economic factors with political considerations. Obviously, the foreign assistance strategy could not begin to cope with all of the complexities of current foreign policy. A serious upgrading, however, could begin to educate U.S. policymakers on the need to integrate economic, political, and strategic factors at all levels of policy up to the presidential level itself.

Further, some basic rethinking needs to be done regarding U.S. foreign assistance strategy. Since its inception, AID and several other such agencies have directed their assistance, in large part, through the recipient governments. Such a policy presents enormous opportunities for political patronage, corruption, and misallocation of priorities on the part of the recipients. If U.S. policy is to foster the development of democracy and the establishment of market institutions, it is a grave error to allow decision making to be held hostage to the host government's own political agenda.

Some years ago, the U.S. government began funding quasi-governmental and nongovernmental U.S. organizations to address this problem. Groups like the Asia Foundation, the National Endowment for Democracy, and the Inter-American Development Foundation were established to tackle political and economic development issues outside of the official executive branch structure. Taken as a whole, these groups have a far better track record than some of the official executive branch agencies, due mainly to their ability to bypass recipient governments, but their funding levels are a fraction of the total foreign assistance budgets.

The next few years will be crucial for a number of countries that are well into the process of democratic development. Others, including Central Europe, Russia, Ukraine, and most of Africa, will require assistance for a much longer period of time but for different reasons. In all of these cases, leadership and assistance from the United States will make a vital contribution to the future of both the recipient countries and the United States itself.

Notes

1. Hernan Buchi Buc, "Reflections on Economic Change in Chile," *Economic Reform Today* 1, no. 1 (1991), published by the Center for International Private Enterprise, U.S. Chamber of Commerce, Washington, D.C.

2. *World Development Report 1991* (New York: Oxford University Press, 1991), p. 5.

The Post–Uruguay Round Free Trade Debate

Ernest H. Preeg

A debate about free trade is under way in the United States, but it is not fully engaged and is ill-defined in conceptual terms, including what free trade means today. There is no question, however, that the debate marks a fundamental shift in orientation for international trade relationships. For almost 50 years, the multilateral trading system, centered on the General Agreement on Tariffs and Trade (GATT), involved a process of gradual trade liberalization among all members. Free trade—the complete elimination of border restrictions—however, was never seriously pursued or considered feasible, even as a long-term objective. Now, in contrast, a metamorphosis is taking place in trade relationships in which free trade has become an explicit objective, on a multilateral as well as regional basis.

One problem with understanding this metamorphosis in trade relationships is that it is caught up in a broader debate over trade policy conducted in more traditional terms between liberal traders and protectionists. The North American Free Trade Agreement (NAFTA) and Uruguay Round agreements, approved by the U.S. Congress in 1993 and 1994, were major steps toward more open markets, and several post–Uruguay Round initiatives, as explained below, lead further in that direction. A growing array of voices and forces, however, is arguing to restrict trade. Political figures, including Democratic house minority leader Richard Gephardt (D–Mo.), Republican presidential candidate Patrick Buchanan, and Ross Perot, decry the loss of U.S. jobs resulting from NAFTA and GATT. Other leading politicians are raising serious concerns about national sovereignty and liberal trade agreements. The Clinton administration has shown little positive interest in the newly created World Trade Organization (WTO), while protectionist interests turn to means other than tariffs to limit foreign competition, such as antidumping complaints. Pessimism runs especially strong among free trade economists, who see the liberal trading system laboriously created since World War II under severe threat. A noteworthy example of such anguish is a recent book, *American Trade Policy: A Tragedy in the Making*, by Anne Krueger, president-elect of the American Economic Association. The purpose of the book is to explain "the tragedy of current U.S. trade policy,"

Ernest H. Preeg holds the William M. Scholl Chair in International Business at CSIS, and is the author of *Traders in a Brave New World: The Uruguay Round and the Future of the International Trading System* (1995).

Copyright © 1995 by The Center for Strategic and International Studies and the Massachusetts Institute of Technology
The Washington Quarterly • 19:1

which has been "increasingly schizophrenic." Krueger concludes that although the open multilateral trading system has served the world well, the United States has failed to exert leadership in support of it.[1] Many of her conclusions are well taken, but the analysis needs to probe deeper into fundamental changes taking place in trade relationships.

The conclusion drawn here is that the liberal trade momentum of recent years will prevail, perhaps even intensify. The rationale for such a conclusion, however, goes beyond reading the short-term political tea leaves and rests largely on the underlying dynamic forces of free trade. The principal purpose of this article, in fact, is to disentangle the evolving free trade relationships from the broader trade policy debate, with particular emphasis on implications for the structure of the world trading system, which are political as well as economic. It begins with an assessment of the free trade process now under way defined in terms of three interacting dimensions: multilateral free trade by sector; comprehensive regional free trade; and the broadening scope of policies included in free trade relationships. This is followed by commentary on the two primary driving forces for free trade, namely the rapidly expanding "dynamic gains from trade" and the private sector leadership role. Finally, a multilateral/regional free trade synthesis is presented that brings together the various components of the debate in terms of what the future course of trade relationships could or should be.

The Three Dimensions of Free Trade

Free trade can be pursued unilaterally, as was done by Hong Kong, simply by eliminating import barriers to all trading partners on a nondiscriminatory or most-favored-nation (MFN) basis. Free trade areas are also permitted, under article XXIV of GATT, among a self-selected group of countries, whereby barriers are eliminated on substantially all of the trade among members while tariffs remain for imports from non-members. If a common external tariff is formed for non-members, such a free trade area is called a customs union. Until the mid-1980s, relatively little trade, except raw materials and some agricultural commodities, was duty-free on an MFN basis, and regional free trade was limited principally to Western Europe. By the mid-1990s, however, free trade on both an MFN and regional basis had grown substantially and further important steps are under active discussion. As defined above, this free trade process involves three dimensions: multilateral free trade by sector; regional free trade agreements; and a broadening scope of policy commitments.

1. Multilateral Free Trade by Sector. The prolonged Uruguay Round negotiations of 1986–93 initially paid little attention to tariff reductions and bogged down over a formula for doing so. Only in 1990, at the initiative of private sector leaders in the United States and other industrialized countries, was the approach of "zero-for-zero" tariff elimination by sector pursued, beginning with the pharmaceutical sector and later extending to eight other sectors, including farm machinery, medical equipment, furniture, and toys. The final Uruguay Round agreement, as a consequence, resulted in more than doubling—from 20 percent to 44 percent—the share of non-agricultural imports by industrialized countries that will be free of duties on an MFN basis.

In 1995, a post–Uruguay Round initiative by the "Quad" countries (the United States, the European Union [EU], Japan, and Canada) was launched to eliminate remaining tariffs in the information technology sector (computers, components, semiconductors, and software), to extend such sectoral free trade later to the telecommunications sector, and to align other technology-related policies as part of a broader global information infrastructure strategy. If this all takes place, as is likely, well over half of non-agricultural imports by these countries will be duty-free.

The WTO has a mandate to develop further sectoral free trade agreements and would be wise to do so. The chemical sector, for example, emerged from the Uruguay Round with tariffs harmonized mostly at a low 5 percent level, and the final move to zero would not be difficult. The automotive sector—troubled by non-tariff barriers in the Japanese market and EU quotas on imports from Japan—has generally low levels of tariffs, which could be phased out in the context of a broader agreement on non-tariff barriers to market access.

This path of MFN tariff elimination by sector, however, faces two major problems in the WTO that will limit the outcome. The first is that the sectors adopted for free trade are those in which multinational companies tend to dominate as they seek to benefit from market rationalization on a global scale, of which more below. Other sectors, including textiles, footwear, and most of agriculture, remain highly protected, with little inclination toward free trade on the part of the industrialized countries. The net result is thus likely to be a very uneven structure of tariffs by sector.

The second problem is that sectoral free trade up to this point is not fully multilateral but is limited to the industrialized grouping. Developing countries played a more active role in the Uruguay Round but did not participate in tariff elimination by sector, and the more advanced developing countries in Asia and Latin America continue to maintain relatively high tariffs. The pharmaceutical and other industries supporting multilateral free trade were disappointed over the lack of participation by developing countries in the Uruguay Round, and they will continue to complain about the "free ride" afforded to such countries whereby they have free access to industrialized country markets while maintaining high protection at home. This asymmetry in market access will create a problem for any future round of multilateral trade liberalization in the WTO.

2. Comprehensive Regional Free Trade. The most active dimension of the free trade debate thus far concerns the proliferation of regional free trade agreements since the mid-1980s, which was triggered by the reversal of long-standing U.S. policy opposing such agreements. The United States first negotiated free trade agreements with Israel, Canada, and Mexico through NAFTA. Then, in 1994, agreement was reached to negotiate free trade in the Western Hemisphere by 2005, beginning with Chile and an interim "NAFTA-parity" agreement with the Caribbean Basin countries, and in the Asia–Pacific region by 2020, with a 2010 date for the more advanced Asia–Pacific countries, including the United States and Japan.

The EU, meanwhile, has been broadening its regional free trade grouping in the wake of the collapse of the Soviet bloc. Austria, Finland, and Sweden joined in 1994, interim free trade agreements leading to membership have been negotiated with the Visegrad four (the Czech Republic,

Hungary, Poland, and Slovakia), and a customs union with Turkey is close to agreement. Further EU expansion to the east and south is anticipated, perhaps eventually including some of the former Soviet republics. Elsewhere in the world, subregional free trade agreements include Australia/New Zealand, the Association of Southeast Asian Nations or ASEAN (Brunei, Indonesia, Malaysia, the Philippines, Singapore, Thailand, and Vietnam), and Mercosur (Argentina, Brazil, Paraguay, and Uruguay).

The most recent proposal, with far-reaching political as well as economic implications, is for a transatlantic free trade agreement (TAFTA), which would reflect the dynamic interaction among the various regional free trade initiatives. U.S. free trade objectives in the Western Hemisphere and the Asia–Pacific region have left the transatlantic relationship, long the backbone of U.S. economic and security relationships, in a subsidiary position—the dog that isn't barking. Europeans are concerned that they may be left out of a dominant economic grouping that embraces the Western Hemisphere and the Asia–Pacific. Indeed, initial proponents of some kind of EU/NAFTA accord were Europeans, plus Canadian prime minister Jean Chrétien. The Clinton administration reaction has been cool to adverse, although some influential Americans with a more strategic perspective of the world economy, including House Speaker Newt Gingrich (R–Ga.) and former secretary of state Henry Kissinger, advocate a TAFTA.[2]

The growing relative importance of regional free trade agreements is apparent in the share of world exports included in them. Trade within the EU and NAFTA alone accounts for almost 40 percent of world exports. EU agreements with the Visegrad four and Turkey, U.S. agreements with Chile and the Caribbean Basin countries, Australia/New Zealand, ASEAN, and Mercosur, raise this figure by another 4 to 5 percent. The further inclusion of Western Hemisphere and Asia–Pacific Economic Cooperation (APEC) free trade agreements would increase the share to 65 percent, and of a TAFTA to over 70 percent. In terms of trade coverage, regional free trade agreements are clearly headed toward a majority position within the overall trading system.

Two noteworthy aspects of the regional trend make such free trade agreements the leading edge for the evolution of the trading system in broader terms. First, they are able to bridge the dichotomy between industrialized and developing countries that has existed in GATT and been carried over in the WTO under the rubric of "special and differential treatment." In the multilateral system, developing countries are not expected to provide fully reciprocal access to their markets, which has been a continuing cause of friction, as noted above with respect to tariff elimination by sector in the Uruguay Round. Regional free trade agreements, in contrast, tend not to make this distinction. Within NAFTA, Mexico is eliminating virtually all border restrictions, in agriculture as well as in industry, from the 70 percent of its imports coming from the United States and Canada, while in the Uruguay Round Mexico maintained MFN tariffs in the 10 to 20 percent range and only agreed to bind many of them against future increase at 40 percent. Extension of NAFTA to Chile and others in the Western Hemisphere should follow the same pattern—little or no special and differential treatment. Similarly, EU membership agreements, earlier with Greece and Portugal, and now with the Visegrad countries and Turkey, are based on the principle of fully reciprocal elimination of import restrictions, even though all of these countries can be considered to some extent less developed.[3]

The second leading edge aspect of regional free trade agreements involves integration or harmonization of other trade-related policies. This broadening scope of policies encompassed by free trade agreements is, in fact, the third and least clearly defined dimension of the free trade debate.

3. The Broadening Scope of Policy Coverage. The definition of free trade can be limited to the elimination of border restrictions on imports—tariffs and quotas—leaving all other related economic policies unchanged. GATT article XXIV is so drafted for regional free trade agreements, and tariff elimination by sector in the Uruguay Round was negotiated on this basis. Trade agreements over time, however, have tended to include a broader and broader scope of other trade-related policies. This reflects, in part, the fact that as border restrictions are reduced or eliminated, other policies become relatively more important in influencing trade flows and thus need to be assimilated in the trade relationship. Even more important, the structure of world trade has changed greatly, particularly since about 1980, creating pressures for a far broader scope of policy response. Key aspects of this changed structure of trade are the subject of the following section of this article.

The broadening scope of policy inclusion in the international trading system has been proceeding on various fronts, through multilateral as well as regional agreements. The multilateral Uruguay Round agreement broadened the mandate of the GATT/WTO to include trade in services, which by definition extended coverage to investment policy for companies delivering services abroad. The Uruguay Round also added the protection of intellectual property rights to the multilateral trading system, as well as expanded coverage of technical standards and certain trade-related investment measures. Finally, the agreement called for further consideration of competition and investment policies in the future, and a multilateral investment agreement is already being negotiated in the Organization for Economic Cooperation and Development (OECD), presumably for later incorporation in the WTO.

The broadening policy scope of trade relationships is most prominent, however, in regional free trade agreements, principally the EU and NAFTA, which constitute the leading edge for the trend toward policy integration. The EU has established the goals of a single integrated market and monetary union, while NAFTA has a more modest but still comprehensive scope of policy coverage, including investment policy, protection of intellectual property rights, financial services, transportation, and side agreements for labor and environmental standards.

Free trade, therefore, has two limiting definitions: at a minimum the elimination of border restrictions and nothing more, or a full economic and monetary union more or less as being pursued by the EU (and as exists among states within the United States). Other free trade agreements, including NAFTA, fall somewhere in between, and where the lines are drawn is based on political as well as economic factors. Why, for example, a monetary union for the EU and not for NAFTA? The reality of deepening economic interdependencies, in any event, increases the relative economic

83

benefits of broader policy integration, and this is most apparent within what are appropriately termed "comprehensive" free trade agreements.

Regional free trade agreements can also create the conditions for dealing with problems in policy areas that cannot be addressed adequately within the multilateral trade system. Antidumping procedures, for example, which are subject to growing protectionist abuse throughout the world, can simply be eliminated inside free trade groupings, as they have been in the EU, provided that antitrust and other elements of competition policy in member states are made reasonably comparable. This step would indeed be highly desirable for NAFTA.[4]

Finally, the broadening scope of trade-related policy integration—and thus the broadening definition of free trade—is being driven as much by market forces as by government design, which is fundamental to understanding where the international trading system is heading over both the short and longer term. These market forces, in turn, can be assessed in terms of two interacting components: the rapidly expanding dynamic gains from trade and the private sector leadership role.

The Dynamic Gains from Trade

International trade is stimulated by "gains from trade," whereby an increase in overall output is achieved as countries specialize in what they do best at the lowest possible cost. Classical trade theory focuses on the "static" gains from trade, in which relative costs and modalities of production remain constant. One country produces clothing more efficiently while another produces wine, and they trade to mutual advantage. When trade barriers are reduced, the relative prices between domestically produced and imported goods change in favor of more imports and, indirectly, more exports. Trade expands as do the static gains from trade. Such gains continue to be reaped as trade barriers are reduced multilaterally in the Uruguay Round, regionally through free trade agreements, and unilaterally as countries pursue economic reforms that include trade liberalization.

There are also, however, "dynamic" gains from trade, whereby national economies increasingly open to international trade become more productive by changing the structure and methods of their production. Such dynamic effects can take various forms. More intensive import competition can force domestic firms to restructure and cut costs, as happened in the U.S. automotive industry in the late 1980s. Increasing returns from large-scale production for export can be obtained not only from longer assembly lines, but also from spreading out the costs of research and development—important for semiconductor and commercial aircraft producers, and critical for the burgeoning computer software industry, in which production costs can be trivial compared with the cost of new product development. Finally, dynamic gains from liberal—or free—trade result from international direct investment and technology transfer stimulated by the more open national markets. Entire new export industries are created, as is happening especially in the more advanced developing countries in Asia and Latin America.

A major driving force for trade liberalization since about 1980 has, in fact, been a veritable explosion in the dynamic gains from trade stemming, in large part, from an unprecedented wave of technological change sweeping the globe. This information-based technological change, still in its early stages, is having a profound impact on the structure of world trade, as well as on national economies. At both levels, the restructuring can be difficult and painful for some firms and workers, but the inherent net dynamic gains, as outlined here, are compelling.

The operative characteristic of this world economy in the process of change is "globalization," that is, the increasing dependence of national economies and companies on external markets. Since the early 1980s, the volume of world merchandise exports has been growing twice as fast as gross domestic product (GDP). GATT Secretariat projections indicate an additional 25 percent growth in exports above this trend line from the Uruguay Round agreement alone. International direct investment has grown even faster than exports since the currency realignments beginning in the mid-1980s. Technology transfer, largely embedded in direct investment, is expanding dramatically. Indeed, the term "international trading system" is misleadingly restrictive. What is really at stake is an integrated process of international exchange in goods and services, investment, technology, and, to a lesser extent, labor.[5]

The telecommunications and financial services sectors play a pivotal role not only as large and rapidly growing sectors of trade in their own right, but because they form much of the infrastructure for the globalization of markets. Telecommunications services provide knowledge about foreign markets and the technical capability for integrated international production and marketing. Financial services delivered through private capital markets are highly integrated on a global scale and provide investment capital to a new breed of international financial entrepreneurs.

A key aspect of the globalization process of particular relevance to the free trade debate is that it is very uneven by region and sector. There is, in fact, a synergy between deepening economic interdependence in certain regions and sectors and an accommodating free trade policy reaction by governments. This synergy centers geographically on the tripolar relationship among the advanced industrialized regions of Western Europe, North America, and East Asia. The share of world trade within and among these three regions rose from 60 percent to 75 percent during the 1980s, and the share of international investment controlled by these countries is even higher. The globalization process has recently been broadening to other "newly industrializing" markets in South America, South Asia, and Eastern Europe, while the "least developed" countries in much of Africa, the Middle East, and Central Asia are conspicuously left behind.

All of the above is illustrative of a rapidly expanding, highly dynamic international economy. A major measurement problem exists, however, that acts to cloud a full appreciation of what is happening, namely, that while the dynamic gains from trade are recognized to be far greater than the static gains, they are also more difficult if not impossible to measure. Many economists tend to limit their assessment of the gains from trade to the more easily quantifiable static gains, and thus to greatly underestimate the full benefits of free trade. For example, the GATT Secretariat estimated the static gains to world trade from the Uruguay Round agreement at $140 billion per year once the agreement is fully implemented, but this figure increases sharply to $512 billion when some of the dynamic effects are included. Even the latter figure, however, excludes the application of new technologies and investment in new export industries stimulated by the Uruguay Round agreement, which are simply not measurable, but which may constitute the most important gains of all over time.

Although economists can ignore dynamic changes that do not fit their established economic models, private sector leaders cannot afford to do so. Indeed, their interests concentrate on highly measurable profits to be gained through trade- and investment-related projects based principally on the dynamic gains from trade, even though not expressed in such terms. As market horizons spread across national borders, business leadership is increasingly free trade oriented as a matter of enlightened self-interest.

The Private Sector Leadership Role

The movement toward free trade, by region and by sector, has resulted in part from the initiative of governments and in part from private sector leadership. President Ronald Reagan had a vision of free trade within North America that he pursued with characteristic tenacity, and the surprise decision of Mexican president Carlos Salinas de Gortari in 1990 to seek a free trade agreement with the United States was critical for NAFTA. Key European political leaders, likewise, were dedicated to the formation of a united Europe in the early postwar years and their successors are now deeply engaged in broadening and deepening the EU. Private sector leaders, however, have also come to play a more active role in developing new market-opening initiatives, most prominently in the United States, but with a growing habit of collaboration among North Americans, Europeans, and Japanese. In recent years, determined private sector leaders have often been out in front of hesitant governments.

Private sectors are, of course, not monolithic when it comes to trade policy. The protectionist interests of some firms compete with the liberal trade objectives of others. Nevertheless, the strong and growing tendency among the majority of private sector leaders is not only for continued trade liberalization, but for definitive moves to free trade on a pragmatic, step-by-step basis. This tendency in corporate policy orientation derives from the globalization of markets described above. Large investments of international scope, with major trade components, require security of market access, the flexibility to adjust production as markets evolve, and a minimum degree of bureaucratic and administrative interference by governments. Free trade at the border and reasonable comparability in other trade- and investment-related policies constitute the best policy framework for multinational business.

A more assertive private sector role in establishing liberal and free trade policy objectives can be traced to the late 1970s, when the U.S. private sector insisted that trade in services be brought within the GATT multilateral trading system. Pressures were brought on a less committed executive branch through the Congress. The U.S. private sector then joined with its European counterparts to press their case with even more reluctant European governments, and the service sector became a primary negotiating objective of the Uruguay Round. Similarly, the U.S. and other industrialized governments were undecided whether to pursue the protection of intellectual property rights in the Uruguay Round. The decisive move came from the U.S. private sector in late 1985, shortly before the Uruguay Round agenda was adopted, first to convince the U.S. government to pursue such an objective as a high priority, and then, together with European and Japanese business organizations, to draw up a statement of specific negotiating objectives that became the industrialized country mandate for the Round.

Tariff elimination by sector in the Uruguay Round, as noted earlier, was largely a private sector initiative as well. Most governments were seeking some formula for across-the-board percentage cuts in tariffs, with little success, when private sector deliberations came up with the simpler concept of sectoral free trade, whereby all companies would end up competing on an equal basis with minimal government interference. The 1995 initiative for free trade in the information technology sector is an even more interesting example of private sector initiative because European governments, in particular, insisted on maintaining high protection for the semiconductor industry up to the end of the Uruguay Round. European companies in the computer sector, however, understand that the resulting higher cost of semiconductors undermines their competitive position throughout this rapidly growing sector.

Comprehensive regional free trade has also been supported consistently by most of the private sector because it permits a broader geographic scope of market rationalization. U.S. private sector support for NAFTA was critical to its success, while European and Japanese firms were not openly opposed, in good part because they, too, can now invest and trade in an integrated North American market. The initiatives in 1994 to achieve free trade in the Western Hemisphere and the Asia–Pacific region also came about through strong and pointed support from private sector leaders in the face of initially disinterested government attitudes in Washington and other capitals. Yet another case in which private sector leaders are out in front of governments is the OECD initiative for an investment policy agreement, which the OECD private sector advisory committee had been advocating strongly for several years before governments finally responded. Looking ahead, the evolution of the concept of a TAFTA will also greatly, and perhaps critically, be influenced by deliberations that will undoubtedly take place among private sector leaders on both sides of the Atlantic.

A Multilateral/Regional Synthesis

The foregoing outlines the principal elements of substance underlying the post–Uruguay Round free trade debate, which can be recapitulated as follows: Important trade relationships are moving toward free trade, within sectors and regions, to the point where free trade could soon be dominant in the overall trading system. At both the sectoral and regional levels, moreover, free trade is increasingly "comprehensive" in that agreements to eliminate trade barriers at the border are linked to commitments on other trade-related policies, principally in the areas of technology, investment, and competition policies. The overall process is being driven by the enormous and growing gains from trade, based largely on the application of new technologies. The net result is a transformation of international trade relationships, writ large to include direct investment and technology transfer, with important political as well as economic implications.

The debate itself concerns the policy response to these rapidly evolving circumstances, and in particular a strategy for reconciling the momentum toward regional free trade with the reinvigorated but still relatively loosely drawn multilateral trading system contained in the newly created WTO. There are many facets to such a strategy, but unfortunately, as stated at the outset, the debate up to this point is not fully engaged and remains conceptually ill-defined. Some oppose further trade liberalization and would like to roll back the Uruguay Round and NAFTA agreements, but their argumentation is essentially episodic demagoguery, mostly related to the short-term effects of the Mexican financial crisis, and little attention is given to the impact on U.S. interests of termination of these agreements. Private sector leaders, for the most part, support specific steps toward free trade on a case-by-case basis rather than in conceptual terms of where the overall trading system is headed. Many in the economics profession, as noted earlier, are predisposed to focus analysis on the limited static effects from free trade rather than on the full impact on world economic relationships. Academic economists also tend to see multilateral trade liberalization and regional free trade agreements as "either/or" competitors, and betray a deep-seated preference for unambiguous, "first-best" multilateralism.[6]

The challenge of formulating a broad trade strategy at this important post–cold war juncture is, in any event, one of international economic statesmanship, and it is in this context that the lack of a fully engaged debate—and leadership—is most disappointing. The strategic vision of post–World War II leaders, which created the Bretton Woods economic system, including GATT, the West European economic union centered on Franco-German reconciliation, and the North Atlantic Treaty Organization security alliance against the Soviet threat, is nowhere to be found. "The vision thing," scorned by the Bush administration, has been virtually excluded from a Clinton administration trade policy dedicated to short-term negotiating objectives. In any event, by mid-1995, trade policy for both American political parties had become largely a tactical matter related to the 1996 election campaign, politically motivated schizophrenia to use Krueger's term. European leaders, meanwhile, are preoccupied with broadening their regional grouping without antagonizing farmers and other special interests, while Japan pursues its economic interests in consistently pragmatic rather than conceptual terms. The lack of interest in strategic thinking about the trading system was clearly apparent at recent economic summit meetings of the group of seven industrialized countries (G–7). At Naples in 1994, the United States proposed a new multilateral trade initiative but without being able to specify what it would consist of, and others understandably rejected it. At the Halifax summit in 1995, trade strategy was simply not addressed.

The principal recommendation to be derived from this presentation is that a full-scale debate on short- and longer-term objectives for the international trading system—writ large to include investment, competition, and technology-oriented policies—should begin. In particular, these objectives should focus on a synthesis between the largely separate multilateral and regional directions of policy currently engaged and work toward a reasonably well-defined, integrated structure. In order to stimulate the debate, the concluding paragraphs outline a four-step scenario for the next several years that would result in such a synthesis, oriented toward free trade relationships of broad scope.

1. Utilize 1996 as an Achievement-Oriented Hiatus. No major trade initiatives can be expected before the U.S. presidential election, but 1996 can be utilized to achieve several significant objectives already in train. Multilateral agreements among industrialized countries for free trade in the information technology sector and for investment policy should be pursued and hopefully completed. NAFTA membership for Chile and an interim NAFTA-parity agreement for smaller Caribbean Basin countries should also be concluded, which will require a difficult but modest dose of bipartisan compromise during an election year. The EU can be expected to continue consolidation of free trade arrangements to the east, especially with the Visegrad countries and Turkey. The WTO faces deadlines to define its role in the trade-environmental policy interface and to complete an agreement to incorporate trade in basic telecommunications services. Broader consultations within the WTO and the various regional groupings could clarify longer-term objectives, but no major breakthrough should be anticipated.

2. Develop a Transatlantic Free Trade Agreement (TAFTA) Proposal for Early Negotiation. Such an initiative would have to begin with wide-ranging discussion of political as well as economic objectives, a dialogue that should not be limited to governments but include legislators and private sector leaders as well. Such dialogue should begin in 1996 so as to reach a more formal stage by 1997. The North Atlantic relationship is ripe for free trade and a TAFTA would reinstate the industrialized democracies of North America and Western Europe together at the center of the overall trading system rather than leaving them as the separate poles of two potentially competing regional groupings in Europe and the Western Hemisphere–East Asia. An early TAFTA initiative is also likely to be a necessary catalyst to engage the broader OECD-plus negotiation discussed under step three.

The substance of a TAFTA would center on the phaseout of tariffs on non-agricultural trade between the EU and NAFTA. Various other trade-related issues, however, would be included on the agenda, many of which are already being discussed bilaterally between the United States and the EU or within the OECD. Agriculture would have to be handled separately to some extent, but this would not be as daunting as many believe. The Uruguay Round, fortunately, changed the EU Common Agricultural Policy from its former incompatibility with the GATT trading system—high domestic price supports, variable import levies, and unlimited export subsidies—to a compatible structure moving in the right direction, namely, a shift toward income support for farmers, fixed tariffs subject to 36 percent cuts, and 21 to 36 percent reductions in export subsidies. Moreover, the Uruguay Round agreement provides for resumed agricultural negotiations within five years with a view to further liberalization. This latter provision would fit a TAFTA scenario, under which a further five-year phased liberalization in agriculture could be adopted in conjunction with a long-term commitment to free trade.[7]

3. Consolidate through an OECD-Plus Free Trade and Investment Agreement. This agreement would be the decisive step to integrate the various regional free trade groupings. The initial objective would be to merge the TAFTA free trade objectives with the yet to be defined APEC 2010 target for free trade. APEC members in the first stage free trade group will include the United States, Canada, Mexico, Japan, Australia, New Zealand, and perhaps South Korea. The TAFTA–APEC 2010 grouping would thus basically coincide with OECD membership and the free trade accord would be combined with the forthcoming OECD investment agreement to create the overall trade and investment agreement. Such an OECD-wide free trade negotiation could also begin directly, skipping the TAFTA phase, but the judgment here is that some serious transatlantic free trade deliberations would be necessary first to establish a more attractive political setting for the broader OECD initiative.[8] The "plus" would be an open-ended arrangement to encourage others to join as they are able to make the transition to free trade, beginning with those countries in East Asia, Latin America, and Eastern Europe already committed to establish free trade with NAFTA or the EU. The net result would be a dominant free trade grouping within the trading system, initially accounting for three-quarters of world exports, with the explicit intent to broaden in scope to include others as their free trade objectives develop.

4. Integrate the OECD-Plus Agreement with the WTO. This process would be more than simply depositing documents at Geneva and would require considerable restructuring of the WTO as it currently exists. As a trading system, it would indeed represent a metamorphosis from a common set of multilateral rules and procedures for all members committed to a gradual process of trade liberalization to a central and dominant free trade relationship with accommodation for others in transition to that status. Special and differential treatment would prevail for least developed countries, but the concept of conditional–MFN, long resisted in GATT, is likely to have to be included in some attenuated form for the more advanced trading nations not part of the inner free trade grouping. Decision making on the basis of one-nation-one-vote, the political Achilles heel in the current WTO, in which 50 percent of the members account for only 1 percent of world trade, is likely to have to be reconsidered. A name change to the World Trade and Investment Organization would also be in order.

These four steps represent a forceful strategy to consolidate and reinforce the movement in recent years toward free trade and to reconcile the separate multilateral and regional free trade policy tracks that have emerged. Some will disagree with the composition of the strategy, others with the free trade direction. In any event, such a strategy for the international trading system would need to be related to national objectives in other areas. The benefits of free trade for the United States would depend, to a large extent, on a corresponding domestic strategy to strengthen the international competitiveness of U.S. industry. The international financial system, which serves to accommodate the rapid growth in trade and investment, deserves a reevaluation in light of recent turmoil in currency markets. Fundamental questions about national sovereignty and the structure of the world political order need to be factored in. This presentation is thus by no means the last word in the free trade debate but, to the contrary, an initial call to full engagement. Let the real post–Uruguay Round free trade debate begin!

Notes

1. See Anne O. Krueger, *American Trade Policy: A Tragedy in the Making* (Washington, D.C.: AEI Press, 1995), pp. 6–7.
2. Speaker Gingrich proposed a TAFTA as well as a free trade agreement with Japan in his first full-length speech on foreign policy at a CSIS meeting on July 18, 1995; Henry Kissinger called for a TAFTA in an op-ed piece in the *Washington Post*, May 12, 1995.
3. The EU subscribes to a policy of regional subsidies favoring its lower-income members, but this does not detract from the fully reciprocal basis of the trade relationship.
4. Antidumping procedures can be eliminated once free trade is established because exports sold at unfairly low prices can be "dumped" back in the exporting country market. The link to competition policy, among other things, is to make sure such dumping back can take place.
5. A full presentation of the restructuring of the international trading system "writ large" is contained in Ernest H. Preeg, *Trade Policy Ahead: Three Tracks and One Question* (Washington, D.C.: CSIS, 1995), chaps. 2 and 3.
6. For example, two leading free trade economists, Krueger again and Jagdish Bhagwati, have accentuated the negative about regional free trade agreements, with Bhagwati concluding that such a policy is a mistake. See their *The Dangerous Drift to Preferential Trade Agreements* (Washington, D.C.: American Enterprise Institute, 1995).
7. Such a further step in agricultural policy by the EU will almost certainly be necessary to permit membership of the Visegrad four without breaking the budget, and a TAFTA initiative could help provide the political setting for such a decision.
8. The idea of OECD-wide free trade, or "GATT-plus," has periodically surfaced over the years, but has never received significant political support. A recent proposal is contained in Gary Hufbauer, *U.S. Trade Policy 1989–1993: Guide Posts for the Bush Administration* (New York, N.Y.: Twentieth Century Fund, 1989). This proposal, however, came at a point of prolonged impasse between the United States and the European Community in the Uruguay Round and was presented as an alternative to the largely discredited GATT, hardly a favorable context for free trade.

II. The U.S. Competitiveness Debate

Competitiveness: Here to Stay

Daniel F. Burton Jr.

COMPETITIVENESS IS A TERM that, for many, captures the challenges facing the U.S. economy. Yet ever since it first surfaced in the early 1980s, it has been repeatedly dismissed as wrongheaded or irrelevant and disparaged as an unwarranted critique of U.S. industry and economic policy. Early critics felt that it was wrong, even slightly unpatriotic, to entertain serious thoughts about systemic challenges to the industrial prowess of the United States. Furthermore, because competitiveness implied that government and industry should seek to work more closely together to strengthen U.S. economic performance, some equated it with a heavy-handed industrial policy that would have the government pick winners and losers in the economy.

Despite these criticisms, competitiveness entered the mainstream of the U.S. economic policy debate. So much so that by the late 1980s, it was dismissed again, this time as just another Washington buzzword that would quickly go out of fashion. It did not. By the early 1990s, the White House and Congress had joined the U.S. private sector in regularly referring to competitiveness as a driving rationale for their policies.

Its impact on the U.S. private sector cannot be overestimated. International competition has forced U.S. firms to conceive of their business in entirely new ways. It has led them to reassess their products, their customers, their markets, and their rivals. It has prompted them to search out new management ideas around the world and to implement them at home. It has driven them to hone their skills against the most demanding customers worldwide. And it is the major force behind efforts to streamline production, improve quality, accelerate cycle-time, and rethink the innovation process.

This revolution in the private sector has not been lost on government officials. With the end of the Cold War, competitiveness has emerged as a new national priority, much as containment was during the past half century. Although a lot of the attention has focused on trade, the competitiveness agenda goes much further, to such areas as technology, education, and investment. Moreover, the urgency of the issue is not limited to the United States; national centers of competitiveness are being established in countries as diverse as Canada, South Korea, Portugal, and Venezuela.

Given all of this activity, it should come as no surprise that competitiveness has attracted fresh attention and criticism. Just as containment was

---

Daniel F. Burton Jr. is president of the Council on Competitiveness, a nonpartisan coalition of 140 chief executives from U.S. business, higher education, and organized labor.

Copyright © 1994 by The Center for Strategic and International Studies and the Massachusetts Institute of Technology

hotly debated in the early postwar era, so is competitiveness today. The past year has witnessed two new critiques. The first surfaced in late 1993 when many voices in the media pieced together anecdotal evidence about U.S. industry's improved performance and announced that the competitiveness challenge was over; the United States had won. With the revitalization of firms from Detroit to Silicon Valley, the press confidently asserted that the problems that plagued the nation's economy during the 1980s—such as poor quality, the high cost of capital, and outdated manufacturing systems—had been overcome. Moreover, with Europe and Japan mired in recession, the United States was once again the unrivaled economic leader of the world. Unfortunately, this view mistakes progress for the endgame. Although there can be no doubt that U.S. firms have made tremendous advances, there is still a long way to go. In a Council on Competitiveness poll of U.S. chief executive officers, labor leaders, and university presidents taken in summer 1994, respondents stated by a two-to-one margin that the toughest competitiveness challenges for the United States still lay ahead.[1]

The most recent attack on competitiveness has come from Paul Krugman, a professor at the Massachusetts Institute of Technology. In the spring 1994 edition of *Foreign Affairs* and in his book *Peddling Prosperity*,[2] Krugman states that competitiveness is an irrelevant and even dangerous concept when applied to national economies. His comments have been widely noted, in part because he helped develop the strategic trade theory that is often associated with competitiveness. Because of his reputation as one of the nation's premier young economists and the scope of his criticism, it is worthwhile to systematically review his argument. In doing so, this article will explain why competitiveness has proven to be such a resilient term and why it remains such a dynamic concept.

At the outset, it should be noted that Krugman has forced economists and policymakers alike to think carefully about competitiveness in terms of both its economic validity and its policy implications. This reassessment is especially important because of the powerful impact that the competitiveness debate is having on U.S. economic policy. If U.S. policymakers are to use it as a way to assess the nation's strengths and weaknesses and fashion appropriate public policy, they must understand not only its lessons, but also its limits.

Krugman, however, pushes his argument too far. Although he raises some interesting points, his conclusion—that competitiveness is a "dangerous obsession"—is not warranted. On the contrary, competitiveness is a valuable concept that can, and has, led to constructive public policy.

In some ways, Krugman's argument is largely semantic. He likes the word "productivity," but not the word "competitiveness." His major complaint is that competitiveness focuses on relatively unimportant issues, like trade balances, and in doing so detracts from the biggest determinant of national economic performance, namely growth in domestic productivity. He believes that this focus is the result of faulty analysis by economists who should know better and leads to bad public policy.

Yet, although international trade has received a lot of attention in the competitiveness debate, so have investment, technology, and human resources, which together constitute the building blocks of productivity. As for the charge that competitiveness leads to distorted public policy, and in particular protectionism, the record of the last decade does not support this claim.

In developing his critique Krugman makes several points, three of which are especially noteworthy and deserve a thoughtful response: (1) countries are not like companies, and any comparison is misleading; (2) competitiveness is a meaningless concept that, at best, is "a poetic way of saying productivity"; and (3) public policies based on worries about competitiveness are sure to lead to trouble. Each of these is considered below.

Countries Are not like Companies

Krugman contends that competitiveness means very different things for countries and companies. Companies compete with each other in a zero-sum game in which one firm's gain is another's loss, but countries do not. Instead, because of the law of comparative advantage, all countries gain from trade with each other. Furthermore, unlike companies, countries produce the bulk of their goods and services for their own consumption, so most of their business will continue no matter how uncompetitive their foreign trade sector may become. As a result of these differences, Krugman does not believe that countries are in any significant degree in economic competition with each other.

This argument assumes a neat distinction between countries and companies that does not exist. The economic output of nations consists largely of the output of firms. Just as countries have a vested interest in how their firms perform, so companies have a stake in the economic vitality of the country in which they are located. The depth of this economic interdependence makes it difficult to separate the fortunes of companies and countries and to say categorically that although firms compete fiercely in the world economy, countries do not.

Krugman's argument also fails to recognize that with talent, technology, and capital mobile around the world, countries are very much in competition with each other for the skills and investment that fuel economic growth. During the 1960s and 1970s, it was popular to speak of the "brain drain" of skilled professionals from the rest of the world to the United States. Today, foreign-born and -bred executives lead many U.S. laboratories and are at the helm of such companies as Ford, Intel, Apple, 3M, and Coca-Cola. A decade ago, in the midst of the third world debt crisis, there was massive capital flight from the developing world to the United States. Today, these trends are just as likely to be reversed, with talent and capital leaving the United States to pursue greater opportunities overseas.

What Krugman objects to most is the notion that rapid growth in other countries reduces the standard of living in the United States. Although some analysts and members of the press may have created the impression that this is the case, the argument for competitiveness does not rest on this assumption. On the contrary, it recognizes that with open international markets rapid growth and a rising standard of living overseas will create greater demand for U.S. goods and services.

What the competitiveness argument does emphasize is that to the extent that U.S. industry can efficiently produce goods and services that are in strong demand around the world, it can increase its exports and command high prices. These, in turn, will contribute to a rising standard of living for U.S. citizens. By contrast, if other countries produce quality goods and services more efficiently than the United States, its exports will come under increasing pressure and it will be forced to compete on the basis of lower prices, which means that its standard of living will suffer. This premise does not contradict the fact that domestic productivity determines the long-term competitiveness of U.S. exports. On the contrary, it highlights the spur of international competition as a major incentive to boost productivity performance. A good example is the transformation of the U.S. automotive industry during the past decade—a transformation that was clearly inspired by international competition.

This fact highlights the need for both firms and governments to be alert to how well their counterparts are doing and try to learn from them. This is one of the more significant lessons of Japan. It is not enough simply to compare a country's present performance to the past; it must also be compared with others around the world. In business, this kind of comparison is often described as "benchmarking against world-class." Such comparisons are powerful because they shed light on innovations that can lead to significant gains in productivity—gains that are vital to companies as well as countries. This lesson has not been lost on the U.S. government, as will be seen below.

It is not necessary to assume that countries and companies compete in identical ways to appreciate the fact that their fortunes are closely linked. Nations enjoy higher standards of living when their firms are relatively more productive and can compete effectively in world markets on the basis of factors other than lower prices. Moreover, countries do compete to attract skilled labor and capital, and they can learn a lot about how to boost their productivity by comparing themselves to their counterparts overseas.

The Poetry of Competitiveness

One of Krugman's biggest complaints is that a preoccupation with competitiveness detracts from really important issues, like productivity, and focuses attention on less significant ones, like trade balances. From the outset, however, the competitiveness debate has emphasized the importance of domestic productivity. *The Report of the President's Commission on Industrial Competitiveness* published in 1985 is generally accepted as the source for the standard definition of competitiveness. Volume 3 of that report clearly identifies productivity—not trade balances—as the central issue:

> A nation's competitiveness is the degree to which it can, under free and fair market conditions, produce goods and services that meet the test of international markets while simultaneously expanding the real incomes of its citizens. Competitiveness at the national level is based on superior productivity performance and the economy's ability to shift output to high productivity activities which in turn can generate high levels of real wages. Competitiveness is associated with rising living standards, expanding employment opportunities, and the ability of a nation to maintain its international obligations. It is not just a measure of the nation's ability to sell abroad, and to maintain a trade equilibrium.[3]

In other words, the mainstream argument for competitiveness does not assert, as Krugman says it does, that "the bottom line of a national economy is simply its trade balance, that competitiveness can be measured by the ability of a country to sell more abroad than it buys."[4] On the contrary, it stresses the pivotal role that productivity plays in a nation's economic performance.

The biggest difference between Krugman and advocates of competitiveness is really one of degree. He tends to emphasize the importance of domestic productivity performance and downplay the impact of international trade on the U.S. economy, whereas competitiveness advocates tend to emphasize both domestic productivity and the impact of international trade. Krugman states that because exports account for only about 10 percent of gross domestic product, marginal changes in exports have an insignificant impact on the economy as a whole. Competitiveness advocates instead highlight the revolutionary impact that international trade has had on the broader economy, including domestic productivity.[5] In doing so, they focus not only on the imports and exports of goods and services, but also on the international flow of ideas.

During the past decade, concern about international competitiveness has had a major impact not only on the U.S. traded goods sector but also on the entire U.S. economy. As firms and workers realized the extent of the challenge of international competition, they have reexamined their approach to production, human resource management, and innovation and reached out to embrace new ideas from around the world.

Quality is perhaps the most obvious example of this trend. Although an American, Edward Deming, was the father of the modern quality movement, his ideas were not put into practice in the United States until it was clear how successful they had been in Japan. Similarly, new inventory control techniques, known as just-in-time production, that were first developed in Japan have had an extraordinary impact on U.S. industry. U.S. human resource management has also been influenced by methods introduced in other countries. The current emphasis on teams, continuous training, and greater employee involvement in the decision-making process all have their roots overseas. These ideas alone have revolutionized much of U.S. industry.

Management of the innovation process in the United States has also been profoundly affected by competitiveness. In seeking to understand why foreign firms were able to move into markets pioneered and once dominated by U.S. firms, many observers were struck by their novel approach to innovation. During the cold war era, the United States developed a view of progress in science and technology as a step-by-step sequential process, a relay race whereby a basic research runner handed the baton to an applied research runner, who handed off the product to marketing specialists, and so on. In their attempt to catch up with the United States, other countries developed an altogether different approach. Instead of a relay race, they viewed research and development (R&D) as a total team effort that subordinated individual heroics to a coordinated team approach and systematic long-term progress. In this respect, they viewed it as more akin to a basketball game in which research was constantly exchanging ideas with engineering, manufacturing, and marketing. This powerful new, concurrent approach to innovation was subsequently borrowed by the United States and has transformed much of its industrial research base.

The adoption of these new ideas has not been limited to a few manufacturing firms in the U.S. traded goods sector. Many companies that are in the 90 percent of the economy that Krugman cites as immune from international competition have also been quick to embrace them. Total quality management, for example, has migrated from manufacturing to many other sectors of the economy and today is found in industries as diverse as insurance and medicine.

It is also important to note that the influence of competitiveness is not limited to the U.S. private sector. The public institutions of the United States, such as its schools, are also focused on the competitiveness challenge. A recent example is the April 1994 report, *Prisoners of Time*, by the National Education Commission on Time and Learning. This report concluded that it is unreasonable to expect U.S. students to achieve world-class academic standards when they spend so much less time on academic subjects than their counterparts overseas. In particular, it noted that in the last four years of secondary school, "French, German, and Japanese students receive more than twice as much core academic instruction as American students."[6] Again, we have here an example of how the benchmark of international competition is fundamentally changing the behavior of institutions in ways that have a powerful impact on the economy of the United States, including its domestic productivity performance. These influences go far beyond the goods and services exchanged in the foreign trade sector.

It is precisely because competitiveness allows people as diverse as managers, researchers, engineers, teachers, and public officials to think about their performance in an international context and to strive to match world-class standards that it is so important. Far from dismissing the importance of productivity, competitiveness emphasizes it and illuminates the means to achieve it. In doing so, competitiveness makes a real contribution to the economic policy debate.

For most people, national productivity is an obscure economic term. Simply saying that productivity is key to economic performance does not shed light on how to achieve it. But when the productivity of U.S. firms is contrasted to that of foreign firms, and the productivity of the U.S. economy to that of other nations, productivity appears in a different light. These comparisons show in stark terms why productivity is so crucial to the U.S. standard of living and, more important, what contributes to it. Large trade deficits and the loss of many high-paying jobs to foreign competitors are not the sum total of the competitiveness problem, but they signal a need to reconsider such issues as quality, education, innovation, and investment that together point the way toward productivity.

Public Policies

Krugman's last criticism is that competitiveness leads to distorted and ultimately destructive public policy. In particular, he claims that it results in a misallocation of resources, protectionism, and an ideological bent that permeates policy decisions in unrelated areas. He further states there is no longer any hope that fears about foreign competition can be channeled toward constructive ends, such as reducing the budget deficit, rebuilding infrastructure, and other much-needed initiatives. His biggest concern is a trade war. In the epilogue to his book *Peddling Prosperity*, Krugman develops a hypothetical example of a competitiveness-inspired trade war that stems from U.S. protectionism "matched by Japanese retaliation and

European emulation. Within two years the results of four decades of negotiations to open world markets are reversed."[7]

These are strong claims. There is no reason, however, to rely on speculation and hypothetical examples to assess their merit. The United States has a decade of experience with competitiveness as a stimulus for public policy. What is the record?

In fact, it is a very good one. First, how has it affected trade? Far from stimulating protectionism and the collapse of the world trading system, the competitiveness debate has been accompanied by a further opening of world markets. President Bill Clinton's most noteworthy trade accomplishments so far are the conclusion of the Uruguay Round of the General Agreement on Tariffs and Trade and passage of the North American Free Trade Agreement. Both of these are designed to liberalize trade, not restrict it. As host of the Asia Pacific Economic Cooperation (APEC) conference in Seattle in November 1993, he also championed the need for open trade within the Pacific region. Krugman's concern about a trade war appears to stem from the tough stance that the United States has taken toward Japan. Here he confuses negotiating tactics with extreme scenarios. Being a tough negotiator is not synonymous with rampant protectionism. U.S. trade policy toward Japan has focused on opening the Japanese market, not protecting U.S. industry from foreign competition. And although the Clinton administration has taken a strong stance in its trade negotiations with Japan, it has also shown flexibility in its willingness to accommodate Japan's current political instability.

A close reading of the policy debate also shows that neither the U.S. government nor the private sector views competitiveness primarily as a trade issue. It has not led U.S. public officials or private sector managers to focus slavishly on trade balances or to regard protectionism as the solution to their problems. A lot more is going on, much of which relates to efforts to stimulate U.S. productivity.

Competitiveness is squarely behind such policies as the Baldrige Quality Award, which was established by the Department of Commerce under President Ronald Reagan to encourage U.S. enterprises to adopt world-class quality standards. To quote the executive director of the Baldrige Award, Curt Reimann, "The focus of the Baldrige Award is enhancing competitiveness."[8] Although Baldrige began with a focus on manufacturing firms, it also includes services and small business, and its program managers are currently exploring the possibility of extending the program to include health care and education. Winners of the award pledge to spread the practice of quality, not just within their own industry, but to firms across the country.

Concerns about U.S. competitiveness are also behind legislation designed to improve U.S. education and training programs, such as the Goals 2000: Educate America Act and the School-to-Work Opportunities Act. Goals 2000 explicitly states that by the year 2000 "U.S. students will be first in the world in science and mathematics achievement." The School-to-Work Opportunities Act takes much of its inspiration from German apprenticeship programs designed to make sure that students are ready for the demands of the workplace when they graduate from school. Will these initiatives succeed? It is too early to tell, but there is no doubt that competitiveness has played a constructive role in focusing the United States on critical domestic education and training problems—problems that if addressed would strengthen U.S. productivity performance and economic growth.

Competitiveness has also had a significant impact on U.S. R&D policy. Here it has prompted a series of programs designed to enhance U.S. industry's ability to develop and commercialize new technology. Some of these programs, such as the information superhighway the Clinton administration is promoting, fall into the category of strengthening the nation's technology infrastructure. Others focus on providing incentives for industry to develop critical technologies with broad application, such as the Advanced Technology Program at the National Institute of Standards and Technology (NIST), launched under President George Bush, and the more recent Technology Reinvestment Program at the Advanced Research Projects Agency in the Department of Defense. Still others, such as the Manufacturing Extension Program at NIST, focus on diffusing new ideas across the industrial base. Federal laboratories have also heeded the call. As they restructure their programs in the wake of the Cold War, they are striving to work more closely with industry to develop technologies that will strengthen U.S. industrial competitiveness.

Competitiveness has even had a salutary impact on management in the federal government. The effort to "reinvent" government was inspired by the competitiveness challenge and prompted Washington to reach out for best practices from around the country and the world in an effort to make government more productive.

Krugman concedes that Washington has been able to draw on competitiveness rhetoric to accumulate support for constructive but politically sensitive policies, such as reducing the federal budget deficit. He believes, however, that competitiveness will not play this role in the future, presumably because he sees it as irrevocably linked with a protectionist trade policy. As the discussion above shows, however, competitiveness continues to influence a wide range of constructive public policies that focus on domestic economic performance, not just trade policy. And even in the trade arena, it is not at all clear that competitiveness is driving the United States inevitably toward protectionism or a trade war with Japan. In fact, the view of mainstream competitiveness advocates and the record of every administration since the early 1980s, when this debate emerged, reflects the strong conviction that the United States must open markets further, not restrict them.

A War of Words

There is no doubt that competitiveness is a broad concept subject to diverse interpretations, which in turn can sometimes create confusion. A careful reading of the competitiveness debate, however, does not support the claim that it is a dangerous obsession that overemphasizes trade, underestimates productivity, distorts public policy, and leads to disastrous protectionism. On the contrary, from the beginning competitiveness has recognized that productivity is key to the economic performance of the United States and has shed light on ways to improve it. Moreover, it has emphasized the importance of open markets and, as the record of the past 10 years indicates, led to a series of very constructive public policies, not protectionism.

Although we can rue the fact that competitiveness is sometimes taken out of context, this does not invalidate it as a concept. In many ways, the competitiveness debate is similar to the cold war debate about containment. Both are sweeping ideas that are difficult to define neatly. Both have led to pitched discussions about definitions and the policy implications that flow from them. And both are too important to ignore. Although containment was couched in foreign policy terms, in the end it had just as much, if not more, to do with the internal fortitude of the United States as a nation—the vigor of its political institutions, the dynamism of its society, the robustness of its economy.

The same can be said about competitiveness. Although the argument may be couched in terms of foreign trade, it is ultimately about the strength and vitality of domestic institutions. Like containment, competitiveness forces the United States to think long and hard about its national priorities in the international arena and to measure its progress against those priorities. This is an essential task for any nation and is much too important to be dismissed by an argument that is largely about semantics.

Because the issue is so difficult for many people to grasp, the private sector Council on Competitiveness developed a Competitiveness Index in 1987 to translate it into terms that were easier to understand. The index consists of a pyramid with four levels (see figure 1). At the pyramid's pinnacle is standard of living; the ultimate aim of a productive nation is to maintain this at a high level. Because how well Americans live is in part determined by how well the United States does in world markets, just below standard of living is trade, or exports. Because the ability of the United States to export at favorable terms is largely determined by its productivity, the third level of the pyramid is labeled productivity. At the base of the

Figure 1
The Competitiveness Index

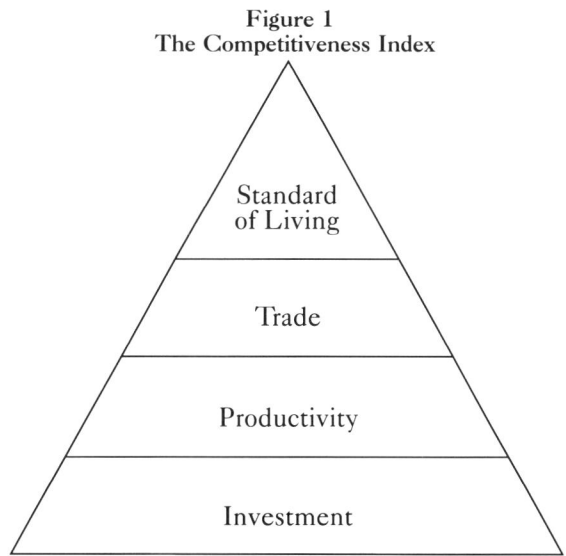

Source: Council on Competitiveness, Washington, D.C., 1987.

pyramid are the building blocks of productivity—the combined investments in education, R&D, and plant and equipment that underpin U.S. long-term economic success.

This pyramid attempts to demonstrate the linkages among these issues. If the United States wants to maintain a strong standard of living, it must have strong performance not only in trade, but also, and especially, in productivity and underlying investments. By showing these linkages in graphic form, the pyramid highlights the means of enhancing U.S. productivity growth. Although the reference point may be international, the agenda is largely domestic. By emphasizing the importance of investments in education, equipment, and technology, competitiveness focuses attention on the essential building blocks of productivity. It is these building blocks that are the real heart of the debate.

In the end, the logic of competitiveness does not lead inevitably to protectionism or the petulant concern that growth in Japan's standard of living diminishes that of the United States. Instead, it lends focus and urgency to the effort to create a world-class economic environment in the United States. It envisions a skilled work force, strong investment incentives, a solid technology base, a first-rate infrastructure, and a streamlined regulatory environment—all in the context of a rising standard of living. In short, it highlights the need to create an environment for investment, innovation, and productivity that is second to none.

The effort to create such an environment has already begun. The firms, schools, workers, and government institutions of the United States are all retooling to the reality of international competition. In some areas, like quality, clear progress has been made; in others, like technology, there are the beginnings of new policies that could yield real benefits in the future; in still others, like elementary and secondary school education, there has been too much talk and not enough meaningful reform. These efforts will take time. It has taken decades for the full scope of the competitiveness challenge to emerge; it will take decades for the U.S. economy to restructure and respond to it.

Although some have tried to paint competitiveness as a divisive, partisan issue, in reality it enjoys broad bipartisan support. The public debate has spanned two Republican and one Democratic administrations, and has grown in urgency with each one. It is not about heavy-handed industrial policy, nor is it about corrosive protectionism. Instead, it is about building partnerships between the public and private sectors that will allow U.S. firms and workers to meet world-class standards. The challenge for groups like the Council on Competitiveness is to outline constructive policy recommendations in such areas as capital formation, human resources, technology, and trade; to develop the political consensus necessary for action; and to make sure that public policy is structured so that it enhances the ability of the United States to compete in world markets.

It is not necessary to equate companies with countries to believe that competitiveness has validity. At bottom it is about much more than the performance of a few sectors or exporters; it is about national aspiration and self-discipline in the international economy. The response of the United States to the challenge this concept offers will have a decisive impact on the health of its economy and its standard of living. Americans would all be the poorer if competitiveness were dismissed as a dangerous, irrelevant slogan.

The views expressed are the author's and do not represent those of the Council on Competitiveness.

Notes

1. Council on Competitiveness, *1994 Competitiveness Index* (Washington, D.C.: Council on Competitiveness, July 1994).

2. Paul Krugman, "Competitiveness: A Dangerous Obsession," *Foreign Affairs* 73 (March/April 1994); *Peddling Prosperity: Economic Sense and Nonsense in the Age of Diminished Expectations* (New York, N.Y.: W. W. Norton, 1994).

3. The President's Commission on Industrial Competitiveness, *The Report of the President's Commission on Industrial Competitiveness*, vol. 3 (Washington, D.C.: GPO, 1985), p. 1.

4. Krugman, "Competitiveness," p. 31.

5. See Ernest H. Preeg, "Krugmanian Competitiveness: A Dangerous Obfuscation," in this issue.

6. *Prisoners of Time*, Report of the National Education Commission on Time and Learning (Washington, D.C.: GPO, April 1994).

7. Krugman, *Peddling Prosperity*, p. 289.

8. Curt W. Reimann and Harry S. Hertz, "The Malcolm Baldrige National Quality Award and ISO 9000 Registration: Understanding Their Many Important Differences" (Baldrige Award, Department of Commerce, Washington, D.C., August 1993).

Krugmanian Competitiveness: A Dangerous Obfuscation

Ernest H. Preeg

PROFESSOR PAUL KRUGMAN, in his recent *Foreign Affairs* article "Competitiveness: A Dangerous Obsession," concludes that "competitiveness is a meaningless word when applied to national economies. And the obsession with competitiveness is both wrong and dangerous." The argumentation is elaborated in the final chapter of his book *Peddling Prosperity: Economic Sense and Nonsense in the Age of Diminished Expectations,* leading to the more explicit judgment:

> So, if you hear someone say something along the lines of "America needs higher productivity so that it can compete in today's global economy," never mind who he is, or how plausible he sounds. He might as well be wearing a flashing neon sign that reads: "I DON'T KNOW WHAT I'M TALKING ABOUT."

The flashing neon sign someone is clearly President Bill Clinton.[1]

This frontal assault on Clinton administration economic policy rests on three interconnected judgments, none of them fully justified, that together lead to an unjustified overcorrection to the shortcomings of Clinton competitiveness policy. The first judgment pertains to the definition of competitiveness as it is used in current policy debate, the second concerns the relative importance of trade to U.S. national economic performance, and the third deals with conceptual issues of the "New Trade Theory." Each is addressed in turn here and then brought together in terms of a policy assessment.

The central theme of this article is that, contrary to Krugman, the world trading system—defined broadly to include the international exchange of goods, services, investment capital, technology, and labor—has a substantial and growing impact on U.S. productivity and growth. The driving force in this relationship is an unprecedented wave of technological change on a global scale that began in the manufacturing sector during the 1980s and is now spreading to virtually all sectors of the national economy. The Krugman writings, in contrast, downplay to the point of negation this central phenomenon of our time, and mislead the reader through unwarranted selectivity in supporting analysis, a tendency to provide easy answers for inherently complex questions, and a highly provocative style of exaggeration and personal attack. The net re-

---

Ernest H. Preeg holds the William M. Scholl Chair in International Business at CSIS.

sult is a dangerous obfuscation of U.S. trade policy interests.

Defining Competitiveness

Competitiveness is an elusive term and has been subject to much abuse. The question is whether it nevertheless has relevance to the current trade policy debate in the United States and other countries. This debate has focused principally on the role of government in supporting technology-intensive industries, and it takes place in the broader context of economic "globalization," whereby national companies are becoming increasingly international in their investment and marketing strategies. The predominant view of corporate leaders is that international competitiveness is indeed important to overall profitability and that trade-related government policies have substantial impact on such competitiveness. If this view is justified, the term needs a clearer definition, including its policy implications. If not, an equally clear explanation should be provided to political and corporate leaders as to why international competitiveness doesn't matter.

Krugman is unambiguously in the latter camp: "The idea that a country's economic fortunes are largely determined by its success on world markets is a hypothesis . . . [that] is flatly wrong."[2] His analysis for rejection, however, digresses from the outset through ridicule of distinguished yet vulnerable straw persons who have misused the concept of international competitiveness. Approximately one-third of the *Foreign Affairs* article is devoted to such attacks on Jacques Delors, president of the European Union Commission, John Major, prime minister of the United Kingdom, Professor Lester Thurow, Ira Magaziner, Clinton health care adviser, and Robert Reich, U.S. secretary of labor. All of the cited presentations can be easily demolished, as Krugman does, but to do so is beside the point, except to impugn the credibility of the three Americans who happen to be influential officials in or advisers to the Clinton administration.

Krugman comes closer to the real target in assessing the definition of competitiveness by Laura D'Andrea Tyson, chair of the Council of Economic Advisers, in her book *Who's Bashing Whom? Trade Conflict in High Technology Industries*, which is recognized as the intellectual basis for much of Clinton's trade policy, particularly vis-à-vis Japan. Competitiveness, according to Tyson, is "our ability to produce goods and services that meet the test of international markets while our citizens enjoy a standard of living that is both rising and sustainable."[3] This statement is very general, but it is nevertheless a valid starting point for a clearer definition of competitiveness. Krugman, however, in a section entitled, "Mindless Competition," attempts to discredit it through rhetorical thrusts and largely misleading information about the relationship between trade, productivity, and national economic performance. The rhetorical devices include prolonged discussion of why international competitiveness has little meaning for a country that has little trade to begin with, a belabored explanation as to why corporate competition between Coca-Cola and Pepsi-Cola is different from competition between countries, and the ultimate straw person admonition: "All are free, if they wish, to use the term 'competitiveness' as a poetic way of saying productivity, without actually implying that international competition has anything to do with it."[4] It is extremely unlikely that anyone has said this, although Krugman asserts, without reference, that a few writers on competitiveness would accept this view.

Krugman's largely misleading information on the relationship between trade, productivity, and national economic performance is the subject of the following two sections of this article and is addressed in the broader context of the debate on international competitiveness that began in the mid-1980s and continues unabated. It centers on the impact of new technology development and application, particularly within and among the advanced industrialized countries. Technology-intensive industry is the issue, as evident in the subtitle of the Tyson book. Most of her book consists of case studies of the cellular phone, semiconductor, telecommunications, commercial jet aircraft, and other industries, concluding that U.S. government support programs have been largely inadequate for these sectors. Her policy conclusions have been subjected to well-founded criticism, of which more below, but there is no doubt that international competitiveness relates principally to the circumstances of a new situation of rapid and broad-based technological change.

The Krugman attack on competitiveness, however, almost entirely ignores the international dimension of technological change currently under way. The *Foreign Affairs* article addresses the issue only in general terms, while discussion in the book of "strategic trade policy" focuses on the example of commercial jet aircraft, which is a special case subject to a bilateral agreement on government subsidies between the United States and the European Union. The critical assessment as to the importance of the broad wave of technological change under way in the world, the so-called information technology revolution, is hedged and more or less dismissed in an earlier section of the Krugman book:

> Economic historians have observed that it often takes a very long time before a new technology begins to make a major impact on productivity and living standards. . . . So a new technology, no matter how marvelous, may have only superficial effects for decades, then flower as it finally reaches critical mass. . . . There were some signs that the "technology payoff". . . the long-delayed economic reward from the widespread use of information-processing technology, was finally beginning in the 1990s. The point, however, is that through the 1970s and 1980s technological advances were impressive but, apparently, not all that fruitful.[5]

The fundamental difference in assessment made here, which is the point of departure for what follows about the meaning of international competition, is that the major impact or delayed reward from information-based technologies was already under way on a big scale during the 1980s for manufacturing industry and is now spreading more broadly in its effects on national economic performance. Such an assessment leads to sharply different conclusions from those in the Krugman texts about the importance of trade and trade-related policies for the U.S. economy in the 1990s. This assessment also leads to the question of how, more precisely, to define international competitiveness in the new situation. The definition certainly requires more than a sentence or two, and the following is my attempt to elaborate more fully what is at stake.

International competitiveness has taken on a broader meaning, beginning approximately in the mid-1980s as rapidly evolving new technologies, especially in the information-technology sector, began to have major impact on both a national and international scale. This technological change is of central importance for productivity gains at the national level, but such gains are increasingly dependent on markets of international scope. Moreover, the truly revolutionary structural change in economic activity now under way requires an expanded definition of "international trade" beyond the traditional focus on the exchange of goods, and should include trade in services and the international flow of investment capital, technology, and human resources. As a consequence, a strong U.S. international competitive performance over a range of technology-intensive industries is both cause and effect of substantially higher national productivity gains initially concentrated in the manufacturing sector and now spreading more broadly throughout the economy. The policy implications of this new international competitive situation are equally far-reaching.

The Importance of Trade

Krugman's contention that trade is of relatively little importance to national economic performance has both a quantitative and a qualitative aspect. Quantitatively, he views trade as very small compared with gross domestic product (GDP), while qualitatively, he assesses the causal relationship between trade and national productivity to be insignificant. A closer look, on both counts, reveals otherwise.

Krugman's contention that trade is a small part of the economy is based almost solely on the observation that U.S. exports are a relatively small 10 percent share of GDP. This simple export/GDP test for the importance of trade, however, ignores two other quantitative dimensions of the overall trade relationship, each of which greatly increases the relative importance of trade to the national economy.

First, imports as well as exports influence national economic performance. Import competition, or the lack thereof through protectionist policies, can have significant impact. A protectionist textile policy, for example, has tended to hold back technological change in the U.S. apparel sector, while import competition in the automotive sector during the 1980s clearly exerted pressure on U.S. companies, both vehicle and parts producers, to cut costs and improve product quality.

Second and probably more important, the relationship between transborder factor movements—investment capital, technology, and human resources—and GDP is ignored by Krugman, but it is obviously of fundamental and growing importance to what is happening in the world economy and its impact on U.S. national economic performance. The restructuring of the U.S. automobile industry during the 1980s, again, was as much influenced by Japanese investment in the United States as by imported vehicles. Technology transfer across borders has been accelerating through foreign direct investment and various forms of corporate alliances.[6] The international movement of human resources also takes various forms, for example through the return to East Asia of a substantial number of engineers, scientists, and managers, educated and trained in California. An evaluation of international competitiveness, in whatever terms, clearly has to include these dynamic elements of interaction between the U.S. and the world economies.

The final misleading quantitative judgment by Krugman is his rejection of the globalization trend that started in the early 1980s:

> It is in fact startling, given the rhetoric of globalization that now pervades economic discussion, to notice that trade was barely higher as a share of GDP at the beginning of the Clinton administration than it was when Jimmy Carter left office.[7]

This simple comparison between two points in time is fully worthy of the term obfuscation. The long-term rise in trade dependence in the U.S. economy from 1960 to the early 1990s is not open to question. The extraordinary yet temporary surge in the trade/GDP ratio at the time Jimmy Carter left office reflected the high oil prices of the second oil shock and domestic recession. From the beginning of economic recovery in 1983 to 1993 there has been a strong, almost steady rise in trade/GDP in the U.S. and the global economies, which is expected to continue. During this 11-year period, the volume of U.S. merchandise exports grew three times as fast as GDP while corresponding world exports grew at twice the rate of world output. Trade in services, international investment, and cross-border technology-sharing arrangements probably grew faster yet. The Krugman rhetoric of non-globalization is simply at odds with reality.

There is no easy way, or perhaps any way, to measure precisely how these various dimensions add up to an overall quantitative relationship between trade—writ large as is done here—and GDP. There is no question, however, that it is of far greater significance than the simple 10 percent, relatively stable export/GDP ratio posited by Krugman.

The foregoing difference in quantitative appraisal as to the importance of trade carries over to Krugman's qualitative assessment of the trade/productivity relationship. Krugman again uses a single measure of how trade competitiveness influences national productivity, a measure preordained to produce an insignificant result. He compares the growth trend in national output—what is actually produced in the United States—with a measure of national purchasing power adjusted so that exports are valued in terms of what amount of imports can be purchased. The difference in the two measures is judged to represent the impact of trade on productivity. Because exports are a relatively small share of national output, however, the export/import price adjustment is also quite small and, in fact, was negative from 1973 to 1990 as a consequence of the gradual slide of the dollar vis-à-vis other major currencies.

The question is whether this numerical test adequately captures the impact of international competition on productivity in the United States, particularly since the early 1980s when the international component of competition in manufacturing and key service sector industries began expanding at a rapid rate. The intuitive response, based on observed corporate behavior, is no, it is not adequate, although a more formal response is elusive. The underlying problem with the Krugman test is that it only addresses the price effects for traded goods and services, and not the trade-induced impact on prices and output for the 90 percent of national output not actually traded. To use the automotive sector as an example one more time, the Krugman test captures the price effects of imported Japanese cars, but not the increased productivity induced by international competition for all other U.S.

and Japanese transplant production in the United States.

One way economists address this major problem is to distinguish between the "static" and "dynamic" effects of trade. Static gains from trade derive from price differences in exporting and importing countries given the existing methods of production, or "constant returns to scale" in technical terms. This is traditional comparative cost theory. The dynamic gains from trade, in contrast, refer to circumstances whereby existing production methods change through capital investment, applied new technologies, cost-cutting restructuring, or other dynamic developments. Indeed, entirely new export industries can be created.

The Krugman analysis, in this context, is couched predominantly in terms of the static effects of trade on national productivity.[8] The contention here, which is explained more fully in the following section, is that the dynamic effects need to be taken fully into account as well, and that they are far larger and more beneficial than the static effects in their impact on productivity. The conceptual underpinning for this crucial point was within the purview of work done during the 1980s by the so-called new trade theorists. Unfortunately, however, these theorists, including Paul Krugman, got sidetracked and never addressed the full and very positive dynamic effects of trade.

The New Trade Theory

A central tenet of the new trade theorists was that trade in certain sectors is subject to conditions of "imperfect competition" and thus a free trade policy is not necessarily the best policy.[9] The focus was on high-technology industries, characterized by very large research and development (R&D) and initial investment costs, a downward-sloping supply curve (i.e., unit costs decline with the volume of output, in part from the learning process of quality control), short product cycles, and various "externalities," whereby benefits are obtained from interactions within the industry or region of production. In some circumstances, as a consequence, the first large firm or firms to market can establish a sustained oligopoly position and reap excessive profits from such market control while late arrivals may never be able to fully compete.

A "strategic trade policy" was derived from this analytic framework, which calls for subsidies and other support for selected technology-intensive products, including a "managed trade" approach of negotiated sector-by-sector quantitative targets for trade. The semiconductor industry received the most exhaustive analysis, highlighting Japanese support of its industry, which threatened U.S. producers at home and in the Japanese market, particularly for DRAM memory chips. The U.S.-Japan semiconductor agreement of 1986, which included a quantitative target for U.S. sales to the Japanese market, resulted in considerable part from the analytic case presented by the new trade theorists.

The most distinguished member of the new trade theorists was Paul Krugman, although he stopped short of endorsing the strategic trade policy response on the grounds that it was extremely difficult to determine which industries to support and by how much, and that the U.S. political process could well turn such a selective industry support program into a protectionist grab bag. Much of the sectoral analysis came from the Berkeley Roundtable on International Economics (BRIE), supported by Silicon Valley and other high-technology industries threatened by Japanese competition. Its most prominent former member is Laura Tyson, whose book cited earlier summed up the case for managed trade. She proposes "aggressive bilateralism" through "bilateral sector specific negotiations" based on the principle of "selective reciprocity," even though she recognizes this as "a dangerous departure from traditional U.S. trade policies."[10] President-elect Clinton made favorable mention of the book when nominating Tyson to the chair of his Council of Economic Advisers, and the sector-by-sector quantitative approach became the basis for U.S.–Japan bilateral trade negotiations through the spring of 1994.

Krugman now unleashes an even harsher attack on strategic traders within the Clinton administration, not only for his reasons stated earlier, but because he believes the strategic traders have distorted and blown far out of proportion the issue of competitiveness as originally developed by the new trade theorists. In this judgment, however, he is only half right, because the innovative work of the new trade theorists was, regrettably, deficient in two central respects, of which Krugman now acknowledges only one. These deficiencies can be referred to as gross overstatement of the oligopoly effect and near total neglect of the positive dynamic effects of trade in technology-intensive and related industries.

The greatly feared oligopoly gains by Japanese companies, to the extent they existed in the mid-1980s, have mostly evaporated. In the semiconductor sector, late South Korean arrivals are undercutting Japanese DRAM exports while U.S. firms remain competitive and may be lower-cost than some Japanese rivals. The long-standing oligopoly position of IBM and Fujitsu for mainframe computers is crumbling in the face of supercomputer competition from one direction and high-powered personal computer networks from the other. Hundreds of millions of dollars of Japanese and European government subsidies for high-definition television proved to be a total loss as U.S.-led private consortia leapfrogged from analog to digital technology. The most prominent new oligopolists are the U.S. firms Intel and Microsoft, with leading-edge microprocessors and software products, although both are subject to fierce and growing competition. Commercial jet aircraft production remains the glaring exception of a sustained oligopoly situation but, as noted earlier, government subsidies, at least, are under constraint through the U.S.–European Union agreement.

Krugman is right, therefore, in decrying a trade policy of managed trade based on the theoretical oligopoly models of the 1980s that have limited practical consequences in the 1990s. But he stops short, as did the other new trade theorists, of fully accounting for the dynamic consequences of the new circumstances of world trade. Yet here is where the true meaning of international competitiveness needs to be confronted. The underlying competitive forces of trade in goods and services, international investment, and technology transfer are having a growing, profound impact on national economic performance throughout the world, including in the United States. Expanded world markets raise the rate of return for investment by lowering production costs through economies of scale and by spreading R&D costs more widely. Competition from imports forces firms to cut costs and accelerate technological innovation to remain competitive. Open trade fosters the wider exchange of technical knowledge among nations as goods and investment capital move more freely.

These are the dynamic effects of trade and they constitute, in the aggregate, an extremely positive-sum game, with substantial impact on national productivity. The fundamental shortcoming of the New Trade Theory work thus far, including the latest contributions by Krugman, is that the overwhelmingly positive dynamic effects of trade are almost entirely ignored.

The reasons for this egregious neglect are hard to explain, and there has recently been some increased professional interest in the subject that has indicated dynamic gains from trade several times larger than the static effects.[11] A large part of the problem, however, is that economists feel more secure and confident when dealing with well-defined analytic models, subject to quantitative testing. This is the situation, for example, for estimating the static price effects of trade or the oligopoly profits for a given firm. But unfortunately the broader dynamic effects of trade do not lend themselves to simple models or quantitative testing because, by definition, they consist of ever-changing conditions of production. And yet, unless fuller account is taken of these dynamic, productivity-enhancing effects, an only partial and misleading conclusion will be drawn, as by the strategic traders obsessed with limited oligopoly profits or by Paul Krugman, who ends up dismissing trade competitiveness as not worth worrying about in the first place. These misleading analytic conclusions in both directions lead to equally misguided courses for U.S. trade policy.

The Policy Implications

Krugman posits two direct and one indirect policy "dangers" from current thinking about competitiveness. The two direct dangers derive from the new trade theory work of the 1980s that has subsequently been distorted and exploited by the strategic traders who advise and populate the Clinton administration. The indirect danger raises more complicated and far-reaching questions.

The first danger is that the U.S. government will misallocate resources through an industrial policy of corporate subsidies to develop selected technologies. This is a justified concern, but it is only a small part of the broad policy objective of government support for new technology research and development. The principal policy instruments to this end are intellectual property rights, across-the-board tax benefits for R&D and/or investment, public procurement practices, and government funding for basic research and public research laboratories, particularly in the agricultural and energy sectors. These policy instruments are, to varying degrees, related to the international trading system as it emerges from the Uruguay Round of the General Agreement on Tariffs and Trade, and certainly play a major role in international competitiveness as defined here. It is not clear how Krugman views the resource allocation implications of these broader policy instruments. They clearly constitute an important incentive to develop and apply new technologies, and they receive broad public support in the United States and elsewhere.

The second and more serious direct

danger is that strategic trade policy has been distorted so as to become the vehicle for solving all trade problems, which can lead to trade conflict and perhaps a world trade war. This has certainly been the case for the U.S. managed trade approach to Japan during the first year of the Clinton administration, as well as for broader statements about unfair trade practices abroad and the need for Tyson's aggressive unilateralism. Krugman documents misguided statements by President Clinton and his advisers, and he is right. Indeed, the anguished chronicler evokes a certain compassion, as the new trade theory Dr. Frankenstein observes the policy havoc the monster he created is wreaking.

The third policy danger stemming from the competitiveness debate, "is its subtle indirect effect on the quality of economic discussion and policymaking." Top government officials become obsessed with the competitiveness doctrine, which "blurs the focus and diminishes the quality of policy discussion across a broad range of issues, including some that are very far from trade policy per se."[12] Health care reform is cited as a specific example of a policy blur of major proportions. This legitimate concern is, of course, a normal danger for all policy-making. Strong advocates of a single cause, utilizing exaggerated and misleading arguments, can greatly distort national priorities and disrupt national policy discussion, particularly when it comes to budget decisions. That is why the Office of Management and Budget, the presumed honest broker, is the most important component of the Executive Office of the President.

This indirect danger in the Krugman context, however, cuts both ways. He elaborates the case wherein the Clinton administration and others have distorted and abused the concept of international competitiveness to ill policy effect, but his own analysis, similarly misguided although in another direction, leads to policy pitfalls of its own. Krugman's trade policy approach includes support for the liberal trading system as it exists, avoidance of unjustified trade conflicts, and aversion to industrial policy trade-distorting subsidies. This is commendable, but implementation of such a policy will inevitably suffer if the underlying analysis concludes that trade has little significance for national productivity and that the ability of U.S. firms in technology-intensive sectors to compete in international markets has little meaning. If this is the case, why resist the strong pressures to protect jobs for industries facing import competition? Why pay the political price for obtaining congressional approval for the North American Free Trade and Uruguay Round agreements? Why not revoke most-favored-nation treatment for countries like the People's Republic of China that flagrantly abuse human rights? A Krugman liberal trade policy of benign neglect would be very vulnerable to protectionist dismemberment.

The fact is that trade, in the broader context described here, does matter a great deal for U.S. national productivity now, and will matter even more in the years ahead. In this context, the policy implications of international competitiveness are very different from those of both the strategic traders and of Krugman.

A full statement of appropriate policy response would require many pages if not chapters, and would extend into areas of policy traditionally considered domestic. The central policy objective is to nurture, with vigor, the unique historical circumstances, cultural values, and policy framework that have made the United States the central driving force for the amazing process of technological change under way and consequent productivity gains. The domestic component of such a policy includes improved educational and worker retraining performance, strengthened telecommunications, financial services, and other technology-oriented infrastructure, and most broadly, a more hospitable investment climate for stimulating the innovation and structural change that constitute the principal U.S. comparative advantage in world trade. The international policy component consists of a further broadening of the world trading system, as begun in the Uruguay Round, to include international investment and technology transfer in a more comprehensive way, a progressive opening of markets on all fronts, and targeted initiatives in areas where grossly imperfect markets can be made less so. The domestic and international components need to be mutually reinforcing just as national and international competition produce a desired synergy for increased productivity and national well-being.

Living and Defunct Economists

Economists can be a strange and insecure lot. There is a deep-rooted professional rivalry between the academics, the business economists, and the policy practitioners as to who best understands the true workings of the economy and what role the government should play in it. Academics, embodying the broadest knowledge of the subject while having the least influence on policy decisions, tend to be the least secure.

Professor Krugman further obscures his substantive presentation by injecting the issue of professional economic competence in a self-serving manner. He contrasts the qualifications for making judgments on international competitiveness of economics professors and a hybrid category of "policy entrepreneurs." A policy entrepreneur, according to Krugman, is a professional intellectual, most likely based in a Washington think tank, who writes and speaks for a broad public audience, and who offers unambiguous diagnoses and easy answers for inherently complex policy questions. "As you might guess, it is mostly policy entrepreneurs who sell books to the general public." In contrast,

> A professor writes mostly for other professors. If he should happen to write for a wider public, no matter how well and simply he may write, he will always have in the back of his mind the reaction of his colleagues, which will inhibit him from saying things that sound good but which he and they know to be wrong.[13]

This stark contrast between the two groups is, to say the least, greatly overdrawn. There is considerable overlap and interchange between them, with at least some reluctance by policy entrepreneurs to say what they know to be wrong, while professors occasionally go off the ill-founded deep end. Indeed, Krugman's article and book both display all of the specified attributions of seasoned policy entrepreneurship.[14]

Debate over such a complex and contentious issue as international competition is bound to be imprecise and at times wrongheaded. Trained economists play a useful role in this process by providing greater analytic discipline and clarity. This does not mean, however, that the professors are always right, any more than that the conduct of war should always be left to the generals. Krugman concludes the *Foreign Affairs* article with the rhetorical question, "If the obsession with competitiveness is as misguided and damaging as this article claims, why aren't more voices saying so?"[15] His answer is that some want to use the specious official arguments for ulterior purposes while others are fearful of disagreeing publicly with the world's opinion leaders. A simpler answer is that the voices may not agree with Krugman. The Clinton administration has misguided the debate in certain ways, but that is a far cry from concluding that "competitiveness is a meaningless term."

A particularly strange attribute of purveyors of the dismal science is their fascination with defunct economists. A current economic development is often presented with reference to a predictive quotation from a long-departed member of the profession. Perhaps in this way the lack of policy influence by living economists is compensated by demonstrating the delayed impact of those who went before. The most-favored quotation of all comes from John Maynard Keynes:

> The ideas of economists and political philosophers, both when they are right and when they are wrong, are more powerful than is commonly understood. Indeed, the world is ruled by little else. Practical men, who believe themselves to be quite exempt from any intellectual influences, are usually the slaves of some defunct economist. Madmen in authority, who hear voices in the air, are distilling their frenzy from some academic scribbler of a few years back.[16]

Krugman uses this Keynesian quote as the epigraph for *Peddling Prosperity*. Indeed, most of the book concerns macroeconomic policy and how Keynesian economics has been resurrected and now enjoys a second coming. Keynes, however, is not a particularly quotable defunct economist in the international economics field. He was something of a protectionist and his extravagant ideas about a world central bank were appropriately shot down by his U.S. counterparts at Bretton Woods.

There is, however, a most apt earlier reading from another distinguished economist that points the way to what is happening in the world economy today:

> Foreign trade tends to produce an extension of productive factors over the expanding market area . . . [which] applies with special force to the development phase of international trade, and particularly to the trade of unequally developed areas.

This economist went on to encourage,

> a more positive analysis than the economists have given us of the economic effects of the enormous and increasing drift of capital and labor over the world's surface.[17]

Professor John Williams wrote this in 1929, which among other things, shows that key aspects of the new trade theory are not all that new. More important, he provides the proper guidance to the economics profession today that trade is a far broader subject than indicated by export and import accounts alone, and that the dynamic effects of international trade and investment, however elusive to measure, are what count most. Williams made no specific reference to international competitiveness, but the term as used here would have been most compatible with the ideas put forward by this academic scribbler of yore.

Notes

1. Paul Krugman, "Competitiveness: A Dangerous Obsession," *Foreign Affairs* 73 (March/April 1994), pp. 28–44; the quotation is from p. 44. Krugman, *Peddling Prosperity* (New York, N.Y.: W. W. Norton, 1994); the quotation is from p. 280, Krugman's capital letters.
2. Krugman, "Competitiveness," p. 30.
3. Laura D'Andrea Tyson, *Who's Bashing Whom?* (Washington, D.C.: Institute for International Economics, 1992). The definition quotation is from p. 1. Krugman misquotes Tyson, substituting "competition" for "markets" ("Competitiveness," p. 31). A critique of the Tyson book, including a more detailed discussion of high-technology trade and the New Trade Theory than contained in this article, can be found in Ernest H. Preeg, "Who's Benefiting Whom? A Trade Agenda for High-Technology Industries," *The Washington Quarterly* 16 (Autumn 1993), pp. 17–33.
4. Krugman, "Competitiveness," p. 35.
5. Krugman, *Peddling Prosperity*, pp. 60, 62–63.
6. For example, the number of technology cooperation agreements worldwide in the biotechnology, information technology, and new materials sectors increased from 317 in 1975–1979 to 2,629 in 1985–1989. See John Hagedoorn and Joe Schakenraad, "Leading Companies and Networks of Strategic Alliances of Technologies," *Research Policy* 21 (1992), pp. 163–190.
7. Krugman, *Peddling Prosperity*, p. 147.
8. For example, in the *Foreign Affairs* article, the lengthy footnote on p. 32, which explains the relationship between national income and trade, is strictly in static terms; the export/import price adjustment captures some dynamic effects of price changes over time, but not most, as explained in the text.
9. A definitive set of papers on the New Trade Theory is contained in Paul R. Krugman, ed., *Strategic Trade Policy and the New International Economics* (Cambridge, Mass.: MIT Press, 1986). An updated assessment can be found in Paul R. Krugman, "Does the New Trade Theory Require a New Trade Policy?" *World Economy* 15 (July 1992), pp. 423–441.
10. Tyson, *Who's Bashing Whom?* pp. 260–261.
11. A summary of recent work on the dynamic effects of trade can be found in U.S. International Trade Commission, *The Dynamic Effects of Trade Liberalization: A Survey* (Washington, D.C., February 1993).
12. Krugman, "Competitiveness," p. 42.
13. Krugman, *Peddling Prosperity*, pp. 11–12.
14. In keeping with current practices of disclosure, the present author reveals that he holds a Ph.D. in economics and has spent most of his professional life as a government policy practitioner, a much shorter time as a policy entrepreneur, and a brief period as a college teacher of economics.
15. Krugman, "Competitiveness," p. 44.
16. John Maynard Keynes, *The General Theory of Employment Interest and Money* (New York, N.Y.: Harcourt, Brace and Company, 1936), p. 383.
17. John H. Williams, "The Theory of International Trade Reconsidered," originally published in *Economic Journal* 39 (June 1929), and reprinted in *Postwar Monetary Plans and Other Essays* (New York, N.Y.: Alfred A. Knopf, 1947), in which these quotations appear on pp. 152–153.

III. New Directions of Trade and Investment

Trade, Investment, and Engagement in the U.S.–East Asian Relationship

Thomas J. Duesterberg

IN NO OTHER region of the world is the promise of prosperity and continued advance of living standards better illustrated than in the East Asia of the Four Tigers, the Association of Southeast Asian Nations (ASEAN), and the newest tiger, the People's Republic of China (PRC). In the last quarter of this century, growth in the East Asian region will average at least double that of the industrialized world. In current circumstances of stagnation in most of the nations of the Organization for Economic Cooperation and Development (OECD), sustained growth of this magnitude inspires awe and a certain disbelief.

It is of more immediate relevance, however, that such growth helps to save OECD members from even further economic deterioration and provides a source of strength by which to regain a viable path of growth and better job creation.

Yet, the current debate in the

Thomas J. Duesterberg is senior fellow of the Hudson Institute and director of its Competitiveness Center. He was assistant secretary of commerce for international economic policy from 1989 to 1993.

Copyright © 1993 by The Center for Strategic and International Studies and the Massachusetts Institute of Technology

United States about trade and economic policy toward East Asia revolves around a narrow effort to reduce the merchandise trade deficit, primarily with Japan but increasingly with the PRC, while contemplating a reduction in the U.S. strategic commitment to the region. Much of the impetus for this debate comes from a highly politicized effort to find a villain for the perceived economic decline in the United States. Barriers to imports and investment in the Japanese and, to a lesser extent, other Asian markets are seen as a major contributing cause of this decline.[1] In addition, the analysis of barriers to U.S. products is coupled with suggestions that the U.S. strategic commitment to the region has not paid visible dividends and consequently should be reconsidered.

The factual and conceptual bases of this type of thinking are rapidly being eroded by the continued evolution of East Asian economies, especially other than Japan. Furthermore, the types of policy responses it suggests—managed trade or a spiral of economic retaliation, and less cooperation or even disengagement in the region—threaten to deprive the U.S. economy of access to the world's premier growth market. A Japan-centered policy not only diverts attention from policies that could pay larger and more immediate benefits, but it will also probably not succeed in its limited goals and could drive other Asian nations away from closer economic cooperation with the United States. At a time when the United States is reducing domestic demand through tax increases and reductions in defense spending, failure to take advantage of the growth potential of export markets in East Asia (or elsewhere, for that matter) would be disastrous. It is clear that growth in the United States in the medium term will depend a great deal on continued growth in U.S. exports, so a sustainable growth and job creation agenda requires an active trade-enhancing component.[2]

Furthermore, economic trends in East Asia are exceptionally favorable for U.S. suppliers and investors, especially in the areas outside Japan. In fact, current trends, if they are not impaired by ill-advised policy choices, could lead to a steady reduction in the overall U.S. trade balance in the region. The strength of the United States in services and in sales by affiliates of U.S. companies established in the region adds to its strong economic position.

In this article I explore the evolution of economic performance in East Asia and argue that the robust U.S. position there can be further enhanced by policy measures that emphasize continued integration through market-opening trade policies and expanded investment ties. I also argue that a narrow focus on Japan distorts the overall policy framework by training attention on the merchandise trade deficit alone, to the exclusion of other factors more central to U.S. economic interests. The set of policy recommendations that follows is driven by the belief that the United States has a unique opportunity at this point in the economic history of East Asia to solidify a strong position in the fastest growing parts of the region, and that this opportunity is jeopardized by efforts to shape policy based on a misguided view of how to solve the merchandise trade deficit with Japan.

Growth in Asia and U.S. Trade

As medium- and long-term growth trends in North America and Europe have moderated or turned downward, the sustained dynamic performance of a growing number of East Asian economies has increasingly drawn attention and comment. A "Japanese model" is often advanced to describe the structure of economic development in the region. High savings, high investment, modest wages, and, above all, dependence on exports and protection of infant industries are the descriptive terms usually associated with this model. Although there is some superficial truth in this description, like all abstractions it oversimplifies the historical, empirical reality of complex economies. More important, however, it retains focus on a static model of Japan and draws attention obsessively to a persistent and seemingly intractable merchandise trade deficit. The reality, especially current reality, is more complex, more varied, and less of a problem to the West than the usual analysis suggests.

Whatever the diverse origins and explanations may be, the economic growth achieved in East Asia in the past 40 years is truly remarkable. Japan increased its share of the total of world output from 1 percent in 1950 to around 17 percent in 1992.[3] A succession of other nations in the region, developing later than Japan, are starting to build impressive records of sustained economic achievement and catapulting themselves into the ranks of the world's leading industrial powers.

Table 1 documents the growth in gross domestic product (GDP) achieved in recent years by the leading economies of the region.[4] Ten-year averages are listed in bold for selected economies in the first two columns to emphasize the sustained nature of performance.

More recently India has undertaken a modest economic liberalization program that has resulted in more robust growth. India grew at a rate of 2 percent in 1991 and 4.3 percent in 1992, and is forecast at 4.8 percent in 1993. Although India must demonstrate a long-term commitment to reform and sustained performance over a longer term to join the ranks of the Asian tigers, its economy is already so large that it can be significant in the trade and investment flows that are the focus of concern in this article. If Vietnam follows through on reform projects, if Cambodia rejoins the ranks of outward-looking economies, and if the Philippines musters the commitment to the market economy that has served its ASEAN partners so well, then the growth prospects of Asia and the rest of the world would be enhanced even further.

According to the projections of the Pacific Economic Cooperation Council (PECC), growth in the region continues to be strong, seemingly unaffected by the slowdown in the rest of the world. A major reason for this, to be explored later, is the increasing importance of regional trade in the overall mix of trade flows in Asia. PECC has issued the forecast summarized in table 2.

Growth of this magnitude is crucial to raising living standards among the huge population of the region. From the narrower perspective of the United States (and Europe as well), such dynamism allows the region to fill the role of "engine of growth" while performance is sluggish in the West. Current World Bank estimates of GDP based on purchasing power parity place the PRC as the third-ranking economy in the world. In the new rankings the Asian economies as a whole are approaching the size of the European Community (EC) and the United States.[5] In 1992, the GDP of the nine dynamic Asian economies was over $5 trillion, while that of the United States was a little under $6 trillion.

Total merchandise trade volume between the United States and Asia ex-

Table 1
GDP Growth Rates in East Asia

	1970–1980 average	1980–1990 average	1990	1991	1992
Japan	**5.21**	**4.19**	3.5	4.5	1.3
PRC	**7.9**	**10.1**	5.2	7.0	12.8
South Korea	**9.0**	**9.9**	9.0	8.3	7.3
Taiwan	**10.26**	**8.25**	5.0	7.3	6.7
Indonesia	**7.7**	**5.5**	7.4	6.4	6.7
Thailand	**7.9**	**7.8**	10.0	7.5	8.0
Hong Kong	**9.3**	**7.1**	2.8	4.0	5.8
Singapore	**7.9**	**6.3**	8.3	7.0	6.1
Malaysia	**7.3**	**6.1**	9.8	8.6	8.5

Source: See endnote 4.

Table 2
Projected Real GDP Growth in Asia

	1993	1994
Japan	2.3	3.2
PRC	10.1	9.5
Hong Kong	5.4	5.5
Indonesia	6.3	6.5
South Korea	6.4	7.6
Malaysia	7.6	7.5
Singapore	6.0	6.1
Taiwan	6.7	6.9
Thailand	7.9	8.4

Source: U.S. National Committee for Pacific Economic Cooperation, *Pacific Economic Outlook 1993–1994* (Washington, D.C., 1993), table I, p. 51.

ceeded U.S.–EC trade as long ago as 1978. In 1992 the United States shipped merchandise worth almost $48 billion to Japan and $67.2 billion to the eight other dynamic Asian economies (the so-called Four Tigers, plus Thailand, Malaysia, Indonesia, and the PRC).

It is worth noting at this point that, in terms of merchandise trade, Japan has already been surpassed as a destination for U.S. goods by this grouping of other Asian nations. This disparity is likely to grow because these economies are growing more rapidly than that of Japan. Japan has an aging and slowly growing economy, while these other nations are demographically vital. Asset deflation in Japan is clearly slowing growth and investment and will dampen growth prospects in the near term. Japanese unemployment has reached 6 percent, if those kept on the payroll without working are included in the rate, giving one indication of the Japanese slowdown.[6] As a result of the dynamism in the eight Asian nations since 1984, the United States has increased its merchandise exports to these countries by an amount greater than the current U.S. trade deficit with Japan. Since 1990, U.S. exports to Japan have been flat while exports to the PRC have been up 55 percent, to Taiwan 32 percent, to Hong Kong and Thailand 33 percent, to Singapore 20 percent, to Indonesia 46 percent, to Malaysia 27 percent, and to South Korea about 5 percent. In the first half of 1993, the U.S. trade balance deteriorated with Europe, Japan, Canada, and Mexico, while improving with the four Asian tigers, again demonstrating the latter's ability to keep growing and importing in a period of global economic weakness.

Commentators regularly draw attention to the merchandise trade deficit the United States has consistently run with Japan and the Four Tigers. In 1992 the U.S. deficit with Japan increased to $49.6 billion. In the same year the U.S. trade deficit with the eight dynamic countries was about $41 billion, while a larger measure of trade with Asia and Africa (excluding Australia and Japan) showed a deficit of $37.8 billion. The numbers are substantially different if we include services in the calculation. The United States exports over $48 billion in services to Japan, Asia, and Africa, and has a total surplus of over $12.6 billion with Japan and $15 billion with Asia and Africa. It also ran a $4.2 billion surplus in merchandise trade and a $1 billion surplus in services trade with Australia.[7] When services trade is added to the total, the overall deficit for Asia, Africa, and Australia drops from $83.2 billion to $54.6 billion.

Clearly, a broader look at U.S. trade performance does not paint as bleak a picture as the obsessive U.S. concern with merchandise trade with Japan suggests. I have argued elsewhere that better U.S. trade performance is due to improved competitiveness, restrained growth in labor costs, and higher productivity.[8] Improved U.S. performance in Asia is also due partly to the fact that unit labor costs in the more advanced Asian countries are rising faster than in the United States. Japan is the only nation to match the United States in keeping productivity up with labor costs in manufacturing since 1982, hence keeping unit costs steady. When calculated in local currency, in South Korea unit labor costs have grown by 47 percent and in Taiwan by 24 percent in a comparable time period. Increases in the value of some Asian currencies further enhance the U.S. advantage. When calculated in terms of U.S. dollars, for example, Japanese costs were ahead by 68 percent, South Korean by 51 percent, and Taiwanese by 80 percent between 1982 and 1990. In the same period, U.S. costs fell slightly.[9]

Continued strong performance by the United States in technology is confirmed by a global $33 billion surplus in advanced technology products in 1992. In addition, Central Intelligence Agency (CIA) data show that the United States leads the world in exports of four of eight high-technology products (microelectronics, computers, aerospace, and scientific equipment) and is second in three others (telecommunications, medicine and biologicals, and organic chemicals), while trailing only Japan and Germany in the eighth (machine tools). In fact, the United States increased its market share in microelectronics, telecommunications equipment, medicine and biologicals, and organic chemicals in the 1980s.[10]

One frequently cited aspect of the debate on trade relations is that Japan and other nations following its development model rely too much on exports for their own growth, and especially rely on the vast and open U.S. market. Although this analysis has some validity when applied to the past, it does not take sufficient account of the rapid changes in East Asia. Most dynamic Asian economies are now relying on their own internal markets and on the intra-Asian market for growth. Dependence on the United States declines as Asian economies move up on the scales of wealth and diversification and as democratization gives a larger voice to the concerns of consumers and environmentalists.

Table 3 shows the exports of the dynamic Asian nations to the United States as compared to GDP. Although the trends vary somewhat, partially due to currency fluctuations, a general pattern is clear. At early stages of development, the U.S. market has played a key role in the economic growth of dynamic East Asian nations. For example, Taiwan in 1985 sent 28 percent of its GDP to the United States in the form of exports. In recent years, the importance of the U.S. economy has diminished, except in the cases of the PRC, Malaysia, and Thailand, three of the most recent entrants to the dynamic Asian economic club. The numbers for Hong Kong and Singapore are skewed due to their role as entrepots.

The decreasing relative importance of the U.S. market and growing importance of regional trade for the dynamic Asian countries are shown in tables 4 and 5.

The trend in merchandise trade shows that, except for the newest tigers, Thailand, the PRC, and Malaysia, the U.S. market is slowly losing its dominance. Table 5 shows the reason for this—the growth in intraregional trade. Others have commented

Table 3
East Asian Exports to the United States as a Percentage of GDP

	1975	1980	1985	1990	1992
Japan	2.25	3.01	4.96	3.09	4.00
PRC	.001	.400	1.44	4.46	5.92
South Korea	7.27	7.34	11.61	8.23	5.29
Taiwan	10.71	17.89	28.21	14.85	11.91
Indonesia	5.80	5.90	4.63	3.15	3.18
Thailand	1.64	2.47	3.75	6.54	6.65
Hong Kong	16.88	18.89	27.74	28.27	28.75
Singapore	13.15	20.47	27.30	32.37	26.12
Malaysia	6.09	9.10	6.38	12.56	14.74

Source: See endnote 4.

Table 4
East Asian Exports to the United States as a Percentage of Total Exports

	1975	1985	1992
Japan	20.16	37.92	28.27
PRC	2.08	15.37	34.46
South Korea	30.29	35.63	22.98
Taiwan	31.12	57.93	29.15
Indonesia	26.17	21.74	12.33
Thailand	11.29	19.87	22.59
Hong Kong	34.41	30.82	23.54
Singapore	13.87	21.17	17.80
Malaysia	15.97	12.76	18.72

Source: See endnote 4.

Table 5
East Asian Exports to Asia as a Percentage of Total Exports

	1975	1985	1992
Japan	20.32	26.63	34.12
PRC	42.85	61.45	74.82
South Korea	33.19	28.77	37.53
Taiwan	36.22	30.86	40.00
Indonesia	56.82	65.47	63.42
Thailand	58.27	42.82	40.49
Hong Kong	25.67	43.79	48.33
Singapore	48.65	50.47	43.67
Malaysia	44.74	64.96	58.16

Source: See endnote 4.

Note: Taiwanese numbers are taken from data supplied by American Express—see endnote 11.

on this phenomenon. For example, American Express analysts calculated that intra-Asian trade grew as a proportion of total trade from 19 percent to 30 percent for nine Asian economies (using the same group I have studied but substituting the Philippines for Japan).[11]

The European Community has also assumed more prominence for Asian exporters. The percentage of Japanese exports sent to the EC between 1975 and 1992 grew from 11 to 19 percent, of Indonesian exports from 5 to 14 percent, and of Thai exports from 16 to 19 percent. The most important change in the direction of trade, however, is the increase in regional trade and the reduced reliance on the U.S. market.

Investment Flows and the Trade Balance

Despite the trend toward greater intraregional trade and greater U.S. merchandise and services exports to dynamic East Asian economies, the United States still has a large trade deficit with the East Asian region. To understand the situation more fully, many analysts have recently turned their attention to the relation between trade and foreign direct investment flows. A review of investment trends in the region helps to show that the maturation of Asian economies will result in continued improvement in the balance of trade.

Attention to the role of foreign direct investment is important for two reasons. First, sales by affiliates of U.S. multinational companies regularly outstrip exports to a given nation by a ratio averaging three to one. In Europe, affiliates of U.S. companies, for instance, will sell almost six times as much as the United States itself exports to Europe. In Asia the ratio is lower for U.S. affiliates.[12] Second, intracompany sales by multinationals now account for about 40 percent of total U.S. trade. Furthermore, recent analysis by the U.S. Department of Commerce shows that the share of the total U.S. trade deficit accounted for by intracompany trade rose from 40 percent in 1984 to 88 percent in 1990, the last year for which comparable data are available.[13] That is, foreign affiliates established in the United States import almost $90 billion more than they export.

Throughout the 1980s, especially after the Plaza Accord, the United States benefited from a large influx of foreign direct investment. The U.S. stock of inward foreign direct investment more than quadrupled in the 1980s, rising from $83 billion to $397 billion.[14] In many ways, this was the result of the U.S. merchandise trade deficit. Instead of holding paper debt, foreigners elected to buy productive assets in the United States. The Japanese were the biggest investors in the United States in this period, their total investment reaching $162 billion by the first quarter of 1993.

Such massive investment flows, especially from Japan to the United States, helped keep the merchandise trade deficit high. As Dennis Encarnation has found, "Japanese multinationals typically invest in majority subsidiaries, which then serve as final markets and intermediary channels for most of their parents'—and Japan's—exports to America." U.S. subsidiaries, by contrast, tend to invest and manufacture abroad largely for sale in the local markets *and* for sale back to the United States.[15] For example, the two largest U.S. imports from Malaysia are electronic circuits and wireless receivers, accounting for about a third of all U.S. imports from that country. Most of these are produced by affiliates of U.S. companies such as Motorola, Seagate Technology, Intel, and Apple that assemble parts, many produced in the United States. The largest U.S. export to Malaysia is electronic circuits, which are assembled there and returned to the United States, if not sold in Asia. The United States has a similar pattern of trade with Singapore. European investors tend to act more like their U.S. than their Japanese counterparts. In general, then, the heavy Japanese investment in the United States in the late 1980s increased the flow of exports to the United States, despite yen appreciation, and helps explain the persistent merchandise trade deficit with that country.

Encarnation, referring to the United States and Japan, has noted that the "single-minded concentration on bilateral trade has already assumed the proportions of national myth, and it has seriously misled observers in both countries." This preoccupation has misled observers because it neglects the real economic importance to a nation of business by its foreign affiliates. It also ignores the global reality that the United States is the world's largest investor abroad and conducts much of its business by selling locally manufactured products using U.S. technology and management expertise. Encarnation estimates, for instance, that local sales by U.S. affiliates plus exports totaled over $1.2 trillion in 1988, and that "U.S. subsidiaries abroad continued to outsell foreign affiliates in America by nearly $1 billion daily."[16] Although one can debate the precision of this estimate, it gives a good indication of the misleading nature of a debate on competitiveness that only looks at merchandise trade. Is the United States less competitive because it assembles electronic circuits in Malaysia that are made at home? The opposite is probably true, as Michael Porter argues:

> World economic prosperity depends on rapid innovation by advanced nations, which creates new products and cedes relatively less productive activities to developing nations. If the rate of innovation slows because an "us versus them" attitude leads to subsidy, protection, and consolidation that blunts incentives, the consequences for advanced and less advanced nations alike are severe.[17]

Competition, then, between Japan and the United States, or between the United States and Asia, includes investment as well as trade flows. Investment trends in the late 1980s and early 1990s, while not decisive, give hope to those who want to see continued improvement in the merchandise trade balance between the United States and Asia. The end of the "financial bubble" and related problems in the banking system have led to a severe slowdown in net investment flows from Japan. In 1991 there was in fact a net capital inflow into Japan.[18] Japan has also slowed the growth of its investment into the eight other dynamic Asian economies while the United States is slowly expanding its investments in the region. Table 6 shows Japanese and U.S. direct investment flows into East Asia.

Japanese investment in the United States peaked in its 1989 fiscal year at $32.5 billion and fell to $13 billion in FY 1992. U.S. investment in Japan, despite numerous informal and formal barriers, averaged $2.3 billion between 1987 and 1992. Globally, the United States still has twice as much invested abroad as does Japan.[19]

Table 6
Comparison of U.S. and Japanese Direct Investment in East and Southeast Asia

(In billion U.S. dollars)

	Japan	United States
1985	1.785	.562
1986	2.289	−.245
1987	4.761	1.831
1988	5.392	1.722
1989	7.918	2.083
1990	6.688	2.182
1991	5.662	4.360
1992	6.029	4.483

Source: U.S. Department of Commerce and Japanese External Trade Organization.

Sources of Growth for the United States in East Asia

Despite the current disparity in the merchandise trade balance, economic trends are moving in ways that benefit U.S. exporters. U.S. investment in East Asia is gradually increasing; higher growth rates in East Asia are gradually reducing disparities in merchandise and the services trade; and U.S. merchandise exports are increasingly competitive. Added to these developments are at least two that are closely linked to the growing sophistication of East Asian economies and the expansion of democracy: the need for massive investments in infrastructure, as production and trade expand, and improvement in the diet of Asians as personal income expands steadily in the region. Both of these factors, if they persist, will complement other developments to create an opportunity for further transpacific economic integration and for narrowing of the merchandise trade and investment balances.

Recent years have seen a flowering of East Asian infrastructure development programs with very large numbers attached to them. Taiwan has a $300 billion, six-year program, and the PRC says its needs dwarf those of its neighbor. Japan announced a 4.3 trillion yen program in parallel with the Structural Impediments Initiative (SII) process last year. Hong Kong is building a $12 billion new airport. South Korea, Thailand, and Singapore also have ambitious investment plans.

Transportation, telecommunications, energy development, and environmental improvement—all occasioned by the enormous expansion of East Asian economies—call for these massive expenditures. The growth of trade itself has made the transport network in East Asia obsolete, vast increases in electric power are needed to fuel the economies of the region and improve standards of living, and environmental degradation resulting from growth requires urgent attention.

One comprehensive estimate of the total infrastructure needs of the region over the next five years was provided by Paul Schulte, an analyst at First Boston in Hong Kong.[20] He estimates total infrastructure needs in nine countries (excluding Japan from and including the Philippines in the list of dynamic economies I have used in this article) at around $627 billion over the next five years. The largest single requirement is for energy development. He notes, for example, that if the PRC continues its current rate of growth it will require new electric generating capacity equal to the entire installed capacity of Japan. Telecommunications and transportation infrastructure are the next largest needs.

On a macroeconomic basis, what is interesting in Schulte's estimates is that the total investment required to meet these politically imperative and economically urgent needs will surpass the huge capacity of Asians to save. He calculates a gap between savings and investment of $158 billion over the next five years in the nine countries covered by his analysis, compared to a surplus of $95 billion in savings over investment between 1987 and 1992. Because Japan, not included in Schulte's analysis, also has a huge investment program (and was a net capital importer in 1991), the sources of capital will increasingly have to be found outside the region, which will either have to run a trade deficit to finance this program or promote greater foreign direct investment. Other solutions to this imbalance, such as putting restraints on foreign trade or forcing more savings on the population, are increasingly unworkable in the face of increasing consumer awareness and the deepening of democracy. Schulte, Encarnation, and David Hale all note the clear implication of such a trend for liberalization of capital markets in East Asia to finance the infrastructure investment. I will return to this theme later, and would only note at this point that the United States probably has a role to play in providing capital to the region, and, because trade follows investment, this provides a clear opportunity to reduce the highly visible merchandise trade deficit.

From a microeconomic point of view, the need for capital goods and investment should also benefit the United States. As noted earlier, the United States has maintained its competitiveness in aerospace technology. Recent purchases by the PRC of Boeing aircraft demonstrate the potential for additional sales to Asia. In the telecommunications area, the United States has improved its competitive position in recent years, partly, as Porter has noted, as a result of the early deregulation of the telephone monopoly.[21] In contrast, Japan's slow deregulation and informal protection of its telecommunications market is resulting in a loss of competitive advantage in this industry to its U.S. and Canadian counterparts.[22] U.S. firms, when not undermined by government interference in contracting, are highly competitive in power plant construction, oilfield development, and public construction. U.S. companies also account for 40 percent of the world market for environmental technology and services. Finally, as studies by McKinsey and many others repeatedly show, the U.S. financial services sector is highly productive and competitive worldwide. The need in Asia for more sophisticated financial services to finance infrastructure development and growth provides a unique opportunity for U.S. suppliers.

U.S. competitiveness in providing infrastructure and capital goods has been recognized by the PRC, Japan, and Taiwan. Each of these countries has explicitly linked its own development program with the desire to placate U.S. concerns over the bilateral deficits.

The other major area offering special potential to U.S. suppliers at this stage of East Asia's economic development is agriculture. Much has been made of the continued demographic dynamism in Asia as a threat to the global environment. Yet we should recognize that, just as in the West, Asian populations reduce their rate of population growth as their per capita income increases. Japan and Hong Kong, for instance, have demographic growth rates of less than 1 percent per year, below that of the United States, and those in Taiwan and in South Korea are declining as these countries move up the income scale. More to the point: Who will provide the additional protein requirements for the enormous Asian population as it advances its standard of living? Related to this is the question of how to meet the need for increased protein requirements in the most environmentally benign fashion.

Asia as a whole has a population of around 3 billion people. Average consumption of high-quality protein is about 11 grams per day, compared to 72 in the United States and 52 in Japan. If economic growth in East Asia, the PRC, and India continues, Dennis Avery of the Hudson Institute's Center for Global Food Issues has calculated that consumption of livestock and poultry will quintuple over the next 20 years.[23] An additional 200 million tons of grain per year would be needed to support increased consumption of high-protein foods in Asia. We are already seeing the results of increased affluence: in recent years, consumption of meat in the PRC has risen by 2.3 million tons per year, India is increasing milk consumption by 2 million tons per year, and Indonesia's poultry consumption is growing by 20 percent annually.

The most economically efficient and environmentally benign way to meet growing demand for better food in Asia would be to rely largely on North American and other existing farming areas that have unusually high-quality land resources. The United States has large tracts of good farmland idled as a result of its supply-management programs. It has the transportation and food processing infrastructure to bring new products to market quickly and efficiently. It does not make sense for Indonesia to clear 1.5 million acres of rainforest to grow soybeans, as the government recently announced it would, when supplies could easily be made available from North American sources. Avery has calculated that direct exports of grain and meat could add more than $50 billion per year to U.S. agricultural sales, and studies at Purdue University estimate a potential gain of $40 billion in processed food exports primarily to Asia because of the U.S. long-term comparative advantage in this sector as well.

Obviously, such gains in agriculture are hypothetical and highly dependent on changes in trade policy and domestic agricultural policies. Indeed, any projection of economic development in the Asian arena is subject to the uncertainties of policy decisions throughout the region. The optimistic scenario for continued growth, increased U.S. exports, and closer economic integration that I have outlined will not unfold automatically as part of some iron law of developmental economics. It must be encouraged and nurtured by policy choices on both sides of the Pacific.

U.S. Economic Policy Toward East Asia

A major assumption of this article is that continued U.S. advances in competitiveness require closer integration of the U.S. economy with the dynamic Asian markets. Economic growth and job creation in the United States will be enhanced if the nation takes advantage of current opportunities to expand its provision of goods and services to these markets and its investment in their economies. To accomplish this requires a number of proactive steps: continued U.S. strategic engagement in the region; a market-opening trade strategy; openness to investment flows throughout the region; domestic policy that does not shackle U.S. ability to export; and encouragement for continued democratization in the region. Clearly, many of these policies are interrelated.

Despite the flurry over the "Tarnoff Doctrine" and the periodic recrudescence of polemics for reducing U.S. military commitment to Asia because of a perceived lack of economic access to the region, most commentators accept the need for an active U.S. security presence and active economic engagement there.[24] Stability and continued economic dynamism in East Asia also require U.S. engagement. Singapore's astute and increasingly blunt Lee Kuan Yew puts the case succinctly: "The American presence, in my view, is essential for the continuation of law and order in East Asia." He also notes that the American presence is necessary to preserve and expand the liberal trading order that is of such obvious benefit to the region.[25] Asians in general accept and welcome the U.S. presence to preserve not only a balance of force in the area, but also a balance of economic influence. Lee Kuan Yew's argument is, however, more sophisticated: the United States can also protect an open trading regime.

Much of the argument over U.S. policy turns not on the link between security and economic considerations, but on how actively to use the leverage provided by engagement to achieve economic goals. Much of the argument is skewed by the priority given to the Japanese relationship and the continued hand-wringing over the merchandise trade deficit. But U.S. economic interests are much broader than this and demand increased attention to the faster-growing economies of the Asian continent and to investment flows. A singular, "laser-like" focus on the merchandise trade deficit with Japan can lead and has led to a policy response emphasizing some sort of managed trade or neo-mercantilist approach, often coupled with a discussion of withdrawal of a military presence from the region.

It is essential, however, to underscore that an active policy of economic engagement in Asia probably cannot succeed if the United States fails to play an active role in the security arrangements of the region. Its leverage dissipates if it retreats into a mercantilist and isolationist policy, especially because the growth of regional trade in Asia has reduced the importance of Asian access to the U.S. market (although such access is still obviously an important lever available to U.S. policymakers).

The second key to a successful economic integration between the U.S. and Asian economies is using U.S. leverage to advance an activist, multilateral, market-opening trade strategy. "The aim of trade policy should be to open markets and eliminate unfair trade practices," writes Porter. He adds that setting "quantitative targets for exports and imports . . . [has] the effect of guaranteeing a market for inefficient firms rather than promoting innovation in the nation's industry."[26] Such elegant principles are unfortunately difficult to implement, but they nonetheless must be rigorously followed if we believe that growth and improvement of living standards can only be accomplished through constant innovation and upgrading of national production.

Again, it is worth noting that the bilateral, Japan-centered approach currently favored by the United States runs counter to its larger interests in Asia. The managed trade solution, unlikely to produce results in Japan, has provoked increasing sympathy in Asia for regional blocs such as the Malaysian prime minister Mahathir Mohamad promotes. The managed trade approach could thus undermine a multilateral market-opening strategy with the more dynamic elements of the Asian region.

The starting point for a market-opening strategy should be the broadest possible geographic theater, with a special emphasis on the sectors that offer the best opportunities for U.S. exporters. A multilateral forum, although presenting complexity in negotiation, offers the advantage of building consensus to settle differences rather than confrontation. The Uruguay Round of the General Agreement on Tariffs and Trade (GATT) provides the best opportunity to advance this strategy in the broad Asian context. The Uruguay Round would, for example, bring agriculture and services such as banking and financial services under the international rules of the GATT for the first time, as well as lowering tariffs significantly in high-technology goods like semiconductors, telecommunications equipment, and pharmaceuticals.

The services agreement in the Uruguay Round is doubly important to the United States and Asia because the latter, especially continental Asia, needs more sophisticated financial services to finance its ambitious infrastructure development plans. U.S. investment in Asia could also be facilitated by liberalization of capital markets. The Round would also establish basic rules of open access and transparency to govern foreign investment. As a consequence, U.S. negotiating leverage in Asia should be directed toward completing the Uruguay Round and obtaining reasonable results in the targeted sectors.

If completion of the Uruguay Round proves to be beyond the diplomatic skills and the political commitment of its 108 members, then regional forums should be employed. To its credit, the Clinton administration has recognized the opportunity offered by the Asia–Pacific Economic Cooperation (APEC) meeting in the United States and has announced plans to use this 15-member group to advance a trade-opening agenda. The group met in mid-November in Seattle at the head of government level. Some combination of sectoral market-opening arrangements or at least framework agreements would be a modest but important contribution to the APEC economic integration process. A set of agricultural, textile, and high-technology sectoral arrangements might be created among nations of the region.[27] Another promising means of regional liberalization would be to consider entry of some Pacific nations—Australia, New Zealand, or Singapore, for example—into the North American Free Trade Agreement (NAFTA), presuming it is passed by the U.S. Congress. Finally, a regional investment agreement modeled on U.S. bilateral investment treaties (the so-called BITs) would be very useful to build confidence in regional integration and facilitate greater regional investment.

Regional or subregional agreements have the benefit of maintaining momentum for trade liberalization and providing clear incentives for other nations to join the process. Japan, for instance, would be hard-pressed to remain on the outside of a NAFTA–ASEAN free trade area, if it were ever to come to fruition. In addition, it would be easier for Japan to join a regional trade agreement, or Korea to join a regional investment agreement, than to give way to bilateral pressure from the United States. Regional agreements of any sort, between Singapore and NAFTA, for example, would also be a spur to completion of the Uruguay Round or larger multilateral arrangements. The example of the EC shows that nations that are hesitant about multinational organizations, such as Austria or Switzerland, feel compelled to participate in regional economic zones.

Despite the best efforts and best intentions of U.S. negotiators, some bilateral problems will remain. Asian markets are in many cases hard to access due to formal and informal barriers. The United States has ample tools at its disposal now to address most sectoral problems that arise with Japan or other Asian nations through U.S. antidumping statutes, Section 301, and specific statutes on telecommunications and government procurement. In addition, the leverage that comes from the U.S. role as ultimate guarantor of security in the region has in the past helped negotiators to resolve most serious disputes. The Bush administration successfully completed sectoral agreements with South Korea, Taiwan, Indonesia, Japan, and the PRC.

What should be avoided in bilateral as well as multilateral negotiations, on the other hand, is use of pressure to obtain "guaranteed outcomes," to manage markets, or to impose political conditions on trade (absent real national security concerns). The Clinton administration's current effort to negotiate guaranteed outcomes with Japan is destined to failure on a number of fronts. Japanese bureaucrats have already worked to undermine any substance to the agreement and to enlist the support of other nations against the U.S. managed-trade strategy.[28] The managed-trade initiative has also elicited a new sympathy for Japan among other East Asian nations and renewed interest in Prime Minister Mahathir's call for a regional trade grouping that excludes the United States and Canada.

To complement a market-opening trade strategy, the United States should maintain its traditional openness to both outward and inward investment flows. U.S. competitive advantage is frequently put into operation by direct investment, resulting in both increased exports and repatriation of profits. Because Asia is at a stage of development requiring large capital inflows, emphasis on liberalizing investment markets and openness to outward investment provide the mechanism for increasing U.S. engagement in the region and may result in narrowing or elimination of the merchandise trade deficit.

The Clinton administration's policy toward outward investment gives some cause for concern. With a singular emphasis on job creation at home, Labor Secretary Robert Reich and others have raised concerns about the value of U.S. investment abroad. According to Secretary Reich, "It is a mistake to associate these foreign investments by American-owned companies with any result that improves the competitiveness of the United States."[29] A more balanced perspective is offered, however, by Jeffrey Garten, nominated to be under secretary for international trade: "U.S. companies will not be competitive unless they can set up in foreign markets, be near their customers and engage in local research."[30] It is not politically comfortable to watch factories moving abroad, but, as Porter has argued convincingly, in order to upgrade its economy continually, the United States must create higher-paying and more productive jobs at home while allowing lower-skill and lower-paying jobs to move abroad.

Several analysts of the relation between trade and investment also advocate closing U.S. investment markets, or establishing a strict principle of reciprocity, as a means of retaliating against closed or difficult investment markets abroad, such as some manufacturing and financial services in Japan and South Korea.[31] Although reciprocity theories are attractive in many ways, especially when explaining foreign economic policy to the American people, it is difficult to envision a fair, rigorous, and nonpolitical application of any rules that could be devised to operationalize the concept. Because U.S. subsidiaries sell much more abroad than do foreign affiliates in the United States, it also does not make sense to risk the already strong U.S. competitive position by undermining the international consensus on open trade flows.

Garten was equally judicious in cautioning the Clinton administration to avoid harming international competitiveness through domestic policy:

> The effort to integrate trade and domestic policy will require great care. Opening foreign markets is essential to the long-term health of the U.S. economy. But hard-won victories can be quickly nullified if American firms are loaded down with new regulatory and financial burdens. The Administration will have to ensure that the new costs of health care, worker retraining and additional taxes do not cripple U.S. industries.[32]

To Garten's list of possible new burdens I would add some affecting agriculture. For if U.S. suppliers are to serve the vibrant new markets in Asia, the supply-management, price-support, and land-use policies that constrain domestic production will have to be reevaluated. Furthermore, production in the United States could be hindered by new restrictions on the use of pesticides and herbicides. The current trend toward no-till agriculture, a response to the soil erosion problem, requires the use of some weed and pest control agents or else production will decline.[33] If the United States cannot supply the new demand, then environmentally sensitive and less productive lands, mostly in Asia, will be brought into production to fill the gap.

A final and perhaps obvious point: promoting democracy and individual welfare in Asia makes eminent sense for U.S. economic interests. Democracy in the region has intensified as nations move up the ladder of income and sophistication in their economies. Part and parcel of this process is increased consumer awareness and demands for improvement in the quality of life. Overall, these processes lead to a larger role for domestic consumption in the national economies, less reliance on export-driven growth, and increases in imports.

I have outlined two regional trends—infrastructure improvement and increasing preference for a high-protein diet—that are likely to increase imports, especially from the United States. Other examples could be given: increased environmental awareness and citizens' action is leading to explosive growth in the environmental products and services market, and increased attention to health care will benefit U.S. suppliers of medical equipment and pharmaceuticals.

Efforts to break down the rigid distribution system that penalizes consumers in Japan, or open the banking market in South Korea that stifles small business and foreign investment, or guarantee intellectual property rights throughout the region to protect entrepreneurs cannot strictly be described as promoting democracy. Nonetheless, these actions empower individuals and help raise their standard of living over the long run. These efforts will therefore lead to a more open system that will ultimately benefit U.S. and other foreign suppliers and will also, as Porter would argue, promote "world economic prosperity."

In addition, U.S. efforts to promote reduction of trade deficits through improved macroeconomic coordination can be linked to the natural evolution in Asia toward increased political power and economic well-being for individuals. The Bush administration made this link more or less explicit in the SII talks, which emphasized the need for a massive infrastructure program and a more open distribution and retailing system to benefit consumers. The Clinton administration has also focused on the need for domestic stimulus, including a tax cut and infrastructure investment in Japan to draw in more imports. President Bill Clinton himself justified U.S. economic policy by an appeal to Japanese consumers while in Tokyo, showing the politician's touch for finding a political rationale for the more abstract concept of macroeconomic coordination.[34] Consumer movements are also linked to deepening of democracy in South Korea and Taiwan.

Obviously, Asian nations will have to cooperate with these efforts to open markets, liberalize investment regimes, and gradually move to an economic regime more oriented toward the consumer or individual. The United States will have no leverage if it disengages from the region, retreats into a mercantilist position, or abandons its leading role in the defense of a liberal trading system. If it pursues the approach outlined here, the Asians, as Lee Kuan Yew puts it, will have to work with the United States: "[T]o get East Asia to stay on course for rapid growth, Japan and all in East Asia have to accommodate the sometimes importunate demands of the Americans."[35] If East Asia stays on course for rapid growth and works with the United States, then the economic future of the United States itself will be considerably enhanced.

The author acknowledges with thanks the research assistance of Alexander Feldman and Cynthia Josef. He also received helpful comments from Richard Fairbanks and Chester Cooper on an earlier version of the paper. The views expressed or implied in this article are solely those of the author. No opinions, statements of fact, or conclusions contained in this article can properly be attributed to Hudson Institute, its staff, its members, or its contributing agencies.

Notes

1. Clyde Prestowitz, Jr., *Trading Places: How We Allowed Japan to Take the Lead* (New York, N.Y.: Basic Books, 1988), was one of the earliest and most articulate proponents of this viewpoint, although the literature is now vast.

2. I explored the argument that U.S. growth is increasingly dependent on export markets in "Global Competitiveness and U.S.–EC Trade Relations," *The Washington Quarterly* 16 (Summer 1993), especially pp. 116–117.

3. David Hale, "The Yen's Role in World Financial Diplomacy: Should We Focus on Trade Flows or Investment Flows?" (Speech to the Japan Society, New York, N.Y., July 14, 1993), p. 15.

4. Economic data presented in this article are derived from diverse sources. Historical growth rates are taken from the Asia Development Bank's *Asia Development Outlook;* from the Central Intelligence Agency's *Handbook of International Economic Statistics 1992;* from *Taiwan Statistical Data Book: 1992;* from data published by the International Trade Administration and the Bureau of Economic Analysis of the U.S. Department of Commerce; and from the OECD's *National Accounts of OECD Countries, 1990,* vol. I. National accounts data are taken from the International Bank for Reconstruction and Development, *World Tables,* as well as the other sources listed here. Most of the trade data are taken from the International Monetary Fund's *Direction of Trade Statistics.* I have used Taiwanese data to fill in gaps and

U.S. data to supplement data on PRC exports to the United States, because the IMF uses PRC data that are distorted. For tables 3 and 4 on exports to the United States, I have used U.S. data for the PRC, while I have used IMF data in other places for purposes of consistency.

5. I have used the term "Asia" loosely. For the purposes of this article I am most concerned with a group of nine dynamic Asian economies: Japan, the PRC, Hong Kong, Indonesia, South Korea, Malaysia, Singapore, Taiwan, and Thailand. These are countries whose economies must be linked more closely to that of the United States, which is the thrust of my argument, because of their size and dynamism. I have largely ignored Australia and New Zealand because the U.S. economy is for all intents and purposes reasonably integrated with theirs. India is beyond the scope of the article for the most part because of its location, its lack of participation in the Asia–Pacific Economic Cooperation (APEC), and my bias that a dynamic Asian economy must sustain good performance over at least a decade. On PRC GDP estimates, see "China's Potential Emerging from Behind the Figures," *Financial Times*, April 26, 1993.

6. "Japan's Unemployment Rate Tops 6 Percent if 'Intra-company' Jobless Are Included," Bureau of National Affairs (Washington, D.C.), *Daily Report for Executives*, July 20, 1993. This summarizes a study by Sumitomo Life Research Institute, Inc.

7. Regional aggregations on trade in goods and services vary widely. I have in this paragraph used data from U.S. Department of Commerce, Bureau of Economic Analysis, *Survey of Current Business* 73, no. 6 (1993), table 10. Unfortunately, the aggregate data on services include Africa, but they are the only consistent regional data on services trade I could find. I do not believe including Africa distorts the numbers inordinately.

8. Duesterberg, "Global Competitiveness."

9. U.S. Department of Labor, Bureau of Labor Statistics, "Output Per Hour, Hourly Compensation, and Unit Labor Costs in Manufacturing, Twelve Industrial Countries, 1950–1990 and Unit Labor Costs in Korea and Taiwan, 1970–1990" (Washington, D.C., December 1991), pp. 8–9, 15–16.

10. Central Intelligence Agency, *Handbook of International Economic Statistics: 1992* (Washington, D.C., 1992), p. 200.

11. American Express Bank, "Asian Trade: New Directions," *Amex Bank Review* 20, no. 3 (1993), pp. 2–3.

12. See Dennis J. Encarnation, *Rivals Beyond Trade: America versus Japan in Global Competition* (Ithaca, N.Y.: Cornell University Press, 1992), p. 16. See also Peter F. Cowhey and Jonathan D. Aronson, "A New Trade Order," *Foreign Affairs* 72, no. 1 (1993), p. 183.

13. See Lester A. Davis, "U.S. Trade in Merchandise and Services by Foreign-Owned U.S. Firms," in U.S. Department of Commerce, Office of the Chief Economist, *Foreign Direct Investment in the United States: An Update* (Washington, D.C., 1993), p. 77.

14. *Ibid.*, table 2–6.

15. Encarnation, *Rivals Beyond Trade*, pp. 97, 180.

16. *Ibid.*, pp. 1, 198.

17. Michael E. Porter, *The Competitive Advantage of Nations* (New York, N.Y.: Free Press, 1990), p. 682.

18. See Hale, "Yen's Role in World Financial Diplomacy," and David B. H. Denoon, *Real Reciprocity: Balancing U.S. Economic and Security Policy in the Pacific Basin* (New York, N.Y.: Council on Foreign Relations Press, 1993), p. 55.

19. U.S. Department of Commerce, *Foreign Direct Investment*, table 2–4. Recent Japanese data are provided by the Japanese External Trade Organization (JETRO).

20. Paul Schulte, "The Asian Miracle Part II: Reversal of Fortune," *CS First Boston-Equity Research Asia*, June 7, 1993.

21. Porter, *Competitive Advantage of Nations*, p. 654.

22. See, for example, Gale Eisenstodt, "Unintended Favors," *Forbes*, August 2, 1993, pp. 104–105.

23. These calculations were taken largely from the work of Dennis Avery, "Soybeans and the Greatest Farm Opportunity in History" (Speech to the "Soybeans in Canada Symposium," Toronto, March 1993); and "The Greatest Opportunity in Farming History" (Speech to the Columbia Farm Credit

Bank, Daytona Beach, Florida, June 1993).

24. See, for instance, Denoon, *Real Reciprocity*, chap. 2; Chalmers Johnson, "Rethink Asia," *National Interest*, no. 32 (Summer 1993), pp. 20–29; and Carnegie Endowment for International Peace, "Rethinking Japan Policy" (Washington, D.C., 1993).

25. "Why American Economic and Security Presence Vital for Asia" (interview with Lee Kuan Yew), *Straits Times*, December 17, 1991; and "Japan's Key Role in the Industrialization of E. Asia," *Straits Times*, February 14, 1992.

26. Porter, *Competitive Advantage of Nations*, p. 669.

27. Cowhey and Aronson emphasize the pragmatic approach of sectoral agreements as consensus among the GATT's 108 members becomes increasingly difficult. "A New Trade Order," pp. 194–195.

28. See David Sanger, "Japan Is Rallying Asian Nations Against New U.S. Trade Policies," *New York Times*, June 7, 1993; and John Bussey, "Japanese Dispute U.S. Comments on Trade Pact's Effect on Surplus," *Wall Street Journal*, July 15, 1993.

29. Quoted in Encarnation, *Rivals Beyond Trade*, p. 215.

30. Jeffrey E. Garten, "Clinton's Emerging Trade Policy: Act One, Scene One," *Foreign Affairs* 72, no. 3 (1993), p. 185.

31. Encarnation, *Rivals Beyond Trade*, pp. 215–217.

32. Garten, "Clinton's Emerging Trade Policy," p. 185.

33. See Dennis Avery, "Poverty Won't Save the Planet," *Hudson Institute Briefing Paper*, no. 142 (July 1992).

34. Carnegie's U.S.–Japan study group places emphasis on macroeconomic coordination to reduce trade friction, see "Rethinking Japan Policy," p. 29.

35. "Japan's Key Role."

Who's Benefiting Whom? A Trade Agenda for High-Technology Industries

Ernest H. Preeg

THE GLOBAL ECONOMY is being transformed by a technological revolution that is central to defining what kind of new world order will emerge from the East–West and North–South orientations of the past half century. The transformation emanates from what is broadly defined as the information technology sector—the amazing growth of computer power—but pervades all sectors of the economy. This high-technology revolution is unprecedented in its pace of change and geographic scope, making the industrial revolution of the late eighteenth century and the agricultural revolution of the early twentieth century leisurely and limited adjustments by comparison. It should be no surprise that governments with traditional nation-state mandates are hesitant and inadequate in their response.

This transformation is increasingly international in character and thus much of the adjustment in national economies is transmitted through the international trading system. The term *trading system*, moreover, now involves a complicated interaction of trade in goods and services, direct investment by multinational corporations, and the international transfer of applied new technologies by various means. The whole process is an extraordinary positive sum game, as demonstrated by the rapid expansion of trade and investment in high-technology sectors as well as by the surges in productivity and economic growth that result from new technology-intensive industries. These massive prima facie gains from trade, however, are difficult if not impossible to measure, as compared with the textbook trade model of exchanging wine for cloth, because they embody a highly dynamic and ever-changing set of relationships.

There is also a counteracting force at play, protectionist in character, that influences how the gains from trade are shared among nations and companies. Most governments, and particularly those of the advanced industrialized countries, apply a wide range of forceful incentives to stimulate technological innovation, including direct subsidies, intellectual property rights (IPRs), preferential public procurement, fiscal benefits, and straightforward trade protection. To the extent these incentives enable applied new technologies to advance more quickly in one country than in another, a na-

---

Ernest H. Preeg holds the William M. Scholl Chair in International Business at CSIS.

Copyright © 1993 by The Center for Strategic and International Studies and the Massachusetts Institute of Technology

tional competitive advantage can be obtained. If one nation's industry achieves a decisive technological lead, it can, in certain instances, maintain a prolonged dominant world market position and reap large oligopoly profits. Moreover, unlike the elusive overall gains from high-technology trade, these market share effects lend themselves to rigorous analysis and quantification.

Recent intensive attention to trade policy for high-technology industries has, in fact, largely ignored the overall positive sum game engendered by trade growth and concentrated on the market share issue. The momentum of political debate in the United States runs heavily in favor of the view that U.S. industry, which launched the information technology revolution three decades ago, is now being adversely affected by the world trading system and that Japan, in particular, is unfairly managing the flow of high-technology trade and investment to its great advantage and at U.S. expense. The net political result is a dangerous trend toward viewing trade in high-technology industries principally in terms of conflict among adversaries rather than of reaping mutual benefits among cooperative trading partners. Last year, three widely cited books bore the subtitles: "Trade *Conflict* in High-Technology Industries"; "The Coming Economic *Battle* Among Japan, Europe, and America"; and "America, Japan, Germany, and the *Struggle* for *Supremacy*" (italics added). Two of the authors now hold or are likely to hold senior positions in the Clinton administration and the third is a valued adviser to it.[1] Another influence on this trend is that unemployed "cold war warriors," who have a zero or negative sum mind-set from a lifetime of geopolitical strategizing, are now retargeting their formidable intellectual firepower on trade and economic issues, with their habitual insistence on defining relationships in terms of adversaries, conflict, and power manipulation.

The crux of the problem, however, is neither personalities nor outmoded political thinking, but rather the lack of a complete national strategy for high-technology trade and investment based on a more accurate assessment of the forces of change that are driving the world economy. There is little question that access to high-technology sectors of the Japanese market for U.S. exports and investment needs to be more comparable with Japanese access to the U.S. market. There is also consensus that U.S. domestic economic policies need to be reoriented toward strengthened educational performance, improved infrastructure, and higher levels of investment for new technology development and application. What is lacking is a broader and more forward-looking trade policy framework within which these immediate objectives are pursued.

The existing international trading system is in a state of flux, contains gaps and inconsistencies, and is in some respects simply ineffective. The multilateral General Agreement on Tariffs and Trade (GATT) deals primarily with trade in goods and has little competence for trade in services, international investment, and technology transfer. GATT commitments in such relevant areas of policy as export subsidies, government procurement, and trade-related investment measures are vague. During the 1980s, primarily at U.S. initiative, the basic multilateral approach to trade policy was expanded to a more complicated "three-track" approach of multilateral commitments, comprehensive regional free trade, and selective bilateral agreements. New technology development remains principally a domestic affair, supported by wide-ranging local as well as national programs, resulting in a communications disconnect between technology and trade policy officials. Policy coherence indeed threatens to become an oxymoron in the discussion of trade policy for high-technology industries.

The United States needs to take a fresh and more systematic look at trade policy for high-technology industries that maintains its focus on national economic performance, deals with immediate market access problems, and builds a stronger, more coherent, longer-term international structure for maximizing the overriding positive benefits of trade and investment. It should include an assessment of recent trade performance, especially for the United States, a more probing look at the analytic underpinning for the special status allocated to trade in high-technology industries, a critique of the existing trade policy framework, and, from all of the foregoing, the elaboration of an action agenda for trade policy over the next two to four years. The following offers some preliminary thoughts on each of these four lines of inquiry.

An Assessment of Recent U.S. Trade Performance

It is generally understood that trade in high-technology industries has been growing rapidly and has become a leading export sector for the United States and other advanced industrialized nations, but there are surprisingly few trade data available to support this view, and there is even less reference to it in policy discussion. A cursory look at what is available on most recent U.S. trade performance, however, is encouraging.

A precise analysis is hampered by varying definitions as to what constitutes high-technology industry, although there is growing acceptance of a relatively narrow definition based on expert evaluation of the content of embodied technology, with possible reference to a high ratio of research and development (R&D) expenditures to sales. On this basis, two similar data bases have been developed. Paolo Guerrieri and Carlo Milana have a multicountry data base at the University of Rome, and the U.S. Bureau of the Census provides the most up-to-date figures for U.S. trade from its Advanced Technology Products (ATP) classification system.

Table 1 presents U.S. trade in high-technology industry from Bureau of the Census data for 1982 through 1992. In the latter year, such industries constituted 23.4 percent of total U.S. exports and 13.5 percent of total imports. The principal sectors for both exports and imports were aerospace, information systems and telecommunications, and advanced electronics. Several observations are pertinent. First, U.S. trade in high-technology industries grew at a high rate of 12.5 percent per year from $54.7 billion to $176.9 billion over the decade, roughly double the rate for total trade. The growth rate for exports was 10.2 percent and for imports an even faster 17.0 percent. Second, the United States sustained a large trade surplus throughout the period, dipping in 1986–1987 because of the overvalued dollar in the early 1980s and the exchange rate adjustment beginning in 1986, but then rising sharply to the $33 to $37 billion range in 1990–1992. In terms of job creation, the increase in the surplus from $16 billion in 1986 to $33 billion in 1992, adjusting for inflation, translates into a net increase in the order of 250,000 presumably high-skill, high-paying jobs. Finally, the ratio of exports to imports declined

Table 1
U.S. Trade in High-Technology Industries

(In billion U.S. dollars)

	Exports	Imports	Trade Balance
1982	39.7	15.0	24.7
1983	42.5	18.5	24.0
1984	46.9	26.2	20.7
1985	51.5	27.1	24.4
1986	53.5	37.2	16.3
1987	62.1	41.8	20.3
1988	76.9	48.9	28.0
1989	83.5	56.4	27.1
1990	93.4	59.3	34.1
1991	100.0	63.1	36.9
1992	105.1	71.8	33.3

Source: U.S. Department of Commerce, Bureau of the Census, Foreign Trade Division, Advanced Technology Products (ATP).

from about 2.5 in the early 1980s to 1.5 in the later years, reflecting growing Japanese and other Asian competition, although the ratio has held relatively stable since 1986.

Table 2 takes a closer look at bilateral trade balances for 1991 on a slightly revised ATP basis. One interesting observation is the geographic diversity of U.S. high-technology trade; the four largest U.S. trading partners listed constituted together only 34 percent of exports and 47 percent of imports. Less surprisingly, Japan is the one country with which the United States had a substantial trade deficit—$7.4 billion—as a result of competitive Japanese industry and structural impediments to U.S. high-technology exports to the Japanese market. The large U.S. surpluses with Canada and Mexico have significance for the pending North American Free Trade Agreement (NAFTA); the com-

Table 2
Bilateral U.S. Trade in High-Technology Industries, 1991

(In billion U.S. dollars)

	Exports	Imports	Balance
Global	101.6	63.3	38.3
Japan	12.4	19.8	-7.4
Germany	8.6	2.8	5.8
Canada	11.0	6.9	4.1
Mexico	2.6	1.1	1.5
(North America)	(13.6)	(8.0)	(5.6)
Other	67.0	32.7	34.3

Source: U.S. Department of Commerce, Bureau of the Census, Foreign Trade Division, Advanced Technology Products (ATP).

Note: The updated Bureau of the Census definition for this table includes software products, not included in table 1.

bined $5.6 billion U.S. surplus means a net plus of more than 100,000 U.S. jobs in high-technology industries, which probably would grow even larger with the implementation of comprehensive free trade among the three neighboring countries.

Other dimensions of U.S. trade performance in high-technology industries concern trade in services and foreign direct investment, but unfortunately there has been no serious attempt to analyze such performance, within the U.S. government or elsewhere. Some proxy indicators are nevertheless revealing. For trade in services, five industry categories related to applied high technology show very rapid growth and a five-to-one ratio of exports to imports.[2] U.S. exports of these services rose from $2.6 billion in 1989 to $4.5 billion in 1991, with a corresponding $3.7 billion trade surplus in the latter year. Another large sector of U.S. services trade—telecommunications—is in overall trade deficit, but more detailed information is needed to sort out high- and low-technology segments. In any event, the largest regional deficit for telecommunications, of $1.3 billion in 1991, is not with Japan or the European Community, but with Latin America, which probably means Mexico most of all. Exorbitant telephone rates charged by the Mexican telephone monopoly on massive southbound calls will be addressed as the NAFTA is implemented. A broad categorization of foreign direct investment that contains a wide range of high-technology industries showed a net outflow of U.S. investment in 1991 of $1.6 billion following substantial net inflows in previous years.[3]

The overall assessment of recent U.S. trade performance in high-technology industries, as presented here, is largely positive. The rapid growth in both exports and imports, with the inherent gains from trade, and the sustained strong surplus position constitute the basic picture. There is, of course, growing international competition in these industries, and there are worrisome clouds on the longer-term horizon. A more forceful policy response, as elaborated below, is needed for U.S. trade policy and even more so for domestic economic policies. But the facts to date on U.S. trade performance for high-technology industries are reassuring in quantitative terms, and a more qualitative commentary, also given below, tends to reinforce this conclusion.

This basic assessment of recent U.S. trade performance, however, is very much at odds with other recent presentations. *Who's Bashing Whom? Trade Conflict in High-Technology Industries*, by Laura Tyson, is the most widely cited example of a more negative assessment, but it follows a pattern found elsewhere.[4] The Tyson analysis of aggregate trade patterns for high-technology industries, drawn from the Guerrieri/Milana data bank, is confined almost entirely to world market shares rather than absolute levels of trade, and the U.S. share declined from 30 percent in 1970–1973 to 21 percent in 1988–1989. All of this decline was due to the coming of advanced industrial age of Japan and the Asian newly industrialized economies, but the shift mostly occurred in the early 1970s, when high-technology trade was far smaller. The U.S. share of global high-technology exports stabilized at 24 to 25 percent during the period 1976–1985, and then declined to 21 to 22 percent from 1985 to 1989. It is possible that the share bounced back somewhat in the early 1990s, based on overall U.S. export performance, although global market share figures for more recent years are not currently available. The only presentation of absolute trade levels in the Tyson book (table 2–8) ends with 1988 data.

The Tyson analysis is thus oriented predominantly toward the zero sum market share issue to the almost total exclusion of the positive gains from overall growth in trade, and even in this context the analysis is somewhat dated because it does not capture the surge in U.S. exports of high-technology goods and services during the past four years. The analysis in any event would not, in itself, justify the one-line, rhetorical assessment at the outset of the book, that "in the full flush of geopolitical triumph, we are teetering over the abyss of economic decline." A fuller explanation of this disturbingly negative conclusion requires a closer look at the analytic underpinning for what is referred to as the "New Trade Theory."

The Analytic Underpinning

A considerable professional literature emerged from the 1980s about the New Trade Theory, with special focus on high-technology industries.[5] The thrust of the new approach is that the characteristics of high-technology industry do not conform with the assumptions underlying classical trade theory of comparative advantage, particularly the assumption of perfect competition, and that therefore free trade is not necessarily the best policy course. For example, if the world market can only accommodate two or three large-scale producers of a new technology-intensive product, a government might protect its "national champion" so that it becomes one of the surviving, profitable producers. An alternative "strategic trade policy" is recommended by some proponents of the new theory, consisting principally of "industrial policy," meaning government subsidy for selected industries of strategic importance, and "managed trade," whereby quantitative targets rather than market access rules determine trade flows.

The New Trade Theory discussion is not really new in that iconoclastic economists can be cited back 50 or 100 years challenging the classical trade theory, but it has now become revolutionary through its potentially sweeping application to the technology-oriented trade and investment flows that are coming to dominate international economic relationships. Disappointment with the New Trade Theory analysis to date, in fact, can be directed principally at its limited scope of inquiry and its preoccupation with particular problem areas that arouse the greatest political attention and that happen to be the easiest to quantify. This major shortcoming can be illustrated by comparing the most prominent problem area addressed thus far, referred to here as the "managed oligopoly syndrome," and the far broader, underlying trade significance of the New Trade Theory, which can be called the "multiple synergy effect."

The managed oligopoly syndrome concerns the experience of several industry sectors during the 1980s, including semiconductors, supercomputers, and commercial jet aircraft, in which one or a few companies threatened to establish, with vital government support, a sustained dominant market, or oligopoly, position. Market characteristics, to varying degrees, included very large companies, huge up-front investment financing, a short product cycle, and sharply declining costs from a "learning curve" as production quality improved. They were classic oligopoly situations in terms of increasing returns to scale and formidable barriers to entry for new firms once the dominant producers became established, but in a highly compressed time frame wherein it was essential to get to market first and in largest quantity.

The most exhaustively analyzed sector was the rapid rise of Japanese semiconductor production, which threatened to dominate the world market for memory storage computer chips, or DRAMs, and some other semiconductor products. Six large, integrated Japanese computer firms made the initial investments while the Japanese market was effectively closed to competitive U.S. producers. As Japanese production expanded, the U.S. market was flooded with low-priced Japanese exports, threatening U.S. producers such as Texas Instruments, Intel, and Motorola with extinction from the DRAM market. A permanent oligopoly by the Japanese firms would lead to higher prices and profits, with broad strategic benefits to the Japanese computer industry. The U.S. policy response culminated in the 1986 bilateral agreement with Japan that curtailed price cutting in the U.S. market and established a target share of 20 percent of the Japanese market for U.S. companies, which was finally reached in 1992.

The 1986 semiconductor agreement is controversial, but something needed to be done to contend with the predatory character of the Japanese market strategy, and a few other examples of the managed oligopoly syndrome also required a strong, largely ad hoc policy response. The preoccupation with such problem situations, however, has obscured the more profound and positive changes under way in the world economy that should be addressed more fully and frontally by the new trade theorists. The term *multiple synergy effect* attempts to encapsulate this broader process of technological innovation that has been sprouting forth over the past three decades. Some combination of factors—human and capital resources, economic infrastructure, intellectual stimulus from universities, government support programs, the quality of lifestyle—caused Silicon Valley and Boston to lead the creative process. Interactions within and between companies and among people in countless ways produced many spillover effects, or synergies, that, in effect, created new comparative advantage in certain high-technology industries. Such technological innovation continues to spread, leapfrogging to other locations, such as Austin, Texas, and the North Carolina research triangle, while gradually pervading the national economy. More pertinent to trade theory, the multiple synergy effect has an international dimension as well, brought about by multinational corporations, the return home to South Korea and Taiwan of engineers nurtured in Silicon Valley, and the accelerating international flow of knowledge about new technological capabilities.

In more formal terms, the basis for international trade, especially for technology-intensive industries, is shifting in composition from trade in goods between relatively self-contained national economies to the international movement of the factors of production—capital and labor—in both of which knowledge of the new technologies is thoroughly embedded. The phenomenon was articulated well in 1929 by one of the earlier iconoclasts, John Williams, who wrote that "foreign trade tends to produce an extension of productive factors over the expanding market area . . . [which] applies with special force to the development phase of international trade, and particularly to the trade of unequally developed areas." He went on to encourage, "a more positive analysis than the economists have given us of the economic effects of the enormous and increasing drift of capital and labor over the world's surface."[6]

This remains the challenge to the new trade theorists for the 1990s. What makes the challenge far more compelling today is the pace and scope of change under way and the critical position now accorded to the international transfer of applied new technologies. Economists need to address problems such as managed oligopoly, cast largely in zero or negative sum terms, but they also need to focus, to a far greater extent than they have to date, on the positive consequences of what is happening in world trade. The question of who's bashing whom requires an answer, but so, too, does the question of who's benefiting whom. The central analytic challenge in the latter case is to formulate and measure the gains from trade within the framework of the new trade theory. How large are they and how are they distributed between nations? Thus far, there is very little in the way of answers. As context for a more complete response, three positive developments over the past two years are noteworthy:

(1) The managed oligopoly syndrome is fading. The reputed advantages of large firm size are under duress. From IBM and General Motors to Fujitsu and Toyota, profits are evaporating and restructuring is the order of the day. The most prominent examples of the managed oligopoly syndrome of the late 1980s are of fading consequence. Japanese DRAM producers face a profit squeeze from new Korean competitors and are losing market share to renewed U.S. production, while the semiconductor industry has shifted emphasis toward more sophisticated microprocessors, with U.S. companies well out in front. The Cray-Fujitsu competitive struggle over the world supercomputer market is broadening to include a new wave of smaller U.S. companies applying lower cost, massive parallel processing (MPP) technology. The threat of early Japanese dominance of the high-definition television (HDTV) market has been shunted aside by several consortia with more advanced digital technology based in the United States. The major remaining contender for managed oligopoly status is the commercial jet aircraft industry, which is at least under the constraint of the 1992 agreement between the United States and the European Community (EC) to limit government subsidies, while accrued oligopoly profits are meager at best. In sum, competition in high-technology markets is apparently intensifying while the prospect of large oligopoly profits becomes more transient and of more limited scope.

(2) The international dimension of the multiple synergy effect is accelerating. This is more difficult to document, but its manifestations are clearly evident. Joint ventures between U.S., Japanese, and European firms, as well as between them and companies in developing and formerly Communist countries, are proliferating. High-technology start-up companies in the newly industrialized countries and government-sponsored industrial parks in the People's Republic of China (PRC), India, and elsewhere, are taking root. A generation of scientists and engineers in Eastern Europe and the former Soviet Union are

being assimilated through direct investment ventures from the West. Advances in telecommunications technology are dramatically lowering the cost and other barriers to the global dispersion of knowledge. Throughout this process, the gains from trade cumulate, however elusive they are to measure.

(3) U.S. technological leadership is resurgent. The United States will never regain the commanding technological lead it enjoyed in the 1950s and 1960s, but the widespread pessimism of only two to three years ago about being surpassed by Japan is greatly muted. Leading-edge developments in the fields of microprocessors, supercomputers, HDTV, software and computer applications across the board, telecommunications, and a wide range of other technologies are firmly concentrated in the United States. The new contenders for outstanding oligopoly profits are Intel with its Pentium microprocessor and Bill Gates's Microsoft juggernaut, and to the extent they face serious challenge to their dominant market position their rivals are American. A more forceful domestic strategy to stimulate continued technological innovation is clearly in order if the United States is to remain at the technological forefront over the longer term, but its existing predominant position is more clearly established today than when the decade began. So, too, as a consequence, is U.S. self-interest in a more open international trading system for high-technology industries.

These recent developments point in the direction of a more competitive and mutually beneficial trading relationship for high-technology industries, including for the United States. The gains from trade appear to be of increasing relative importance compared with maldistributed oligopoly profits. A more precise assessment, however, awaits further empirical research by the new trade theorists.

The Existing Trade Policy Framework

The international trading system changed fundamentally during the 1980s, and in the process attention to technology-intensive industries grew steadily, although not in a systematic way. Change involved both a broadening of the multilateral trade framework and new initiatives in regional and bilateral relationships. In spring 1981, U.S. Trade Representative William Brock proposed, as a matter of urgency, an ambitious new round of multilateral GATT negotiations to deal with the changing realities of world trade, and trade in high-technology industries was targeted as a priority area. Others questioned such a priority, and by the time the GATT Uruguay Round was finally launched at Punta del Este in September 1986, the United States had dropped its proposal to single out high-technology trade as a specific negotiating objective.

The Uruguay Round negotiations are still under way, 12 years after the Brock call to action, but, at this writing in summer 1993, they are hopefully in the home stretch, and the draft final agreement includes a number of provisions with potentially important consequences for high-technology trade, even if they are not specifically identified as such. Import barriers would be reduced on many high-technology as well as other products. A framework agreement and improved access for trade in services would facilitate the international transfer of applied new technologies. Basic obligations for the protection of IPRs would be brought within the international trading system. R&D and other government subsidies, as they affect exports, would be subject to more specific limitations. Changes in the areas of antidumping procedures, public procurement practices, and trade-related investment measures could have an impact on high-technology trade.

The systemic change in trade relations during the 1980s went beyond attempts to broaden the multilateral framework, however, and involved a restructuring to what is now referred to as a three-track system. The multilateral first track is now complemented by a growing network of comprehensive regional free trade agreements and by a series of more structured bilateral agreements for particular trade issues or sectors. The change in U.S. trade strategy from an overwhelmingly multilateral orientation to the three-track approach was decisive for the global system. At the regional level, the U.S.–Canada and North American free trade agreements are initial steps toward further agreements in the Western Hemisphere and perhaps beyond. The most prominent U.S. bilateral initiatives have been an almost continuous series of negotiated agreements with Japan, the U.S.–EC agreement on subsidies for commercial jet aircraft, a market access agreement with the PRC, and numerous bilateral commitments on IPRs.

The implementation of U.S. trade policy thus now consists of managing the multilateral, regional, and bilateral tracks in parallel, with the hope that they will be mutually reinforcing toward broadly established, longer-term goals, but there have been some inconsistencies and conflicting objectives among the tracks. A full analysis of this three-track trade strategy has been elaborated elsewhere,[7] and comment here is limited to a brief status report as to how the three tracks have been interacting for six selected issues of particular importance to high-technology trade.

(1) Intellectual property rights (IPRs). This is the best example of a mutually reinforcing three-track approach. In the Uruguay Round, a multilateral agreement on standards and procedures has been pursued in the face of prolonged resistance from many developing countries, particularly India and Brazil. Some difficult issues remain unresolved, but a comprehensive multilateral agreement is a prominent part of the draft final Uruguay Round text. In parallel, the United States achieved substantial results in bilateral negotiations with the most flagrant violators of IPRs, mostly in Asia, under the threat of sanctions through Section Special 301 of the 1988 Omnibus Trade Act. Indeed, some developing countries switched from opposition to support for a multilateral Uruguay Round accord in part as the lesser evil in face of intense U.S. bilateral pressures. At the regional level, within the NAFTA context, Mexico has adopted a new law on IPRs that serves as a model for other reluctant developing countries.

(2) Government subsidies for R&D. This issue has also been pursued on all three tracks, in a largely consistent way, but the goals are less clearly defined and U.S. policy has recently become somewhat muddled. The U.S. objective in the Uruguay Round has been to tighten up the GATT subsidy code so as to minimize or eliminate permissible government subsidies for exported goods. Almost all other countries have insisted on some exemptions, and the draft final text, with

148

respect to R&D subsidies, would permit up to 50 percent subsidies for basic industrial research and 25 percent for applied research. At the regional level, low or reduced levels of subsidies in Canada and Mexico were an underlying condition for a free trade agreement. Bilaterally, the U.S.–EC agreement on commercial jet aircraft established a 30 percent limit on government-financed support for development, with specified repayment terms, which is similar to, although not the same as, the limits in the Uruguay Round draft. The Clinton administration's proposal to greatly increase government subsidy for new technologies with commercial potential, however, raises a question about U.S. objectives in the GATT and about trade policy generally.

(3) Competition policy. This is an important area of trade policy where the three tracks are on separate roadbeds with only a limited degree of convergence. The GATT "trade remedy" approach for anticompetitive practices by exporters is the threat of imposition of antidumping duties by the importing country. The Uruguay Round draft agreement attempts to limit current abuses of antidumping procedures, particularly when used with protectionist effect. At the regional level, the U.S.–Canada and NAFTA agreements do not address the substance of the issue but have more expeditious dispute settlement mechanisms and leave for possible future discussion more harmonized national approaches to competition policy. At the bilateral level, a more direct attempt at convergence of national policies is under way with Japan through stricter enforcement of Japanese antitrust laws. The basic issue is whether to continue the contentious antidumping approach as a defense against anticompetitive behavior abroad or, as within the EC, to harmonize national competition policies and free trade to the point where antidumping procedures can be suspended.

(4) Trade-related investment measures (TRIMs). This is a significant policy area for high-technology industries in which U.S. objectives at the multilateral and regional levels are to some extent in conflict. At the Punta del Este conference, the U.S. delegation held firm through the final night of negotiations to get TRIMs included as a priority item for negotiation. The primary U.S. objective was to eliminate "performance requirements" in many developing countries, whereby foreign investors have to undertake domestic content, export, or other commitments as a condition for obtaining approval to invest, which can be highly distorting to trade. In the late 1980s, the EC went even further in applying TRIMs to Japanese and other Asian investors by requiring that specified advanced technology components or operations be provided from within the Community and not through imports. Such requirements also run counter to the U.S. Uruguay Round objective. At the regional level, however, the United States, first in the U.S.–Canada agreement and then more broadly in the NAFTA, insisted on regional content requirements as a condition for third country investor benefits from free trade—a "rules of origin" test with trade effect comparable to other such TRIMs. TRIMs at all levels not only distort trade but can be especially onerous for high-technology industries because of the paperwork and government intrusion involved in certifying regional content or other requirements when

inputs leading to final assembly are so widely dispersed, nationally and internationally.

(5) Public procurement. This is probably the most important trade-related issue for high-technology industries in view of the hundreds of billions of dollars of contracts involved, but it is also, and perhaps for that reason, the least advanced in terms of a cooperative trade policy approach on any of the tracks. The GATT public procurement code calls for international competitive bidding while permitting members to exclude specified sectors from the code, as they generally do for key sectors such as power generation, transportation, and telecommunications. At the regional level, the objective of competitive bidding among member state companies is being pursued in the EC, but at a slow pace, while the NAFTA does provide substantial new commitments. Bilaterally, the United States has been negotiating with Japan, the EC, and others on a selective basis, with only modest results. The telecommunications sector is the most frequent target for such negotiations.

(6) Telecommunications. This sector is not only at the forefront of many applied new technologies but is also the sector in which the full range of trade policies influencing high-technology industries most clearly interact, including the five issues addressed above. In 1981, Trade Representative Brock may have been more successful in explaining the need for a sector negotiation for telecommunications than he was for high-technology industries in the abstract. In any event, that is what the U.S. Congress did in the 1988 trade act, pressing for bilateral as well as multilateral negotiations toward more open and competitive markets for U.S. companies. The stimulus for action was the market asymmetry created when the United States broke up and privatized AT&T in 1984, thereby giving greatly increased market access to foreign suppliers while most other countries retained highly protected government telephone monopolies. A trend toward privatization of telecommunications services is under way throughout the world, but U.S. negotiations, multilaterally and bilaterally, have thus far produced only modest results. A major unresolved issue in the Uruguay Round draft text on trade in services is resistance by the United States to making a binding commitment on most-favored-nation (MFN) treatment for primary telecommunications services while other major countries maintain government monopolies for such services that render meaningless a corresponding MFN commitment on their part. The telecommunications sector will surely play a prominent role in post–Uruguay Round trade deliberations.

This is a mid-1993 snapshot of key trade policy issues that influence high-technology industries as they interrelate within the evolving three-track trade strategy. If the NAFTA should fail, the regional free trade track would drop out of the strategy for the foreseeable future. If the NAFTA were to be implemented and the Uruguay Round fail, trade policy would take on even stronger regional and bilateral orientations. If both the NAFTA and the Uruguay Round were to fail, there would be considerable disarray, a likely flurry of bilateral initiatives to confront long-simmering disputes, and generally negative political fallout. The following section, in contrast, is based on the assumption of a successfully concluded NAFTA and Uruguay

Round, both approved by the U.S. Congress by about mid-1994.

A Trade Policy Agenda

The United States needs a comprehensive, post–Uruguay Round trade strategy for high-technology industries that relates immediate policy goals to a broader strategy for continued technological innovation, investment, and trade growth. Recent trade policy has been excessively short term in orientation, with an inherent tendency to ad hoc results, while broader strategic thinking is suspect as too long term and thus of questionable relevance. Such an orientation is also reflected in the policy proposals of the Tyson book. It judges the GATT system of multilateral rules to be "largely irrelevant," and therefore "for the foreseeable future" the proposals it offers constitute "a stopgap measure to defend American economic interests." This measure takes the form of "aggressive unilateralism," through "bilateral sector specific negotiations" based on the principle of "selective reciprocity," even though this is recognized as "a dangerous departure from traditional U.S. trade policy."[8] How this stopgap proposal relates to other, longer-term objectives of U.S. trade policy is left largely unspecified beyond a general call for the successful completion of the Uruguay Round.

A complete trade strategy for high-technology industries should be elaborated for the politically relevant time frame of the next two to four years. It would consist of three basic components: the national economic strategy, the macropolicy adjustment process among national economies, and trade policy more directly. The presentation here is limited to brief comments on the first two and more extended thoughts on the composition of the trade policy agenda.

The current wide-ranging debate on national economic strategy will have far more impact on future U.S. competition in high-technology industries than any likely adjustments in trade policy, and most key issues involved, including educational performance, strengthened infrastructure, and the rising cost of health care, have little if any direct connection with the international trading system. One exception is the "industrial policy" objective of increased government subsidies to develop selected technologies for commercial application, which could conflict with GATT obligations and reduce U.S. ability to limit subsidies by others. The overarching issue of the national economic debate is whether to induce a shift of resources from the binge in private and public consumption of recent years to productive investment, including much higher levels of R&D. If the shift does not occur, a longer-term decline in U.S. technological leadership and export competitiveness is all but inevitable.

Macropolicy adjustment through concerted fiscal, monetary, and exchange rate policies should be the principal vehicle for reducing excessive trade imbalances. When one nation drifts greatly out of line, as is currently the case with the Japanese trade surplus, finance ministers should act promptly and effectively to reduce the imbalance. Precise quantitative commitments are not reasonable, but general targets can be agreed, as well as the need for exchange rate adjustment if other policy actions prove inadequate. The lack of prompt and effective macropolicy adjustment should also be clearly recognized as increasing trade protectionist pressures in general terms and most particularly for politically sensitive sectors such as high-technology industries.

Within this broader context of national economic strategy and macro-policy adjustment, a comprehensive trade policy agenda should be developed for high-technology industries that integrates priority sector-specific stopgap measures with a broader set of goals to bring the surging forces of international trade and investment into a more cooperative and less conflictual policy framework. The conceptual model continues to be the interacting three-track structure, in which specific objectives on each track reinforce each other toward convergent longer-term goals. The IPR example was cited earlier, wherein actions at the multilateral, regional free trade, and bilateral levels all worked toward the long-term goal of adequate standards effectively enforced on a global basis. In other areas of policy, however, it can be far more difficult to formulate the ultimate objective as well as the means for converging toward it. Moreover, for the next two years there is likely to be a hiatus in new initiatives on the multilateral and regional free trade tracks, giving even greater prominence to bilateral actions.

At the multilateral level, a successfully concluded Uruguay Round will not go into effect until January 1, 1995, and the GATT or a successor Multilateral Trade Organization (MTO) will be preoccupied for at least a year thereafter with initial implementation of the many substantive and procedural provisions of the final Uruguay Round agreement. Some unresolved Uruguay Round issues and selected new issues, most notably the relationship between trade and environmental policies, will also heavily burden the work program. For these reasons, as well as the effect of a large and unwieldy membership, the principal objective for high-technology trade within the GATT/MTO over the next two years should be full and rigorous implementation of the relevant provisions of the Uruguay Round agreement.

Similarly, regional free trade objectives will be limited to implementation of the NAFTA and of EC directives emanating from the EC '92 market unification program. Negotiations for additional free trade agreements by the United States beyond the NAFTA are unlikely to begin before 1995, because the president will first have to obtain new legislative authority in 1994. Earlier regional initiatives for Asia–Pacific economic cooperation are likely to be modest in content in view of the diversity of political and economic interests among the participants, including the PRC and reluctant members of the Association of Southeast Asian Nations (ASEAN).

Bilateral trade initiatives, in contrast, will receive increased attention, particularly with the anticipated renewal of Section Super 301 authority by the U.S. Congress, and high-technology industries will be the focus of much bilateral attention. A dispute with the EC over public procurement in the telecommunications sector is already engaged; a sector-specific agenda for Japan is being formulated; and the large trade deficit with the PRC will require some form of response to achieve greater market access for U.S. exports. Some market opening abroad through bilateral initiatives should be forthcoming, but the process will be politically contentious and the results limited to a few priority industries. The prospect for negotiating new quantitative sectoral targets with Japan, in particular, is less favorable than in the past because much of Japanese industry is now struggling with more costly credit, a sagging domestic market, and a strengthened yen.

The time is right, in fact, for a broader initiative toward a more open and balanced trading relationship for high-technology industries, to be jointly undertaken by the major industrialized countries that constitute the driving force for new technology development and its international transmission. It is now far clearer than it was in 1981 that an integrated approach for trade and investment is not only desirable but necessary. The various accomplishments on all three tracks over the past 12 years have contributed to this realization and prepared the way for a more ambitious step at this time.

The obvious launching pad for such an initiative would be the Group of Seven (G–7) economic summit process. The summit leaders would direct the formulation of an integrated framework of policy commitments for trade and investment in high-technology industries, perhaps couched more broadly in terms of the conditions for industrial competition, but with the emphasis on technology-related issues. Much of the technical preparatory work would be carried out by the Organization for Economic Cooperation and Development (OECD), which would also provide a bridge to the larger grouping of industrialized democracies. Early OECD membership for Mexico and South Korea, as can be expected, would bring these two important newly industrialized countries into the process. The G–7/OECD orientation for the initiative would not constitute a new "fourth track," because the ultimate policy commitments would best be incorporated within the multilateral trading system, and the G–7/OECD catalytic role in expediting negotiations might better be described as "three-track-plus."

The substantive scope of the initiative would include the six major areas of policy outlined in an earlier section, as well as other related issues, including technical standards, foreign investment in broader policy terms, and national security interests as they affect trade policy commitments. An integrated approach for the telecommunications sector would play a central role not only because of the various interacting issues currently being addressed on all three tracks, but because this sector constitutes the basic economic infrastructure for information technology–based industries. In boldest terms, the initiative could envisage trade and investment free of border restrictions with a high degree of harmonization with respect to the internal conditions of competition and the forms of government support for new technology development.

The initiative could be officially adopted at the time of the summer 1994 summit meeting in Italy, but that would require an early start in preparations by the seven policy-level "sherpas." Considerable preparatory work on most of the issues involved is already under way in several OECD committees.[9] Early consultations with private sector leaders would also be essential because they are generally out in front of governments in their understanding of the significance of new technological developments across national borders. The real work in fleshing out a detailed blueprint of international commitments that would incorporate policy relationships evolving at the multilateral, regional, and bilateral levels would in any event come in the year or two after the political launching at the summit. The principal role of the summit leaders would be to articulate the far-reaching benefits of a more integrated trade relationship, for world peace as well as prosperity.

The Vision Thing

The foregoing policy agenda for high-technology industries is couched in technical terms of what should be done over the next few years to bring trade relationships into a more balanced and cooperative relationship. Its full implications, however, can only be judged when related to a longer-term vision of where the world order of nations is or should be heading. The "vision thing" was openly disparaged during the Bush administration and has been shunted aside by the rush of immediate events during the initial months of the Clinton presidency. Charting a longer-term course through the confused and treacherous waters of the post–cold war world order is nevertheless the ultimate challenge, and the form of economic relationships that evolves among the advanced industrialized democracies will be critical to the outcome.

The underlying political message of the discussion here on trade in technology-intensive industries is that the most hopeful prospect for a more stable and prosperous world order is through a deepening and broadening of the current tripolar grouping of advanced industrialized democracies in Europe, North America, and East Asia. This might evolve in various ways, with the future course of East Asia least clear, but there should be no doubt that if the relationship within this grouping should degenerate into economic conflict, battle, and a struggle for supremacy, there will be little hope for coping with the far more daunting global challenges of population growth, environmental degradation, ethnic wars, and the proliferation of weapons of mass destruction.

The international trading system is the warp and woof of the relationship among the advanced industrialized democracies as well as their principal bridge to the rest of the world. There are profoundly positive opportunities to be realized as new technological capabilities are shared across borders, but the process needs to be managed with clear vision that balances longer-term mutual gains with the immediate national interests at stake. In simplest terms, it means giving the question of who's benefiting whom preeminence, even though not to the total exclusion of that of who's bashing whom.

The author is organizing a new CSIS project on the subject of this article. In this context, comments on the article will be gratefully received.

Notes

1. Jeffrey E. Garten, *A Cold Peace: America, Japan, Germany, and the Struggle for Supremacy* (New York, N.Y.: The Twentieth Century Fund, 1992); Lester Thurow, *Head to Head: The Coming Economic Battle Among Japan, Europe, and America* (New York, N.Y.: William Morrow, 1992); and Laura D'Andrea Tyson, *Who's Bashing Whom? Trade Conflict in High-Technology Industries* (Washington, D.C.: Institute for International Economics, 1992). Tyson is chair of the President's Council of Economic Advisers and Garten's nomination as under secretary of commerce was awaiting Senate confirmation when this journal went to press.

2. Computer and data processing services; data base and other information services; research, development, and testing services; construction, engineering, architectural, and mining services; and industrial engineering.

3. The figures are based on an earlier U.S. Department of Commerce classification for high-technology industries, in terms of the Standard Industrial Classification (SIC),

which is no longer used for trade data as presented in tables 1 and 2.

4. Two volumes of frequently cited papers are Paul R. Krugman, ed., *Strategic Trade Policy and the New International Economics* (Cambridge, Mass.: MIT Press, 1986), and Martha Caldwell Harris and Gordon E. Moore, eds., *Linking Trade and Technology Policies* (Washington, D.C.: National Academy of Engineering Press, 1992). To the extent these papers assess U.S. trade performance, they generally tend to a pessimistic assessment based on the experience of the mid- to late 1980s.

5. The Krugman book from the previous endnote is a standard reference. An updated assessment is contained in Paul R. Krugman, "Does the New Trade Theory Require a New Trade Policy?" *World Economy* 15 (July 1992), pp. 423–441.

6. John H. Williams, "The Theory of International Trade Reconsidered," originally published in *Economic Journal* 39 (June 1929), and reprinted in *Postwar Monetary Plans and Other Essays* (New York, N.Y.: Alfred A. Knopf, 1947), in which these quotations appear on pp. 152–153.

7. See Ernest H. Preeg, *The American Challenge in World Trade: U.S. Interests in the GATT Multilateral Trading System*, CSIS Significant Issues Series 11, no. 7 (Washington, D.C.: CSIS, 1989), chaps. 4–7.

8. Tyson, *Who's Bashing Whom?* pp. 2, 5, 255, 261.

9. These are described in Geza Feketekuty, *The New Trade Agenda* (Washington, D.C.: Group of Thirty, 1992). Feketekuty is chairman of the OECD trade committee.

Trade and the Environment

*Kenneth Berlin and
Jeffrey M. Lang*

PLANNING FOR THE post–cold war era may be less about marshaling armies under the United Nations (UN) banner than about enhancing coordination among diverse forms of market economies in an economy that is increasingly global. It will be essential to this effort to establish coherence in the present maze of policy issues, international agreements, and international institutions that affect the everyday interchanges between the world's nations and peoples. Nowhere is the need for coordinated effort clearer than in the clash between environmental protection measures and the international trading system.

Although environmental concerns have played an important role in setting domestic economic policy for many years in industrial nations, such concerns were, until recently, largely ignored in the formulation of international economic policy. Concern about the impact of environmental degradation on international economic growth and sustainable development has been increasing so rapidly, however, that in June 1992 it became the theme of the largest gathering of heads of state (110) in history—the 1992 Earth Summit in Rio de Janeiro, Brazil.

Environmental issues have burst upon trade and environmental communities ill-prepared to address the interrelationship between their divergent concerns. Most people with expertise in either trade or environmental matters have very different academic backgrounds and experience. In the United States, trade and environmental laws were written in different committees of Congress and responded to quite different constituencies. The two types of law, moreover, were administered, at least until recently, in different departments and agencies of U.S. and foreign governments, and these bodies rarely communicated with one another. The different perceptions of the two disciplines are summed up in their respective connotations of the word protection. It is a pejorative word in the trade community, an exemplary one in the environmental community.

In addition, because of their different experiences, people in the trade and environmental communities have very different expectations of what is attainable. Environmentalists expect a responsive system of laws that has programs and sanctions to enforce compliance. Because of the limitations national sovereignty places on international actions, trade policy special-

---

Kenneth Berlin is a lawyer in Washington, D.C., specializing in trade and environment issues. Jeffrey M. Lang was until 1990 chief international trade counsel of the Senate Committee on Finance. Both have provided counsel on the NAFTA to several environmental groups.

Copyright © 1993 by The Center for Strategic and International Studies and the Massachusetts Institute of Technology
The Washington Quarterly • 16:4

ists have not developed the kind of activist institutions that environmentalists expect. They tend to be advocates of open trade and at the extreme are skeptical in general about government regulation of economic activity.

The conceptual barriers created by the different academic and experiential worlds in which most people in the environmental and trade communities have worked are particularly difficult to overcome because many in both communities are idealistic in their belief that the welfare of society depends to a significant degree on whether their values prevail over competing concerns. There is thus a critical need for both sides to break down the dogmas and barriers that separate them by learning to understand each other's disciplines.

This article tries to give U.S. policymakers a framework for reaching accommodation between trade and environmental concerns by analyzing the interactions of these two policy systems and defining a procedure for accommodation. It begins by setting forth background information that trade and environmental communities must understand about each other's disciplines. It then divides trade and environmental conflicts into five categories and recommends action to resolve the conflict within each of the categories. The categories are: the application of product standards to goods sold within a nation's borders; the application by a nation of import restrictions on products because production processes in the exporting nation do not meet the importing nation's standards; the role of government subsidies for pollution control equipment; the special case of fish, wildlife, and plants; and the impact of trade on patterns of development and thus the environment.

Trade and the Environment in the 1990s

The profile of international environmental issues has been raised in recent years because a number of environmental problems appear to defy solution at the national level. The best known of these problems relate to threats to public health and the environment caused by the cross-border discharge of pollutants, their effect on the atmosphere, and their discharge into the oceans. Although these concerns have been articulated for some time, fears escalated after acid rain became an issue and the possibility of a disaster in plants that generate nuclear power became recognized in North America and Europe. These fears gathered momentum as people became aware of the threat to the earth's atmosphere caused by ozone depletion and the potential threat of global warming posed by emissions of greenhouse gases, particularly carbon dioxide. Although there is debate about the seriousness of the global warming crisis, it and many of the issues described above are now being addressed in either bilateral or multilateral agreements.

These environmental concerns began to come to a head in the late 1980s, when scholars began to express increasing alarm that efforts to bring the developing world into the trading system were likely to have horrific effects on the environment.[1] The most important of these is the rapid depletion of "renewable" natural resources. In the last 20 years, for example, the world has lost nearly 500 million acres of trees (mostly, but not entirely, in tropical forests), and this is likely to have a significant impact on the sustainability of development in the developing world. It is also having a devastating impact on species survival, with the rate of species extinction accelerating so rapidly that it is increasingly possible that a million or more species will become extinct in the next 30 to 60 years if the trend is not reversed. Because of the interrelated chains of life that exist in the world's environment, such massive extinctions could cause the collapse of many ecosystems on which humankind depends for food, medical and scientific resources, and the atmospheric cycle of oxygen generation. Paleontologists have estimated that it took the environment 20 *million* years to heal fully after the last great episode of mass species extinction.[2]

These issues led in large part to the concern that occasioned the Rio Summit—the fear that the world's development may not be sustainable at its current and projected rate. In the United States this fear is not limited to environmentalists. Concern that development may not be sustainable because of environmental degradation led *Business Week* in its cover story on the Rio Summit to state that unless environmental issues are addressed, the world's "prosperity" is at stake.[3] This threat has also been recognized by many corporate leaders. The chief executive officer of Dow Chemical, Frank P. Popoff, for example, has stated that "there can be no economic development without environmental responsibility."[4]

Debate over the North American Free Trade Agreement (NAFTA), during which the difficult question of whether Mexico is adequately enforcing its environmental laws has been raised, has brought this aspect of the trade/environment conflict into focus. In much the same way, the attempts of the European Community (EC) to arrive at a trade relationship with Central Europe and the former Soviet states to the east may sharpen the focus on the same concerns.[5]

The clash between the developed and the developing countries over these issues could be profound. Many in the developing world believe that it is too costly to address environmental issues in the way the developed world would like. Moreover, many in the developing world believe that the developed world is asking them to make sacrifices and forgo short-term economic development policies that the developed world was itself not willing to forgo. It is difficult to ask any people, particularly those in developing countries, to adopt remedies for the long-term consequences of development at the expense of short-term economic needs.

The view from the developed world is different. People are genuinely worried about the impact of environmental degradation on the sustainability of the current economic system. Even classical economic welfare analysis, although strongly supporting the position that free trade is advantageous, concludes that trade and trade liberalization may not benefit a country's general welfare if the cost of the goods sold or produced as a result of trade does not fully reflect the environmental cost of the goods,[6] and where, as a consequence, the benefits from increased trade are not sufficient to outweigh the negative effects of the reduction in environmental quality.[7]

Equally important as a potential source of conflict between the developing and developed worlds is the fact that many in the developed world are concerned about environmental degradation because of deeply held beliefs that transcend economic concerns. For some, the choice is a conservative one; they believe that society should tolerate very little risk of degradation of the environment because of what they perceive to be the overwhelming seriousness of the consequences. For others, the concern is a moral one, based on deeply held values about the right of species to survive. As we have been learning during the NAFTA debate, those who hold these views will not easily be reconciled to a trading system that does not seek to prevent or at least ameliorate the impact of increased trade upon the environment.

Finally, there also appears to be a growing shortage of patience in the developed world with the demands of the developing world. Despite the free trade rhetoric of the conservative governments of the period, the recession of 1982 resulted in negative growth in total world exports in the early 1980s and slow growth in the rest of the decade. One result was increased resentment on the part of industrialized nations against the sheltering protectionism of part IV of the General Agreement on Tariffs and Trade (GATT) and the other GATT exceptions developing countries have been granted since the 1960s. The suspicion, now confirmed by the World Bank, that if gross domestic product (GDP) per capita is calculated on purchasing power rather than on market exchange rates the incomes in a number of advanced developing countries are much higher than is generally believed, will fuel the feeling that developing countries must meet the environmental standards of the industrialized countries to get full membership in the global trading system.

Global concern about the environment is paralleled by concern in the international trade community about the impact of protectionist policies on international economic growth. Here again, the concern is profound and goes beyond anxiety over the negative impact that protectionist policies will have on short-term economic growth. Instead, the trade community's concerns arise from a deeply held conviction, stemming largely from events occurring between World Wars I and II, that protectionist trade policies poison relations between nations by lowering economic growth rates. Under Secretary of State Sumner Wells expressed this sentiment in 1941:

> Nations have more often than not undertaken economic discriminations and raised up trade barriers with complete disregard for the damaging effects on the trade and livelihood of other peoples, and, ironically enough, with similar disregard for the harmful effect on their own export trade. . . . The resultant misery, bewilderment, and resentment, together with equally pernicious contributing causes, paved the way for the rise of those very dictatorships which have plunged almost the entire world into war.[8]

Wells's views remain relevant today, even without a threat of world war, and they are widely held. Recognition of the need to buttress emerging democracies in the developing world and the formerly Communist states in Eastern Europe and Asia is a current example. Wells's views, moreover, reflect classical economic analysis and the view of many, but not all, in the trade community that free trade increases general world economic growth even if not practiced on a completely reciprocal basis by all the parties in the international trading system.

The current system of trade regulation is organized largely through the GATT and a system of bilateral trade agreements. The principal goal of the GATT is to foster free trade and reduce policies that distort trade. Where agreed-upon trade rules are violated, the GATT provides only one sanction—retaliation through the withdrawal of trade concessions previously given. This limited choice of sanctions has caused conflict between the trade community and those with other agendas, such as environmental protection, because advocates of an open trading system are reluctant to see the trade sanction used in any way other than to punish actions specifically inconsistent with trade rules.

An open trading system is, however, not the only goal of the GATT. The GATT also regulates international business transactions and accommodates concerns other than pure free trade.[9] These accommodations include those made for national foreign and military policy; national economic policy; other domestic regulatory policies, such as policies to protect health and the conservation of natural resources; and openly protectionist measures including customs duties, quotas, tariff rate quotas, and many others, which have been gradually reduced, but not abolished, by the GATT process. In each case, the rules of the trading system, or at least the ideal of unrestricted and open trade in goods, have been bent or superseded to allow national purposes to be achieved.

Although the GATT has accommodated some environmental concerns, these accommodations are rudimentary. They are set out in article XX, which contains a series of general exceptions including measures to protect public morals; human, animal, or plant life or health; and the conservation of exhaustible natural resources.[10] The GATT, however, never mentions the word environment, and the references in article XX to animals and plants (the reference to "natural resources" refers to mineral resources) have been interpreted narrowly and cover only a fraction of the environmental issues that are regarded as important today because of their impact on the environment or on sustainable development.[11]

During this period of quiescence within the GATT regarding environmental issues, the trade community's concern has, in contrast, been growing about the subterranean labyrinth of what are called non-tariff barriers to trade. Such non-tariff barriers emerged as significant distortions to trade as tariffs were reduced under the GATT system. Because article XX provides one justification for such barriers, there has been an exhaustive effort over the last 20 years to narrow the scope of the article's exceptions as they relate to all kinds of standards. These efforts have been directed at questionable safety and health regulations, but the rationales on which they are based apply equally to measures implemented to protect the environment.

Efforts to reduce non-tariff barriers to trade have proceeded in great part through the drafting of a "Standards" code, which reached fruition during the Tokyo Round in the 1979 agreement on technical barriers to trade. The basic goal of the Standards Code is to ensure that government-imposed rules and voluntary standards, such as requirements on packaging, labeling, marking, and methods of certifying compliance, do not themselves create and are not applied to create "unnecessary obstacles to trade." The Standards Code provides in article II that:

> Parties shall ensure that technical regulations and standards are not prepared, adopted or applied with a view to creating obstacles to international trade. . . . They shall likewise ensure that neither technical regulations nor standards themselves nor their application have the effect of creating unnec-

essary obstacles to international trade.[12]

Efforts to strengthen the Standards Code continue as part of the Uruguay Round. Negotiators in December 1991 produced a draft agreement known as the "Dunkel Draft." The Dunkel Draft further tightens restrictions on standards by adding to the first sentence of the Standards Code a restriction on the adoption and application of standards and technical regulations not only with a "view to" creating obstacles to international trade, but also with the "effect of" creating such obstacles. This is an important change because regulations, including environmental regulations, can have an effect on international trade, even when they were not adopted with a view to creating such obstacles.

The environmental standards that a country sets for sale or production of a good within its own borders affect foreign commerce in a variety of ways. For example, if the United States bans sales of products containing a chemical that is found in a product being imported, that product cannot be sold in the United States. Similarly, if the United States requires that its internal production facilities meet specified environmental standards, international investment in the United States is affected. This is the case even if the restrictions meet the standards of the GATT's articles I and III, that is, the ban applies equally to imported and domestic products. In addition, the Dunkel Draft expands on the Standards Code's necessity requirement, adding the language:

> For this purpose, technical regulations shall not be more trade-restrictive than necessary to fulfill a legitimate objective, taking account of the risks non-fulfillment would create. Such legitimate ob-

jectives are, *inter alia*, national security requirements; the prevention of deceptive practices; protection of human health or safety, animal or plant life or health, or the environment.[13]

As will be described below, environmental standards issues have been addressed in the NAFTA in a manner substantially different from the accommodations reached in article XX of the GATT or in the Standards Code and Dunkel Draft.

Individual countries have also endeavored to reduce non-tariff barriers by seeking determinations by GATT dispute resolution panels that a specific measure implemented by another party constitutes an impermissible non-tariff barrier to trade.[14] The most important GATT panel decision on the environment was reached in the dispute known as the tuna/dolphin case.

The tuna/dolphin case arose after the United States banned the importation of tuna products from Mexico because Mexican tuna fishermen were incidentally killing what was regarded under a U.S. statute as an unacceptable number of dolphins. Deaths to dolphins from tuna fishing had been an issue in the United States since the early 1970s, and as the cause of the deaths switched from U.S. fishing vessels to those of other nations, the U.S. law was amended to cover foreign fishing fleets.

The GATT panel found for Mexico, basing its decision on the historical view in the trade community that although a country can under certain circumstances regulate a product entering its territory for health or safety reasons, it cannot prevent a product from entering the country because it does not like the way the product is produced. The ruling, however, caused a storm of outrage in the environmental community of the United States. Aside from fear of the general nature of the precedent, the decision appeared particularly ominous because the panel equated industrial methods of production with the "taking" of species and because it considered restrictions on taking on the high seas outside a nation's territory as the equivalent of objecting to a protected method of production within a nation's territory. Environmentalists distinguish between living things and goods, and between the global commons and national territory. Because of the controversy, the Mexicans have been convinced not to seek to implement the ruling.

Harmonization of Standards versus Border Measures

Because of their concern with non-tariff barriers, trade policy agencies in industrialized countries have historically been strong, even unbending, advocates of the global "harmonization" of product standards and have sought such standards in the Standards Code and elsewhere. Environmentalists, on the other hand, have opposed harmonization of environmental standards, fearing that it will reduce regulation to the lowest common denominator and thus reduce environmental protection.

Opposition in the environmental community to harmonized environmental standards has expressed itself domestically in the analogous context of federal and state environmental laws, where almost every federal environmental statute permits states to enact even stricter standards. Although this failure to preempt stronger state laws affects trade within the United States in the same way that varying national laws affect international trade, business interests have failed to bring about greater harmonization within the United States despite constant efforts to reach that goal. It is thus very unlikely that harmonized international environmental standards would ever be accepted in the United States. Moreover, and perhaps more important, there are compelling practical obstacles to harmonization.

The key issues in the harmonization debate can be summarized under the rubric of "sound science." In other words, should national product standards meet objective, scientific criteria, and should standards be applied only to the extent necessary to achieve an appropriate level of protection, taking into account technical and economic feasibility? Such tests, for example, are set forth in the general standards provisions of the Dunkel Draft and in the sanitary and phytosanitary articles of the NAFTA.[15] The requirement for scientific criteria, however, is left out of the general standards provisions (which apply to environmental standards) found in chapter 9 of the NAFTA.

Environmentalists would agree that it is prudent policy to base all decisions by governmental entities on the best information available, including scientific information, but they legitimately question whether there are objective, scientific standards according to which environmental decisions can be "harmonized." The fundamental environmental decisions at issue in the harmonization debate—which chemicals to regulate, at what level of concentration, and at what exposure level—are not ultimately scientific decisions. Instead, they are decisions on how much risk a community is willing to bear. Although risk can be estimated, there is no scientific answer to the question of what level a society should bear. That, instead, is a political and moral decision that each society must face with no help from science. And countries do not agree on what constitutes an acceptable risk.

Indeed, the answer to the question of how much risk U.S. citizens are willing to bear within the United States varies from community to community. The internal debate has been so contentious that it has ultimately had to be resolved through the political process rather than through administrative decision making. In 1990 the Congress broke a 13-year administrative deadlock over which substances to regulate as hazardous by adding 172 chemicals and 17 compounds as hazardous air pollutants to a list that had previously numbered only 8 substances.

Moreover, seeking to determine whether a regulation is a disguised barrier to trade through sound science is clearly asking the wrong question. If a regulation is applied equally to domestic and foreign-made products, and if its scientific basis is found deficient, the absence of sound science says nothing about whether the regulation was intended as a disguised barrier to trade. No one would argue, for example, that the Clean Air provisions were intended as a disguised barrier to trade, even though one could question the scientific basis for the listing of many of the substances. The proper test, the one used in chapter 9 of the NAFTA, is whether the regulation had a "legitimate objective," because this test directly relates to the disguised barrier-to-trade issue.

A similar problem arises with the "necessity" or "least restrictive alternative" requirement. Here the problem is a political one because, although economists may agree that the first-order solution is to use some form of market mechanism like a pollution tax,[16] the best theoretical approaches are often not possible to implement for a political reason, and instead some less economically desirable solution has to be chosen. It is doubtful that any society will accept a finding by a dispute resolution panel that its approach, based on political feasibility, is not "necessary," particularly with respect to the type of politically explosive issue that environmental harm often raises. Permitting countries to implement politically feasible, but less than ideal, environmental regulations should cause little trade tension.

Although internal product standards should not be subject to either scientific or necessity tests, they should remain subject to articles I and III of the GATT and to a legitimate purposes test similar to the one in the NAFTA.[17]

The Production Process and Trade Sanctions

The obverse side of the issue of domestic standards is whether a country should be allowed to restrict the import of industrial goods (animal and plant products are discussed separately below) because they (or some other products) were produced in the country of export without adequate environmental standards. Differing national environmental standards can have a profound effect on international trade because production will be cheaper in countries with lax environmental standards, potentially giving exports from those countries a cost advantage in the importing country. Weaker environmental standards also encourage a flow of investment to the country with the lax standard. Nevertheless, most trade policy makers and international economists oppose letting one country restrict imports from another that has lax standards because they argue that policymakers should not interfere with the market advantage gained by a country that is willing to tolerate higher levels of pollution, and because they believe that the United States would not tolerate a similar interference with its exports. (Remember that exports contributed one percentage point to GNP growth in the period 1987–1992 and were responsible for nearly all the jobs created in that period.)[18]

Environmentalists, however, are not reluctant to use import restrictions to achieve their objectives. They argue that the market advantage of the country with the lax standards results from a breakdown in the ability of market mechanisms to include the costs of pollution in the price of a product. They are concerned about cross-border effects of pollution resulting from lax standards. And generally they would like to see more effective environmental laws everywhere. Thus, it is quite natural for U.S. environmental advocates to see the huge capacity of the United States to absorb imports—$500 billion a year in economic activity, about one-tenth of all importing done in the world—as a ready source of leverage to achieve environmental objectives.

Great practical difficulties, however, face a nation that attempts to develop a scheme to restrict the import of goods from nations that do not meet the importing nation's environmental protection standards or even fail to enforce their own environmental laws adequately. This can be seen clearly by examining how the United States goes about regulating industrial discharges of pollutants.

In the United States, the focus of the effort to control pollution is at the plant level through either setting discharge limitations or by requiring specific types of pollution control equipment. Because the age and technical sophistication of the existing plant base often differs dramatically both within and between industries, a set of regulations that required all plants to respond in the same manner could wreak havoc, forcing many facilities out of business. Moreover, the ability of a new facility to meet discharge limitations is often superior to the ability of an old facility to retrofit to meet such standards. The United States has therefore adopted a multifaceted approach to regulating pollutants that takes these differences into account.

The U.S. Clean Water Act, for example, required that industrial facilities meet four different standards that became effective between 1977 and 1989, depending on the age of the facility and the type of pollutant involved. Similarly, compliance schedules in the Clean Air Act amendments of 1990 run for as long as 20 years (these are extensions of earlier deadlines that were not met). In some cases it is likely that there will be further extensions of these schedules.

U.S. environmental laws thus tend to set relatively long-term compliance schedules that are designed to enable facilities to achieve compliance on a step-by-step basis. This flexibility, however, raises great practical difficulties for those arguing that there should be restrictions on trade from foreign facilities that do not meet U.S. standards. First, as indicated above, there are often a series of standards, not one standard, that are applied under a prolonged implementation schedule. Second, to complicate the matter further, U.S. standards often differ between states, yet there are no interstate standards on production requirements, and it would be difficult to articulate why this variability is acceptable in the United States but not between countries. Third, as the above examples demonstrate, it would be far too disruptive to foreign production, particularly in developing countries, to mandate that they immediately achieve U.S. levels of pollution control technology. At a minimum, a long period of transition would be necessary.

In addition, such an approach could create a nightmare of trade restrictions. If the stricter pollution standards for an industry could be used to justify a trade restriction, then each industry in every country would have to be compared to see which had the stricter level of pollution control. There would be no end to such comparisons.

As both a practical and policy matter, therefore, trying to implement unilateral, blanket restrictions on trade because the environmental standards in one country are not as strict as those in another would be counterproductive. Nevertheless, different standards unquestionably have an impact on trade patterns, and lax environmental standards in an exporting country harm the competitiveness of U.S. products vis-à-vis imports from that country and encourage, to at least some extent, U.S. industries to shift their production abroad. Some of this harm results from the failure of market mechanisms to measure the cost of pollution in the cost of production of goods accurately. As a result, the question remains whether there are bilateral and multilateral approaches to this problem that can be implemented fairly and without triggering a trade war.

We suggest approaching the industrial process standards issue as a two-step process. During the first step, the international community would take steps that build on existing international agreements, precedents in the GATT, or national laws. During the second phase, the international community would begin negotiations of process standards on a case-by-case basis beginning with substances of global concern. As this process proceeds, we believe that it will become apparent that there is a need for the creation of a counterpart of the GATT for the environment.[19] From a trade and environmental perspective, it will be far more productive to address process standards and many other environmental issues through negotiations and to impose sanctions only through an agreed upon multilateral framework than through unilateral action.

The logical starting point for addressing process standards is existing international agreements that affect industrial production, including those relating to ocean and cross-border pollution, ozone depletion, and global warming (species issues are considered below). Most of these agreements require steps to be taken that will improve pollution control throughout the world and thus should raise the pollution control standards of many U.S. competitors.

Most of these agreements are also likely to be revisited with the goal of strengthening their provisions. To address the competitiveness issues described above, the United States should propose in these negotiations minimum standards that protect the environment and, by reducing disparity in standards, reduce trade distortion and thereby foster U.S. competitiveness. Consistent with the approach in U.S. law, these minimum standards can and should be implemented over a reasonable period calculated on their cost and their level of difficulty. Moreover, consistent with existing agreements such as the Montreal Protocol on chlorofluorocarbons, it should be a goal of U.S. policy to make the agreements enforceable through trade sanctions against nations that do not comply with an agreement or, in the case of multilateral agreements, nations that do not become signatories and refuse to implement equivalent standards.

In addition to addressing process standards issues through renegotiation of existing agreements, the United States should address these issues by seeking in future GATT negotiations an agreement that authorizes trade barriers to enforce these multilateral agreements, much the way GATT activities were to be coordinated with international financial decisions under the original GATT agreement.

Moreover, this agreement ought to authorize national regulations aimed at ameliorating environmental harm in the global commons, on condition that the country imposing the condition "pay" for the action with compensation elsewhere. The idea is similar to article XIX of the GATT, which permits contracting parties to raise their custom duties temporarily to allow for adjustment to import pressures, provided they "compensate" the adversely affected exporters with offsetting trade concessions—a sort of self-imposed retaliation for their import barriers. The Dunkel Draft proposes that the free trade interest of structural adjustment be served by allowing three years of such temporary import barriers without "compensation." A suggested approach in the environmental area would authorize environmental barriers to continue for a limited period without compensation, subject to the parties' convening a working group to study the reasons behind the barrier and, it is hoped, to negotiate an end to the allegedly offensive practice.

Although it might at first be considered harmful to environmental interests to allow such barriers only on sufferance, they would provide a useful middle ground because considerations of national sovereignty and free trade pressures will make any other approach difficult to justify or even administer. Used strategically, such temporary barriers might be an engine to bring about improved environmental management, particularly with respect to the global commons, in which all nations have an interest.

It is in these limited senses that the next round of the GATT could be the "environmental" round. It is unlikely and probably undesirable for the GATT to be in the business of environmental improvement itself; as a thoughtful student of the field has said, combating protectionism is a full-time job for the GATT.[20]

Another step in the approach to regulating process standards is to address head-on the most contentious issue in the United States concerning these standards—the fear that differing standards will encourage investors to relocate to countries with lax environmental standards. This could be accomplished by requiring that a nation's environmental standards be met on all cross-border investment. Such an approach would be more acceptable than approaches setting other categories of process standards because such regulation would apply to nationals of the country imposing the conditions on investment, not of the country with the weaker environmental standards. In addition, as is indicated above, singling out investment in new plants and in plant upgrades is consistent with U.S. law, which treats such investment differently from regulation of existing facilities.

This issue is being addressed seriously in the business community, where many companies are setting environmental standards for their investments outside the United States. Following the initiative of these companies, it would be logical for the

United States to suggest bilateral and multilateral negotiations to establish investment standards. Recent studies conducted in connection with the NAFTA indicate that, despite the concern over the issue, most investments in Mexico that are likely to result from the agreement will not, in fact, be stimulated by weaker environmental standards or enforcement.[21] New environmental investment standards, therefore, while removing the threat that the pollution haven issue poses to free trade negotiations, should not significantly reduce investment in developing countries. At the same time, developing countries will receive the benefit of environmentally sound investment.

During the second stage of process negotiations, the international community would address the more difficult problem of addressing differing process standards that affect the environment and cause distortions to trade, but do not affect another nation directly and affect the global environment only to the extent that there is a negative cumulative effect on the overall environment from numerous situations where harm is being done to the local environment. Such negotiations would have to take place in the context of a global agreement on the environment pursuant to which countries would agree to address environmental problems that affect both competitiveness and the environment. An example would be regulation of particularly dangerous and difficult substances to deal with such as dioxin and certain solvents.

One final approach to this problem deserves comment because it has been discussed in the context of the American-proposed environmental "side-agreement" to the NAFTA. This is the idea of agreeing to apply trade sanctions to a government's failure to enforce its own environmental process laws. This approach presents an opportunity to move local standards upward without necessarily harmonizing them. The approach is attractive for this reason, and we think it is workable, but as a practical political matter it requires several qualifications. First, the relief must be postponed to allow for means other than trade sanctions to work. These methods include independent fact-finding and opportunities for governments to propose schedules for upgrading enforcement of their own laws—in other words, attenuating the remedy. Second, because not all countries are at the same stage of developing environmental law and environmental law enforcement, the standard for applying sanctions must be hard to meet, that is, a "persistent pattern" of nonenforcement has been suggested in the NAFTA negotiations. And finally, the trade sanctions must be related to the environmental damage done, not the harm to foreign industry. Otherwise, this remedy will be confused with antisubsidization penalties and could become a protectionist weapon. Antisubsidization in environmental action is the subject of our next section.

Environmental Subsidies

Closely related to the issue of retaliation against countries with lax environmental standards is the issue of how to respond to environmental subsidies. Such subsidies can have a very significant impact on trade because if the government of one country subsidizes the installation of pollution control equipment while another makes its industry bear all the cost, industry in the latter country will suffer a competitive disadvantage.

Consistent with its GATT obligations, a country may be able to impose countervailing duties against imports from a country that provides subsidies to companies for installing pollution control equipment. Thus, pro-environmental subsidies might be subject to challenge. In contrast, failure to pass laws to protect the environment might not be accepted as a "subsidy" subject to countervailing duties in the absence of affirmative action to serve as the basis for the duty, even though the failure to pass laws protecting the environment can provide as great a competitive advantage as the passing of affirmative subsidies. This would have an adverse effect on the environment and would not reflect wise or acceptable policy.

The negotiators at the Uruguay Round considered the issue of subsidies and in earlier drafts permitted environmental subsidies as an exception to regular GATT obligations. Although exceptions for research and regional aid remain in the Dunkel Draft, the exception for environmental subsidies was deleted, partially at the insistence of the United States. This position should be reconsidered. As described above, inherent in the concept of environmental regulation is the necessity of granting facilities and thus countries time to improve their pollution control efforts. The costs that countries will incur during this period will be staggering. Conservative estimates of the costs that U.S. companies will incur in complying with the new Clean Air Act amendments, for example, are $20 billion a year for an indefinite period of time. In many countries, private firms simply will not be able to bear these costs without assistance, and, in fact, many countries may not be able to bear these costs without aid.

Thus, if U.S. policy seeks to clean up the global environment rapidly, the United States may be faced with the less than ideal situation of permitting other countries to subsidize the installation of pollution control equipment. To minimize the impact of this concession, the United States could seek to limit permissible subsidies to developing countries and former Communist countries in Eastern Europe and Asia for a specific period of time, much as reduction of tariff, government procurement, and services barriers will be phased in under the new GATT agreements expected in December 1993. Eventually, as standards improve, the distortions in trade arising from the subsidies will be reduced.

Any exemption for subsidies should also be limited to subsidies for the installation of pollution control equipment, not for their operation and maintenance. Operation and maintenance subsidies raise an entirely different issue from capital subsidies. Operation and maintenance of pollution control equipment can be costly, but once such equipment is installed, a firm should be able to recover those costs from its sale of goods. To permit subsidies in such a situation would permit permanently uneconomical operations to compete against goods that are not subsidized. This is not necessary, environmentally or otherwise, and such subsidies should remain subject to countervailing duties.

The Case of Renewable Natural Resources

As the tuna/dolphin case described previously indicates, renewable natural resources, particularly marine resources, migratory wildlife, endangered species, and forestry resources, constitute an important component of world trade. The first three of these categories have been the subject of numerous international agreements, dating back to at least 1900.[22] The reason for this is straightforward: fish and wildlife resources have always been considered by many individuals in the United States and many other countries as being of more than local concern and, more often than not, of international concern.

The first great battle in Anglo-American law over the status of wildlife resources resulted in a determination that wildlife was not "owned" by any person.[23] Over time this decision has translated in U.S. political culture into a view that fish and wildlife resources are part of a common heritage and are thus of more than local concern. Beginning around 1900, it became clear that marine and migratory species could not be protected by national measures alone, and a series of international treaties relating to these species resulted. Endangered species and tropical forests also came to be thought of more and more frequently as being of international concern, even when they are found only within one nation, because the benefits they are perceived to offer—their scientific, medical, and ecological value—are of significance to more than merely the nation in which they are found.[24]

Protection of extraterritorial species has been part of U.S. domestic law since the Lacey Act of 1900. U.S. law has included restrictions on international trade in migratory, endangered, and other species and, in some cases, trade sanctions for violation of international agreements or U.S. law relating to species, including the sanctions that led to the tuna/dolphin decision. Moreover, emotions about species, particularly marine mammals and endangered species, run deep among strong political forces that regard species protection as a moral issue that allows little room for compromise.

Regulation of renewable natural resources and regulation of the production and sale of industrial goods thus raise different issues. As a result, efforts to place the former in the same category as conventional "production" issues will lead to direct confrontation between the trade and environmental communities. This result can be avoided by the simple device of recognizing that fish, wildlife, and plants are subject to different standards from those for industrial goods, and that bans on importation of fish and wildlife should be accepted so long as they are applied equally to domestic and foreign products.

Although there are many international fish and wildlife agreements, they can create trade issues because they are not always consistent with the GATT. In such situations, the GATT should almost always give way to international environmental agreements because, compared to the GATT, these environmental provisions are more specific, very limited in scope, often later in time, and most of all, more popular. Such deference is incorporated, in part, in article 104 of the NAFTA, which provides that certain listed environmental agreements take priority over the provisions in the agreement itself. A similar provision should eventually be incorporated into the GATT.

Trade, the Environment, and Development

The final and perhaps most fundamental way in which trade and the environment intersect is with respect to the impact of trade agreements on patterns of development. Indeed, as we suggested earlier, this is a major reason why the intersection between the two disciplines is receiving so much attention. Agreements such as the NAFTA are likely, for reasons other than the environment, to cause at least some shifting of industrial production from the United States and Canada to Mexico. Trade agreements, moreover, can and do create greater opportunities for exploitation of natural resources. These shifts in patterns of industrial location and development underlie the unease many environmentalists feel about freer trade.

There is reason for this concern. Assume, for example, that a developing country insists that all new investors in industrial facilities install pollution control equipment comparable to that which would have been installed in the United States. Such measures, nevertheless, would be only partially effective if the country did not also have an adequate infrastructure to handle waste from even modern industrial facilities.

Potential harm to the environment from trade must, however, be balanced against the benefit to the environment from industrial development that provides a nation with the resources it needs to protect the environment. A recent study, for example, found that as a general matter nations begin to protect the environment when their annual per capita income starts to exceed about $5,000.[25] Today only 28 countries, with approximately 15 percent of the world's population, fit within this category on an exchange rate basis.[26]

This dilemma cannot be resolved without returning to the issue of the cost of protecting the environment. It is costly, particularly to developing nations, not only to install pollution equipment but also to protect natural resources and to build the infrastructure necessary to ameliorate the impact of increased development resulting from freer trade. As indicated above, the industrialized nations will have to bear some of this cost. It would be advisable for the international community to address this issue directly as was attempted, although with relatively little success, at the Rio Summit.

Proposals were considered this year in connection with the NAFTA that a customs duty be established among the NAFTA parties, with the funds to be used to lessen the impact of the trade agreement on the environment and U.S. labor. This type of proposal should be given serious study as soon as possible as a potential way to ameliorate the impact of trade on the environment. A one-half of 1 percent duty on all imports by all countries, for example, would have little impact on trade patterns because the duty would be small enough to have little impact on the competitiveness of goods. Such a fee would raise approximately $26 billion,[27] assuming world trade of approximately $5.2 trillion. As an alternative, a percentage of the duties already being assessed by nations could be allocated to the fund, which might have the collateral benefit of encouraging governments to reduce duties more quickly than they are now inclined to do.

Such a duty might also provide the last and most difficult incentive necessary to increase confidence in the trade and environmental communities that development is sustainable and thus to assure cooperation between these communities in resolving trade and environmental issues.

Conclusion

There is a tendency in the trade community to treat the environment as just another roadblock on the path to open trade. It is not; the environment will not go away. Concerns about the impact of global commerce on the environment will have to be accommodated in the trading system.

There is a counterpart tendency in the environmental community to see trade as appropriate leverage to achieve a wide variety of environmental objectives. This, also, is not true. Global economic integration would and should proceed, albeit with sensitivity to environmental concerns.

The intersection of trade and the environment can be managed in the global policy system, but that intersection is complex because the two disciplines are themselves highly complex. This article has suggested the framework for the necessary process as well as some specific ideas for the critical provisions.

Notes

1. H. Jeffrey Leonard et al., *Environment and the Poor: Development Strategies for a Common Agenda* (New Brunswick, N.J.: Transaction Books, 1989). Leonard states in his overview of the book:

    Poverty and environmental destruction are becoming inseparable twins less because the absolute numbers of people have grown than because the poorest people (who have the least access to investment capital and technology) occupy the lands that need the most infrastructure, management, and external inputs if their utilization is not to result in land degradation and environmental destruction. (p. 19)

2. Edward O. Wilson, *The Diversity of Life* (Cambridge, Mass.: Belknap Press of Harvard University Press, 1992), p. 31.

3. Emily T. Smith, "Growth vs. Environment," *Business Week*, May 11, 1992, p. 69.

4. Jerry Alder with Mary Hager, "Earth at the Summit," *Newsweek*, June 1, 1992, p. 21.

5. Japan does not seem to have experienced this problem yet, perhaps for the same reasons that the U.S. relationship with the Caribbean nations and the EC relationship with the African, Caribbean, and Pacific countries did not really raise these issues. Regarding the U.S. relationship with the Caribbean, see the provisions of the Caribbean Basin Economic Recovery Act, 19 U.S.C. §§ 2701–2706, and, as to the EC experience, the Lomé Convention, XXIX I.L.M. 788 (July 1990). In both cases, industrialized countries provide unreciprocated trade benefits to developing countries. The countries that receive these benefits evidently pose little threat to most domestic industries in the donor countries.

6. Kym Anderson and Richard Blackhurst, *The Greening of World Trade Issues* (New York, N.Y.: Harvester Wheatsheaf, 1992), p. 19. This book contains a series of essays written by leading international economists that are revised versions of papers commissioned for the GATT Secretariat's annual report, *International Trade 1990–91* (Geneva, 1991).

7. *Ibid.*

8. U.S. Department of State, Commercial Policy Series 71 (Pub. no. 1660) (Washington, D.C., 1941).

9. The leading treatise on the GATT has in fact described international trade transactions as being among the most regulated of all economic activities. John Jackson, *World Trade and the Law of GATT* (Charlottesville, Va.: Michie, 1969), p. 2.

10. Such measures are exempt from the GATT under article XX only if they are "not applied in a manner which would constitute a means of arbitrary or unjustifiable discrimination between countries where the same conditions prevail, or a disguised restriction on international trade."

11. See generally Steve Charnovitz, "Exploring the Environmental Exceptions in GATT Article XX," *Journal of World Trade* 25 (October 1991), p. 37.

12. Agreement on Technical Barriers to Trade, 26th Supplement, GATT Basic Instruments and Selected Documents (Geneva, 1979).

13. The Dunkel Draft states in a footnote that "this provision is intended to ensure proportionality between regulations and the risks non-fulfillment of legitimate objectives would create."

14. Under the GATT, a sophisticated system of negotiation known as dispute settlement has developed to assist in the resolution of concrete differences between GATT contracting parties. Central to the process is a system of appointing and charging a panel of experts (usually, but not always, experts

in GATT matters, but not, as far as can be determined, experts in environmental matters) to gather facts and analyze them to reach a decision about which party's interpretation of the GATT is correct. To the concern of many outside the trade community (and perhaps some within it), GATT panels conduct their proceedings entirely in secret.

15. NAFTA, articles 754, paras. 3 and 5; 755. The NAFTA also provides that international sanitary and phytosanitary standards should be applied only where those standards do not reduce the level of protection of human, animal, or plant life.

16. See Anderson and Blackhurst, *The Greening of World Trade Issues*.

17. Note that this analysis of standards applies only in the environmental context. It does not make any determination about traditional health and safety standards. The ideas developed in the 1979 GATT Standards Code and in the Dunkel Draft may be appropriate in the broad area of industrial standards that do not relate primarily to environmental conditions, but this article makes no judgment on that question.

18. Bruce Kasman, "Recent U.S. Export Performance in the Developing World," *FRBNY Quarterly Review* 64 (Winter 1992–93).

19. This idea has been suggested by a leading scholar in the field. See Edith Brown Weiss, "Environment and Trade as Partners in Sustainable Development," *American Journal of International Law* 86 (1992), p. 729.

20. Steve Charnovitz, "Environmentalism Confronts GATT Rules," *Journal of World Trade* 27 (April 1993), p. 53.

21. Gene M. Grossman and Alan B. Krueger, *Environmental Impacts of a North American Free Trade Agreement*, Discussion Papers in Economics, no. 158 (Princeton, N.J.: Woodrow Wilson School, Princeton University, November 1991).

22. The Convention for the Preservation of Wild Animals, Birds and Fish in Africa was signed in 1900. It required export licenses for certain species because of their rarity and danger of extinction. See Charnovitz, "Exploring the Exceptions," p. 39. A recent survey listed 170 international agreements to protect the environment and wildlife. U.S. International Trade Commission, *International Agreements to Protect the Environment and Wildlife* (Washington, D.C., January 1991).

23. See William Blackstone, *Commentaries on the Laws of England: A Facsimile of the First Edition of 1765–1769*, vol. 2 (Chicago, Ill.: University of Chicago Press, 1979), p. 14.

24. See generally Wilson, *Diversity of Life*.

25. See Grossman and Krueger, *Environmental Impacts*.

26. World Bank, *World Development Report 1991* (New York, N.Y.: Oxford University Press, 1991), p. 205.

27. Although this figure seems very large, it is only a small proportion of the aid that was considered necessary at the Rio Summit to ensure sustainable development in the developing world.

The Natural Resource Wars: Let Them Eat Trees

Richard E. Bissell

THE FOREIGN ASSISTANCE community has been witness in the last decade to a debilitating war over the developing world's natural resources. As public debate would have it: Who has first claim on our natural heritage—people, to grow food, or mother nature, to preserve her integrity?

The concerns about feeding people are dramatic. With the projected growth of population in the twenty-first century—to a range of 11 to 15 billion from the current 5.5 billion people—food needs will easily double and possibly triple. Concerns about conserving the environmental heritage are equally stark. Linear projections of the loss of biodiversity and rate of pollution of the earth's water and air generate a vision of a natural world that is significantly diminished.

For developing countries, the collision between these two imperatives has been escalating over the last decade and it has damaged efforts to meet both. Each side has had reasons for its attacks on the other. Debates have been polarized to extremes. The result has been a severe contraction in the commitment of foreign assistance agencies such as the U.S. Agency for International Development to developing food production. And the effort to meet new environmental challenges has been inadequate.

People in the United States and other developed countries have too little appreciation of this conflict over natural resources. The wealth of the countries of the Organization for Economic Cooperation and Development (OECD) allows them to have their food and save the environment too, notwithstanding fights over the timber resources of the U.S. Northwest. Developing countries pose a stark and much more common challenge. Unless foreign assistance donors fund outcomes that will bring both sides nearer together, developing countries are likely to get the worst of both worlds. Bringing a "sustainable" perspective into both camps has been proposed as the bridge to peace.

Past experience in developing countries would suggest that the answers will have to be long term in nature, with strong doses of research, institution building, and technology transfer, but focused and launched in a short- and medium-term time frame in order to avoid losing a generation of potential progress to the current confusion. Perhaps most troubling is that too few

---

Richard E. Bissell is distinguished adjunct professor at American University and visiting fellow at the Overseas Development Council. He is a former assistant administrator for the U.S. Agency for International Development (1986–1993).

Copyright © 1993 by The Center for Strategic and International Studies and the Massachusetts Institute of Technology

people are willing to acknowledge just how few answers are in hand for the problems posed by the food-environment nexus. Whatever it is called—sustainable agriculture or environmentally sensitive development—the need for action and long-term research investments will have to be met simultaneously. Developing countries gain nothing from the polarization of the natural resource fields; integration to improve their people's lives is essential.

How Did We Get in This Fix?

The field of agricultural research has a long scientific tradition, focused on the issue of increasing output rates. The main questions it has asked have been: How can we maximize the production of food products from a given piece of land? How can we bring new land into production that has previously been in a natural state? The answers to both questions—one on intensity of production and the other on extensiveness of production—have delivered to mankind staggering improvements in food access over many centuries. Malthus was wrong, if only because he did not appreciate the room for technological change in food production.

The field of environmental science is no less ancient, but it has only recently been given a name and appreciated for what it brings to the issue of preserving and sustaining our natural environment: plants, animals, soil, water, air, light, and the biological processes that unite these elements. For some, the environmental sciences are focused on preservation and maintenance: How can we preserve the ecosystems we inherit for succeeding generations? How can human activities be bounded in a way that will provide for the survival of the environment? Mankind's capacity to adjust has proved the prophets of environmental doom wrong so far, but people no longer accept the goal of staving off catastrophes; the public wants a positive vision to remove the environmental sword of Damocles they see hanging over their heads.

Convergence of these two fields is fraught with difficulties, whether conceptual, logical, political, economic, or cultural. What they share, however, is a basic rooting in a long-term view. Agriculture, as a domesticated version of nature, still shares the need for space and time associated with the environment. Plants and animals cannot be produced like plastic widgets, despite the promise of biotechnology. And where the capacity to absorb new technologies is limited, the time element is even greater. In those countries where millions or billions of people still subsist on family farms, there is only a short distance from farm practices to a return to nature.

The goal of food production is not inherently damaging to the environment, if conducted in a "sustainable" manner. Indeed, farmers since time began have been sensitive to the interaction of their activities with the natural resource base in which they work. The goal of production, most simply stated, means that farmers want to harvest enough food for their own table and cash needs and to have seed for the next year. Farmers understand that in growing crops, they are essentially "mining the land" if they give nothing back. Thus, depending upon the particular ecoregion in which they are working, farmers will either farm land only a few years, rotate among different fields, or fertilize to maintain the productivity of the land. Even today, traditional swidden farmers who work on 30 percent of the world's arable land—supporting some 300 million people—still harvest a crop or two, and then move on to clear other land and leave the farmed land to return to nature for a time. Farmers do not have a vested interest in damaging the long-term value of the land; on the other hand, what damage they do to the land may be invisible until it accumulates to the point of irreversibility. For example, when the land is salinized from overirrigation, it is too late, and the land has to be abandoned. If well informed about long-term maintenance, farmers will implement it as long as they can meet their immediate production needs as well.

Tapping these mutual concerns has not been easy in recent decades, owing to fundamental changes in both disciplines. For the agriculturalists, tremendous population growth and migrations of poor people in developing countries in and out of rural areas create conflict and tension. For environmentalists, the growing ability to measure changes—whether harmful or benign—as a result of improved science generates a sense of alarm about human sources of environmental alteration. The growing demands of the environmental community pose challenges around the world to the ability of agricultural producers to meet needs, both at the household level and the national level. The resulting clashes are shrill, only sometimes articulate, and too often focused on mobilizing political strength instead of solutions.

One source of that clash has been the very different measures of success used by the two schools of thought. Agriculture, for example, relies extensively on measures of production, that is, production efficiency per hectare, economic value of output as a function of the cost of inputs, total production in relation to optimal caloric availability, and so forth. The environmentalists, on the other hand, tend to measure losses rather than gains, with attention focused on quantitative measures of forest reduction (both natural and total), soil erosion, groundwater depletion, reduction of the ozone layer, species loss, or loss of tillable land to salinity. The tone established by these kinds of measures naturally leads to clashes. Their logical implication is that natural resource conservation (as a production-limiting factor) becomes a lower priority for the farming community. For the environmental community, the logical temptation is to oppose improvements in production, given the (possibly unknown) side effects on natural resources. Hostility rather than compatibility is thus generated.

If there is one theme running through these tensions, it is that science has recently done a much better job of measuring losses where the environment is concerned than it has in fully analyzing alternative approaches to food production. The race for benchmarks and measures has left the agricultural community on the sidelines, still largely focused on the same measures of productivity that predated the environmental revolution.

In political terms, too, the environmental and farm communities have diverged fundamentally. The traditional strength of the agricultural community in democracies is well known. In some countries, it derived from the attachment of political elites to the land, and in others it was a reflection of powers reserved to subunits (as in the states of the United States) that by their sheer numbers were able to maintain significant clout for the farming community. Owing to electoral systems in all of the major democracies, the farmers have substantial political influence. In most developing countries, the farmers suffer from an inverse proposition: they have next to no power relative to their urban counterparts.

The environmental constituencies in developed countries have been able to seize the high ground politically by pointing to the continuing large global surpluses in food (even if badly distributed between rich and poor) and the problems of the natural environment blamed upon human activity and economic growth. Some of the power of the environmental political movement derives from fear—of the health effects of industrial activity, of long-term damage to the earth both in the air and underground. For some, the principal struggle is with the anthropocentric traditions of many cultures in the world, where nature exists only to serve man, and if man alters nature, it is mankind's right to do so. The international efforts to formalize those political agendas, ranging from the Brundtland Commission of 1979 to the United Nations Conference on Environment and Development (UNCED) in 1992, have served to both strengthen and to smooth out some of the national inconsistencies in the international political agenda on the environment.

The net effect of these viewpoints has been to put the environment and agriculture on a collision course. Nevertheless, in political terms, what is now important is that both communities have embraced the phrase "sustainable agriculture" as compatible with their goals; politically, however, the phrase has not yet been given a mutually acceptable content. It is progress that leaders on both sides have adopted the phrase for speeches; the question now is its meaning.

In economic terms, the hurdles to adoption of sustainable agriculture are still enormous. The power of the marketplace remains firmly in the hands of production agriculture. The nature of economic structures does not yet give environmental criteria an equal place with the traditional measures of income generation and productivity. Work has been undertaken to develop new measures of national income that would treat the natural resource base as a depreciable asset,[1] and several officials high in the Clinton administration have indicated that they consider it a priority to see such new approaches to depreciation included in national statistics.

In the meantime, demographers argue for avoiding measures that would undermine the trend toward rising productivity in global agriculture. In the developing countries in particular, where intensity of agriculture is much less than in the developed countries, there remains considerable room for greater yields on good land in order to meet the population growth likely to continue in the twenty-first century and to thereby avoid the continued shift of poor farmers onto low-yield lands. On this issue, the best case suggests a stable population in 2040 at least double the current population on the earth (11 billion versus today's 5.5 billion), and a number of scenarios go half as high again. In such a case, calculating the need for food is not merely a matter of arithmetic (i.e., twice the number of people need twice the volume of today's food supply), but also of quality because if incomes grow, richer people will demand more food and of higher quality. A target of 11 billion people then would require three times today's production of food for twice as many people.

In developing countries in particular, economists fit such numbers into investment needs that leave little room for the environment. What price can one put on clean water for people whose annual income is $400 compared with the need for food each day? The need for electric power in developing countries over the next decade is likely to require as much as $120 billion each year.[2] How much of that generating capacity would poor people be willing to give up in order to install smokestack scrubbers and reduce air pollution? Probably not much, given the tiny amount of electricity available to them now.

Finally, there are contradictions within the environmental and farming communities. Neither community is uniform, and there are crosscutting allegiances among the participants that reflect cultural approaches to organizing their lives. Respect for the conservation of the environment can be as strong in subsistence farmers as it is in environmentalists fighting the harvesting of natural forests. Issues that divide along cultural lines have to do with religion, with the relationship of man with nature, and with the nature of communities (their permanence, their attitudes toward change, and the role of agriculture in broader status structures). The rapid and pervasive urbanization of the world is creating unprecedented tensions around agriculture and the farming communities. A country such as Mexico has experienced a series of revolutions in the last two centuries caused in part by the issue of the poor's access to land; today, with an estimated 15 million people in Mexico City, the needs of the urban poor are beginning to outweigh the needs of the average farmer on a national scale. Thus, cultural issues do not provide a clear-cut division between the environmental and farming communities; but the issues do weave through the two communities in ways that impede rapid responses to their common concerns.

Emergence of the Common Vision

Like many global organizing concepts, "sustainable agriculture" suffers from too many parents, each of whom has a different definition of what it means and how to carry it out. Solutions would be much more manageable if there were a single, accepted vision. The variety of approaches ensures that it will take time to reach agreement. But such a development does not mean it should be abandoned. Instead, the many parents of the concept give it a strength it would not otherwise have.

What is important is that the different definitions of sustainable agriculture are not mutually exclusive; indeed, they depend on each other for their success in ways that are only now emerging, especially in developing countries. Although the proponents of each may not admit their interdependence, research is making it increasingly clear that only a multidimensional understanding of sustainable agriculture makes sense. The natural world inhabited by farmers and environmentalists has many dimensions, and it is important to find a way to include them all in a concrete approach to third world sustainable agriculture.

The simplest version of sustainable agriculture is one that includes six elements. They form the constellation in figure 1.

The six elements of sustainable agriculture are drawn from a variety of disciplines. Each has taken a place in new approaches to sustainable agriculture that are now being applied in developing countries. For example, ag-

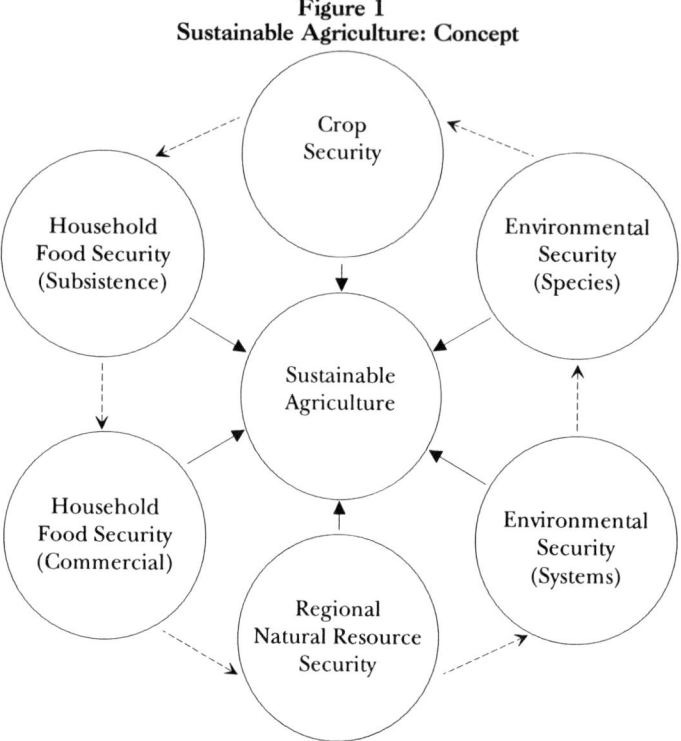

**Figure 1
Sustainable Agriculture: Concept**

riculture has traditionally focused its basic research on crop security, with an emphasis on improving germ plasm (the genetic blueprint for plants) and the inputs associated with crops to maximize the product per hectare. Commercial food security has also been a major focus for agriculture, with an emphasis on policy and economics as well as market development. As one moves around the circle, the environmental sciences become more prominent, both at the systemic and species level. Each element is strongly dependent on those on either side, and the circle as a whole makes up an interdependent framework for sustainable agriculture.

Crop Security. This element captures the issue of yield increases and maintenance. In terms of techniques, questions of selective breeding and *ex situ* germ plasm (preserved in a laboratory) have been essential to advances in food production. Within the field, agronomists have focused on various elements that influence yield, namely, the relation of specific crops to nutrients, soils, water, and pests and diseases. The growth of environmental consciousness in this element has been steady over time, not only in the recognition of the importance of *in situ* germ plasm (preserved in its natural habitat) as a resource for future species improvement that cannot be anticipated in current *ex situ* collections, but also through the formalization of improved input management. The emergence of "integrated pest management" as a discipline, with its dramatic application to Indonesian rice crops, exemplifies the merged concerns of different communities. The most recent variation of crop security has emerged in genetic engineering to develop synthetic varieties with special growth and resistance characteristics.

Household Food Security (Subsistence). This element deals with poverty and the need to combat it in the least developed socioeconomic environments through food production for the family. Estimates are that 1 billion people are chronically undernourished around the world, and most of them live in rural areas. Such farming households are sometimes extremely destructive of the natural environment (and the role of new homesteaders in the tropical forests has been well documented), although others with established patterns of livelihood can have the most symbiotic relationship with nature. Even as condemned a practice as "slash and burn" can be carried out with positive or negative effects on the environment. What these subsistence households look for from the crop security dimension is not so much spectacular outputs as durability and steadiness of yields in the face of plagues, drought, heat, and varying soil adversity. Given their poverty, they are generally unable to take advantage of expensive inputs such as fertilizer or hybrid varieties, and instead need reliable, preservable crops that can be consumed on the farm.

Household Food Security (Commercial). This element focuses primarily on the income potential of agriculture. Because the crops grown will not, in the main, be consumed on the farm, the need to increase yields and grow commercial quantities that can be moved to cities and other markets is essential. Commercial farmers usually have access to some kind of credit and thus are able to increase inputs to reduce yield gaps. They invest in irrigation systems in order to increase yields and the number of annual croppings from a given parcel of land. Their approach is more scientific because they have more education and thus have better access to new ideas, technologies, and supplies for meeting challenges on the farm. Even as farmers attempt to escape from subsistence agriculture in order to gain the benefits of higher cash income, they also know that it is a riskier course for the household, and many will create a blended farming operation, with some areas planted to commercial crops and others saved for the household's needs. The full commitment to commercial farming comes only when the technologies have proved reliable over a period of years and where conditions can either be controlled (e.g., irrigation) or are predictable.

Regional Natural Resource Security. This element brings an understanding of the long-term endowments of the environment to practitioners of sustainable agriculture. Soil and water quality are particularly crucial elements in these calculations, but they can encompass any issues described by economists as "externalities," depending upon how broadly the regional system is defined. Some farmers are aware of natural resource security by virtue of well-established traditions and lore in their culture. For others, it has to be measured through site surveillance techniques that are rapidly becoming available in developing countries (such as satellite-based, resource-mapping programs). Agricultural extension systems have been invaluable in the twentieth century in keeping farmers aware of natural resource changes that may be occurring throughout an area and thus giving them time for preemptive action to maintain crop yields. As the farmers seeking commercial food security meet problems in closing yield gaps, they turn increasingly to experts in natural resource security for answers, and their interaction is essential to the success of both. For developing countries, with only minimal extension services, the need to understand clearly the interactions of agriculture and the environment *before* applying scarce resources is essential.

Environmental Security (Systems). This element expands the perspective of regional natural resource security to include the unseen interactions of various sites as well as the global variables that will influence both the sustainability of the environment and food production. The emerging concept of biospheres or ecoregions has done much to give meaning to the security of environmental systems. More popularly, the attention given, for example, to increases in CO_2, toxic pollution of water systems, and global climate change from volcanic eruptions shows that people have become more aware of their systemic vulnerability. The search for environmental security related to systems has spurred a great deal of science in both forestry and agriculture in order to understand the feedback effects on the overall biosphere of different environments shaped by man. For instance, the role of forests as carbon sinks for the earth has stimulated greater research into the part played by different kinds of forests: temperate/tropical, natural/farmed, old growth/new growth, and so forth. Analysts of environmental systems are above all concerned about stability, and the focus of their work is the role of man-made effects that may destabilize known biological interactions.

Environmental Security (Species). This area brings to light one specific aspect of the biosystem's stability: the identification and conservation of natural germ plasm, both flora and fauna. Maintaining biological diversity is a uniquely important aspect of natural resource conservation in the context of sustainable agriculture because the maintenance of germ plasm *in situ* becomes essential for future agriculture, because current custodians of *ex situ* collections only maintain what they value at the present time. Thus the need to maintain the random collection of genetic material found in nature reflects the understanding that we cannot predict what will be important in the future. The interaction of biodiversity with systemic environmental security emerges in the realization that *in situ* germ plasm does not exist in a vacuum. Environmentalists have thus brought a special perspective to the process of maintaining biological diversity. And the presence of the greatest diversity in developing countries has created a special mandate for foreign assistance programs to help in this area. The need for sustaining the context of species as well as the germ plasm itself has led to well-publicized conflicts with users of the resources, such as farmers. And there are analysts who argue that the best way of conserving those resources is through developing commercial, sustainable exploitation of *ex situ* resources,[3] growing nontraditional, commercial-value products, or, as a last resort, using tourism to give value to the *in situ* sites.[4]

These six elements do not yet willingly come together in a single constellation. The fact that they bump into each other constantly, however, is proof that they may eventually develop working relationships within the durable concept of sustainable agriculture. Their interaction is clearest in developing countries, where programs and systems to pursue both directions are most fragile, and where for this reason the six thrusts of sustainable agriculture show the greatest interdependence.

These six elements are not separate disciplines. In research terms they are interdisciplinary. In development terms, it is necessary to call upon many different specialties to bring them to life. The development community has become increasingly vocal in recent years with regard to its stake in the outcome of investments in sustainable agriculture. The economic community has now opened up the issues of "externalities" and has thus created an opening for other disciplines to proclaim their concern with the outcome of investments.

At the grassroots level, for instance, people do not segment their lives in the manner of scientists or bureaucrats. As one researcher put it,

> Rural people see their environment as a whole, whereas government agencies continue with the traditional sectoral approach. For the people to respond adequately to government policies, the policies must reflect their holistic outlook. . . . Ad hoc inter-ministerial committees may not be an effective substitute in the long term.[5]

How far should one go in creating a holistic approach? Beyond agriculture and the environment, one can also consider health, job creation, education, and communications, just to name a few.

Implementing the Common Vision

The pressure is growing on donors and on developing countries to go beyond the mitigation of risk of environmental damage or simply supporting work that is "good for the environment." At a certain point, systematic investments need to be made in sustainable agriculture, along with publicizing an easily understood rationale as to why any particular endeavor advances the overall interest of the community. Political support for that program will be stronger the more donor-supported efforts begin to integrate the full range of the vision.

One of the foreign assistance community's largest programs is the multidonor Consultative Group on International Agricultural Research (CGIAR). In this case, donors support a very large investment (about $250 million annually), and a long-term program as well. The issue of justifying long-term investments has been explored elsewhere,[6] and the difficulties in the development field of making such long-term judgments are well known. Not only do massive current needs exist that have a call on resources, but in the area of sustainable agriculture there are numerous technological breakthroughs that are possible that cannot be predicted or even foreseen, and these may affect the value of research investments made today.

The CGIAR has made a very clear policy commitment to integration of agriculture and conservation of the environment. At the semiannual meeting of the CGIAR in May 1993, V. Rajagopalan, chairman of the meeting and vice president of the World Bank, opened with the following statement:

Feeding the people is, of course, an essential component of poverty alleviation. But the challenge to research is to expand food supplies to feed an increasing population without causing irreparable damage to the natural resource base on which food productivity depends. The World Development Report described the situation aptly when it said that "the key is *not* to produce less but to produce differently." For international agricultural research, this is not an option. It is a compulsion. The overwhelming challenge we face is that of truly integrating crop improvement with natural resource management. Productivity increases achieved through crop improvement, the creation of varieties that are resistant to pests and disease, which in turn decrease dependence on pesticides, the availability of unrestricted access to genetic resources, the management of tropical forests, and research into the productive use of marginal land inhabited by the poor, all need to be combined in production systems that are truly sustainable.[7]

The International Agricultural Research Centers (IARCs), many receiving core funding from the CGIAR, have organized their work on sustainable agriculture with a view to comprehensive coverage of natural resource issues. The CGIAR's 18 constituent centers have taken both collective and many independent approaches. On the one hand, each center has attempted to ensure the sustainability of production (consistent with the natural resource base) for the commodities in their mandate. More recently, the CGIAR collectively has organized its research programs on natural resource issues around a set of "ecoregional zones," in which centers are expected to work collaboratively (among themselves and with national research institutions in developing countries) on the strategic and applied issues that arise in particular agroecological environments.

The work of several of the research centers illustrates how food production and environmental goals can be incorporated into a single strategy. But each center is unique, just as each ecological site is unique, and so these illustrations are meant to be no more than that. These areas of emphasis illustrate the extent to which the foreign assistance community is beginning to develop long-term strategies.

Policy Studies. The International Food Policy Research Institute (IFPRI), by its mandate to cover food policies in general, has certain natural entry points in its research program where the issues of food production and environmental goals are of greatest importance. According to its director general Per Pinstrup-Andersen,

> Our interest is dictated by the growing international concern with protecting the environment and the recognition that, in the developing world, the issues of poverty, agricultural productivity, and depletion of natural resources are inseparable.[8]

At a policy level, the challenge is particularly acute; third world policymakers now need to face all three issues at the same time, rather than being able to address them sequentially.

IFPRI has done much pioneering work on household food security (subsistence), and it is a primary source of research on the household response to the challenge of sustainable agriculture. The future work at IFPRI will focus on three ecoregional zones: forest margins of the humid tropics, fragile rain-fed lands, and highly intensified irrigated areas. IFPRI has also begun to focus on urban nutrition. For household food security (commercial), the nature and predictability of urban food markets is of central concern. And without adequate connections between farmers and urban markets, the farmers who cannot generate enough income will migrate to the cities with predictably serious environmental consequences in urban areas where health and sanitation issues can become acute. IFPRI is beginning to explore these policy issues in an attempt to meet the needs of the very poor and the environment at the same time.

In its work on sustainable resource management, IFPRI looks at various strategies for "achieving sustainable increases in rural livelihood," among them:

- management of common property resources;
- protection of watersheds;
- preventing pollution of rivers and groundwater; and
- meeting local consumer needs for natural products, especially from the forests.[9]

Research on each of these areas will not be evenly distributed in developing countries because, as IFPRI points out, "many developing countries still have to demonstrate their openness to policy choices with a long-term bias toward better management of natural resources."[10] To some degree, researchers will be able to substitute the involvement of nongovernmental organizations (NGOs) and community groups for governments not interested in this work, but over the long term, the commitment of governments will be essential to take advantage of the research being launched. After all, nearly all research to date identifies land tenure and property rights as a central issue, and that cannot be resolved unless governments are willing to act.

Animal Agriculture. Sustainability potentially takes on a different complexion when livestock are added into the equation. Much anecdotal evidence about damage by livestock to the environment has been derived from the droughts of the African Sahel and the expansion of forage in the Amazon. Despite that reputation, livestock management in various developing countries shows a much more mixed record: the impact of such practices depends entirely on how they are managed. A recent benchmark review of livestock in Africa by Winrock International made it clear that stable agricultural systems that include livestock—whether traditional pastoralists in arid areas or more intensive forage systems in semiarid zones—show strongly positive relationships between livestock and natural resources management.[11] But if the environment is under various forms of stress, livestock can become yet another stress.

Nearly 20 percent of the resources of the CGIAR as a whole have recently gone into livestock research globally. Because livestock contribute some 25 to 30 percent of farm output in developing countries, the CGIAR may be, if anything, underinvesting in these research issues.[12] As the intensity of livestock management increases in response to population growth and public need for meat and milk, the natural resource constraints will grow. On the one hand, livestock competes with conservation needs (forests and wildlife) in humid and arid zones; on the other hand, intensification of livestock will have to deal with soil infertility, water scarcity, and easily overburdened ecosystems.[13] The CGIAR, through the International Livestock Center for Africa (Addis Ababa)

(ILCA), the International Laboratory for Research on Animal Diseases (Nairobi) (ILRAD), and other centers, thus has to wrestle with livestock issues in sustainable agriculture that range from the strategic scientific work of the latter to the applied farming systems of the former. Each has a place in any strategy for sustainable livestock practices.

The livestock centers, for instance, have been working jointly on the identification of native cattle breeds in Africa that are naturally resistant to trypanosomiasis. Through a process of isolating the relevant gene, and then crossbreeding the resistant cattle with more productive non-African breeds, it is expected that farmers will be able to support their agricultural needs with fewer cattle, even in areas infested by the tsetse fly. ILCA, in particular, has been working on the development of a breed of "multipurpose" cattle, able to meet all a farm's needs for traction, milk, manure, and meat. In that way, the burden on the plant environment would be reduced.

Plant Genetic Resources. The International Board for Plant Genetic Resources (IBPGR), and gene banks in many of the IARCs, testify to the importance of crop security in the work of the CGIAR. Just as the IBPGR was established in Rome in 1974 after the Stockholm Conference, so work on genetic resources is being strengthened by the results of the 1992 UNCED conference. The IBPGR is about to be recast as the International Plant Genetic Resources Institute.

The IBPGR's objectives have been clear and straightforward for the last two decades and were recently reaffirmed in the context of its medium-term plan for 1994–1998.[14] The top priority is the ability to assist developing countries in expanding capacity to both identify and conserve germ plasm, as well as to make it accessible to users. The second priority is to expand networks of conservers and users of plant genetic resources. Its other priorities are to develop new technologies, strategies, and information systems for those interested in this area. In terms of the biodiversity universe, the IBPGR has consistently focused on *ex situ* conservation, saved both for posterity and, to give it economic value, for current users.

The reputation of the centers was established through the application of selective plant breeding in the 1970s, when short-stem rice and wheat were developed. The resulting higher production led to the original "Green Revolution," particularly in Asia. That early work in plant breeding now pays off year after year as plant scientists develop varieties with resistance to pests and diseases (and thus reduce the need for chemicals), varieties able to grow in degraded soils (and thus allow worn-out land to be brought back into production), and varieties that continue to increase productivity of staple grains (and thus reduce the need to expand acreage). Today, the centers are witnessing the emergence of a "Greener Revolution," combining the needs of farmers with the agenda of the environmental community.

Water Resources. The mandate of the International Irrigation Management Institute (Sri Lanka) (IIMI) is at the center of a major environmental issue. The priority of water, and associated natural resources such as watershed management and soil erosion, was evident in the 1992 UNCED meeting. A special global meeting on water was held in Dublin in January 1992, prior to the Rio Summit, to ensure that the momentum of the UN water decade just completed was not lost and that the dual nature of water would be considered—as a factor in natural resources conservation and as an essential consumable for mankind.

IIMI was established well before Rio to deal with the spread of irrigated agriculture in Asia. It focused particularly on the management issues associated with irrigation, both at the national and the local level. In terms of the mandate of IIMI—"to foster the development, dissemination, and adoption of lasting improvements in the performance of irrigated agriculture in developing countries"—the institute is widely recognized as doing first-class work. The challenge is substantial, given that the productivity of irrigated agriculture needs to rise by as much as 3 percent each year,[15] yet irrigation is already the single largest user of water, accounting for about 80 percent of global water withdrawals. In effect, IIMI sees its mandate as both fostering food production and meeting environmental concerns about future water supplies. The impact of IIMI's work in both areas will be substantial.

In *Agenda 21*, UNCED argued that

a key strategic principle for holistic and environmentally sound management of water resources is that local communities must participate in the planning, investment and management of agricultural water use and water conservation.[16]

In one sense, UNCED was merely confirming reality. As a percentage of total irrigated area, farmer-managed irrigation already prevails in India (64 percent), the Philippines (63 percent), and Nepal (67 percent). Although many applaud this move to locally managed systems, and farmers have a much more direct interest than governments in the maintenance of their irrigation systems, IIMI also points out that such a trend does not relieve government of central responsibilities, especially with regard to equity and environmental sustainability.

Agroforestry. The International Center for Research on Agro-Forestry (ICRAF), founded in 1978 but not incorporated into the CGIAR until 1991, brings some extraordinary assets to the strategic research enterprise. The role of trees in farming systems is itself essential. Also important is the systematic approach taken by ICRAF to technology transfer. ICRAF has developed broad working relationships with national research systems and extension agencies, originally in Africa and now all over the world, and aggressively pushes to measure the extent to which national and local systems take ownership of technologies through training, planning, budget allocations, and local information.

In the area of natural resources, ICRAF has laid out a set of programs and issues of special concern to the environmental community:

- management of fragile semi-arid ecosystems, with a focus on reforestation of desert margins;
- integration of research on natural resource management in the East and Central African highlands; and
- organizing an international research program on slash-and-burn agriculture, and finding alternative land-use patterns.

The East African highlands are already showing considerable stress from a lack of fallow time, overburdened as they are by a growing population. ICRAF has taken the lead, with other centers, in developing inexpensive means of maintaining soil fertility, initially through nitrogen-fixing legumes such as leucaena, now through a variety of species. Working directly with farmers, its scientists are able to determine whether the various purposes of the program, both environmental and agricultural, can be met and ideas disseminated by local institutions, such as the Kenyan Agricultural Research Institute and the Ministry of Agriculture. If the ideas make sense for the local farmers, and developing country governments ensure their spread throughout the farming community, a new technology can be considered a success.

When Is Development Sustainable?

How will donors know when they are having an impact through their support of programs in sustainable development? Whatever the measures may be, they have to be scientifically verifiable, explained in nontechnical English, and transferrable to the developing country's specific environment. The tests of impact are thus simultaneously empirical, anecdotal, aesthetic, and systemic. In effect, it will no longer be sufficient for scientists investigating any given element of sustainable agriculture to evaluate their own performance—or even to be judged solely by their specialized peers. Instead, the future of sustainable agriculture will be ensured by the impact of individual projects and by assessment of the programs by the steadily expanding group of its constituencies.

Those engaged in sustainable agriculture tend to miss the effects on their own work of activity in other specialized fields. Both science and development are organized to evaluate on a specialized basis. It is far easier to know "microresults" than to measure the big picture.

Given the importance of site-specificity, all agree that the emergence of new capacity to measure impact at the national level is extremely important. Bottom-up information from farmers is crucial for better understanding the gains or losses from new technologies. But there is a natural reluctance to expand the scope of research too far. The World Bank argues that agricultural projects are inherently more difficult to evaluate than other sectors because agricultural development impinges on major social and environmental problems; institutionally, an enormous range of governmental agencies are involved along with NGOs; rural ministries tend to be the weakest in a government; and the outcomes from agricultural investments are unusually risky (both in terms of production and prices).[17] As the bank moved to incorporate issues related to agriculture into rural "area development" projects, their internal success rate dropped from about 50 percent unsatisfactory in 1974–1989 to about 65 percent unsatisfactory in 1989–1990. In effect, the larger the scope of the project, the greater the likelihood of failure—presumably due to uncontrollable factors.

Given the importance of understanding systemic feedbacks at the household and regional levels, most agree that it is important for social scientists to be involved in analyzing successes and failures. There are clearly reservations, however, about taking social science criteria too seriously. For instance, many resist using monetary household income as a proxy for well-being, because of the widespread focus in development on rural households, which consume most of what they produce within the family. Rural and urban incomes will never be comparable in that environment.[18] Some IARCs have developed close relationships between the crop scientists and social scientists, however, ensuring that the feedback from social science impact studies can be substantial.

Few agree on how to consider the impact of time on outcomes—even though time is an essential element of sustainability. An argument has been made that sustainability cannot be understood in a time frame of less than 25 to 30 years; at one level, that is not a contentious issue, because plant breeding always has a long-term payoff.[19] On the other hand, we cannot wait for 25 years to judge the impact of work on sustainable agriculture. That ambiguity is frustrating for economists, who wish to know the anticipated time period in order to calculate a discount rate for investments today. It is also frustrating for those making resource allocation decisions today whose forecasts may be evaluated on the basis of variables whose effect cannot be predicted now. The latter issue needs to be defused soon in order to reduce its paralyzing effect. A "no regrets" approach would dictate going ahead with initiatives that have the potential to achieve some progress, even if they do not meet the maximal demands of some constituencies. In the real world, after all, decisions on resource allocation and research plans can only be made on the basis of a given point in time, using current projections of population levels, food needs, and impact on the environment. If those variables change, iterative changes can be made in the research and application of approaches to sustainable agriculture. Technological breakthroughs, whether in agriculture or more likely in another field, will undoubtedly emerge over time as welcome solutions to current dilemmas.

If the agricultural community is going to include environmental issues among its concerns, the reverse ought to be true as well. Substantial benefits could develop if scientists who knew the agricultural implications of their work were included in research on biodiversity and natural resource systems. Just as the Institute for Biodiversity (InBio) has prospered in Costa Rica by having closer relations with pharmaceutical research institutes, so other biodiversity programs could gain from partnerships with IARCs and national research programs. The development of cross-constituencies is the fundamental point, and it has to be reciprocal. Important issues that need to be incorporated into research designs are equally neglected by both communities, such as population/demographic factors. The different effects of sedentary and migrant populations on natural resources are substantial. The research focus of the agricultural and environmental communities needs to be broadened to include those "externalities" through working relationships on systems issues, whether agricultural or environmental. In that way, there need be no dilution of specialized research goals (such as crop security), while the dynamic contributions of those now excluded, such as demographers and anthropologists, can still be captured.

Setting Priorities for Sustainable Agriculture

Defining a vision for the future of food production in an endangered natural environment is only the first step. And the second step cannot be simply to go ahead with development programs without some plan for measuring achievements along the path toward sustainable development. Developed at the design stage, such evaluation tools, based on research from both agricultural and environmental scientists, will not only provide for more focused application of limited foreign aid resources, but also help developing countries to correct their course along the way.

Only in rare, highly focused cases does the world of development need new institutions for these tasks. If anything, there is a great risk of fracturing the current effort even more by the creation of new international bodies. Instead, the principal effort needs to be applied to modifying and expanding the mandates of existing institutions. This article has highlighted the shift and potential further expansion of the role of the CGIAR in the field of agriculture. Similar analysis could be done for local, national, and international institutions throughout the field.

The need for integration in the field of sustainable development is so imperative, combined with the current restrictions on funds for foreign assistance, that narrowly specialized institutions are likely to see their support shrink. Their contribution will still be essential, given the way the scientific task is defined, but their share of the overall pie will have to yield first place to the growing networking of programs and institutions in support of bringing "sustainability" to reality.

No single country will provide the leadership for this endeavor, even though the United States has provided much of the scientific and conceptual effort in the past. The role of multilaterals in defining the future course will be essential, whether the World Bank, the UN Development Program, the UN's Food and Agriculture Organization, the UN Environmental Program, or the regional banks. The developing countries themselves have pressed the case for integrating the effort hard, so that the values of development and conservation can be made compatible. And ultimately, sustainable agriculture will make sense only if the farmers of the Third World practice it.

The natural resource wars have produced no winners so far. Unless they get together to work jointly on a Greener Revolution, there will only be losers. The first need is for long-term investments in this new revolution. There are no instant solutions, and research must begin now if we are to improve people's lives in the twenty-first century. The scale of resources needed to invest in the Greener Revolution is likely to be much higher than the original revolution, if only because there are many more variables to consider. Finally, no solutions to the Greener Revolution will be implemented—however elegant they may be scientifically—without the world's farmers. The farmers are those who deal with the earth every day; how and where they do so will determine the success of sustainable development.

The author gratefully acknowledges the support of the United Nations Development Program in the preparation of this article.

Notes

1. Robert Repetto et al., *Wasting Assets: Natural Resources in the National Incomes Accounts* (Washington, D.C.: World Resources Institute, 1989).

2. U.S. Department of Energy and U.S. Agency for International Development, *National Energy Strategy 1992. Analysis of Options to Increase Exports of U.S. Energy Technology* (Washington, D.C.: GPO, 1992).

3. Walter V. Reid et al., *Biodiversity Prospecting: Using Genetic Resources for Sustainable Development* (Washington, D.C.: World Resources Institute, 1993).

4. Jeffrey A. McNeely, *Economics and Biological Diversity: Developing and Using Economic Incentives to Conserve Biological Diversity* (Gland, Switzerland: International Union

for Conservation of Nature and Natural Resources, 1988).

5. Eldad M. Tukahirwa, *Uganda: Environmental and Natural Resource Management Policy and Law. Issues and Options* (Kampala: Makerere University Institute of Environment and Natural Resources, 1992), p. 3.

6. John K. Lynam and Robert W. Herdt, "Sense and Sustainability: Sustainability as an Objective in International Agricultural Research," *Agricultural Economics* 3 (1989), pp. 381–398.

7. CGIAR, "Chairman's Opening Remarks" (CGIAR Mid-Term Meeting, San Juan, May 24, 1993), p. 5.

8. Per Pinstrup-Andersen, "Presentation of IFPRI's Medium-Term Plan" (Paper presented at the CGIAR Mid-Term Meeting, San Juan, May 28, 1993), p. 3.

9. IFPRI, "Research Program 1994–1998: Environment and Production Technology Division" (Washington, D.C., February 1993), p. 1.

10. IFPRI, "Medium-Term Plan for 1994–1998" (Washington, D.C., February 1993), p. 8.

11. Winrock International, *Assessment of Animal Agriculture in Sub-Saharan Africa* (Morrilton, Ark., 1992), pp. 17–18.

12. See CGIAR, "Progress Report by the Livestock Strategy Working Group," Document AGR/TAC:IAR/93/6/Rev. 1 (Presented at the CGIAR Mid-Term Meeting, San Juan, May 1993).

13. See Winrock International, *Assessment of Animal Agriculture*, pp. 29–31.

14. International Plant Genetic Resources Institute, "Medium-Term Programme and Budget Proposals (1994–1998)" (Rome, February 17, 1993), pp. 5–6.

15. IIMI, "Medium-Term Plan, 1994–1998: Draft" (Colombo, October 1992), p. 1.

16. Quoted in *ibid.*, p. 25.

17. International Bank for Reconstruction and Development, Agriculture and Rural Development Department, *Agricultural Sector Review Paper* (Washington, D.C., 1992), p. 30.

18. David R. Lee, Steven Kearl, and Norman Uphoff, eds., *Assessing the Impact of International Agricultural Research for Sustainable Development: Proceedings from a Symposium at Cornell University, June 16–19, 1991* (Ithaca, N.Y.: Cornell International Institute for Food, Agriculture, and Development, 1992), p. 13.

19. *Ibid.*

Trade Battles as Investment Wars: The Coming Rules of Origin Debate

Jeri Jensen-Moran

AS STATES STRENGTHEN their economic ties on a regional basis—toward a greater Europe, the Asia–Pacific Economic Cooperation (APEC) forum, and now a Free Trade Area of the Americas (FTAA)—there is broad appreciation of the benefits—increased trade, enhanced investment, and stronger economies.[1] With no global trade agreement successor to the Uruguay Round in sight, U.S. policymakers and industry groups have shifted their attention away from globalism to the regional economies, with the natural expectation that these arrangements will increase economic welfare and global living standards.

As yet, however, little scrutiny has been given to one problematic side effect: the danger that just as nations negotiate free trade agreements in key regions throughout the world, they may erect a series of regional trade barriers that become a source of "new protection," preventing products from moving freely between regions and subverting the broad vision of global trade liberalization.

The risk arises from the rules of origin negotiated to implement these liberalizing agreements—the rules necessary to implement bilateral or regional trade agreements and ensure that other countries cannot take advantage of the tariff reductions negotiated among the partners. They are also the rules customs officials use every day for all trade to determine where a product comes from in order to assess tariff treatment.

Rather than the straightforward, technical tools they were meant to be, rules of origin in key economic sectors can instead operate as industrial policy, compelling producers that want to take advantage of liberalized regional trade to invest directly in the region in order to meet high domestic content requirements. In effect, rules of origin become vehicles of forced investment, facing companies located outside the free trade area with a stark choice: invest in production facilities within the region, or don't trade with it at all. The resulting investment provides high-

---

Jeri Jensen-Moran wrote this article while serving as director for Inter-American Economic Affairs at the National Security Council under the auspices of a Council on Foreign Relations International Affairs Fellowship. She is currently director of the Trade Promotion Coordinating Committee (TPCC) Secretariat in the U.S. Department of Commerce.

Copyright © 1995 by The Center for Strategic and International Studies and the Massachusetts Institute of Technology
The Washington Quarterly • 19:1

wage jobs and technology to the locality, but it also distorts trade and investment patterns and undermines the long-term competitiveness of the companies and countries involved.

As a consequence, trade battles are becoming investment wars as governments recognize they must attract capital, desirable industries and high-skilled jobs in order to succeed in the global economy. As regional arrangements proliferate,[2] rules of origin have been looked to increasingly as a means to force investment in economic sectors perceived as critical, sensitive, or at least politically powerful. And, in contrast to the win-win outcome the United States traditionally associates with trade negotiations and enhanced trade ties, the fight for premier investments takes on a zero-sum quality in the competition for scarce capital.

These investment wars promise to raise the stakes—and the significance—of the next round of global trade negotiations and competition for world market share. Already the European Community (EC) (after February 1992 the European Union) has used origin rules as instruments of commercial policy in its Single Market as a way to force investment and protect critical high-tech industries. The United States followed in the North American Free Trade Agreement (NAFTA), using rules of origin not only to prevent the use of Mexico as an export platform into the U.S. market by Japan and other countries, but also to stimulate investment and encourage sourcing from the NAFTA partners.[3]

Now the global trade system has reached a crossroads. Its member states will soon begin three negotiations that will determine the role of rules of origin in the future and, consequently, what the contours of the global economy will be for U.S. companies. The three negotiations will aim to create a Free Trade Area of the Americas by 2005 and an APEC free trade area by 2020, and to begin the harmonization of all nonpreferential rules of origin three years after the completion of the Uruguay Round. Although issues surrounding APEC are less pressing because negotiations are several years off, negotiations in the Western Hemisphere and the World Trade Organization (WTO) are just over the horizon.

As Washington enters these negotiations, U.S. government and corporate leaders face a number of wrenching decisions.

- Do U.S. political leaders want their industries to produce the most competitive exports in the world, sourcing from the most economic locations with simple, transparent origin rules? Or do they want to ensure that domestic or regional businesses are the first to benefit from the increased trade from the agreement?
- Do U.S. industries want to source worldwide and pursue a flexible and global corporate strategy with unlimited access to other regional markets and as little administrative burden as possible? Or do they want their investments protected and their local or regional preferences maintained?
- Does the United States want to accumulate capital and high-skilled jobs at home through regional arrangements? Or will it conclude that regional arrangements are not the place for beggar-thy-neighbor investment policies that discriminate against foreign firms that merely export into the region?

How these issues are resolved in these upcoming negotiations—both within the United States and internationally—could permanently define the economic landscape for corporate strategy and ultimately trade and investment flows for the twenty-first century.

This essay examines these questions by offering brief examples of the effect of rules of origin in current regional trade agreements to demonstrate the powerful effect these rules can have. The essay then considers the most fundamental question of all: What role should rules of origin play in future U.S. trade policy?

The European Community

The EC was the pioneer of using rules of origin as a trade policy tool to encourage EC content, EC sourcing, and hence investment in EC manufacturing facilities throughout the creation of the Single Market in 1989–92. Unlike the case of NAFTA, where encouraging investment was an important, but not always primary, objective in the design of origin rules, EC practices were directly tied to an industrial strategy to define acceptable forms of direct investment, create desired types of jobs, and transfer desired kinds of technology.

Semiconductors

The case of semiconductors in the EC is the premier example of a regional forced-investment strategy. After several years of allowing semiconductors assembled in the EC to be considered of EC origin, and therefore not subject to the high 14 percent semiconductor tariff, the rule was suddenly changed in 1989 with little warning. Now the process of diffusion, or wafer fabrication, had to be performed in the EC for integrated circuits to be considered of local origin. In other words, foreign producers had to make an investment of at least $300 million in order to remain competitive in the EC market, versus an investment in an assembly and testing facility of $50 million.

After the origin rule was announced in 1989, investment in semiconductor manufacturing facilities in the EC dramatically increased, even though at the time investment in Europe was not cost-competitive relative to Asia or the United States. In 1987, Dataquest recorded 102 semiconductor fabrication facilities in Europe; by 1990 the number had increased to 124, an increase of more than 20 percent. U.S. fabrication facilities have now moved to Europe. U.S. companies (both merchant and captive) have approximately 40 fabrication facilities in Europe, while European companies have approximately 30. Of the top 10 U.S. companies, 7 currently have fabrication facilities in the EC. There were, of course, other good reasons for U.S. semiconductor companies to locate facilities in the EC, but at the time of the EC origin decision, the U.S. industry performed most of its diffusion operations in the United States. Thus the effect of the origin rule change was to shift, and in some cases divert, investment and jobs out of other countries, including the United States.

The reaction of Intel is the best example of the effects of forced investment policies on U.S. jobs and research and development (R&D). Intel was one of the few U.S. semiconductor producers that traditionally exported to rather than invested in Europe, although Europe represented nearly a quarter of its $2.9 billion annual sales. After the EC semiconductor origin decision, Intel decided to expand its computer systems business in Ireland (a $400 million computer complex including a wafer fabrication facility, an assembly and test center, and an investment of several million dollars for employee training and R&D). Intel tied its decision to invest in Ireland directly to the European origin decision, stating it had already lost "hundreds of thousands of dollars" in sales to Japanese manufacturers who no longer felt comfortable using Intel chips in electronic goods bound for Europe. This was because "European governments tend to favor local content and automotive and telecommunications companies balk at purchasing foreign-made technology products."

Automobiles

Automobiles provide an example of EC use of origin rules in combination with other restrictive policies—in this case voluntary restraint agreements—to limit market access and encourage investment.

Technically, the EC does not have a special rule of origin for automobiles. According to U.S. industry sources, however, EC application of the rule has not always been straightforward. Sometimes the EC has applied the equivalent of a value-added requirement as high as 75 percent in the case of Japanese companies, although there is no written rule to this effect.

Proposals have been made in the past for the EC to adopt a written rule of origin based on a value-added determination. Some European car company and trade association proposals reached as high as 80 percent. Indeed, the United Kingdom and France almost reached agreement on an 80 percent local content rule in the case of the Nissan Bluebird. The Italians pushed for a 60 percent rule, citing previous U.S. proposals to increase origin requirements from 50 to 60 percent under the U.S.–Canada Free Trade Agreement (FTA) as precedent. The United States argued these proposals would adversely affect the $1 billion U.S. automobile parts export industry.

The U.S. Big Three automobile companies are heavily invested in the EC (General Motors [GM] and Ford have above 90 percent content in Europe already). It is therefore unlikely that any high origin requirement imposed now or proposed in the WTO by the EC would adversely affect any major U.S. automobile producer; still, in terms of jobs and the location of new industrial activity, a high domestic content rule would have a significant effect at the margin. And it could affect U.S. exports of U.S.–manufactured vehicles containing Japanese content and vehicles produced at U.S. subsidiaries of Japanese automobile companies. U.S.–manufactured Hondas and Geo Prizms, for example, would find it difficult to make a 75 percent origin requirement because they only use about 40 percent U.S. content. They would therefore be considered Japanese vehicles by the EC, subject to EC quantitative restrictions that will be in effect through 1999.

The Legacy from NAFTA

In NAFTA, the United States used rules of origin for at least two purposes—discouraging free riders to the agreement and encouraging investment in certain sectors in the NAFTA partners. A third purpose—to protect the relative position of U.S. suppliers of components—was also paramount. In automobiles, electronics products (printers, copiers, television tubes), textiles, telecommunications, machine tools, forklift trucks, fabricated metals, household appliances, furniture, tobacco products, and other sectors, NAFTA rules of origin required that a substantial portion of these products' inputs originate in the NAFTA countries.[4] In some cases, other countries have complained that these rules raised levels of protection above pre-NAFTA levels.

Telecommunications

The telecommunications rule accomplished several goals for the industry: it was easier to administer than under the U.S.–Canada FTA, and was both more flexible *and* more restrictive. The rule requires that in order to be considered a NAFTA product, the essential component of office switching equipment—printed circuit board assemblies (PCAs)—be packaged in North America. But the rule allows 1 of every 10 PCAs to be stuffed outside the NAFTA partners, to allow some flexibility.

The industry believes the rule is accomplishing its goal of discouraging Japan and other countries from investing in assembly operations in Mexico for export to the U.S. market. Moreover, AT&T has shifted some production from Asia to Mexico, and concurrently increased its high-end investment in the United States with an eye toward increasing sales to the Mexican market. In order to export to the United States and to become a more competitive supplier of the newly privatized Telmex, competitors Ericsson and Fujitsu will have to increase their existing investment in Mexico significantly.[5]

Color Televisions

The NAFTA rule for color televisions—the largest consumer electronics sector in Mexico—was similar in concept to that of computers, in that it required the major component of televisions (the television tubes) to be of North American origin in order for the sets to be considered North American. The notion behind the NAFTA rule was to rationalize North American production by attracting television tube production—the source of the highest-paid jobs in the industry—in North America, while allowing assembly elsewhere.

The industry has found the rule to be enormously effective in generating tube exports and attracting investment in tube manufacture. Before NAFTA there was no North American manufacture of projection television tubes. In the two years since NAFTA was signed, five factories have been planned or established in North America. U.S. exports of tubes have increased 50 percent, primarily to Mexico but also, surprisingly, to Asia.

By creating a premium on North American tube manufacture, NAFTA has encouraged Hitachi, Mitsubishi, Zenith, Sony, and Samsung to expand or begin tube production in North America. The rules have also helped in reducing the ability of Japan to circumvent existing antidumping provisions.

Computers and Flat Panel Displays

The history behind the computer rule presents a good example of the dilemma negotiators confront when rules of origin are used as a policy tool: how to balance the competing interests of promoting domestic production of critical technologies with allowing U.S. companies to source competitively.

U.S. negotiators originally proposed a rule designed to create a flat panel display industry by encouraging the production of computer components by tightening the U.S.–Canada FTA rule for computers. The rule would have required two of three key components (motherboard, flat panel display, and hard disc drive) to be North American for a computer to qualify for NAFTA preferences. At the time, there was almost no North American production of the product.

197

U.S. negotiators, driven by a belief that Congress would not support a NAFTA that did not encourage at least 60 percent of computer parts to be sourced in North America, pushed the proposal. And yet, ironically, industry trade associations led by IBM were adamantly opposed. Although computer makers would have had the option of sourcing the other two components from North America, this would have been difficult, and sometimes impossible for U.S. producers. The rule would have been the equivalent of at least 60 percent value content, and would have forced IBM to completely alter its North American operations, which account for almost half of its sales.

After a contentious battle between industry and government representatives, U.S. negotiators backed down. Instead, as part of a package deal that would tighten origin rules for printers, color televisions, fax machines, photocopiers, and line telecom equipment, U.S. negotiators proposed a rule that would require only the motherboard to be North American for the next 10 years. In January 2004, the rule disappears when a common external tariff of 3.9 percent on computers goes into effect.

This rule, with provision for a common external tariff that will eventually eliminate the need for a rule of origin altogether, has been considered extremely successful by the industry. It has become a prototype for future free trade agreements for other sectors. IBM, for example, is so pleased with the NAFTA rule that it is proposing a broader version of it to be applied on a worldwide basis.

Automobiles

The automobile sector was one of the most visible examples in NAFTA of restrictive origin rules. The articulated purpose behind the high rule for automobiles was to limit the use of the agreement by Japan to export into the U.S. market; increasing jobs and investment was rarely discussed as a factor.

Yet the rule was clearly designed to increase investment in the automobile sector and has been successful in doing so.[6] The industry sought a high rule because the three Japanese car manufacturers with assembly plants in Canada—Honda, Toyota, and Suzuki, which export 80 percent of their output to the United States—made it clear they had the means to meet a 60 percent value-content requirement under the U.S.–Canada FTA. A higher threshold would have forced the Japanese producers to move their transplants to the United States, where the parts industry is far larger than in Canada or Mexico. Canada, predictably, was adamant that the 50 percent value-content requirement should be maintained.

The U.S. opening position in the negotiations was 65 percent.[7] In the final days of the negotiations, Canada and Mexico agreed to 62.5 percent under a revised formula, along with an agreement that the new formula would be applied retroactively to Honda exports from Canada in order to resolve a dispute over back duties allegedly owed the U.S. Treasury because Honda was not meeting the rule of origin under the U.S.–Canada FTA.

From the point of view of the Big Three, the rule has been successful: not only has Japan been prevented from exporting to the U.S. market from Mexico, but investment in North American production of vehicles and parts has increased. All Japanese companies producing in North America have made known their plan to comply with the more stringent 62.5 percent rule so they can trade freely within North America. Automobile factories in the NAFTA partners have relied more on "domestic" components and less on imports from Japan, and multinationals with operations in both Europe and North America have shifted European production to North America.

Policy Implications: The Future of Rules of Origin

An analysis of the most notable cases where origin rules have been used for trade policy ends gives rise to a number of observations, all supporting one fundamental conclusion: the United States should abandon its reliance on rules of origin as a long-term trade strategy.

1. Origin rules can be effective in attracting foreign investment and protecting national companies.

In the case of the EC, U.S. and other foreign direct investment in semiconductor manufacturing facilities went up dramatically after origin requirements were changed, even though investment in Europe was not cost-competitive relative to Asia or the United States. Sourcing decisions of U.S. and other foreign firms were affected by the EC's ad hoc origin determinations on printed circuit board assemblies, and the uncertainty generated from EC proposals for restrictive rules on automobiles inspired U.S. companies to modify their strategies.

These practices will become increasingly relevant as the EC continues this strategy in its association agreements with the Central Europeans.[8] And we have already seen in the opening skirmishes in WTO negotiations that the EC intends to attempt to multilateralize many of its restrictive rules in the upcoming Uruguay Round harmonization exercise.[9]

After almost two years of operation of NAFTA, it is evident that in those sectors where restrictive rules were negotiated, the rules were effective not only in preventing other countries from benefiting from tariff preferences, but also in encouraging both U.S. and foreign producers to alter their corporate strategies and move (often high-end) investment to the NAFTA partners. This was true at least in the cases of telecom equipment, color televisions, printers and copiers, machine tools, automobiles and textiles.

2. Negotiating regional agreements in which industrial policies are embedded creates "investment wars" that, unlike the original trade-creating agreements, are not a win/win situation and distort trade and investment flows.

Not only do jobs and investment shift to possibly uneconomic locales, one region's desire to force investment can hurt another region's desire to increase exports. To the extent that governments rely on rules of origin to accomplish trade policy goals, companies have an additional calculus in their analysis of whether to expand their investment at home and increase exports, or instead focus production abroad to increase their certainty of access to key markets.

These practices of drawing high-skill, high-wage activities away from other countries through rules of origin have a particularly adverse effect on the United States, whose exports are concentrated in high-technology products. If, for example, the EC had not changed its rule of origin to require diffusion, would Intel have instead expanded its facilities in the United States and continued to serve its market in Europe through exports? What are the effects of these practices on small exporters—whose only option may be to export—or on companies, like Hewlett-Packard, that still rely on exports for more than half their sales? Does regionalism mean that corporate strategies that emphasize exports will become a thing of the past, and that companies must invest within their target regions, rather than merely export to them, in order to be assured market access?

3. *The negotiation of the NAFTA rules of origin demonstrates a policy contradiction: the interests of exporters (who want neutral origin rules that allow them to source the lowest-cost components) are pitted against companies wanting a guaranteed market for their product.*

In NAFTA, the difficulty of negotiating rules of origin that pleased all industries was clear. There was a stark trade-off between creating an incentive to source from North American partners (as was called for by the printed circuit board industry, the original U.S. computer proposal, and the cases of textiles and automobiles) and allowing multinationals to source globally, from the most economic and efficient source (telecom, computers, textile exporters).

4. *As long as trade negotiators are left to broker this contradiction, the trade and investment contours that result from the agreements will reflect the most politically powerful industries, rather than the most strategic or competitive.*

NAFTA clearly demonstrated how rules of origin can become a "viper's nest for special interests,"[10] in the context of regional agreements. Even if there were an accepted method to determine which industries should be favored for strategic economic purposes, trade negotiators would still have to respond to the political constituencies necessary to get the agreement through Congress. That is why the rules of origin under NAFTA were drawn to favor IBM and AT&T at the expense of the less savvy printed circuit board industry (where job potential was demonstrated), in favor of textiles at the expense of the importers and retailers, and in favor of the Big Three automobile producers at the expense of Japanese transplants in the United States. Xerox and Zenith succeeded in obtaining special rules that favored their existing corporate strategy as opposed to less politically astute domestic producers in other industries.

It may be that the agreement did in fact succeed in encouraging the most jobs and attracting the most important technology. If it did, however, the outcome was largely a coincidence.

5. *The conflict for negotiators—should they negotiate rules that stimulate exports by allowing firms to obtain low-cost components, or should they negotiate rules that encourage investment and U.S. sourcing—will heighten in future negotiations in which U.S. industry has more at stake and producer interests are less compatible.*

This tension will not be fully apparent in negotiations over Chile's accession to NAFTA. The Chilean market is one-hundredth the size of the U.S. market, with a high degree of complementarity between U.S. and Chilean industries. It is therefore unlikely that significant rule of origin changes will be necessary to cope with the dynamics of this new partner. Although it is possible (although improbable) that Chile would make a pitch to strengthen origin rules to attract investment in high-tech sectors, it is more likely it will find existing NAFTA rules sufficient, or in some cases too restrictive.

The real reckoning will come when the NAFTA partners look to add countries with larger markets, with industries more competitive with U.S. products (such as in Argentina or Brazil) and with more complicated and polarized industry interests (such as the

Caribbean Basin countries). For example, the automobile industry has already hinted it will want a rule even higher than 62.5 percent when negotiations begin with Mercosur, because the Brazilian market is much bigger and, unlike Chile, a competitive supplier of automobile parts. The Big Three will find allies in business interests in Brazil, which are likely to call for rules that encourage high levels of local production.

The lesson from NAFTA should be that balancing competing economic interests in fashioning regional rules of origin is hard to do and will become increasingly difficult in future integration efforts. As was the case in printed circuit boards and flat panel displays, it was not an easy call to determine where the line should be drawn for components that must be sourced within North America and components that can be sourced globally. In future negotiations, the policy contradictions experienced in NAFTA will be raised to a fever pitch, and trade negotiators will carry the heavy burden of attempting their resolution.

6. NAFTA rules of origin should not be applied throughout the hemisphere in a Free Trade Area of the Americas.

All three NAFTA partners have taken the position that NAFTA origin rules should not be altered to accommodate Chile. In the short run, this position is unlikely to change as we look toward the FTAA. From a U.S. perspective, any signal that the United States would contemplate changes to the agreement risks tipping a delicate balance of concessions among the NAFTA partners, provoking constituencies and Congress to pursue their own agendas, and complicating U.S. efforts to maintain NAFTA's high standards in other areas and its broad scope.

But from an economic perspective, extending NAFTA origin rules throughout the hemisphere will contribute to the trade bloc nature of the agreement and be extremely distortive. Not only would there be an administrative nightmare for companies and the U.S. Customs Service, but each country added to the agreement would have to source most of the components of its cars, textiles, machine tools, and electronics from the NAFTA countries, even though cheaper or better components are available in other, geographically closer countries.

7. Each new set of rules of origin has a domino effect on the next negotiation, as each region tries to outdo the last in establishing high sourcing requirements.

We saw this when NAFTA went one step beyond the EC, broadening the swath of industries considered "critical" to include a hodgepodge of electronics and other products. It is likely that EC positions in the WTO harmonization negotiations will be influenced by some NAFTA rules; in any case some of the most restrictive NAFTA rules in the electronics sector are being discussed as possible U.S. proposals in the WTO negotiations. Maintaining NAFTA rules in future integration efforts could give credibility to those in other regions (such as the countries of the Association of Southeast Asian Nations, where restrictive origin rules still apply) to attempt to preserve and possibly extend these rules multilaterally.

8. From both a policy and industry perspective, the best approach may be to move toward a customs union in various sectors in the negotiations with Chile.

Just as states within the same country trade freely, countries within a customs union no longer require rules of origin, because all apply the same tariff to products outside the union. Negotiating a common external tariff in some product sectors in the Chile talks will facilitate movement away from rules of origin and help dislodge rather than strengthen the various vested interests that will push hard to tighten the agreement as it expands.[11]

The EC has reached this conclusion and will move toward a common external tariff for 15 countries. APEC has supported a work program that looks toward a customs union for preferential rules. Policymakers may not recognize the inconsistency if the United States were to propose the extension (or strengthening) of NAFTA rules in the Western Hemisphere while supporting the notion of moving toward a customs union in the APEC context.

9. The U.S. objective in the negotiations under the WTO is to harmonize multilateral rules that meet overall U.S. economic interests, especially in critical high-tech sectors. This means neutral rules that do not encourage investment in one industry sector at the expense of the competitiveness of another.

EC positions in the negotiations are expected to be at odds with U.S. interests. Negotiators for the Uruguay Round harmonization exercise should not be captured by the temptation to outdo the EC in developing proposals in the high-tech area and adopt positions that mimic past EC practices. Such a course could backfire by creating industry constituencies to harmonize global rules at more restrictive and less transparent levels, hardening industry positions and making it more difficult to develop neutral multilateral rules.

Conclusion

Regional agreements, particularly NAFTA, are likely to define the future trade and investment parameters for U.S. business in the hemisphere and possibly elsewhere in the coming decade. These agreements will indeed move the United States forward—and in fact take it further toward liberalization in many key areas (intellectual property, investment, services, and market access) than it would otherwise go in a multilateral negotiation (if there were one) in the near term.

Unless, however, policymakers deal squarely with the policy contradictions embedded in NAFTA as they look to it as a model for future trade agreements, the United States may discover at the end of the day that it is still some distance from its goal of freer trade and investment. Such contradictions will inevitably emerge as the rules of origin necessary to implement these agreements are negotiated.

Using origin rules to accomplish trade policy purposes brings into stark conflict two economic priorities—attracting capital and high-skilled jobs via forced investment, or attracting capital and high-skilled jobs via providing an economic environment that allows companies to trade and invest freely. It presents a similar dilemma for companies that want both the flexibility to source globally to produce competitive exports and the guaranteed market share regional agreements can provide.

As countries are added to NAFTA and the Uruguay Round harmonization exercise advances, these contradictions will become even more difficult to finesse, industry views on appropriate rules will be even more polarized, and the challenge of avoiding harm to the competitiveness of U.S. companies even more formidable for U.S. negotiators. Consequently, policymakers should not be confident they can replicate the NAFTA success throughout the hemisphere in the case of rules of origin, and should look instead toward a course that will help move them out of the business of industrial policy. If the United States steps away from its reliance on these tools, it would be in the long-term interest of its own industries and could serve as a useful example to other regions in the multilateral arena.

Both industry and policymakers should think first of more sustainable means of encouraging investment and domestic sourcing. The incentive to invest in partner countries to a regional arrangement should come from the economic advantages of the agreement itself—lower trade barriers, harmonization of standards and customs procedures, and other features, rather than the requirement that products be sourced largely from the partner countries. In the long run, rules of origin will in any case become a less powerful and relevant tool as tariffs fall and burdens on compliance and sourcing patterns multiply.

Ultimately, the best investment, technology, and jobs will flow to countries that offer the best manufacturing environment, including education, training, productivity, and growing markets. Otherwise, trade wars will become investment wars, where rules of origin are manipulated to divert trade and investment in suboptimal ways, producing a domino effect as each region tries to outdo the others in establishing high sourcing requirements. Such a course could also contribute to the difficulty of negotiating neutral origin rules in the Uruguay Round, where the fate of the most competitive U.S. industries in the next century will be at stake.

The views expressed here are solely those of the author and do not represent the views of the Council on Foreign Relations or any agency of the U.S. government.

Notes

1. See J. Frankel et al., "Continental Trading Blocs: Are They Natural or Super-Natural?" Paper no. 4588 (National Bureau of Economic Research, Cambridge, Mass., May 1994). Also Paul Krugman, "Is Bilateralism Bad?" in E. Helpman and A. Razin, eds., *International Trade and Trade Policy* (Cambridge, Mass.: MIT Press, 1991) and "The Move Toward Free Trade Zones" (paper prepared for a symposium on "Policy Implications of Trade and Currency Zones" sponsored by the Federal Reserve Bank of Kansas City, Jackson Hole, Wyoming, June 1991).

2. The next round of agreements will cover about half of world trade. The FTAA and APEC alone cover 48 countries—almost 50 percent of the world's gross domestic product (GDP) and roughly 40 percent of its population. When the European Union is added, regional agreements will cover 53 countries, 70 percent of the world's GDP, and 47 percent of its population.

3. There is an important distinction between the use of rules of origin as a trade policy tool by the EU and NAFTA. The NAFTA partners used *preferential* origin rules to stimulate investment and jobs, while the EU relied on *nonpreferential* rules. Preferential rules are those rules that apply to parties to a regional agreement, while nonpreferential rules apply to non-participating countries. Although it is expected that members of a preferential arrangement will use origin rules to protect tariff benefits, it is now (post Uruguay Round) illegal under the General Agreement on Tariffs and Trade (GATT) for countries or regions to use nonpreferential rules for commercial purposes.

4. For example, auto imports must meet a 62.5 percent rule to receive NAFTA benefits now; under the U.S.–Canada FTA, autos could be imported duty-free if they contained at least 50 percent Canadian–U.S. inputs.

5. Canada and Mexico ranked as the first and second largest export markets for U.S. telecommunications equipment in 1992, collectively representing more than a quarter of U.S. telecommunications exports.

6. A rule demanding NAFTA production of more than two-thirds of the product's cost forces investment in production of the vehicle's power train (engine and transmission, estimated at about 35 to 40 percent) or, if the power train is not produced in North America, manufacturers have to

source almost all other parts from the NAFTA partners.

7. Two of the Big Three auto companies sought a 75 percent origin rule in NAFTA; GM, however, resisted and consensus was eventually reached to seek 70 percent, but to agree to no less than 65 percent.

8. The EU has also negotiated relatively restrictive preferential origin rules with its association partners in Central and Eastern Europe. Generally the rules require at least 40 percent value-added, and sometimes as much as 60 percent in critical sectors, in order to be considered as originating in the EU. If, as expected, these origin rules are established throughout the region, some U.S. companies will find it difficult to maintain market access without changing their sourcing patterns.

9. The United States succeeded in limiting many of the EC practices described above in a multilateral agreement in the Uruguay Round that provides discipline over the use of nonpreferential rules of origin as a policy tool. The agreement established principles and procedures to guide GATT contracting parties in formulating origin rules, such as nondiscrimination, transparency, and predictability. It also established a three-year work program to harmonize nonpreferential origin rules among GATT countries.

10. Gary Hufbauer, "Comment" on Paul Wonnacott, "Beyond NAFTA: The Design of a Free-Trade Agreement of the Americas" (paper presented at a conference on "Capital Flows and Regionalism," Center for International Economics, University of Maryland and American Enterprise Institute, Washington, D.C., June 12–13, 1995). Indeed, if you look at the number of pages of exceptions to origin rules in the U.S.–Canada FTA and NAFTA you can quantify (in terms of inches) the increasing perfection of special interest lobbying in these agreements.

11. Some have suggested sectoral customs unions as a long-term solution to the hemispheric problem, which avoids the disadvantages of customs unions (such as the tendency for barriers to stick at high levels). See Wonnacott, "Beyond NAFTA," and Hufbauer, "Comment."

IV. The New Regional Dimension

Engineering Regional Trade Pacts to Keep Trade and U.S. Prosperity on a Fast Track

Paula Stern and Raymond Paretzky

AT THE END of World War II, the United States as victor chose to incorporate its adversaries into a global economy that made the whole world better and stronger. The victory that the nation won in World War II and in the Cold War that followed must now be followed by still a third victory: the development of new long-term strategies for the post–cold war international economy. The choice in this new era of global economic cooperation and healthy global economic competition is not whether to trade or not to trade; the question is how to trade. The United States now has an opportunity to demonstrate its leadership once again, by leading the effort at the negotiating table to build a world trade structure.

Ironically, the trade strategy that is least appreciated—but that is most appealing—is to build on the successes of the North American Free Trade Agreement (NAFTA) and expand on these successes to include other countries. Although important aspects of NAFTA have been obscured lately by the hyperbole of both proponents and critics, the NAFTA template has many positive and helpful features that can be applied universally. These include high economic and legal standards; broad coverage of areas of great importance to the United States such as intellectual property rights, investment, services, labor, and the environment; enforcement rules with teeth; and open accession. These features can be extended beyond the Americas to enrich relations with U.S. trading partners worldwide and to reinforce and deepen the multilateral World Trade Organization (WTO).

A Trade Architecture for the Twenty-First Century: Alternative Trade Policy Approaches

A variety of alternative strategies will be available to the United States in the

---

Paula Stern, president of The Stern Group, Inc., an international trade advisory firm, and senior fellow of the Progressive Policy Institute, is a former chairwoman of the U.S. International Trade Commission and a member of the President's Advisory Committee on Trade Policy and Negotiations (ACTPN). Raymond Paretzky practices international trade law as an associate at Kaye, Scholer, Fierman, Hays & Handler in Washington, D.C.

Copyright © 1995 by The Center for Strategic and International Studies and the Massachusetts Institute of Technology

coming years. Each has advantages, but each has fatal limitations.

One approach would be to pursue exclusively multilateral trade negotiations, such as the recent Uruguay Round, which led to the establishment of the WTO, the successor to the General Agreement on Tariffs and Trade (GATT). A new multilateral trade round is not imminent, however: the world seems exhausted from the last seven-year negotiation process, and the job of getting the WTO up and running and completing the financial and telecommunications services negotiations still takes precedence. It will probably be years before the next big multilateral agreement on world trade. Thus, while it would be preferable to build on the WTO, U.S. negotiators must meanwhile pursue other means to that end. As detailed below, building on NAFTA, initiating agreements with as many nations as possible as soon as feasible, is a promising approach, much as the U.S.–Canada FTA helped jump-start the Uruguay Round negotiations, and even as NAFTA itself helped the Uruguay Round to bring closure and coverage in areas such as intellectual property and services.

The antithesis of the multilateral approach is for the United States to pursue a series of unilateral trade actions, such as under its "section 301" law. Reliance solely on this approach, however, is both inadequate and overly broad. It is inadequate because the WTO dispute resolution system has effectively replaced section 301 for many areas of dispute between the United States and its trading partners. It is overly broad because the "aggressive unilateralism" associated with section 301 causes friction with U.S. trading partners without advancing world prosperity.[1]

A third approach for the United States would be to enter into a series of separate regional agreements. Many proposals of this type have been advanced, including the Bogor Declaration of the Asia–Pacific Economic Cooperation (APEC) leaders and the proposed transatlantic free trade agreement (TAFTA) between the United States and the European Union (EU). This method, however, is too slow, requiring a series of painstaking negotiations or discussions, each one beginning from scratch. On closer examination, moreover, some of these regional schemes are limited to hortatory declarations about the future, with little concrete action to show for a results-oriented U.S. policy. Also, advancing different arrangements with the myriad of regional groupings is likely to lead to a proliferation of different standards for each region or country grouping, which would have a chilling effect on business people trading globally. Finally, the raison d'être of any regional economic grouping should be to advance prosperity beyond the level achieved by multilateral institutions such as the WTO. If the standards adopted by a regional grouping are lower than those of the WTO or than those the United States has achieved in bilateral agreements with individual trading partners, then the grouping risks diverting rather than advancing economic prosperity.

Thus, although the United States will no doubt continue the pragmatic course of combining a variety of approaches, when it comes to regional trading the best choice for U.S. trade policy makers is to build on NAFTA. In November 1993, Congress cast a decisive, bipartisan vote for more open trade.[2] By approving NAFTA, Congress put the United States on a positive course toward opening world markets to trade and investment; at the same time, Congress advanced labor (blue) and environmental (green) goals to ensure that U.S. firms that abide by higher standards in these areas would not be competitively disadvantaged. NAFTA's backers argued forcefully and effectively for a strategy of global engagement—for expanded trade opportunities for both U.S. consumers and businesses. Now, the opportunity exists to follow this strategy beyond North America to other regions in Latin America, Asia, and Europe.

Applying the NAFTA approach universally would signal that the admission price to free trade with the United States is the same for all nations. This strategy of extending NAFTA also makes clear that regional initiatives that involve committing the United States to maintain open markets have a place in U.S. trade policy, particularly with emerging democracies, but only when the arrangements *exceed* multilateral standards for trade liberalization. In this way, expanding NAFTA is consistent with the U.S. objective of bringing the benefits of regional agreements into a multilateral context.

The United States faces the growing challenge of competition with emerging nations of the world. Just as it assimilated war-devastated Japan and Europe into a healthy trading system, and just as it forged an agreement between a developing nation, Mexico, and an advanced nation, Canada, now the United States must tap into the fastest growing regions of the world, Asia and Latin America, and into other emerging economies in Eastern Europe and elsewhere. In pursuit of the nation's own interests, the United States should welcome to NAFTA all countries that wish to open their markets reciprocally to trade and investment, and to undertake at a minimum the NAFTA labor and environmental standards.[3] These commitments, made by a growing number of nations, could eventually become the basis for broader multilateral agreements.

Ultimately, expanding NAFTA to include many if not all of the United States' other trading partners will result in a new world template, a WTO at a higher level.[4] NAFTA has higher economic and legal standards than the WTO; broader coverage than the WTO in many areas, such as intellectual property rights, investment, and services; and more coverage than the WTO to tackle labor and environmental issues that particularly arise with the creation of trade pacts between developed and developing nations. Furthermore, NAFTA has more effective enforcement mechanisms than the WTO, and NAFTA's open accession clause means that NAFTA, unlike other major trading areas, is not bound by geography. The United States must avoid the pitfalls of piecemeal regional trade policy making, a practice that leads to a hodgepodge of regional trading areas with trading policies that are neither uniform nor desirable. Instead, the United States should bring the many advantages of NAFTA to its relations with its trading partners throughout the world.

NAFTA's Track Record

Both critics and proponents of NAFTA have exaggerated its potential short-term impacts, but its most important features are the new areas it covers and its more comprehensive nature. Overlooking these, foes predicted its passage would result in a flood of cheap foreign goods, an exodus of U.S. firms and investment to south of the border, and a net loss of 550,000 U.S. jobs over 10 years. But the critics were wrong; in the first year after NAFTA's passage, three-way trade among the NAFTA nations soared 17 percent, growing over $50 billion.[5] U.S. merchandise exports to Canada and Mexico grew more than twice as fast as U.S. exports to the rest of the world, accounting for 50 percent of the total 1994 gain in U.S. exports.[6]

And there is much potential for these trends to continue if NAFTA's reach continues to grow. Over the next five years, 12 Big Emerging Markets (BEMs),[7] accounting for about half of the world's population, are expected to experience import growth double that of industrialized countries.[8] The Commerce Department projects that U.S. exports to these BEMs by the year 2000 will be as large as combined exports to the EU and Japan.[9] In the longer term, annual U.S. exports to Asia (exclusive of Japan) are projected to increase by $154 billion over the next 15 years, and exports to Latin America will increase by $144 billion over the same period; each $1 billion in new U.S. exports means 17,000 new U.S. jobs.[10]

Implementing NAFTA, Plus

The Clinton administration inherited the Bush administration's regionalist plan to follow up NAFTA by holding free trade talks with Chile to reward its remarkable return to a democratically elected government pursuing economic privatization, liberalization, and deregulation. As a global power, however, the United States should be thinking of how to broaden the NAFTA model and apply it beyond Latin America to capitalize on economic opportunities for U.S. industry and agriculture worldwide. Because of the open-accession clause that governs eligibility of future NAFTA members, it is possible to open NAFTA beyond just one country or one region (which was the Bush administration's original intent).

There are two principal ways to build on NAFTA. One is by accession: adding countries, such as Chile, one at a time. The second is by merger: merging with existing groupings of countries, such as the Mercado Común del Sur (Mercosur) or the EU. These methods are not inconsistent; whichever is more appropriate for the country or group of countries at issue can be used.

The Americas

The Western Hemisphere affords the most obvious opportunities for further expansion. Besides Chile, other nations or groups of nations that could beneficially be added to the NAFTA framework include the Mercosur nations (Brazil, Argentina, Paraguay, and Uruguay), the Andean Group (Colombia, Venezuela, Bolivia, Ecuador, and Peru), the English-speaking nations known as Caricom, and the Central American nations.[11] Latin America and the Caribbean now form the second fastest growing region in the world, and U.S. exports to the region have tripled in the past decade, creating over 600,000 new U.S. jobs.[12] By 2010, the United States will export more goods and services to Latin America than to Europe and Japan combined.[13]

The Mercosur nations, in particular, would mesh extremely well into the NAFTA framework. In 1994, the Mercosur nations and Chile had global imports of $65 billion, and these five countries and the three NAFTA nations together represent *95 percent* of the hemispheric market.[14] In 1994 in Miami, the Summit of the Americas endorsed a Free Trade Area of the Americas (FTAA) by the year 2005, and the same group's June 1995 Denver Trade Ministerial meeting established seven FTAA working groups, with four more slated to follow in March 1996.[15] The president of Brazil,

Fernando Henrique Cardoso, met with President Bill Clinton in April 1995 to discuss means by which Brazil and the other Mercosur nations could make substantial progress toward achieving an FTAA by the year 2000.[16] The most optimistic scenario is that Mercosur and NAFTA could merge before the end of this century.

However, although virtually all Latin nations have signed trade and framework agreements with Washington that could lead to negotiations for expanded trade, the benefits granted Mexico will only be offered to other economies that undertake serious and sustained reform effort, and these benefits—and the disadvantages that would accrue to any nation that opts out of the process—provide a compelling inducement to adhere to the reform course. Brazil, for example, the dominant member of Mercosur, would have to improve both its internal political reform efforts and the functioning of its economy before it—and consequently Mercosur—could join NAFTA. Moreover, Brazil may wish to focus its energy on building up Mercosur rather than merging Mercosur with NAFTA.[17] In the meantime, Mercosur and NAFTA continue to grow together: NAFTA member Mexico also has free trade deals with Chile and with Mercosur, and Chile and Colombia are applying to join both NAFTA and Mercosur.[18]

Asia

In Asia, Singapore, Korea, and Taiwan have at different times all expressed interest in joining NAFTA. A bridge between NAFTA and Asia could ultimately develop into a Pacific area free trade agreement (PAFTA), although some APEC countries would resist this idea.[19] The allure of the "Asian economic miracle" and the attendant idea of a "Pacific century" have become almost clichés. But the breathtaking reality of the economies of Asia—Japan; the Four Tigers (South Korea, Singapore, Taiwan, and Hong Kong), which are averaging almost 6 percent annual growth over the course of a generation; China, in the period since 1979; and the "new tigers" of Malaysia, Thailand, Indonesia, and possibly Vietnam—remains a monument to Asian export-growth approaches to development that have shattered the North–South paradigm. To put the Asia–Pacific economy in context, whereas in 1980 the Asian economies produced 21 percent of world output, in 1994 they produced over 30 percent of world output, even as North American production remained at approximately 25 percent of world output over the same period.[20] In the November 1994 Bogor Declaration, APEC leaders established a goal of free and open trade and investment within APEC by 2010 for industrialized member countries and by 2020 for developing member countries.

East Asia has clearly become an engine of the global economy and a defining reality of the post–cold war international system. The challenge for the United States is how to balance competing interests and best utilize its many assets—economic, political, and strategic—to provide sustained and consistent leadership as a first among equals and to help shape the emerging order in the Pacific with Washington woven into its political and economic fabric. U.S. exports to Asia already account for over 2 million U.S. jobs, and one projection shows that Asia, excluding Japan, will be the largest U.S. export market in the world by the year 2010.[21] Bringing together Asia and NAFTA thus has enormous potential to bring dramatic growth in trade and investment for both the United States and its NAFTA partners and for the dynamic economies of Asia.[22]

Europe

There has recently been a great deal of talk about a merger between the EU and the United States to form a transatlantic free trade agreement. President Clinton and Prime Minister John Major of Great Britain discussed this possibility at a meeting in Washington earlier this year, and Germany's foreign minister, among others, has urged that the idea be studied further.[23] The trade considerations with respect to this idea are mixed. On the one hand, a number of sectors would like to see total elimination of trade barriers. On the other hand, certain sectors, most notably agriculture, are likely to remain stumbling blocks to a true free trade arrangement with the EU. Notwithstanding the obstacles, however, the structural similarities, economic interdependence, and balanced trade relations of the North American and European economies argue in favor of allowing a TAFTA to remove the remaining barriers to free trade between these two strong regions.[24]

The economic argument in favor of a TAFTA is not the only one. The end of the Cold War has broken an important link across the Atlantic, and a strong geostrategic argument can be made that there is a need to find other means to maintain this alliance. U.S. undersecretary of commerce Jeffrey Garten, for example, recently warned that the United States and EU could drift apart unless a "new economic architecture" replaces the security links that the end of the Cold War has weakened.[25] Similarly, in congressional testimony in July 1995, Henry Kissinger testified that a TAFTA would "foster cooperation among the nations of the North Atlantic," now that security is no longer their primary unifying bond.[26]

A critical flaw in some versions of a TAFTA that have been proposed is that this economic merger would create an entity that could be perceived as a "rich man's club" and/or a "white man's club." To solve this problem, the union must permit the inclusion not only of the United States' NAFTA partners Canada and Mexico, but also the developing economies of Eastern Europe, thus creating a *true* transatlantic free trade agreement. A broader-based TAFTA will bring political and economic benefits to both the developed nations and the developing ones, much as the NAFTA template approved by Congress added Mexico to the free trade union of the United States and Canada and created rewards for all three countries.

Fast Track, Labor, and the Environment

Despite the many attractive countries and regions available for building on the achievements of NAFTA, U.S. domestic politics threaten to derail the NAFTA bandwagon—indeed, any serious effort to advance trade liberalization—before it can even get rolling. The most serious current domestic obstacle to expansion of NAFTA is the controversy over fast track and its relation to labor and the environment.

Realistically, bold trade initiatives, including the expansion of NAFTA, cannot move forward unless the executive branch and the Congress put aside their differences and reenact fast track legislation, that is, legislation that authorizes the administration to submit a trade agreement to Congress for an up or down vote, without the possibility of amendment. There are several reasons for this. First, fast track enhances the U.S. ability to speak with one voice when addressing other sovereign nations. Second, by giving a president credibility with U.S. trading partners, fast track lays the groundwork for a comprehensive trade strategy as opposed to reactive, ad hoc management of individual trade disputes. Third, fast track allows for rapid U.S. action in response to fast-moving global events. Fourth, fast track establishes a mechanism for the executive branch and the Congress to consult closely on trade talks. Finally, fast track allows U.S. negotiators to channel and use pressure from domestic interests to help negotiate improved dispute-settlement arrangements or new international rules with U.S. trade partners.

The main objection to the renewal of fast track is that some in Congress do not want to permit the executive branch to negotiate labor and environmental objectives as part of a trade package. This objection is puzzling: fast track laws passed in 1974[27] and 1988[28] included labor rights among their negotiating objectives, and in May 1991, an exchange of letters regarding NAFTA negotiating objectives—including environmental issues—was worked out between Republican president George Bush and Democratic congressional leaders Richard Gephardt (D–Mo.) and Dan Rostenkowski (D–Ill.). The inclusion of labor and environmental issues in fast track negotiations is thus neither a new issue nor a partisan one.

Purists argue that the issues of trade, labor, and the environment should each be considered in separate policy frameworks. But as the NAFTA side agreements demonstrated, policies on these three areas have begun to be closely interrelated, which is why the NAFTA model is so useful. To build the necessary domestic political support for future expansion of NAFTA, Congress and the White House must strike a balance to advance worker and environmental goals as well as trade and investment expansion.[29] Trade expansion is a boon to average working families, who get greater choices, lower prices on imported goods, and higher-skilled, higher-paying jobs in firms serving fast-growing overseas markets. Trade protection, on the other hand, favors less dynamic business, financial, and labor interests.

Furthermore, new organizations, or reinvigorated old ones, are needed to handle the increasingly controversial issues surrounding environmental concerns and international labor standards. The value of the 75-year-old International Labour Organization (ILO) should be reevaluated now that it is no longer used as a debating forum for cold war adversaries. Likewise, the time may have come to form a new global environmental organization to establish widely accepted, international environmental rules to replace the jumble of different standards and approaches adopted by individual nations.

Since the United States and its GATT trading partners formulated the objectives of the Uruguay Round a decade ago, many important new issues have emerged, including environmental protection, international recognition of worker rights, and the harmonization of competition or domestic antitrust policies (which also relates to the unfair trade practice of dumping). These issues must be addressed in a balanced, reasonable way to help establish common rules for global competition in an era of economic interdependence.

Leading the Way

The battles over NAFTA and GATT show that U.S. political leaders, despite much pulling and shoving, still understand the requirements of national success in the global economy. The experience of the United States since World War II shows that if it does not lead the way, it puts U.S. businesses, workers, and consumers—even U.S. leadership in a secure world—at risk. It is time for the president and the Congress to rebuild a bipartisan public consensus to achieve new authority for the executive branch to negotiate future arrangements based on the NAFTA model. NAFTA's high economic and legal standards and broad subject matter coverage fulfill the necessary purpose of any regional economic grouping: to advance prosperity by adopting standards *higher* than those of multilateral institutions. These features make NAFTA the ideal to which other regional groupings should aspire, and show how much the United States can achieve if it chooses to lead the way.

This article is adapted from congressional testimony delivered by Paula Stern during hearings on fast track legislation in May 1995.

Notes

1. Although there are times when judicious use of section 301 is certainly warranted, before targeting any industry for protection or bilateral trade discussions the United States should review the relationship of that industry to *overall* U.S. trade goals.

2. Indeed, it has been noted that between NAFTA and the WTO, 1993–94 may have been the high watermark for internationalist policies in the United States.

3. As we discuss in more detail below, although the NAFTA labor and environmental standards are flash points for critics of NAFTA and the fast track process by which it was approved, the U.S. goal of higher labor and environmental standards worldwide has historically been an area of consensus among U.S. decision makers and could be crucial again in forging the domestic political coalition that will be necessary to expand NAFTA and free trade generally.

4. NAFTA and other regional pacts are sometimes criticized for undermining the WTO by promoting trade diversion. In most cases, however, the positive income effects of regional pacts outweigh the negatives of trade diversion. See Gary Hufbauer and Jeffrey J. Schott, "Toward Free Trade and Investment in the Asia–Pacific," *The Washington Quarterly* 18 (Summer 1995), p. 45, n. 5. Moreover, regional pacts are currently the only viable routes to trade liberalization, and the WTO could ensure that regional pacts advance rather than hinder global free trade by reviewing the provisions of such pacts for compliance with WTO multilateral norms.

5. U.S. Department of Commerce, NAFTA Facts, Document No. 4003 (Washington, D.C., February 17, 1995).

6. *Ibid.* Moreover, although NAFTA accounts for 29 percent of total U.S. goods trade, it accounts for only 9 percent of the total U.S. merchandise trade deficit. Critics, of course, are anxious to attribute the January 1994 Mexican financial crisis to NAFTA. NAFTA, however, is a trade agreement, not a monetary agreement, and was silent on macroeconomic or monetary coordination. Not only would Mexico probably have experienced the peso crisis even if NAFTA had not existed, but NAFTA has prevented Mexico from raising tariffs against increasing U.S. imports, as it might have done had the agreement not been in place, and many of NAFTA's features will lead to important long-term gains.

7. The twelve BEMs are China, Hong Kong, Taiwan, India, Indonesia, South Korea, Turkey, South Africa, Argentina, Brazil, Mexico, and Poland.

8. U.S. Department of Commerce, "U.S. Global Trade Outlook 1995–2000" (Washington, D.C., 1995), p. 64.

9. *Ibid.*, p. 13.

10. Remarks of Ambassador Mickey Kantor, United States Trade Representative, prepared for delivery to the Commonwealth

Club, San Francisco, California, July 27, 1995.

11. Leaders at the Summit of the Americas in December 1994 called on hemispheric governments to establish a free trade area from Canada to Tierra del Fuego by 2005. See Georges Fauriol and Sidney Weintraub, "U.S. Policy, Brazil, and the Southern Cone," *The Washington Quarterly* 18 (Summer 1995), p. 123.

12. Testimony of Ambassador Charlene Barshefsky, Deputy United States Trade Representative, before the International Trade Subcommittee of the Senate Finance Committee, August 1, 1995, p. 7.

13. Remarks of Ambassador Mickey Kantor.

14. Félix Peña, "New Approaches to Economic Integration in the Southern Cone," *The Washington Quarterly* 18 (Summer 1995), p. 113.

15. Final Joint Declaration, Summit of the Americas Trade Ministerial, Denver, Colorado, June 30, 1995.

16. The enthusiasm of the Mercosur nations for free trade groupings is not confined to the Americas: Mercosur has also begun discussions with the EU regarding the formation of a joint free trade area.

17. It also must be recognized that Brazil and the other Mercosur nations may prefer routes toward free trade in the Americas other than accession to NAFTA. By steering Mercosur toward South America rather than North America, Brazil ensures that it will remain the dominant member of an important subregional grouping in a manner that would be impossible were Mercosur to merge with NAFTA. Moreover, North America is not necessarily the most logical focus of Mercosur's attention; each of the four Mercosur nations currently exports more to other Latin American nations than to the United States. See Fauriol and Weintraub, "U.S. Policy, Brazil, and the Southern Cone," pp. 130–132, and James Brooke, "Brazil Looks North from Trade Zone in Amazon," *New York Times*, August 9, 1995.

18. "Hemispheric Trade," *Journal of Commerce*, July 12, 1995.

19. The 18 members of APEC, created in 1989, are Australia, Brunei, Canada, Chile, China, Hong Kong, Indonesia, Japan, South Korea, Malaysia, Mexico, New Zealand, Papua New Guinea, the Philippines, Singapore, Taiwan, Thailand, and the United States.

20. U.S. Department of Commerce, "U.S. Global Trade Outlook 1995–2000," p. 25.

21. Testimony of Ambassador Charlene Barshefsky, p. 7.

22. Predictably, proponents of expanding trade in the Americas are wary of simultaneously pushing NAFTA into Asia. These critics contend that overtures to Asia will signal that the United States is not serious about expanding free trade and encouraging democracy in this hemisphere, and will fan the flames of domestic protectionism. See Fauriol and Weintraub, "U.S. Policy, Brazil, and the Southern Cone," p. 134. However, emphasizing that any new member must abide by the strenuous requirements of NAFTA (including its labor and environment side agreements) should help allay moderate protectionist pressures.

23. Guy de Jonquières, "Warning on EU–U.S. Free Trade Area," *Financial Times*, April 24, 1995.

24. For further discussion of the arguments favoring a TAFTA, see Thomas J. Duesterberg, "Prospects for an EU–NAFTA Free Trade Agreement," *The Washington Quarterly* 18 (Spring 1995), p. 71.

25. Caroline Southey, "US Reaches Out for New Trade Relationship with Europe," *Financial Times*, April 26, 1995.

26. Testimony of Henry Kissinger before the Senate Foreign Relations Committee, July 13, 1995. House Speaker Newt Gingrich (R–Ga.) has also promoted the idea of shoring up the North Atlantic Treaty Organization by bringing its members together in a free trade area. See, e.g., his speech to the National Press Club, July 5, 1995.

27. The law listed as a negotiating objective "the adoption of international fair labor standards and of public petition and confrontation procedures in the GATT." Trade Act of 1974, Pub. L. No. 93–618, §121(a)(4), 88 Stat. 1978.

28. "The principal negotiating objectives of the United States regarding worker rights are—
(A) to promote respect for worker rights;
(B) to secure a review of the relationship

of worker rights to GATT articles, objectives, and related instruments with a view to ensuring that the benefits of the trading system are available to all workers; and (C) to adopt, as a principle of the GATT, that the denial of worker rights should not be a means for a country or its industries to gain competitive advantage in international trade." Omnibus Trade and Competitiveness Act of 1988, Pub. L. No. 100–418, §1101(b)(14), 102 Stat. 1125.

29. It has been noted in the Asia–Pacific context, but is true more generally, that the United States will be able to continue leading efforts to liberalize world trade only if the domestic policy agenda is controlled by a coalition of traditional free traders and moderate social agenda proponents. Hufbauer and Schott, "Toward Free Trade and Investment in the Asia–Pacific," p. 42.

Toward Free Trade and Investment in the Asia–Pacific

Gary Hufbauer and Jeffrey J. Schott

The Asia–Pacific region stands at the beginning of what promises to be a long and rewarding march toward free trade and investment. The successful November 1994 meeting of the Asia–Pacific Economic Cooperation (APEC) forum at Bogor, Indonesia, launched the process of regional integration. Eventually this process should yield a rich harvest of liberalization.

We first summarize the Bogor vision. We then assess Asian partiality toward "do-it-yourself" liberalization, and evaluate the "toe-in-the-water" negotiations initiated by the APEC member countries. Next we speculate on the durability of the APEC process. We conclude with a discussion of the implications of APEC developments for the new World Trade Organization (WTO).

The Bogor Vision

At Bogor the grand vision of free trade was proclaimed and endorsed by 18 APEC presidents and prime ministers. The APEC leaders committed their countries to achieving "the long-term goal of free trade and investment" in the Asia–Pacific region by the year 2010 for industrialized economies and by 2020 for developing economies. The Bogor Declaration does not spell out detailed steps by which to achieve that goal; instead, much of the ongoing work of the various APEC meetings in 1995 will be devoted to formulating a plan of action. In this sense, the APEC approach is very Asian with its broad consensus style, and very unlike North American and European regional pacts with their detailed liberalization schedules.[1]

The Bogor Declaration is silent as to which countries are committed to the earlier target date, but that group obviously encompasses the United States, Japan, Australia, New Zealand, and Canada. Singapore and Taiwan also have volunteered to meet the 2010 target. Within the next decade, two other "tigers," Korea and Hong Kong, are likely to be counted among the industrialized economies. Together, these countries produce more than 80 percent of the current aggregate gross domestic product of the APEC region.

The big question is the status of

Gary Hufbauer and Jeffrey J. Schott are senior fellows at the Institute for International Economics, Washington, D.C.

Copyright © 1995 by the Institute for International Economics. All rights reserved.
The Washington Quarterly • 18:3

China in the year 2010. Some parts of China, notably Hong Kong, Guangzhou, and Shanghai, will clearly be industrial areas in 2010. Other parts of China will not; nevertheless, most APEC members will be reluctant to give the industrial parts of China an extra 10 years to liberalize. Conceivably, by the year 2010, China will see its own interests as best served by embracing free trade and investment.

In terms of historical comparisons, the Asia–Pacific countries in 1995 are approximately where the European states were in 1950 when their leaders laid out a vision of economic unification. Similar landmark moments of visionary anticipation can be found in the history of other regional pacts—the Association of Southeast Asian Nations (ASEAN), the Australia–New Zealand Closer Economic Relations Trade Agreement (ANZCERTA), the U.S.–Canada Free Trade Agreement, the North American Free Trade Agreement (NAFTA), and the Mercado Común del Sur (Mercosur).

Typically, once the founding fathers had announced a vision, many missteps interrupted the march toward free trade and investment. After the Treaty of Rome was signed in 1957, Europe alternated between phases of Europessimism, when nothing seemed possible, and Europtimism, when all barriers could be swept away. Similar mood swings have already gripped NAFTA, from the halcyon days of 1994, when everything went well in the Mexican economy, to the peso crisis of December 1994, when everything went sour.

Roller-coaster moods are almost inevitable in the Asia–Pacific context. Political turmoil in China, speculative booms and busts in stock exchanges, violent exchange rate swings, trade imbalances, and commercial frictions will all put strains on the APEC group.

Proponents of APEC free trade and investment would do well to ponder the ill-fated Latin American Free Trade Area (LAFTA). As with APEC, the LAFTA rhetoric was grand, the geographic and cultural distances were vast, and it was hard to agree on concrete steps. There is, however, a big difference between LAFTA and APEC: APEC is constructed on a solid foundation of market economics, whereas LAFTA was erected on the shaky stilts of statism. Moreover, LAFTA members generally pursued import-substitution strategies that led them to compete rather than cooperate with their integration partners. By contrast, Asian countries pioneered the strategy of export-led growth. But these distinctions alone will not guarantee APEC's success in the years ahead. Leaders will need to take advantage of propitious moods to move integration forward; and they will need to rely on economic integration as a bulwark against protection when bleak moods cloud the region.

The political component of APEC integration has a decidedly different flavor from major integration efforts of the past. In Europe, economic unification was seen as protection against World War III and a bridge to better political relations, especially between Germany and France. In ASEAN, the first two decades were largely devoted to easing political tensions surrounding territorial disputes. In Mercosur, long-standing and bitter rivalries between Brazil and Argentina are being put to rest by economic integration. By sharp contrast, neither the U.S.–Canada FTA nor NAFTA had a comparable political agenda. Canada and Mexico laid aside their antagonisms toward the United States before embarking on free trade talks.

The Asia–Pacific lies somewhere between the extremes of Europe and

North America. For the moment, Asia–Pacific tensions largely spring out of economic differences rather than ideological or territorial disputes.[2] For the moment, more important than conflicting claims to the Spratly Islands are the challenges posed by Japan's persistent trade surpluses, China's explosive growth as an exporter of manufactured goods, and exaggerated U.S. concerns that trade with Asia will depress the wages of unskilled U.S. workers.

Although economic questions are now at the forefront, big security questions will not forever remain on the back burner. Unless Japan, North and South Korea, China, India, and Pakistan resolve their various and complex tensions, they may instead build nuclear submarines and missiles. The U.S. security umbrella over Asia will not be folded away soon, but neither will it last another 20 years. Realizing all this, Asia–Pacific leaders are farsighted in trying to build a preemptive network of economic relations to dampen political antagonisms.

Do-It-Yourself Liberalization

The decade between 1985 and 1995 saw lots of do-it-yourself liberalization in the Asia–Pacific region, even while the Uruguay Round was slogging to a difficult conclusion. The United States substantially dismantled its "voluntary" import restraint measures between 1985 and the early 1990s. The fraction of all U.S. imports subject to exceptional protection dropped from 20 percent to 10 percent. Mexico dramatically cut its tariffs and dismantled most of its licensing restrictions before the NAFTA negotiations were launched. China liberalized its entire economic apparatus, including severe foreign exchange restraints that limited imports, and an array of barriers that restricted foreign investment. South Korea cut tariffs and relaxed quotas. ASEAN nations put out the welcome mat for foreign investors.

Reflecting on this record, most Asian political leaders subscribe to the view that unilateral liberalization will continue. Their logic is straightforward. Many domestic business firms can be counted on to lobby for lower trade barriers, both as purchasers of industrial inputs and as distributors of imports in the local market. Expanding cross-border investment will give open markets a further push as multinationals seek to facilitate transactions in their own components and to widen markets for their final products. The formerly closed banking sectors of Japan and Australia illustrate these tendencies: once the large Japanese and Australian banks began to do a good volume of business in New York, London, and Hong Kong through their foreign subsidiaries, they nudged their own governments to relax domestic barriers.

Following this logic, the process of regional integration in APEC could well continue along the do-it-yourself path. Progress toward free trade and investment in the APEC region might evolve through an incremental process in which individual countries ante up commitments to liberalize barriers to trade and investment, with each country setting its own pace for reform within the transition periods established by the APEC summit leaders. Such an approach would differ sharply from the traditional negotiation of a free trade agreement, in which negotiators work out in advance the schedule of trade concessions that all countries implement step by step.

But we are skeptical that do-it-yourself liberalization will achieve the Bogor vision. Casual empiricism tells us that very few countries manage to get their average tariff equivalent import barriers below the 10 to 20 percent range, or to level the high peaks of protection (such as U.S. apparel quotas), without the assistance of multilateral negotiations.

Apart from the United States, Canada, New Zealand, Hong Kong, and Singapore, nearly all APEC members have average tariff barriers above 10 percent and lofty peaks exceeding 30 percent. In most APEC countries, peak tariffs protecting sensitive sectors (e.g., automobiles and parts) will remain intact even after implementation of the Uruguay Round cuts. In many cases, average tariffs will also remain above 10 percent. We will be very surprised if APEC countries manage, on a do-it-yourself basis, to assault the political-economic complex behind high average barriers and exceptionally lofty peaks.

Toe-in-the-Water Negotiations

Indeed, the APEC leaders recognized in the Bogor Declaration that negotiations must be part of the APEC process, and they took initial steps to promote the goal of free trade and investment in the region. Specifically, they resolved to facilitate regional trade by developing new arrangements on customs procedures, standards, and administrative barriers to market access. The Bogor Declaration also envisages cooperative programs to strengthen regional economic infrastructure in areas such as energy, transportation, information, telecommunications, and tourism.

The declaration recognizes that some lesser developed APEC countries may not be able to move forward in these areas at the same pace as the industrialized members, and specifically endorses a "variable speed" approach to regional integration. In this regard, the declaration states that "economies that are ready to initiate and implement a cooperative arrangement may proceed to do so while those that are not yet ready to participate may join at a later date."

Regarding investment, APEC ministers endorsed an extremely weak set of nonbinding investment principles but directed government officials to try to improve them. As they now stand, the APEC principles do *not* (1) include a firm commitment to national treatment; *nor* (2) constrain the use of investment restrictions; *nor* (3) prohibit investment incentives such as tax holidays and outright grants.

The APEC leaders agreed on a number of institutional measures to help support the ongoing regional integration initiatives. First, the Bogor Declaration agreed to examine a proposal to establish an APEC dispute mediation system, which would "supplement the WTO dispute settlement mechanism," particularly in areas not yet subject to WTO rights and obligations (e.g., investment and competition policy).

Second, the declaration established a new private sector advisory body, the Pacific Business Forum (PBF), and extended the mandate of the Eminent Persons Group (EPG). The APEC leaders requested that the EPG and the PBF provide ongoing advice to them in three broad areas. Their role is to:

- monitor and assess the progress of the implementation of the APEC commitments;
- develop further recommendations on initiatives that could be taken to achieve the long-term goal of free trade and investment in the region; and
- review "interrelationships between APEC and the existing subregional arrangements (the ASEAN Free

Trade Area, ANZCERTA, and NAFTA) and to examine possible options to prevent obstacles to each other and to promote consistency in their relations."

Third, the APEC leaders agreed to continue their annual ministerial and summit meetings. The next APEC summit will take place in Osaka in November 1995. Subsequent meetings will be held in the Philippines in 1996, in Canada in 1997, and in Malaysia in 1998.

Fourth, the APEC countries emphasized that regional initiatives should complement and reinforce the multilateral trading system and should be carried out "in a GATT-consistent manner." The Bogor Declaration commits the APEC countries to accelerate the implementation of Uruguay Round liberalization, to deepen and broaden the Uruguay Round results, and to "endeavor to refrain from using measures which would have the effect of increasing levels of protection." In other words, the leaders all but promised a standstill on new forms of protectionism.

Finally, the Bogor Declaration resolved that APEC liberalization should not evolve into an "inward-looking trade bloc that would divert from the pursuit of global free trade," and that APEC reforms should also be extended to trade between APEC and non-APEC economies (particularly developing countries) "in conformity with GATT/WTO provisions." In the last section of this essay, we explore the implications of this important commitment for the multilateral trading system.

Durability of the APEC Process

After Bogor, is all for the best in the best of all possible worlds? Has Dr. Pangloss been reincarnated as an Asia–Pacific guru? Will APEC maintain its momentum toward free markets over the next 20 years?

APEC has 18 members, but 3 of them individually hold the power to limit the speed and scope of the APEC agenda. These three are the United States, Japan, and China. Each of the big three can block the APEC ambitions of the other two. At the same time, each of the big three can launch, but not conclude, APEC initiatives. All three will have to concur before concrete steps toward liberalization can be taken.

The problems facing the United States as a negotiating partner are larger than most observers in Asia appreciate. Distinct political groups are now competing for control of U.S. trade policy, and these groups cross political party lines. First, there are the establishment voices, represented by the likes of the Business Roundtable. These voices continue to push for open markets everywhere, the quicker the better. For the moment, they are in the ascendant in the Clinton administration, but they no longer dominate the trade policy scene as they did five years ago. They were dealt a severe blow by the December 1994 crisis in Mexico and the implied rebuke to NAFTA.

Second, there are the social agenda advocates who want to see trade policy used as a lever for worldwide environmental protection, labor standards, and human rights. These advocates made themselves felt in the 1993 NAFTA debate. Until congressional elections swept Republicans into power in November 1994, the social activists were gaining prominence in the U.S. trade policy scene. For the time being, they have lost influence.

Finally, there are the neo-protectionists, led by billionaires Ross Perot and Roger Milliken, who want to limit U.S. trade with developing countries as a means of shoring up the wages of the bottom third of the U.S. workforce. The neo-protectionists lost the NAFTA fight, and they lost the Uruguay Round battle, but they have been defeated, not routed. They have strong sympathizers in both political parties.

If the United States is to participate in broad-spectrum APEC negotiations, a coalition of establishment free trade forces and moderate social agenda advocates will have to maintain control of the policy agenda. The domestic question is whether such a coalition can prevail over the neo-protectionists and immoderate social agenda groups. The international question is whether a moderate social agenda can simply be accepted by China and other Asian countries. We offer an optimistic yes to both questions. But if the bottom third of the U.S. workforce continues to lose economic ground (no matter what the reasons, and they may have little to do with international trade), if endangered species begin to disappear in Asia, if overly repressive measures are used to preserve the Chinese social order, then a prolonged stalemate could limit U.S. participation in serious APEC negotiations.

For Japan, the central dilemma is quite different. At this juncture, Japan's tariffs are very low, and its quotas are confined to agricultural products. For the most part, Japanese trade barriers reside in a host of opaque regulations and private cartel practices. A recent study suggests that the resulting tariff equivalent barriers run between 30 and 100 percent for many important products.[3] The central question facing Japanese leaders is whether they can negotiate a radical deregulation of their domestic economic system. Another five years of very slow growth might persuade the Japanese establishment to put competition policy on the APEC agenda and to attack the cartels that have so long been a hallmark of the Japanese economy. But if Japanese growth rebounds to the 3 percent range, it seems unlikely that the conservative Japanese system will allow competition policy to be placed on the APEC negotiating agenda. And without this contribution, Japan will bring little to the negotiating table.

Finally there is the great unknown, China. Very few Chinese officials have mastered the details of trade policy and its interaction with the domestic economy. Right now, those few are totally overwhelmed with immediate issues: trying to impose common tariff and nontariff rules in the various provinces; addressing bilateral trade disputes with the United States; and negotiating China's accession to the WTO.

What will be China's attitude in 5 or 10 years? That depends. First and foremost, it depends on whether China's new leaders ignore Deng Xiaoping's famous adage about the color of cats, and instead place political goals ahead of economic objectives. For example, repression of dissidents, abrasive integration of Hong Kong, or an aggressive embrace of Taiwan would sharply diminish the chances for meaningful Chinese participation in economic negotiations. Second, China's international role depends on the workings of its economic engine. If China can grow at 7 percent or more without extravagant inflation, and if the investment rush continues, the Chinese authorities may think they can afford to be indifferent toward APEC negotiations. Rapid growth, however, probably requires a continuation of the Chinese export boom. And booming Chinese exports will only increase the number of friction points with other APEC members. In turn, trade friction will give Chinese leaders a strong incentive to address their problems within the APEC context.

Putting these considerations together, it is easy to foresee obstacles in the path of APEC integration. A pessimist can envisage a long list of bilateral problems—such as competition policy, intellectual property disputes, human rights, environment, and labor issues—that could obstruct regional initiatives. On the other hand, powerful ideas can motivate political leaders to overcome major obstacles. In the sphere of economic integration, we have seen this happen in Europe, in North America, and now in Latin America: such names as Jean Monnet, Konrad Adenauer, and Charles de Gaulle; George Bush, Brian Mulroney, and Carlos Salinas de Gortari; and Carlos Saúl Menem and Eduardo Frei Ruiz-Tagle come to mind. At bottom, it is this factor that leads us to bet on a successful APEC process and achievement of free trade and investment by 2010.

What will the APEC of 2010 achieve, besides elimination of tariffs and quotas? On this we place three bets. Our first bet is that intellectual property protection, a wide range of services, government procurement, and other "new" issues will get equal attention with barriers to trade in manufactured and agricultural goods. The reason is that the Uruguay Round made considerable headway on traditional barriers and do-it-yourself liberalization will make more. But as for the new issues, the Uruguay Round ended with lots of unfinished business. Moreover, with the ongoing revolution in communications technology, it is only a matter of years before the less developed APEC nations discover the vistas that are open to them in services trade. Any work done on a computer can soon be done anywhere in the world. Skilled personnel in developing nations do not need to migrate to North America or Japan; they can sell their services by satellite. In terms of international trade flows, this is a revolution equal to the steamship.

Our second bet concerns environmental and labor issues, the so-called social agenda. We do not expect APEC to host a large-scale negotiation on environmental issues. Rather, APEC members will rely on new efforts in the WTO to bridge the gap between trade and environmental interests. As a result, environmental issues are likely to provoke intra-APEC trade disputes and retaliation only in the most grievous instances (typified by the ban on the ivory trade). APEC will encourage cooperative ventures (both intergovernmental and between the public and private sectors) to support environmental infrastructure projects, however, as well as technical assistance funded by the richer APEC countries.

We think the labor agenda, insofar as it is addressed in APEC negotiations, will be limited to a few core issues: child labor, prison labor, and extremely unsafe working conditions. To a large extent, the social agenda of labor and environmental groups will be met by an International Standards Organization 9000 type of process: multinational firms will certify (subject to independent audit) that the goods they ship to industrial country markets were manufactured with due respect for the environment and labor.

Our third bet concerns the widening of APEC. The current membership roll is frozen until the end of 1996, but India, Russia, and many others have already expressed interest in joining the club.[4] The existing big three APEC members are uneasy about admitting two new giants. On the other hand, no one wants to give offense to powers as large as India and Russia. A likely compromise is for APEC to insist that these countries, and other new applicants, achieve a high degree of external and internal liberalization before their candidacy is considered. In fact, if India promised to meet the 2010 target for free trade and investment by industrial countries, it would become a very attractive member.

Implications for the Multilateral Trading System

The successful conclusion of the Uruguay Round should silence Lester Thurow and his followers who, for years, have argued that "GATT is dead." But it does not mean that all efforts at trade reform should now be centralized in Geneva. If anything, a revitalized multilateral system makes it easier to accommodate expanding regionalism in the Asia–Pacific (and in Europe and the Western Hemisphere). These free trade initiatives should not pose a serious threat to the world trading system as long as progress continues to be made on multilateral trade reforms in the WTO.

There are two broad reasons why expanding regionalism *complements* the reinvigorated multilateral trading system. First, regional pacts often produce deeper liberalization than multilateral negotiations, which involve a larger number of countries and thus must necessarily cater to a broader range of interests. The benefits of such reforms can be accorded to nonmember countries (as many countries have done with their unilateral reforms, and as Mexico has done with key aspects of NAFTA), or can be targeted for credit in future WTO talks.[5]

Second, regional pacts often act as negotiating laboratories for new issues that have not yet advanced on the multilateral trade agenda. For example, provisions on trade in services in the U.S.–Canada and Australia–New Zealand Free Trade Agreements helped inform and guide the Uruguay Round negotiators; and the NAFTA investment chapter provides useful precedents for both the current development of investment guidelines in the Asia–Pacific region and for future negotiations in the WTO. Regional pacts tend to broaden and deepen GATT trade reforms, and in so doing often provide useful models for strengthening multilateral disciplines.

As a matter of GATT/WTO law, as spelled out in GATT article XXIV and article V of the General Agreement on Trade in Services (GATS), preferential trading areas are permitted to engage in conditional most-favored-nation (MFN) treatment. In other words, provided that APEC negotiations meet WTO requirements, individual APEC countries may discriminate against nonmembers in the application of their APEC reforms. Individual APEC countries may choose to implement their trade reforms on an MFN basis, or they may decide to limit the APEC preferences to other APEC members. In short, the APEC leaders recognized that, in a free trade arrangement, each country maintains sovereign control over its trade policy vis-à-vis outsiders.

Nonetheless, because the unconditional MFN approach is regarded by many APEC countries as a core tenet of "open regionalism," the Bogor Declaration sidestepped the issue of multilateral versus regional application of APEC reforms. Because most APEC members want to provide unconditional MFN treatment to developing countries, the issue of discrimination really boils down to how trade with Europe will be handled.

If all APEC members liberalize on an unconditional MFN basis, thus extending the benefits of APEC reforms to the European Union (EU), it is likely to have the perverse effect of impeding rather than accelerating the pace of European liberalization. The EU is in the process of adding three new members (Austria, Sweden, Finland) and laying the groundwork for the membership of Poland, Hungary, and the Czech and Slovak Republics after the year 2000. Beyond are the demands of Russia, Ukraine, and Turkey for better access to the European market, both for goods and for workers. Meanwhile, Europe has created a social safety net that markedly reduces its capacity to change. Taking these forces together, it is hard to imagine that the EU will soon press for a fresh round of WTO talks. Simply put, left to its own devices, Europe would free ride on APEC reforms and maintain its current trade restrictions against North America and Asia.

If, however, APEC reforms were not automatically extended to the EU, but rather offered on a reciprocal basis, the threat of discrimination in such a large trading area could propel the EU into pushing for new multilateral trade negotiations in Geneva in order to dilute or eliminate the APEC preference margins. The leverage to get the EU to the negotiating table in the WTO would probably come from the United States, Japan, and perhaps a few others.

In short, regional trade initiatives can "ratchet up" reforms to a broader multilateral accord. Indeed, before the end of this century, the competitive liberalization generated by APEC and the Western Hemisphere, in conjunction with the continuing expansion of the EU, could well spur a new round of multilateral trade negotiations as the EU attempts to negotiate the global extension of APEC reforms, and APEC and Western Hemisphere countries push for a sharp reduction in European trade barriers.

The opinions expressed are those of the authors and do not necessarily represent the views of the Institute for International Economics, its director, or members of its Board of Directors or Advisory Committee.

Notes

1. In some respects, the Bogor Declaration is akin to the Punta del Este Declaration that launched the Uruguay Round of negotiations under the General Agreement on Tariffs and Trade (GATT): it is an agreement to negotiate to achieve a target level of liberalization. It is available from the APEC Secretariat in Singapore or the U.S. State Department.

2. In some ways, China is more capitalist than Australia. Indeed, a major problem is that China cannot contain its bandit entrepreneurs—especially software pirates!

3. Yoko Sazanami, Shujiro Urata, and Hiroki Kawai, *Measuring the Cost of Protection in Japan* (Washington, D.C.: Institute for International Economics, 1994).

4. Vietnam is likely to enter APEC via ASEAN membership.

5. Concerns do arise that preferential trading pacts run counter to the spirit of GATT by promoting trade diversion. In most instances, however, regional pacts generate positive income effects that more than outweigh the adverse effects of trade diversion. Moreover, the size and scope of potential diversion is small because average MFN tariffs in industrial countries are low.

The Depth of Economic Integration between Mexico and the United States

Sidney Weintraub

DESPITE THE contentious debate in the United States over approval of the North American Free Trade Agreement (NAFTA), there was a school of thought—call its practitioners the "inevitablists"—that was of the opinion that the agreement was not a big deal because it merely ratified the integration taking place in any event in North America. The inevitablists made some concessions on innovation. They recognized that the Mexico–Canada integration was new, but saw it as relatively trivial; and they conceded that perhaps NAFTA had important political, even if not economic, content.

Then, within a year of its entry into force, economic integration between Mexico and the United States was discovered to be both less significant than the NAFTA proponents had hoped, and also much more profound than the inevitablists had dreamed. The financial crisis that erupted on December 20, 1994, when Mexico attempted to modestly devalue the peso—from 3.5 to 4.0 pesos to the dollar, or by about 14 percent when measured in terms of what a peso was worth—showed that the financial consultation between the United States and Mexico wrought by NAFTA was primitive. But the fallout from the trauma that followed, and that continues to this day, shows the underlying integration between the two economies to be in fact deep. President Bill Clinton, when he sought legislation to deal with the consequences of the devaluation, estimated that depth as being worth $40 billion of credit from the U.S. taxpayer. Although in the end the U.S. credit was only $20 billion, its importance is still profound.

Would the rescue package have been as large without NAFTA? I will argue here that it would not. Absent NAFTA, would the United States have exerted so much pressure on the International Monetary Fund (IMF) to join in the rescue effort with what turned out to be an extraordinarily large credit by previous IMF standards? I will argue that it would not. Would the Mexican response have been the same had NAFTA not been

---

Sidney Weintraub holds the William E. Simon chair in political economy at CSIS and also the Dean Rusk Chair in international affairs at the Lyndon B. Johnson School of Public Affairs at the University of Texas at Austin.

Copyright © 1995 by The Center for Strategic and International Studies and the Massachusetts Institute of Technology

in existence? Again I will argue that it would not.

What follows looks first at the causes and the nature of the financial meltdown; then at its meaning in the context of U.S.–Mexican integration; and finally at the fallout. I will draw two competing conclusions. The first is that the existence of NAFTA made a marked difference in how Mexico and the United States reacted to the crisis; or put differently, that NAFTA added much depth to the integration of the two economies. The second is that even this extra depth is insufficient.

Causes of the Collapse

The NAFTA negotiators and observers were conscious of the important role of exchange rates and financial policy in the economic integration arrangements in North America, but they were not sure how to tackle the most thorny of these issues.[1] The NAFTA bargain included a gradual opening of financial markets, especially in Mexico, but this did not deal with underlying financial policy issues. The expectation was that each country would pursue a sound, non-aggressive macroeconomic policy. This, in practice, would be buttressed by regular meetings among the three central banks and treasuries. The management of exchange rate and financial policies was left to non-binding consultation rather than embodied in the kind of formal undertakings that have been adopted in the European Union, from the exchange rate snake to the proposed economic and monetary union.

The reason for this looser arrangement is embedded in the nature of North American integration. The technique chosen was a free trade area (FTA) in order to bring the three countries together economically while minimizing the political content. Neither Canada nor Mexico would have accepted a customs union (CU) with a common external tariff (CET) and a common commercial policy. Their fear was that commonality in these areas would mean adopting U.S. tariffs and U.S. commercial policy, such as an economic embargo of Cuba. Nor was the United States, for its part, interested in the deeper integration implied by a CU; as it was, the opposition to NAFTA focused heavily on U.S. loss of sovereignty.[2]

The lack of any formal exchange rate understandings did not, at first, appear to have any great significance. There was no evidence of exchange rate rigging in order to stimulate exports or impede imports. The Canadian dollar, following the implementation of the Canada–U.S. Free Trade Agreement on January 1, 1989, soared in value to close to parity with the U.S. dollar as a consequence of tight domestic monetary policy. The Canadian dollar has since depreciated substantially, but this stems from Canada's flexible exchange rate formula and not from manipulation. In Mexico, the peso was devalued sharply in 1987—well before NAFTA came into effect on January 1, 1994—and then allowed to appreciate until the devaluation of December 20, 1994. The exchange rate was used as the anchor for Mexico's anti-inflation policy, not as a trade tool.[3] If anything, in both Canada and Mexico, their appreciating exchange rates once their respective trade agreements with the United States went into effect were anti-export promotion. Depreciation of the U.S. dollar could not be a major tool for promoting exports to Mexico and Canada because their currencies were, in effect, pegged to the dollar.

In retrospect, this loose attention to monetary and financial policy was an error. Mexico engaged in policies that were unwise. This can be seen clearly in retrospect but arguably they should have been seen as unsound at the time. The policy measures that led to the financial collapse at the end of 1994 have been widely analyzed and a summary review should be all that is needed here.[4]

Mexican exchange rate policy after 1987 was geared primarily to the anti-inflation effort. The technique was to maintain the peso within a band with respect to the dollar, using market intervention for this purpose. The peso was devalued by small amounts daily, but the cumulative depreciation did not compensate for the difference in inflation between Mexico and the United States. Consequently, the peso, which was deliberately undervalued when the anti-inflation *pactos*, as they were called, began in 1987, gradually became overvalued. It is hard to be precise about the degree of overvaluation by December 1994, but purchasing power parity calculations placed it at between 10 and 20 percent.

The deficit in the current account of Mexico's balance of payments has increased considerably over recent years and it reached roughly 8 percent of gross domestic product in 1994. Nevertheless, in most years prior to 1994, the deficit was more than fully covered by capital inflows. Indeed, in January 1994, Mexico's net international reserves reached $29 billion, a substantial figure in the Mexican experience.[5] There was much commentary in Mexico and from Mexico watchers outside the country that a current account deficit as high as 8 percent of gross domestic product (GDP) made Mexico vulnerable to shocks. This turned out to be accurate, but the monetary authorities contended at the time, and do so even to this day, that slowing the economy was not called for in the circumstances.[6]

What is much harder to explain is why corrective action was not taken as Mexico suffered shock after shock during 1994 and its international reserves began to decline. Thus, when Luis Donaldo Colosio, the presidential candidate of the Partido Revolucionario Institucional (PRI), was assassinated in March, reserves fell by more than $10 billion in the following month. They fell again by almost $3 billion in June and July when the then secretary of government, Jorge Carpizo MacGregor, made an abortive effort to resign over alleged irregularities in the preparations for the August national elections. And, finally, reserves plummeted by more than $6 billion in November and December because of events surrounding the murder of José Francisco Ruiz Massieu, the number two officer in the official PRI hierarchy, and the later charges against his brother Mario for obstructing the investigation and stashing away millions of dollars in U.S. bank accounts.

The almost complete exhaustion of Mexico's reserves by December made the devaluation necessary. They had fallen to less than $6 billion, hardly enough to intervene decisively in markets to maintain the old exchange rate. The advocates of exchange rate fixity have a weak case when they argue that Mexico should not have devalued its currency in December; their case is much stronger when they argue that corrective action should have been taken much earlier.

One reason it is difficult to assess the degree of overvaluation of the peso in 1994 was that Mexico's exports were showing robust growth. Total merchandise exports grew by 17 percent in 1994; manufactured exports grew by even more, by 21 percent that year. Unfortunately, total imports also

229

were growing—by 21 percent in 1994—leading to a trade deficit of $18.5 billion, or $5 billion more than in 1993. Only about $3 billion of that deficit was with the other two countries of NAFTA. The rest of the deficit was in trade with Asia and Europe—$15 billion worth in 1994—to which regions Mexican exports grew by only 4 percent in 1994.[7] As one senior Mexican businessman put it in a conversation with me: "Our trade problem is with countries that penetrate our market but don't buy as much as a bottle of tequila in return."

The crisis that followed the devaluation manifested itself in a major liquidity problem. A good part of the government's cash flow needs were financed by the sale of Mexican Treasury bills known by their acronym—cetes. Following the assassination of Colosio, there was a shift in purchases of government debt away from cetes to another Treasury instrument with its own acronym—tesobonos. Both were peso instruments, but the difference between the two was that payment of tesobonos was indexed to the dollar. All told, Mexico increased tesobono debt by $26.4 billion in 1994. Both instruments were short term, frequently for 28 days, which meant that there had to be constant auctions, weekly in fact, to sell these instruments to redeem maturing obligations. But in the aftermath of the devaluation, there were few takers, even at astronomical interest (or discount) rates. Because tesobonos were indexed to the dollar, when cashed in they represented a form of capital flight.

The features that brought on the liquidity crisis were the dollar indexation, the paucity of reserves to meet requests for payment of the tesobonos, the lack of confidence in Mexico's finances following the devaluation, and the inability to roll over the maturing debt. It was this combination that prompted President Clinton to propose a $40 billion credit to Mexico to provide assurance to purchasers of Mexican debt that they would be paid. In the end, President Clinton extended a credit of $20 billion from the Exchange Stabilization Fund administered by the U.S. Treasury, augmented by $18.5 billion from the IMF, plus $10 billion from various central banks working through the Bank for International Settlements. Not all these funds were made available at once. The stated rationale for the large rescue effort was that a Mexican default would have adverse repercussions throughout the international financial structure.

As of June 1995, Mexico had drawn down a portion of the available credit—$10 billion from the U.S. credit and the first tranche, or $7.76 billion, of the IMF funds. Tesobonos are no longer being issued, but cetes are being sold at high, but declining, interest rates at the weekly auctions. The peso seems to be holding at between 5.75 to 6.00 to the dollar. Interest rates remain high, but the financial stabilization program, other than inflation reduction, seems to be working—slowly, to be sure, but the financial situation was better after May than earlier. In addition, a rescue effort to prevent wholesale commercial bank failure appears to have served its purpose.

Mexico's current account deficit is well on its way to correction. Mexico had a trade surplus for the first quarter of 1995. This rapid turnaround in the current account results from a combination of a domestic slowdown that is limiting imports and providing an incentive for producers to find foreign markets, and the depreciated exchange rate. Real wages have fallen drastically, helping companies whose markets are outside Mexico. If portfolio capital inflows do not recover in 1995—and they are unlikely to do so—then Mexico must reduce or eliminate its current account deficit because it cannot be financed.

Solution of the deeper problem, that relating to the real economy—production and employment, and still very high inflation—lies ahead. Sketchy evidence indicates that bankruptcies are rising due to the declining domestic market and high interest rates. Unemployment has increased by an estimated 500,000 persons and there are few places for the one million or so persons who will enter the labor market in 1995. The government estimates that the informal sector now constitutes about one-third of the economy. The government projects that the worst of the overall decline in the real economy will be over by the end of 1995. There is no solid way to evaluate this projection, although more evidence will be available in the coming months.

By way of summary, these financial developments and their repercussions throughout the Mexican economy can be put in a NAFTA context:

- Mexico's trade and current account turnaround depends crucially on an open U.S. market, and NAFTA, as long it remains in existence, assures this access. More than anything, Mexico needs a healthy U.S. economy during at least the next few years.
- The trade reversal—from a U.S. to a Mexican surplus—is a consequence of Mexican monetary and financial policy reverberating back on the real economy. Put differently, the current trade picture is an outcome of policies barely dealt with in the NAFTA accord as signed.
- When the financial crisis erupted, the U.S. government felt compelled to mount a rescue effort much more substantial than any previous assistance provided to Mexico.
- When Mexico acted to deal with its problems, it did not resort to trade restrictions against its NAFTA partners, quite unlike what had been the norm on previous occasions when Mexico faced a balance-of-payments crisis.
- And one final point that will be developed further: despite all the signs of financial vulnerability in Mexico, the precise provisions of NAFTA on this score turned out to be irrelevant—but the trade provisions of NAFTA are now more important to Mexico than ever.

Depth of Mexican–U.S. Integration

It was by no means a foregone conclusion that the United States would come to Mexico's rescue as massively as it did. Indeed, if the original Clinton proposal for legislation had been left for resolution by the Congress, the initiative almost surely would have failed or been so encumbered by non-economic conditions as to be unacceptable to Mexico.[8] There was much unease even among supporters of the rescue package that it would repay the holders of tesobonos in full.[9] After all, these persons had invested in Mexican debt instruments to obtain high interest income and they should be expected to take their losses as well as benefit from their speculation.

The interesting issue to analyze is how NAFTA, because it was in place, influenced the actions of the two governments in this crisis. How will the existence of NAFTA affect future relations between the two countries in the recovery period and after Mexico emerges from its current turmoil?

The inevitablists have an incontrovertible point on their side in that the industrial integration between Mexico and the United States was proceeding apace before NAFTA. This took its most intensive form in the growth of the maquiladora industry. The special feature that most stimulated the establishment of maquiladora plants was the ability of companies to set up production facilities in Mexico to import semifinished products in-bond, that is, without payment of import duty, and then to reexport the elaborated product back to the United States while paying the duty only on the value added outside the United States.[10] NAFTA institutionalized industrial coproduction between Mexico and the United States across the board and even improved on the maquiladora structure by the promise of eliminating any import duties—on the import of the original input into Mexico and on its reexport either back to the United States or into the customs territory of Mexico proper.[11] By 1991, some 35 percent of U.S. manufactured exports to Mexico and 39 percent of U.S. manufactured imports from Mexico were between affiliates of the same company.[12] The proportions are higher today. This intrafirm trade is based on coproduction.

It is doubtful that production integration would have advanced as far as it has absent the institutionalization of duty-free trade between the two countries. NAFTA provided a legal basis for the growth of coproduction. It meant that when Mexico found itself in a balance-of-payments crisis, its extrication could not be achieved by raising import barriers against goods from the United States—which is precisely what Mexico did in the aftermath of the devaluation crisis with respect to imports from countries with which it did not have free trade agreements. NAFTA, in other words, removed one major degree of sovereign freedom in Mexico's response to its crisis.

Consider what the consequences would have been had Mexico reacted to the current financial crisis as it had to earlier balance-of-payments crises, by raising import duties or reimposing import licensing on goods from the United States. The adverse impact on U.S. merchandise exports would have been direct. Under those circumstances, the ability to provide a credit of as much as $20 billion would have been politically unthinkable. What has happened instead is that the decline in U.S. exports to Mexico will occur as well, perhaps just as sharply, but it will be indirect—as a consequence of the decline in Mexico's GDP and the sharp depreciation of the peso.

As already noted, Mexico's trade balance turnaround is also facilitated by the growth of exports. Here again, NAFTA provides assurance of Mexico's access to the U.S. market. The market will determine the bilateral trade outcome and not administrative or regulatory action by Mexico.

The existence of NAFTA thus had a major influence on the buildup to the financial and related economic crisis and the response of both Mexico and the United States to it. First, the legal assurance of free trade stimulated investment for coproduction between the two countries. Mexico became an increasingly important part of the production strategy of U.S. companies. The U.S. market became an increasingly important aspect of Mexico's export growth. Influential industrialists from both countries have a vested interest in not interrupting these linkages.

Then, when the crisis erupted, each side was constrained in the response it could make. Mexico could not impose increased import barriers on U.S. goods. Had it been able to and had it done so, the atmosphere for a massive rescue loan would have been poisoned. Rather, the market, working through the demand decline in Mexico, coupled with the price effect of the exchange rate change, is altering the trade balance—at least for now. This is a post–NAFTA scenario. During earlier Mexican crises, the typical scenario involved the imposition—or the reimposition during the administration of José López Portillo—of import restrictions.

The existence of NAFTA also influenced Mexican reaction to the crisis in the financial field. The negotiation of the financial provisions of NAFTA had been highly contentious. Mexico agreed to open its banking, securities, and insurance activities to foreign investment, but only over a transition period running through 2000 and, in some respects, beyond that to 2004 and 2007.[13] Then, when the crisis erupted, the Mexican authorities speeded the pace of financial liberalization, in part to attract investment to shore up domestic weakness. Presumably this liberalization could have been done without NAFTA, but this would have been unlikely. NAFTA provided a framework for action. The opening of the financial market was not carried out in a vacuum, but could be portrayed as a speedup of what was contemplated in any event.

Here, as with the trade response, the action taken was starkly different from what had been earlier practice. In 1982, as his administration was coming to a close in the midst of an earlier financial crisis, President López Portillo nationalized Mexico's private banks and imposed exchange controls, all in the name of preventing capital flight. This time, the action was precisely the reverse. This time, the financial system was opened more widely.[14]

The shift in Mexican policy that prompted the conclusion of NAFTA obviously had its political as well as economic ramifications. In the leadup to NAFTA, President Carlos Salinas de Gortari quite radically altered the style with which Mexico interacted with the United States. He established close relations with President George Bush; the two men met as presidents or president-elect on 11 occasions.[15] In order to establish the right atmosphere for the NAFTA negotiations, there was a deliberate effort on the part of Mexico to prevent contentious disputes from contaminating the overall relationship. Thus, the kidnapping in 1992 orchestrated by U.S. officials on Mexican soil of the Mexican doctor Humberto Alvarez Machaín, who was believed to be implicated in the torture and death of the U.S. Drug Enforcement Administration official Enrique Camarena, was treated without tantrums or interruption of other negotiations going on at that time. So, too, was the Mexican response to U.S. inaction after a panel of the General Agreement on Tariffs and Trade (GATT) ruled in Mexico's favor that the U.S. embargo against tuna imports from Mexico, carried out under U.S. law because of the dolphin kill by Mexican tuna fishing boats, was inconsistent with GATT provisions.

Those familiar with apoplectic Mexican responses to earlier U.S. actions that impinged on Mexican sovereignty must recognize the change in diplomacy inherent in these reactions. The two examples cited were pre–NAFTA. The campaign by Governor Pete Wilson of California and the subsequent approval by the electorate of proposition 187 occurred in November 1994, after NAFTA was in place. Proposition 187 was designed to deny certain public services, particularly education and non-emergency medical treatment, to illegal aliens in California. There was a strong reaction in Mexico, epitomized by the sacking of a McDonald's restaurant in the Zona Rosa in Mexico City and affirmed in public opinion polling, that this was a deliberate anti-Mexican action denying the basic rights of Mexican nationals.

Mexico, however, was restrained in its response, in part because of its traditional doctrine of non-interference in the internal affairs of other states, but also because of the changes in the bilateral relationship wrought by NAFTA. Several diplomatic notes, written in a calm tone, were sent to the U.S. State Department noting that California was usurping federal authority in the United States. A key element of the Mexican response was to suggest a formal study by the two governments of the entire immigration issue. A study, not an explosion. The terms of reference have been agreed to by the two countries and the persons to direct this study on both sides of the border have been chosen. Whatever the content of the final study, and regardless of its impact on U.S. immigration policy, the Mexican response to proposition 187 fits into the new pattern of post–NAFTA behavior. Restraint, not rabid denunciation, is now in fashion—and NAFTA surely has contributed to this.

It is significant that Mexico's economic response to the current crisis was not to jettison the economic model that led to NAFTA, but rather to reinforce it. The speedy opening of the financial market is the most dramatic indication of this. Mexico raised tariffs selectively, but not on imports from free trade partners. There was no moratorium or default on outstanding obligations, including the tesobonos, despite great temptation. Mexico's concern was not only that this would have set back the eventual renewal of capital inflows, but also that it would have destroyed NAFTA. It is accepted wisdom in official Mexico that NAFTA, because of its assurance of access to the U.S. market, is an essential element of Mexico's recovery.

The trade data for 1994 demonstrate that it was not NAFTA—not two-way trade with the United States—that stimulated Mexico's large trade deficit. More than 80 percent of the deficit was in trade with Asia and Europe. The recovery, however, depends crucially on increased exports to the United States. Economic relations between Mexico and the United States were deep before NAFTA. The United States was the major source of Mexican imports and the major market for Mexican exports. The United States, on average, provided two-thirds of Mexico's direct investment. NAFTA accelerated this integration by institutionalizing reasonable certainty of treatment. It is quite clear that Mexico's response to its current crisis was shaped in large part by the existence of NAFTA. NAFTA, in other words, has added much depth to the relationship.

The Crisis Fallout

The official basis given for the substantial U.S. financial support of Mexico was that this was necessary to stabilize global financial markets. Whatever the merit of this explanation, it soon became clear that the U.S. rescue was tailored to Mexico only and did not establish a rule for U.S. behavior toward other countries that might find themselves in similar straits. For Mexico, yes; for Argentina or Brazil, should this prove necessary, no—not with the United States playing such a prominent role.

This position is not remarkable.

Even apart from the existence of NAFTA, Mexico is a neighbor. Instability there quickly crosses the border in the form of migrants. Yet, it is impossible to avoid the concern that what happened in Mexico could be replicated in some fashion in other countries. This issue arose in the meetings of the Interim Committee of the IMF in Washington, D.C., in April 1995. Fernando Henrique Cardoso, the president of Brazil, raised this concern during his official visit to the United States that month.

The Mexican financial crisis is also affecting the potential expansion of free trade elsewhere in the Western Hemisphere. There is little stomach in the U.S. Congress—and little either in the executive branch—to proceed now beyond Chile in fashioning a Free Trade Area of the Americas (FTAA). The agenda for the June meeting of hemispheric trade ministers in Denver stemming from the Miami Summit of the Americas concerned itself with important, but more prosaic, matters, such as examining the consistency of rules of origin in the various economic integration arrangements that exist, and how to facilitate customs clearances. The idea of an FTAA is not dead, but it is clearly on hold. The Mexico financial experience has concentrated minds about the perils of economic integration between a highly developed country like the United States and developing countries in the hemisphere.

Two issues require some sorting out. The first deals with the kind of surveillance and early warning systems that might be devised internationally in this era of instantaneous and substantial capital flows. The second concerns the kinds of exchange rate provisions that might be included in future economic integration agreements in the Americas, particularly between the United States and other countries.

On the first—the international surveillance arrangements—there is clearly groping. The Interim Committee of the IMF concluded that the IMF has a role, as it had in the Mexican case, but there is no consensus that more resources should therefore be made available for this purpose. There is even less agreement about the precise surveillance role of the IMF before a country is in crisis. It is not easy to determine what should be done if the IMF is convinced that a country is heading into dangerous waters. Should the IMF go public? That could worsen a crisis. Should it make its views known in private discussions? They can be ignored. Should it make its later rescue efforts contingent on a country's response to earlier warnings? That might mean standing aside in grievous situations.

The Mexican case provides a good example of these dilemmas. We do not have full reporting on IMF–Mexican interaction during 1994. What we do know is that informed observers both inside and outside Mexico were concerned over Mexico's growing current account deficit, its overvalued exchange rate, the growth of its dollar-indexed debt, the loss of foreign reserves, the relatively loose monetary policy in the run-up to the August national elections, and the hiding of fiscal expenditures by taking them off budget and passing them through the intermediary of development banks.[16] Did the IMF raise these issues? How? And with what response? Did the U.S. Treasury raise these matters? Both the United States and the IMF later contributed heavily to the rescue package despite these lapses in Mexican policy.

Difficult or not, it seems clear that the international community, once burned in the Mexican case, cannot ignore the possibility of a replication of the financial meltdown in other developing countries. My guess is that this issue, because of its complexity, will be on the international economic agenda for some time to come. In the interim, countries may themselves consider how to reduce their vulnerability to a vote of no confidence by money-market players. One way is to reduce reliance on volatile capital inflows by, for example, raising domestic savings rates. This is more easily said than done. Chile has accomplished this, but it stands just about alone in the Americas. Raising its savings will have to be part of Mexico's policy in the years ahead. But, this will not be achieved quickly, if at all, and will not obviate the need for the international community to deal with future crises.

The second issue is a narrower one for the United States—how to deal with exchange rate issues in future economic integration agreements. Monetary union, the goal in the European Union, is not a real option between the United States and other countries in the Americas, at least for now. There have been recommendations for rigidly fixed exchange rates in the Americas—like Argentina's, which is buttressed by that country's currency board—but there is no agreement on this course of action in the hemisphere. Mexico has explicitly rejected this path and is leaning toward a flexible exchange rate system.

As with an international surveillance rescue program, the exchange rate issue is not ripe for decision. At a minimum, we can expect the inclusion of some hortatory words on exchange rates in any future U.S. integration agreements (such as not using exchange rates in a predatory manner), plus some understandings on frequent consultations between central banks and treasuries.

My guess is that the derogation of sovereignty already inherent in economic integration agreements—on commitments relating to tariff and non-tariff barriers, opening financial markets, binational panels for dispute resolution, and others—will have to go further by encouraging some degree of interference in a partner's financial policy if it is seen as exposing itself excessively to shocks. I do not accept the argument made by the U.S. Treasury that if it had taken action to alert Mexico to the dangers of its policies, this intervention would only have become a self-fulfilling prophecy. The prophecy was fulfilled by the failure to take action. This is a sensitive issue, but it almost certainly will be addressed if and when the hemisphere moves ahead toward an FTAA.

One final commentary on hemispheric free trade. There is little prospect, other than for Chile, of full-scale negotiations for accessions to NAFTA during 1995 and 1996. The goal agreed at the Miami Summit was to conclude negotiations for an FTAA by 2005. This objective does not necessarily require accessions to NAFTA, but can instead be achieved by some form of amalgamation of the various integration arrangements in the hemisphere. This would require understandings between Brazil and the United States—or, put in economic integration terms, between Mercosur and NAFTA. This, in turn, would require both sides to maintain a policy of open trading regimes behind low or nil barriers.

The hemisphere presents a mixed picture on this score. The United States has not retrogressed in any substantial way in its commitment to keep its market open, but there is much resistance to going beyond what now exists, at least in the form of more free trade arrangements. Brazil, at least rhetorically, has stood by its commitment to an open trade regime, but then in March 1995 it raised import tariffs on 109 items, the most important of which was for automobiles, from 32 to 70 percent. Argentina stuck by its fixed exchange rate of one peso equals one dollar in the fallout from the Mexico crisis, but it also raised tariffs by 3 percent under the label of a statistical tax. Venezuela is going through an economic crisis and is giving little consideration to free trade issues.

Yet, on the whole, there has been no abandonment of the open market goal in the hemisphere. There certainly has been no widespread advocacy of the old import-substitution model. Latin American and Caribbean countries remain highly export oriented. The Mexican experience has not dealt the objective of the FTAA a mortal blow.

The views expressed in this article are those of the author and do not necessarily reflect those of either CSIS or the University of Texas at Austin. Financing for travel to the Latin American Centre of Oxford University to present an earlier version of this paper was provided by the Mexican Center of the Institute of Latin American Studies at the University of Texas at Austin and by the University itself.

Notes

1. My own writings have dealt with these policy issues. One example is Sidney Weintraub, *NAFTA—What Comes Next?* (Westport, Conn.: Praeger for the Center for Strategic and International Studies, 1994), p. 8.
2. I will give only one dramatic example of this sentiment. See Pat Buchanan, "NAFTA Is about a New World Order; ... It Is about a Loss of American Sovereignty," op-ed, *Washington Times*, September 22, 1993.
3. The Mexican peso, as this is written in June 1995, is valued at close to 6 to 1 with respect to the U.S. dollar. The Mexican authorities undoubtedly would be pleased if it stabilized at around that level because it gives some impetus to exports.
4. I reviewed the financial developments even as the situation was changing daily in "The Mexican Economy: Life After Devaluation," *Current History* 94 (March 1995), pp. 108–113.
5. Banco de México, *Informe Anual 1994* (Mexico City: Banco de México, 1995), p. 60. Data in the following paragraphs come from this publication.
6. Singapore, on average, had a current account deficit of 14 percent of GDP between 1970 and 1982; Malaysia of 8.4 percent between 1981 and 1985; and Thailand of 6.9 percent between 1990 and 1993. *Ibid.*, p. 47.
7. These trade data merit an aside. Many opponents of NAFTA in Mexico point to the agreement as the cause of Mexico's growing current account deficit. The trade data show the reverse, that NAFTA provided dynamism to Mexican exports to North America. The trade shortcoming was the lack of dynamism of exports to Asia and Europe while these two regions were taking advantage of Mexico's newly open market. This helps explain Mexico's action following the financial collapse of raising its tariffs against countries with which it had no free trade agreements. Whatever the wisdom of these protective measures, they were consistent with Mexico's GATT obligations.
8. Some of the conditions proposed were for Mexico to sever relations with Cuba, privatize Pemex, and seal its border against Mexicans emigrating to the United States without authorization. These suggestions came from both Republicans and Democrats. My own interpretation is that the authors of these political conditions knew they would be unacceptable and used them as stalking horses to kill NAFTA itself.
9. I include myself in this group.
10. The most important early book to analyze the coproduction inherent in the maquiladora system was Joseph Grunwald and Kenneth Flamm, *The Global Factory: Foreign Assembly in International Trade* (Washington, D.C.: Brookings Institution, 1985).

11. I noted in a study before NAFTA came into being that "the way to examine the maquiladora industry is as a transition from enclave to an integral part of the national industrial structure [of Mexico]." See Sidney Weintraub, "The Maquiladora Industry in Mexico: Its Transitional Role," Working Paper no. 39 (Commission for the Study of International Migration and Cooperative Economic Development, Washington, D.C., 1990), p. 11.

12. Data from the U.S. Department of Commerce, cited in Weintraub, *NAFTA—What Comes Next?* pp. 45–46.

13. Gary Hufbauer and Jeffrey Schott, in *NAFTA—An Assessment*, rev. ed. (Washington, D.C.: Institute for International Economics, 1993), pp. 64–65, state the following: "While the pace of liberalization of the Mexican financial services market is slower than we recommended, the NAFTA reforms do establish significant new opportunities for US and Canadian firms right from the start." They graded the financial services results in relation to their recommendations before the fact as B+.

14. During a press conference in New York in May 1995, Guillermo Ortiz, Mexico's finance secretary, was asked whether Mexico contemplated imposing exchange controls. He responded that he would not dignify the question with an answer. The passage of 15 years, a new economic philosophy in Mexico, plus the existence of NAFTA, do make a difference.

15. The information comes from a doctoral dissertation in progress at Georgetown University by Rafael Fernández de Castro that focuses on the institutionalization of relations between Mexico and the United States as a result of NAFTA. Several of the examples used in the following paragraphs come from this work in progress.

16. These expenditures, which were channeled mostly through Nacional Financiera and Bancomext (Mexico's export-import bank), amounted to more than 4 percent of GDP in 1994.

U.S. Policy, Brazil, and the Southern Cone

Georges Fauriol and Sidney Weintraub

THE REFORM ACTIVISM of the Southern Cone nations (defined here as Argentina, Chile, Paraguay, and Uruguay) and Brazil's renewed sense of confidence are at the heart of South America's resurgence. That resurgence has become a significant catalyst for the convergence of the interests of North and South American countries and is redrawing the fundamentals of economic relationships in the Western Hemisphere. Yet, even with trade at the center of long-term U.S. economic strategy globally, Washington appears to be groping for policy balance and for consistency in its approach to the hemisphere in general and to South America's new relevance in particular.

The prevailing assumptions of U.S. policymakers engender a sense of confidence over the long run about Latin America. Democratization and economic reform have proceeded at a quick pace. The benefits that have ensued for the United States, particularly in terms of increased trade and investment flows, have been tangible. The Miami Summit in December 1994 ratified these trends and established common markers toward which further progress would evolve.

The "Spirit of Miami" calls on the governments of the region to establish a free trade area from Canada to Tierra del Fuego by 2005. Although ambitious, this target is made more credible by at least three important developments: (1) the hemisphere is awash with subregional efforts to encourage freer flows of trade and investment: the two most influential forces are the North American Free Trade Agreement (NAFTA) in the North and the Mercado Común del Sur (Mercosur) in the South; (2) an internal process of political reforms (democratization) and economic liberalization has transformed Latin America into a dynamic center of market economic experiments; and (3) perhaps most significant, much of this forward movement has been possible due to a remarkably committed political and technocratic leadership. Economic news from Chile, Argentina, and now Brazil has become a topic of conversation on Wall Street as much as in Washington or at dinner tables across the country.

Yet, as remarkable and encouraging as this Latin American experience may be, it has been brief and punctuated

---

Georges Fauriol is director of the CSIS Americas Program. Sidney Weintraub holds the William E. Simon Chair in Political Economy at CSIS and is the Dean Rusk Professor at the Lyndon B. Johnson School of Public Affairs at the University of Texas at Austin.

Copyright © 1995 by The Center for Strategic and International Studies and the Massachusetts Institute of Technology

by setbacks. These difficulties have been all too easily ignored by U.S. policymakers. Washington's rhetoric has seen growth and stability as firmly planted—at least until the recent Mexican peso crisis and the ensuing turbulence in South American markets. That crisis has underscored the degree to which Latin America's future into the twenty-first century will not follow a straight course but rather a series of zigzags and corrections. The "end of history" is not at hand in the Western Hemisphere.

The NAFTA debate, immigration and refugee flows from Mexico and the Caribbean Basin, and the financial crisis at its doorstep have drawn the attention of the U.S. public, but attitudes toward Latin America as a whole remain narrowly focused and ambivalent. Well into the late 1980s, U.S. relations with the region were inconsistent across a broad range of issues, most notably regarding democracy and human rights, trade policy and protectionism, environmental policies and other concerns. There was increased attention to Central American insurgencies in the past decade, but after years of disappointments, the U.S. image of Latin America remained blurred by a lack of immediacy and the perception that it had limited strategic relevance.

Looking just at South America, both Argentina and now probably Brazil are coming out of the fog of years of either political or economic breakdown—or both. This region—Brazil plus the Southern Cone (Argentina, Chile, Uruguay, and Paraguay)—is undergoing a transformation whose outcome could significantly alter the way the United States pursues hemispheric policy into the next century. The emerging customs union that has been formed in the southern part of the hemisphere—Mercosur—brings together Argentina, Brazil, Paraguay, and Uruguay. This development is to some degree the result of a new coherence in the region's domestic political systems, headlined by President Carlos Saúl Menem and his turnaround of Argentina since 1990 and the hopes placed in the recent election of Fernando Henrique Cardoso in Brazil. For its part, Chile is institutionalizing its sound economic management and stable governance. As it explores some form of association with Mercosur, it is pressing forward with entry into NAFTA. The evolution of both Mercosur and NAFTA are at the heart of the Miami Summit's goals of hemispheric free trade.

That goal may be achieved, but the hemisphere is hardly of one mind about trade policies. The United States generally looks at NAFTA as the point of departure, yet also has a global agenda of its own. The reemergence of Brazil suggests a stronger South American pull toward Mercosur. Others, perhaps following Chile's example, may prefer to keep their options open and in effect trade with the world. Most likely, economic cooperation will increase and hemispheric free trade will first move along flexible lines of what is being called "open integration."

As complex as all of this may be, the U.S.–*South* American trade agenda is relatively well demarcated, although its close cousin, the region's domestic economic liberalization agenda, is not. Implementing financial balance through macroeconomic reform and restructuring, fiscal discipline, and privatization provides the bases for the region's new international competitiveness. The combination of market reforms and renewed growth in South America has been beneficial for the United States. But such dramatic results are achieved only through strong political leadership, which Chile and Argentina have benefited from and Brazil is only now acquiring.

The other major component of the South American relationship with the United States is fundamentally political and these days falls under the general rubric of democratization or "governance." The resurgence of democratic governance undergirds the hemispheric consensus on trade liberalization. It generates a sense of unity not readily found in other regions of the world. This move toward democracy and unity provides the United States with a generally positive Latin American agenda and allows Washington to draw from it diplomatic and strategic advantages. The U.S. economy benefits from an economically revitalized and politically stabilized Latin America, and particularly South America. In turn, the region needs Washington's continued accommodation on trade and investment issues and on economic development. It also counts on continuing U.S. strategic protection.

The ability of countries such as Brazil and Argentina to exploit this expanding environment suggests a maturing relationship with the United States. But the overall convergence of interests will hide an occasional divergence of strategy. Brazil's increasing momentum in Mercosur and Cardoso's election imply some complications for the NAFTA-based U.S. trade outlook. Likewise, actual trade negotiations with Chile or Argentina may bring out greater U.S. political demands than these countries have been accustomed to deal with. Finally, functional integration of the hemisphere's trade, let alone its economic agenda, leaves out the likely swings in domestic political orientation. Such swings may occur first and foremost in the United States, whose emerging populist electorate has its rough equivalents in Brazil and the Southern Cone.

What ultimately drives U.S. policy is the realization that this region of the world has become a permanent fixture in U.S. economic and diplomatic priorities. The fact that exports to Brazil and Argentina have grown by 64 percent and 79 percent respectively between 1984 and 1994 tells only half the story.[1] Although the natural tendency for the United States—necessary in a superpower—to lead unilaterally has been tempered in recent years toward more measured leadership, forthrightness continues to be welcomed by governments in the region. This came out in the preparation for the Miami Summit, whose agenda as drafted by Washington did not match Latin American expectations and was modified with input from both sides. This form of mature relationship is going to become even more significant as the United States interacts more broadly and deeply with key South American nations. The latter will expect clearly defined U.S. policy, akin to what they perceive to be Washington's style when it interacts with Europe and the Pacific community.

The Foundations of U.S. Hemispheric Interests

U.S. priorities toward Brazil and the Southern Cone overlap with a broader range of issues applicable to Latin America as a whole. Among these, one set represents a primarily U.S.–Mexican/Caribbean Basin focus on immigration and refugee flows and residual security issues (Cuba, the Panama Canal, and Haiti-like operations). Although there are pockets of South American migrant communities in the

United States (Colombians, or the residuals of past political crises such as the one in Chile, for example), these are numerically small and do not constitute a critical mass. Likewise, there are no bilateral security concerns likely to draw significant U.S. military power into South America, especially in the case of Brazil and the Southern Cone.

A second set of issues stretches further into the Andean region and begins to overlap with Brazil and the Southern Cone: narcotics, organized crime, and raw materials and energy security. Drug trafficking, its links to money laundering, and its connections to global organized crime are contentious issues in the U.S.–South American agenda. The Southern Cone, particularly Paraguay, has not been immune from these problems, and Brazil is knee-deep in it as both a transshipping point and a large-scale consumer of narcotics. In this latter sense, the United States and Brazil have a growing number of concerns in common. The area of raw materials and energy security ranks as a residual U.S. interest in the case of Chile (copper and other minerals), and more broadly as a matter of regional strategic self-sufficiency. Brazil abounds in a broad range of mineral and natural resources, and both Brazil and Argentina have relatively developed oil and gas industries.

A third set of issues is not the exclusive domain of relations between the United States and Brazil and the Southern Cone but its growth in importance increasingly confirms U.S. interest in Latin America as a whole: democratization, trade integration, domestic economic liberalization, environmental policies, and hemispheric technological and security postures. These functional issues are the ingredients of a strategic proposition, namely that the consolidation of the hemisphere's mutual political and economic interests, and the institutions to support them, is in the U.S. interest. This is not new to U.S. policy, but the U.S. commitment to this objective as far as the hemisphere is concerned may be stronger and more realistic than it has been elsewhere. Such a commitment implies a degree of sustained policymaking that U.S.–Latin American relations have rarely benefited from, especially regarding U.S. ties with Brazil and the Southern Cone, where the agenda is now wide, varied, and challenging.

The free market values that undergird this environment in Latin America as a whole are at the heart of Washington's articulation of global strategy after the Cold War, in which Jeffrey Garten's "cold peace" reigns.[2] After subordinating economic policy for 40 years to Western strategic imperatives, a brutally competitive global economy in the 1990s has the United States reordering its priorities. Without a global ideological context, this need for reordering is what is left of the policy conceptualization of the 1980s. The difficulties of the past decade in Central America and the Caribbean, and on a regional basis with the debt crisis, gave rise to the notion of the "lost decade." A more constructive interpretation is that the response to these difficulties provided the foundations for the development of a regional consensus that now serves the hemisphere well. A remarkable community of policy opinion has grown up in favor of liberal or market economic reform, together with a deepening of the notion of representative democracy and a surge of regional self-confidence. This evolution has positively transformed the Latin American vision of the U.S. role in the region and has focused the hemisphere on the opportunities of the future rather than the defects of the past.

In retrospect, a defining moment of this new atmosphere was embodied in President George Bush's Enterprise for the Americas Initiative (EAI) of June 1990. Providing a framework for an enhanced hemispheric trade and market economy community, the EAI did not have a fixed timetable but at its best provided a welcome focus in an area of growing regional consensus, namely, economic policy. More recently, there is no doubt that NAFTA was creative and even visionary policymaking, but the resulting regional trade "vision" papers over the complexity of the rest of U.S. policy in the hemisphere into the next century. This affects particularly Washington's relations with Brazil and the Southern Cone.

When it came into office, the Clinton administration was given the opportunity to build on two helpful policy cornerstones: the EAI and NAFTA. For its part, Latin America itself seemed wholeheartedly supportive of these initiatives. But the initial reconceptualization that followed suggested a broadening beyond those two economic markers. Early definitions by senior National Security Council aides and also Vice President Al Gore in Mexico City in late 1993 articulated a policy linkage between the trade agenda and domestic political and socioeconomic trends within Latin American countries. The supporting argument was that the region's market reform process could be sustained only if it remained credible. For that to happen, governments would also have to address the social inequalities made more apparent by the economic reforms. Tied to this was the challenge that the Latin American countries should adopt a more accountable political process, a code word for addressing corruption.

The triad upon which the Clinton administration then anchored its hemispheric vision—economic liberalization and free trade, democratization, and sustainable development/alleviation of poverty—remains well intentioned and ambitious. But the consensus that was to ensue from it among the hemisphere's democratically elected leaders meeting in Miami almost never came to pass.

U.S. policy initially appeared not to take fully into account the degree to which core U.S. interests and a practical Latin American consensus were both strongly linked to the first leg of that triad. Latin America has become one of the largest and most dynamic regions for U.S. economic expansion. More important, most Latin American governments have pursued profound economic liberalization policies at considerable sociopolitical cost, taking a common approach to the region's future viability. As Mexico's recent peso crisis underscored, trouble in one country has immediate regional and potentially global repercussions.

The Mexican crisis has fed the ambivalence of the U.S. public about foreign policy in Latin America, not to mention the specifics of the U.S. relationship with *South* America. The 1992 U.S. presidential election campaign provided some hints of what may be repeated in 1996. Views about Latin America will be influenced by the electorate's concern for budgetary restraints and a nervousness regarding overseas exposure of any kind. In garbled fashion, these concerns shaped the debate of Latin American policy issues during the first two years of the Clinton presidency—highlighted by the divisive fight over NAFTA ratification. Two other elements can now be added: a potentially profound reassessment of immigration-related laws, exemplified by California's proposition 187 and the relevance this will have for this country's Latino community; and the confused message of Mexico's peso crisis, suggesting to some the dangers inherent in U.S. integration with Mexico and the cautionary flags this crisis should raise with regard to the growing U.S. exposure to Argentina, Brazil, and South America's other political and economic experiments.

The U.S. public's anxiety about these four factors presents a challenge for U.S. policymakers, whose views of Latin American policy have historically been crisis oriented. Political stability, democratization, economic and debt crises, trade-related disputes, and narcotics trafficking have more or less defined Washington's agenda with Latin America over the past decade. Which issue has been in the forefront has varied by country and by time period. But significantly, none of this interaction has involved a particularly positive, forward-looking agenda, nor has it often provided any encouragement for a second look by either policymakers or corporate boardrooms.

Four brief vignettes relating to *South America* help to explain this negative outlook. (1) In the early 1980s Argentina's catastrophic Falklands/Malvinas conflict forced the United States to chose between its South American relationships and the imperatives of its strategic alliance with Europe. (2) U.S. ties with Brazil, fragile since the Carter administration's missteps, gradually lost much of their residual salience as increasingly acrimonious trade and investment disputes dominated the bilateral agenda. (3) The Andean region's narcotics trade mushroomed into the Drug War and, more significantly, became the defining image of South American affairs in the minds of most Americans. (4) To cap it all off, the debt crisis became a shorthand definition for the general unattractiveness of most Latin American markets. This unhappy picture was confirmed by the decline in U.S. trade and investment flows, which were stagnant during the crisis-ridden 1980s. Only in the early 1990s did developments in Chile, now joined by Argentina and perhaps Brazil, begin to accumulate into a critical mass that could attract positive interests.

In contrast to the more visible set of issues linking the United States to Mexico and the wider Caribbean Basin area, there are in early 1995 no seriously contentious issues in Washington's agenda with Brazil and the Southern Cone. Yet the outlook will remain affected by prickly issues of the past. Illustrative are concerns over environmental policy that have affected the tone of the U.S.–Brazilian relationship in particular. In the 1990s, the environmental question overlaps with tensions over human rights and the political interest shown by Americans in the Amazon's indigenous populations. Closer cooperation with Brazil in other policy areas is likely to encounter some resistance from U.S. constituencies because of these concerns.

On the other hand, continued U.S. interest in Brazilian and Argentine behavior regarding nuclear power is on a more promising path. On the shortlist of nuclear threshold nations, and offering at best a less than comfortable picture regarding research programs, both countries have since the early 1990s modified their approach. Safeguards are more comprehensive, and the confidence-building measures between the two countries are extensive. Symbolic of these developments is the fact that Argentina, Brazil, and Chile are now full parties to the Treaty of Tlatelolco, which is at the heart of the Latin American nonproliferation regime and its nuclear-weapon-free zone. Progress under the treaty has enormous dividends for U.S. policy globally, making Latin America a rare success story in what has been a particularly serious post–cold war challenge.[3]

Another facet of U.S. security concerns, sales of conventional arms, has been reawakened as a result of the aging of South American hardware and pressures from a U.S. defense industry unhappy with the prospect of losing yet another decade of sales in South America to European manufacturers. Argentina, Brazil, and Chile, among others in the region, are candidates for purchases of refurbished F–16 jet fighters and supporting equipment. This demand for armaments comes at a time of both reduced defense budgets in countries now led by democratically elected governments and slowing sales by U.S. industry worldwide. But U.S. policy and congressional perceptions are still governed by an aversion to selling advanced weaponry in Latin America, although Secretary of Defense William Perry's visit to the region in late 1994 led to some wishful thinking that flexibility in this area might be possible over the next decade.

Overall, much of the agenda is now being driven as much by a new tone in U.S. policy as by a repositioning of South American diplomacies. Of these, Argentina's Menem government has covered the most ground, providing previously unimaginable diplomatic and even military support of U.S. policy (in the Persian Gulf War and the Haitian embargo and subsequent intervention against the Cuban government, among other cases). The recent formation of a U.S.–Argentine task force on defense cooperation comes in the wake of joint strategic war-gaming and further confirms the unprecedented and nearly "automatic" alignment with the United States.[4] The revival of Brazilian policy expected under the Cardoso government is likely to be welcomed nervously in Washington. On the one hand, Brazil's independent stance on the region's free trade process may ultimately hamper U.S. hopes of achieving its hemispheric objectives. But on the other hand, Brazil's superior capabilities and latent regional leadership aspirations suggest growing competition on some aspects of U.S. policy in South America.

Looking North from South America

The United States has a tendency to set forth hemispheric policy without fully taking into account the views from the south. President Bush's EAI received rave reviews in Latin America when it was proclaimed, but it was not preceded by extensive consultation with the other countries involved. Vice President Gore, when he invited all other democratic countries in the hemisphere to a summit meeting in 1994, gave no forewarning of what was to be discussed. Then, as noted earlier, the United States started framing the summit agenda based on the view from Washington. This did not work. The Latin Americans saw trade as the centerpiece, and an agenda along these lines was worked out *after* consultation with them.

A mature relationship requires informed consent from both sides, from the United States to the north and the Latin Americans to the south. Old habits no longer work, especially when the agenda is reciprocal trade as opposed to a unilateral U.S. bestowal of favors. The difference between now and earlier times, between granting U.S. aid under the Alliance for Progress and trade preferences under the various programs through which this is done (the general system of preferences, the Caribbean Basin Initiative [CBI], and Andean preferences), is that the United States today insists on reciprocity. Such a demand requires negotiation.

The trade agenda is not uniform throughout the hemisphere. The countries located in the northern part rely primarily on the U.S. market for their merchandise exports. This dependence reaches its zenith in Canada and Mexico: each sends upwards of 70 percent of its merchandise exports to the United States. It drops off but remains high for the countries of the Caribbean, Central America, and the northern rim of South America. Their dependence generally exceeds 40 percent, and rarely drops below 30 percent. Then, in the southern part of the hemisphere, no country's reliance on the U.S. market exceeds 30 percent.

In trade terms, therefore, it is not surprising that the Southern Cone countries and Brazil look south within South America, and east and west to Europe and Asia, as much as they look north to the United States as they frame their trade agenda. Mercosur has a trade as well as a political and geographic logic. Each of the four countries exports more to other Latin American countries than to the United States.

Trade is only one reason for seeking affiliation with NAFTA; attracting foreign investment is another. A close relationship with the United States is perhaps even more important to most hemispheric countries. But in pursuing a hemispheric agenda centered on NAFTA, the United States was acting in its traditional mode of policy development based on a partial view from Washington. The end result of the Miami Summit brought some reality to the position of the United States, which had to recognize that accession to NAFTA was only one path toward a free trade area in the hemisphere and not necessarily the first choice in the Southern Cone and Brazil.

It was remarkable as well that the United States conceived of the summit agenda without highlighting its trade aspect. U.S. rhetoric included endlessly repeated assertions that trade was to be the "centerpiece," but the early draft agenda belied the words. The agenda as promoted was diffuse; trade yes, but also governance and sustainable development, with no clear sense of priorities. It was as though the U.S. framers of the original agenda had not grasped the profound transformation undergone by South American countries during the 1980s away from insistence on import-substituting industrialization in favor of export-promoting development.

The new game for the key countries in Latin America was to expand foreign sales more than to protect the internal market. The United States may not have been ready for the new outlook after the fierce fight to obtain approval of NAFTA and then the Uruguay Round of the General Agreement on Tariffs and Trade, but reality could not be erased by ignoring it. What the United States discovered was that after President Bush floated it, the idea of hemispheric free trade was out of the box.

Challenges

Two of President Bill Clinton's major achievements during his first two years in office were in the trade field—approval of the NAFTA accord and then of the Uruguay Round. In both cases, the sales pitch in Congress and to the general public was that these would lead to an improvement in the U.S. trade balance, essentially trade as mercantilism. Then, when the 1994 figures revealed the largest U.S. merchandise trade deficit in its history, $166 billion, a lot of explaining was necessary. This took the form of the use of familiar clichés, such as the closed Japanese market, Chinese theft of U.S. intellectual property, and unfairness by other countries in their trade policies. Although there is much merit in each assertion, the administration did not rely on straightforward economic analysis to explain that a large budget deficit and a low savings rate requiring capital imports to maintain investment levels explain the trade deficit better.

As a consequence of this failure to acknowledge reality, U.S. trade policy is hostage to perennial conflicts that may alter the composition and geographic elements of the deficit without essentially affecting its overall level. Hemispheric free trade in this context is justified by showing that it will generate larger regional trade surpluses and not that it will stimulate more two-way trade. Now that the devaluation of the Mexican peso is sure to reverse the U.S. trade surplus on which the rationale for NAFTA was based, this line of argument makes suspect not only that agreement, but also the proposal for hemispheric free trade.

Two other aspects of hemispheric trade policy present significant challenges for the United States. The first is how to move ahead to achieve hemispheric free trade; a commitment has been made, but the willingness to follow through is uncertain. The second is to factor in the thinking of the South Americans on how to achieve free trade.[5]

On the first—leadership on hemispheric free trade—the U.S. position is awkward. The executive branch lacks fast-track authority, a necessary precondition for satisfactory negotiation. Obtaining this authority will be difficult. The mainstream of the Democratic Party opposes further opening of the U.S. market and there can be no negotiation without this reciprocity. And even if this problem can be overcome with the help of Republicans in Congress, the parties disagree on how closely to tie sanctions on environmental and labor matters to trade policy.

U.S. policy on NAFTA now seems to be to proceed with negotiations with Chile, but to hold the applications of all other prospective NAFTA adherents in abeyance for an indefinite period. The compromise necessary to secure fast-track authority for Chile is itself far from assured. If fast-track authority is uncertain for hemispheric free trade, then it is even more problematic in the global context. This is because the Western Hemisphere is the one region in which the mercantilistic argument has some resonance. Excluding Canada, with which the U.S. merchandise trade balance has been in deficit for many years, the Western Hemisphere is a region of U.S. trade surplus. The bulk of the U.S. trade deficit is with Asia—Japan, China, and Taiwan primarily.

The second challenge—to factor in Latin American thinking as the United States formulates hemispheric policy—presents equally formidable problems. The United States cannot shut itself in economically as the rest of the hemisphere looks outward and still have a viable hemispheric policy. Nor can the United States have a policy acceptable to the rest of the hemisphere without taking into account the aspirations of other hemispheric leaders.

Intraregional trade is booming in South America as a result of policy changes that have lowered import barriers and made possible preferential arrangements among the countries of the region. By far the most important subregional arrangement in Latin America is Mercosur and there trade is growing rapidly, especially between Brazil and Argentina, the two largest countries. Mercosur has been a customs union since January 1, 1995, which means that it has a common external tariff (CET). The CET is not yet in place for some key imports, such as computers, automobiles, and capital goods, but there are understandings for gradual movement to the roughly 15 percent average applicable for other products.

One consequence of choosing the customs union rather than the free trade approach is that individual Mercosur countries cannot accede to NAFTA because this would violate the CET. Mercosur, if it is to survive, must negotiate as a unit. Thus the first priority is for its members to consolidate Mercosur and only then decide the nature of its affiliation, if any, with NAFTA.

Brazil has been encouraging other South American countries to associate with Mercosur, not necessarily by joining as full members, but by reaching a free trade agreement with the grouping as a whole. Chile is engaged in precisely such a negotiation and Bolivia has indicated it may do the same.

There are thus two important and potentially competing subregional groupings in the hemisphere, NAFTA and Mercosur, each with a dominant member, the United States and Brazil respectively. Although Brazil is encouraging other South American countries to associate with Mercosur, the United States presents the image of a reluctant partner, with the exception of a potential link with Chile.

Most South American countries would prefer not to make a choice between subregional groupings. Like Chile, they would like affiliations with both, but few now have this option. Most countries would welcome an aggressive U.S. policy promoting hemispheric free trade, but they are not sure this will be forthcoming. Most countries would welcome U.S. leadership in hemispheric economic policy as long as this involved consultation with them, but the disconnect between the executive and the legislature in the United States precludes this for now.

The foregoing discussion deals with trade policy, but trade, although important in and of itself, is also a metaphor for other issues. Trade policy is the leading edge of U.S. interaction with other countries of the hemisphere. In the absence of much foreign aid, trade defines the key alliances of the day. It, more than other items on the agenda, makes possible the cooperative achievement of other objectives.

The other main themes of the Miami Summit agenda are also important in and of themselves, but they are linked in the minds of most Latin American countries with access to the U.S. market. The United States was able to obtain Mexican commitments on environmental issues only when they were made a condition of NAFTA. Other Latin American countries are likely to tell the United States to keep out of how they manage their environmental programs if cooperation brings no trade opportunities.

The democracy theme also carries much force in the hemisphere today. The State Department regularly parades the fact that all countries in the hemisphere, save one, now have democratically elected governments. True enough, as long as the definition of democracy is flexible, but these countries turned to democracy mostly of their own volition. It is hard to determine if the United States is using the democracy theme as a club in the hemisphere (hold elections or be excluded) or promoting it as a goal. If as a club, its efficacy is limited to this hemisphere, as the 1994 Asia–Pacific Economic Cooperation (APEC) meeting in Indonesia demonstrated in its call for free trade in that region, replete with nondemocratic nations, by 2020. Following that meeting, Latin Americans are somewhat cynical as to whether the United States really cares deeply about promoting democracy if this conflicts with expanding exports.

Yet this triad of objectives—economic liberalization and free trade, democratization, and sustainable development/alleviation of poverty—is generally accepted in the hemisphere. The commitment to the latter two varies by country, but all three are taken as valid. All three are also themes expounded widely by the United States, but with more vigor in this hemisphere than anywhere else in the developing world. Thus, failure to advance on all three in Latin America will compromise progress elsewhere in the world.

But it is worth repeating that progress on trade issues is for the moment the sine qua non for U.S. influence on most other issues, from the protection of human rights, to cooperation in stemming narcotics traffic, to being taken seriously in the environmental field. Progress on trade in this hemisphere will be taken as a sign that the United States has the will to negotiate more widely on trade issues, whether globally or in APEC.

Success in U.S. trade policies has an underlying institutional context. The Miami process is anchored to existing organizations, such as the Organization of American States and the Inter-American Development Bank, and pressures will build to ensure that the former, not previously strong in the trade field, reconfigures itself in line with the trade tasks assigned to it at the Miami Summit. The same holds true for a set of specialized institutions, ranging from human rights to regional defense concerns. The mood in the U.S. Congress may not be all that sympathetic to regional bureaucracies, which, despite arguments from Latin Americans, may end up being viewed as partially unnecessary. The interest that countries such as Brazil and those of the Southern Cone assign to this question will affect U.S. attitudes.

Policy

The spirit of Miami has weakened after the Mexican financial meltdown. The United States has no stomach for admitting countries other than Chile to NAFTA, and the strength of even this commitment is uncertain. Yet two considerations should be kept in mind: (1) the economic-financial situation in South America is not identical to that in Mexico; and (2) economic integration there will probably move ahead even if the United States is not an active player.

As a policy matter, therefore, the process ratified at Miami should move forward. The Mexican economic situation will change and so will the U.S. mood toward integration. It may take several years for this to come to pass, but it would be unwise for the United States to send a message to the hemisphere's component countries that it is not receptive to their imperative of augmenting exports.

The current U.S. preference to defer concrete steps toward hemispheric integration beyond the commitment to Chile dictates that the U.S. posture should be flexible on how hemispheric integration comes about. Brazil is determined to strengthen Mercosur; this goal should be respected. Argentina concurs but is nervous about putting all its eggs in the Brazilian (Mercosur) basket: U.S. policy should take this into account. All the variations in attitude in the Andean countries and the Caribbean Basin also require a flexible and nuanced U.S. trade policy in the hemisphere.

Many in the United States remain ambivalent about expanding NAFTA into the Pacific. To do so would be unwise at this time. It would send the wrong message to the countries in the Western Hemisphere about U.S. priorities. Beyond that, protectionist sensitivities in the United States are apt to be greater in free trade arrangements with Asian than with most hemispheric countries. Finally, moving to the Pacific in the aftermath of the Miami Summit would signal a downgrading of priorities other than trade there, particularly that of encouraging democracy. Besides, the Pacific has its own institutional mechanism in APEC.

For better or worse, priorities in the hemisphere have changed away from an overwhelming concern with security issues to economics, away from aid to trade, away from official to private capital flows, away from import substitution to export promotion, away from one-sided favors from the United States to reciprocity. The United States can be influential in the hemisphere only if its policies reflect the majority aspirations in Latin America. Because the hemisphere's political and security agenda—combatting the narcotics trade, dealing with organized crime, slowing illegal immigration, encouraging environmental protection, shaping regional institutions, and taking into account remaining security issues—continues to be occasionally troublesome, cooperation on these issues will be eased provided that U.S. economic policy and the requirements of countries in the Western Hemisphere are compatible.

Notes

1. The figures are taken from U.S. Department of Commerce, International Trade Administration, 1995.

2. Jeffrey E. Garten, *A Cold Peace: America, Japan, Germany, and the Struggle for Supremacy* (New York, N.Y.: Times Books, 1992).

3. This issue is particularly well documented in John R. Redick, Julio C. Carasales, and Paulo S. Wrobel, "Nuclear Rapprochement: Argentina, Brazil, and the Nonproliferation Regime," *The Washington Quarterly* 18 (Winter 1995), pp. 107–122.

4. See Margaret Daly Hayes, "By Example: The Impact of Recent Argentine Naval Activities on Southern Cone Naval Strategies," no. CRM 94/111 (Center for Naval Analyses, Alexandria, Va., November 1994).

5. See Sidney Weintraub, *NAFTA: What Comes Next?* (Washington, D.C.: CSIS, 1995).

Prospects for an EU–NAFTA Free Trade Agreement

Thomas J. Duesterberg

SEVERAL SEMINAL EVENTS in the early 1990s have set the stage for renewed thinking about a free trade agreement (FTA) between countries that subscribe to the North American Free Trade Agreement (NAFTA) and to the European Union (EU).

- The completion of the Uruguay Round negotiations of the General Agreement on Tariffs and Trade (GATT) inevitably raises the question of crafting the next logical step in the ongoing process of trade liberalization.
- The need to find new and lasting foundations for the U.S.–European relationship in the post–cold war period has led to consideration of a more formal treaty or agreement relationship between the two.
- The proliferation of regional trade groupings around the world has also spawned new thinking about ways to avoid dissolution or erosion of the traditionally close transatlantic relationship.
- European leaders are starting to consider trade liberalization as one component of a badly needed program to revitalize economic competitiveness in their countries in the face of persistent unemployment and stagnation in many high-technology industries.

Thinking about a transatlantic FTA is not without precedent. In the 1970s and 1980s U.S. congressional leaders such as Al Ullman (D–Ore.) and Bill Bradley (D–N.J.) suggested some form of FTA between the United States and the European Community (EC). In 1989, economist Gary Hufbauer argued that a free trade and investment agreement for the Organization for Economic Cooperation and Development (OECD) zone would be the next logical step in trade liberalization following completion of the Uruguay Round.[1] And following the demise of the Cold War and the Warsaw Pact, U.S. Secretary of State James A. Baker III began a dialogue with the European Commission and its president, Jacques Delors, on a new transatlantic charter. Discussion of the possibility of a U.S.–EC trade liberalization agree-

---

Thomas J. Duesterberg is senior fellow of the Hudson Institute and director of its Competitiveness Center. From 1989 to 1993 he was assistant secretary of commerce for international economic policy.

Copyright © 1995 by The Center for Strategic and International Studies and the Massachusetts Institute of Technology
The Washington Quarterly • 18:2

ment was at least part of the Baker–Delors dialogue.

By the end of 1994, two additional events had drawn attention to the need to find new foundations on which to strengthen the U.S.–EU relationship in an era of growing economic and political regionalism. The Uruguay Round was finally ratified and Europe began to prepare for the Intergovernmental Conference on institutional reform to be held in 1996 as required by the Maastricht agreement. In 1994, the U.S. ambassador to the EU, Stuart Eizenstat, stated that an FTA could be a possible pillar of the new U.S.–EU relationship, the new Canadian prime minister, Jean Chrétien, floated the idea of a broad European–North American free trade accord, and the head of the European Commission Delegation to the United States, Andries van Agt, also called for a transatlantic FTA.[2] Van Agt rightly emphasized the need for the United States and the EU to pay special attention to nurturing their long-standing and vital relationship at a time when the focus is on regional agreements anchored separately on either side of the ocean.

This article will suggest some of the economic and political considerations involved in an FTA between the NAFTA area and the EU. In the post–cold war era, which is characterized by rapidly expanding economic integration, it is increasingly difficult to separate domestic economic and political considerations from those more narrowly focused on international diplomacy, but for the purposes of this article, this separation facilitates analysis and exposition.

Economic Factors

The North American and European economies are already integrated to an extent unmatched by any other interregional relationship in the world. The NAFTA and EU areas together account for slightly over 50 percent of the total world economy and for over 40 percent of world trade. More important, the two-way relationship is deep, broad, and well balanced.

In 1993 U.S. exports to the EU stood at $97 billion and EU exports to the United States at $98 billion. The United States sold $54 billion in services to the EU and the EU sold $46 billion in services to the United States. Total NAFTA exports of goods to the EU were $116 billion in 1993 and EU exports of goods to NAFTA were about $120 billion. Europe and North America exchange a wide range of goods, from raw materials to high-technology products to services, in a reasonably balanced pattern of trade.[3]

Increasingly in the modern world economy, trade follows investment.[4] And, due to the long and close economic relationship between Europe and North America, direct investment between the two is extremely well developed. In 1991, U.S. direct investment in the EU totaled $232 billion, and sales by U.S. affiliates in Europe reached $741 billion. EU investment in the United States was $188 billion, and sales by EU affiliates in the United States totaled $600 billion.

Almost 15 percent of products sold in Europe are made by U.S. companies either in Europe or for export from the United States, and slightly more than 13 percent of the products sold in the United States are European in origin. European affiliates employ over 2.9 million workers in the United States, and U.S. affiliates in the EU employ over 2.4 million workers.[5] Although Canada also has extensive export and foreign direct investment relations with Europe, the United States is the largest foreign investor in Europe, and European countries represent almost

60 percent of foreign direct investment in the United States. In contrast to Japanese companies, both U.S. and European companies are more likely to buy components and do research in the country in which they have invested.[6]

The large cross-border trade flows and huge direct investment positions are roughly in balance between the two regions, reflecting the structural similarities of their economies and the relative lack of trade and investment barriers, apart from some significant sectors to be discussed later. Tariffs are already largely at the negligible level of 5 percent or less, except for a few "tariff peaks." The Uruguay Round agreement will reduce tariffs applicable to U.S.–EU trade by almost 50 percent when implemented. Over 40 percent of all goods will enter the United States and the EU duty free, including goods from such significant sectors as construction and agricultural equipment, steel, beer, medical equipment, pharmaceuticals, paper, and furniture. Nearly 100 percent of U.S., EU, Canadian, and Mexican tariffs are bound and hence cannot be altered without negotiation with trading partners.

The Uruguay Round agreement also saw progress in previously contentious areas of dispute between the United States and the EU. Most notable is the area of agriculture: subsidies and tariffs will be cut by more than one-third; the two sides agreed to settle disputes within the new World Trade Organization (WTO)—the successor to the GATT once the Uruguay Round takes effect; and they agreed to further negotiations to reduce remaining trade-distorting subsidies in the future. Agreement to include trade in services under WTO rules will also reduce some tensions between the two. In addition, Europe and the United States made progress in solving long-standing differences in the areas of telecommunications and heavy electrical equipment.

In these conditions of economic interdependence, balanced trade, and relative lack of trade frictions, then, it would make sense for both consumer and producer interests to remove remaining impediments to trade through a comprehensive FTA. Given the already extensive cross-border investment in the transatlantic region, the importance of intracompany trade flows in overall trade in goods, and the growing importance of services trade (where the right to invest in or establish a business in the host country is often important), it would also make economic sense to remove the few remaining barriers to investment as part of an FTA. Harmonization of product standards within an FTA would also enhance the efficiency benefits derived from such an agreement.

In addition to the benefits to consumers of removing tariffs and increasing product choice, exposing industry on both sides of the Atlantic to greater competition would also lead to efficiency gains for industry, which, in turn, would increase competitiveness outside the EU–NAFTA area. Such gains would be especially important for Europe, which is experiencing a sustained period of stagnation and long-term unemployment related to its high cost structure and lagging technology. European economies are also losing market share in extra-EU trade, a trend likely to continue according to OECD projections. The increasing regionalization of trade in the EU is a partial reflection of these factors, which place its products at a competitive disadvantage in Asian and, increasingly, in North American markets. As a share of total exports, EU member-state exports to other member states have risen from about 50 percent to over 63 percent since 1970, while the proportion of total gross domestic product (GDP) represented by exports to non-EU destinations has fallen from 11 percent to 8 percent in the last decade.[7]

Increased integration with the North American market would in the short to medium term require a restructuring of European industry similar to what took place in the United States in the 1980s. The European Commission has recognized Europe's structural competitiveness problems and signaled that the use of trade liberalization arrangements should be an integral part of the drive to rebuild international competitiveness as a basis for more robust long-term growth.[8] European industries such as automobiles, metals, mining, transportation, financial and cultural services, and electronics are likely to be affected by increased competition within an EU–NAFTA free trade agreement, but U.S. industry would also be forced to become more efficient. U.S. industries such as textiles, some household goods, some agricultural processing, and higher-end automobiles might also be required to restructure. In the longer run, however, such restructuring would enhance the competitiveness of the affected sectors in world markets and build a basis for overall productivity gains. Indeed, these latter features probably constitute the principal economic benefit of a transatlantic FTA, especially for the EU, which is in search of a workable path to more solid and sustainable growth and job creation.

Finally, an EU–NAFTA agreement would give North American companies access to East European markets equal to that enjoyed by EU countries under the network of Association Agreements that the EU has set up with developing countries to promote trade and investment. EU companies would at the same time gain access equivalent to that of Americans and Canadians in Mexico under a transatlantic FTA.

There are three principal areas where negotiation of an FTA would meet entrenched opposition. First, the agricultural sector on both sides has been protected and subsidized since the Great Depression of the 1930s and has been a source of trade tension throughout the period since World War II. Recent negotiations for the Uruguay Round, NAFTA, and, on the European side, the Association Agreements, show the nearly intractable nature of opposition to trade liberalization among agricultural interests and those that sympathize with them. Reducing protection and subsidy in this sector, according to analyses by the World Bank and others is, however, likely to have the broadest benefits for consumers and overall economic efficiency, especially in Europe. In the somewhat inelegant language of World Bank economists, the argument is as follows:

> Moreover, since agricultural protection is implicitly a tax on manufacturing, with its removal resources flow into the urban sector where Europe and Japan have a comparative advantage. The food-exporting OECD countries are aided significantly by agricultural trade liberalization, although gains for the U.S. are small.[9]

The World Bank estimates, for example, that the partial agricultural trade liberalization envisioned in the Uruguay Round will account for $190 billion of the total $213 billion per annum added to world GDP by implementation of the Round, with OECD countries receiving $120 billion of the agricultural benefits.[10]

Another factor mitigating some of the problems in agricultural liberalization stems from the recent elections in the United States. The changed political configuration may give new political impetus for reduction of agricultural support programs and build some support for trade liberalization as compensation.

The second area of potential difficulty is in high-technology goods. In recent years, some products like commercial aircraft, telecommunications equipment, computers, semiconductors, and environmental technology have been protected and subsidized to some extent on both sides of the Atlantic, although, until the arrival of the Clinton administration, the Europeans had a more extensive and explicit high-technology industrial policy. Even convinced proponents of free trade like Martin Bangemann create exceptions for an industrial policy featuring "national champions" to keep Europe competitive in what are considered the high-growth industries of the future.[11] Protection in this arena is often buttressed by restricting access to government research programs by foreign firms. At the insistence of the Clinton administration, the scope of government subsidies sanctioned by the GATT/WTO was considerably widened in the Uruguay Round. Given the recent actions by sitting governments, protection of high-technology sectors appears likely to be a continued source of friction in the future. Forging a workable dispute settlement mechanism to cover this area would also be a big challenge.

The third area of difficulty is represented by the "tariff peaks" and tariff preferences that both the EU and NAFTA countries maintain, even after the Uruguay Round. On the U.S. side this involves textiles, apparel, specialty agricultural products, ceramics, and glassware, while on the EU side high tariff walls are maintained for large trucks, some semiconductors, wood, aluminum, many value-added agricultural products, and fish. The United States, the EU, and Canada all maintain tariff preferences with southern trading partners in their respective hemispheres. Political instability and the looming threat of immigration have led some of the southern EU countries and Germany to push for additional concessions for North African trading partners.[12] Canada is also concerned about EU tariff peaks in the natural resource area. Elimination of these barriers may be easier in a bilateral negotiation than it was in the Uruguay Round, although the current preoccupation with reducing unemployment and economic insecurity on both sides of the Atlantic suggests that the task will continue to be difficult.

We might also note that, presuming that investment rules are part of an FTA negotiation, there may be some friction regarding the right of establishment and ownership restrictions in some services areas. Areas of friction would include transportation, finance and banking, and cultural services. The cultural services dispute that was carried over from the Uruguay Round is likely to be exacerbated by the advance of new information services in the economy of the twenty-first century. If the EU extends its limits on foreign content as a proportion of broadcast time to some of the newer information services like interactive video, interactive data bases, or interactive shopping, then the differences between the two sides will widen even further.

Although it is difficult to assess the balance of economic benefits from an EU–NAFTA free trade and investment agreement, it is not likely that the perceived economic benefits to either side would be significant enough on their own merits to justify the transitional problems they would entail at this time. This is due primarily to the following factors:

- trade and investment ties are already so well developed that additional gains in the advanced manufacturing sector from deepening the economic relationship are likely to be small;
- the biggest gains to overall economic efficiency would be generated from agricultural liberalization, which is the most difficult sector;
- the EU is still grappling with the economic dislocation and institution building required by Maastricht; and
- the U.S. leadership is so concerned with job creation and new government support for industry that further expansion of free trade with industrialized countries is not high on its agenda.

The current domestic political environment on both sides of the Atlantic, in which the fear—or reality—of economic stagnation and unemployment is high, also leads policymakers to be wary of taking on the short-term pain of dislocation due to trade opening. In addition, both sides, despite the considerable effort made to complete the Uruguay Round, have in recent years perceived their own economic destiny more in terms of expanding and deepening regional ties than of broadening international trade liberalization.[13] Some European leaders, at least those in Brussels, London, and Bonn, are beginning to reconsider existing economic policies and to push for new ones that emphasize private sector initiative and flexibility and more open competition as the foundations of growth. But this tendency is far from dominant. In these circumstances, any discussion of a possible EU–NAFTA agreement must be considered also in terms of what Zbigniew Brzezinski calls the "geopolitical" situation. Noneconomic factors in favor of an EU–NAFTA free trade and investment agreement may be more compelling, in fact, than the economic considerations.

Political Considerations

After the exhausting and dauntingly complex negotiations of the Uruguay Round, many analysts look to some variation of an EU–NAFTA trade and investment agreement as the next logical step in maintaining momentum for global trade liberalization. If one accepts the so-called "bicycle theory," constant progress in terms of trade opening is needed to protect the international system from reverting to ever-present protectionist dangers. Although most trade theorists would prefer to keep trade liberalization within the institutional structure of the WTO, the very size of this organization and the difficulty of the next steps in the trade agenda make success in this forum problematic. Not the least of the problems for the 124-member WTO will be determining how to handle the new "trade plus" issues such as trade and the environment or trade and worker rights.

An EU–NAFTA arrangement could serve the purpose of keeping the bicycle moving because it could probably be achieved more easily than a major, multilateral WTO agreement or any other regional agreement. Negotiations by either Europe or North America with an Asian partner will be extremely difficult because of the economic, cultural, and political differences that divide Asia from Europe.

In addition, despite the recent commitment of the Asia–Pacific Economic Cooperation (APEC) group to negotiating a free trade agreement by 2020, accommodating the diverse economic and cultural differences among its 18 members will not be easy. Some analysts now believe that the rapid pace of growth in Asia will soon reach limits based on inability to increase total factor productivity.[14] If this analysis proves sound, it would weaken the rationale for placing priority on the Asian market. By contrast, the long affinity between North America and Europe and their balanced economic relationship would facilitate an EU–NAFTA negotiation process.

Not the least of the political benefits of such an agreement would be the reduction of trade tensions between the two trading areas that have at times in the postwar period threatened the very foundations of the Bretton Woods regime. The international trading system was founded and nurtured by the North American–European axis, and further deepening of that system inevitably has to be driven by these two partners. Japan has shown little creativity in or commitment to building a leadership role for itself in global trade liberalization efforts and is unlikely to do so in its present political circumstances. Indeed, adding Japan to the EU–NAFTA equation would greatly complicate any negotiation and probably doom it to failure.

An EU–NAFTA agreement would have some ancillary politico-economic benefits for both parties. As Hufbauer has pointed out (admittedly in connection with an agreement encompassing all of the OECD), this type of agreement would "soften the edges of emerging regional trade blocs."[15] Europe, North America, and Asia have all seen growth in intraregional trade in recent years, although it has been relatively lower for North America. Intraregional trade accounted for about 46 percent of trade in the Americas, 51 percent of Asia–Pacific trade, and 70 percent of European trade in 1991. Some regional tensions have resulted, and these have been underscored recently by trade frictions between the United States and major Asian partners. An EU–NAFTA alignment might exacerbate tensions with Asia in the short run, but it is hard to fathom how the major trading nations of Asia (especially Japan, South Korea, Taiwan, and Singapore) could long stay out of a new bloc that comprised 40 to 50 percent of world GDP and trade. Many Latin American nations are already anxious to gain accession to NAFTA, and a transatlantic agreement would whet their appetite even more.

In a geopolitical sense, moreover, the EU–NAFTA alignment could eventually be a means of bringing Japan fully into the world trading *and investment* system as practiced by Europe and North America. Again, this presumes that Japan would in effect have no other choice but to join the new arrangement. EU leaders like Sir Leon Brittan have indicated growing interest in finding acceptable methods of U.S.–EU cooperation by which to convince Japan to move in this direction more decisively. Inclusion of investment rules would be especially important where Japan is concerned because that nation's trade imbalance is at least partially explained by its extremely low level of foreign direct investment.[16] Other Asian nations and the emerging market economies of Latin America would have to follow as well. In this important sense, the EU–NAFTA agreement would simply be an interim step in deepening the global trading system and a proxy for the next step in the sequence of progressive "rounds" of trade liberalization. It would substitute in some respects for the difficult task of multilateral negotiations involving all 124 GATT signatories.

An EU–NAFTA free trade and investment agreement would also allow the world's oldest liberal democracies and founders of the international economic system to cement their bilateral political ties and reestablish the leadership role in world trade that seemed to be threatened in the early 1990s by initiatives suggesting a return to various forms of national or regional protection. Such moves as the EU automobile restraint agreement with Japan, use of antidumping duties against commodity exports from the countries of the former Council for Mutual Economic Assistance (COMECON), threatened resumption of Super 301 legislation, and increased reliance on subsidies for "national champion" industries were some of the manifestations of the rejuvenated protectionism. Countering these tendencies would be of crucial assistance in erecting the institutions and global ties needed to chart a new world order in the post–cold war era. It would also help reassert clear leadership in global affairs by a large grouping united by democratic and liberal economic principles. At the very least, a closer economic relationship would provide an excellent building block for reconstructing transatlantic political ties in a new era.

Some would argue that, especially given the possibility of failure of an EU–NAFTA negotiation due to the opposition of entrenched economic interests and the new economic nationalism, it is not worth the risk of starting such a negotiation because it might also drive Asian nations into their own trading bloc. Prime Minister Mahathir Mohamad of Malaysia has been promoting an exclusive Asian trading bloc for a number of years. Japan and other Asian nations have increasingly diverted their investment toward Asian partners in recent years, partially in response to the expansion of European and North American regional trading areas. Recent U.S. trade démarches toward Japan, China, and other Asian nations have led to broader sympathy for Mahathir's proposal in Asia. Other events in recent years, such as U.S. differences with Singapore, uncertainty over U.S. Korean policy, and perceptions of U.S. meddling in domestic issues, have reinforced the tendency, best expressed by Lee Kuan Yew of Singapore, to question U.S. leadership in this region.[17]

From the U.S. perspective, one could also question the wisdom of risking the increasingly important U.S. economic and political relations with the fast-growing, market-oriented economies of both Asia and Latin America. A North American–European negotiation might raise the old specter of a "rich man's club" or, worse, a "white man's club." Expanding NAFTA or deepening trading relations with APEC while pursuing an FTA with Europe are not necessarily contradictory initiatives, but as a practical matter the U.S. government has only limited personnel and political resources with which to undertake the complex negotiations involved in an FTA with any one significant trading partner, let alone two. Asian nations, too, would probably be wary of U.S. motives in negotiating regional arrangements with Europe at the same time as with them.

From a more narrowly strategic economic point of view, North American trade with Asia is much larger than with Europe, and North American trade and investment are both growing more rapidly with the emerging nations of Asia and Latin America than with Europe.[18] Total cross-border merchandise trade between Asia and the United States surpassed equivalent U.S. trade with Europe starting in 1978, and total U.S. exports to the Americas are about twice the level of U.S. exports to Europe. Trade and investment barriers are also much higher in Asia and Latin America, so that the economic benefits to North America of liberalization would be greater for these areas than for Europe. According to estimates made by the Office of the U.S. Trade Representative, total U.S. exports to Latin America and Asia (excluding Japan) in the year 2010 will be $232 billion and $248 billion, respectively, while U.S. exports to the EU will only reach $128 billion.[19] Nor is the United States alone in recognizing the growing importance of Asia and Latin America. The Canadian minister for international trade, Roy MacLaren, spoke in May 1994 in favor of an expansion of NAFTA to emerging economies in both Latin America and Asia.[20] Many U.S. and Canadian policymakers, then, see more economic benefit in opening developing country markets than in further liberalization of transatlantic markets. Political and strategic considerations are thus more dominant in the United States than in Europe, where there is clearly some long-term competitiveness gain to be derived from a transatlantic FTA.

Concentrating efforts on an EU–U.S. agreement, finally, might slow down momentum for bringing the new democratic, market-oriented countries of Eastern Europe and Latin America into the respective regional free trade areas that have developed in the last few decades. One could argue that, in current historical circumstances, the political mission of Europe to bring East European states (and perhaps some constituent elements of the former Soviet Union), and of North America to bring the new market-oriented democracies of Latin America, firmly into the democratic, free market system is best accomplished by expansion of the two regional free trade areas. The EU also has ample unfinished business in completing the Maastricht and Single Market programs and the next phase of expansion to Austria and the Nordic countries. Moreover, West European traders are already dominant in Central and Eastern Europe, and North Americans are dominant in Latin American markets. Both the EU and NAFTA thus stand to lose market share in their respective hemispheres if a transatlantic FTA equalizes access.

Concluding Observations

The intergovernmental conference process in Europe and the U.S. presidential election in 1996 will provide a good opportunity for political leaders to sort through some of the difficult choices they face in deciding the next steps in building a sustainable set of institutions and, possibly, agreements to anchor the U.S. relationship to the European Union. A decision to initiate a process leading to an EU–NAFTA trade and investment agreement would require subsuming many short-term and parochial economic interests under a larger vision of political and economic leadership by a transatlantic partnership in the post–cold war world. These two regions have risen above such narrow interests in the past, especially in the immediate postwar period when they established the Bretton Woods system, and are certainly capable of doing so in the future.

At this point in the political history of both North America and Europe, however, the strong leadership needed to take this step is not apparent. Nor is the economic rationale for this decision so compelling as to risk the transitional economic dislocation that would inevitably occur in both areas. What is lacking now, perhaps, is the crisis atmosphere that sometimes, as Hegel stated in a famous epigram ("the Owl of Minerva takes flight only as the shades of night are falling"), engenders heroic wisdom and leadership.[21] Perhaps if economic stagnation, technological lag, and weak job creation performance in Europe persist much longer, the crisis will be serious enough to compel difficult remedial action.

If the current generation of leaders does decide that the next steps in trade liberalization would prove too cumbersome in the WTO and that closer transatlantic cooperation requires a firm economic foundation, then an EU–NAFTA free trade agreement offers one mutually beneficial path to cooperation. Even then, however, difficult questions on the modalities of an agreement would quickly arise. What would be the scope, the timing, the form, and the breadth of the agreement? What would be the relationship of this new agreement to the WTO and to the network of existing regional trading relationships?

Because the economic rationale for some form of agreement is not totally persuasive, leaders would probably be well advised to adopt modest short-term goals while setting in motion a process that has the intended effect of providing leadership to the entire world in advancing a trade liberalization agenda. For example, if recent experience in the Uruguay Round is any guide, agriculture should not be high on the near-term agenda, especially because that agreement provides for further negotiations in the WTO five years after it comes into effect. New areas like trade and the environment and labor standards would also be divisive and should be avoided at the outset of the process.

Instead of a comprehensive negotiation from the start, a more realistic approach might take on a defined basket of issues, such as investment, tariff peaks, intellectual property rights, financial services, subsidies, and government procurement, where the two sides have roughly convergent economic interests. Presuming that eventual inclusion of Japan in the agreement is an agreed goal, these areas are also critical to the trade-opening agenda with the world's second largest economy. The negotiation could be placed in a larger context of setting a goal for a comprehensive free trade and investment agreement in a time frame not exceeding a decade. Whatever the form and timing, the agreement should be crafted to be compatible with the WTO and indeed to point the way toward future liberalization within the WTO. In this way, Europe and North America could reestablish the clear leadership role in world economics that no other country or regional grouping can play, and go a long way toward buttressing their leadership in political affairs as well. Not the least of the benefits would be to give a new foundation to a transatlantic relationship badly in need of rejuvenation.

The original version of this paper was presented to the Working Group on the Post–Uruguay Round Agenda of the European Institute on June 8, 1994, in Washington, D.C. The views expressed or implied here are solely those of the author. No opinions, statements of fact, or conclusions contained in this article can properly be attributed to the Hudson Institute, its staff, its members, or its contributing agencies.

Notes

1. Gary Clyde Hufbauer, *The Free Trade Debate: Report of the Twentieth Century Fund Task Force on the Future of American Trade*

Policy (New York, N.Y.: Priority Press Publications, 1989), pp. 149–154.

2. Stuart Eizenstat, "Excerpts of Remarks to the European Institute Working Group on the Trans-Atlantic Joint Action Initiative," Washington, D.C., May 12, 1994. Van Agt's call for an FTA was reported in the *Washington Post*, November 18, 1994, p. B-1. Chrétien's remarks were briefly summarized in "Euro-American Trade Pact Urged," *Wall Street Journal*, December 5, 1994, p. A–11.

3. A recent report on the transatlantic relationship emphasizes the deep and balanced economic relationship and its role as a pillar in the international trading system. See Robin Gaster and Clyde Prestowitz, Jr., *Shrinking the Atlantic: Europe and the American Economy* (Washington, D.C.: Economic Strategy Institute, 1994).

4. This relationship is documented and analyzed in Lester Davis, "U.S. Foreign Trade in Merchandise and Services by Foreign-Owned U.S. Firms," in U.S. Department of Commerce, Economics and Statistics Administration, *Foreign Direct Investment in the United States: An Update* (Washington, D.C.: U.S. Department of Commerce, 1993), pp. 77–89.

5. See Marianna Knight and Margaretha Dehandschutter, eds., *Jobs and Investments of European Firms Operating in the United States* (Washington, D.C.: European Chamber of Commerce in Washington, 1993), executive summary.

6. See Dennis J. Encarnation, *Rivals beyond Trade: America versus Japan in Global Competition* (Ithaca, N.Y.: Cornell University Press, 1992), passim.

7. For a longer discussion of European competitiveness problems, see Thomas J. Duesterberg, "Global Competitiveness and U.S.–EC Trade Relations," *The Washington Quarterly* 16 (Summer 1993), pp. 115–127. For sectoral and national level data on Europe's competitiveness problem and its declining share of world trade, see Terence Roth, "Gordian Knot," *Wall Street Journal*, September 30, 1994, p. R–4. On the theoretical and empirical bases for the relationship of competition to economic efficiency and global competitiveness, see Michael E. Porter, *The Competitive Advantage of Nations* (New York, N.Y.: Free Press, 1990), especially chaps.

7–9, which cover developments in the European and U.S. economies.

8. See the European Commission report, "An Industrial Competitiveness Policy for the European Union," *Bulletin of the European Union*, supplement 3/94 (Luxembourg: Office for Official Publications of the European Commission, 1994), executive summary.

9. Ian Goldin, Odin Knudsen, and Dominique van der Mensbrugghe, *Trade Liberalisation: Global Economic Implications* (Washington, D.C.: OECD/World Bank, 1993), p. 79.

10. *Ibid.*, p. 17.

11. See Martin Bangemann, *Meeting the Global Challenge: Establishing a Successful European Industrial Policy* (London: Kogan Page, 1992), especially chaps. 1 and 5.

12. See William Drozdiak, "France, Germany at Odds over EU's Direction," *Washington Post*, October 30, 1994, p. A–35.

13. For a good exposition of the deep foundations of "mercantilism" in Europe, see Martin Wolf, *The Resistible Appeal of Fortress Europe* (Washington, D.C.: American Enterprise Institute, 1994), chaps. 3–5.

14. See Paul Krugman, "The Myth of Asia's Miracle," *Foreign Affairs* 73 (November/December 1994), pp. 62–78.

15. Hufbauer, *Free Trade Debate*, p. 149.

16. In 1990, the total foreign direct investment (FDI) stock in the United States was $397 billion, in the United Kingdom $205 billion, in Germany $132 billion, in Canada $108 billion, in Singapore and Mexico about $29 billion each, and in Australia $70.2 billion. Japan had only about $10 billion in FDI stock, ranking it close to Greece and Sweden and well out of the top 15 countries in this regard. Figures are from *Foreign Direct Investment in the U.S.*, tables 2–5 and 2–6.

17. See Fareed Zakaria, "A Conversation with Lee Kuan Yew," *Foreign Affairs* 73 (March/April 1994), pp. 109–127.

18. I have discussed the importance of emerging Asian economies to U.S. trade policy in Thomas J. Duesterberg, "Trade, Investment, and Engagement in the U.S.–East Asian Relationship," *The Washington Quarterly* 17 (Winter 1994), pp. 73–90.

19. These figures ignore the U.S. trade in services, which is considerably larger with the more complex European economy than with either Asia or Latin America. See David Sanger, "U.S. Is Shifting Trade Emphasis Away from Asia: More Growth Predicted for New Markets," *New York Times*, November 4, 1994, pp. D–1, D–2.

20. John Urquart, "Canadian Trade Minister Says NAFTA Should be Opened Up to Other Nations," *Wall Street Journal*, May 31, 1994, p. C–18.

21. The quotation is from G.W.F. Hegel, *The Philosophy of Right*, trans. T. M. Knox (Oxford: Oxford University Press, 1967), p. 13.

V. The Global Power of Financial Markets

Surrendering to Markets

Erik R. Peterson

AS ANALYSTS CONTINUE to grapple with identifying the forces transforming the post–cold war world, they will need to focus on a phenomenon that ultimately will affect the international system more profoundly than U.S.–Soviet competition: the international financial markets. The new clout of global markets, more than any other feature of the current global topography, has the potential of generating an overarching and onerous "discipline" on countries worldwide in the years ahead. In events as diverse as the collapse of the Exchange Rate System in Europe three years ago, to the many unsuccessful interventions in support of the dollar over past years, to the financial implosion in Mexico in December 1994, the new global hegemon has already served notice. As Thomas Friedman has put it:

> Whichever country has the most stable government, the most efficient economy, the most Westernized legal system, the most convertible currency and the most educated labor force, gets rewarded with investment capital from the super [global] markets. Those countries that don't get their house in order are left as roadkill on the global investment highway.[1]

This essay addresses the increasing power of the global markets and the implications of that power for nation-states and the international structures they have designed to deal with international financial stability. It is based on the premise that some governments have already been forced to surrender important economic policy-making prerogatives to the markets—and the others will soon forfeit theirs as well. The key question is not if, but rather when and how, the ongoing surrender to the new discipline of global markets will occur. The essay concludes with some ideas about the implications of this phenomenon for the United States in particular.

Reign of Markets

There are important reasons to suggest that the rapid expansion and as rapid integration of markets across the world are cutting deeply into the capacity of governments—even those presiding over the largest economies—to control the economic activity within their frontiers. Four trends in particular stand out.

First, *the rate of global economic and financial integration is accelerating.* Trade and finance linkages are expanding so

---

Erik R. Peterson is vice president and director of studies at CSIS. He also directs the Center's International Financial Contingencies Group and is co-editor with Gerrit Gong of the CSIS monograph series on "East Asia Economic and Financial Outlook."

rapidly that residual—or resurrected—barriers to trade of merchandise and services and the flow of capital are becoming enormously costly for those countries that seek to perpetuate them. The explosion of merchandise and services trade over recent years is well documented; merchandise exports have increased from 11 to 18 percent of global output over the past 20 years, while trade in services as a percentage of total world trade has moved from 15 to 22 percent over the past 15 years.[2] Trade integration, expressed as the share of trade volume in gross domestic product, is projected by the World Bank to increase steadily among developed and developing countries alike; the percentage for the countries of the Organization for Economic Cooperation and Development is expected to rise from less than 30 percent in 1986 to over 40 percent by the year 2004, while the corresponding level for developing countries could move from approximately 30 percent in 1986 to over 50 percent.[3]

The rate of increase in global financial linkages has been even more profound. We have reached a historical intersection in which the forces of regulatory disarmament, the development and dissemination of information technologies and capacities, and new thinking in theory and applications in finance have combined to propel global financial integration to unprecedented levels of growth.[4] The builddown in capital controls in the advanced economies following the disintegration of the Bretton Woods pegged exchange rate system in the early 1970s[5] and, more recently, the renunciation of controls in many developing countries have been a major factor in expanding international capital mobility. Technology, of course, has also played a dominant role. High-speed computer coverage and tracking across markets worldwide on a 24-hour basis have reinforced the integration of markets. The downward price curve in marginal transaction costs in the uninterrupted hunt for arbitrage and other investment opportunities in diverse markets has also been a contributing factor. Finally, the state of the art in financial innovation and the remarkable complexity of the instruments that have emerged, and are emerging, create new linkages in themselves.

Another key factor driving integration is the significant extension of securitization to many other capital markets—part of what Henry Kaufman has referred to as the "Americanization" of global finance. Kaufman emphasizes the importance of the adoption by other capital markets of well-established practices in the U.S. securities market, including repurchase agreements, scheduled auctions, and higher levels of involvement by foreign investors.[6] In parallel, the proliferation of managers of large portfolios has expanded the volume of cross-border flows. Said Kaufman in 1992:

> The ultimate evolution of the risk-taking financial entrepreneur is the portfolio manager who can go long or short in any market, in any currency, and on a leveraged or an unleveraged basis. . . . [w]hen full leverage is employed by this breed of managers, I suspect that they can command portfolios totaling upwards of $500 billion.[7]

The symptoms of this rapid growth in global financial linkages are acute. Daily foreign exchange trading, according to the Bank for International Settlements (BIS), was in the $10 billion to $20 billion range in 1982; 10 years later, the corresponding figure was $880 billion. The magnitude of daily trading in government bonds and equities in 1992 added another $223 billion in daily turnover, bringing the total for foreign exchange, government bonds, and equities trading volume for that year to over $400 trillion. There can be little doubt that current levels (as yet unreported) are significantly well above the 1992 levels, and that the trajectory of global financial integration is continuing to push the system toward a convergence of risks and rewards in the global market.

Integration of foreign exchange markets is mature, but substantial upside potential exists in the areas of bonds (government and corporate) and equities. In the case of bond trading, this applies to new issues as well as secondary markets. Growth in the pace of integration can therefore be sustained or increased in the years ahead—assuming continued liberalization of policies and expansion of technologies. Both of these assumptions are safe bets.

Second, *the days of segmented markets are numbered.* Economic activity no longer conforms to geographical boundaries, and the factor mobility made possible by technology and information flows has ushered in a world in which borders count for substantially less. The fact is that geographical borders simply no longer conform to concentrations of business activity. Kenichi Ohmae, writing in his recent book *The End of the Nation State: The Rise of Regional Economies,* is less subdued in his conclusions about the obsolescence of states; he concludes that "reflexive twinges of sovereignty make the desired economic success impossible, because the global economy punishes twinging countries by diverting investment and information elsewhere" and that "the nation state has become an unnatural—even a dysfunctional—organizational unit for thinking about economic activity."[8]

The issue of borders and economic activity aside, one of the key features of the late 1980s and early 1990s was what can be referred to as the "quiet" revolution—a revolution overshadowed by the momentous events in the former Soviet Union. Regulatory shifts in developing countries are not the stuff of headlines, but the virtual renunciation of residual statist policies in many key developing countries during this period had a no less significant effect on the welfare of billions of lives across the world. They have recast the fundamental nature of the world economic system by opening new areas of the world to capital flows and investment opportunities and are changing the balance of global economic power in the process.

In many key countries, most notably in Asia and Latin America, nationalism and expropriation have been replaced by privatization, trade protection by trade liberalization, price controls by fiscal reform, and policies designed to deter foreign investment inflows by policies to attract them. The external financial imbalances that characterized many developing countries in the early 1980s have been improved. In short, many developing countries have engineered sweeping macroeconomic stabilizations and, in the process, done much to resurrect internal investor confidence as well as their standing in the international capital markets. At some future point, when global markets are even better positioned to impose higher levels of discipline on the entire spectrum of economies worldwide, this adjustment by developing countries will be recognized as a key factor in the ascendance of those global markets.

It should be stressed that many of these changes—especially in the area of domestic policy reform and trade liberalization—were unilateral, or homegrown, although the shock of the debt crisis in the early 1980s was certainly a major catalyst in the redefinition of policies. Some structural adjustments were encouraged by conditionalities on assistance imposed by the International Monetary Fund (IMF), but it is fair to say that many of the reforms and enacting policies were self-generated in recognition that market forces—rather than development assistance—were the key to renewed economic vitality. This culture of advocating market forces and advancing market policies is at the center of the ongoing changes. And despite the economic and political turbulence that has accompanied this new culture in many countries, the costs associated with retreating to statism or command economies will eventually generate costs even more onerous.

The coincidence of historical events —the nearly simultaneous liberalization of policies in much of the developing world and the introduction of market policies in much of the former Communist world—has brought a large portion of the world on-line in the international economic system for the first time in many decades. As David Hale, chief economist of Kemper Financial Services, has often stressed, the confluence of political and economic circumstances has injected three billion persons into the global capitalist economy.

Third, *the magnitude of global capital flows is exceeding the capacities of even the most powerful governments to manage the pressures they generate.* Technologies now allow massive shifts of capital in the space of nanoseconds, and the integration of markets across the world has multiplied the number of targets for that deployment of investment. One result of this capital mobility is that economic decision-makers can no longer fashion and implement policies that are based on the traditional levers of macroeconomics in isolated economies. National economies, observes Alan Greenspan, are exposed to "shocks from new and unexpected sources, with little if any lag."[9] As integration continues, policymakers run the growing risk of being left behind.

Consider, for example, the takeoff in daily foreign exchange volume mentioned previously. In 1983, when average daily volumes in the New York, London, and Tokyo exchanges were at about the $39 billion level, the combined central bank foreign exchange reserves of the United States, the United Kingdom, Japan, West Germany, and Switzerland were some $139 billion. Less than a decade later, in 1992, the ratio had reversed itself. As figure 1 suggests, market turnover had expanded by 1,600 percent, to $623 billion, or over double the size of the combined reserves of the five countries. In less than a decade, the reserves-to-market-turnover ratio had plummeted from 3.5:1 to 0.45:1.[10] The implications of this shift in the financial balance of power are staggering and give empirical meaning to the view that markets, and even some individuals, now play a role in the international markets formerly reserved only for countries.

As market growth and integration continue, it is difficult to imagine that governments will be able to maintain fine-tuning control over their interest rates and currencies. Shifts in interest rates will be vulnerable to offsets by international flows, while attempts to intervene on behalf of currencies will be met with a similar immediate and overwhelming response. Market forces, in effect, will progressively play the role of neutralizers unless policy decisions reinforce what the market

Figure 1
Central Banks and the Foreign Exchange Market

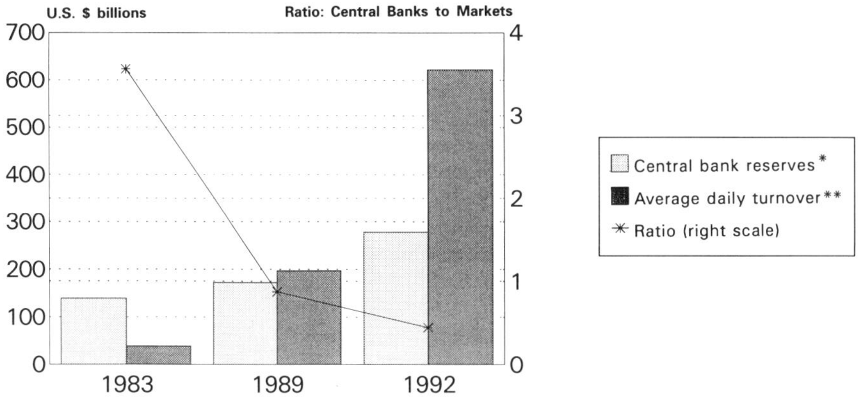

Sources: OECD, BIS, McKinsey.
*United States, United Kingdom, Japan, West Germany, Switzerland
**New York, London, and Tokyo markets

perceives as moves toward higher efficiencies and "sound fundamentals."

Furthermore, the potential exists that governments could be supplanted in some of their most time-honored functions as regulators of economic activity. Currency and check payment systems are good examples of areas in which governments could soon come under assault. A number of new commercial network-based systems are now being developed that could ultimately subjugate the monetary system as we now know it. "E-cash," the rubric used to describe the various emerging electronic money systems, has the potential to circumvent—and gradually replace—the current anachronistic banking system by allowing payments to be made more quickly, efficiently, and inexpensively. Such innovations would enable the massive electronic networks in place to exploit a monetary system that is outdated and more impractical by the day.

How much longer can governments and central banks maintain their long-standing monopoly over money systems when they continue to rely on physical check-clearing and other antiquated procedures? Not much longer, unless they undertake a significant retooling of current structures. James G. Cosgrove, vice president and general manager at AT&T, does not overstate the trend when he asserts that "electronic business will literally change the way business is done worldwide [by triggering] another revolution similar to the Industrial Revolution."[11] If they fail to respond to this order of change, governments run the risk of being stripped soon of their most basic traditional roles in overseeing their economies.

Fourth, *governments are increasingly incapable of keeping up with the march of technology and information flows.* At issue is the speed and efficiency with which governments can respond to the introduction of new technologies and information streams. With the ever-diminishing time needed for new technology cycles to appear, there is every reason to doubt whether governments can shorten their own policy and regulatory cycles to keep pace. Already, there is a substantial—perhaps insurmountable—lag in key sectors driven by technology in the United States. The situation appears to be no different in other advanced economies, and it is even more pronounced in the post-Communist and developing economies.

In the area of finance, governments across the world are already fighting a losing battle. As complexities of financial instruments continue to escalate, and as execution periods are reduced to nanoseconds, the potential for meaningful regulation becomes more nearly moot. The well-publicized controversies in the United States involving derivatives are a case in point. For many U.S. policymakers, the experiences involving losses by prominent companies because of speculative derivative exposure were a signal that a sinister element had infiltrated the financial system. The subsequent Orange County fiasco fanned the flames, and among other things sparked calls for the prohibition of derivatives altogether. This represents a clear case in which the understanding of the role of derivatives as a well-established hedging mechanism was lost on some key decision makers. It also highlights how far behind policymakers are in their capacity to address the complexities and speeds of these kinds of instruments.

As integration advances, economies will also become increasingly vulnerable to forces that are beyond the control of their governments. The "tequila effect" set into motion by the financial crisis in Mexico in December 1994 demonstrated in no uncertain terms how connected financial systems are and what indirect effects actions by second- and third-party countries or other non-state players can have at home.

End of the Nation-State?

"[I]n terms of real flows of economic activity, nation states have *already* lost their role as meaningful units of participation in the global economy of today's borderless world," writes Ohmae.[12] The statement, of course, is extreme. It is far too early to write off governments as important players in the global economy. Across the world, they retain significant powers to control the nature of economic activity in their territories and, in some cases, outside their frontiers.

But for the reasons set out in the previous section, there is reason to believe that by definition governments are ill-equipped to maintain their traditional sovereign prerogatives with respect to decision-making on economic policies. Technology and information streams are outpacing them. The new complexities and time frames are stretching their capacity to respond. And growing linkages with other financial systems dramatically limit their capabilities in fashioning national responses to what is a global phenomenon. The countdown to the surrender to the new global markets is under way.

This is old news for many smaller countries that for years have faced the wrath of markets. To the extent that they have persisted in clinging to statist or non-market economic policies, many have already been faced down by international market forces at huge economic and social cost. What followed in many countries was the striking renunciation of discredited policies and practices and the introduction of antithetical positions.

More significantly, the power of the global markets is now stripping away the policy prerogatives of the largest economies. As the collapse of the Exchange Rate System in 1992 demonstrated, major economies as advanced as those in Britain and Italy are by no means impervious to the new constellation of market forces. More pressures on the advanced economies are to come so long as they carry high deficits and other financial imbalances.

In the final analysis, for advanced, transitional, and developing countries alike, what matters is how the surrender of governments to the global markets is carried out. Either leaderships resist the markets at high cost to their economies, or they seek to redefine the core functions of governance over economic activity while taking into account the forces generated by the new global economy. The outcome, in social opportunity cost terms, depends on the efficiency with which governments yield to markets and the manner in which they seek to redefine their core competences in the face of the imminent reign of market forces.

Whither Global Structures?

In the lead-up to the June 1995 summit of the group of seven industrialized countries (G–7) in Halifax, Robert E. Rubin, U.S. treasury secretary, argued that one of the key challenges facing the world is:

to develop effective multilateral mechanisms to deal with the problems that may arise from the vast increase in the speed and size of the international financial markets, and to minimize systemic risk in those markets. Our institutions must be made as modern as the marketplace.[13]

To meet this challenge, Rubin pointed to the need for "greater and more timely disclosure of financial data to the markets" and for the development by the "international economy" of "enhanced mechanisms to rapidly mobilize relatively large amounts of conditional assistance when problems of sufficient importance develop."[14] These factors were at the core of the decisions at the summit to expand a special "emergency financing mechanism" under the IMF's General Agreement to Borrow (GAB) and to put new surveillance conditions into place at the IMF.

Clearly, these actions are designed to correct for the financial instability engendered by the December 1994 crisis in Mexico. Among other things, that episode served to illustrate the vulnerabilities of the monitoring system and the difficulties associated with mobilizing large pools of capital to dampen the effects of financial meltdowns in various markets. The fact is that early warning on Mexico failed. As Henry Kaufman has observed:

the governments of the major industrial countries and the key multilateral financial institutions —the International Monetary Fund and the World Bank—were conspicuously silent in cautioning either the Mexicans or the investor community about financial problems . . . none of the leading officials made even nuanced statements suggesting that investors think twice about investing in Mexico.[15]

Furthermore, the prolonged process that was necessary for the United

States (apart from its own domestic political constraints) to marshal a sufficiently large pool of capital revealed the political and economic limits of the current "multilateral mechanisms." The IMF's contribution to the rescue package stretched the capacities of the organization.

The question now needs to be asked: Will these adjustments lead to greater stability and less systemic risk? At this point, it is by no means clear that significantly greater transparency will result from the disclosure standards under consideration. Unless managed carefully, those standards could have precisely the opposite effect. At the time of this writing, there have been calls for the IMF to publish its confidential economic reviews and to certify disclosure of financial data. Even if, as expected, the IMF is successful in resisting these initiatives, the possibility exists that analysts in the Fund might dilute their conclusions in the expectation that they will be made public.[16] At issue is the redefined role for the IMF in the post-Mexico world financial system. Can the organization operate effectively as the global equivalent of the Securities and Exchange Commission, with the GAB as a standing executive committee?

There are also serious questions about the "international financial peacekeeping" role that the enhanced GAB will assume. One would hope that the GAB members might be more effective in their decision-making process than their counterparts in the security sphere, but there are no guarantees. A financial Bosnia could arise in which the members are unable to agree on the specific criteria that make states eligible for a bailout—no matter how onerous the conditions on support may be. For a recent precedent of political fallout on financial issues, one need only look back to the experience of the Mexico support package. In the early phases of the crisis, Washington ruled out raising the matter with the other G–7 states out of concern that they would be unable to agree on a solution. And the European G–7 states abstained on the U.S.–IMF–BIS package that finally surfaced. An important related issue is potential GAB support for third-party states that are subject to the derivative financial impact of developments outside their countries. Will the GAB fund cover the "tequila-effect" level of countries as well as the principal source of financial instability? The "moral hazard" issue adds additional layers of complexity in the use of the fund.

Assuming that countries will be willing to expand their commitments on the G–7 formula, which is no sure thing, there is the issue of size. The GAB, according to reports, will be expanded from its current level of $29 billion to approximately $60 billion. In the context of the capital flows now encircling the planet, that amounts to small change. It translates into about three months' worth of foreign direct investment flows; to about two days' worth of cross-border trade in securities; to less than 20 hours' worth of global output; to some 7 hours of global trade in government bonds; and to about 85 minutes of trade in foreign exchange.

The G–7 response can therefore be characterized (yet again) as too little, too late. The Halifax formula was mostly reactive insofar as the expanded GAB facility is designed to respond—to the extent that it can—to crises that are imminent or actual. The attempt to create a proactive response was encumbered by uncertainties that the revised monitoring system would

Surrendering to Markets

help avert future Mexico-style situations. When weighed together, these considerations raise more fundamental questions about the capacity of the leading global economies and the international financial organizations to make "our institutions as modern as the marketplace," as Rubin suggested. It is arguable that what remains of both the G–7 and the Bretton Woods system is becoming equally obsolete in the emerging global financial system.

As an organization, the G–7 does, of course, have merit as a means of more systematic communication between the advanced economies on a range of issues of common interest. Beyond that, however, its role as a forum for leadership initiatives in the global economy has become negligible at best.

At the core of this marginalization, argues Fred Bergsten, is "the growing consensus among members that the group cannot influence events much anyway."[17] One key factor in this consensus, asserts Bergsten, is that "immense flows of private capital have intimidated the [G–7] officials from any efforts to counter them."[18] The more fundamental issue is *whether* those flows can be countered.

In the face of the inertia that has characterized the organization over recent years, there is little doubt that officials in the member countries will come under increasing pressure to reconfigure the structure and mandate of the G–7 in the coming years. Now that Russia has become a de facto member, it is perhaps only a matter of time before an analog to the associational membership status of the North Atlantic Treaty Organization's Partnership for Peace appears in the G–7 context. The scope of the G–7's competence may also be expanded to include political and security issues.[19] All this could—and, in all likelihood, will—lead to even less of a focus for the G–7 with respect to the changes in the global markets.

The same applies to the IMF and the other multilateral development banks. In 1989, IMF managing director Michel Camdessus noted that while his predecessor, Jacques de Larosière, had to fight hard to persuade ministers to pursue responsible economic policies, he himself was faced with policymakers who *wanted* to enact the right policies.[20] This reflects the early surrender to markets and market forces by many of the developing countries, and the recognition by officials in those countries that external trade and financial linkages were essential to the success of their adjustment programs. We are moving beyond the time when IMF conditionalities were necessary for countries to enact responsible policies:

> Policymakers are confronted more and more with a new discipline, the need to maintain the confidence of markets, both domestic, and increasingly, international. In this setting sound economic policies command a rising premium. To an extent, globalization is having the effect of "endogenizing" policy reform in developing countries. Greater integration into the world economy raises the payoffs to increased competitiveness but also compounds the losses from failure to act.[21]

The new reality is that the IMF and the other international financial institutions now take second place to the global markets as the source of reward or punishment for policies. That point is borne out by the volume of flows. The percentage of official financing of total foreign capital inflows has fallen

273

significantly over recent years. With it comes the marginalization of the multilateral institutions designed to preside over the global economy.

The point is that the current leadership structures for the world economic and financial system are becoming progressively more dysfunctional and ill-equipped to deal with the volumes, speeds, and complexities of the global marketplace. In short, day by day they are failing the Rubin test—to make "our institutions as modern as the marketplace."

The Predicament for Washington

The United States faces enormous challenges in positioning its economy in response to the changes sweeping the global system. How effectively it meets those challenges will determine whether Washington can maintain its international leadership role—not only in the area of economics and finance, but also in the realms of foreign policy and international security.

The immediate challenge, of course, is to address the acute deficits dragging the country down as it enters the twenty-first century. As costly as those deficits are, and as tumultuous their implications economically and politically, they will become even more burdensome in the years ahead as the global markets exact higher premiums for policy practices that are the opposite of "sound and prudent." If current domestic trends are allowed to persist, U.S. leaders could soon be forced into triage decision-making on economic issues. They will face an economy disabled by huge government deficits and mounting national debt, by low savings, reinvestment, and research and development levels, by a Social Security system collapsing under the weight of the imminent demographic bubble, and by even more pronounced external economic imbalances and a steadily declining dollar. Another key concern is the regulatory framework that the U.S. government is imposing on its private sector. Year by year, U.S. companies are losing competitive advantage because of the regulatory burdens and the oppressive litigation environment they must face.

With the onset of the information-based economy, it is also incumbent on policymakers, academics, and the private sector to recast their understanding of economics in the global context. The fact is that global economic and financial integration is fundamentally altering the menu of prerogatives and options available to policymakers, and new approaches to managing that altered equation need to be weighed carefully. House Speaker Newt Gingrich (R–Ga.) recently put it this way:

> What you need are good observers, who then codify what they are observing. You do not need good economists who try to translate a failed system and fail, not because it was bad, but because it no longer relates to the objective correlation of what is happening around them.[22]

This kind of reassessment is indeed critical. U.S. policy prerogatives continue to be built on assumptions based on a highly segmented economy, on the assumption that governments can in fact keep pace with markets, and that policies grounded in politics rather than sound economic fundamentals are immune to adverse market forces. Even the most basic of concepts need to be revisited and scrutinized in the context of the emerging global economy. Such a reappraisal of global economic forces must recognize the new power brokers—the traders behind computer terminals worldwide—who can either reinforce or decimate economic strategies in nanoseconds. What happened in Mexico could happen in the United States someday soon if the current anti-market policies are allowed to fester.

The implications of the coming hegemony of global markets, of course, transcend the narrow constraints placed on U.S. policymaking. They will also have an impact on the U.S. capacity to carry out effective security and foreign policies abroad and will determine the extent to which Washington can maintain its world leadership role.

To borrow Albert Einstein's remark about the atom, "Everything has changed but our ways of thinking, and if these do not change we drift toward unparalleled catastrophes." Obviously, the United States has not yet reached that threshold with respect to its position in the emerging global economy. But continued shortsightedness and parochialism in its political leaders could indeed bring about dire consequences. There are increasingly alarming indications that political elements on both sides of the aisle are drifting toward isolationism and economic nationalism, the enunciation of which could ultimately impose massive costs on the United States and its future.

Lost on those political figures is the fact that in an age of global integration, segmented, domestic policy responses no longer apply. A policy of global engagement, tailored to the new role of global markets, is critical to any strategy for domestic economic renewal. Robert Rubin put it this way: "We have to help Americans understand that their economic well-being is directly related to this country's engagement with the global economy."[23]

Gerald Corrigan of Goldman Sachs encapsulated these challenges to the United States in testimony before the U.S. Senate Committee on Banking, Housing and Urban Affairs:

> [I]n the face of myopic trade policies, efforts to regulate or control capital flows, or continued large-scale government dissavings in the form of budget deficits at the national level such as in the United States, the period ahead could prove to be extraordinarily difficult. . . . In the fullness of time . . . the marketplace will treat harshly even the largest of nations that fail to conduct their economic and financial affairs in a sound and prudent fashion.[24]

As the competition for global capital reaches even higher levels, the global markets will soon be in a position to pass judgment by attaching a premium to capital flows to the United States. In the short term, it means more costly capital to sustain U.S. economic activity. Americans will have to pay a higher price to finance their external deficits, especially when investors have a greater choice of high-return investment options across the world. It will mean driving capital formation offshore, and with it the possibilities for economic gain from innovation and commercial follow-through.

In the longer term, that means the risk of forfeiting the leadership role the United States has carved out for itself over the past several decades. If U.S. leaders insist in enfeebling the United States by carrying large and growing external deficits, how can they expect to maintain U.S. dominance in the age of markets that is upon us?

If the United States is destined to lead in this new age of global finance, it must devise and enact a strategy that brings its economy into equilibrium, that recognizes the growing power of global market forces, that stresses international economic engagement as the key to domestic renewal, that adapts to the onset of the knowledge revolution in economic activity, and that positions the United States for continued prosperity and economic dynamism in the next century. But if the economic and financial challenges confronting the country are allowed to fester, U.S. policymakers will effectively renounce their country's international leadership position and the welfare of future generations of Americans.

Notes

1. Thomas Friedman, "Yesterday's Man," *New York Times*, March 19, 1995, p. E–15.
2. World Bank, *Global Economic Prospects and the Developing Countries* (Washington, D.C.: The World Bank Group, 1995), pp. 1 and 14–22.
3. *Ibid.*, p. 18.
4. For two interesting views of the longer-range impact of these changes, see Andrew Freeman, "The Future of Finance: Capitalism Without Owners?" in Richard O'Brien, ed., *Finance and the International Economy* (New York, N.Y.: Oxford University Press for the American Express Bank, Inc., 1994), pp. 28–40, and Charles S. Sanford, Jr., "Financial Markets in 2020" (paper delivered at the Federal Reserve Bank of Kansas City meeting on "Changing Capital Markets: Implications for Monetary Policy," Jackson Hole, Wyoming, August 20, 1993).
5. See, for example, John B. Goodman and Louis W. Pauly, "The Obsolescence of Capital Controls? Economic Management in an Age of Global Markets," *World Politics* 46 (October 1993), pp. 50–82.
6. See, for example, Henry Kaufman, "Structural Changes in the Financial Markets: Economic and Policy Significance," *Federal Reserve Bank of Kansas City Economic Review*, Second Quarter 1994, pp. 6–8.
7. *Ibid.*, p. 9.
8. Kenichi Ohmae, *The End of the Nation State: The Rise of Regional Economies* (New York, N.Y.: The Free Press, 1995), pp. 12 and 16.
9. Alan Greenspan, speech presented at Federal Reserve Bank of Kansas City meeting on "Changing Capital Markets: Implications for Monetary Policy," Jackson Hole, Wyoming, August 19, 1993.
10. See Bank for International Settlements, Monetary and Economic Department, *Central Bank Survey of Foreign Exchange Market Activity in April 1992* (Basle: BIS, March 1993), and "The Global Capital Market: Supply, Demand, Pricing and Allocation," McKinsey Global Institute, Washington, D.C., November 4, 1994, pp. 6–14 to 6–16.
11. As quoted in "The Future of Money: E-Cash Could Transform the World's Financial Life," *Business Week*, June 12, 1995, p. 66.
12. Ohmae, *The End of the Nation State*, p. 11.
13. Robert E. Rubin, speech at the Center for Strategic and International Studies, Washington, D.C., June 6, 1995.
14. *Ibid.*
15. Henry Kaufman, "Why Alarm Bells Didn't Ring Over Mexico," *Wall Street Journal*, January 26, 1995, p. A–14. Kaufman also pointed to the decision by many financial institutions "to emphasize near-term over longer-term profit opportunities and to utilize their researchers in this pursuit." He concludes that "[w]hat is needed to safeguard the objectivity of the analytical process are strong research leaders who are represented in the highest level of management and who are encouraged by top management to support honest analysis, even if it might endanger some near-term profit opportunity."
16. See, for example, Bob Davis, "U.S. Backs 'Preventative' Role for IMF to Deter Mexico-Style Financial Crises," *Wall Street Journal*, June 7, 1995, p. A–10.
17. Fred Bergsten, "The Corpse at the Summit," *Washington Post*, June 11, 1995, p. C–4.
18. *Ibid.*
19. See, for example, William E. Whyman, "We Can't Go on Meeting Like This: Revitalizing the G-7 Process," *The Washington Quarterly* 18 (Summer 1995), pp. 139–165.
20. As cited by John Williamson, "The Progress of Policy Reform in Latin America,"

in Williamson, ed., *Latin American Adjustment: How Much Has Happened?* (Washington, D.C.: Institute for International Economics, 1990), p. 353.

21. World Bank, *Global Economic Prospects and the Developing Countries*, p. 1.

22. Newt Gingrich, "Our Role in the World" (speech at the Center for Strategic and International Studies, Washington, D.C., March 28, 1995).

23. As quoted in "A Wall Streeter Makes His Debut on the World Stage," *Business Week*, June 19, 1995, p. 52.

24. E. Gerald Corrigan, Testimony before the U.S. Senate Committee on Banking, Housing and Urban Affairs, September 28, 1994.

Risk and Volatility

Roy C. Smith

DURING THE PAST 20 years financial markets have changed and developed at an astonishing pace. The markets have expanded, globalized, integrated, disintermediated, and innovated at a rate unknown to history and in doing so have escaped the bonds of control traditionally provided by government officials and regulators. Market forces and disciplines now rule the global economy, wielding the power of a vast pool of highly liquid capital. Huge volumes of financial transactions occur daily—foreign exchange trading, for example, is over $1.0 trillion *a day*. The combination of world stock and bond markets and markets in financial futures, options, and swaps options generates additional trading volume in the range of $10 trillion to $20 trillion on an annual basis. The reach of this new and enlarged pool of funds has extended far beyond the traditional limits of the developed industrial countries to affect dozens of third world "emerging market" countries. Only the most die-hard socialist and dictatorial regimes have been un-affected by the hopes and promises of the new world's capital pool, which, like the old-time advertisement for Sherwin Williams paint, now "covers the globe."

Markets and Volatility in Perspective

But all this market activity has a dangerous side. Investors can change their minds—suddenly and often provoking severe consequences—proving that a free market can also be cruel one. Recent history has offered a number of examples:

- The stock market crashed worldwide in October 1987, triggered by a 508-point decline on the New York Stock Exchange. Equity values around the world fell by an average of nearly 30 percent.
- In December 1989, a 5-year, 60 percent drop in prices on the Tokyo Stock Exchange began, after a 10-year sixfold increase. The market decline spread to real estate and other financial assets, ultimately bankrupting hundreds of companies, forcing the worst banking crisis in Japan's history and driving the real economy into recession.
- Following a 200-point market drop in October 1989, the U.S. high-yield debt market began to collapse. By mid-1990 the entire market was virtually illiquid, which contributed to the failure of the leading firm in that sector, Drexel Burnham.

Roy C. Smith is Professor of Finance and International Business, The Stern School of Business, New York University, a Limited Partner of Goldman, Sachs and Co., and author of *Comeback: The Restoration of American Banking Power in the New World Economy* (1993).

Copyright © 1995 by The Center for Strategic and International Studies and the Massachusetts Institute of Technology

- In September 1992 the British pound was forced into a sudden devaluation as a result of an attack by "speculators," despite earnest intervention efforts by the central banks of Britain and Germany of about £15 billion. George Soros, a prominent hedge fund operator, is reported to have made over $1 billion for his investors by selling the pound.
- Subsequent attacks on other European currencies in 1993 forced the realignment of the stabilization bands of the European exchange rate mechanism to 15 percent from 2.25 percent, a change that renders the mechanism inert and has virtually halted progress toward the Economic and Monetary Union of the European Union (EU).
- In December 1994, the Mexican government announced a change in the stabilization rate for the peso, which resulted in a sharp market reaction leading to the collapse of the peso-dollar exchange rate, and the peso's devaluation by more than 50 percent. This in turn resulted in the proportionate collapse of the Mexican stock market, and stock markets in almost all other emerging market countries fell by 10 percent to 30 percent within a month.
- Due to excessive exposures in downward markets in mortgage-backed securities and internal control problems, Kidder Peabody, a leading U.S. investment bank, reported large losses, and was sold by General Electric to Paine Webber in a liquidating transaction.
- Similar failures befell the highly prominent British merchant banks Baring Brothers and S. G. Warburg during 1994 and early 1995 and resulted in the forced sale of both banks to foreign banks.
- In early 1995, Orange County, California, declared bankruptcy as a result of $1.7 billion of trading losses from leveraged positions in government securities and derivatives.
- A major derivatives scare occurred in the United States, following the failure of a large hedge fund specializing in mortgage-backed securities, and the replenishment by other funds of capital lost to investing in derivatives. Bankers Trust, a leading derivatives dealer, was sued by its customers for causing losses, and this resulted in the loss of approximately one-third of the bank's market capitalization.

These events have been alarming to investors and regulators around the world. Some, it is understood, were the result of poor management practices by the principals involved and should not be regarded as systemic. These included a number of situations that, however poorly they reflected on the judgment of the persons involved, seem to have been created by the simple availability of the casino-like marketplace, which drew in players that should not have been there and whose involvement should have been checked by supervision. Other episodes seem to have unfairly affected governments trying their best to put into effect the sort of policies that attract and retain capital. In all of these situations substantial consequences were felt by investors in the securities or currencies affected. But in none of these cases did a worldwide financial crisis result in which markets and/or banking systems failed to function and money was not available where it was needed to sustain ongoing financial activity.

In other words, the free market continued to operate, with all its benefits and costs, and its inherent, self-righting disciplines. Technology, deregulation, and increased competition in financial services have led us to a world in which market forces are more powerful than national or international regulatory systems currently in place. The market offers many advantages in efficient capital allocation but are the risks associated with these advantages worth the possible collapse of the whole system? To answer this question, we need to understand volatility better and the ways in which financial regulators and the market itself have adapted to live with it.

Where the Volatility Comes From

Before the Smithsonian Agreement in 1971, which ended the fixed exchange rate regime of the Bretton Woods era, currency values were maintained by government economic policies that often included substantial controls on capital and trade. Because of these controls, the volume of foreign exchange trading was largely restricted to that required to finance international trade and direct investment. The system was thought to be manageable, stable, and disciplined and therefore a positive contribution to world economic growth and safety. The International Monetary Fund often points out that in the period between 1957 and 1971, the average growth rate in the group of seven industrialized countries (G–7) was 4.9 percent, and from 1971 to the present, only 2.5 percent.[1]

Many factors exist to explain this change in growth rates, although there does not appear to be a consensus around any single explanation. Ending the fixed rate system is often put forward as one, but it must be dismissed on the grounds that the change was involuntary—uncontainable market forces, circumventing the disciplines and controls put in place to manage the system, had already begun to build up sufficient strength to undermine the old regime. Because of the growth of the world economy since 1944 and the unwillingness of many countries to suppress their own economies in the interest of world cooperation, the system was not working well in 1971. The United States periodically ran balance of payments deficits, which supplied useful liquidity to foreign markets, but also resulted in a large buildup of offshore dollars. These dollars were acquired by central banks that began to redeem them for gold at the official rate of $35 per ounce, which rightly seemed a bargain price to many of them at the time. These actions, however, alarmed the U.S. government, which feared the sudden loss of its gold reserves, and the Nixon administration decided to "close the gold window," thus refusing to honor its obligations under the system and effectively ending it for good. Market forces, even in those days when they were substantially restricted, had in fact devalued the dollar from its 1944 level.

Acknowledging these forces by changing to a hands-off system, in which the market set the price of foreign exchange every day, was thought by most policymakers at the time to be a very dangerous and undesirable move. World trade would drop, many predicted, because of the uncertainty of the value of the currencies to be paid or received by traders when goods ordered earlier were finally delivered. Nonetheless, the change had to be made.

The system that replaced Bretton Woods was in fact no organized system at all but a free market for currencies that evolved on its own to reprice every currency relative to every other every day. The new system was tailored to accommodate market forces not to block them, and accordingly, it was not long before the countries of the Organization for Economic Cooperation and Development began to dismantle their controls on cross-border capital flows, which were no longer necessary. With the controls gone, institutional investors in the United States, Britain, and Japan were free to make unrestricted investments overseas for the first time since the 1930s. Corporations, too, were free to make direct investments abroad, something they had in general been restrained from doing for many years. As new suppliers and users of capital entered the international arena, primarily through the Eurocurrency market that developed in London, the volume of transactions began to rise until it reached today's levels.

Benefits and Costs

Despite much prediction to the contrary, the free market system has worked well in several respects and has produced a number of related, if unexpected, benefits. World exports, for example, instead of declining, as predicted, actually increased fourfold from their 1975 level.[2] Even in the trade-deficit-bound United States, exports have kept up with the world trend and increased as a percentage of gross domestic product.[3] Indeed, world trade has increased substantially as a percent of world output since 1987.[4]

The dismantling of controls on capital flows also contributed to a much increased activity in world foreign direct investment, which in 1993 was more than eight times its 1975 level.[5] This increased investment has contributed to the increase in trade, technology transfers, and the development of multinational corporations.

Further, deregulation of capital controls led to a substantial increase in international portfolio investment around the world, providing the basis for the pooling of assets and the integration of markets. This in turn has caused convergence in market practices, regulation, and efficiency. It also led directly to the market reform movement in Europe during the late 1980s, beginning with Britain's "Big Bang," which reorganized and modernized stock exchange and financial markets. Such reorganizations allowed full participation by foreigners and competition in financial services increased significantly, resulting in more efficient markets, greater innovation, and lower costs of financing.

Ultimately, these markets became competitive with bank lending, resulting in greater usage of capital markets and significant changes in corporate control and governance practices. The increased capacity of the capital markets also allowed major corporate reorganizations through mergers and acquisitions to occur on a large scale for the first time in European financial history.

The more active capital markets also provided opportunities for superior risk-adjusted returns for pension funds and other institutional investors, which in turn has enabled these institutions to attract an increasing portion of their national savings. Based on estimates of InterSec Securities Corporation and The Investment Company Institute, global pension and mutual funds should reach a combined value of about $15 trillion in 1997, of which approximately 10 percent, or $1.5 trillion, is expected to be invested in foreign securities, where it will contribute to market efficiency and liquidity. In 1975, by comparison, only a negligible amount of a much smaller pool of such assets was invested in overseas markets.

This vast international investment

flow has made privatization programs possible on a huge scale. Such programs, in which governments sell state-owned enterprises to the public via share offerings, have been central to the economic reforms necessary to revitalize ineffective economic systems in semi-socialist countries (such as were found in Western Europe in the 1970s), developing countries, and former Communist states. Several hundred billion dollars have been raised by such programs, which have been adopted virtually everywhere in Europe and Asia since the British under Margaret Thatcher began the effort in the early 1980s. Several hundred billion dollars worth of privatization programs remain to be completed over the next decade.

Today's investors, however, are very proactive and performance oriented. They must be to retain the funds entrusted to them to manage and to attract others away from competitors. They are interested in undervalued securities, new markets, and instruments that will help to improve performance. They are traders willing to move in and out of markets quickly, and so stay ahead of their competition. They thrive on information. Because they must operate at a large scale in order to have any effect on their relatively large portfolios, their impact on markets is considerable, especially in smaller or emerging markets. Hedge funds and others of the more aggressive among these investors sometimes appear to have become dangerous to the system. They move money around without regard to the consequences, into and out of currencies, for example, which may destabilize a worthy effort by European governments to create a monetary union, and into and out of countries like Mexico, or Turkey, or India, accepting no responsibility for the effect that such rapid movements have on the local economy. Of course, that is what free markets do—they adjust to changed economic conditions as they see fit, without asking for permission.

Systemic Risk

The worst fear is that all of this frenetic investing will ultimately cause the global financial system to fail, as it did in 1929, triggering events that led to the Great Depression of the 1930s. Such a failure could be initiated by a market break similar to 1987, followed by the failure of a number of insured depositary institutions that were either involved in the market directly or exposed to those that were. It is not difficult to extend the scenario from there to a massive credit crunch, unemployment, and demands for increased social welfare and other public services. A major recession in the United States could easily be transferred to its trading partners.

Although concerns about a systemic collapse should not be dismissed lightly (regulators appropriately worry about such things all the time), they should be kept in perspective. Indeed, in different ways the world experienced a major systemic shock with the failure of the U.S. savings and loan banks (S&Ls) and some other banks in the 1980s, which required the intervention of the federal deposit insurance institutions to the extent of several hundreds of billions of dollars. Unlike the 1930s, when thousands of banks failed, helping to push the country into the Great Depression, this time no such result occurred. The crisis was confined to the Federal Deposit Insurance Corporation. It had little effect on either the United States or the world economy.

Also, about 10 years later, a second potentially systemic crisis occurred when the stock market and real estate bubble enveloping the economy of Japan burst and the government had to face up to the damage. Massive loan losses and bankruptcies were the result (estimated in total to exceed $500 billion), which significantly dried up the real economy in the aftermath, creating a low-growth economic condition that lasted several years. The crisis, however, did not spread to other countries. The government intervened in many ways to manage the crisis, including slowing down the deregulatory efforts needed to conform to world financial practices, and steps are under way to deal with the bad loans. The financial system in Japan now appears to be recovering, although slowly.

The lesson from this, and the U.S. S&L crisis, may be that the global financial system may be tougher than it looks and much less susceptible to self-inflicted damage than generally thought; certainly it is tougher than it was in the 1930s.

Weakened Banks

The banks that failed, or were forcibly recapitalized, in the United States, Japan, and Europe in the 1980s and 1990s did so because of traditional loan losses, often undertaken as part of an aggressive and unwise growth strategy that was not sufficiently restrained by regulators, not because they were speculating in securities. Their failures were not the direct consequence of increased securities market activity, volatility, and risk.

But the fate of the banks may have been indirectly caused by these characteristics of the securities markets. For the past 20 years or so, while the markets were building up to their present levels of energy, a substantial degree of competitive displacement has occurred. The banks have been steadily losing market share to market-based financial institutions, and they have found it increasingly difficult to compete with financial markets to attract depositors' funds (in competition with money market funds) or customer loans. A consequence of this disintermediation has been a loss of profitability, which the banks made up for by taking greater lending risks, that is, by turning to lower-quality credits and loans secured by real estate and securities. As a result the world's major banks lost credit standing, in turn causing further disintermediation and a continuation of the cycle. In 1980, for example, there were more than 60 large banks in the world rated triple A by Moody's Investors Services; today there are only five (none of which is American or Japanese).

Thus because of disintermediation caused by deregulation, innovation, and market reforms, a vast amount of money has moved from banks and other depositary institutions around the world into financial markets, where it is currently subject to daily changes in security prices. Further, at the end of 1994 six U.S. investment banks had assets greater than those of Bankers Trust, the most active commercial banking trader of corporate securities and derivatives, and two such firms, Salomon Brothers and Merrill Lynch, had assets twice as great. This much exposure in the financial system to market risk makes many people very uncomfortable and produces cries for its curtailment, even though its potential to cause systemic damage to the global financial system may indeed have been reduced by removing the funds from the bank deposit insurance safety net.

By far the most damage to national and international financial systems has been the result of the failure of banks, savings institutions, and finance companies, which are linked by a global payment system, and the moral hazard of deposit insurance. Because of these linkages, losses and other liquidity problems can affect the entire banking system in one country and thus in others linked to it. Bank losses, too, can be extremely large before they are reported, because of historical cost accounting practices and poor surveillance by banking regulators of the several thousand banks under their control.

Failures of securities firms (there have been quite a few since 1975), however, rarely have much effect on the overall financial system. These firms finance their inventories by borrowing securities valued at their market value as collateral. The firms are also required to mark their inventories to market every day, so losses are not hidden. Further, they are not eligible for the federal financial safety net and accordingly are less affected by moral hazard problems. When failures occur, the firms' capital is lost, but creditors are rarely exposed for very much.

Free Markets and Volatility

The increased level of volatility and financial risk apparent in the system today, however, is a consequence of many changes in the world economy that are beneficial and that tend to increase growth and efficiency. Volatility can flourish only in a free market environment, in which capital may come or go, depending on price levels for essentially the same commodity in different marketplaces. Securing the lowest prices through competition is one of the principal virtues of free markets, the one that ensures that capital will be allocated efficiently.

As unfree or impeded markets are made free to gain efficiency, volatility increases. A totally unfree market may be inefficient, but it is not volatile. As it becomes free to change prices based on supply and demand, it does so, increasing its volatility. The volatility may continue to increase as other, related unfree markets are persuaded to convert to freedom, and the markets are linked. At its peak, volatility may inhibit some trading, increase exposure to market risks, and result in failures of some financial intermediaries, creating a relatively disorderly environment for some financial transactions. But, after a time, the markets become better understood, more often used and more efficient in processing transactions. Volume increases and buy and sell orders become offsetting. More market-makers appear. As this happens, volatility decreases. This continues until some event occurs that injects major discontinuities into the system, choking up the market's ability to function efficiently and reintroducing volatility as a consequence. We have had much experience of sudden external events that have introduced new volatility into the markets, such as the oil crises of 1973 and 1979, the fall of the Berlin Wall, the Persian Gulf War, and various financial crises. There is little anyone can do to prevent these events from happening every so often, but markets have adjusted fairly quickly and have thrown off the added volatility before long.

Nevertheless, learning to live with freer markets and greater volatility has meant accepting increased amounts of uncontrollable money flows, an increase in so-called speculative trading (i.e., for financial investments, which now greatly exceed traditional investments in property, goods, and services), and greater risk to those acting as market-makers. But it has also meant a much increased pool of investment funds available to those deserving of access to them, and a rapid increase in the financial information gathering and technology of hedging and risk management necessary for those seeking to act as intermediaries and investors. These changes, of course, have been accompanied by an equally rapid obsolescence of older, more traditional competitive practices, and in the true spirit of Schumpeter, the rise of new players and the fall of old ones.

Evidence of Volatility

Contrary to conventional expectation, if we look, for example, at historical measures of volatility for three common indices of financial activity—the returns on 20-year U.S. Treasury bonds, the trade-weighted foreign exchange value of the dollar, and the Standard and Poor's 500 Company stock price index—we will see for all three indications of *declining* volatility since the mid-1980s, although several exceptional events took place during this period that increased volatility for a time.

Treasury Bonds. Volatility of U.S. Treasury bonds was effected by the change in Federal Reserve policies related to management of the money supply in 1979, which resulted in a spiking of U.S. interest rates through the early 1980s, and, subsequently, in a sudden shift-to-quality effect following the 1987 stock market crash, which caused rates to decline sharply. As a result, there was a sharp increase in volatility from 1980 to 1983, followed by a runoff until 1987, when another upward adjustment occurred that was followed by a steady, gradual decline. Today U.S. bond market volatility is back to the levels of 1980 (see figure 1).[6]

The Dollar. The dollar was substantially devalued after the Plaza Agreement in 1985, and by 1987 had returned to its 1980 levels relative to a trade-weighted index of currencies published by the Federal Reserve. From 1987 through 1995, the trade-weighted dollar has not fluctuated very much, although it has gradually declined to date from its 1987 level. Using a trade-weighted dollar more accurately reflects the significance of changes in value of the dollar, but because the index incorporates a number of currencies, the volatility associated with the index is relatively low, especially as compared to the dollar against individual currencies such as the yen or the deutsche mark (see figure 2).

The Stock Market. The S&P 500 index experienced significant volatility after the market crash of 1987, from which it has since steadily declined. Today the volatility of the S&P 500 is at its lowest level in 10 years (see figure 3).

These three analyses indicate that the actual levels of volatility in the most important financial markets are not especially high, and indeed are significantly lower today than at any time since 1987. These results may seem surprising because the years since 1979 have been deemed by many observers to be those in which most of the volatility-enhancing and destabilizing changes to financial markets have occurred. The simplest explanation is that the increasing volume of transactions, including a variety of hedging transactions in derivative markets, has made the markets in these standard investment media more efficient and therefore reduced volatility.

Effects on Traders

Modern market developments have profoundly affected traders and their institutional investor clients, for whom, properly managed, volatility is

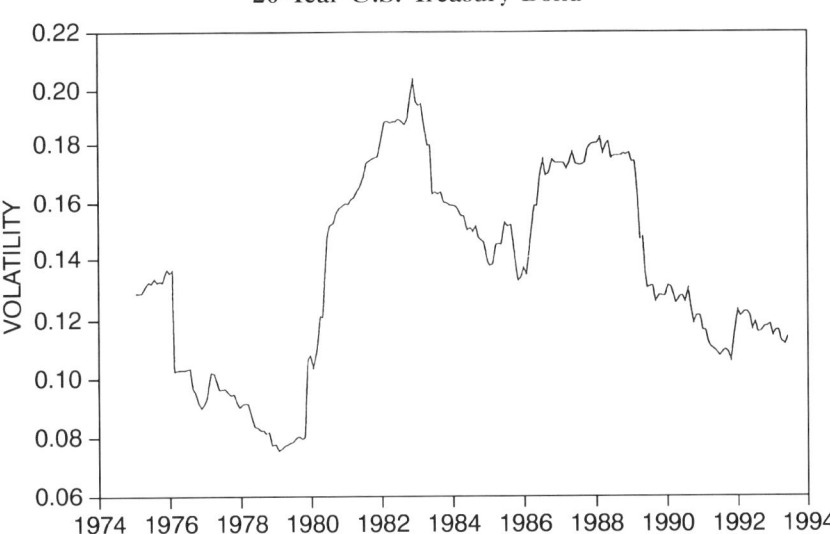

Figure 1
Yield Volatility for Last 36 Months
20-Year U.S. Treasury Bond

a friend. Market-makers prefer large price changes to generate volume and the opportunity for inventory profits. Proprietary traders are usually arbitrage traders, who invest in one thing and fund it with another, hoping that the spread in values between the two will close, creating a profit. The more volatile the markets are, the more arbitrage possibilities will exist, and the quicker they will be resolved. Arbitrage, of course, has its risks, but sophisticated players work the percentages and believe the more different arbitrages they handle the better.

Traders complain that, in low volatility conditions, spreads between bid and ask prices and on potential arbitrages narrow significantly, making it much harder to make the same amount of money for risk exposures undertaken. Lacking such opportunities, the determined trader may try to replace the lost profits by riskier investment strategies, such as investing in uncovered positions on future price levels. Such investments can be much riskier than hedged or arbitraged positions. During 1994, a year in which U.S. interest rates were raised by the Federal Reserve several times in succession, virtually all of the principal trading houses in the United States and Europe did poorly—normally they would make money when rates change steadily. As volatility declined across most of their principal markets, and efforts to catch up by undertaking greater (and riskier) uncovered investments did not produce the desired results, many firms, including such skilled traders as Salomon Brothers, Goldman Sachs, J. P. Morgan, S. G. Warburg, Baring Brothers, and Bankers Trust, lost large amounts in their trading operations. For all of these firms, trading comprised between 40 percent and 80 percent of noninterest

Figure 2
Federal Reserve Board Trade-Weighted U.S. Dollar

Index (March 1973=100)

[Chart showing index declining from ~160 in 1985 to ~85 by week ending 5/24/95]

Source: Federal Reserve Board.

earnings. In two of these cases, these losses, together with other market-related factors, significantly destabilized the firms, resulting in a merger with a stronger firm.

Investment bankers discovered a similar problem in the new issues markets. Although large volumes of new securities were created in domestic and overseas markets in 1994, the business was much less profitable than in the previous year. This was partly due to a continuous narrowing of underwriting spreads, or commissions, accompanied by an increase in the amount of risk taken by aggressive underwriters in competition with others. Comparable results were experienced in the mergers and acquisition field, where despite large volumes of transactions, commissions were down due to greater competition.

Effects on Investors

Most institutional investors today follow modern portfolio theory, in which volatility is a pseudonym for risk. The more volatile a security, the riskier it is to own, but ironically it has been amply demonstrated that it may be less risky for a portfolio as a whole to

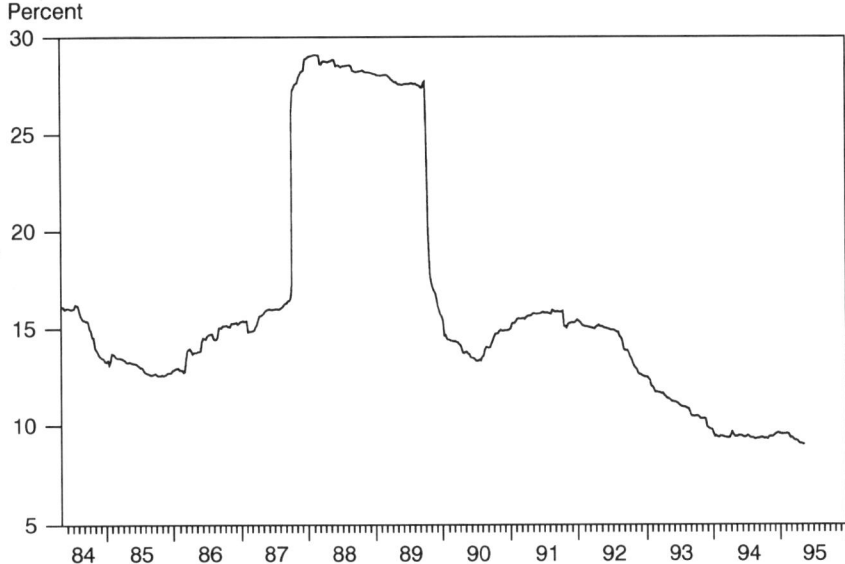

**Figure 3
S&P 500 Volatility**

Note: Annualized standard deviation of S&P 500 2-year daily price performance.

own a limited amount of risky securities, so long as each of the securities is independent of the other, that is, its price movement is not correlated with the others. Thus, the benefits of diversification can be achieved, in which for a given level of return, a portfolio with some risky investments in it may actually have less risk than a portfolio consisting of securities of average risk. The practical effect of this is to encourage portfolio managers at large financial institutions to look for new, risky but uncorrelated investments to make. These have been found in recent years in high-yield debt securities, in leveraged buy-out funds, real estate partnerships, venture capital, investment grade foreign securities, in foreign exchange and other financial derivative contracts, and most recently in securities of below-investment-grade emerging market countries. By adding such holdings to one's portfolio, the portfolio itself will increase its probability of beating market returns while lowering risks. Thus the search is on, more or less permanently now, for new, uncorrelated, risky (therefore volatile) investments. As these are found, and large amounts of institutional investment capital flows into them, their prices rise and they become more correlated with similar securities that these investors might buy. Although good for the early investors, later-stage investors may find limited value in such securities because both the profit and the diversification potential have been dissipated.

Ironically, the great flow of institutional capital into emerging markets in Latin America and Asia, which produced average gains of 48 percent in 1992 and 20 percent in 1993, produced losses of 20 percent in 1994 and even worse results in early 1995, when emerging markets almost everywhere were affected by panicky rushes for the exits following the Mexican market collapse at the beginning of the year. Indeed, what the investors learned was that these emerging markets were substantially correlated with each other because of the behavior of the investors. Correlated, these investments offered the opposite of portfolio diversification—an unusual and much undesired concentration effect. Having produced such results, it is unlikely that portfolio investors will return to emerging markets with their prior enthusiasm. Whatever it is, however, something new will appear on the horizon to offer a chance at superior investment performance to aggressive money managers.

Living with Volatility

To an important degree, volatility has been bled out of the markets by an increasing volume of transactions, but it has been reintroduced voluntarily by non-bank financial intermediaries as these struggle to compete with each other by increasing the risks they are prepared to take on behalf of returns for their clients or investors. Such risks become of great importance to the stability of the financial system as the size of the exposures of the intermediaries increases.

These risks are at present addressed at several levels of regulation and control, each of which is intended to provide some protection against systemic collapse while not impeding the general movement toward greater competition in all aspects of banking and finance. The levels involve capital adequacy regulations, requirements for disclosure of market risks, and self-management.

Capital Adequacy

The banking industry, involving substantial government interest as lender of last resort and guarantor of deposits, has experienced radical regulatory change, along both competitive and safety axes. In the past, a bank was considered safe if it had a lot of capital and did not do much with it. Banks were made safe by protecting them from competition by regulation and by allowing them to make large profits for their services. That they were safe but not very competitive did not contribute much to national economic growth. During the 1970s, however, banks began to compete aggressively with each other for lending business, and regulators began to be concerned that excessive risks would be taken by overeager or unsound banks. They were right; the banks did overindulge, and many failed or were rescued as has been discussed above. Regulators went back to the drawing boards—they wanted vigorous competitive financial activity, but not at the cost of safety.

So, in 1987, the Bank for International Settlements (BIS) brokered a completely unprecedented agreement among the banking regulators of all the member countries of the EU, Switzerland, the United States, and Japan that set a common standard for the minimum capital adequacy for banks. The agreement required banks in all the countries to be required to assess the credit risk of all on– and off–balance sheet holdings and to provide sufficient capital from two permitted tiers to back those assets. This meant that all the world's major banks would be subject to virtually the same capital adequacy requirements to assure their safety. As long as they met these requirements (with some margin) they could be as competitive as they liked; if they fell short, they would be restrained from many activities. In January 1998, the agreement is to be modified to include additional capital for market-risk exposures as well, based on "value at risk" as measured by the banks themselves or by applying a standard model. Securities firms are not yet subject to the same capital adequacy minimums, but proposals exist for them to become so, and they are subject to stock exchange and other capital requirements.

Increased Disclosure

Banking and securities regulators, rating agencies, and auditors are also increasing their requirements for disclosure of information concerning holdings of derivatives and other volatile securities. It is assumed that before much longer all major banks and non-bank securities dealers will be required to disclose similar information as to values at risk and to demonstrate the availability of capital to support them. The additional disclosures are important. Although these may be obscure to most investors, they will be clearly understood by rating agencies, the credit departments of other banks, and regulators. These disclosures can affect published bond ratings and market prices of extant securities, and hence they will be effective as a regulatory device.

Self-Management

Finally, all major trading firms, especially after the example of Kidder Peabody and Baring Brothers, which perished because of rogue trader and internal control failures, are investing heavily in new forms of internal risk management systems. Such systems include risk identification, measurement, reporting, and management, and they extend to all cash market securities as well as futures, options, swaps, and forward contracts. The Group of Thirty, an unofficial association of bankers, has proposed certain procedures for managing risks associated with derivatives, as has the Derivatives Policy Group, an association of the six leading Wall Street non-bank derivatives dealing houses. These proposals do not have enforcement powers, but many leading firms are adopting them voluntarily, which in many cases involves substantial new investments in control systems and procedures.

One step many firms have taken is the creation of a stand-alone, credit-enhanced subsidiary to carry the firm's inventory of swaps and some other derivative investments. These subsidiaries are backed by enough capital and securities carried at market value to qualify for AAA ratings. They are necessary for firms with lesser ratings (all investment banks are rated below AAA) to be able to trade freely with all counterparties. Without the AAA subsidiary, the firms would experience more limited trading capability and higher costs of financing. Accordingly these high-grade subsidiaries limit systemic risk to some extent.

Firms also are aware that the reason that failures occurred at Kidder Peabody and Baring Brothers (and at Salomon Brothers during the case of the rigged Treasury auction bids) was fundamentally because of the loss of managerial control. Thus, much effort is being made to shore up systems and keep them up-to-date. Most firms have installed risk-adjusted controls affecting every trader in the firm, improved compliance systems, and new programs to identify exposure risks while they are still manageable. The firms are also endeavoring to prevent actions that result in sizable client litigation such as that experienced by Bankers Trust in the case of Gibson Greetings and Proctor and Gamble in 1994. Regulators are not able to keep up with the latest in risk-taking techniques, so they must rely on the firms themselves to see their self-interest in controlling such risks.

Today, the market risk exposures are confined to a modest number of wholesale financial service providers in the United States and Europe. Globally, the top 20 firms providing wholesale financial services (including several commercial banks) accounted for approximately 80 percent of the market. Keeping track of these players, most of whom today are subject to capital adequacy or similar tests, is not difficult. In addition, all of these firms must maintain public credit ratings from the leading rating agencies, which scrutinize the firms closely.

Still, accidents can happen. Traders can forget themselves in the heat of competition and then increase risks to cover up. Firms can underinvest in control systems and procedures or make a variety of other mistakes that their partners and shareholders will be unable to detect or prevent. When all goes wrong in this industry, however, there are no depositors to guarantee. Securities belonging to customers are segregated and themselves insured by SIPC, the Securities Investment Protection Corporation, an insurance concern owned by the industry. Losses are borne by only the stockholders, subordinated lenders, and then creditors as in any other bankruptcy. There have been occasions, such as during the crash of 1987, when the Federal Reserve has organized the advance of credit to the securities industry to stem the tide in a market crisis, but there has never been a case of an individual broker/dealer or investment bank being rescued by the government.

The Market Regulates Itself

What now appears to be clear is that, for the past several years, the market has placed a cost on participants that have not lowered their market risks voluntarily and provided adequate capital to support their trading activities. The cost appears in the form of lower debt ratings and stock price multiples. This cost has increased as derivative and other potentially volatile holdings have increased, as the regulators have grown more concerned with market risk, and as certain accidents have occurred. A trader not absorbing his share of such costs (a free rider) will be found out by the required disclosures and by deteriorated credit ratings and will be unable to trade in any volume great enough to do damage to the system. Fearing inappropriate forms of regulation introduced by poorly informed regulators, the industry has volunteered a variety of self-regulated solutions to risk containment. The BIS, for one, has agreed that many of the risk-modeling procedures of major traders are far superior to those it might otherwise prescribe and accordingly has allowed such models to be used for calculating market risk.

Financial market risk and volatility are by-products of deregulation and efforts to increase competition. They can be contained by regulatory steps and required disclosures already undertaken and subject to periodic updates. This kind of regulation is now generally consistent all over the world, affecting all significant competitors equally. The markets periodically create a variety of new products and services that lower the cost of capital to issuers and increase the returns to investors. Most of the market risk is borne by the firms that manufacture and sell the products and services and whose shareholders' capital is directly at risk. The government is not required to bail out any customer of securities firms (nor is it required to guarantee non-depositor customers of securities subsidiaries of commercial banks), nor has it ever done so. The securities firms are large and therefore could have a large impact on the financial system as a whole, but most of their liabilities are secured by securities at market value. The capital of such major firms is rarely more than a few billion dollars, thus suggesting that the cost to the system of a single failure, or a series of connected failures of securities firms, would at worst be far less than the cost incurred in another major banking or S&L crisis.

Existing regulation in the securities industry and coordination between the Securities Exchange Commission, the commodities authorities, and the Federal Reserve seem adequate relative to the identifiable risks. Most of the effort to regulate has been directed at intermediaries, rather than at the end users of securities and derivative transactions. Certain regulated end users (S&Ls and insurance companies, for example) might be restrained by their own regulators, but the rest of the market, consisting of sophisticated wholesale market investors, should be permitted to look after itself. Otherwise, the three-tiered approach to regulation by capital adequacy, disclosure, and self-management appears to be enough to balance the real threat to the financial system against the need for a free market and lots of competition.

In one important area, however, governments should beware. The lines between banks (and their entitlement to the safety net) and non-bank financial service firms is rapidly blurring. Reform of the Glass–Steagall Act must recognize that the securities business, although perhaps not so risky to the financial system, is very risky for its principals. So far, the securities market has been ineligible for the safety net, but should it become eligible inadvertently as a result of abolishing the differences between banking and securities businesses, the increased exposure to securities market risks on the part of the government and its taxpayers could be very substantial. At present the reliance is on regulatory "firewalls" to separate banking and securities to avoid this possibility. The administration and the Federal Reserve, both strong supporters of Glass–Steagall reform, must realize that they have a very large bet on the integrity of the firewalls they are proposing.

The author gratefully acknowledges helpful suggestions from Richard Levich and Steven Figlewski.

Notes

1. IMF International Statistics, quoted in Commission Report, *Bretton Woods: Looking to the Future* (Bretton Woods Commission, July 1994).

2. Ernest H. Preeg, *Trade Policy Ahead: Three Tracks and One Question*, Significant Issues Series 17, no. 2 (Washington, D.C.: CSIS, 1995), p. 7.

3. Council of Economic Advisers, *Economic Report of the President* (Washington, D.C., February 1995).

4. "Battle Lines," *Economist*, December 24, 1994.

5. Preeg, *Trade Policy Ahead*, p. 7.

6. Volatility is better observed when daily price changes are averaged with other price changes over a longer period of time, such as two or three years as in figures 1 to 3.

Is It a Yen or a Dollar Crisis in the Currency Market?

David D. Hale

ANY ASSESSMENT OF the state of global finance in the mid-1990s and any prediction of the future of the global economy must take account of the changing balance of forces in the currency market, where a dramatic shift is under way. The following questions stand out as particularly important. Why is the yen so strong? How are its appreciation and the dollar's weakness changing the roles of the two currencies in the global financial system, and with what effect for capital flows? What will be the consequences for the United States if the dollar's reserve currency role erodes significantly? And finally, what policy can the United States pursue to maintain the dollar's status as the world's leading reserve currency? This article sets out to answer these questions.

Yen Appreciation

During the late 1980s, one of the best sell signals for Japanese equities was the explosive growth of the Tokyo stock market's capitalization compared to other countries. As a result of the dramatic share price gains of those years, Japan's stock market capitalization reached a level equal to 45 percent of the world total or nearly 50 percent higher than the U.S. share. At the start of the 1980s, Japan's stock market capitalization was equal to only about 15 percent of the world total while the U.S. share was about 54 percent. As a result of the bear market that began in 1989, Tokyo's share of global stock market capitalization has fallen sharply and is now at a level equal to only about 27 percent of the world total or close to that of Europe. The U.S. share, by contrast, has returned to nearly 45 percent (see figure 1).

As a result of the yen's 20 percent appreciation during 1994, the nominal dollar value of Japan's gross domestic product (GDP) has risen to a level that is now equal to 84 percent of U.S. GDP. If the yen appreciates to 70, Japan's nominal dollar GDP will exceed U.S. GDP despite the vast differences in the two countries' resource endowments. Compared to Japan, the United States has a land area 24 times greater, a population more than twice as large, and a 13 percent share of world trade

---

David D. Hale is chief economist of Kemper Financial Services, Inc.

David D. Hale

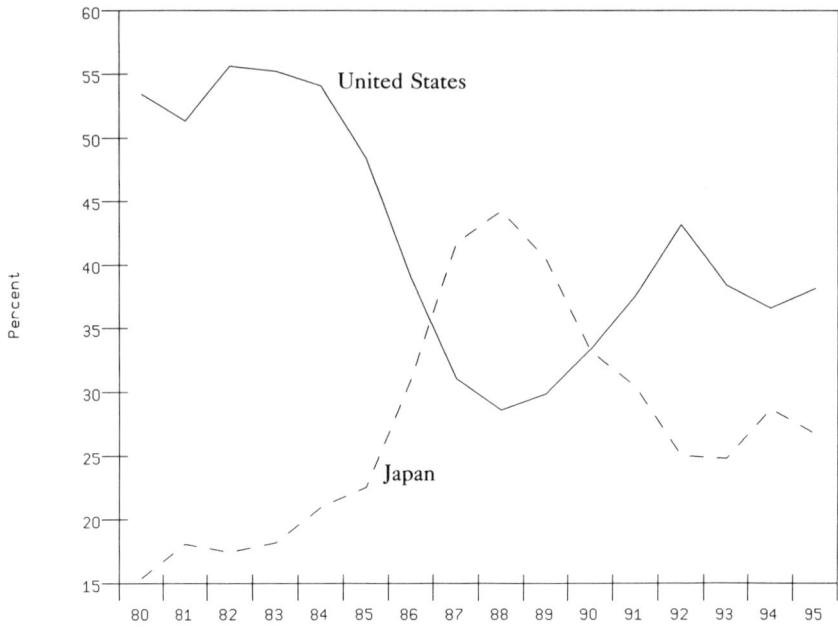

Figure 1
Share of World Market Capitalization
United States (line) versus Japan (dash)

Note: If the yen reaches an exchange rate of 70, the nominal dollar value of Japan's GDP will exceed U.S. GDP despite the fact that the United States has a land area 24 times greater than Japan's and a population twice as large. In the late 1980s, Japan briefly had a larger stock market capitalization, but that phenomenon was in retrospect a good sell signal because the Japanese market soon began a multiyear slide that caused it to lose over two-thirds of its value. The high nominal dollar value of Japan's GDP may also be regarded as a sell signal at some point.

versus 9 percent. As with the Tokyo stock market bubble of the late 1980s, this upsurge in Japan's nominal dollar GDP should not be regarded as a sign of Japanese economic strength. Rather it is a symptom of economic imbalances that are threatening to push Japan into a state of hyperdeflation. In fact, it is widely expected that the nominal yen value of Japan's GDP will decline during the second quarter of 1995 for the first time ever in the post–World War II era.

The yen's appreciation during 1994 resulted from a systemic recycling crisis in Japan's balance of payments. Japan is generating a far larger trade surplus than its private sector is willing to recycle into long-term foreign investments, while foreign private and official investors have been bidding for Japanese financial assets in order to diversify their portfolios away from the dollar. As a result, Japan has faced a double balance of payments adjustment challenge during the past 18 months—it has had to recycle both its own surplus savings as well as capital inflows from foreign investors purchasing yen-denominated securities.

Since 1990, Japan's current account surplus has grown from $35.7 billion to about $130 billion, but long-term capital outflows to non-yen assets have fallen sharply. In 1994, total long-term capital outflows were about $81.8 billion but almost $65 billion of this sum went to purchase yen-denominated Eurobonds in Luxembourg and London. Total investments in U.S. securities declined to $14.4 billion from $22 billion in 1993 and levels as high as $40 billion to $50 billion during the 1980s. As a result of the severe recession now occurring in Japanese corporate profits, foreign direct investment (FDI) also remained at the depressed level of $17 billion compared to $30.7 billion in 1991 and $48 billion in 1990.

In 1994, the primary channels for recycling Japan's current account surplus were bank lending and central bank purchases of foreign securities. Japan's international bank lending rose to $670 billion in 1994 from $608 billion in 1993 and $599 billion in 1992, with practically all of the gain occurring in yen-denominated loans. Japan's central bank also purchased over $27 billion of foreign securities in order to restrain the yen's appreciation during periods when private capital outflows stalled.

The yen rose steadily in 1994 despite the central bank intervention because Japan had to recycle foreign investor demand for yen financial assets, not just its own current account surplus. According to official data, foreign monetary institutions purchased over $29 billion of yen securities during 1994 compared to $3 billion in 1993 and $1 billion in 1992. Although no data are available about the source of these official purchases, they appear to represent portfolio shifts by Asian central banks concerned about their countries' large yen liabilities (e.g., Thailand and Indonesia) as well as diversification away from the depreciating dollar.

Japan's financial recycling problem during 1994 was also magnified by foreign investor demand for Japanese equities. In early 1994, there was significant foreign buying of Japanese equities because many international fund managers had perceived that Japan was overdue for a catch-up rally with other world equity markets. Foreign purchases of Japanese equities shot up to $48.9 billion in 1994 from $20 billion in 1993 and $8.7 billion in 1992. As a result of the deflationary recession engulfing the Japanese economy, foreign demand for Japanese equities has slumped during recent quarters but it could revive at some point if foreigners decide that Japan offers better prospects for profit growth than other countries of the Organization for Economic Cooperation and Development (OECD). The foreign ownership share of the Tokyo market is now at 8 percent compared to a range of 6.0 to 8.5 percent during recent years. Foreigners own about 9 percent of the shares in Japanese manufacturing industry but have much lower weightings in banks and service companies. Because the return on equity in the Japanese corporate sector was only 3.0 percent in 1994 compared to over 8.0 percent in the late 1980s, Japanese companies will have potentially significant profit leverage during the next economic recovery. Such opportunities will attract foreign investors and limit the magnitude of future yen corrections even if Japanese interest rates have to fall to 0.5 percent later in 1995 in order to produce an economic upturn.

The sharp decline in Japanese demand for foreign assets has resulted from the large losses Japanese investors have experienced on their foreign investments since the mid-1980s. On the basis of exchange rate movements since 1986, they appear to have lost about $600 billion on their total foreign investments and close to $500 billion on their U.S. investments. In the late 1980s, Japanese investors were able to compensate for losses on their foreign investments with the large capital gains they earned from their holdings of domestic equities and real estate. But since 1990, there has also been a sharp correction in domestic asset prices that has eliminated the reserve cushions at many Japanese financial institutions for offsetting foreign exchange losses. In fact, some Japanese life insurance companies have experienced such large capital losses that they could probably be classified as insolvent.

Japanese demand for U.S. securities has also suffered from regulatory changes in the life insurance industry. In the 1980s, the Japanese life insurance companies were the largest foreign buyers of U.S. Treasury securities. They were attracted by the high yield compared to yen securities and the fact that many life insurance products had yields linked solely to coupon income, not capital gains. As a result of the large foreign exchange losses of the life insurance companies, Japanese regulators are now imposing higher reserve ratios on foreign bonds and equities than on yen-denominated securities. Japanese life insurance companies have therefore scaled back their foreign investments from over 15 percent to less than 7 percent of total assets and reduced the dollar share of their foreign currency exposure to 51 percent from 65 percent in 1988. This cautious approach to foreign investing is unlikely to change in the near future because the Japanese life insurance industry is suffering from large losses on domestic equities and real estate as well as foreign securities. Because Japanese insurance companies are by far the country's largest investor group (they have assets of 174 trillion yen or $2.2 trillion), their investment strategies have profound consequences for Japanese capital flows and exchange rates.

In recent years, some of the reduced capital outflow from the life insurance companies has been offset by foreign bond purchases from Japan's postal savings bank. It has total assets of 79.9 trillion yen and 3.5 trillion yen of foreign securities. But as these investments have so far been unhedged, the postal savings bank has large unrealized losses on its foreign assets and recently sought permission to begin hedging them. Such hedging could generate new dollar selling during the next few quarters.

The other major conduit for Japanese capital outflows is the securities investment trusts. At the peak in 1990, they exported over 5 trillion yen per annum but in 1994 their foreign investments were only 3 trillion yen. As they have short-term investment horizons, they can shift funds among various asset classes very quickly. After concentrating on U.S. assets during the 1980s, the security trusts significantly increased their exposure to Europe during the early 1990s and to the emerging markets during 1993–94.

The only category of Japanese capital outflow that appears likely to expand during the near future is foreign direct investment (FDI). As a result of the recession in Japanese corporate profits, this type of investment fell from a peak of $69 billion in 1989 to $13 billion in 1993 before reviving to $17 billion in 1994. The yen appreciation of 1994 caused many Japanese companies to announce that they would shift more production offshore, so foreign investment is now expanding at a $35 billion annual rate. In addition to yen appreciation, there is a strong case for the Japanese corporate sector to expand its FDI because Japanese multinational firms still have only about 10 percent of their production outside Japan compared to 20 percent for U.S. multinationals.

In the late 1980s, about half of Japanese FDI went to North America, about 22 percent went to Europe, and only 12 percent went to East Asia. In 1994, the East Asian share of Japanese FDI rose to 21 percent while the U.S. share shrank to 39 percent and the European share fell to 17 percent. East Asia is likely to absorb a growing share of Japanese FDI because Japanese firms regard the region as an important export base for the whole world, not just the local markets. According to recent corporate surveys, Japanese firms plan to export only about 5 percent of their output at U.S. plants to third countries outside the neighboring region compared to over 33 percent at their East Asian operations. In the 1980s, the major beneficiaries of the Japanese FDI boom in East Asia were Thailand, Malaysia, and Indonesia. In the case of Thailand, one in seven manufacturing workers is now employed by a Japanese firm. These countries should continue to benefit from expanded Japanese FDI in the region but more of the next investment wave will probably go to China and the Philippines because they are better positioned to attract FDI today than they were five years ago. Labor costs have risen sharply in Malaysia and Thailand since the 1980s compared to China, while the Philippines has finally begun to resolve problems with energy supplies and economic management that retarded its performance in the years immediately after the fall of the Marcos government. As a result of the cheap dollar, Japan will also boost FDI in the United States but the growth will occur primarily through greenfield investment whereas in the 1980s many Japanese firms joined in the merger and acquisition boom through takeover bids (see figure 2).

Despite the large decline in Japanese equity and real estate prices since 1990, FDI in Japan has remained very modest. It was only $800 million in 1994 compared to a peak of $2.7 billion in 1992. Until recently, Japan had many official restrictions on FDI but in recent years the major barrier to investment has been the perception of foreign companies that Japan is an expensive country in which to operate. Foreign companies therefore own only about 1 percent of Japan's capital stock compared to 10 to 15 percent for many other OECD countries, including the United States.

The low level of FDI in Japan has been an important contributing factor to Japan's trade tensions with other countries because in the modern era trade flows often follow investment. U.S. multinational firms, for example, have total sales in the British market of $149 billion, with 84 percent of the sales consisting of locally produced goods, 3 percent consisting of licensed sales, and 14 percent consisting of exports from the United States. In the case of Germany, sales by U.S. multinational companies are $91 billion, with 79 percent consisting of locally produced goods, 3 percent licensed sales, and 19 percent exports from the United States. In Japan, by contrast, U.S. multinational corporations had sales of $113 billion, consisting of 43 percent locally produced goods, 18 percent licensed sales, and 37 percent exports from the United States. If U.S.

David D. Hale

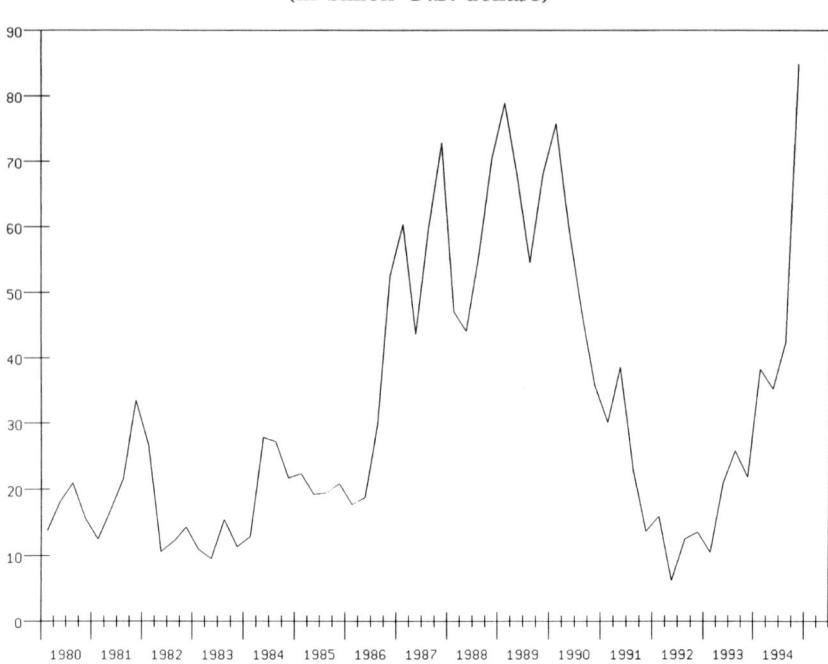

**Figure 2
Foreign Direct Investment in the United States
(in billion U.S. dollars)**

Note: Foreign direct investment in the United States has been rising since 1992 and should expand further because of the profit recovery occurring elsewhere and the weakness of the dollar.

firms had larger operations in Japan, the share of exports might decline but the total level of trade would probably be higher because these firms would source many of the components for local production in the United States. In fact, the per capita sales of U.S. multinational companies in Japan are only about $921 compared to $2,600 for Britain and $1,500 for Germany, despite the much higher level of personal income in Japan. Instead of U.S. exports to Japan benefiting from more U.S. FDI there, the major boost to U.S. trade with Japan appears to be coming from Japanese FDI in the United States itself. Japanese multinational firms purchase nearly 70 percent of their U.S. imports from their North American affiliates whereas European firms purchase far more of their American imports from U.S. firms. Despite the dollar's recent depreciation (shown in figure 3) the intracorporate share of U.S.–Japan trade is likely to remain high because it is doubtful that U.S.

Figure 3
Yen/Dollar Exchange Rate and 1970–Present Trend of Yen/Dollar

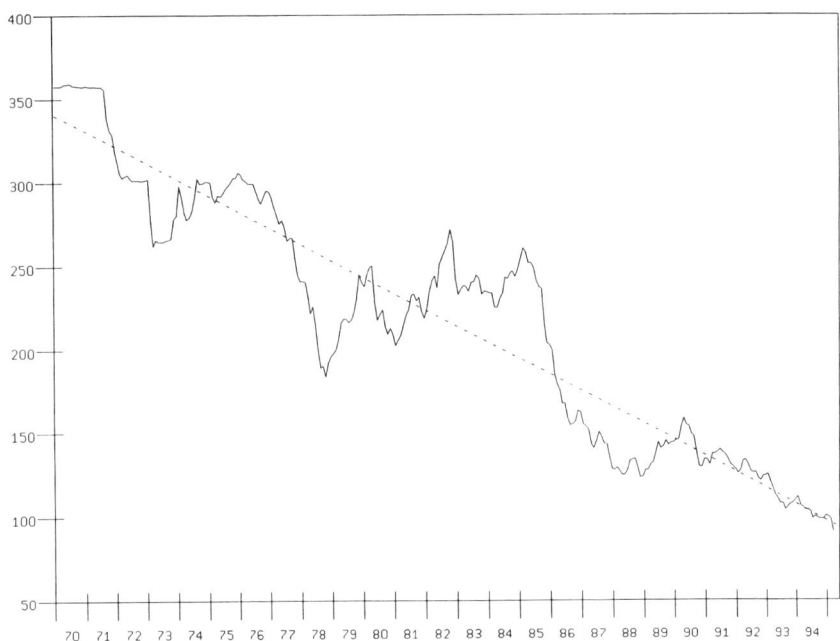

Note: This figure shows the 25-year trend line of the yen against its actual level.

firms will boost their investment in Japan significantly with the yen at 80 to 85 to the dollar.

How Will Japan Adjust?

Japan can adjust in a number of ways to the imbalance between the country's large trade surplus, the growing foreign demand for the yen securities, and the new caution of Japanese financial institutions toward foreign portfolio diversification.

First, the yen can appreciate until there is a significant erosion in the size of Japan's trade surplus. The yen appreciation of the 1990s has encouraged a large rise in import penetration within Japan but it has not significantly reduced the trade surplus because import prices have fallen while export growth has benefited from the recovery in the world economy. The yen's current value against the dollar will probably boost the trade surplus in the short term by lowering import prices but it should curtail export growth by more than previous yen rallies because profit margins were already very slim before the yen's latest rise. Most Japanese manufacturing firms had been budgeting for a yen in the 95 to 105 range during the next 12 months while price deflators for Japan's high-technology tradeable goods industries suggest that their products will suffer a major loss of competitiveness when the yen exceeds 95.

Second, the yen could appreciate to levels at which foreign assets become so cheap that Japanese investment institutions conclude that the potential returns from them will more than offset the risk of currency depreciation. The problem for Japanese investors is that the U.S. dollar has already violated numerous support levels that were once regarded as sacrosanct, including 150 yen to the dollar, 100 yen to the dollar, and more recently 90 yen to the dollar.

Third, Japan can reduce interest rates in order to lower the return on its money market assets and bolster the value of bonds and equities. Such capital gains could bolster the reserves of Japan's investment institutions and thus increase their tolerance for the risk of diversifying into foreign assets. The problem with this solution is that a rally in Japanese equity prices will probably also encourage large short-term capital inflows to purchase Japanese shares. In mid-April 1995, during the week after the Bank of Japan reduced interest rates to 1.0 percent from 1.75 percent, there was a moderate stock market rally in Tokyo but it did not attract external support because most foreign investors perceived the government's economic policy package to be inadequate. If interest rates fall further, or the government introduces a stimulative fiscal package, foreign investors could become more aggressive buyers of Japanese equities.

Finally, Japan could attempt to reduce its trade surplus by accelerating deregulation of its economy. Although import penetration has risen sharply since the late 1980s, the increase has occurred from a very low level and Japan still appears to have more non-tariff barriers to manufactured imports than other industrial countries. In 1993, the Clinton administration embarked upon an ambitious round of multiyear trade talks with Japan in order to open markets through a mixture of microeconomic reform and more aggressive use of targets to promote import penetration. The Japanese government has responded by announcing its own deregulation package, but most observers believe that it will have only a modest effect on the trade imbalance compared to the appreciation of the yen.

The Clinton administration is now attempting to significantly improve U.S. access to the Japanese auto market as well as to boost the domestic content of Japanese autos manufactured in the United States. The Japanese claim that many of the U.S. demands are an intrusion on their inspection rules and traditional methods of distribution, but with the yen at 82 to the dollar some Japanese industrialists are encouraging the government to offer concessions in order to lessen upward pressure on the currency. As the foreign share of the Japanese auto market is only 4 percent today compared to 80 percent before World War II, any significant breakthrough in the level of import penetration would have a major impact on the trade account in autos. But in the short term, such trade conflicts could push the yen higher because of investor perceptions that a higher yen will have a far greater impact on the willingness of Japanese investment firms to export capital to the United States than on the bilateral trade imbalance. Some officials in the Ministry of Finance (MOF) have also suggested to journalists that they might encourage Japanese investment firms to sell dollar securities if U.S. trade pressures become intolerable.

What remains to be seen is whether investors will at some point rethink their assumptions about the relation between trade tension and exchange rates. In the case of the auto dispute, for example, Japan is protesting the U.S. sanctions at the World Trade Organization (WTO). Many trade lawyers fear the WTO will take Japan's side in the run-up to the U.S. 1996 presidential election and thus encourage U.S. protectionists to argue that the new global trade rules are unfair. In such a scenario, the United States could become even more antagonistic toward both Japan and the WTO, jeopardizing its authority only two years after completion of the General Agreement on Tariffs and Trade. Because Japan is the industrial country most vulnerable to increasing protectionism in North America and Europe, such trade tensions might encourage selling of the yen in the expectation that Japan's current account surplus could decline sharply in response to growing American and European trade barriers, not just exchange rate appreciation.

Before the financial boom of the late 1980s, Japan's sensitivity to oil shocks and trade conflicts caused investors to regard it as a vulnerable country. In recent years, this perception of vulnerability has eroded because of the country's large trade surplus and big foreign investments. But the fact remains that Japan is highly vulnerable to external shocks and depends far more heavily upon international rules for both access to markets and military security than other countries. The large losses Japan has incurred on its foreign investments and the recent deflation in domestic asset prices also illustrate the limitations of a high savings rate on the process of wealth accumulation if the money cannot be productively deployed because of rigidities in the financial system that limit competition. If and when investors resume perceiving Japan as vulnerable, they could rethink their assumptions about the relationship between trade tension and exchange rates.

As a result of the paralysis now gripping Japanese investment institutions, the solution to the yen recycling crises during 1995 and 1996 is likely to consist of an eroding trade surplus driven by exchange rate overvaluation, further cuts in Japanese interest rates designed to boost Japanese asset prices and capital outflows, and a revival of Japanese FDI to both East Asia and North America.

This adjustment path will give the yen a bias toward being commercially overvalued for some time but it will not prevent volatility in the value of the yen in a trading range above 100 to the dollar. The yen will fluctuate in response to changing investor perceptions of the speed at which the trade surplus is likely to contract, the willingness of Japanese institutions to resume exporting capital, and the degree of monetary restraint in the U.S. economy compared to Japan. Ironically, recovery of the Japanese financial system and asset prices could depress the yen by encouraging renewed capital outflows whereas in most other countries the restoration of a healthy banking system would be considered the prerequisite of a strong currency. The yen could also be vulnerable to political tensions in the Western Pacific from time to time. North Korea is still ruled by an authoritarian Communist regime and has developed a small nuclear arsenal. The United States has tried to persuade the regime to curtail its nuclear arms program in return for access to Western nuclear technology, but the negotiations over disarmament have been inhibited by North Korea's attempt to create divisions in the U.S.–

South Korean alliance. If the United States felt compelled to impose economic sanctions on North Korea or threatened to use force against the country, investors would probably sell all currencies in the region, including the yen. The growing military power of China and its increasingly assertive stand over the Spratly Islands also could remind investors of Japan's limited military power and continuing dependence upon the United States for military security.

As with the rise of the deutsche mark as a regional reserve currency in Europe, Japan does not have to be a major military power in order to promote greater international use of the yen for denominating trade and finance. But if Japan does become an independent military power during the next century, its new status will pose two threats to the dollar. Investors will not only perceive Japan to be a more independent country. They will also expect the Bank of Japan to be less supportive of official intervention on behalf of the dollar during periods of crisis than was the case when Japan depended upon the United States for security, and currency intervention might have been regarded as an implicit form of burden sharing.

The Role of Reserve Currencies

As a result of the dollar's persistent weakness against the yen and the D-mark during recent years, there has been recurring discussion about the dollar losing its role as a reserve currency. Because the U.S. share of world output has declined from almost 50 percent after World War II to only 25 percent recently, it is not unnatural that the world should move toward a multipolar currency system compared to the dollar-denominated one that evolved during the Bretton Woods era.

In fact, it is somewhat surprising that the dollar's share of global foreign exchange reserves still exceeds 60 percent despite the large decline in the U.S. share of world output.

The dollar remains the leading reserve currency because the United States still satisfies most of the requirements for being the anchor country of the world monetary system. In the past, reserve currency countries have typically had six key economic characteristics. They have had large economies accounting for over 25 percent of world output at their zenith. They have had low inflation rates that made their currencies a reliable store of value. They have had robust and open capital markets capable of recycling savings on a global basis. They have had strong central banks capable of supporting the financial system as lenders of last resort during periods of crisis. The foreign trade sector has played a modest role in their economy and thus limited the power of economic interest groups that might want to encourage currency depreciation in order to bolster trade competitiveness. The country has typically had a savings surplus that permitted it to export capital to other countries. In addition to these economic characteristics, the key reserve currency countries have also been major military powers.

Britain before the World War I and the United States during the first two decades after World War II were model reserve currency countries. In the late nineteenth century, Britain accounted for about one quarter of world output independent of its empire and its share of world output was still 14 percent at the start of World War I. Britain also had foreign assets equal to almost 150 percent of its GDP in the United States, Latin America, Australia, South Africa, and other countries in the empire. The investment income from these assets encouraged Britain to adhere to free trade policies despite the fact that it had a large manufacturing sector and accounted for 16 percent of world trade, the largest share of any country at that time. In the 1990s, the United States retains many of the characteristics of Britain in the late nineteenth century. It accounts for about one quarter of world output and 13 percent of world trade, while the New York financial markets are still the largest in the world. But as a result of the large federal budget deficits of the 1980s, the United States has ceased to be a net creditor vis-à-vis the rest of the world. It now has a net international investment deficit exceeding 10 percent of GDP and is projected to continue running current account deficits of $150 billion to $200 billion per annum for several years. If such large current account deficits persist, the United States will ultimately have a significant deficit on external investment income, not just merchandise trade. Britain, by contrast, was a creditor country until the cost of financing World War II forced it to sell most of its foreign assets to the U.S. government. The large U.S. merchandise trade deficit has also caused Washington to emphasize commercial factors in its exchange rate policy far more aggressively since the late 1980s than did Britain in the early twentieth century.

The British pound remained an important reserve currency long after the British economy fell behind the U.S. economy in size and New York replaced London as the world's leading financial center. But in the 1950s and 1960s, Britain attempted to prop up the role of sterling in the world financial system through comprehensive exchange controls and financial diplomacy. In the mid-1960s, for example, the U.S. government provided secret loans to Britain in order to support the pound sterling as a quid pro quo for Britain maintaining its military base in Singapore for longer than the newly elected Labour government of Harold Wilson had originally intended. The pound ceased to be an important reserve currency only during the 1970s because of high inflation in Britain and the global shift to a floating exchange rate system in which the dollar became a far more useful intervention currency than the pound. But London retained a major role in the global financial system as a recycling center for Eurodollars.

The dollar's global financial role has not diminished significantly even though the United States has lost its creditor status because both U.S. and foreign financial institutions have been able to recycle other countries' surplus savings through dollar-based forms of financial intermediation. The dollar continues to be a useful medium of exchange and unit of account for global trade and financial transactions because of the flexibility and sophistication of dollar financial markets in the United States and elsewhere. In the past, national currencies have not assumed a major global role simply because a country had a high savings rate and surplus liquidity. This role has also required a financial infrastructure capable of promoting the currency as a medium of exchange beyond the country. In the 1970s, for example, the members of the Organization of Petroleum Exporting Countries (OPEC) had massive surplus savings but their currencies did not emerge as important denominators of trade and finance because they lacked the financial institutions and capital markets necessary to play such a role. They simply enhanced the role of the dollar despite its large devaluation in 1971–73.

Until recently, Japan was ill-equipped to serve as the anchor country for a reserve currency despite the fact that it had a high savings rate. There were no markets for either corporate or government short-term securities, the sale of corporate bonds within Japan was prohibited, the MOF encouraged financial resource allocation through the banking system rather than capital markets, and there were numerous withholding taxes on the domestic securities that foreigners were allowed to buy. But since the mid-1980s, the MOF has permitted large markets to develop in Japan for corporate commercial paper and bonds as well as a wide range of derivative instruments. Japanese banks have also taken advantage of their capital power to expand significantly in foreign markets. With the yen's recent appreciation, all of the world's top 10 banks are Japanese.

As a result, the role of the yen in the global financial system has increased significantly during the past decade and will probably continue to expand in the future. The yen share of the Eurobond market has grown from 5 percent in 1980 to 13 percent in 1993. The yen-denominated share of Japanese banks' international loans has expanded from only 10 percent in 1980 to 43 percent in 1990 and 65 percent in 1994. A large share of these loans were made to the foreign division of Japanese companies but many non-Japanese companies now have yen loans as well. The yen's share of global foreign exchange reserves is still only about 9.0 percent on a global basis but it is significantly higher in several East Asian countries with significant financial links to Japan. The yen share of foreign reserves now appears to be at 30 percent or higher in Indonesia, Taiwan, Singapore, and the Philippines. It is in the 15 to 25 percent range in China, Korea, and Malaysia. According to preliminary data from the International Monetary Fund (IMF), the dollar's share of global foreign exchange reserves rose slightly during 1994 because of heavy Japanese central bank intervention to restrain the yen's appreciation, but the dollar's share of other countries' reserves clearly fell. The IMF data may also understate the yen's reserve currency role because they do not include Taiwan's large foreign reserves, which are now more than 20 percent invested in yen securities. The yen's role as a denominator of trade is expanding as well but the rate of change has been more modest than the yen's role in denominating financial transactions. In 1993, the yen was used to denominate about 40 percent of Japan's exports and 21 percent of Japan's imports compared to 33 percent and 10.6 percent respectively in 1987. In Japan's trade with Southeast Asia, by contrast, the yen is used far more extensively to denominate transactions. In 1993, it was used to denominate 52.5 percent of exports and 25.7 percent of imports compared to 41 percent and 11.5 percent respectively in 1987.

Despite the significant increase in the yen's role as a denominator of trade and debt, no country has yet chosen to link its exchange rate specifically to the yen. In East Asia, most countries continue to maintain currency links to the dollar or to currency baskets in which the yen still has only a small weighting. As a result, econometric studies of the link between interest rate movements in Tokyo and other countries in the region continue to show relatively weak linkages compared to New York. These studies indicate that Indonesia and Korea have become more sensitive to Japanese interest rates than previously but the impact is still not large compared to the effect of U.S. interest rates on Canada or Australia.[1]

In the mid-1980s, the United States launched talks with Japan on financial liberalization in order to encourage more widespread use of the yen as an international reserve currency. At the time it was thought that the yen's limited international role caused its exchange rate to be commercially undervalued compared to the dollar. The Japanese government was not anxious to promote the yen's international role because of concerns about losing control over the exchange rate, but it did accept far more liberalization of the financial system in order to enhance its efficiency and ability to be globally competitive.

In mid-1994, the Ministry of International Trade and Industry (MITI) produced a report on the yen as a reserve currency and offered several suggestions for enhancing its international role. They included:

- Improve the market for treasury bills, for which demand has increased as investors seek shorter-term investments. The MOF currently issues mostly long-term bonds as a matter of policy.
- Improve the environment for international legal and accounting services.
- Establish institutions able to rate the financial condition of Japanese companies with international credibility.
- Relax restrictions on the issuance of corporate bonds and commercial paper.
- Expand the secondary market for corporate bonds by improving the settlement system.
- Reduce costs for financial transactions in Tokyo, which are high compared with costs in other global money centers and represent a factor about which market participants have become more conscious in this belt-tightening era.

Few of the proposals in the MITI report were new. In the mid-1980s, the U.S. government itself had proposed several of the suggested reforms in order to promote international acceptance of the yen as a currency for denominating trade and financial transactions. But although Japan has permitted significant liberalization of its financial system since the "yen-dollar talks" of the mid-1980s, the MOF's tax bureau has resisted suggestions to reduce withholding taxes on privately owned Japanese domestic securities. As the Japanese system of writing does not allow the use of personal signatures (individuals have stamps), many tax officials do not want to eliminate withholding taxes until a system of taxpayer identification numbers can be introduced. Further changes in the tax system, as well as continued liberalization of the financial system, will be an important prerequisite for the yen to play a larger global role because both companies and governments will be reluctant to depend upon a yen-denominated payments system unless it offers more efficiency, flexibility, and transparency than have been available in the past. Further development of markets for short-term financial instruments and derivatives will be especially important because of the need for yen creditors and debtors to hedge currency risk effectively. Recent yen borrowers, such as the governments of Italy and Spain, appear to have hedged through the currency swap market but some of the Asian countries that received concessional yen-denominated development loans during the 1980s are reported to have suffered large exchange rate losses because they failed to hedge.

When the British pound and the U.S. dollar were the world's leading currencies, both countries had open capital markets and liberal trade policies. Britain had a far larger current account surplus than the United States as a share of GDP but it was increasingly dominated by investment income that was easily recycled to the rest of the world through the London capital market. Because Japan evolved under an economic model that was much less open than the U.S. or British experience, it does not yet have the same symmetry between trade and capital flows as previous creditor powers. The Japanese goods market has numerous non-tariff barriers, while Tokyo financial markets are much less transparent and open than London or New York in the past. The severe overshooting of the yen during 1994 and early 1995 has been a by-product of these rigidities. They have produced a systemic recycling crisis that is being resolved through yen appreciation. But even though Japan's economic traditions pose numerous obstacles to the emergence of the yen as a major denominator of international trade and financial transactions, the yen's international role will probably continue to grow for a number of reasons.

First, because Japanese institutions have suffered large losses on their non-yen assets, they will encourage more international borrowers to use the yen as a denominator of bonds and bank loans. As the world's largest capital exporters, the Japanese can influence the currency in which debt is denominated.

Second, Japan's trade surplus will probably shrink by 30 to 40 percent during the next few years because of yen appreciation and a shift to more stimulative economic policies in Japan itself, but Japan will continue to be the world's largest capital exporter. The recent movement toward current account surpluses in several European countries is a temporary cyclical phenomenon while the United States will continue to run at least moderate current account deficits unless there are radical pro-savings tax changes in Washington during the next administration. Such changes are possible, but they will probably not cause the United States to return to a current account surplus until the end of the century at the earliest. According to OECD estimates of exchange rate competitiveness, the United States enjoys more international competitiveness today than at any other time in the modern era but it cannot return to a current account surplus without a higher savings rate. Unless the United States boosts its level of savings, the dollar's depreciation will encourage higher inflation, not just an export boom, and thus erode the economy's competitive position again.

Third, it is increasingly doubtful that the countries of Western Europe will be able to move quickly toward establishing a monetary union. Several countries have such large fiscal deficits that it will be difficult for them to satisfy the Treaty of Maastricht's criteria for monetary union anytime in this century. The new French government of Jacques Chirac appears to be more committed to promoting employment growth than maintaining the previous government's support for an exchange rate link between the D-mark and the French franc. In fact, some of Chirac's advisers favor the more rapid admission of Poland, Hungary, and the Czech Republic to the European Union (EU) as an offset to German power. Until recently, most French officials opposed widening EU membership because of the potential cost to the farm budget as well as a long-standing belief that the best way to control German power was a deepening of the EU through monetary integration. But Germany does not have the surplus savings of Japan or a financial community with the dynamism of London and New York, so it is doubtful that the D-mark will play a larger international role than it does currently. The failure of the Europeans to create a central bank and common currency will therefore leave the yen as the dominant alternative currency to the dollar.

Fourth, the yen's global role should benefit from the dynamic growth occurring in the economies of East Asia and the region's increasing commercial and financial links to Japan. Although the level of trade between them is growing rapidly, the share of intraregional trade is still smaller than it was in the early twentieth century, when Japan had an empire encompassing Korea and Taiwan as well as large investments in China. Many countries in East Asia now obtain 25 to 35 percent of their imports from Japan but send only about 5 to 10 percent of their exports in return. The highest ratios of exports to Japan to total exports are Singapore at 10.8 percent, Malaysia at 9.4 percent, Indonesia at 7.0 percent, and Thailand at 5.3 percent. Korea, Taiwan, China, and the Philippines still send less than 5.0 percent of their exports to Japan. The United States, by contrast, consumes 20 to 30 percent of the exports of several East Asian countries. During the next quarter century, Japan's FDI boom in the region should promote more growth of regional trade while reducing the region's current heavy dependence upon the United States as an export market. The growth in bilateral trade between Japan and countries in East Asia will promote more widespread use of the yen as a denominator of trade. The role of the yen in denominating financial instruments and official foreign exchange reserves should also benefit from the rapid growth occurring in the region's level of foreign exchange reserves. In 1994, for example, the countries of East Asia (the members of the Association of Southeast Asian Nations, as well as China, Korea, and Taiwan) had over $355 billion of foreign exchange reserves or 27 percent of the world total compared to $200 billion (22 percent of the world total) in 1990 and $63.6 billion (14 percent of the world total) in 1985. Ten years ago, most Asian countries kept less than 10 percent of their reserves in yen whereas today some have levels as high as 40 to 50 percent. The high savings rate of the countries in East Asia will help to promote the growth of the yen as a reserve currency simply because they are generating the current account surpluses that produce large foreign exchange reserves. The U.S. dollar, by contrast, does not enjoy such an advantage in its own region. At the peak last year, Latin America's foreign exchange reserves were about $110 billion or 8 percent of the world total while every single country in the Western Hemisphere was a net debtor with savings rates far below those prevailing in East Asia. The D-mark also has benefited from the higher savings rates Europe enjoys compared to the Western Hemisphere. As a result of its large public spending on unification, Germany has shifted to a current account deficit during recent years but most of the countries around Germany have current account surpluses, including the countries with large budget deficits such as Italy. The countries in a potential mark zone will have a current account surplus of $80 billion in 1995, while the countries in a potential yen zone will have a surplus of $100 billion. In the Western Hemisphere dollar zone, by contrast, there will be a current account deficit of nearly $250 billion despite Mexico's move to a small current account surplus.

Until recently, the low savings rate of the Western Hemisphere was not a constraint on the dollar's global financial role because of the strong U.S. trade and commercial links with East Asia. But if the U.S. share of East Asian trade and investment continues to diminish, the dollar's role will fade as well. What remains to be seen is whether the countries of East Asia will pursue special policies to bolster the dollar's role because they are worried that the region will become overly dependent upon Japan. With the possible exception of Malaysia, most East Asian countries want the United States to remain a major power in the region because of their apprehensions about the future ambitions of Japan and China. As with the balance of payments offset programs in Germany, which the United States developed to compensate for its defense spending there, the foreign exchange market could also at some point emerge as a vehicle for burden sharing and bolstering the dollar's role as a reserve currency in Asia.

The fifth factor that could encourage the yen to emerge as a more important reserve currency is the increased willingness of Japanese officials to discuss the idea and consider policy changes that could actually encourage the yen to play a larger role in the world financial system. The 1994 MITI report on the yen's international role did not have any visible impact on Japanese policy, but the yen appreciation of early 1995 caused the prime minister to ask Toyoo Gyohten, chairman of the Bank of Tokyo and former vice minister of finance, to launch a study group on the yen's international role. As Gyohten is one of Japan's senior international financial statesmen, his study group is likely to have a greater impact on official attitudes than the MITI report. In the annual June reshuffle of the Japanese bureaucracy, the ministry also promoted Eisuke Sakakibara to the position of director general of the International Finance Bureau. In the past, Sakakibara has been a prolific writer about Japan's role in the global economy, the contrasts between the Japanese and U.S. economic systems, and why Japan should be more assertive in promoting its form of capitalism over the Anglo-Saxon alternative. In a book published in 1993 and entitled *Beyond Capitalism*, for example, Sakakibara warned of the challenges that could confront the Japanese form of capitalism as the economy internationalized.

> Even though Japan did not introduce capitalistic concepts in any significant way, its market mechanisms and competition have functioned extremely efficiently. Its economic efficiency may even be greater than that of a more purely capitalistic country such as the United States, for example, and there would seem to be precious little merit in capitalizing now. In fact, such an attempt might only succeed in bringing in the disadvantages of the capitalistic system, such as a wider gap in income distribution, rampant money worship, and the vulgarization of culture, or superficial fashions, thereby accelerating the corruption or demise of the system. Such trends already exist today with the Recruit Scandal and a growing pornographic presence

in the media, etc., and there is a pressing need now to take a fresh look at the basic tenets that underpin the Japanese socioeconomic system.

Of course, upholding basic tenets and returning to origins does not mean holding on blindly to the existing regime in toto. The systems formed and firmly implanted in the 60-some odd years of Showa have taken a beating over the years, and many have drifted a long way from their original purpose. Moreover, because economic expansion has taken place at a rapid pace, existing interests have become incorporated into the system. Thus, rather than recognizing wider national interests, there is undeniably a strong systemic trend now toward protecting and maintaining existing interests within the status quo.

The question is whether the basic tenets of the Japanese mixed economy—in other words, anthropocentrism, or a system of true equality and participation—can be maintained as the system becomes more open and transparent in response to the trend toward deregulation and internationalization.

Itami, for one, argues the following: Post-war Japanese corporate society has become a different animal than capitalistic corporate society in other countries to date. It has created a classless, democratic corporate society. Hence its success. Should that not continue to be the doctrine of Japanese companies in the future? Would this not enable Japanese companies to cross both temporal and geographical borders? Yes, there are many aspects of the specific business management system that need to change. Yet, there is no need for the prototype to change, nor should it be changed.

It is precisely in order to uphold the basic tenets of the system and to maintain the prototype that its antiquated parts should undergo an extensive overhaul, thereby preventing imminent decay and stagnation. Instead of trying to turn Japan into some cheap, capitalist society in the name of deregulation and internationalization, for example, bold, structural reform is required to maintain the impartiality of the public sector and the democratic features of the Japanese firm. To this end, there is a need to reexamine—in the light of their basic ideology and today's new climate—systems that have become dominated by vested interests and have lost sight of their original purposes. Yet this is a mammoth task.[2]

In contrast to many of his predecessors in the International Finance Bureau, Sakakibara believes that the time has come to actively promote the emergence of the yen as a reserve currency. He intends to promote abolition of the withholding taxes and other impediments to the use of the yen as a global currency. As with many other Japanese intellectuals, Sakakibara believes that Japan should now "normalize" its international status by assuming more of the roles of a great economic power. Although Sakakibara is more outspoken than most Japanese officials about the need to project a new Japanese economic vision, he is by no means alone in favoring a greater international role for the yen. Since Japan emerged as a major capital exporter during the 1980s, a variety of officials and academics have begun to speculate about a new role for the yen.

As Republican congressional adviser David Asher explained in a recent paper:

In December 1992 former BOJ Executive Director Nakagawa Yukitsugu wrote a revealing article in the Institute for International Policy Studies *(Sekai Heiwa Kenyuujou)* newsletter describing his "¥1 bills to the dollar dream." Noting that both Paul Volcker and Fred Bergsten advocated a lower "target zone" for the dollar versus the support for *endaka*, he explained that if *endaka* occurred, due to Japan's "superior fundamentals," the Yen could take on the status of a reserve currency equal to the dollar. Then he presented his "dream" of bringing the Yen to 100 to the dollar and then redenominating the currency. ¥100 coins would be replaced by ¥1 bills and the prewar sen (penny) would be brought back. With ¥1 equaling 1 dollar he speculated Japan's power and prestige would escalate dramatically. Although he called this a dream, he hinted that he "had the feeling it could soon become a reality." Wonder why he had this feeling.

Scared by NAFTA and the EC, both Japanese foreign policy and financial elites were looking for a means of ensuring Japan's "comprehensive security" in the face of the growing "regionalization of the world economy." For *Gaimusho* intellectuals, such as Ogura Kazuo—who published an article on "Asian Regionalization and Japan's Choice" in *Gaiko Forum*, December 1992—a strong Yen was an important means of ensuring that Japan would gain even more power of international affairs in Asia. For MOF leaders like Vice Minister Chino—who published an article on "Asian Economic Development and Capital Markets" in *Fainansu*, January 1993—a strong Yen was a means of "restoring Asia's old glory." It appears that the key to both men's thinking was the increased direct and portfolio investment power in Asia that *endaka* entailed, especially vis-à-vis China. From the standpoint of Japan's Asian expansionism, rather than a tragedy, a Yen bubble was a saving grace.[3]

It is interesting to note that Ogura Kazuo was recently promoted to the post of deputy vice minister for economic affairs at the Ministry of Foreign Affairs after serving as Japan's ambassador to Vietnam. The coincident promotion of both Sakakibara and Ogura in the annual 1995 bureaucratic reshuffle at Japan's key ministries provides further confirmation of the far-reaching generational changes occurring in official attitudes toward Japan's role in the world.

The changes occurring in Japanese attitudes toward the role of the yen are a natural outcome of the country's new creditor status. But inasmuch as they are occurring simultaneously with increasing resentment at U.S. demands for microeconomic reform and trade liberalization, there is also a risk that they will be interpreted as a threat by some Americans. Sakakibara stresses that he wants to promote a new international role for the yen in consultation with the U.S. Treasury so that the U.S. government is not alarmed by the development. But as the current dispute over the auto trade will testify, it is far from clear that both sides will be able to manage such a transition in an orderly way. In fact, it is possible to construct scenarios in which the yen's evolution as a reserve currency could intensify the economic conflicts that are already straining U.S.–Japan relations. In the case of the United States, Americans might perceive that Japan was trying to dethrone the dollar's reserve currency status so as to enhance its ability to resist U.S. trade pressures by threatening to divert capital from the U.S. financial markets. The U.S. government has so far been able to pursue a policy of benign neglect toward the dollar because foreign central banks have been prepared to support it when private investors withdrew, but if the dollar were not the world's key currency, the loss of private funding for the current account deficit would probably provoke a large rise in the level of U.S. interest rates. In the case of Japan, there is a risk that discussion about the yen's emergence as a reserve currency will encourage further appreciation of the exchange rate, intensifying the recession in many of Japan's manufacturing industries. As unemployment increases, there could be great public hostility toward the United States, and Japanese politicians might increasingly attempt to use the United States as a scapegoat for the country's recession, despite the fact that many American proposals for microeconomic reform are essential to reviving the country's economic growth. The dispute over the auto trade got out of control because both the U.S. and Japanese sides misread each other's willingness to compromise under pressure. If the new generation of bureaucratic leadership in Japan now intends to promote a wider international role for the yen and greater independence for Japan, it will be important that the United States and Japan do a better job of communicating effectively about the consequences.

The final reason why the yen could become a more important reserve currency is because the U.S. government appears to care little about defending the dollar's traditional role in the international financial system. In contrast to the 1950s and 1960s, U.S. policymakers are now far more concerned about the dollar's role as a denominator of U.S. trade than about its role as a global reserve asset. This change in perceptions has been a by-product of the large U.S. trade deficit and the growing belief in Washington that U.S. international economic policy should now focus on promoting trade, not defending the currency relationships that were a by-product of the role of the United States at the center of the Western security system during the Cold War. In the 1960s, by contrast, the United States actively promoted balance of payments offset programs with countries such as Germany to generate trade and capital flows large enough to compensate it for its military role in Europe. The United States was deeply concerned to protect the dollar's value in the conduct of its foreign policy, not just its economic policy.

Some U.S. officials believe the dollar's international role produces positive economic benefits for their country and is worthy of more support than it has often received during recent years. In a 1994 speech, Lawrence B. Lindsey, a governor of the Federal Reserve, even attempted to quantify some of the seignorage benefits of the dollar's global role:

> I believe that the benefits to the United States of having a leading international role for the dollar are enormous, and go well beyond those that are readily quantifiable. . . .
>
> Let us begin by considering the most basic value of a currency to its issuer: seignorage. The capacity of a country to issue currency means that, in effect, a portion of government spending can be financed by a permanent interest free loan. Holders of currency exchange real goods and services in return for what is, to all appearances, little more than a piece of

paper. In reality, the value of the currency flows from the services which that piece of paper can provide as a medium of exchange and a store of value. At first blush, the exchange of real goods and services for paper would appear to be as close to the proverbial "free lunch" as an economist could imagine. In practice ... the price of the supposedly free lunch is real constraints on policy to convince holders that the currency has value.

An illustration of the amount of benefit which seigniorage can provide comes from the experience of the U.S. dollar during the 1980s. By 1981, after two bouts of inflation in less than 10 years and serious concerns about the future of the U.S. role in the world, the ratio of dollars in circulation to U.S. GDP had fallen to just a bit over 4 cents of currency per dollar of GDP. Twelve years later, after a painful disinflation and sustained efforts by the central bank and successive Administrations at rebuilding the United States's international economic credibility, there were slightly more than 5 cents of currency for every dollar of GDP.

The extra penny per dollar of GDP amounted to $64 billion in extra seigniorage resulting from an increased willingness to hold dollars. Total currency in circulation had risen by nearly $200 billion over this period. Most of this increase was used to provide a medium of exchange for a higher level of nominal GDP. The extra $64 billion, roughly the equivalent of half a year of corporation income tax collections, was and continues to be largely held by foreigners outside the U.S. economy.

These extra resources understate the real financial benefits. Most use of the dollar as a store of value is represented by interest-bearing holdings of government paper. While the government and taxpayer do not get the "free lunch" from these instruments that currency provides, the liquidity and convertibility of these instruments which stems from the role of the dollar as a reserve currency certainly carries some value. As a result, the yield of these instruments is lower than what it otherwise would be if the dollar did not have its current role. How much is involved is uncertain. But each basis point— one hundredth of a percentage point—off the yield on government paper is worth $350 million annually to the American taxpayer.[4]

There is no precise way to quantify all the seigniorage benefits that have resulted from the dollar's global role. If foreign central bank holdings of dollar securities in official foreign exchange reserves were equivalent to the U.S. share of world GDP, they would be worth only about $250 billion to $300 billion compared to the $600 billion to $650 billion currently in central bank portfolios. Such reduced demand for U.S. securities would obviously increase U.S. interest rates but the magnitude of the adjustment would depend upon a variety of factors, including the interest rates available on bonds in other currencies. The huge foreign ownership of dollar-denominated banknotes, by contrast, is clearly an interest-free loan to the U.S. economy worth about $210 billion or 3 percent of GDP. It is also a uniquely U.S. form of seigniorage. Bundesbank officials estimate that only about 30 percent of D-mark banknotes circulate outside Germany, while Japanese officials guess that only about 10 percent of yen-denominated currency circulates outside Japan.

Currency Market Crisis

As a result of the widespread intellectual support for floating exchange rates, awareness of the economic and political benefits resulting from a country's reserve currency status has faded from debates about exchange rate policy compared to the 1960s and 1970s. When the dollar declined against the yen and D-mark during early 1995, for example, most U.S. officials said that the dollar's weakness was not a domestic problem and thus did not require a policy response. Many market participants also perceived that some U.S. officials privately favored a weak dollar against the yen because it would be a potentially useful bargaining chip in negotiations over the automobile trade. The stance of the Clinton administration is not totally new. In 1971, Treasury Secretary John Connally used the threat of dollar depreciation as a bargaining chip against Japanese trade negotiators, but in that period it was widely perceived that the Bretton Woods fixed exchange rate had caused the dollar to become commercially overvalued. The mid-1990s is the first period in which investors widely perceive that the U.S. government is willing to use currency depreciation as a trade bargaining tool despite the fact that practically everyone considers the dollar to be commercially undervalued. The U.S. Treasury denies that it favors a weaker dollar, but investors believe that the U.S. Trade Representative and the White House have welcomed dollar depreciation as a means of intimidating the Japanese manufacturing industry into supporting more rapid market liberalization.

U.S. officials also failed to support the dollar during the first four months of 1995 because they did not perceive the dollar's weakness to be the result of domestic economic problems that required immediate policy action. Rather, they perceived the dollar's decline to be the result of the peso crisis in Mexico, the financial recycling problem in Japan, intra-European capital flight from high-deficit countries such as Italy to the German D-mark, and market disappointment at the sudden slowdown in the U.S. economy after a year of surprisingly robust growth during 1994. The slowdown in the U.S. economy was an especially important factor because if there had not been a pause in U.S. growth momentum, the dollar's weakness would probably have caused bond yields to spike toward 9.0 percent instead of declining below 7.0 percent. In such a scenario, U.S. policymakers would have had to choose between raising short-term interest rates another 50 to 100 basis points or running the risk that domestic investors—not just foreign investors—would lose confidence in Federal Reserve policy. The Japanese government suggested that the U.S. Treasury should start issuing yen-denominated Treasury bonds in order to stabilize the dollar but the Clinton administration declined because such bonds conjured up memories of the foreign currency debt issued by the Carter administration during the dollar crisis of 1978–79. In the Carter era, the dollar fell sharply because the Federal Reserve moved far too slowly to restrain inflation whereas U.S. inflation in mid-1995 is running in the 3.0 to 3.5 percent range despite a capacity utilization rate of 85 percent.

When the United States did not raise interest rates during March and April 1995, the weakness of the dollar compelled Germany and Japan to lower their interest rates. Germany also eased its rates because of the strength of the D-mark against other European currencies and a slowdown in its domestic monetary growth, but as a result of the sharp decline in Germany's surplus manufacturing capacity since 1993 it is doubtful that the Bundesbank would have pursued any easing this year in the absence of the D-mark's appreciation. There were a few signs of economic recovery in Japan during the first quarter, but the upturn was expected to be the most subdued in modern Japanese economic history because of lingering credit quality problems in the banking sector and the impact of the strong yen on corporate profitability and investment. The Bank of Japan would have been prepared to leave interest rates unchanged with the yen in the 95 to 105 range, but once it dropped into the 80 to 85 range there was so much risk of deflation that the bank had to ease. Because the true inflation rate in Japan is probably minus 2 to 3 percent, Japan still has higher real interest rates than the United States despite the fact that nominal money market yields have dropped to only 1.0 percent. Deflation has become so pervasive in Japan that the popular press has coined a new slogan for it—price destruction.

The U.S. policy of neglecting the dollar during the first quarter was risky. The U.S. economy is operating at high levels of resource utilization and the $200 billion trade deficit has resulted in part from domestic supply shortages that will produce accelerating inflation if the United States loses access to surplus manufacturing capacity in other countries. But, so far, the markets have vindicated the U.S. policy because of investor perceptions that growth in U.S. output will remain subdued for several quarters and thus restrain inflation in the face of the declining dollar.

The U.S. strategy of forcing Japan and Germany to reflate their monetary policies has been very bullish for stock markets. The New York market has rallied to record high levels while many of the emerging markets that fell sharply during the first quarter have begun to recover. The Japanese market has also stabilized while many European markets have experienced moderate rallies. If, by contrast, the United States had raised interest rates to support the dollar, there would have been major stock market corrections in several countries and the Tokyo market might have broken through its 1992 low of 14,000. In fact, the Japanese market is caught in such a vicious liquidity trap that it will probably drop to new lows unless the government announces a major bank rescue package.

As a result of the yen's appreciation, the Japanese finance minister has spoken publicly about the need to establish new rules for restraining exchange rate movements, but there was little support for such an initiative at the meeting of the group of seven industrial countries (G-7) in Washington in April 1995 because the major industrial countries have divergent views about why the dollar has been weak. The Germans and Japanese believe that the United States should have raised interest rates while U.S. officials contend that monetary policy in Japan is too deflationary. As the international monetary system has neither rules nor a policy surveillance process to guide G-7 policy coordination, there was no way for the major industrial countries to agree on any policy course except to threaten further intervention if exchange rates continue to overshoot.

This ad hoc approach to international policy coordination is likely to persist for some time because there are still fundamental disagreements between the major industrial countries about the role of exchange rates as policy targets. In medium-sized countries with large foreign trade sectors, the exchange rate will usually be a more dominant policy concern than in a country as large as the United States. In the case of the United States, the exchange rate will become an important consideration when restraining inflation is a priority but it will not be a significant policy constraint when the U.S. economy is weak.

What policy actions can the United States pursue to bolster foreign confidence in the dollar and prevent further erosion in its status as a global reserve currency? In a regime of floating exchange rates, it will be difficult for it to take actions specifically designed to bolster the dollar's global role without giving a more deflationary bias to domestic monetary policy. The optimal policy course for boosting the dollar's status as a reserve currency would be for the United States to introduce a new fiscal policy that boosted domestic private savings and reduced the country's need to borrow externally. If the nation could raise its private savings rate by 2 to 3 percent, it would cease to need foreign capital and could even reemerge as a moderate capital exporter.

As a result of the Republican takeover of the U.S. Congress in November 1994, intense discussion is now beginning on Capitol Hill about radical tax reforms to bolster private savings through the introduction of much lower marginal tax rates on some categories of income. Several members of Congress also favor replacing the income tax with a national consumption tax or shifting to a flat rate income tax. The Clinton administration has not articulated any strategy for raising the national savings rate except reducing the federal budget deficit through increases in marginal income tax rates and selective spending cuts. It is, therefore, doubtful that the president would be prepared to let the Republicans undertake a radical overhaul of the federal tax system. But if the Republicans can capture control of the White House in 1996 while retaining their new majorities in the House and Senate, there could be a reform of the U.S. tax system in 1997 even more far-reaching than those that occurred in 1986 and 1963, when marginal income tax rates were slashed to their lowest levels in the postwar era.

Although the debate about tax policy is widely regarded as a domestic affair, it will have important international implications. If the new administration and Congress could agree on policies to bolster private savings, there would probably be a significant dollar rally in the expectation that the U.S. need for external savings would diminish in the future. The rally against the yen might be especially large because many Japanese economists expect that country's savings rate to decline during the early years of the next century in response to the aging of the country's population. The public sector deficits of Germany, Italy, and other European countries will also swell in the early years of the next century because of aging populations and the high cost of funding retirement programs.

Many economists are skeptical that changes in tax policy will be able to bolster U.S. private savings because the income tax reductions of the 1980s were followed by a decline in household savings. But it is important to note that much of that decline resulted from the behavior of pension funds. About half of the U.S. population and practically all high-income people save for retirement through tax-deferred pension programs. In the United States, pension funds are usually target savers that accumulate assets in order to achieve actuarial objectives. If there are significant rallies in equity prices, such as occurred during the 1980s, corporations will often reduce contributions to pension programs because the capital gains on their existing assets will allow them to achieve their actuarial targets with smaller outlays. The United States needs to reorganize its retirement programs in such a way that large capital gains do not discourage new savings while broadening the share of the population belonging to pension programs.

Fluctuations in Canada's personal savings rate during the past two decades suggest that private savings will respond to reforms in the tax system for pensions and individual retirement accounts. It also should be noted that the U.S. savings rate was higher than most other industrial countries before World War II. Other countries' savings rates rose sharply after the war because they had to rebuild and thus offered generous tax allowances for depreciation, postal savings accounts, equity capital gains, and many forms of retirement savings. The United States lagged because there was no perceived savings problem until the country started importing capital on a large scale during the 1980s. As a recent IMF study notes:

> Long-run historical data on saving patterns suggest that before the 1920s most industrial countries, including Australia, Canada, France, Japan, and the United Kingdom, had very low gross national saving rates—in the range of 10–15 percent of GDP. The exception was the United States, which as early as the 1870s had a saving rate of almost 20 percent. While the U.S. saving rate stayed remarkably constant over most of the twentieth century until the 1980s, virtually all other industrial countries and fast-growing developing countries have seen their saving rates move up to the 20 percent range. A few, such as Japan, China, and some of the newly industrializing Asian economies have had rates that exceeded 30 percent.[5]

The United States also could help to reduce its need for external savings by controlling the growth of federal spending and reducing the government deficit, but the U.S. fiscal position is actually far superior to that of many other industrial countries. The ratio of U.S. government debt to GDP has risen by over 25 percent during the past 15 years but it remains well below the ratios now prevailing in much of Europe and Canada. Although deficit reduction should still be an important policy objective, the focus of the next big debate about U.S. fiscal policy should be on boosting private savings.

The factors that have caused the dollar to fall sharply since January 1995 are the by-product of the extraordinarily complex interdependence that has developed between the United States and Japan during recent years. The United States has been correct not to tighten monetary policy in order to protect the dollar at a time when Japanese monetary policy has been pushing that country toward hyperdeflation. But the weakness of the dollar has resulted from structural savings imbalances, not just cyclical divergence in monetary policy, and the core structural problem now alarming the markets is the effect of the low U.S. savings rate on the current account balance and future external indebtedness. The United States is a low-savings country in a low-savings hemisphere but it has ambitions to be a large-scale capital exporter to the exciting high-growth countries set free by the end of the Cold War. The United States lacks the private savings to achieve this objective. Moreover, the U.S. Congress was so consumed by the problem of deficit reduction in winter 1994–95 that it was unwilling to provide emergency financial assistance to Mexico after December's shock peso devaluation. The Clinton administration is therefore turning to the high-savings economies of East Asia in order to find new capital for the IMF so that it can more effectively play the lender of last resort role in future crises.

If East Asia and Japan are to be the major lenders to the IMF and other international organizations in the future, they will ultimately expect to have more influence over their policies. An expansion of Asia's voting rights does not have to threaten the United States but it will represent an erosion of American influence that could be damaging in a future crisis. In the year 2010, for example, the IMF might be less responsive to U.S. requests for emergency loans to help a country in the Western Hemisphere than it was in the case of Mexico in 1995. Indeed, most European countries abstained in the vote on Mexico's relief program earlier this year in order to show their displeasure at the Clinton administration's effort to provide such large-scale assistance to a neighboring country.

The shift to a more multipolar currency order could also create the risk of new financial accidents because of greater imbalances in the currency exposure of large corporations and financial institutions. The dollar is still so dominant in global finance that fluctuations in its value have created problems for only a few countries with large yen debts in East Asia. But if the yen were to account for 30 to 40 percent of international bank loans and bonds and the German D-mark another 15 to 20 percent, significant exchange rate movements might produce more bankruptcies and financial accidents than have occurred so far.

The bipartisan congressional coalition led by Senator Pete V. Domenici (R–N.M.) and Senator Sam Nunn (D–Ga.) now proposing a radical overhaul of the federal tax system has probably given little thought to the international consequences of its proposals. The Contract with America of Representative Newt Gingrich (R–Ga.) has an almost totally domestic focus and many Republican House members often sound isolationist on issues such as foreign aid because over half of them were elected after the end of the Cold War. But the issue of private savings is of critical importance to the future outlook for the trade account of the United States, its economic relationship with other countries, and the status of the dollar as a reserve currency. As a result, the major determinant of the dollar exchange rate against the D-mark and the yen in 1996 may not just be the investor's traditional concerns about interest rate differentials, business cycle divergences, and trade deficits. There will also be growing focus on the debate about national tax policy during the run-up to the 1996 presidential election and the ability of the next U.S. administration to restore the traditional role of the United States as an external creditor by enacting a more radical pro-savings overhaul of the federal tax code than has occurred at any time since the introduction of the income tax in 1913.

Conclusion

The yen is likely to play a greater role in denominating global trade and financial transactions than it has in the past because of Japan's new role as the world's largest capital exporter and the tremendous expansion occurring in the wealth of East Asia. But as a result of the dynamism, efficiency, and transparency of the U.S. financial markets, the dollar will continue to be the world's primary medium of exchange, although there will be more competition from the yen because of the changing economic circumstances of the United States and Japan.

Several factors will encourage an expanded role for the yen. Japan now has external investments exceeding 15 percent of GDP whereas the United States has a net external investment deficit equal to 11 percent of GDP. The Japanese have lost over $600 billion on their non-yen financial assets since 1985 and thus have become more reluctant to provide credit in the form of dollar liabilities. Japan is developing increasingly strong commercial and financial links with the countries of East Asia while many of those countries now have over half of their external debt in yen-denominated instruments. These countries currently account for about 28 percent of global foreign exchange reserves compared to half that level in the early 1980s and many keep 25 to 50 percent of their reserves in yen. Because they have much higher savings rates than countries in Europe and the Western Hemisphere, their share of world foreign exchange reserves is likely to continue expanding and thus further bolster the role of the yen. The United States, by contrast, is in a low-savings hemisphere that will run an aggregate current account deficit of close to $250 billion in 1995 despite the Mexican financial crisis. U.S. officials have also become much less concerned about sustaining the dollar's global role as a reserve currency despite the large seigniorage benefits that the United States has derived from it. Foreigners own about 60 percent of dollar-denominated currency ($210 billion), while foreign central banks still keep over 60 percent of their foreign exchange reserves in dollar securities. The factors that will help to sustain the dollar's role as the dominant medium of exchange for global trade and finance are the large size of the U.S. economy, the ability of the United States to recycle other countries' surplus savings through its financial system, and the efficiency and transparency of the dollar payments system compared to others. The high level of commercial and financial integration between the United States and Japan has also forced the Japanese government to spend over $50 billion supporting the U.S. exchange rate during the past year. In the absence of such intervention, the dollar's share of global foreign exchange reserves would probably be 5 percent less than the 61 percent level that prevailed during the early 1990s. The major threat to the dollar's dominance would be the emergence of a new European currency, but there is unlikely to be a European monetary union until the second or third decade of the twenty-first century.

Notes

1. See Jeffrey Frankel, "Is a Yen Block Emerging?" in Robert Rich, ed., *Economic Cooperation and Challenges in the Pacific* (Washington, D.C.: Korea Economic Institute of America, 1995).

2. Eisuke Sakakibara, *Beyond Capitalism* (Lanham, Md.: University Press of America, 1993).

3. David Asher, "The Yen Bubble and the Coming Collapse: Price Keeping Operations and the Distorted Price of the Yen," Joint report of the Mike Mansfield Center for Pacific Asian Affairs and the Pacific Basin Institute (Washington, D.C., and Santa Barbara, Calif., June 1995).

4. Lawrence B. Lindsey, "The Future of the Dollar as an International Currency" (remarks at a conference on "Monetary Arrangements in the Americas after NAFTA," Mexico City, May 25, 1994).

5. IMF, *World Economic Outlook, May 1995* (Washington, D.C.: IMF, 1995), p. 67.

VI. The Governance Agenda

Goodbye, G–7

W. R. Smyser

THOSE WHO BELIEVE that great things spring from humble origins can reinforce their convictions by marking the date of March 25, 1973, when one of the century's most important institutions was created in an inauspicious, informal, and almost casual manner.

It was on that day that George Shultz, then U.S. secretary of the treasury, invited the British, French, and German finance ministers to meet with him in the White House Library to talk about the future of the world monetary system.

The circumstances surrounding the invitation could not have been more dramatic. A year and a half earlier, in August 1971, when the U.S. dollar was under assault from all quarters, President Richard Nixon on the advice of Treasury Secretary John Connally had closed the "gold window," announcing that the United States would no longer sell gold at the price of $35 per troy ounce set in the Bretton Woods agreements of 1944. In the wake of Nixon's announcement, international currency and commodity markets had heaved and buckled as finance ministers and central bankers tried to come to grips with a new world in which exchange rates were out of government control and in which international finance and business threatened to collapse in confusion and uncertainty.[1]

By early 1973, many solutions had been tried and found wanting. Countless meetings under countless auspices had been held, either reaching no agreement at all or setting up some fleeting arrangements soon ignored by governments, banks, and traders. New exchange rates had been set and scuttled. Markets would boost currencies one week and drive them down the next. Various groups of states, such as the Group of Ten and the Committee of Twenty, tried to find new formulas that would stabilize international finance and trade. But their meetings settled nothing as each state tried desperately to protect its own currency, its own trade, and its own domestic well-being.

Some states tried to "float" their currencies, letting markets set the price. Some tried "dirty floats," in which they would try to influence and limit market trends. Others tried to continue fixed exchange rates across the board or for certain transactions. The West Europeans established a joint float known as the "snake," but within less than a year it had turned into the "worm" as one currency after another had to be withdrawn.

The Americans and the Europeans railed at each other, with the Europeans accusing the Americans of having neglected their responsibilities and the Americans accusing the Europeans (and especially the Germans) of having failed to make the adjustments

---

W. R. Smyser is a Washington consultant in political economy and strategy. His most recent books are *The Economy of United Germany* (New York: St. Martin's, 1992) and *Deutschland Gegen Amerika?* (Freiburg: Rombach, 1992).

that they should have made to preserve the Bretton Woods system. Both were right, but winning the argument did not and could not solve their problems.

In this chaotic atmosphere, those who met in the White House Library began quiet and purposeful deliberations. Soon joined by the Japanese finance minister, they set about discussing global financial problems in the broadest terms and looking for sensible and commonly acceptable solutions. The central bankers also began attending. Far from the crowds and the speculators, meeting in one city or another and often on the fringes of other gatherings, they all agreed during the coming months on steps to help right the international monetary system. Their governments carried out those agreements, and the system returned to balance.

As the exchange rates and the financial markets stabilized, and as the existence and the purpose of the rescue meetings became known, the little band of finance ministers was formally designated as the Group of Five, or the G-5, the new guardians of value and stability. But several of them still preferred the name they had given themselves from their first meeting, the "Library Group," for it conveyed a sense of wisdom and sagacity in the face of panic and upheaval. It evoked the image of a small group of thoughtful people united in deep understanding and common commitment, remaining high above the foibles of the world and immune to the passions of the mobs, the profiteers, and the politicians.

What emerged from that original Library Group was to become for a time one of the most influential institutions of the twentieth century, bringing into a common forum the leading states of the industrial world and their most powerful personalities.

Like all institutions, however, it has evolved in ways that could not be foreseen and that no longer serve its original purpose. It now needs to be examined anew, therefore, to see if it still has something useful to offer its members and the world as a whole, and to see what changes it must undergo in order best to serve either its original purpose or whatever it must now be called upon to do.

To conduct that examination, we shall look at the record of the G-5 and its successor, the G-7, at what they have achieved and what they have not achieved, and how they fit into the new world that has succeeded the Cold War.

The Summits

Two years after the original meeting of the Library Group, two of its members, Helmut Schmidt and Valéry Giscard d'Estaing, had become chancellor of Germany and president of France respectively. They decided that it would be good to supplement the G-5 meeting of finance ministers with an annual meeting at the very highest levels. They had three reasons:

- International financial affairs remained crucially important as well as potentially fragile, and they needed to be discussed at the most senior levels.
- Too many top-level international gatherings tended to concentrate on political and military affairs, which were important but would be meaningless if their economic underpinnings collapsed. A senior forum for economic matters would bring matters into balance.
- Gerald Ford, then president of the

United States, seemed amenable to reason and influence, and it would be useful to discuss these topics with him in person.

Giscard therefore invited the chiefs of state and government of the G–5 to the first of the economic summits, at Rambouillet outside Paris. Hoping still to maintain a discreet and scholarly atmosphere, he left a frustrated press corps 25 miles away in Paris. The meeting produced some serious conversations and helped to restore international confidence after the first oil shocks and the deep and widespread recession of 1973–1974.

With that meeting, the G–5 institutionalized the annual summit format. Several years later, Canada and Italy joined, and the summits became the best known if perhaps not the most important element of the international economic coordinating mechanism.

The summits take place every year, usually in the summer, with a well-established sequence of host countries (France, the United States, Great Britain, Germany, Japan, Italy, and Canada). They have been held in settings intentionally away from capitals (like Puerto Rico or Williamsburg), in capitals themselves (like Tokyo, Bonn, or Ottawa), or in splendor (like Versailles or Venice).

The summits, like the meetings of the finance ministers, reflect the notion that international cooperation or at least international mutual understanding in fiscal, financial, monetary, and commercial matters is useful and perhaps even essential for the stability of the world monetary and trading system. Theoretically, agreement at the most senior levels should assure coordination and should reduce the risks of financial disarray. Thus, a powerful philosophy regarding the importance of international economic coordination lies behind the summits, whatever theatrics may wait outside the doors.

Without a single dominating state to guide and manage the system, as the United States had been expected to do under the Bretton Woods agreements, the members of the G–7 have tried to achieve the same results by working together. Coordination was to be a virtue in its own right, so important to the system that it would take precedence over the normal nationalist impulses. For, even if those impulses might promote a quick gain for one at the expense of others, they would over the long run jeopardize even those who might have enjoyed a short-term victory. As d'Artagnan said, "one for all and all for one."

The national envoys who prepare the meetings and the documents are known as "sherpas" (after the Himalayan summit guides). They try to establish an agenda of vital questions and then to discern areas of agreement or at least mutually acceptable communiqué language. The sherpas now have almost full-time jobs as advance men, resting and concentrating on their regularly assigned responsibilities for a month or two after each summit and then beginning the preparations for the next. Their main objective has been to find language that makes each summit and each participant appear important and successful. They are also charged with finding communiqué language that obscures differences instead of solving them.

The summit that came closest to the original ideal of mutual coordination was the 1978 summit in Bonn. Carefully planned and directed by Helmut Schmidt, it was intended to demonstrate the virtues of cooperation. Schmidt even postponed a domestic economic stimulus package of his own in order to be able to introduce the package as a summit response to U.S. president Jimmy Carter, who wanted Germany and Japan to become "locomotives" for international prosperity. In exchange, Carter was to raise U.S. oil prices and Japanese prime minister Takeo Fukuda was to stimulate the Japanese economy.

Schmidt was deeply disappointed by the results. Carter could not carry out his commitment and may not even have tried very hard. Fukuda did not stimulate the Japanese economy as much as he had promised. Germany stood alone in carrying out its share of the bargain and in what turned out to be an ill-timed stimulus. When the second oil shock came shortly thereafter, the waves of inflation and recession that followed destroyed Schmidt's chancellorship, along with the ideal that international coordination could be effective and reliable.

No summit ever again achieved the kind of agreement that the 1978 summit had achieved, for no national leader was ever again ready to take responsibility for assuming that others would carry out their parts of any accord. With that, one of the original purposes of the summits was neutralized even as the summit process had barely begun.

Despite that failure, the summits continued. They had become institutionalized. International cooperation, even if it was no longer as grandly conceived or as achievable as earlier expected, was still regarded as a useful objective. Moreover, as the 1980s began with severe recessions in several G–7 states, the leaders wanted to be able to tell their constituents that they were doing everything possible to bring back prosperity. Nobody dared or wanted to terminate a process that provided soothing reassurance and the semblance of unanimity, even if both the reassurance and the unanimity were bought at the price of obfuscation. Instead, they changed the agenda.

The G–7 During the 1980s

During the 1980s, the G–7 summits added political matters to their agenda, thus going well beyond the original economic agenda and even against the intent of the founders of the summit format. Although Ronald Reagan as U.S. president had originally disdained the summit and pursued his own policies, he warmed to the process when he found himself surrounded by other like-minded figures. With Margaret Thatcher as prime minister of Great Britain, Helmut Kohl as chancellor of Germany, and François Mitterrand as president of France, the senior leaders of the West wanted very much to use the summits not only to discuss economic matters but also to coordinate their thinking on such major political and strategic questions as the East–West conflict, international terrorism, armament, and arms control.

Without Giscard and Schmidt, who really believed in the central importance of economic coordination and who had faith in their own expertise, the European and American summiteers were generally happier to talk about global political issues. Moreover, they had no wish to change their economic policies to suit others. The Japanese prime ministers, who might have had a greater interest in economics, were also ready to speak about other subjects because they always found themselves under pressure either to stimulate their economy, reduce the trade surplus, or help to finance policies in which they had little interest. So they were happy to sit, listen, and add their voices when necessary without changing their policies either.

The 1980s summiteers thus found themselves comfortable with broad talk about common political and strategic purposes accompanied by separate descriptions of their own, often divergent economic objectives and policies phrased in a way that suggested cohesion. The sherpas found that they had to prepare not only an economic but also a political communiqué, and that the two subjects often vied for interest and attention not only in the summit setting but also in the separate bureaucracies at home.

With the changes in personalities and interests, the very nature of the summits changed. Not only did their agendas become broader, but their objective became very different from that of the Library Group. They no longer believed that it was necessary or wise to change their separate national policies for the sake of the system as a whole.

As national leaders lost the fear that they would hang separately if they did not hang together, the original ideal of coordination was honored more in the breach than in the observance. Although several of the summit members pursued similar economic policies along the supply-side spectrum, the G–7 leaders saw the summits mainly as opportunities to outline their own visions and to exchange ideas about the shape of the non-Communist world as a whole. The G–7 summit ceased to be an economic coordinating mechanism and became a clubby opportunity for informal talks among world leaders, talks that were often useful but that strayed far away from the original purpose of the summits.

Nonetheless, the summits found a new and important role. They became the main place at which the most powerful states of the industrial world could discuss and coordinate their broad interests and policies. The G–7 and the summits became the governing board of what might be termed the global concert. The summits were the regular meeting places of those who guided the Western polity and economy during the latter phases of the Cold War.

As the need and the will for economic coordination declined, the new reason to devise concerted policies was to be the common struggle against Moscow and against various outlaw powers such as Libya. That incentive was to prove a more powerful impulse for cooperation than the economic motive on which the G–7 had been founded.

The G–7 summit in effect assumed a function that the founders of the United Nations (UN) had originally envisaged as the role of the UN Security Council. With the Security Council emasculated by the Soviet veto and by the absence of Germany and Japan, the G–7 and the global concert became the institutions that could make the most important security as well as economic decisions. Whereas the Security Council included the victors of World War II, the G–7 summit included those who were to be the victors of the Cold War.

This did not mean that the summits took over the formally assigned military functions allotted to the Security Council in the UN Charter. Those functions lapsed for the duration of the Cold War, with individual states or international alliance systems taking care of their own protection. But the G–7 assumed the broader function of being the center of global political discussion.

The importance of having Germany and Japan within the G–7 and not in the Security Council cannot be overestimated. Despite the limitations on the exercise of their military power, and although they had no nuclear weapons, consultation with those two states on major global decisions was increasingly necessary and their involvement in any international action came to be essential to the success of that action. They controlled more resources than any other state except the United States. Germany's economy gradually came to dominate Europe. German decisions prevailed in the European Community. Japan in turn came to dominate much of Asia. No major international decision could be made without their concurrence and their support. And the G-7 became the vehicle that brought Germany and Japan back to global influence in a way acceptable not only to themselves but also to others.

The UN Security Council might have voted for military action in the Persian Gulf in 1991, but the action could not have been carried out as fully and effectively if Germany had not offered discreet logistic support for U.S. forces and if Japan and Germany had not helped to finance the operation. The two states were roundly condemned in the British and American press for their failure to commit forces, but their contributions were as important as those of any state other than the United States. And coordination for German and Japanese financial contributions was carried out through G-7 channels, not through the UN.

The ever greater power and authority of Japan and Germany in the G-7 have also put some of the smaller G-7 powers into a subordinate category, especially in economic matters. As the European Exchange Rate Mechanism (ERM) began to take hold around the mid-1980s and the German Bundesbank became the central bank for much of Europe, the G-7 became the G-3, with the United States, Germany, and Japan as the ruling economic powers of the world.

During the 1980s, the G-7 system split into two separate structures related more in name than in reality and serving different and not always complementary purposes. The summits became political and representational. Economic coordination moved back to the finance ministers (including the U.S. secretary of the treasury), who had dealt with it before Rambouillet.

The most ambitious financial meetings of the 1980s were not any of the summits but rather the two ministerial meetings held at the Plaza in New York during September 1985, and at the Louvre in Paris during February 1987. At the first meeting, the finance ministers agreed that the U.S. dollar had become too strong because high U.S. interest rates and investment opportunities had raised the demand for the American currency. They agreed to coordinate an effort to reduce the dollar's value. At the Louvre, after the dollar had declined by about one quarter of its value, the ministers agreed to stabilize the new exchange rates and to set informal (and never officially announced) trading ranges for their currencies.

Like other efforts at coordination, however, the Plaza and the Louvre fell short of their objectives. The Plaza meeting even occurred under somewhat false pretenses, for the value of the dollar had actually peaked well ahead of the meeting itself. And the ranges agreed at the Louvre could not be, and were not, defended for long. Different states and central banks soon returned to their usual practice of following policies dictated by internal economic considerations or by such arrangements as the ERM. In particular, American and German policies diverged sharply, with the Americans and Germans shifting their interest rates in an uncoordinated set of maneuvers that contributed to the stock market crash of Black Monday in October 1987.

On other occasions, when the finance ministers and central bankers met and agreed—as they have often done—that interest rates were at the right levels, separate central banks shortly thereafter either raised or lowered their rates. In early 1991, the Bundesbank raised the flagship Lombard rate within weeks after a G–7 meeting. The embarrassed bank president had to let it be known that the action was forced by the heads of the regional banks, against his recommendation. The regional bankers had acted for domestic reasons, and the international agreement was not as important to them as their domestic needs.

Almost the same thing happened in 1992. After an April G–7 meeting at which interest rates were pronounced to be properly set, the Bundesbank raised its short-term rates and the U.S. Federal Reserve did the opposite. Soon thereafter, the U.S. dollar began to fall. Even after being propped up by joint interventions, it came to rest at a new low against the deutsche mark. The Japanese government, which had pledged at the April meeting to introduce a growth package, only did so five months later after the Nikkei index had collapsed to a new low.

In 1992 as in 1991, no major country or central bank acted in accordance with the agreements purportedly reached in the meetings of the G–7 finance ministers, except to the extent that the agreement suited its own immediate interests. Nor did any of the G–7 governments lower their budget deficits, although they had all pledged to do so.

With these developments, the ministerial G–7 format has, like the summits, lost its original purpose. More important, it risks losing its credibility. Since the mid-1980s, the ministerial "decisions" have been little more than paper exercises. They increasingly serve only to show that the Bundesbank's Central Bank Council (*Zentralbankrat*) could do more to set global interest rates than the G–7 ministerial. In fact, global financial markets have long since recognized that the Bundesbank has virtually become the G–1 for the global financial system, and they watch the Central Bank Council meetings with far more attention than the G–7 gatherings in order to forecast the likely course of interest and exchange rates. Even the U.S. Treasury and Federal Reserve must keep an eye on German policies to protect the dollar.

Monetary harmonization, which the ministerial G–7 had been intended to assume during the 1970s and 1980s, has been virtually abandoned by the ministers. It is now mainly attempted by the deputy finance ministers, who meet every two to three months in less publicized settings than their ministers, and by the International Monetary Fund (IMF). Because the executive director of the IMF has deputies from each of the G–7 countries, and because those deputies function as ambassadors for their finance ministries, the IMF is actually as efficient a place for coordination as any other. Central bankers, of course, maintain their own links apart from the finance ministries and the IMF, and they are best organized to conduct interventions when rates become unstable.

The G–7 summit has suffered the same decline in its authority as the ministerial meetings, especially in the economic realm. The summiteers themselves value their informal chats, but the formal outcome of any summit has been agreed well in advance and is neither determined nor even much affected by those talks. Most summit "decisions" have been meticulously negotiated in advance, with the increasingly lengthy and platitudinous communiqués having been carefully drafted for weeks or sometimes months. Even the sherpa proceedings have become intricately orchestrated, and woe to the sherpa who suggests a new way of doing things or who steps out of the established pecking order.

The three most recent summits have shown the decline of the summit's authority clearly and painfully:

- At Houston in 1990, the G–7 principals agreed to complete the negotiations for the Uruguay Round of the General Agreement on Tariffs and Trade (GATT) by the end of the year, but those negotiations were not completed by that deadline. The summiteers disregarded their own "decision," failing to follow it with effective instructions to their negotiators.
- At London in 1991, the G–7 leaders remained so divided and cautious about providing aid for the post-Soviet Confederation of Independent States that they almost certainly encouraged the coup against Mikhail Gorbachev a month after the summit. Although they professed wanting to support Gorbachev, they left him embarrassed and gave his opponents an argument against him.
- At Munich in 1992, the political communiqué was irrelevant to the real problems facing the global community, and the statement on Yugoslavia encouraged the combatants by showing no resolve to act. Russian president Boris Yeltsin's requests for aid were greeted more sympathetically than Gorbachev's had been the year before, but his request for membership in the G–7 was rejected by the group. No agreement was reached to complete the Uruguay Round, despite some ritualistic communiqué language about the importance of completing it in 1992. This failure was particularly striking because agreement was tantalizingly close. The remaining difference between the European and the American positions was over a few percentage points in a European Community (EC) pledge to reduce its export subsidies, and the difference could have been bridged in a minute if the summiteers most directly affected had shown the political will and determination to compromise for the sake of coordination.[2]

The Munich summit not only underlined the futility of the G–7 format. It also showed how far the summit and the entire G–7 process had come from the thoughtful, responsible, and intimate approach of the Library Group. It drew hundreds of official participants and hangers-on, thousands of correspondents, more thousands of protesters, and what seemed like an army corps of security personnel. It may have had no genuine purpose and no discernible result, but it certainly brought out a crowd.

It was not, however, the G–7 format itself that was to blame. It was the unwillingness of any of the member states to change their domestic economic policies in order to achieve international policy coordination. During the 1970s, governments could perhaps still hope to coordinate internationally without adjusting what they did at home. As the 1980s advanced, however, states could no longer draw a barrier between their domestic and foreign economic policies.

With foreign and domestic policies interlinked, international economic coordination can only work if states are prepared to change their domestic policies to suit a common global purpose. And this, to date, they have been unwilling to do. Until they are actually ready, the G–7 will remain a forum without a purpose and the G–7 meetings can coordinate nothing more important than the market interventions that are necessitated by its failure to reach real agreements.

No G–7, a New G–7, or What?

Given the changes in the world, all established institutions must be reevaluated and reexamined to determine whether they can still perform useful roles in the new situation. In such a reexamination, the G–7 mechanism now receives a failing score. It is not functioning as originally conceived or even as currently envisaged.

The G–7 members no longer share a common purpose or a common fear. They have come to live with divergence, and perhaps even to like it. Governments, central banks, and summiteers do what best suits them. They see little reason for cooperation and even less reason to adjust their separate policies for the sake of a common goal, no matter how worthy and desirable that goal may appear.

Under those circumstances, it is fair and even necessary to ask whether the G–7 structure, including the ministerials and especially the summits, should be discontinued.

The G–7 ministerial, the original Library Group, deserves the most immediate scrutiny, for it is theoretically in continuing existence and able to meet whenever needed. And yet there are reasons to wonder whether it is really effective or whether it might now actually contribute to instability rather than to stability.

As shown above, the ministerial format cannot now be taken seriously. The ministers and the central bankers may meet, but they do not take their commitments to heart. They ignore the statements that they themselves have issued. They seem to forget at home what they pledge abroad.

The two most important finance ministers and central bankers, the American and the German, cannot even commit their own central banks and governments on the two things that are most frequently discussed at G–7 meetings:

- As shown in 1991 and 1992, most members of the Bundesbank's Central Bank Council do not feel obliged to follow summit or ministerial G–7 decisions when they act on interest rates. The Bundesbank has been going its own way more and more, and other European central banks have no choice but to follow. In the area in which German policy has the greatest relevance to the world as a whole, the summits have no influence on German policy.
- By the same token, no U.S. secretary of the treasury can carry out any commitment he or she might make about the U.S. budget deficit, the area of U.S. policy that is of deepest concern to global capital markets, because the U.S. budget has since 1974 been the exclusive prerogative of the U.S. Congress. The president can neither spend funds that the Congress has not appropriated nor impound funds that the Con-

gress has appropriated. The budget "commitments" of the U.S. administration have no meaning although they are as much a staple of G–7 discussions and communiqués as German interest rate "commitments."

In September 1992, as France was preparing to vote on the European Community's Maastricht treaty, the G–7 finance ministers reached what has been to date their nadir of futility. The Bundesbank was maintaining a draconian monetary policy that was strangling European and even American growth and straining global currency markets. Even as the English pound and the Italian lira were dropping out of the European Exchange Rate Mechanism and as Sweden raised its short-term interest rate to 500 percent, the ministers and central bankers were unable to resolve the crisis or even to calm the markets. They could not reestablish European equilibrium. They reached no enforceable agreement to limit the fiscal deficits of the G–7 members themselves. Nor could they reach agreement on rescheduling Russian debt. They thus added nothing to either Western or Eastern stability.

One can also wonder whether G–7 meetings are really necessary for most purposes. The IMF has become a much stronger institution than it was in the 1970s. It has gained experience and confidence. It arranged and continues to manage the credits to Russia. It has excellent contacts throughout the world, and it can accomplish most financial tasks quickly and efficiently. In fact, the G–7 have increasingly had to ask the IMF to solve problems because they have themselves been unable to act.

The risk of global economic storms and perhaps even of economic catastrophe still threatens, however. Powerful deflationary forces are sweeping across the global economy. Most of the G–7 states are now either in recession or in phases of exasperatingly slow growth. The issues that the ministers and central bankers must address and resolve are more crucial than ever. The potential for financial disaster cannot be dismissed, given the collapse of the Japanese equity markets, the pressures on several European currencies, the persistent U.S. deficits, the uncertainties confronting the new Russian ruble, and the fragile prospects for credit repayment by East European and former Soviet states.

This, however, underlines even more the importance of not using the G–7 ministerial mechanism for petty purposes. The G–7 ministerials are now losing credibility, not gaining it, and there may come a day when they will need all the credibility that they can muster. To continue meetings that have no purpose or effect is not only useless. It is even dangerous, for it undermines the most precious commodity that such meetings can offer the world: the capacity to inspire confidence in the face of crisis.

It would be best for the G–7 to suspend the meetings of ministers and central bankers until the G–7 members are really prepared to change their domestic policies to avert or survive a global crisis. At that point, if the credibility of the G–7 institutions has not been diluted, the very fact of their meeting can help to calm markets. Their decisions might then even carry weight, as they do not now.

The G–7 ministerial should thus be shelved until it is really needed and until it can make a positive difference. In the meantime, other institutions can carry the process of regular international coordination. And the ministers can still meet informally, as they do now, either at IMF meetings or at such gatherings as the Economic Forum at Davos, in Switzerland.

The summits present a different problem from that of the ministerial meetings, for they are no longer financial meetings. But, like the meetings of the ministers, they have become increasingly diluted and are no longer taken seriously even by their participants. As the ministerials are no longer coordinating financial policy, the summits are no longer coordinating either political or economic policy.

There is an old and valid rule to the effect that institutions should be dissolved when they no longer link words, actions, and responsibilities. That rule applies especially to institutions that commit the most senior authorities of any government. And it must now be applied to the G–7 summits.

Like the ministers' meetings, the summits have become dangerously deceptive. They attempt to create the impression that global economic coordination exists, but the world is moving rapidly toward separate trading blocks and toward competing currencies managed with no regard to the global consequences. Coordination, except for market interventions, has to all intents and purposes collapsed.

The summits and the surrounding rhetorical exercises thus create a lulling effect at a time when the alarm bells should be ringing in every chancellery and in every finance ministry and central bank. They are also wasting the time and fraying the authority of some of the world's senior statesmen.

The international trading system is in deep trouble. After the Uruguay Round fiasco in Munich, President George Bush returned to Washington to complete the North American Free Trade Agreement (NAFTA) with Canada and Mexico and to announce increases in U.S. agricultural export subsidies. Although there is still hope for completion of the Uruguay Round, the countless delays and the centrifugal tendencies that they have encouraged must be seen as a warning that half a century of global commercial coordination may be coming to a halt.

As indicated above, the international financial system is under immense pressure. The passage from the European Exchange Rate Mechanism to the European Monetary Union has combined with German unification to drive the Bundesbank toward interest rate policies that threaten to undermine European and global prosperity. The U.S. dollar, the staple international currency in which major global commodities are denominated and traded, is hitting new lows and may be gradually or brutally displaced by the deutsche mark for a number of transactions. The crisis of September 1992 is almost certainly not the last. The European Monetary System's currency, the ecu, is hostage to intra-European disagreements about the future of the EC itself. The narrow French majority for the Maastricht treaty promises more uncertainty about the future of Europe, even as it diminishes the authority of European leaders to deal with that future.

New global political and defense problems are also multiplying although the Cold War is over. Nuclear proliferation and escalating international arms sales raise the specter of a world ever more deeply saddled with crushing defense expenditures and with tempting collections of military hardware. Ethnic difficulties are multiplying everywhere, especially in Europe and Africa. The failure of the international aid system to deal with desperate human needs is most starkly evidenced in Somalia and Yugoslavia but is by no means confined there.

The summit format has proven largely irrelevant to solving these problems. It does not even address them seriously any more. Instead, the sherpas appear to be under instructions to devise acceptable communiqué language that permits the meetings to proceed smoothly without facing difficult and disagreeable issues trenchantly.

The summits' main purpose of the 1980s, to serve as a coordinating mechanism for the free world, has also became a dead letter. In fact, the demise of communism has even removed the G–7's main incentive to work as a group. It is little wonder that the three summits since the breaching of the Berlin Wall have been futile.

There is also some question whether the G–7 summit format is still needed to give Japan and Germany a voice in the major political and defense councils of the world. The UN Security Council has been revived somewhat. Japan and even Germany have expressed an interest in applying for permanent membership. Although this would require also adding others, especially from the Third World, and perhaps amending the veto rules somewhat, it could certainly be achieved.

There are, however, three major reasons to maintain some kind of summit format despite the futility of recent meetings. The first is that periodic informal talks among chiefs of state and government do serve a useful purpose if they are used for genuine discussions. The second is that the post–cold war problems should be discussed at the most senior levels if there is to be any hope of finding solutions. The third is that a successful world order can only be built if the most important states agree on it and are prepared to help to build it together.

But the summit that can serve those purposes must be different from the G–7 summit that the world has come to know. It must have a new agenda and a new membership.

The first order of business for the G–7, therefore, should be to begin to devise a summit format that can move away from the empty rituals of the last several gatherings in order to deal with the new world.

On this basis, three steps should be taken:

- The Tokyo Summit now scheduled for 1993 should be announced in advance as the last meeting under the present format and with the present agenda. The G–7 should appoint a cabinet-level working committee—not the present sherpas—that will recommend a new format at the Tokyo meeting.
- Under that new format, the agenda of the summits should be fundamentally changed to give more time for informal discussion about the organization of the future world in light of the changes that have taken place since 1989.
- The summiteers should set three goals: First, to devise new international financial and monetary arrangements that can handle the potential crises that might arise and that one can already foresee; second, to devise a global security system that can hope to gain some control over the multiplication of weaponry; and third, to plan for the new trading system that must be developed as soon as the

Uruguay Round is safely completed or—even more important—if it should fail.

These economic and political topics are now fully linked, because it is now obvious that global trade and especially the Western states will have to find a way to accommodate the products that come from the states formerly behind the Iron Curtain if those states are not to collapse economically and politically. This may not be possible without profound economic and perhaps even societal adjustments everywhere.

Summit meetings can offer good opportunities to address the future shape of the world, because it goes without saying that this subject will require at least as much senior-level mutual understanding as the Cold War did. But that is for a summit different in format from the present meetings, with new agendas, new ways of proceeding, and new attitudes.

It must also be a summit with a different membership. If the world's problems are to be fully discussed, they must be discussed in the company of those states that are most able to carry out the summit decisions. Russia should be invited to become a full summit member at the first new summit after Tokyo and to attend the meetings not as a penitent debtor but as the great power that Russia has been for centuries and can be expected to remain. It is to everybody's advantage for Russia to resume the process of economic growth and linkage to the West that it had begun before 1914 rather than to remain in the limbo to which Lenin and Stalin consigned it.

As soon as possible after that, and subject to political developments in Beijing, the People's Republic of China (PRC) should also be invited to the summit meetings. The PRC now has one of the world's fastest growing private sectors, a considerable trade surplus, and the potential for explosive advances in modern industry. It has the world's largest population, and it must join the global economic and political system to help that system function effectively. No summit can carry out any decisions that it may make if the PRC does not agree to them.

Once the PRC joins, the summit will be the G-9, and it will again be the central coordinating mechanism of the world. It should not need to practice artificial consensus building or to pursue some abstract facade of unanimity. Nor should it occupy itself with the many petty or short-lived issues that now pepper summit communiqués and that should be handled in other organizations and at other levels.

Instead, it should be the body in which the major powers make certain that they work together to build a truly new world order with some sense of community and some sense of urgency. It should also be the forum in which they can meet free of the protocol of bilateral visits and can come to understand each other well enough to avoid having future crises turn into disasters. These are immense tasks, which cannot and must not wait forever.

Russia and the PRC should not, however, be invited to the G-7 monetary and financial forum. That forum should remain, even in abeyance, a place for those who hold the financial balance of the world. The ministerial and the summit should remain split, as they are now. Russia and the PRC at this point belong in the senior political forum, not the monetary arena.

There is a precedent for this type

of arrangement. Italy and Canada joined the summit meetings at the beginning of the 1980s but were not invited to join the G-7 financial ministers and central bankers until the Louvre meeting in 1987.

The new G-9 can then go back to the principles of the original Library Group. The summiteers can talk quietly and informally, far from the glare of publicity and—one must hope—imbued with a deep desire to shape a political and economic world in which all can exist and thrive. And, like the Library Group, they should base their deliberations on the simple truth that none can succeed if others fail.

If they are organized on those foundations, the meetings can contribute to global political and economic stability at a crucial time. The G-7 ministers and central bankers can hope to stave off financial crisis. The G-9 leaders can establish a new international framework for peace. Together, they can help to make certain that the triumph that ended the Cold War does not turn into a tragedy.

Notes

1. The material for this article is drawn from a number of sources, including publications of various G-7 governments and central banks, books on international economics, published newspaper accounts and official reports of G-7 meetings over the last several years, and talks with members of the G-7 process at various levels. I am particularly indebted for the date in the opening paragraph to Paul Volcker and Toyoo Gyohten, *Changing Fortunes* (New York: Times Books, 1992), pp. 126, 347–348.

2. The English language version of the 1992 summit documents is in U.S. Department of State, *Dispatch* 3, supplement no. 5 (August 1992), pp. 1–10. That *Dispatch* supplement also contains, on pp. 11–15, a useful summary of the 1980s summit declarations. The German version of the summit documents is in Presse- und Informationsamt der Bundesregierung, *Bulletin*, no. 77 (July 11, 1992), pp. 729–742.

The Japan–U.S. Bilateral Relationship: Its Role in the Global Economy

Raymond Vernon

THE CONVENTIONAL WISDOM of 1990 portrays Japan and the United States on a collision course. According to a view shared widely in both countries, the United States is on the way down, and Japan is on the way up. The United States is giving up to Japan its mantle of technological superiority, dominance over international finance, and leadership as the home of the world's leading enterprises.

My views differ from conventional wisdom in two critical respects. First, the future of U.S.–Japanese relations is far from being so fully determined; and although it is filled with risks and dangers, the future still offers opportunities for collaboration and cooperation. Second, the strong disposition of U.S. and Japanese representatives to use bilateral discussions in an effort to settle their differences is dangerous and misguided, a practice more likely to precipitate the risks than to realize the opportunities in their relationship.

Raymond Vernon is Clarence Dillon Professor Emeritus of International Affairs and Herbert F. Johnson Professor Emeritus of International Business Management, Harvard University. His most recent book is *Beyond Globalism: Remaking American Foreign Economic Policy* (New York: The Free Press, 1988).

Japan Ascendant

The perception of Japan as the ascendant partner in the bilateral relationship has been prevalent for a decade or longer, and was foretold fully in a remarkable book by Herman Kahn that was published 20 years ago.[1] Kahn foresaw that the Japanese economy would grow to be one of the largest in the world, when measured by its gross national product, with per capita incomes that rivaled those of Europe and the United States. He anticipated that Japan and the United States would continue to share some interests, as they have, including a joint concern for global economic growth, protection of the global environment, and the maintenance of defense capabilities sufficient to hold China and the Soviet Union in check. Kahn also envisaged the possibility that the two countries would develop a partnership to preside over the non-Communist Pacific area, with Japan playing the role of economic overlord, and the United States the role of political and military leader. This is an idea that occasionally emerges in today's political discussions. Finally, although Kahn regarded nothing as absolutely certain, he did foresee stressful bilateral relations between Japan and the

United States, especially in areas in which the two countries would continue to compete.

It would be a mistake not to give Herman Kahn his full due as a seer, but there is little risk that his prescient views will be forgotten. Other effective publicists on both sides of the Pacific, including Ezra Vogel, Clyde Prestowitz, and James Fallows, since have affirmed the rightness of Kahn's remarkable projections. When trying to fathom likely developments in the U.S.–Japanese bilateral relationship, however, one must do more than extrapolate the past. Two sets of changes must be taken into account in appraising the ways in which that bilateral relationship will develop in the 1990s. The first set emanates from within each of the two countries, the second set from changes in the global environment.

Japan's Changing Interests. Kahn's expectation that Japan would prove a dominant actor in the non-Communist Pacific area obviously is consistent with the reality of the 1990s. Japan is a dominant power in the Asian Development Bank, and a dominant investor and trader in Southeast Asia. In addition, Japan's growing influence on the Pacific coasts of North and South America adds to its strength in the Pacific region.

Missing, however, is a lesson that every economic power eventually is obliged to learn. A nation that exports a substantial part of its savings and develops a considerable market abroad acquires stature and power in the process. Still, as that nation's stake in foreign countries grows, its autonomy declines. Unlike the exploitative hegemon of history, the modern hegemon intertwines its own well-being with that of the foreign countries with which it deals. On reflection, that proposition may seem self-evident, but it is overlooked too easily.

In Japan's case, a surge of exports to North America in the first half of the 1980s sharply altered the geographical composition of its export trade. In a brief period, the North American share of Japan's exports was lifted from about 25 to about 36 percent, where it since has remained. In the latter half of the decade of the 1980s, Japan was pouring its capital into the United States at the rate of about $60 billion annually, so that its aggregate stake in the U.S. economy reached about $300 billion by the end of the decade.

In power terms, the effect of these trends was evident. Because the United States had become dependent on Japan's savings, Japan was in a position to inflict great pain on the U.S. economy. Japan only could use that power, however, if it were prepared to risk giant losses, including a massive impairment of capital and a loss of critical markets.

Meanwhile, Japan's increasing stake in other areas has reduced its autonomy further. Between 1983 and 1987, Japan's long-term capital commitments in the European Community (EC) grew by over $140 billion, increasing at about the same rate as in the United States. At the same time, Europe provides Japan's largest market outside of the Pacific Rim, accounting for about 16 percent of Japan's exports.

Herman Kahn's picture of Japan's future, therefore, needs to be refined in major ways. Japan is indubitably a Pacific power, but its new status in the world is inescapably a source of weakness, as well as strength. As with Britain and the United States in earlier eras, the change in Japan's status has required an increase in its global commitments. Like the United States and Europe, Japan's future is intertwined deeply with that of the rest of the world.

Japan's Changing Policies. Japan's policies have evolved in ways that reflect its changing interests. Until the early 1970s, the country's foreign policy was essentially passive or reactive. Japanese foreign policy consisted mainly of fending off measures that restricted Japanese exports, resisting pressures to open the Japanese market, conducting foreign economic relations through bilateral deals when possible, and spending on military objectives and on foreign aid only to the extent necessary to avoid the acute displeasure of the United States. Where global institutions and global programs were concerned, Japan left initiatives and responsibilities to others.

Japan's growing economic interests in the 1970s and 1980s, however, have given the country a major stake in the maintenance of effective international regimes for the conduct of trade, payments, and investment. Today, it would be hard to find a country with a stake greater than Japan's in furthering the central objective of the International Monetary Fund (IMF), the General Agreement on Tariffs and Trade (GATT), and the Organization for Economic Cooperation and Development (OECD). That objective is to maintain in the world a system of open and stable markets.

After 1971, with the abandonment of fixed exchange rates, the stability of the U.S. dollar and European currencies became matters of deep concern to Japan. In the two decades since, Japan has found itself a key player in every major global arrangement relating to exchange rates: in the IMF, where the country has developed a decisive role in the financing of heavily indebted developing countries; in the OECD, where Japan's concurrence in agreements on export financing has proved critical; in the Bank for International Settlements, where its concurrence on issues of solvency and supervision of international banks has been indispensable; and in the U.S.–Japanese–German triangular consultations on measures to stabilize the U.S. dollar, where the yen–dollar relation has been paramount.

Japan's greatly augmented role in world affairs has been accompanied by new initiatives and greater assertiveness in international bodies. Occasional references in the Japanese media to the so-called mad dog Americans have matched in their ugliness occasional U.S. references to Japan as a so-called enemy to be contained. In a turnabout long overdue, Japan has taken the United States to task in the GATT, alleging that U.S. threats to deny Japan access to U.S. markets are a violation of GATT provisions. Japan's special commitment of $10 billion to supplement World Bank and IMF funds for heavily indebted developing countries has been another illustration of an initiative that would have been unlikely in the 1970s.

To be sure, some surveys see the new accents in Japanese policy as a ringing affirmation of Kahn's view of Japan as an emerging superstate. Kahn, however, saw Japan as using its power to dominate the Pacific, and not to become a participating member in global institutions. Indeed, I have been unable to find a single reference in the Kahn opus to either the IMF or the GATT. A Japan that finds itself anxious to improve the world's economic institutions is bound to take a different direction in its foreign policies than a Japan bent mainly on the domination of the Pacific.

This is not to say that Japan will

turn its back on opportunities to build up its influence in the Pacific or elsewhere. Like the United States in Latin America, Japan almost surely will try to carve out a special place for itself in Southeast Asia; and, like the United States, it almost certainly will discover the limitations of such a strategy. Like the United States, too, Japan also will revert to bilateral negotiations whenever it feels such an approach would serve its interests. In the U.S. case, such bilateral approaches mainly have served to clamp down the flow of goods from exporting countries. In contrast, in the Japanese case, they principally will aim to secure preferential access for Japanese products in foreign markets. In spite of such regional and bilateral efforts, however, Japan seems pushed inexorably by its growing global interest of supporting multilateral organizations, such as the GATT, OECD, and IMF, as channels through which Japan may shape its economic relations. Japanese influence in such organizations is bound to increase, but its interest in influencing their future will not be vastly different from those of the United States and Europe.

Japan's Internal Developments. Four decades ago, John Foster Dulles was referring to Japan as "a basket case," and scarcely a dissenting voice was to be found. Today, the only observers who are prepared to pay any attention to the possibility that Japan may stumble are the Japanese themselves. The rest of the world seems persuaded that Japan has mastered the secret of perpetual growth without pain.

Herman Kahn was one of the earliest of those who were convinced that Japan could overcome practically any difficulty. Although in most respects history is on his side, Kahn has yet to be proved correct on one issue. His 1970 guesses were much too sanguine about the ability of the Japanese to use their high incomes to create a livable environment.

As Kahn had predicted, the Japanese have been making many determined environmental efforts, including the introduction of vigorous antipollution measures, the upgrading of sanitary and health facilities, and the improvement of retirement plans. Despite efforts to curb urban air pollution, however, Tokyo's atmosphere has remained one of the world's most polluted. Despite elevated income levels, most Japanese live in cramped houses and apartments, suffer long commutes to work, have limited access to parks, beaches, and other outdoor commons, and face prohibitive housing costs.

These shortfalls appear to be a source of discontent among young Japanese, especially those who have traveled abroad and formed firsthand impressions of living conditions in Europe and North America. They have learned quickly that Japan's high per capita income, as a measure of its living amenities, is altogether misleading. The high internal prices of consumer goods reduce Japanese incomes by about one-third, when compared with the United States, while the paucity of leisure time and shortage of living space widen the amenities gap even further.

To the outside observer, two added factors seem relevant in gauging the reactions of the Japanese people. One is growing restiveness among Japanese women with the restraints on the economic and social roles they usually are required to accept; the other is increasing concern among Japanese wage earners over an inescapable increase in the national tax burden. The Japanese workforce has realized that the tax burden cannot fail to mount, as the society undergoes dramatic aging in the coming decades. The fact that the percentage of Japanese citizens over 65 years of age will have risen from 10 percent of the population in 1984 to 21 percent in 2015, for instance, carries striking implications. Accordingly, the years ahead point to some significant changes in Japan's economic performance that would affect measurably the country's bilateral relationship with the United States.

One possible scenario is that the savings rate of Japanese households, which has been declining slowly in the past decade, will continue to fall. That development could come about as the aging Japanese population demands more amenities. If that occurs, the Japanese economy would lose some of the critical cushion that previously has allowed it to maintain a high rate of investment, without risking a high rate of inflation.

Another possibility is that the Japanese public may resist further increases in military expenditures and foreign aid, believing that the economy cannot afford such expenditures. A reaction of that kind would be even more likely if the Soviet Union and the People's Republic of China continue to maintain a relatively unthreatening posture toward Japan, and if the tensions between the United States and Japan regarding trade and technology issues continue to grow.

At the same time, however, the Japanese government likely will be highly sensitive to the need to nurture and protect the vested interests that Japanese banks, insurance companies, and manufacturing enterprises rapidly are establishing all over the world. Like the United States, the United Kingdom, and Germany, Japan will come to recognize that the well-being of its citizens increasingly will depend on how other economies are faring. Accordingly, the Japanese tendency to pull away from the United States in response to domestic pressures could be diluted or offset by Japan's need to collaborate with the United States on projects in order to protect their joint interests in world markets.

U.S. Frustrations

The central problem of the United States is to reconcile an unchanging desire to remain the world's leading military and political power with a growing national realization that U.S. economic and technological resources are limited.

The East European revolution inspired by Mikhail Gorbachev could provide the United States with a graceful way out of this dilemma, allowing it to shrink dramatically the U.S. defense establishment and to redeploy a so-called peace dividend to meet some neglected needs at home and abroad. The United States likely will make such shifts slowly and cautiously. Worries over Gorbachev's durability will serve to curb such efforts as will vested U.S. economic interests, including the cities, states, single enterprises, and whole industries that have a stake in maintaining a large defense establishment.

The frustrations that the limited resources of the United States generate for its leadership are bound to continue. While East Europeans face the severest trial and greatest opportunity of their modern history, the United States only can scrape together a few hundred million dollars to affect the outcome. While Japan marshalls $10 billion to help developing countries reduce their overhanging debt and enthusiastically supports a major expansion in IMF quotas, the U.S. government is obliged to plead poverty. U.S. housing and education needs are underfunded chronically, and the growth of U.S. domestic industry depends increasingly on European and Japanese business investments.

Yet, retreating to an economic or military "Fortress America" is not a realistic U.S. option. The United States cannot yet bring itself to modify its leadership image on the political and military front. Besides, U.S. firms based in foreign countries and foreign firms based in the United States have become so critical to the U.S. economy as to prevent such a withdrawal. With most large U.S.-based multinational enterprises typically relying on foreign subsidiaries to generate 30 to 40 percent of the parent company income, one can anticipate that such enterprises will support a continued U.S. presence abroad.

The so-called Fortress America possibility is obsolete, rendered inoperative by the modern technology of transportation and communication. There is no longer any serious hope of relying alone on U.S. technology in order to build the world's most advanced fighting force. Nor is there any serious hope of controlling the movement of capital and technology across U.S. borders. The formidable problems encountered in attempting to control the movement of people and goods across U.S. borders attests to these difficulties.

Apart from international links in the fields of investment and technology, the United States also is anchored to the rest of the world by the U.S. dollar. The dollar serves double-duty, being the world's key currency at the same time that it serves the U.S. economy. In the latter 1980s, for example, foreign governments' holdings of U.S. dollars exceeded $300 billion, and were showing no signs of shrinking. At that time, the dollar claims of banks outside of the United States came to something like $2,000 billion. Nor can the U.S. government easily alter the situation, because U.S. banks and other financial intermediaries would struggle to avoid having the U.S. dollar withdrawn from its leading role. The United States, therefore, is both master and slave in its role as the provider of the world's leading currency.

The idea of a Pacific partnership with Japan does not seem to offer much prospect of resolving these U.S. dilemmas. Such partnership, although attractive, cannot provide easy answers to the country's complex frustrations regarding the mismatch between limited resources and global interests. Europe, Canada, and Latin America continue to occupy a dominant position in the external economic interests of the United States. Moreover, until *perestroika* is on a much firmer footing within the Soviet Union, Europe will continue to occupy a central position in U.S. military interests.

The United States, therefore, seems committed inescapably to the pursuit of a policy that attempts to be global in its reach rather than autarkic or regional. The inevitable inconsistencies and contradictions of U.S. economic policy likely will prove even more pronounced, as the country attempts to maintain a global position without adequate resources to sustain it. Still, it is difficult to picture a set of circumstances that will persuade the policymakers to accept more limited horizons for the exercise of their influence.

Mismatched Policy-making

During the decades ahead, for the United States, Japan, and all other industrialized countries, an increase in the exposure of national economies seems inescapable. With the globalization of markets, the multinationalization of enterprises, and the increase in environmental concerns, Japan and the United States are bound to engage in more frequent and concerted dialogue. Most bilateral interchanges likely will prove relatively routine and trouble-free. Governmental agencies with specialized functions, such as tax collection, bank supervision, or air traffic control, will continue to develop and explore their cross-border contacts, operating at various levels of their respective bureaucracies.

Some bilateral issues, however, will be lifted out of such humdrum channels and dealt with at higher levels. As a rule, these will be domestic policy issues, such as the protection of Japanese rice farmers from competition or the promotion of the U.S. aircraft industry. In these and other instances, it will be a challenge for both countries to avoid rancor and bitterness.

The high level of tension that heretofore has characterized practically all such bilateral U.S.–Japanese negotiations perhaps could be explained by the intrinsic importance of the subject matter under discussion. Similar heated debates between the United States and Germany or France, however, have generated far less tension. Understandably, many Japanese believe that the underlying problem carries racial overtones. I am convinced, however, that the explanation is to be found in the fundamental incompatibility of Japanese and American styles of conducting their bilateral discussions.

Historians and sociologists repeatedly have explored factors that have produced the obvious mismatch, and some of their observations are worth recalling. On the U.S. side, the highly fragmented distribution of power in the federal government provides the backdrop. When President Bush speaks with Prime Minister Toshiki Kaifu about trade matters, he speaks only for the executive branch, not the U.S. government. As foreign governments have been slow to learn, that fragmentation pervades the three main branches of government, including the executive branch. Although that fragmentation of governmental power reflects American values, it gives an ephemeral and uncertain quality to U.S. economic diplomacy. What one agency might present as a position of the United States may, in the end, prove to be only an opening gambit unsupported by the rest of the U.S. government. For example, a 1987 proposal made by the U.S. trade representative for all governments to abolish agricultural import restrictions over a ten-year period could not possibly have had the firm commitment of the U.S. Department of Agriculture, much less that of the Congress.

Another U.S. value that creates confusion is the idea that a professional bureaucracy should operate under the firm control of its political masters. This is a laudable principle, fully consistent with the notion that the legitimacy of any government derives from the mandate it receives from the electorate.

The application of that exemplary principle, however, generates some difficult international problems. The new crop of cabinet ministers and bureau chiefs ushered in by new administrations are transient recruits from law firms, universities, newspapers, and state governments, assigned to temporary duty in Washington. As a rule, such political leaders do not remain in their jobs for longer than two or three years. Accordingly, one political scientist aptly has described the U.S. government as a "government of strangers." Such politicians have a limited capacity for consensus-building, and few of them spend much time attempting to build the internal agreements necessary for the development of international positions.

Still, the results of a revolving-door bureaucracy are not all bad. With little time to spare, little effort to build consensus, and, sometimes, little appreciation of all the difficulties in their own proposals, U.S. officials are much quicker than those in most other governments to launch new initiatives in response to international problems. Often, the ability of officials to launch a new policy or redirect an old one depends on extraneous factors, such as the official's force of personality or access to the president, rather than on the merits and durability of the policy. As a consequence, the capacity of the system to pursue an unwavering course over time has been limited.[2]

Contrast these patterns of operation with those of the Japanese government. The permanent Japanese bureaucracy has a much more powerful hand in the shaping of governmental policies. True, that power does not go unchallenged altogether in Japan. Even before a succession of scandals in the late 1980s began undermining the power of the Liberal Democratic Party (LDP), the Japanese *Diet* and political parties appeared to be gaining rapidly in strength, relative to the bureaucracy. Moreover, U.S. scholars energetically debate whether the dominant financial, industrial, and commercial enterprises of Japan may be exerting more power in the framing of national policies than the Ministry of International Trade and Industry (MITI) or the Ministry of Finance.[3] However that debate resolves itself, it is indisputable that the Japanese bureaucracy plays a dramatically different role in Japanese policy-making than that of its U.S. counterpart.

Nevertheless, the Japanese bureaucracy secures its power at a high price and retains it through the deeply ingrained practice of touching all bases before any international position is taken. Occasionally, Japanese negotiators will take an action that seems to breach that rule; but that is the exception and usually is taken under great pressure from the opposing government.

Operating under an imperative for consensus, the style of Japanese negotiators differs markedly from that of their U.S. counterparts. In most international gatherings and to the vast annoyance of the Americans, the Japanese participants usually do no more than observe and report. Occasionally, they will make formal gestures of open-mindedness and goodwill, but subsequent meetings often reveal that they were without real substance. Meanwhile, within the Japanese establishment, a national position slowly is being hammered out among the competing interests. As a rule, the final product of those internal battles is devoid of principle, reflecting only a small shift in the center of gravity of the interests that contributed to it. When the Japanese negotiators eventually produce the mouse that is the product of their protracted discussions, the U.S. instinct is to cry foul.[4]

One hardly could find two less compatible styles of policy-making. On the Japanese side, one finds a long trail of commitments in principle, embodied in treaties and agreements, followed by a snail-like movement in the general direction defined by the principles. On the U.S. side, traditional adherence to such principles is obscured by the mercurial shifts that repeatedly shock the Japanese.

An examination of the past 40 years illustrates the bewilderment and frustration that the process has produced. From 1952 to 1957, U.S. policymakers repeatedly urged the Japanese to reduce their trade barriers, in accordance with GATT provisions. In 1957, however, the pressure was turned on Japan to curb its increasing exports of textiles to the U.S. market, in gross violation of the spirit of the GATT. Throughout the 1960s, the United States supported a regime of fixed exchange rates and convertible currencies. Then, in 1971, the United States abandoned fixed rates, and violated its commitments to Japan by slapping a discriminatory 10 percent duty on Japanese imports. In 1986, after decades of inveighing against the evils of the so-called managed trade proposals put forward by France and others, the United States demanded an agreement from Japan to guarantee U.S. semiconductor producers a share of the Japanese market. In 1989, after a century of supporting the principle of national treatment for foreign-owned businesses, the United States abruptly began to discriminate against Japanese-owned enterprises that were seeking to do business in the United States. Meanwhile, after interminable representations from the U.S. side, the Japanese began the slow and laborious process of modifying their practices in the general direction the United States had sought for so long.

Because these disconcerting patterns appear to be the consequence of well-entrenched institutions and values in Japan and in the United States, it would be unrealistic to assume that either country will alter significantly its behavior in the immediate future. The challenge, therefore, is to find a way to deal with their shared problems, and by means that would not require the bilateral confrontations of the past.

Beyond the Bilateral

Over the years, the bilateral discussions between the United States and Japan have fallen into a familiar pattern. Rarely have they involved an exploration of common problems and opportunities. Typically, they have had their origins in a complaint by the United States that Japan was behaving unfairly toward U.S. interests and a demand that Japan should change its practices. That opening gambit has been followed by a long, drawn out succession of meetings on the U.S. complaint, followed by a series of apparent Japanese concessions.

Some of the issues on the agenda of bilateral U.S.–Japanese discussions have been of primary concern to the two countries, and have not affected the interests of other countries. The most contentious issues, however, have involved substantial interests of other countries as well.

Many of the complaints have been based on the contention that Japan was violating a particular provision of the GATT. Subsequent U.S. proposals for remedy affected the interests of third countries. For instance, in proposing to Japan that it should set aside some proportion of the Japanese semiconductor market for U.S. exports and should stop dumping its computer chips in third-country markets, the United States obviously was stepping on the toes of other countries.

Even issues not governed by any agreement have had direct effects on the interests of third countries. In the so-called structural discussions between the United States and Japan launched in 1989, each country raised issues regarding the other's economy that were global rather than bilateral in their impact. The United States questioned Japan's restrictive distribution system, its strong propensity to exclude foreign service companies, and its tortuous antiforeign local ordinances. In turn, Japan pointed to the dangerously low U.S. savings rate, U.S. underinvestment in education, and the heavy U.S. emphasis on short-run financial returns.

With bilateral discussions between Japan and the United States so heavily handicapped by incompatibilities of structure and style, an obvious alternative would be to search for multilateral opportunities. For example, both the semiconductor issue and the structural discussions would have been far more appropriate in a multilateral forum. To be sure, the provisions in the Omnibus Trade and Competitiveness Act paint the United States into a corner by forcing the president to deal with Japan on a bilateral basis. But, the early 1990s will produce a number of major occasions for the reconsideration of U.S.–Japanese relations in a multilateral setting. These are opportunities that both countries would do well to seize.

One such occasion is the round of negotiations accompanying the European Community's remarkable program for completing the integration of its internal market by 1992 (EC–92). On many issues arising in connection with that process the interests of Japan and the United States are on the same side. Both countries, for instance, want to persuade the Europeans to maintain as open a border around the new Europe as it will be possible to negotiate. A temptation for the United States will be to accept any EC arrangement that will seem to serve U.S. interests in the short run, even if the arrangement is opportunistic, and even if it slights Japanese interests.

The problem is illustrated by the EC's principles in granting foreign banks the right to do business inside the European market. Those principles have been drafted in such a way as to raise the possibility that U.S. banks eventually will gain greater access to European markets than their Japanese competitors.[5] Presented with an opportunity to better its competitive position over the Japanese, the U.S. side may prove unable to resist the temptation to "take the money and run." Yet, the occasion could be used much more fruitfully by attempting to develop a global *modus vivendi* on such issues, including an international mechanism to adjudicate disputes over banking issues.

The multilateral approach to issues such as these already has generated some impressive successes, as illustrated by the various governmental agreements that have been reached since 1975 to increase the safety of international banks. These agreements, sponsored by the Bank for International Settlements, have brought the EC, United States, and Japan together in a series of unprecedented accords on measures to tighten up the supervision and increase the capital of such banks.[6]

Another opportunity for shifting the bilateral issues between the United States and Japan into a more promising environment is provided by the ongoing negotiations sponsored by GATT under the title of the Uruguay Round. Although the United States traditionally has been the principal proponent for strengthening GATT powers, it has tried almost invariably to avoid recourse to the GATT in handling bilateral U.S.–Japanese disputes. Presumably, the idea has been that the coercive powers of the United States in the bilateral relationship would be stronger than those that the United States could exercise in GATT. That never has been a self-evident proposition, and it may be even less so in the future.

It would be too much to expect that either Japan or the United States would give up bilateral channels wherever they thought something could be gained by the maneuver. Still, the case for shifting U.S.–Japanese discussions to multilateral channels is already strong, and will increase in strength if the dispute-settling mechanisms of international agencies can be reinforced. In recent years, there has been a visible movement in this direction, as quarreling parties have been turning increasingly to such mechanisms. A notable step was taken in that direction when Japan uncharacteristically invoked the GATT mechanism to complain about U.S. threats to apply the super-301 provisions of its trade law, under which the United States reserves the right to determine unilaterally what is fair in trade practices.

Conclusion

Bilateral relations between Japan and the United States promise to remain critical for both countries in the foreseeable future. On economic issues, however, the bilateral approach inescapably will continue to generate interactions of a destructive kind. What may prevent such developments from turning into more active hostility is that neither country can inflict great harm upon the other without imposing great costs upon itself in the process.

Likewise, there are few bilateral issues that do not intimately affect third countries as well. As a result, most of the disputes that arise between Japan and the United States involve issues in which third countries have a legitimate interest, suggesting the desirability of shifting to multilateral settings wherever the choice exists.

In the case of Japan and the United States, however, the reasons for avoiding bilateral efforts to resolve large problems or disputes are strengthened greatly by the basic incompatibilities in the decision-making processes of the two governments. As a result, when the United States and Japan engage in two-way conversations, it appears that they cannot hear each other.

Inadequate as existing multilateral institutions may be for the development of policy and the settlement of disputes, therefore, they are measurably superior to the bilateral channels of Japanese–U.S. relations. Japan already shows small signs of recognizing this critical point, and it is time for the United States to recognize it, as well.

An earlier version of this paper was delivered to a conference of the CSIS Pacific Forum on "An Agenda for the United States and Japan on Northeast Asia," November 26–29, 1989.

Notes

1. Herman Kahn, *The Emerging Japanese Superstate* (Englewood Cliffs, N.J.: Prentice Hall, 1970).

2. Raymond Vernon and Debora L. Spar, *Beyond Globalism* (New York: Free Press, 1989), p. 15 et seq.

3. Richard J. Samuels, *The Business of the Japanese State: Energy Markets in Comparative & Historical Perspective* (Ithaca, N.Y.: Cornell University Press, 1987), pp. 231–237.

4. Clyde V. Prestowitz, Jr., *Trading Places: How We Allow Japan to Take the Lead* (New York: Basic Books, 1988), pp. 46–70.

5. For a description of the relevant provisions, see Sidney Key, "Financial Integration in the European Community," International Finance Discussion Paper No. 349, Federal Reserve Board, Washington, D.C., 1989.

6. Ethan B. Kapstein, "Resolving the Regulator's Dilemma: International Coordination of Banking Regulations," *International Organization* 43:2 (Spring 1989), pp. 323–347.

Governing Global Finance

Ethan B. Kapstein

EVERY AGE HAS its defining phrases, and globalization is surely one of ours. Increasingly, we are told, industries of all kinds are losing their national identity as they roam the planet for capital, markets, labor, and technology.[1] With this international expansion, the ability of states to control domestic economic activity has eroded, and sovereignty is undermined. Economist Charles Kindleberger took these developments to their logical extreme when he asserted in 1969 that "the nation-state is just about through as an economic unit."[2]

This tension between states and international markets is hardly of postwar vintage. Writing in 1939, a professor at the Fletcher School of Law and Diplomacy, Eugene Staley, asserted that "fundamental technological changes are pushing mankind in the direction of world-wide economic integration and interdependence, but . . . political tendencies . . . have strongly resisted that trend." He called for "the creation of a permanent International Economic Organization in which economic groups as well as governments would be represented" as a first step toward ameliorating relations between states and international markets.[3]

Thirty years later, Richard Cooper renewed interest in the conflicts between nation-states and the international economy with his classic work, *The Economics of Interdependence*.[4] Cooper argued that states were finding it difficult to strike a balance between increasing economic interdependence on the one hand and the pursuit of legitimate national objectives on the other. He concluded that the achievement of domestic goals in an international economy would require increased policy coordination among the major industrial powers.

Today, the state remains remarkably resilient in the face of powerful international economic forces. In this article I argue that states have responded to economic globalization through the expansion of international cooperation. Ironically, this cooperation rests on the bedrock of home country control. Rather than look to some supranational or multilateral entity to supervise global economic activity, states have taken it upon themselves to identify their national firms and to regulate them. If they are unable to do so, their firms are generally not permitted by international agreements to operate beyond national boundaries. Overall, I label the state response to globalization one of "international cooperation based on home country control."

Ethan B. Kapstein is codirector of the Economics and National Security Program at the John M. Olin Institute for Strategic Studies at Harvard University. A former international banker, he has written widely in the field of international political economy.

Copyright © 1994 by The Center for Strategic and International Studies and the Massachusetts Institute of Technology

In what follows I focus on the case of international banking, for no sector of the economy is more global in its orientation and operations. If I can show that states have created a political structure with which to supervise international banks, it is likely that they have responded to the challenges posed by other economic sectors as well. In short, banking would seem to provide a "hard case" for those of us who continue to view nation-states as the most important actors in the world economy.

The Globalization of Financial Markets

The globalization of financial markets dates back to the 1970s. Unlike previous postwar decades, the 1970s were characterized by a unique combination of inflation, floating and erratic exchange rates, and volatile interest rates. The major commercial banks in the industrial countries responded to these shocks in three prominent ways: innovation of financial practices and instruments; speculation in financial markets; and globalization of assets and liabilities. These responses were further encouraged by widespread financial deregulation throughout the Western world.

The data suggest the extent to which banking has gone global since that time. International bank lending grew from $40 billion in 1975 to well over $300 billion by 1990, while bond lending rose almost tenfold, from $19 billion to over $170 billion, during the same period.[5] Banks have placed branches throughout the world, and many now earn the bulk of their earnings outside their home country. By 1990, London was host to over 500 foreign banks, which held over 87 percent of the international assets booked in the City.[6] The capitalization of foreign stock exchanges also grew dramatically during this decade and a half, with major markets emerging in Tokyo, London, Paris, and Frankfurt; in 1992, the United States accounted for only 35 percent of all stock market capitalization.[7]

Further, with the liberalization of capital flows in the 1970s and 1980s, transfers of funds from one market to another became virtually unregulated. These transfers were the creatures of investors and the private sector and responded solely to the profit motive. Allen Myerson of the *New York Times* emphasized this point when he asserted that "The world's currency markets . . . are no longer governed by central bankers in Washington and Bonn, but by traders and investors in Tokyo, London and New York."[8]

The technological processes that have spawned these markets and sustained their operations were also apparently beyond state control (although it should be recalled that technological change itself has been consistently encouraged by capitalist states).[9] In many accounts of financial globalization, pride of place has been given to the "technological revolution," which made the growing sophistication of the marketplace a function of bringing to the banking sector the latest in information technology, including telecommunications and computers.[10] According to one scholar, "one of the basic forces behind recent global financial evolution is technological change. Underlying the revolution in global finance is a revolution in communications and information processing which if anything may accelerate over time."[11] Indeed, according to Michael Dertouzos of MIT, "There are so many [computer] networks and subnetworks. . . . It could mean that there is no longer any meaning to international boundaries."[12]

This confluence of increasing interdependence, the expansion of international banks, and technological change—in short, the globalization of finance—poses not just a major policy challenge to public officials, but also an analytical challenge to students of international economic relations. It suggests that traditional approaches to analyzing the international political economy are missing a large chunk of contemporary reality and must be revised or, perhaps, tossed into the dustbin of history. If the state is losing control of its economic borders, and if firms are losing their national identity, then maybe we do need, as John Gerard Ruggie has asserted, a "postmodern" vocabulary for describing the contemporary international economic system.[13]

One way of countering this assertion would be to deny the fact of globalization, or to minimize its importance. After all, Janice Thomson and Stephen Krasner remind us that "Challenges to state-centric paradigms are nothing new in the study of international affairs." They demonstrate that the international microeconomic changes of the postwar world have been deeply embedded in political macroprocesses. Regarding the global economy, to the extent that international integration has occurred (and by some measures the level of interdependence today among the major industrial nations is *lower* than it was at the turn of the twentieth century; for Western economies, trade as a percentage of gross national product has risen somewhat since 1913, but foreign investment as a share of GNP has fallen dramatically),[14] it has been a consequence of political decisions taken by the United States and other industrial powers at the end of World War II.

My approach, however, is somewhat different from those just described. Unlike Thomson and Krasner, I take seriously the challenges that changes in the international economy have posed for nation-states; unlike Ruggie, I do not believe we need a postmodern vocabulary for describing those challenges or the state response to them. To be sure, I accept the proposition that states have created the political conditions that have made globalization possible. But having said that, I would also agree that the promotion of economic change has had unintended consequences for those who have promoted it, creating a fresh set of problems that could not have been accurately predicted by policymakers.[15]

For nation-states, financial globalization has complicated the formulation of both economic and foreign policy; indeed, it has largely eradicated the distinction between the two. First, on the economic side, public officials have discovered that it has become increasingly costly to defend economic policies against market pressures, given the unimpeded flow of international financial transactions. Such policies are immediately translated by foreign exchange traders into currency valuations, and consequently into a money flight into or out of the country. Several European states—notably Britain—were reminded of this lesson during 1992 and 1993, when the pound sterling (among other currencies) was battered by the financial markets and ultimately forced to leave the Exchange Rate Mechanism (ERM) of the European Community (EC). These developments, in turn, created severe tensions in the Community after the summit at Maastricht, particularly between Germany and Britain.[16]

Second, domestic financial systems can no longer be sheltered against the collapse of international banks or foreign stock exchanges, as graphically illustrated by the developing world debt crisis of the 1980s and the October 1987 stock market crash that began in New York and then quickly spread overseas. Wall Street economist Henry Kaufman has observed that the major disruptions to financial markets "have come repeatedly on the international side in the past 20 years."[17] In the regulatory arena, states have found that they can only achieve their domestic objective of maintaining a safe and sound financial system through information sharing and policy coordination with other countries; in short, through international cooperation.

Concomitantly, the ability of states to use multinational corporations, including international banks, for the promotion of political ends has seemingly eroded. Now that these enterprises stand at the hub of the world's trade and investment networks, they have become less responsive to their national authorities; indeed, according to some observers, they no longer possess a national identity at all. Robert Reich brilliantly captured this insight with his question, "Who is Us?"[18] Reich asserted that large corporations take a global—as opposed to national—view in searching for markets, employees, and new technology, and as a result their national identity no longer matters to them.

States have responded to the political and economic challenges of financial globalization, I argue, by promoting *international cooperation based on home country control*.[19] As noted above, states that wish to enjoy the benefits of an open economy while protecting their national financial institutions from systemic shocks have found it necessary to develop an array of cooperative arrangements. Cooperation with respect to international banking has evolved since 1974 from the founding of a bank supervisors' committee by the Group of Ten (G-10) industrial countries (the so-called Basle Committee), to the convening of annual meetings and "summer schools" of bank regulators, to the articulation of internationally accepted principles and rules of banking supervision.[20] The effect of this cooperation has been to promote policy convergence among the major industrial nations with respect to banking regulation, and in some cases—such as the Basle Accord on bank capital adequacy, which is discussed in greater detail below—it has resulted in the development of uniform standards that all international banks must meet.[21] Nonetheless, I also argue that international cooperation remains far from complete, and tensions among states with respect to banking supervision remain.

International cooperation among central bankers rests not on multilateral or supranational agreements, however, but on home country control. Home country control refers to a model of governance in which the responsibility for defining national financial institutions (that is, for determining "who is us?" or which firms are headquartered in the home country) and regulating them is placed on the state. Under home country supervision, states look to one another, as opposed to some supranational or multilateral entity, to legislate and enforce any agreements that have been collectively reached. As a result, the linkages between states and their national banks have not been broken by globalization, and in some respects they have even been strengthened.

The Politics of International Cooperation

This article is concerned with the actions that states have taken to cope with the economic and political consequences of globalization. In framing a policy response, public officials must face both systemic and domestic constraints; that is, they must confront both the international system and their own societies as they fashion public policies.[22] Systemic constraints are posed by the relative position of the state in the international system. Weak states are generally less capable of influencing international outcomes than great powers, and in the case of banking, powerful states are those, like Britain, Germany, Japan, and the United States, that possess large and dynamic financial markets; the sources of power lie in their ability to provide international lender of last resort services to the financial system, to grant market access to financial institutions, or, alternatively, to threaten closure. To be sure, as the monopoly supplier of the world's reserve currency, and as home to the world's largest financial marketplace, the United States holds a unique position in the international monetary and payments systems, with a singular ability to set the global agenda and advance its preferences.

Yet there are limits even to the exercise of American power, and these are imposed not only by other states like Japan and Germany, but by domestic political actors as well. Indeed, any account of national policy making in the world economy would be incomplete without reference to domestic politics.[23] In conceptualizing domestic politics, I argue that the ability of societal actors, like banks, to influence state policies depends in large measure upon the formal and informal institutional networks that bind them to the central authorities.[24] This perspective reveals that banks are uniquely situated in the domestic political economy in this respect because of their roles and responsibilities in money creation, the granting of credit, and the harboring of household savings. Banks are able to draw on a set of formal, institutional linkages to public officials in voicing their concerns and policy preferences (although it should be noted that financial actors do not always speak with one voice), because every nation-state possesses regulatory structures that link banks with supervisory and monetary authorities. In the United States, for example, representatives of commercial banks serve among the directors of the Federal Reserve banks in each district, giving them a voice in both monetary and regulatory policies; the "mom and pop" store on the corner, in contrast, lacks such a voice when it comes to financial policies. Raymond Vernon has labeled the relationship that links organized business interests and government one of "constrained capture."[25]

As Vernon's phrase suggests, it has long been recognized that regulators respond to the industries they supervise. Indeed, the traditional view in economic theory is that the regulators have, ironically, been captured by their industry. In George Stigler's famous phrase, "regulation is acquired by the industry and is designed and operated primarily for its benefit."[26]

Subsequent analysis has suggested that the story is more complicated than that. According to Sam Peltzman, Stigler's colleague at the University of Chicago, regulators are bureaucrats who are seeking to resolve conflicting public and private sector interests in such a way as to enhance their own power within the domestic political system. This, in turn, leads to some policy outcomes that appear inconsistent.[27] Central bankers, for example, are concerned with maintaining a safe and sound financial system, but they have also been forced by societal actors to accept policies, like prohibitions on interstate banking, that appear to be at odds with that objective. The success of banking supervisors in maintaining or enhancing their power in the political system will ultimately be a function of their ability to solve the complex regulatory challenges with which they are confronted.[28]

To illustrate the Janus-faced nature of public officials (including central bankers and banking supervisors), who must look to domestic politics on the one side and international politics on the other, and the contending pressures acting upon them, let us briefly examine the Basle Accord on bank capital adequacy, which had its origins in the regulatory response to the debt crisis of the 1980s.[29] The Basle Accord would, on its face, seem to be of rather limited interest to students of international economic relations, given its narrow and technical focus. Yet it provides powerful illumination for seeing the response of both public officials and bankers to financial globalization.

In early 1983, as part of its debt management strategy, the Reagan administration went to Congress to seek an increase in the U.S. contribution to the International Monetary Fund (IMF). The request was not greeted warmly. As Senator Jake Garn (R–Utah) responded, "There will be legislation. . . . The price of $8.4 billion in the Congress is going to be legislation . . . so we can go home and say we didn't bail out the big banks."[30]

The Congress demanded that the bank supervisors report back to them with a new package of regulations. Among the new regulations, the authorities called on those international banks with heavy exposure to the developing world to increase their capital-to-assets ratio. This seemed entirely reasonable, given the nature of the risks that the banks then faced.

But in the hearings that followed, the banks warned that unilateral regulations would place them at a competitive disadvantage in the international marketplace. Japanese and French banks, for example, had much lower capital requirements than did the Americans, making it possible for them to offer lower prices on their services and thus win market share. As Representative Charles Schumer (D–N.Y.) stated, "we cannot put our banks at a competitive disadvantage to German, Japanese, or other banks."[31]

The bankers' pleas created a dilemma for Congress. Its members felt strongly that U.S. bank capital levels should be raised, but they wanted to encourage foreign banks to do the same. Congressmen were certainly concerned about the safety and soundness of the international financial system, but they were also paid to worry about competitiveness and American jobs. The obvious solution to this dilemma was to promote international convergence of banking regulations, especially with respect to capital adequacy, and Paul Volcker was requested to cajole his fellow central bankers into accepting common capital standards.

Volcker dutifully went to Basle and made the congressionally inspired pitch, but his colleagues' collective response was one of shock. How could the industrial countries formulate a single capital adequacy standard for their international banks, given the differences in banking, legal, and accounting structures? German banks, for example, had a "universal" banking structure that combined investment and commercial banking, while American financial institutions were segmented. The notion of an international standard was thus summarily rejected, and Volcker hoped that the issue would simply disappear.

But fate conspired against him. In May 1984, the eighth largest bank in the United States, Continental Illinois, required a $6 billion infusion from the Federal Reserve system in order to meet its financial obligations. In the aftermath of this crisis, Congress again called upon the regulators to tighten capital standards.

This time, the Federal Reserve responded by developing a new capital adequacy standard, drawn largely from the types already in use in Western Europe. This was a "risk-weighted" standard that tied capital requirements to the riskiness of the bank's portfolio. In January 1986, the Federal Reserve requested American banks to provide balance sheet statements on the basis of risk-weighted calculations.

But as before, the bankers protested this unilateral attempt to raise their capital levels. They said that they would lose their ability to compete internationally because the major commercial banks in other countries usually had lower capital requirements. Thus, the Federal Reserve found itself exactly where it had been during the IMF hearings in 1983.

Realizing that a multilateral approach was again doomed, Volcker traversed the Atlantic to London, where he met with the governor of the Bank of England, Robin Leigh-Pemberton. The Federal Reserve had borrowed from the British in developing its new capital adequacy standard. Volcker therefore proposed that the two countries ally to articulate a "US/UK" accord, with both countries agreeing to have a single measure of capital adequacy that would apply to their respective international banks. This would have the effect of bringing the two largest financial centers in the world into a single standard, and over time other countries might accept the US/UK rule as well. The US/UK Accord was announced in January 1987.

Once more, however, the bankers expressed their displeasure. An agreement between London and Washington went part of the way in alleviating their concerns about international competitiveness, but where were Germany, Japan, and France in the agreement? Until all the major players were involved, the U.S. bankers would continue to fight the agreement through direct lobbying at the Federal Reserve and indirectly through Congress.

As a next step, the Bank of England and Federal Reserve pressured Japan into accepting the agreement. The tacit threat made was that Japanese financial firms would lose access to the U.S. and British markets if they did not accede, and at this time the Federal Reserve had on its desk several applications from Japanese firms for expanding their operations in the United States. Eventually, Tokyo joined on, although important modifications were made to the US/UK Accord in the process.

By 1987, the remaining members of the Basle Committee recognized that they were faced with a fait accompli. Now that Tokyo, London, and Washington were committed to a single capital adequacy standard, the weaker financial powers would have no choice but to sign on. Again, a period of intensive negotiation followed, but on December 10, 1987, the Basle Committee announced that its members had reached agreement on a proposal for "international convergence of capital measurements and capital standards." The Basle Accord represented the most far-reaching international agreement among banking supervisors ever achieved.

The Basle Accord powerfully illustrates how domestic and international politics converged to create a demand for cooperation among central bankers. The need to balance concerns over safety and soundness with those of competitiveness presented public officials with an obvious dilemma. In a global economy, both sets of concerns had to take into account the actions of foreign governments and enterprises, and no satisfactory solution could be reached in the absence of international agreements.

Why Home Country Control?

It must be emphasized that international agreements, like the Basle Accord, ultimately rest on home country control. That is, the capital adequacy of financial institutions is not monitored by the Basle Committee, the IMF, or other multilateral organization, but by national regulatory authorities. To be sure, it seems counterintuitive on first glance that home country control would be maintained, much less strengthened, in a world of global finance, but a deeper understanding of the issue reveals its logic.

First, as finance has globalized, states have seen an increasing number of foreign banks settle on their territory. This forces the national authorities to ask whether or not they wish to provide discount window and lender of last resort services to these foreign banks. In those cases where banking operations are being conducted out of branch offices, with the headquarters clearly based overseas, the answer is "no"; they would usually prefer that the banks' own national supervisors provide emergency assistance.

Second, home country control forces states to take responsibility for the enforcement of those regulatory standards, like capital adequacy, that are adopted domestically or in international forums. In the absence of a supranational central bank or regulatory agency with enforcement powers, only state authorities can punish banks for improper behavior and force them to conform to domestic and international norms. By demanding home country control of one another, states are seeking to ensure that regulatory agreements are enforced. The tacit threat that states are making to one another is that, in the absence of such enforcement, the national banks of that country will not be permitted to operate overseas.

Third, to the extent that central authorities seek to use national firms for the advancement of broad domestic and foreign policy interests, they will wish to maintain control over these institutions. Money is a critical power resource in both domestic and international politics, and money is usually intermediated by financial institutions. Control over the flow of funds, in the form of targeted loans or loan guarantee programs, for example, is an important tool of "economic statecraft."[32]

From the perspective of firms and other societal actors, home country supervision also has its advantages. Only the state can defend corporate interests in international negotiations over trade, investment, and market access.[33] Agreements over such things as the opening of banking establishments and the right to sell insurance are not decided by corporate actors; they are determined by diplomats and bureaucrats. Further, given complaints in recent years, especially in Western Europe, over the "democratic deficit" that occurs when international institutions assume the tasks once reserved for national governments, home country control ensures that domestic political actors will continue to have a voice in policy deliberations; in this regard home country control may be linked to the political demand for "subsidiarity," namely, for decision making to devolve to the lowest possible political level.[34]

Yet home country supervision also leaves critical problems of financial governance unresolved, and these may be called the problems of control, capability, and competitiveness. First, despite the emphasis placed on home country supervision, countries continue to disagree over the appropriate division of responsibility between home and the host states when it comes to regulating international business. In the EC, recent banking legislation has diminished the authority of the host; in the United States, especially following the BCCI scandal, the opposite has occurred. This conflict about where the dividing line should be drawn between home and host countries continues to animate international negotiations over banking regulation, just as it has troubled all efforts to regulate multinational business.[35]

Second, home country control does not address the fact that different states have differing capabilities when it comes to international banking regulation; some states are more capable than others. Greece and Luxembourg have fewer resources than France and Britain when it comes to regulating complex financial institutions, and if this is the case it suggests that not all home countries will be regarded with equal confidence. In the EC particularly, the differing capabilities of the member states may cause problems for regulators in host countries.

Finally, home country supervision, as we have seen, has competitive consequences for national firms that operate in the global economy. If state A imposes a set of unilateral regulations on its national firms, the less regulated firms in state B may gain a competitive advantage. One implication of this development is that firms have called upon state actors to level the playing field in the regulatory arena. This, in turn, has reinforced the need for international cooperation among banking supervisors. Still, in the absence of complete harmonization, differing regulations will continue to have competitive effects.

In sum, international cooperation based on home country control represents the political structure that states have built to provide global finance with a framework in which to operate. The structure may be shaky, but thus far it has withstood some powerful shocks, most notably the debt crisis of the 1980s. More to the point, one must ask whether markets—global or not—can operate at all in the absence of such political frameworks. Clearly, the answer of this author is a resounding "no."

Conclusion

This article has presented an argument concerning the state's response to globalization. Unlike many contemporary scholars and journalists, I do not believe that the world economy now operates in some "extranational" realm, beyond the nation-state. On the contrary, international trade and investment flows have multiplied because nation-states have seen these trends as being in their economic and political interests. Indeed, states have even cooperated in order to provide the global economy with some regulatory structures. In the absence of these structures, international competition might produce outcomes that are in nobody's interest.

This is not to say that economic globalization has been without cost for public officials. As I have shown, the challenge for bank supervisors has been to strike a balance between conflicting systemic and domestic demands, and in so doing they have hit upon the formula of international cooperation based on home country control. To be sure, that formula represents only an imperfect response to the challenges posed by international finance, but in a world of nation-states complete policy convergence is unlikely to obtain. So long as central banks have a national as opposed to supranational character, home country control will remain the cornerstone for any international regulation.

This article is drawn from the author's forthcoming book, Governing the Global Economy: International Finance and the State *(Cambridge, Mass.: Harvard University Press, 1994).*

Notes

1. See, for example, Robert Reich, "Who is Us?" *Harvard Business Review* 68 (January–February 1990).
2. Cited in Andrew Walter, *World Power and World Money* (Hemel Hempstead, Herts., England: Harvester Wheatsheaf, 1991), p. 12.
3. Eugene Staley, *World Economy in Transition* (New York, N.Y.: Council on Foreign Relations, 1939), p. vii.
4. Richard N. Cooper, *The Economics of Interdependence* (New York, N.Y.: McGraw-Hill, 1968).
5. Walter, *World Power and World Money*, p. 198.
6. Organization for Economic Cooperation and Development, *Banks Under Stress* (Paris: OECD, 1992), p. 119.
7. Linda Corman, "Lands of Opportunity," *Fidelity Focus* (Fall 1992), p. 9.
8. Allen Myerson, "Turmoil in the Currency Markets," *New York Times*, September 17, 1992, p. D–1.
9. See Janice Thomson and Stephen D. Krasner, "Global Transactions and the Consolidation of Sovereignty," in Robert Art and Robert Jervis, eds., *International Politics* (New York, N.Y.: HarperCollins, 1992), p. 310.
10. See, for example, Walter Wriston, *The Twilight of Sovereignty: How the Information Revolution Is Transforming Our World* (New York, N.Y.: Scribners, 1992).
11. Walter, *World Power and World Money*, p. 201.
12. Quoted in Charles Radin, "US Data Highway Gathers Speed," *Boston Globe*, December 26, 1992, p. 10.
13. For an articulation of this view, see John Gerard Ruggie, "Territoriality and Beyond: Problematizing Modernity in International Relations," *International Organization* 47 (Winter 1993), pp. 139–174.
14. Thomson and Krasner, "Global Transactions," p. 310.
15. For a classic account of this issue with respect to the nineteenth century, see Karl Polanyi, *The Great Transformation* (Boston, Mass.: Beacon Press, 1944). In the modern world, a simple example is provided by the rise of Japan and the economic challenge it poses for the United States; such a challenge was, of course, unthinkable during the late 1940s and early 1950s.
16. During summer 1993 a Deutsche Bundesbank memo critical of British economic policy leaked to the press, and the British government responded sharply.
17. Henry Kaufman, "Fundamental Precepts Guiding Future Financial Regulation" (Talk delivered before the International Organization of Securities Commissions, London, U.K., October 27, 1992).
18. Reich, "Who is Us?"
19. For an academic treatment of international cooperation, see Robert Keohane, *After Hegemony* (Princeton, N.J.: Princeton University Press, 1984).

20. For a review of these interactions, see Peter C. Hayward, "Prospects for International Cooperation by Bank Supervisors," *The International Lawyer* 24 (Fall 1990), pp. 787–801.

21. See Ethan B. Kapstein, "Supervising International Banks: Origins and Implications of the Basle Accord," *Princeton Essays in International Finance* 185 (December 1991).

22. Robert Putnam examines this issue in terms of a "two-level game." See Putnam, "Diplomacy and Domestic Politics: The Logic of Two-Level Games," *International Organization* 42 (Summer 1988), pp. 427–460. For a study that uses two-level games in the international banking issue-area, see Glenn Tobin, "Global Money Rules" (Ph.D. diss., Harvard University, 1991).

23. There is a rich literature on this topic. See, for example, Stephen D. Krasner, *Defending the National Interest* (Princeton, N.J.: Princeton University Press, 1978).

24. For a good summary of the institutionalist perspective, see G. John Ikenberry, "Conclusion: An Institutional Approach to American Foreign Economic Policy," *International Organization* 42 (Winter 1988), pp. 219–243.

25. Raymond Vernon, personal communication, February 26, 1993.

26. Cited in James Q. Wilson, *The Politics of Regulation* (New York, N.Y.: Basic Books, 1980), p. 358.

27. Sam Peltzman, "Toward a More General Theory of Regulation," *Journal of Law and Economics* 19 (August 1976), pp. 211–240.

28. Some observers, however, believe that central banks should *not* play a regulatory role, owing to the capture problem. Should they be viewed as captured actors, they could no longer claim "independence." See "A Central Bankers' Charter," *Economist*, October 10, 1992, pp. 16–17.

29. This section draws on Kapstein, "Supervising International Banks."

30. *Ibid.*, p. 12.

31. *Ibid.*, p. 13.

32. See David Baldwin, *Economic Statecraft* (Princeton, N.J.: Princeton University Press, 1985).

33. See "The Global Firm: R.I.P.," *Economist*, February 6, 1993, p. 69.

34. For a good introduction to these debates, see *Economist*, "An Expanding Universe," July 7–13, 1990; this served as the magazine's annual survey of the European Community.

35. See Raymond Vernon, *Sovereignty at Bay* (New York, N.Y.: Basic Books, 1971).

Reengineering Regulation: Maintaining the Competitiveness of the U.S. Capital Markets

J. Carter Beese, Jr.

THROUGH MOST OF the twentieth century, U.S. companies have succeeded in creating highly structured organizations, developing and refining the art of mass production. These organizations were ideally suited to the economic environment of the era after World War II. Giants like Ford and General Electric fed an insular and hungry customer base that had a seemingly unrelenting appetite, starved by the Great Depression and the war.

More recently, however, the environment in which these companies operate has turned upside down. As Michael Hammer and James Champy note in *Reengineering the Corporation:*

> Advanced technologies, the disappearance of boundaries between national markets, and the altered expectations of customers have combined to make the goals, methods, and basic organizing principles of the American corporation sadly obsolete.[1]

With customers no longer in fragmented markets, inefficiencies once tolerated can no longer be ignored. Companies that are unable to respond quickly to changing market demands and deliver quality products at reasonable prices face eroding market share as savvy consumers choose the "better mousetrap" from a wide range of international providers.

For corporations to remain successful, Hammer and Champy prescribe nothing short of a complete redesign of processes, organization, and culture. Management must rethink its activities from end to end, focusing on the processes that create value for the customer.

An examination of the U.S. capital markets reveals that many similar forces identified by Hammer and Champy are at work. These markets have developed a well-deserved reputation for fairness, depth, and liquidity that has attracted investment capital from at home and abroad. In the process, they have provided the fuel for

---

J. Carter Beese, Jr., is vice chairman of Alex. Brown International and a senior adviser at CSIS, where he is chairman of the CSIS Capital Markets Regulatory Reform Project. From March 1992 to November 1994, he served as a commissioner of the SEC.

Copyright © 1995 by The Center for Strategic and International Studies and the Massachusetts Institute of Technology
The Washington Quarterly • 18:4

the country's explosive economic growth throughout the post–World War II era.

With the twenty-first century approaching, however, the preeminence of the U.S. capital markets is no longer assured. The forces of technological change, international competition, and more demanding consumers have combined to create a global marketplace for capital in which the U.S. market now competes. Today, issuers and investors are free to conduct their business in virtually any corner of the globe, and they are doing so. Moreover, they are able increasingly to circumvent national boundaries and regulations through financial engineering, using derivatives to create synthetic exposure in virtually any market.

These developments significantly complicate the task of capital markets regulators. In a world where capital knows no boundaries, Darwin's law of survival of the fittest applies. The cost and quality of regulation have become competitive factors. Where investor protection is provided in an efficient and cost-effective manner without overly burdening issuers, markets will thrive. Where excessive regulatory burdens impose unnecessary barriers to the capital formation process, however, markets will wither.

If the U.S. capital markets are to meet this challenge and remain preeminent in the world, the regulatory system underpinning them must undergo its own exercise in reengineering—a top to bottom reexamination with a focus on creating value for the issuers and investors who serve as its consumers. The Securities and Exchange Commission (SEC) has been fortunate over its 60-year history to regulate captive markets that were relatively insensitive to regulatory expense. In this environment, the United States developed the highest quality regulatory system in the world, but also one that is high cost.

Going forward, cumbersome and overly costly regulation will no longer be an option. Only eliminating inefficiency and retooling the system for the modern marketplace can ensure that the U.S. markets will continue to provide the fuel for sustained economic growth.

This article examines the forces that are transforming the capital markets around the world. Focusing upon the impact of these changes on the regulatory process, it highlights the need for a fundamental review of capital markets regulation. It reviews some of the important steps that regulators have already taken to meet the challenge of the global marketplace and suggests other possible areas for more fundamental reform.

Background

Two hundred years ago, a group of bankers began meeting under the shade of a buttonwood tree on New York's Wall Street. In an effort to bring order and stability to their activities, the group signed an agreement binding themselves to certain regulations and restrictions in their dealings with one another. The resulting entity eventually became known as the New York Stock Exchange and the American capital markets were born.

Although today's markets trace their roots to the colonies, the regulatory system that surrounds them is much younger. Like most components of the American financial regulatory structure, the capital markets regulatory system and the SEC were created out of crisis—in this case, the abuses that led to the crash of 1929.

At that time, legislators and regulators could wield effectively monopoly power over the domestic markets. Securities activities respected national boundaries and activities. Activities that were perceived to be undesirable could be restricted with relative certainty. There was little threat that capital would move offshore or that exotic derivative products would be used to circumvent regulation. When Congress decided that banking and securities should be separated and the walls of the Glass–Steagall Act were erected, market participants had few choices. J. P. Morgan restricted its activities to banking while its investment bankers established Morgan Stanley & Co.

For decades, this environment enabled the SEC to respond quickly and effectively to problems as they arose. Take the case of rule 10b–5. In 1942, the SEC's main office (then in Philadelphia) received a call from the Boston regional office. The president of a company in Boston was buying up the stock of his company at $4 per share and telling people that the company was performing poorly. In fact, the company was doing quite well and was about to announce that earnings would quadruple in the next year.

The SEC staff looked at the securities statutes and regulations and decided that there was nothing that they could do about the problem. As a result, the staff members drafted a rule and took it to the Commission for a vote that very same day. Rule 10b–5, on which all of the Commission's subsequent insider trading cases have been based, was born.

Although often developed through ad hoc responses to particular issues, this regulatory regime has proven resilient. It has been successful in ensuring fairness in the markets and maintaining the confidence of investors. The proof is in the results. In 1992, over $950 billion was raised through securities offerings in the United States. In 1993, that figure topped $1 trillion. By way of comparison, only approximately $75 billion was raised through securities offerings in Japan in 1992.[2]

Changing Environment

Over the last decade, however, the same factors that have buffeted private industry have collectively worked to revolutionize the capital markets. Together, these forces have driven the globalization of the capital markets and eliminated the monopoly power of domestic regulators.[3]

Disappearance of Boundaries Between National Markets

The decade of the 1990s will doubtless be remembered as the decade of cross-border capital flows. In recent years, the world's markets have become more international with each passing day. Japanese investors purchase assets ranging from Rockefeller Center to U.S. Treasury bills. London hosts firms from Deutsche Bank to Internationale Nederlanden Groep. Both investors and issuers find the world increasingly at their feet, and neither has been shy about taking advantage.

Table 1 illustrates the growth in transactions by foreign investors in U.S. equity securities. In 1980, foreign purchases and sales of U.S. securities together amounted to slightly over $75 billion. Fourteen years later, in 1994, that figure topped $700 billion. Total foreign trading in U.S. equity securities has grown at a compounded annual rate of over 17 percent.

It is important to view these data in context. Although foreign trading in U.S. securities has grown significantly, the dollar volume of trading by all investors has grown during the period,

Table 1
Aggregate Foreign Purchases and Sales of Securities in the U.S. Markets

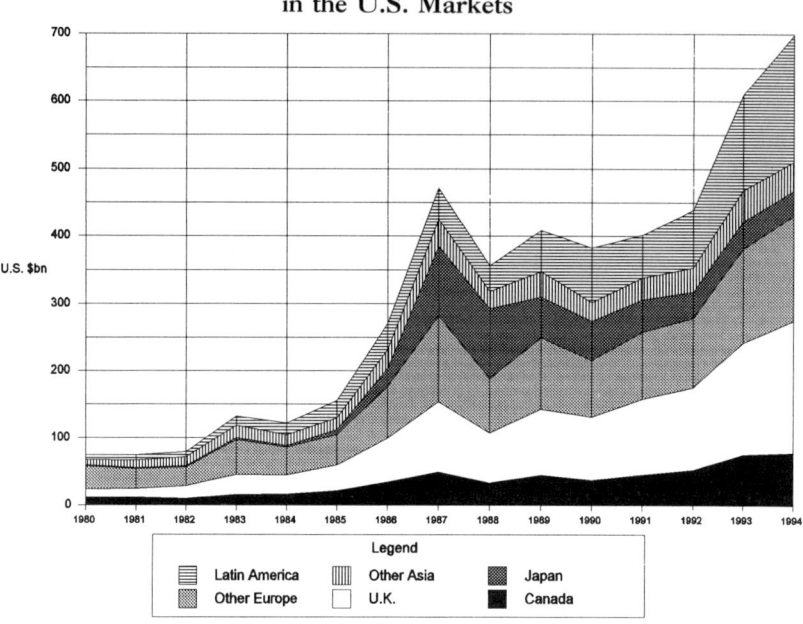

Source: U.S. Treasury Bulletin

albeit at a slower rate. Trading volume on the New York Stock Exchange has grown at a compound annual rate of 14.27 percent during the same period.[4]

Viewed over the last decade, however, the comparison is more dramatic. Since 1984, the volume of foreign trading in U.S. securities has risen at a compound annual rate of 18.95 percent, while New York Stock Exchange volume has grown 12.34 percent annually.[5] Foreign participation has outstripped domestic market growth by over 50 percent.

For their part, U.S. investors have shown a similar desire to participate in the globalization trend. Table 2 illustrates the growth in aggregate U.S. purchases and sales of securities in foreign markets. Fifteen years ago, that figure stood at $17.9 billion. By 1994, it had grown to over $850 billion. The compound annual growth rate for the period exceeded 30 percent.

Again, these data are not without limitations. Changes in exchange rates and particularly the decline in the dollar tend to overstate the extent of U.S. participation in foreign markets. Still, the rate of growth in U.S. participation has been most pronounced in the United Kingdom and the Latin American markets. Against the currencies of these countries, the dollar has actually retained much of its value or increased it in recent years.

The development of the emerging markets has played a major role in the globalization trend. Political and social changes in the last decade have com-

Table 2
Aggregate U.S. Purchases and Sales of Securities in Foreign Markets

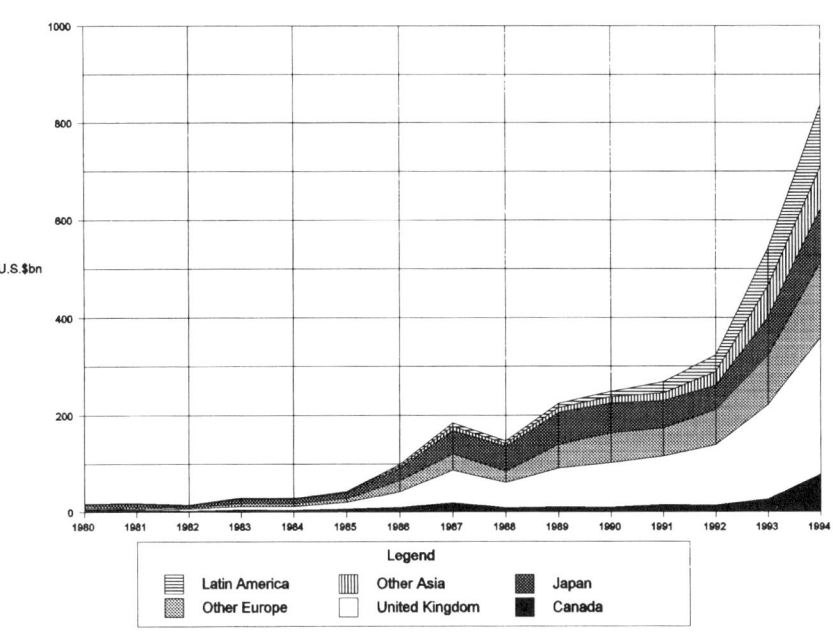

Source: U.S. Treasury Bulletin

bined to open markets from Eastern Europe to the Pacific Rim. The market capitalization of the 21 countries that make up the International Finance Corporation's composite emerging market index grew from $352 billion in 1988 to over $1.1 trillion in 1993. Another two dozen emerging markets in Eastern Europe and Africa have market capitalizations that now approach $75 billion.[6] By way of comparison, the total capitalization of all the stock markets in the industrialized countries has grown from $9.4 trillion to about $12.5 trillion in the same five-year period.[7]

As these new markets have grown, they have attracted considerable foreign investment. According to research by Barings Securities of London, net capital flows to developing country equity markets rose to $52 billion in 1993 from only $14 billion in 1992 and $1.3 billion five years ago. The developing countries also improved their access to the debt markets. In 1993, they were able to sell $84 billion of bonds in the international markets, approximately tripling the $28.6 billion sold in 1990.[8]

Adding momentum to the international trend are large issuers that face capital constraints in their home markets. In particular, the wave of privatizations currently taking place around the globe often exceeds the capital capacity of their home markets. Recently, the Argentine government sold nearly half of YPF, a state-owned oil and gas company. Of the $3 billion raised, only $400 million came from Argentine investors, with much of the rest being raised in the United States through American Depository Receipts.[9] Such enormous transactions require global offerings whereby individual tranches can be offered in multiple markets.

Private companies are also looking abroad for low-cost capital. Daimler Benz, which attracted headlines in 1993 with its listing on the New York Stock Exchange, is now listed on exchanges in eight countries—Germany, Switzerland, the United Kingdom, the United States, Japan, Austria, France, and, most recently, Singapore. Gerhard Liener, the company's chief financial officer, has stated that the company intends to have 5 percent of all of its shareholders in Asia by the year 2005 and would like to be the first foreign company listed on the Shanghai Exchange.[10]

Taken together, the evidence paints an accurate picture of a world in which capital flows freely around the globe. National boundaries that used to define markets are gradually losing their significance. Instead, investors and issuers alike have increasing freedom to chose from among an ever-widening range of opportunities from New York to Jakarta and Chicago to Singapore.

Advanced Technologies

Advances in technology have also played a pivotal role in revolutionizing the functioning of the world's capital markets. As computers and advanced telecommunications equipment have become available, the investment community has proven to be a huge customer. The head of CS First Boston recently estimated that the firm has spent over $800 million on technology in the last three years alone.[11] Likewise, the New York Stock Exchange has installed over $1 billion worth of new technology on its trading floor since 1985.[12]

The effect of modern technology is to make global investment possible. Telecommunications provides unprecedented access to distant markets. From an execution standpoint, portfolio and risk managers now allocate assets among markets at the stroke of a computer key. At the same time, news services and data transmission provide access to essential information from around the world on a real-time basis. It is no longer necessary to have a physical presence in a given area in order to monitor events that affect one's investment.

While telecommunications provides access and information, computer technology enables market participants to harness the information flow and take advantage of global opportunities. Managing complex portfolios and geographically dispersed investment exposure depends upon cutting-edge computer modeling. Dennis Weatherstone, former head of J. P. Morgan, demanded to be updated at each day's end on the institution's net global exposure in the numerous countries in which the company conducts business. Only through computer modeling could such reports ever be prepared.

Computer technology has also accelerated the pace of financial engineering and new product development, particularly in the area of derivatives. It is now possible to slice and dice cash flows along virtually any dimension. In the process, market participants easily circumvent national boundaries, taking or hedging exposure in a particular market or currency at times without ever crossing the borders of a particular market.

Altered Expectations of Customers

The third development transforming the capital markets is the ever-increasing sophistication of market participants. From the investors' perspective, a major trend in the United States over the last 20 years has been the growth of institutional investment through pension funds, mutual funds, and insurance companies. Between 1975 and 1993, the share of the U.S. equity market owned through mutual funds has more than doubled, from about 4 percent in 1975 to almost 11 percent in 1993. During the same period, the value of U.S. equity securities owned by private and public pension plans increased more than tenfold from $132 billion to $1.6 trillion. The present holdings of one of the nation's largest pension plans are almost equal to the amount that was held by all public pension plans collectively in 1975.[13] These institutions are able to seek out and evaluate the ever-widening range of global opportunities.

At the same time, advances in portfolio theory have helped to broaden investors' horizons. Volumes of research have proven that it is possible to reduce risk relative to return through portfolio diversification. Much of the attractiveness of global investing can be traced to these roots. In the past, a well-diversified portfolio consisted of stocks, bonds, and other domestic assets. Today, investors seek to add international exposure as they strive to reach the "efficient frontier" where return is maximized relative to a given level of risk.

The impact of these developments has been significant and continues to grow. According to InterSec Research Corporation, U.S. pension funds alone had $262 billion invested in non-U.S. equities in 1993, or 7.2 percent of their assets.[14] The group expects further diversification and projects that figure to grow to $630 billion, or 11.5 percent of total assets, by 1998.[15]

Adjusting to the New Environment

Together, technological change, internationalization, and more demanding consumers have thrust the U.S. capital markets into an intense global competition where their continued preeminence is hardly assured. Although the U.S. markets have increased significantly in absolute size, their percentage of the world's total equity market capitalization has dropped from approximately 90 percent to only about 30 percent. At the beginning of 1980, the U.S. equity market was four times larger than its nearest competitor. By 1994, that advantage had been more than halved.[16]

The decline has not thus far been detrimental. The competitive position of the U.S. markets following World War II was not sustainable, and certainly, some of the recent shift can be traced to the decline of the dollar. Moreover, positive market development overseas has helped to fuel global economic growth, particularly in the emerging market countries. The benefits of such development accrue to all nations around the world.

The days of regulating fragmented markets, however, are over. Today, investors seek out and choose among an ever-increasing range of international opportunities across the globe. If they do not desire to invest directly, derivative product specialists stand ready to create exposure synthetically in any market.[17]

In this international environment, the United States can no longer afford to adopt the perspective of the 1930s and regulate from its borders inward. Forcing market participants to accept overly costly regulations now runs the risk of driving capital overseas.

The flow of capital out of the United States and into the Eurobond market should be a warning to U.S. policymakers about the impact of excessive regulatory costs. In 1963, the United States instituted a 30 percent withholding tax on interest paid on bonds sold in the United States to foreign investors. In response, the market for dollar-denominated bonds for non-U.S. citizens moved from New York to London and the Eurobond market was born. Despite the subsequent repeal of the withholding tax, the market has largely remained overseas.[18]

In the future, regulation must add value in excess of its cost in order to attract and retain investment capital. The goal is not to engage in a regulatory "race to the bottom." Investors properly demand and value protections that promote liquidity, transparency, and fairness before they will put their hard-earned savings at risk. At the same time, however, a market that tends toward regulatory overreach will drive away issuers and create incentives for capital to move abroad. Thus, like the capital flows that it regulates, U.S. policy now more than ever needs to seek out the optimum risk-adjusted return.

Recent Developments

In recent years, the SEC has taken some significant steps to reduce excessive regulatory burden without compromising quality. These steps have proven successful in attracting overseas participation in the U.S. markets.

In 1990, recognizing the increasing role of sophisticated investors in the marketplace, the Commission adopted rule 144A. Pursuant to this rule, issuers can sell securities in the U.S. markets to certain investors without registering the offering with the SEC. The marketplace has developed a disclosure regime that is generally accepted for the purposes of rule 144A transactions, and this regime is much less rigid than the disclosure requirements prescribed by the SEC for full public offerings.

Operating in this less structured environment, the market for rule 144A offerings by foreign issuers has flourished. From the adoption of rule 144A in 1990 through the end of 1993, foreign issuers from 43 countries used the rule to sell their securities, particularly companies from Europe and Latin America. In total, 300 foreign issuers have used rule 144A to sell over $25 billion of securities.

More recently, the SEC has taken steps to streamline the registration process for foreign issuers. In April 1994, the SEC amended its rules so that more foreign issuers are eligible to use short form prospectuses and the shelf registration process. Also, several rule changes have been adopted to accommodate U.S. accounting standards to the needs of foreign issuers. The comprehensiveness of U.S. standards has been a significant entry barrier to foreign issuers seeking to tap the U.S. markets. New changes require foreign registrants to reconcile financial statements for only the two most recent fiscal years, and any interim periods, rather than five years as previously required. Likewise, cash-flow statements may be presented in accordance with International Accounting Standards and without reconciliation to GAAP. In December 1994, additional changes were adopted in areas such as reporting currency and accounting for hyperinflationary markets.

These efforts have borne fruit. In

spite of 1994 being a difficult year for public offerings in general, over 100 foreign issuers entered the U.S. capital markets for the first time. This represents a record for new listings. By year's end, there were 662 foreign reporting companies representing 40 countries listed on a U.S. exchange or quoted on NASDAQ, more foreign listings than in any other market.

More Sweeping Reform Is Needed

Looking to the future, more structural regulatory reform is essential if the U.S. markets are to remain competitive. During my tenure as an SEC commissioner, I became increasingly concerned regarding the lack of an overall blueprint for financial regulation. The traditional ad hoc approach to new issues is as costly as building a new house by change order.

The entire regulatory system would benefit from reexamination and a shift in focus toward weighing the costs, as well as the benefits, of regulation. Outlined below are examples of the types of issues that warrant attention. Ultimately, however, these and other discrete issues must be viewed in the context of a broader review that takes into account international competition, asking such fundamental questions as: Is there a sufficient governmental interest to warrant regulation? Do market forces adequately protect the integrity of the marketplace? In those instances where regulation is necessary, is the form and substance of the current regulatory regime the most cost-effective?

At the most general level, the legal structure that was put in place in the 1930s creates excessive redundancy and overlap. The laws that have set up barriers to prevent banks entering the securities markets and securities firms entering banking may have been a good idea in the 1930s. Today, the Glass–Steagall and Bank Holding Company Acts impose arbitrary barriers that stifle competition and innovation in the financial services industry and disadvantage U.S. institutions vis-à-vis their foreign competitors. In a marketplace where investors and issuers have their choice of a wide range of products across a wide range of markets, institutions that are artificially constrained to individual segments cannot possibly keep pace.

More specific efforts include steps to make the U.S. markets more attractive to foreign investors. One major step would be to eliminate the current disincentive in the tax code for foreign investors to invest in U.S. mutual funds.[19] U.S. tax laws now subject foreign investors in U.S. mutual funds to withholding taxes that are not imposed if the investor purchases securities directly or through a foreign fund. This tax provision has led the mutual fund industry to establish funds offshore to attract these investors. Foreign investment demand is therefore satisfied by U.S. funds and their foreign competitors in places like Bermuda and the Cayman Islands. Although the growth of offshore mutual funds has been impressive, these funds will never reach as wide an audience of foreign investors as would otherwise be possible because they lack the seal of approval provided by the U.S. regulatory system. The U.S. mutual fund industry has been free from major scandals and enjoys tremendous public confidence because of the commitment to investor protection shared by both the mutual fund complexes and their regulators. Unfortunately, the current tax laws inhibit the ability of U.S. mutual funds to utilize this advantage to attract foreign capital to the U.S. markets.

Likewise, there are measures that should be considered to eliminate disincentives for issuers to participate in the U.S. markets. Perhaps the most important is addressing the tremendous costs imposed on the U.S. capital markets by frivolous securities litigation.[20] Today, SEC oversight of the capital markets is supplemented by the right of private citizens to file securities fraud claims and to seek their own remedies. Although the private right of action is an important adjunct to SEC enforcement and is vital to maintaining investor confidence, the system has become unbalanced. One in eight firms on the New York Stock Exchange is sued for fraud every five years.[21] The total cost of class action securities suits has almost tripled from $529 million in 1989 to $1.4 billion in 1993. The threat of such litigation has become a major barrier to foreign issuers considering participation in the U.S markets.

At the root of the problem is an incentive structure that serves to encourage lawsuits, regardless of their merit, while discouraging resistance by companies that are falsely accused. Filing a suit involves minimal expense and little downside risk. The result is a veritable race to the courthouse whenever a company's stock price drops as lawyers vie for certification in a potential class action suit. At the same time, due to the expensive nature of the discovery process, the plaintiffs' (and their attorneys') incentive to sue is largely matched by the defendants' incentive to settle.

Addressing this problem requires addressing the imbalanced incentives currently in place. Serious consideration should be given to making plaintiffs responsible for the defendants' litigation costs in frivolous securities suits. Moreover, liability should be limited to an amount proportionate to the defendant's level of responsibility except in cases of intentional fraud. These changes would go a long way toward separating the meritorious cases from the frivolous, while at the same time safeguarding the right to sue for genuine wrongdoing.

Conclusion

In the aftermath of the Great Depression, the United States has developed the world's highest quality regulatory system, providing the underpinnings for the development of the deepest and most liquid markets in existence. The environment in which these markets operate, however, has fundamentally changed. International competition, technological change, and more demanding consumers are collectively working to erode the significance of national boundaries and create a global marketplace.

For business, these developments have required fundamental restructuring and reorientation toward creating value for the consumer. To quote again from *Reengineering the Corporation*, American business cannot survive by "entering the twenty-first century with companies designed during the nineteenth century to work well in the twentieth."[22]

For capital markets regulation, the challenge is similar. Much of the regulation administered or developed by the SEC and the nation's other fragmented financial regulatory agencies is a product of a different time and a different environment. Today, it is no longer feasible to approach regulation with a rear-view mirror. New market developments are at least as challenging today as they were in the 1930s. As a result, more than fine-tuning and ad hoc responses are needed. A functional approach to financial regulation that is both cost-effective and competitive in a world of global and cyber-markets should be our goal. Such a focus is essential for the United States to prevent significant erosion of its market share.

Notes

1. Michael Hammer and James Champy, *Reengineering the Corporation: A Manifesto for Business Revolution* (New York, N.Y.: HarperCollins Publishers, 1993), p. 11.
2. Testimony of SEC chairman Arthur Levitt before the Senate Committee on Banking, Housing, and Urban Affairs, September 28, 1994.
3. See Joseph A. Grundfest, "Internationalization of the World's Securities Markets: Economic Causes and Regulatory Consequences," *Journal of Financial Services Research* 4 (1990), pp. 349–378, which provides a thorough analysis of the forces transforming international capital markets.
4. *New York Stock Exchange Factbook* (1994).
5. *Ibid.*
6. Daniel F. Adams, "Financial Markets and World Economic Growth: Perspectives Towards the 21st Century" (Remarks at the 1994 Conference of the International Organization of Securities Commissioners, Tokyo, October 19, 1994).
7. David D. Hale, "Stock Markets in the New World Order," *Columbia Journal of World Business* 29 (June 1994), p. 14.
8. See *ibid.*, note 7.
9. "Plunging into Foreign Markets," *Economist*, September 17, 1994, p. 87.
10. Richard House, "A Question of Control," *Institutional Investor*, international ed., 20 (April 1, 1995), p. 36.
11. Allen D. Wheat, "Glass–Steagall Versus the Market: The Market Wins," *Investment Dealers Digest* 61 (supplement) (May 22, 1995), p. 21.
12. Philip Maher, "The New Wall Street: On to the Millennium," *Investment Dealers Digest* 61 (supplement) (May 22, 1995), p. 10.
13. Testimony of SEC chairman Arthur Levitt.
14. Caren Chesler, "Where the Investors Are: Anywhere but Close to Home," *Investment Dealers Digest* 61 (supplement) (May 22, 1995), p. 98.
15. A survey by Broadgate Consultants, Inc., in New York found that over 80 percent of institutional investors plan to increase their foreign equity portfolios over the next five years.
16. Securities and Exchange Commission, Division of Market Regulation, *Market 2000: An Examination of Current Equity Market Developments* (Washington, D.C., January 1994), exhibit 6.
17. See testimony of SEC commissioner J. Carter Beese, Jr., before the House Committee on Banking, Finance, and Urban Affairs, October 28, 1993, for detail regarding regulatory treatment of derivative products.
18. Merton H. Miller, *Financial Innovations and Market Volatility* (Cambridge, Mass.: Blackwell, 1991).
19. See J. Carter Beese, Jr., "Mutual Funds, The Next Great U.S. Export," *Wall Street Journal*, September 22, 1993, for analysis of mutual fund tax treatment.
20. For analysis of securities litigation reform, see testimony of J. Carter Beese, Jr., and the CSIS Capital Markets Regulatory Reform Project before the Subcommittee on Securities of the Senate Committee on Banking, Housing, and Urban Affairs, March 2, 1995.
21. Comments of Bill Ezzell in "CEO Litigation Roundtable," *Chief Executive Magazine*, January 1995, p. 18.
22. Hammer and Champy, *Reengineering the Corporation*, p. 30.

The Bundesbank: America's German Central Bank

W. R. Smyser

FEW AMERICANS PAID attention when Hans Tietmeyer became the president of the German Bundesbank in Frankfurt on October 1, 1993. A few newspapers and economic magazines carried brief reports of the event, but even they did not point out that Tietmeyer's appointment deserved the same attention as the appointment of a prominent American to a senior position.

They should have done so. For the Bundesbank has begun to have a deep and pervasive influence on the economy of the United States. It is now to all intents and purposes America's second central bank, a bank that is beginning to introduce conservative German economic philosophy into the workings of the U.S. economy.

One might not have come to that conclusion upon hearing or reading Tietmeyer's accession speech. He concentrated on the Bundesbank's primary responsibility for the German currency and the German economy. He stressed the bank's domestic German function above all others, although he noted that the bank also had to think about Europe as a whole.

But Tietmeyer's concentration on Germany should not have deluded his listeners. The financial world no longer draws a boundary between domestic and foreign economic policy. The two merge into each other and shape each other as global markets carry the effects of any country's domestic policies into the economies of other countries as well. This ever more powerful reality gives the policies of the Bundesbank a much wider arena than Germany itself, an arena that reaches well across the Atlantic.

Tietmeyer at first glance hardly seems like a man who carries such awesome responsibilities. He does not surround himself with a retinue of acolytes, courtiers, and hangers-on. His manner is courteous and even somewhat diffident. He smiles easily and warmly. It is not immediately apparent why traders would follow every move that he and the Bundesbank's *Zentralbankrat*, or Central Bank Council, make, or why they would sometimes describe his bank in terms that invoke the image of a grim reaper of global finance.

It is only when one hears Tietmeyer talk that one can begin to grasp his importance. Then it becomes evident that he is a man of profound, even unshakable conviction. He will place special and perhaps unconscious stress

---

W. R. Smyser is a Washington consultant in political economy and strategy. His most recent books are *The German Economy* (New York, N.Y.: St. Martin's Press, 1993), and *Germany and America* (Boulder, Colo.: Westview Press, 1993).

Copyright © 1994 by The Center for Strategic and International Studies and the Massachusetts Institute of Technology

on words like value, stability, predictability, or responsibility, words that to him obviously form an entire architecture of belief.

It is this conviction that sets Tietmeyer apart, especially from most Americans, and that gives him his influence. In a world of shoddy compromises, transient fads, and instantly gratifiable urges, Tietmeyer—like his colleagues—believes in eternal truths.

As president of the German Bundesbank, Hans Tietmeyer is in the best possible position to act upon his beliefs. The Bundesbank is now the dominant central bank of Europe and the anchor of the European Monetary System (EMS). The world must increasingly respect and follow its policies.

As the bank's president, Tietmeyer also has a strategic role and responsibility. Contrary to the situation during the Cold War, when military realities determined global strategy and dominated economic considerations, economic realities now determine national influence and shape the world. The Bundesbank's policies, although ostensibly confined to the monetary realm, can have as profound a strategic effect as one or another state's military policy used to have.

Tietmeyer and the Bundesbank thus deserve a longer look—to see what drives them, to understand the dominance they now exercise over Europe, and then to examine the growing influence that they have over the American economy and over the United States.

The Bundesbank in Germany

Tietmeyer does not act alone, although he is the president of the Bundesbank. He is only one member of the Central Bank Council. He must act within the laws and guidelines of the bank. But those laws and guidelines only reinforce his own convictions.

The Bundesbank has its own philosophy, rooted deeply in German history and in Germany's long-term needs. At the core of that philosophy lies a resolute determination to fight inflation, which the bank and most Germans regard as the most pernicious curse that can be visited upon a land.

The nightmare of the Bundesbank and of the German nation is the historical experience of the Great Inflation of 1923 that destroyed the German middle class and laid the foundations of social bitterness and ethnic hatred on which Adolf Hitler built his drive to power. The record of that inflation is best conveyed by showing changes in the exchange rate for the German mark against the U.S. dollar between 1914 and 1923 (see table 1).

It remains impossible, even 70 years after the event, to find a German who does not have either a direct personal

Table 1
U.S. Dollar Quotations for the Mark, July 1914 to November 15, 1923
(monthly averages)

July 1914	4.2
January 1919	8.9
July 1919	14.0
January 1920	64.8
July 1920	39.5
January 1921	64.9
July 1921	76.7
January 1922	191.8
July 1922	493.2
January 1923	17,972.0
July 1923	353,412.0
August 1923	4,620,455.0
September 1923	98,860,000.0
October 1923	25,260,308,000.0
November 15, 1923	4,200,000,000,000.0

Source: Gordon A. Craig, *Germany, 1866–1945* (Oxford: Clarendon Press, 1978), p. 450.

or a family recollection of the destruction wrought by that inflation. Germans speak of jobs, homes, or savings lost forever, of heirlooms that their families sold in a desperate attempt to recoup only to find that the money they had received had lost its worth within days. They speak of a lifetime's work wrecked in moments.

Germany again felt the ravages of inflation after the dark hour of capitulation and disgrace in 1945. Its currency was worthless. The standards of value and the means of exchange were cigarettes, nylon stockings, or Parker pens—the goods of the occupation and of the occupiers. To end this inflation, Ludwig Erhard, with the backing of the Western occupation forces, established the *Deutsche Mark*, the D-Mark, as the new currency in 1948, and the new Federal Republic created the Bundesbank in 1957.

A brooding sense of the fragility of value and a visceral fear of the kind of total loss that can destroy lives and families remain deeply ingrained in the German psyche even to this day. In the heart of every German, and especially in the heart of every Bundesbanker, lies the absolute determination not to let it happen again. They have made certain that the D-Mark has remained the most stable money in the world since its foundation 45 years ago, losing less of its value than any other major currency.

It would be a mistake, however, to attribute the loathing that the German people and the Bundesbank feel toward inflation only to those experiences. But those experiences have hammered home a solid German conviction regarding the fundamental principles that should guide economic policy.

The leaders of the Bundesbank believe that only stable prices will promote real well-being over the long run, and that holding prices steady must be the principal objective of any central bank. The members of the Central Bank Council fully recognize that this theory runs counter to many notions (such as Keynesianism) regarding the constructive role that flexible monetary and fiscal policy can play in smoothing out the business cycle and especially in stimulating growth at appropriate times. They will even use or condone such instruments briefly on occasion. But they hold fundamentally to their own theory, and they denounce alternative theories—as Tietmeyer himself has done—as "Anglo-Saxon siren songs."[1]

The Bundesbank believes that low inflation encourages much sounder growth than demand management and especially demand stimulation can achieve. Low inflation keeps long-term interest rates low (even as short-term rates may rise to slow down an economy that risks overheating). Low inflation helps to promote investment in productive facilities instead of in gold or other nonproductive assets. This is particularly true in Germany, where most financing is done on the basis of long-term bonds and bank loans, and where the Bundesbank's reputation has created a climate of expectations of low inflation.

One of the veteran members of the Bundesbank's directorate, Otmar Issing, reiterated the bank's long-standing philosophy on this matter to an American audience in late August 1992:

> The quintessence of the research conducted in the past few decades is that a lastingly high rate of economic growth cannot be achieved through large budget deficits and a passive monetary policy which tries to keep central bank [short-term] interest rates low. On the contrary, a disci-

plined fiscal policy which keeps government debt within narrow limits and a counter-inflationary policy are the decisive cornerstones of a successful economic policy geared to long-term objectives.[2]

The Germans also believe in the importance of foreign trade and foreign sales. In an inflationary global environment, a country that has stable prices will over the long run be more competitive than one that has not, even if the latter may gain some temporary advantage by devaluing. Sooner or later, whether through domestic pressures for wage and price increases or through disadvantageous shifts in their international terms of trade, other countries will face higher production costs, especially if they must (like the Germans) import most raw materials.

The notion is simple but it has been successful for most of German postwar history: take care of the value of money and prosperity will take care of itself.

To make certain that the members of the Central Bank Council of the Bundesbank have no doubts about their priorities, the *Gesetz über die Deutsche Bundesbank*, the law that established the bank in 1957, states categorically that the bank's mission is "the preservation of the value of the German currency." In fact, Tietmeyer will insist, and rightly so, that he is not the master but the servant of the Bundesbank, and that what matters are not his views or even those of the Central Bank Council but the awesome historical and political responsibility that has been conferred upon them to keep the German economy and polity on a safe and steady path.[3]

What is most striking about that council is that it is dominated by men who do not think that it is their primary task to direct the global economy, no matter what effect their decisions may have on others. Prior to German unification, the council consisted of the 11 heads of the banks of the separate German states (*Länder*) and the 7 Frankfurt-based members of the bank's directorate, giving the majority and effective control to those concerned with conditions internal to the German states instead of to those who might have had a wider perspective at the center of the bank's national and international operations.

By contrast, in the U.S. Federal Reserve the members of the Board of Governors can outvote the regional presidents in the Federal Open Market Committee (FOMC). That can lead to a situation, as for several years in the 1970s, where the Federal Reserve Board of Governors might permit an upsurge in inflation for what the Bundesbank would regard (and then regarded) as political reasons. This former Federal Reserve policy is still cited by many Germans as an example of ill-conceived monetary behavior based on short-term considerations, and it contributed to the establishment of the EMS (see below).

The state bank presidents have retained their power since German unification. Of the 17 members of united Germany's new Bundesbank council, only 8 can be from the directorate. The majority of 9 state bank presidents will keep the council firmly in their own hands, and they will in turn keep the council's decisions oriented primarily toward German stability.

The Bundesbank does not serve the political interests of the German government. It is more independent than most central banks, especially in Europe. In its independence it resembles the U.S. Federal Reserve, on which it was very closely modeled to avoid a recurrence of Hitler's domination of the Reichsbank during World War II.

Although Chancellor Helmut Kohl appointed Tietmeyer to the Bundesbank's council in 1991, and many observers have expected Tietmeyer to help Kohl win reelection in October 1994 by lowering short-term rates quickly to stimulate the German economy, Tietmeyer and his colleagues will base their decisions on economic conditions and not on political preferences. Former German chancellor Helmut Schmidt received his own lesson in Bundesbank political independence when Karl-Otto Pöhl, whom Schmidt had appointed to the presidency of the bank, followed policies that had the side effect of damaging Schmidt's own political fortunes.

The single most important event now shaping the Bundesbank's decisions is the high price of German unification. The German government has pursued policies that have not only raised production costs in eastern Germany but have also necessitated high subsidies from western Germany. It conducted the exchange of former East Marks for D-Marks at an unrealistic rate; it permitted the takeover of East German firms and institutions by West German firms more committed to promoting their own interests than to the rapid development of new production in eastern Germany; and it decided to sustain a number of uneconomic if traditional eastern German production lines for which there was no justification. The annual West-East transfers of government funds that these policies necessitated have run over DM 150 billion for several years, and they will probably remain at that level through much of the 1990s. The German government has run a huge public-sector budget deficit to cover those costs, preferring the economic risk of inflation to the political risk of raising taxes.

The Bundesbank has tried to counter the potential inflationary effects of this government policy by tightening credit, raising short-term interest rates, and taking other steps that put the German economy into a deep recession beginning in 1991. Nevertheless, inflation at the end of 1993 was still running at an unacceptable rate of almost 4 percent, money growth was almost 7 percent, and the budget deficit was not under effective control.

Under those circumstances, the Bundesbank has acted upon its obligations as it sees them. It has persisted in pursuing a policy of tight money to rein in a potentially escalating price spiral. Although it gradually began to relax its grip during the last six months of 1993, it remained sufficiently obdurate to prevent a resumption of German growth during that year. There is only a slight prospect of measurable German economic growth during 1994.

The Bundesbank in Europe

Bundesbank policies now reach well beyond Germany, however. Under the EMS, the D-Mark has become the lead currency of Europe, widening the bank's influence even as it widens the bank's responsibilities.

The two new European institutions that have given the Bundesbank its wider influence were those created in the late 1970s. They are the EMS itself and its Exchange Rate Mechanism (ERM). The former, which includes all the countries of the European Community (EC), is the basic structure for a European currency (the ecu, or European Currency Unit) and for European monetary cooperation. The latter, the ERM, is essentially a fixed exchange rate mechanism in which a number of EC members link their currencies to the ecu and to the D-Mark. Not all EMS members are in the ERM, largely because they have not been able to match the discipline of the D-Mark.

The EMS and ERM were established in order to give Europeans a monetary alternative to the dollar when U.S. policy stimulated inflation and the price of gold rose to $800 per troy ounce. President Valéry Giscard d'Estaing of France and Chancellor Helmut Schmidt of Germany, responding to an appeal by the president of the European Commission, Roy Jenkins, designed the EMS and won widespread acceptance for it from other governments. They wanted to create a stable continental currency within an unstable global system dominated by what they regarded as the self-serving Americans. In their view, the U.S. government was taking advantage of the dollar's status as a global currency in order to print cheapened dollars that other states and central banks would have to accept —whether they wanted to or not— because they needed dollars for their international transactions and for the purchase of commodities denominated in the U.S. currency.

Schmidt and Giscard d'Estaing concealed their plan from the Central Bank Council of the Bundesbank until it was close to realization because they knew that the council wanted to continue to concentrate all its energies on saving Germany from disaster and did not want to assume responsibility for managing European as well as German currency in a highly unstable international environment. The Bundesbank only agreed to the EMS because it saw no alternative. It remained very skeptical toward any European currency system during the early 1980s.

Over time, however, the Bundesbank began to accept the EMS and the ERM. It did so in part because the Central Bank Council became convinced that having such a system might become necessary to shelter Germany itself. It also did so because several European governments and central banks—most particularly the French—made clear that they would be prepared to emulate Bundesbank policies in order to help establish a climate of monetary responsibility across Europe no matter what happened in the United States. But the Bundesbank in turn made clear that it would not bend its standards, that it would only support a European currency system that established a truly solid currency, and that it would only accept as members of that system those that were prepared to guarantee domestic and continental monetary stability.

The EMS/ERM system was at first marked by repeated devaluations of other European currencies against the D-Mark. But these devaluations either ceased or became insignificant during the last half of the 1980s as the Bundesbank's anti-inflation policies became more widely appreciated and as a number of EC/EMS governments and central banks in France, Italy, and Spain proved willing and able to match the policies of the Bundesbank and to accept its discipline.

German policy has become so widely accepted that, when the EC decided in October 1993 to move toward European Monetary Union (EMU) and to establish a European Monetary Institute in January 1994 and a European Central Bank by the late 1990s, Frankfurt was chosen as the site for both those institutions.

With that choice, the Europeans essentially voted to convert their continent into a de facto realm of German monetary policy.

Monetary stability has not come without a price, however. When the Bundesbank raised German short-term interest rates sharply in reaction to the German government's unification policy, as noted above, the effect was felt throughout Europe because of the EMS and ERM. Other European central banks had to match the Bundesbank's higher interest rates if they wanted to keep their currencies aligned with the D-Mark.

This posed a particularly severe problem for some European countries, including France, Italy, and especially Britain, where a larger proportion of credit is financed with short-term rates than in Germany. Those countries do not benefit as much as Germany from the lower long-term rates that a firm anti-inflationary policy promotes, and they suffer more than Germany from the recessionary effects of higher short-term rates. The Bundesbank had been aware of the structural problem that the different credit patterns might generate for the EMS and ERM. That was one of the reasons the bank was reluctant to undertake European responsibilities. But the Bundesbank has not been able to find a way to adjust its policies to overcome that structural dilemma.[4]

As short-term interest rates rose throughout the ERM economies after 1990, West European growth began to slow significantly. Some central banks were politically unable to continue to match the Bundesbank's policies and lowered their short-term interest rates to try to boost their economies out of recession. Two ERM crises followed, in September 1992 and August 1993. Several European currencies were forced to devalue. Two major currencies, the British pound and the Italian lira, were even forced to drop out of the ERM. Nonetheless, a significant group of governments and central banks has been prepared to pay the immediate price of following the Bundesbank's discipline in order to obtain the long-term advantage of lower inflation.

The Bundesbank's victory is not complete, however. The prospects for the EMU and for a European Central Bank have made the Bundesbank even more determined than before to create not only monetary discipline but an anti-inflationary mode of policy and philosophy throughout Europe. The bank has insisted that any European states that want to join the EMU must demonstrate their commitment to stable money by pursuing strict and unbending anti-inflationary policies. With the German government, it persuaded the other members of the EC at the European Council's summit of December 1991 at Maastricht to establish a series of criteria that EC members have to meet before they can join the EMU. The criteria are so rigorous that only 3 out of the 12 EC member states have met them, and at the end of 1993 no state (not even Germany) was fully in compliance.

The bank's policy toward the EMU is simple and logical. At present, the Bundesbank is the de facto central bank for Europe, although only Germans sit on its board. When a de jure European bank is established, other nations will also be represented. And those others, by controlling *European* money, will also be controlling *German* money. It is little wonder that the Bundesbank insists on the most stern criteria, for it cannot contemplate losing control over the value of German money that it is sworn to defend, except to another institution that will be at least equally rigorous. In fact, it may even be illegal for the Bundesbank to surrender its authority over German money if it is not absolutely persuaded that the successor bank will carry on the Bundesbank's legal mandate to preserve the value of German currency.

The move toward a European common currency thus has two mutually reinforcing effects that stiffen the bank's policy even as they magnify the impact of that policy. First, it compels the bank to be stricter than ever in order to create what it terms a "stability zone" all over Europe. The bank must not only think of the immediate situation but must also try to begin creating a European system dedicated to stability and value. In the process, the bank has cast a prolonged pall over the continent. As of the end of 1993, Europe remains in the grip of a long recession that shows no sign of having bottomed (except perhaps in Britain), and the EC is suffering from a jobless rate averaging over 11 percent. Germany is suffering along with the others, in part because of the continental reach that the EMS and ERM give to Bundesbank policies. In the past, the policies of the Bundesbank might have restrained German domestic demand but might still have permitted German exporters to find markets all over Europe. Through the EMS and the ERM, restrictive Bundesbank policies now affect the continent as a whole, stifling German growth in any direction.

Second, it gives the bank's policies a powerful sounding board and thus a stronger international effect. Although the bank still insists that its primary concern must be the stability of German money, the decision of other European states to match the bank's policies has helped not only to give a much wider effect to Bundesbank policies but also to establish a zone of direct Bundesbank control over much of the continent. Bundesbank policies now have more far-reaching and more powerful consequences. The D-Mark, as one author observed, has "obviously . . . replaced the dollar as the currency standard in Europe."[5]

The United States under Bundesbank Influence

The rise of the Bundesbank and of the D-Mark has three different but mutually reinforcing effects on the U.S. economy. The first, which affects exports directly and U.S. growth indirectly, is already manifest. The second, which affects the entire structure of the economy, is more important but less identifiable although it is becoming visible. The third, which is the imposition of a new discipline on the U.S. fiscal process, remains conjectural—but the better part of wisdom would be not to test it.

1. Curtailing U.S. Exports and Slowing Growth in the United States. This development has been a subject of deepening concern to the U.S. administration and to U.S. economists, especially as the influence of Bundesbank policies across all of Europe has become more evident and as exports have become more important to the U.S. economy.

The United States has been the world's leading exporter for most of the past five years, but its sales are weakening in Europe because of stagnation there. U.S. exports to Europe, which were rising strongly throughout 1990 and 1991, began to decline during 1992 and especially in 1993. In the first half of 1992, the United States still had a trade surplus of $5.2 billion with Western Europe, but in the first half of 1993 that surplus had turned into a deficit of $2.3 billion. The decline in European sales helped contribute to the slow American growth rate of most of 1993.[6]

This slowdown in exports has been especially damaging because the export sector of the U.S. economy has produced the fastest American job growth over the past five years, accounting in many of those years for nearly all new employment. Moreover, many of the industries whose exports to Europe have been curtailed are among the most dynamic in the United States.[7] They include electronics, computers, aircraft, and industrial chemicals, as well as the agricultural sector.

U.S. concern about German policies has led to frequent American criticism of Bundesbank policies. The Americans have complained repeatedly in meetings of the Group of Seven (G-7), and they have voiced their concerns more insistently as U.S. exports have become more directly affected. On the other hand, U.S. officials have also welcomed signs of Bundesbank relaxation. Secretary of the Treasury Lloyd Bentsen commented after a modest Bundesbank short-term rate reduction in October 1993 that the cuts would "help strengthen world growth and create jobs."[8]

As the United States becomes more of an exporting nation, it must not only concern itself with international trading rules but it must also watch and try to predict Bundesbank policies ever more carefully in order to see what will happen to an important and growing part of the U.S. economy.

2. Beginning to Shift the Basic Thrust of U.S. Macroeconomic Policy. The second effect is both wider and deeper than the first. It is measured not in export statistics but in the progress of the economy as a whole, because monetary policy can reach into the heart of a nation more deeply, more insidiously, and more permanently than any other aspect of a nation's activities.

What is happening in the U.S. economy is easier to describe than to evaluate or to explain. It has begun to show signs reflecting more traditional German than American characteristics. Like the German economy over the past two decades, the U.S. economy is now showing dampened personal consumption and retail sales but relatively stronger sales of producer and investment goods.[9] Like the German economy, it is beginning to rely less on the internal market and is beginning to strive for greater exports (although—as indicated above—it is frustrated by the recession in Europe). The growth in domestic consumer demand across the board, traditionally the sparkplug of U.S. growth, appears suppressed and tentative even as construction, some types of consumer durables, and producer goods are picking up strongly.

Beyond that shift, the U.S. economy is showing slower growth than it used to manifest when it emerged from recession. It is also producing fewer jobs than before. It is, however, less obviously subject than before to inflationary pressures. In short, it is behaving like an economy subject to high short-term interest rates and to low long-term rates, the policies and the philosophy typical of the Bundesbank.

There are a number of potential explanations for this phenomenon. One is that the U.S. economy must now pay off the debt burden that it has carried over from the 1980s, needing a period of slow growth to get back to a steady course. But another explanation may lie in the fact that the yield curve and U.S. interest rate patterns are indeed starting to match the patterns usually in effect in Germany.

383

For, although the U.S. Federal Reserve has brought short-term rates down to well below their 1989–1990 peaks, it has still kept them high enough to discourage inflation although that has meant giving up some immediate consumption stimulus.

Economists have increasingly come to recognize that in an interdependent economic world with floating currency exchange rates and free capital movement there would be a tendency for the situation in one country to have a deep effect upon another. This seems paradoxical because floating was intended to make it theoretically possible for states to coexist even as they pursued different policies, but it reflects the fact that in the real world states prefer to avoid constant devaluations and are therefore obliged to match each others' policies at least to some extent. Economists have also begun to recognize that in such a world there is only one real interest rate and that decisions made in one country can thus shape the economy of another.[10] In that situation, the tone for the entire system can be set by the central bank with the most restrictive policy, provided that it is strong enough and is determined to hold to that policy.

Statistics have confirmed this tendency, demonstrating that policies in one country could have some effects upon other countries. A study conducted in 1986 tried to measure such relationships. It showed that the effects of U.S. policy on others were greater than the effects that might be felt in the other direction.[11]

Any study conducted in 1986, however, would have preceded the full functioning of the EMS and ERM. It could not have weighed the reinforcing effect that German macroeconomic influence over much of Western Europe would give to Bundesbank policy. One must therefore begin to recognize that Bundesbank policies in Europe could already begin to have as much effect on the United States as American policies might have on Europe.

Although the relationship may be conjectural, it has not escaped notice. The most obvious instance of that attention came in 1987, when Secretary of the Treasury James A. Baker III blamed the U.S. stock market crash of October 1987 on a slight upward shift in the Bundesbank's interest rate governing money market funds, the "Repo" rate. But Baker was neither the first nor the last U.S. treasury secretary to complain about the Bundesbank.

Beyond the real and perhaps measurable effect of outside forces on an economy, there is the effect of such forces on national policy itself. Here, one can certainly suggest some new and important realities, because the combined weight of Bundesbank policies and their West European reinforcement undoubtedly has an effect upon the thinking of the U.S. Treasury and the U.S. Federal Reserve and probably an effect upon their policies as well. It may well have helped to persuade the Federal Reserve to exercise greater discipline through monetary policy in recent years. Although officials of the Federal Reserve do not comment on this topic openly, they will state in private conversation that the decisions of the FOMC are influenced by such external considerations as German interest rates. They will thus indicate that Bundesbank policies and their European reinforcement do have an effect on U.S. policies.

Bundesbank officials who come to the United States report similar comments not only by Federal Reserve officials but also by observers of the Federal Reserve's behavior in foreign exchange markets and interest rate policy. The FOMC and the U.S. Treasury watch the Bundesbank carefully, and they cannot ignore German decisions. They must particularly pay attention if they do not want the dollar to suffer devaluation.

The Federal Reserve has been pursuing its own anti-inflationary policy, not only out of concern about the Bundesbank but also because of its own convictions. It has warned for some years that U.S. inflation had to be brought under control and it reacts to U.S. budget deficits with the same concern—although not with the same strident condemnation—with which the Bundesbank reacts to German deficits. The new reality of Bundesbank influence must mean, however, that the Federal Reserve may be less able to reverse policies if and when it wishes.

The wider Bundesbank influence goes well beyond the traditional U.S. concern about the slowing effect of Bundesbank policies on European growth or even the more recent concern about the slowing effect on U.S. growth, because the U.S. economy may be beginning to reflect the impact of Bundesbank policies on the very thinking of U.S. government and central bank officials. The Bundesbank does not yet reach as deeply into American thinking as into European thinking, but it nonetheless has an effect here as well as across the Atlantic.

All this suggests that the effects of floating foreign exchange rates are different from those originally expected. When floating first became widespread during the 1970s, there was a general belief that floating rates would export inflation—largely because the U.S. dollar was then the dominant currency and because the United States was conducting a persistently inflationary policy.[12] But the effect may well be the opposite when a bank with a strongly disinflationary policy—such as the Bundesbank—becomes more influential in global monetary policy. With the EMS reinforcing Bundesbank policies, the effect of floating may well have become disinflationary and perhaps deflationary.[13]

When the Bretton Woods system with the dollar-gold link collapsed in the early 1970s, one could observe that a principal reason for the system's collapse was abuse by the United States of its prerogative as the anchor of the system to compel other countries to follow its policies.[14] That can no longer be said in 1993, because the United States no longer has such influence and power. Indeed, the power and influence may be starting to go in another direction as German policies begin to have an effect in the United States.

The common policies pursued by the Bundesbank and a number of other European central banks have imposed some limits on the freedom of maneuver of the U.S. Treasury and the Federal Reserve although those limits cannot be truly evaluated until the Federal Reserve decides that it must try to move toward an expansionary policy. At most, they have significantly curtailed U.S. freedom of action, helping to shape U.S. policy and beginning to have a noticeable influence on the U.S. economy and on those who attempt to direct that economy. At the very least, they have given financial and central banking officials in the United States something to think about and even to worry about.

3. Deepening the Potentially Dangerous Consequences of U.S. Fiscal Irresponsibility. The third effect of the Bundesbank's policies reinforces the need for more discipline in the U.S. fiscal process. The single greatest dilemma for the U.S. Federal Reserve, as for the future of the U.S. dollar, is the U.S. federal budget deficit. Such a deficit, anathema to every central bank but especially the Federal Reserve and the Bundesbank, requires constant attention. It absorbs domestic savings (in the U.S. case, now over three-quarters of those savings), consumes an ever growing portion of the federal budget (by now, close to 20 percent) for interest payments on the federal debt, and can over the long run only be financed by importing foreign capital. In the absence of such capital, it can only be financed by printing money, spurring inflation, and depreciating the currency (as has long been done in Italy). Some economists have written that coordination of fiscal policy is as necessary as coordination of monetary policy for true economic cooperation, but it has never been achieved.[15]

The U.S. federal deficit began its steady climb in 1975, when it rose over the $50 billion annual level for the first time since World War II. As the U.S. government saw the dollar beginning to fall, it declared "benign neglect." Some foreign capital came in to help finance the deficit, which had risen close to $80 billion by 1979 and 1980, but the dollar decline continued. As international investors feared the dollar's collapse, gold boomed, oil prices rose in the "oil shock" of 1979, and foreign currencies rose. The dollar weakened and a dollar crisis loomed. But there was no genuine alternative haven except gold or collectibles, and a crisis was averted—or at least delayed.

When Paul Volcker was appointed chairman of the Federal Reserve Board, he put an end to inflation by raising short-term interest rates to record levels. He drew foreign capital to the United States by those interest rates and by renewing international confidence in the dollar. The tax cuts of the early 1980s helped by stimulating an investment boom in the United States, attracting even more foreign capital. The dollar weakness passed. The potential crisis did not come. Foreign capital, including German, helped to finance the U.S. budget deficits of the 1980s. The dollar was able to retain its position as the principal global means of exchange, as the major reserve currency, and as the currency in which global commodity prices are calculated.

Fifteen years later, the danger of a dollar crisis must again be examined even if that crisis has not arrived. The U.S. deficit has continued to rise, having been over $250 billion every year from 1989 to 1993. The current "deficit reduction" plan, although a step in the right direction, is intended merely to curtail the rate of growth. It does not truly cut the deficit, which is expected to begin rising even more rapidly during the last half of the 1990s. Yet even the modest efforts that have been made to control the deficit are already under challenge as ever more spending and "investment" proposals are unveiled in the U.S. Congress and the administration.

Financing the U.S. deficit will become increasingly difficult, much more difficult than during the 1970s and 1980s, not only because the deficit itself will be higher but also because some foreign capital—such as Japanese or Middle Eastern—that helped to finance the earlier deficits will not be available as before. This increases the risk that the deficit cannot be funded.

But there is an even more important distinction between the 1990s and the 1970s or 1980s. A true alternative currency is now beginning to emerge, albeit slowly. The D-Mark, under Bundesbank management, is already used for 23 percent of global currency reserves, as against 55 percent for the dollar. Other EMS currencies constitute almost another 10 percent of global reserves, even if they are concentrated in Europe. And the managers of the U.S. deficit must recognize that the growth of the D-Mark not only increases the likelihood of a dollar crisis but also increases the likelihood of an outcome that is deeply disruptive to the dollar, the U.S. economy, and the global economy as we know it today.

The D-Mark is still not truly ready to assume the international role of the dollar for several reasons:

- The German economy is too small to carry such a burden. Its total gross domestic product is about $1.7 trillion (3 trillion D-Marks), less than a third of the U.S. $6 trillion economy.
- The D-Mark still has limited acceptability. It cannot yet be used for most international commodity transactions although it is already more widely used than before—especially in Europe.
- The German financial system is neither as extensive nor as flexible as the American, in part because the Bundesbank has done all it could to maintain conservative financial structures. Although the German government and financial community are now attempting to narrow the gap in order to increase the importance of Frankfurt as a European financial center, D-Mark holdings cannot be used for as many different transactions or investments as dollar holdings.
- The D-Mark is not as liquid as the dollar. With fewer in circulation, even small shifts in supply and demand can generate exaggerated price movements that frighten traders. That may not be as important a barrier as in the past, however, because other EMS currencies could perhaps be used as surrogates.

All these considerations, however, could pale into insignificance if there were a true loss of confidence in the capacity of the U.S. Treasury and the Federal Reserve to manage the dollar. At that point, if global capital were to flee the dollar, and given the stability record of the Bundesbank, the main havens of choice would be the D-Mark itself, any instruments denominated in D-Marks, or any currencies linked to the D-Mark. The D-Mark could be propelled to ever higher (and probably unsustainable) levels of value by investors and speculators convinced that the days of the dollar as the sole or even the principal international medium of exchange and store of value were over.

Even if there were no general crisis of confidence and only the Bundesbank itself were to withdraw its freely disposable funds from the United States, the effect would be noticeable. Those funds now amount to over $40 billion, and they are all kept in short-term instruments in order to remain highly mobile. Private German capital in the United States is well over $120 billion.[16]

Markets do not act logically. If the dollar began to become an unattractive holding, either because the United States appeared determined to print its way out of debt or because of a sharp decline in U.S. short-term interest rates that might be interpreted as an effort to inflate away that debt, the search for alternatives would begin in earnest. And, in contrast to the past, such alternatives are beginning to emerge.

Equally seriously, the dollar's role

as an international medium of exchange might come under challenge. Mineral and raw material exporters such as the Organization of Petroleum Exporting Countries or the states of the former Soviet empire could begin to insist on being paid in a basket of currencies that would include the D-Mark and perhaps some other truly hard currencies as well as the dollar. And those who lend money to the United States could insist on having the loans repaid in D-Marks or another currency that they regard as stable.

Thus, the market forces of the world would impose their own harsh discipline on the United States as they have done on others that did not discipline themselves. The dollar's role as an international currency could begin to erode, and could even erode very quickly, if other governments and central banks were no longer prepared to accept it. That would dramatically increase U.S. vulnerability to global financial shifts, from which Americans have been largely sheltered by the dollar's unique role.

The Bundesbank would not welcome such a development, even if its own policies might have helped to bring it about. The bank is loath to undercut the dollar. Bundesbankers know, as every other central banker knows, that the scenario outlined above could bring about the collapse of a system that has served them and others well. Even if the system itself survives, any dramatic upsurge in D-Mark strength would jeopardize German exports, and a rush into the D-Mark would undercut the bank's capacity to manage the currency. But the Bundesbank will not respond by weakening the D-Mark but by attempting to strengthen it so that new holders do not in turn flee from it. A basic constant in Bundesbank thinking over the past 50 years has been a determination to avoid a run on German currency. This has created the makings of a vicious cycle, where ever-larger holdings of D-Marks in foreign hands have led the bank to protect the value of the currency ever more fiercely and where this attitude has in turn encouraged ever more investors to hold D-Marks.

Therefore, the policies that the bank will continue to pursue—like the policies it has pursued since 1957—will not prevent a crisis from deepening unless the U.S. government changes its policies. The Bundesbank firmly believes that it is right, and it will assert that responsibility for any dollar crisis rests with the failure of the United States to put its own house in order and not with those who have acted properly and responsibly.

The Bundesbank's performance in the EMS/ERM crises shows why the bank cannot be expected to sacrifice its assets to save the dollar even if it did not welcome a dollar crisis. The bank has displayed a strong judgmental bias. It has been prepared to separate the sheep from the goats and to support only those whom it felt deserving of support. During the crises, the bank was perfectly prepared to let the British pound, the Italian lira, and the Spanish peseta fall. Helmut Schlesinger, then president of the Bundesbank, even told a press conference that some currencies had to fall. But the bank supported the French franc as long as possible and then agreed to a generous arrangement for widening the ERM bands in order to let the franc remain in the system. It thus rewarded the long French effort to help build and sustain the system.

The bank's statements about the crises were totally unapologetic, warning ominously (and accurately) that the bank would not help those whose policies did not deserve it and that it would insist that those it chose to help should have a commitment to "stability."[17] As the *Financial Times* observed, governments can no longer rig domestic markets or conduct other maneuvers to ensure that investors buy their bonds and hold their currencies. They must conduct policies that inspire confidence.[18]

It would be illusory for Americans to believe that even their own vast resources would suffice to stop the action of the global currency markets during a crisis. Those markets have reached dimensions unimaginable 10 or 15 years ago. Every day, currencies of a value of over $1 trillion are traded. During any kind of currency crisis, the amount rapidly rises close to $1.5 trillion. At that rate, the value of the entire U.S. gross domestic product is traded in four days, and that of the rest of the world in barely two weeks. Therefore, what the U.S. Treasury and the Federal Reserve must try to do is to prevent a crisis from ever happening. In current terms, that means making certain that the dollar does not appear less attractive than the D-Mark.

What the Bundesbank has done by the pursuit of virtuous policies is, paradoxically, dangerous both to Germany itself and to Germany's U.S. ally. By offering an alterative currency, it has provided an avenue of flight for those who wonder whether, when, and where to flee. At this point, such a flight must still be regarded as conjectural. But any serious U.S. official must regard even the existence of a D-Mark option to the dollar as an ominous warning against a careless move, because any such development, and all that would flow from it, would change the world that the Western allies built after World War II and that they and others have known and enjoyed ever since.

Policy and Strategy

Shifts in global economic power and the relative weights of global currencies are like shifts in the great tectonic plates on which the continents of the world rest. They are slow and ponderous. They can and do remain invisible for a long time even as they are creating entirely new realities under the surface. Then, one day, they manifest themselves as suddenly and as violently as earthquakes or volcanic eruptions. When they do, they precipitate financial and monetary crises in which long-established relationships change dramatically, in which currencies surge or collapse, and in which hyperinflation or depression can be born or accelerated. Those upheavals are usually denounced as the work of speculators, but in reality they are only the visible manifestations of movements that have been long at work and of forces that are much too massive for governments or central banks to keep under control.

Those tectonic plates are now shifting irreversibly toward configurations that will install the Bundesbank as an ever more powerful global financial institution. It is not yet clear whether they will over time install it as *the* dominant institution or only as one of the two or three dominant institutions. Whichever it may be, the Bundesbank will have risen to that eminence because it has pursued policies to which global markets have responded and may increasingly respond. Capital flows toward places where it is managed with care and protected. Other things being equal, it will flow toward strong and stable currencies.

Among the ironies of the Bundesbank's growing influence and of the effects of that influence on the United States are the potentially negative consequences for U.S. strategic and foreign policy. An American public that is uncomfortable with the performance of the U.S. economy may well want to reduce the cost of U.S. global commitments, including those to Europe and to Germany.

The Bundesbank's policies may therefore over the long run reduce the readiness of the United States to shelter the new united Germany and may compel the German government to look more to its own or to European defenses. To that extent, the effect of Bundesbank policies may not serve German national interests. It would also, of course, constitute one of many instances in which economic reality and policy are now increasingly shaping and even determining strategic and security policy.

A number of U.S. members of Congress have insisted that the U.S. Federal Reserve should release information about FOMC meetings and take other steps that might put its work under greater political inspection and perhaps control. But even the U.S. Congress cannot change reality. Nor can it alter the basic relationship of currencies throughout the world. If the Congress does indeed compel the Federal Reserve to abandon the fight against inflation and for the dollar, it would promote parity between the dollar and the D-Mark and make the Bundesbank the leading central bank in the world.

Whatever may be the full consequences of the Bundesbank's influence, however, one result is already evident. Policies made in Frankfurt are beginning to shape the U.S. economy directly and indirectly to varying and not always predictable degrees.

They are affecting and even shaping U.S. economic policy and the U.S. economy itself. Americans are not accustomed to such outside influence, especially from a nation that they regard more as a junior than as a senior partner, but they cannot escape the new reality and the new obligation for self-discipline. They must decide whether they wish to accept the new authority or whether they are prepared to do what is necessary to counter it.

The Bundesbank is like an old-fashioned grandfather. It is not unfriendly, but it is stern. It rewards and it punishes. It also insists on self-discipline. Until the United States finds a way out of its present economic dilemma, the bank will have a potentially enormous influence on its fate. And the United States can only escape that outside influence by forcing itself to do some of the hard things that the bank would do. In effect, as long as the Bundesbank is there, and as long as the markets are drawn to it, Americans must think about the consequences of their actions far more carefully than they are used to doing.

It has become a commonplace since 1990 for Americans and others to observe that the United States is the world's sole remaining superpower. But, even while this is being repeatedly asserted, the United States may actually have lost its economic independence.

The United States did not lose that independence in a day. The developments described in this article have taken place over a long time. The rise of multiple international financial centers is even in the U.S. interest. And—it is important to remember—Bundesbank policies may well be correct in objective terms. But Americans may chafe at the adjustments and accommodations that must now be made, at the restraint that must now be exercised, and at the necessary shifts in their economic policies, priorities, and behavior. They will especially resent the discipline to which they must subject themselves, not least because that discipline originates from outside the United States.

The United States now has two central banks. One is American, the Federal Reserve. The other is German, the Bundesbank. The two banks function in an uneasy and not always obvious partnership. They must watch each other constantly and carefully. They must cooperate as much as possible. They must be very sensitive to the impact that their actions have on each other. And they must be even more sensitive to the reaction of the markets to their policies.

The Bundesbank did not seek the role in which it now finds itself. It has always wanted only to do what is best for Germany and for the German people. But it cannot now escape that role without being untrue to itself. The very success of its policies, in a world with ever wider and ever more open financial markets, has given it far greater responsibilities and far greater burdens than it has sought. And among those burdens, ironically, are the effects that its policies have on Germany's most important friend.

Notes

1. Interview with Hans Tietmeyer in Deutsche Bundesbank, *Auszüge aus Presseartikeln*, October 8, 1993, p. 3.

2. Otmar Issing, "Policies for Long-Run Economic Growth—The Contribution of Monetary Policy" (Speech delivered at a conference in Jackson Hole, Wyoming, August 27–29, 1992). Reprinted in Deutsche Bundesbank, *Auszüge aus Presseartikeln*, August 31, 1992, p. 3.

3. The best sources of information on the Bundesbank, from which this discussion is mainly drawn, are the publications of the bank itself. They are among the most thorough of any central bank, containing not only an impressive array of statistics but many articles describing the performance of the German economy as well as specific financial issues. In the course of the articles the bank also reveals much about itself. Also see Ellen Kennedy, *The Bundesbank* (London: Chatham House, 1991); David Marsh, *The Bundesbank* (London: Heinemann, 1992); and W. R. Smyser, *The German Economy* (New York, N.Y.: St. Martin's Press, 1993), chap. 3.

4. See Tietmeyer's speech on European monetary issues printed in Deutsche Bundesbank, *Auszüge aus Presseartikeln*, December 3, 1993, pp. 1–4.

5. Yoichi Funabashi, *Managing the Dollar: From the Plaza to the Louvre*, 2d ed. (Washington, D.C.: Institute for International Economics, 1989), p. 121. An expanded analysis of the relationship between the D-Mark and the EMS is on p. 126.

6. *Washington Post*, October 27, 1993, p. F-4.

7. *Washington Times*, October 26, 1993, p. B-7.

8. *Financial Times*, October 22, 1993, p. 1.

9. For a statistical reflection of this slow and uneven U.S. recovery from recession, see *Survey of Current Business*, October 1993, pp. C–8 to C–20.

10. Joseph E. Gagnon and Mark D. Unferth, "Is there a World Real Interest Rate?" International Finance Discussion Paper no. 454 (Board of Governors of the Federal Reserve System, Washington, D.C., September 1993).

11. Stanley Fischer, "International Macroeconomic Policy Coordination," in Martin Feldstein, *International Economic Cooperation* (Chicago: University of Chicago Press, 1988), p. 16.

12. See Jacob S. Dreyer, Gottfried Haberler, and Thomas D. Willett, eds., *Exchange Rate Flexibility* (Washington, D.C.: American Enterprise Institute, 1978), for an extended discussion of this likelihood.

13 For an analysis of potential EMU effects on the U.S. economy see Matthew B. Canzoneri, "The Effect of European Monetary Union on American Economic Interests and Monetary Policy," Testimony before the Subcommittee on Domestic Monetary

Policy of the Committee on Banking, Finance, and Urban Affairs, U.S. House of Representatives, July 25, 1991.

14. Raymond Vernon, "A Skeptic Looks at the Balance of Payments," *Foreign Policy*, no. 5 (Winter 1971–72), p. 60.

15. See Robert Solomon, "Background Paper," in *Partners in Prosperity: Report of the Twentieth Century Fund Task Force on the International Coordination of National Economic Policy* (New York, N.Y.: Priority Press, 1991), pp. 107–108.

16. Deutsche Bundesbank, *Monthly Report*, July 1993, p. 46.

17. See Deutsche Bundesbank, *Annual Report, 1992* (Frankfurt: Deutsche Bundesbank, 1993), pp. 79–84, for the statement on the 1992 crisis. For the bank's statement on the 1993 crisis, see Deutsche Bundesbank, *Monthly Report*, August 1993, pp. 19–26.

18. *Financial Times*, September 9, 1993.

U.S. Policy Toward the Multilateral Development Banks

Donald R. Sherk

THE CLINTON ADMINISTRATION faces many challenges in refashioning an international strategy for the United States suited both to changing times around the world and the nation's own domestic political and economic agenda. As it reassesses the place of various policy instruments in this overall strategy, and evaluates the amount of political and financial capital it is willing to invest in each, there is a real risk that the multilateral development banks will receive lower priority in the years ahead. This is a prospect that must be faced with a clear understanding of its implications, not just for its consequences for global development aspirations but also for the political and economic interests of the United States.

This essay reviews key questions confronting the Clinton administration in crafting a policy toward the multilateral development banks (MDBs). It begins with an assessment of the state of the MDBs in the 1990s, underscoring the widespread expectation that despite a number of political and managerial problems they continue to make a significant contribution to shared global goals. It then turns to the issue of leadership of these institutions, where two challenges stand out. One is the ascendancy—with important limits—of Japan. The other is the troubled U.S. role, and the possibility that a waning U.S. commitment will create a leadership vacuum with profound consequences for the work of the MDBs. The essay closes with recommendations for a new administration trying to advance U.S. economic interests while also paring unnecessary expenses.

The Multilateral Development Banks

The multilateral development banks include a number of different institutions: the International Bank for Reconstruction and Development (known to most people as the World Bank); the three regional development banks, namely the Inter-American, the African, and the Asian Development Banks; and the recently launched European Bank for Reconstruction and Development. A number of subregional development banks also exist but the five mentioned here

---

Donald R. Sherk is vice president for multilateral and corporate client services at Development Alternatives, Inc., and adjunct fellow at CSIS.

are the most important and represent what is most often thought of when the term MDBs is used. The World Bank was founded in 1944, and the four regional development banks came into existence in subsequent decades and were modeled on it. They are each based upon international agreements that establish a charter and institutional structure to support development objectives in the less developed country members.

As a group, they have come to occupy an important position in the post–World War II international economic architecture. Their principal function has been to mediate between the major capital markets and the project financing needs of the Third World. In addition, they mobilize concessional resources and provide technical assistance and economic policy advice to their borrowing members. Collectively they can currently lend over $45 billion which, when combined with local financing and other co-financing, can stimulate an aggregate investment flow into developing countries of over $100 billion yearly. Prior to their creation, the world depended exclusively on private capital flows, which were shown to be inadequate in the extreme during the global depression of the 1930s.

Their successes over the years are numerous and can be traced in their annual reports. But success has not prevented criticism. The criticisms of the MDBs change with time, reflecting trends in contemporary world opinion. In one thorough review by the U.S. Treasury of a decade ago, 19 separate criticisms of the banks were identified and analyzed.[1] The criticisms were varied, ranging from "MDB projects benefit the rich," "MDBs primarily serve the interests of the private banks," and "bilateral aid is superior to multilateral aid," to "MDB members lack control over the institutions" and "MDB staff are overpaid." These and other criticisms were reviewed by Treasury staff who concluded that, for the most part, the criticisms were overblown or were being corrected, and that taken together they did not represent an adequate case for phasing down U.S. support of the institutions.

In recent years, however, there has been a quantum leap in criticism of MDB operations and policies. Charges levied against them include: lending to dictatorial regimes or regimes that violate human rights; lending for projects that damage the ecosystems of the borrowing countries or that fail to improve the recipient country's ecology; lending to inefficient state enterprises that are incapable of competing in the private economy; and lending without listening to the people who have the most to gain or lose from the implementation of a project and without seeking to involve them in the project's design. The World Bank itself has taken on the task of self-criticism, concluding that it embodies an institutional culture that tends to promote lending for the sake of lending at the expense of sound implementation and supervision.[2]

Most observers of the banks agree that they could do a better job of running themselves. Bureaucratic inertia and the forces of the status quo have reduced the flexibility and creativity of these institutions. But these are deficiencies at the margin and not at the core of the institutions—they raise questions about how more effectively to use the MDBs but not about their overall importance and promise.

Looking to the future, one of the key challenges will be to cope with the rigidities in the funding process.

Ordinary, market-based lending operations are financed through periodic capital increases that, except for a small amount of funds paid in, consist of callable capital guarantees used by the banks to back their own bonds sold in the capital markets. The bonds of all of the MDBs are rated AAA, the top rating given, by the major investment rating firms. With this rating their bonds are attractive investments for pension funds and insurance companies that respect the commitment of the major shareholder countries to support the banks. The banks also offer loans at concessional, non-market rates. These funds are replenished every three or four years by contributions from member countries to so-called soft loan windows, which are targeted lending programs to the lowest income countries with specific program goals.

Keeping these replenishments on track has proved difficult in recent years. Arrearages have been a fact of life for most of the last two decades. The United States bears the brunt of responsibility for this problem; it has been current in its obligations to the banks only once in the last 10 years. Its behavior can be explained in part by an increasingly ideological approach to the MDBs in the early years of the Reagan presidency, when numerous demands were made for changes in bank policy. Its failure to deliver pledged amounts of funding contrasts significantly with the practices of almost all the other member countries of the banks.[3]

Replenishments have also been bedeviled by the larger issue of coping with the changing economic power of the principal shareholder nations. Negotiations of MDB funding replenishments are conducted according to a traditional, multilateral, burden-sharing exercise whereby the agreed-upon sum of additional funding is allocated among member contributors according to their respective shares of capital. The distribution of shares in any of the banks is very difficult to alter, because if one country wishes to change its percentage shareholding, all other countries must agree to a revision in their own. But the distribution of shares does change. Japan has experienced a steady rise in the shares it holds in most of the MDBs. There is, however, no smooth way to accommodate a large increase in the shares one country holds or, equally, a large cutback in the holdings of a major contributor.

The largest challenge confronting the banks in the years ahead relates to their leadership. These institutions do not function well in the absence of leadership—they are not merely managerial enterprises. The principal shareholder countries play a critical role in supplying management oversight and policy direction in addition to their capital. Yet leadership appears at the moment to be in short supply. Many observers have expected and desired that Japan would assume a growing role in the operations of the MDBs as its weight in the global economy has increased—and they have been disappointed. Many have also lamented the apparent vacuum of leadership provided by the United States and fear that an inward turn in U.S. politics and sharpening economic pressures will drive the United States into an essentially reactive role, unwilling or unable to make the necessary investments of fiscal and political capital to sustain a leading role in the banks. Expectations of and disappointments with the roles of Japan and the United States are of course connected, but it is not nearly so simple a matter as Japan picking up where the United States has left off.

Japan

Japan is the second leading shareholder (behind the United States) in three of the MDBs and holds equal shares with the United States in the Asian Development Bank. Japan has typically participated in the MDB pledging sessions in such a way as to support what the banks' management believes its financial requirements to be over the coming years. Japan has told its G–7 partners that it will attempt to manage its large balance of payments surplus by "recycling" funds to the developing world through its contributions to the MDBs and through co-financing many of the MDB projects. From 1988 to 1992 Japan co-financed projects with the World Bank worth more than $11 billion. Japanese co-financing with the Asian Development Bank over the same period amounted to over $2 billion. Japan has never been in arrears to any of the banks, quietly delivering its pledged amounts on time and with its customary minimal fanfare.

Most of the G–7 countries have nevertheless called upon Japan to play a larger role in helping shape the international economy and the Japanese have begun to formulate their own agenda in the MDBs. Although evidence for this remains scattered, there appears to be a change in attitude within the Japanese Ministry of Finance (MOF) with respect to how much responsibility it should take for the policies of the banks. In the past it was normal for the Japanese executive directors on the boards of the MDBs to be reluctant to speak their minds regarding specific policy debates conducted by the boards. If they spoke at all the statement tended to be quite conservative and, for the most part and on most issues, supportive of the positions advanced by bank management. Subjects on which they would make comments were often limited to aspects of the administrative budgets, borrowing and financial policy issues, and questions pertaining to staffing. They almost never engaged in any discussion about specific countries, nor were they willing to go against the management with respect to a specific loan proposal. In large part their interventions reflected a generally high level of satisfaction with bank operations and a desire on the part of Japan to be a "good multilateral partner."

To date, the Japanese Ministry of Finance has not experienced much difficulty in obtaining the necessary financial support for the banks from the Diet. When called upon to justify Japan's support of the banks the MOF has defended them as important components of the international economic system and convenient and cost-effective ways to assist developing countries. Japan also looks to the MDBs as important instruments in helping recycle some of its large balance of payments surpluses and in helping it to meet its pledges to various economic summits. Japan's bilateral aid programs, the Overseas Economic Cooperation Fund (OECF), the Japanese International Cooperation Agency (JICA), and the Japan Export-Import Bank have neither the capacity to move large sums of money bilaterally nor the historical tradition of doing so. As a consequence, Japan has seen an opportunity to recycle substantial amounts of funds through the MDBs via the co-financing route. Add to this the limited personnel in the Japanese foreign assistance structure, a basic unfamiliarity with certain parts of the globe (Latin America, Africa, and Eastern Europe), and a lingering sensitivity to significant visibility in third world countries, and Japan can make a compelling case to support the operations of the MDBs.

Japan's view of the role of the United States in the MDBs is complex. The Japanese acknowledge the long-standing supportive relationship that the United States has demonstrated over the years of the MDBs' existence. They also appreciate that certain aspects of bank policy would probably not have been advanced as well or as quickly if it had not been for U.S. pressure. For example, the much greater attention to environmental considerations of loan proposals now evident in each MDB is seen to be the direct result of U.S. pressure on the MDB bureaucracies. The Japanese also applaud the detailed review of each proposed project conducted by the U.S. Treasury prior to board consideration. But most knowledgeable Japanese feel, when they speak candidly, that the United States throws up so many issues and proposals for change that they cannot "digest all that comes from the U.S."[4] The Japanese clearly feel that the World Bank is too much under the influence of the United States and that it is time for them to begin asserting themselves more vigorously on bank policy issues.

This is seen most clearly in the different views held on the proper role of the state in development. Most of the Japanese officials handling MDB matters believe that the United States is excessively fixated on privatization. For the Japanese, just because an enterprise belongs to the state or has partial state ownership is not reason enough to insist on privatizing it. Their view is that the most successful models of development are those in which the state and the private sector work together harmoniously.

A recent exchange of papers between the Japanese OECF and the World Bank is clear evidence of this dispute regarding the proper role of the state in development.[5] The OECF paper suggests that the bank, in its approach to structural adjustment, is excessively concerned about the allocative efficiency of the market mechanism and at the same time gives too little weight to other important factors. These other factors include, according to the OECF: (1) the need to sustain growth through government-instigated investment promotion measures; (2) the need for appropriately selected infant industry protection measures; (3) the judicious use of subsidized interest rates; and (4) the need for a more cautious approach to privatization.

The World Bank's very polite response challenged each Japanese point and concluded that the capabilities of governments in most developing countries were not sufficient to implement successful industrial promotion campaigns; utilize targeted, subsidized, interest rate systems; prepare and carry out protection regimes for infant industries; and adequately improve the efficiency of most state enterprises in place of privatization. The bank concludes, "Consequently, it appears that for most developing countries, relying on imperfect markets—rather than imperfect governments—has the greater chance for promoting sustainable growth."[6]

Looking to the future, it appears unlikely that Japan will emerge quickly as the leading force in the MDBs with a well thought out and clearly articulated global strategy for them and a willingness to invest significant political capital to implement that strategy. Rather, Japan's steady emergence as a more vocal and important participant in the decision-making process should be expected—and encouraged.

The United States

The larger leadership question relates, of course, to the United States. It has played key roles in the establishment of each of the MDBs save for the African Development Bank. In the case of the World Bank, the United States and the United Kingdom combined forces to draw up the blueprint in 1944. The Inter-American Development Bank (1959), the Asian Development Bank (1966), and the European Bank for Reconstruction and Development (1991), all started with active U.S. involvement and leadership. When the African nations decided to open their bank's capital to non-African nations, the United States moved quickly to acquire the largest non-African shareholding and now stands third in terms of shares behind Nigeria and Egypt.

The historic role played by the United States in bringing the MDBs into existence and nurturing them over their nearly half century of operations conveys special responsibilities for the future. The United States clearly has significant influence over the policies of the MDBs. The real question is how that influence is used and for which developmental issues, and how much of that influence might be dissipating as a result of changing economic circumstances. Other leading shareholders, especially Japan, look to the United States for leadership in supporting the banks' continuing development activities. For the present at least they would be hard pressed to find a substitute for the United States.

But the pressures upon the United States to withdraw or reduce substantially its support for the MDBs are clear. The United States faces real budget constraints and the new administration has been elected with a mandate to focus its energies and the nation's resources on the U.S. domestic economy. The years ahead promise to be a time of unprecedented fiscal stringency and budget cuts. Moreover, decisions about whether and how to provide development assistance will be taken against a backdrop of growing public antipathy to foreign aid.

What would be the impact of a significantly impaired leadership role by the United States at the MDBs? The institutions would probably survive, but their effectiveness in promoting development would undoubtedly be impaired.

One early manifestation would be in the replenishment debate. As the dominant shareholder the United States usually determines what the eventual replenishment level will be. In the World Bank, Inter-American Development Bank, and European Bank for Reconstruction and Development the United States is currently the largest shareholder (17.4, 34.7, and 10 percent respectively). In the Asian Development Bank the United States and Japan each have 12.3 percent of the capital (a parity that has existed since the bank's beginning in 1966). In the African Development Bank the United States is the largest non-African shareholder at 5.9 percent. As argued above, a reallocation of these ratios is difficult to manage under the fairly rigid MDB financial system.

A diminution of U.S. commitment might also have a negative impact on MDB bond ratings. Because the U.S. capital market is still the largest and most open, U.S. government support of the MDBs is the most important element in those ratings.

The central role played by the United States in funding the MDBs also has the effect of making the future of the banks disproportionately dependent upon the internal political process of one country, their largest shareholder. This implies that a key determinant of the future of U.S. policy toward the MDBs will be the attitudes of the U.S. Congress.

In this regard, a pattern of behavior is well established. Congressional preoccupations are often elevated to the status of legislative amendments which, although they have no direct effect on the charters or bylaws of the banks, do affect how the U.S. administration manages its participation in them. Through the years the U.S. executive directors to the MDBs have been required to use their voice and vote in specific ways mandated by the amendments made in Congress to the bank funding legislation.

During the past decade U.S. executive directors have even been required to vote against or abstain on loan projects that were objected to by specific legislators. U.S. opposition has been directed against loans for citrus, sugar, tourism, copper, soybeans, and cattle raising, as well as loans promoting state enterprises, for environmentally suspect projects, and for tobacco. Loans to socialist economies, to countries engaging in expropriation of U.S. assets, and to abusers of human rights have also been opposed. Across the banks the United States has of late voted against or abstained on between 100 and 150 loans. The U.S. executive directors have been predominately voting alone, and it is the rare exception to have the United States supported in its vote by one or more other shareholders. Only once in the last 10 years has the U.S. vote on a loan led to the withdrawal of the loan by bank management.

It is frequently claimed by officials of other bank members that the U.S. Congress intrudes too far into the affairs of these multilateral institutions, which are established on the principle that the leadership and governance of the banks will be shared through consensus and negotiation. But in the absence of widespread U.S. public support for the MDBs it is too easy for Congress to hold the policies of the banks hostage to its demands or, in particular, to those of one or a few well-placed members. Because most Americans do not really understand why the United States is a member of these institutions or why their tax dollars should support them, Congress rarely comes under pressure to expand funding for the banks. On the contrary, most members of Congress are placed on the defensive, having to justify to their constituents why they voted in favor of MDB funding. This lack of broadbased support for the MDBs by the American public makes U.S. policy and the level of U.S. financial participation in the banks very susceptible to influence by whatever interest group can capture the attention of a specific representative or senator.

Often, the topic of special legislative concern is less important than how much influence can be mobilized to promote that issue into an amendment of the MDB legislation. Some of the issues involved in the past yearly funding battles have concerned lending to specific countries that at the time were not in particular favor in the United States, such as Afghanistan, Nicaragua, Chile, Vietnam, the People's Republic of China (PRC), and Ethiopia. Also on the list of disputed issues are: appropriate technology; subsidized interest rates; local cost financing; lending to state enterprises; involvement of nongovernmental groups; environmental review; lending for specific commodities such as palm oil, sugar, citrus, or copper; lending to countries having poor human rights records; cofinancing with commercial banks; foreign investment rules; and poverty alleviation.

The Bush administration requested from Congress an overall MDB appropriation for fiscal year 1993 of $1.6 billion. These funds were to cover all the various lending windows of the MDBs including the World Bank Group (International Bank for Reconstruction and Development, International Development Association, and International Finance Corporation), the Inter-American Development Bank Group (Inter-American Development Bank, Fund for Special Operations, Inter-American Investment Corporation), the Asian Development Bank and its soft loan equivalent the Asian Development Fund, the European Bank for Reconstruction and Development, and the African Development Bank and Fund.

Of that amount a House–Senate conference committee appropriated only $1.4 billion. The difference added to an existing shortfall for FY1992, making a combined FY92/93 shortfall of $364 million. This shortfall represents the overall status of U.S. arrearages to the MDBs, and it means that although the administration has participated in various MDB pledging sessions it has been unable to get congressional support for full funding.

The United States stands at an important crossroad with respect to the MDBs. How should the new administration respond to these problems? A renewed commitment to leadership of the MDBs would entail a decision to craft a new bipartisan consensus in Congress in support of U.S. leadership in the banks, a major educational campaign aimed at the American public, and a willingness to work in the G–7 process to fashion appropriate policies for the MDBs.

The alternative is to acquiesce to budgetary pressures, cut deeply the U.S. financial commitment, and try to ride out the resulting economic and political storm until U.S. economic health is restored. A related question will be how much of its political capital the White House can "afford" to devote to an effort to support multilateral foreign assistance, given the need to demonstrate fiscal discipline. But clearly, continued reductions in funding or, equally, significant delays in funding will be less and less tolerated by other key shareholders of the banks. U.S. influence in the banks will gradually erode as other major nations move into the vacuum created by a reduced U.S. role.

Is there a credible case for continued active U.S. leadership of the MDBs that can be made with sufficient persuasiveness to ensure the flow of funds from Congress and the underlying foundation of public support? There is, but to date it has not been well articulated. The case should build upon the obligations genuinely felt by many Americans to help countries less fortunate than their own. It should build also upon the banks' recognized role in helping keep the developing nations on the path toward more open economies and expanded domestic investment. But it should also clearly spell out what economic gains for U.S. industry stem from U.S. participation in the MDBs. A dynamic, thriving, and export-led U.S. industry can utilize U.S. membership in the banks in ways that will help stimulate greater growth and new markets. Far too little attention has been paid by successive administrations to how to use the banks for immediate economic benefit. U.S. businesses can gain in a variety of ways including competing for consulting, procurement, and construction contracts under MDB-financed loans; utilizing the banks' published reports on economic conditions in their borrowing member countries; pursuing business opportunities in combination with other national firms that work on MDB projects; sharing in the two-way transfer of technology that takes place under MDB loan and technical assistance activities; and being involved in the early stages of development of countries newly opening up to foreign business, such as the states of the former Soviet Union. In short, U.S. jobs, productivity, research and development, investment, and business arrangements are all capable of being promoted via U.S. involvement in the MDBs.

Conclusion

Underlying the Clinton administration's pending decisions about its commitment to the MDBs is a set of larger decisions about American purposes in the post–cold war world, the place of global economic development in long-term U.S. goals, the utility of development assistance in promoting domestic U.S. economic goals, and the character of leadership that the new president and his team intend to provide. Abandonment of the commitment to the MDBs in the name of short-term fiscal prudence would serve U.S. interests badly on each score. The United States can maintain its leadership in the MDBs but to do so will require a major selling job, domestically and also with key partner nations abroad.

U.S. partners in the MDBs understand that the U.S. role in the banks is open for renewed discussion and is likely to continue to evolve in the years ahead. Most countries appreciate that the MDBs owe much to the long-term support given to them by the United States. They also understand that there is no alternative to U.S. leadership if the banks are to continue to play a positive role. Many expect that with the passing of the Cold War the United States will be more forceful in asserting its right to share in the traditional benefits of MDB membership, such as procurement for U.S. suppliers and consulting opportunities. The major MDB shareholders are also sympathetic to the U.S. need to hold constant or reduce slightly its annual contributions to the MDBs, although they hope that this will be done in close consultation with the MDBs themselves and with key member countries. The administration can also anticipate a receptive attitude toward financial innovations that allow the MDBs to operate more like commercial banks and that reduce need over time for direct budgetary support in the magnitudes now provided.

The new administration can build on these attitudes to craft a new partnership at the banks or, through a decision to ignore the banks, it can watch these attitudes sour and poison U.S. relations with both lenders and borrowers at each of these institutions.

Notes

1. See U.S. Department of Treasury, *United States Participation in the Multilateral Development Banks in the 1980s* (Washington, D.C., February 1982).

2. The World Bank's "Wapenhans' Report" describes a worrisome deterioration in the quality of the bank's portfolio observed over the last decade. The report attributes this deterioration in part to a "lending culture" that permeates the bank. The report suggests, as have other bank critics, that an institutional pressure exists to make

new loans as opposed to ensuring that old loans are properly implemented and supervised and that their results are sustainable.

3. One needs to bear in mind that in a unitary governmental system the amount pledged to a multilateral institution can be assured in full if it is included in an approved annual budget. This is not guaranteed in the U.S. system, where the executive and legislative branches assume different roles in the multilateral funding process.

4. In another context I interviewed nine current or former members of the MOF who had been part of the machinery making policy on the MDBs for their views on U.S. policy toward the banks. This comment was made by one of those individuals, who asked not to be identified.

5. "Issues Relating to the World Bank's Approach to Structural Adjustment—Proposal from a Major Partner," OECF Occasional Paper no. 1 (Tokyo, October 1991). The World Bank's response was in the form of a memorandum to the Japanese alternate executive director, Kiyoshi Kodera, from the bank's chief economist, Lawrence H. Summers, dated April 3, 1992.

6. World Bank memorandum, p. 14.

Promoting Higher Labor Standards

Steve Charnovitz

FOR MANY DECADES, the United States has promoted higher labor standards throughout the world.[1] U.S. interest in this area began during the negotiations for the Treaty of Versailles and was reinforced two decades later in the Atlantic Charter. Over the years, this policy has had a mixture of motivations. One was to thwart communism through pluralist institutions like free trade unions. Another was to seek fairness in international trade. A third was to improve the prospects for foreign economic development.

The Clinton administration has actively sought to upgrade labor standards in other countries. Its first initiative was to negotiate a side agreement on labor to the North American Free Trade Agreement (NAFTA). Then in 1994, the administration proposed taking up "worker rights" in the new World Trade Organization (WTO).[2] This effort became embroiled in controversy after many nations disagreed with the administration that the relationship between trade rules and worker rights should be examined. The contentious debate that ensued has cast doubt on the longtime assumption that governments should work together to raise labor standards.

The purpose of this article is to show how higher labor standards can be promoted in a non-protectionist way. The first section provides historical background on the issues. The second discusses the role of the International Labour Organization (ILO) and makes recommendations for its reform. The third explains why the international trading system will not be able to avoid the issue.

Labor Standards and the World Economy

Unlike the response to some global challenges, such as terrorism, in which cooperation among countries is essential, nations can carry out their labor policies autonomously. The rationale for an international labor regime is that coordinating national actions may make it politically easier for individual countries to achieve optimal regulation. An analogous situation exists with the international trade regime. The General Agreement on Tariffs and Trade (GATT) has helped governments pursue trade policies that are in their own national economic interest.

Steve Charnovitz is policy director of the Competitiveness Policy Council in Washington, D.C. He was previously a legislative assistant to the Speaker of the U.S. House of Representatives and an international relations officer at the U.S. Department of Labor.

Copyright © 1995 by The Center for Strategic and International Studies and the Massachusetts Institute of Technology

The strongest case for the creation of an international regime is to address transborder physical spillovers. Disease control, telecommunications, and ozone protection are examples of such regimes. Some international regimes are not engendered by physical spillover, but rather by economic spillover. International cooperation is sought because the policies of one country can affect the economy of another. The international trade regime, for example, seeks multilateral action to lower tariffs and trade barriers. The international labor regime seeks multilateral action to raise employment standards. Both regimes lay down rules for competition among governments.

Despite economic common sense, continued progress in trade and investment liberalization may not occur. Politicians must develop and retain voter support for open economic borders. In the United States, there are many pockets of resistance to free trade on the grounds of job loss, unfair competition, and the immorality of buying products from countries and corporations that mistreat their workers. Attention to labor standards, therefore, may be a way to reduce opposition to new trade agreements.

Almost all proposals for incorporating labor standards into international rules have been based on the use of international labor standards, not the domestic labor standards of the importing country. International labor standards are the policies and principles for guiding national lawmaking to which numerous nations have agreed. In many instances, such as ILO conventions, the ratifying countries regard them as international law.[3] Indeed, the ILO sometimes refers to its body of conventions as the "International Labour Code."

There are international labor standards to (1) outlaw forced labor; (2) permit freedom of association; (3) uphold the right to organize and bargain collectively; (4) regulate the use of child labor; and (5) regulate dangerous workplace conditions. There are also ILO conventions on many other issues (e.g., discrimination and sickness benefits), but, for the purpose of this article, only the standards listed here will be discussed. Contrary to popular perception, there are no international labor standards regarding minimum wages or wage adequacy.

All governments have labor standards and embody them in national or subnational law. Businesses generally support reasonable labor standards because, in their absence, an employer seeking to provide decent workplace conditions would face competitive pressure from less scrupulous employers. Labor standards are justified because of well-recognized imperfections in labor markets (e.g., information on occupational risks) and because markets must be undergirded with certain legal (or natural) rights. As the U.S. Council of Economic Advisers explains, "Core labor standards represent fundamental human and democratic rights in the workplace, rights that should prevail in all societies whatever their level of development."[4] Few would question the need for labor standards by arguing that an unregulated labor market can yield an optimal outcome.

In any good labor standard, the social benefits of the regulation exceed the social costs. For some labor standards, the individual benefits of the regulation to the employer may exceed its individual costs (e.g., workplace hazards). But for the most part, higher labor standards probably add to the cost of production. Whether labor standards redistribute income depends on the ability of employers to pass through these higher costs to workers in the form of lower wages.

The impact of ILO standards on economic development and growth has not been sufficiently studied. There is some evidence that freedom of association promotes economic development.[5] In its study of East Asian countries, the World Bank cited the examples of Hong Kong and Japan to show that countries need not repress unions to achieve high economic growth.[6] The Organization for Economic Cooperation and Development (OECD) is carrying out a new research program that may illuminate this issue.

The idea that national labor policies needed to be coordinated began to dawn in the nineteenth century. This recognition led to the creation of the ILO as part of the Treaty of Versailles 76 years ago. The ILO was one of the earliest intergovernmental economic institutions and the first intergovernmental social institution. It is the only surviving organization from the original League of Nations and was the first specialized agency of the United Nations (UN). Its membership now includes over 170 countries.

The ILO was established for two reasons.[7] First, the governments involved believed that "the failure of any nation to adopt humane conditions of labour is an obstacle in the way of other nations which desire to improve the conditions in their own countries."[8] The persistence of low labor standards in some nations could make it harder politically for other nations to raise their labor standards. Through cooperation, nations could upgrade their labor standards together.

Second, the governments believed that fair labor standards were important to commercial policy. The Treaty of Versailles called on governments to endeavor to secure humane conditions of labor at home and "in all countries to which their commercial and industrial relations extend."[9] In other words, the concern was that just as competition needed to be regulated within a domestic market, it also needed to be regulated in the international market. As the U.S. War Labor Policies Board explained in 1919, "nations with higher labor standards are handicapped in competition with nations having lower standards."[10]

The idea that labor standards in one nation can adversely affect those of another is under challenge today. Looking back seven decades, it seems clear that the "obstacle" noted in the Treaty of Versailles was not as overpowering as the authors of that provision presumed. Nevertheless, as national economies become more interdependent and as barriers to capital (and perhaps labor) mobility are removed, there may be increasing pressure to lower certain labor standards to achieve greater competitiveness.[11] The power of unions to resist this pressure has been attenuated by their minimal transnational bargaining and the growing financial and political clout of multinational corporations.[12]

Although the first meeting of the ILO in 1919 was held in Washington, the United States did not join the organization because the U.S. Senate failed to approve the Treaty of Versailles. It was not until 1934 that President Franklin D. Roosevelt and Secretary of State Cordell Hull took important steps to abandon the postwar isolationism of the United States by joining the ILO and by initiating the Reciprocal Trade Agreements program. The United States withdrew from the ILO in 1977 following an increased politicization of ILO conferences, but rejoined in 1980 after the

ILO undertook corrective action to regain a focus on labor matters.

The ILO is unique among international organizations in being tripartite. Its delegates consist not only of government officials, but also of employers and workers from each member nation. For the United States, the U.S. Council for International Business represents the employers and the American Federation of Labor–Congress of Industrial Organizations (AFL–CIO) represents the workers.

The ILO carries out four main activities. First, it passes resolutions on international economic and social policy. Second, it provides technical assistance to labor ministries. Third, it writes labor conventions that impose binding minimum standards on nations that ratify them. From the very beginning it was recognized that these conventions needed to be sensitive to the differential needs of developing countries. Fourth, it reviews national adherence to ILO conventions. This latter function includes an adjudication process that permits complaints to be registered by nongovernmental organizations. Although the original ILO treaty provisions contemplated the use of economic and legal enforcement, such tools were never employed.[13] Instead, the ILO seeks to use moral suasion and exposure to convince countries to raise labor standards.

Concerns about "social dumping" (and the term itself) go back to the 1920s. Social dumping is the exportation of products at prices below what the costs of production would be if international labor standards were followed. At one time, several countries had trade remedy laws to respond to social dumping. For example, Austria provided for a dumping duty on foreign goods from countries that had not ratified and were not following the ILO Convention on Hours of Work (no. 1).[14] The ILO has never advocated such social dumping duties.

The issue of social dumping received attention at the UN Conference on Trade and Employment of 1946–48, which wrote both GATT and the more comprehensive Charter for the International Trade Organization (ITO). Although both agreements permit antidumping duties, neither permits social dumping duties. Instead, the ITO included an article on "fair labour standards," which provided that

1. The Members recognize that measures relating to employment must take fully into account the rights of workers under intergovernmental declarations, conventions and agreements. They recognize that all countries have a common interest in the achievement and maintenance of fair labour standards related to productivity, and thus in the improvement of wages and working conditions as productivity may permit. The Members recognize that unfair labour conditions, particularly in production for export, create difficulties in international trade, and accordingly, each Member shall take whatever action may be appropriate and feasible to eliminate such conditions within its territory.

2. Members which are also members of the International Labour Organization shall cooperate with that organization in giving effect to this undertaking.

3. In all matters relating to labour standards that may be referred to the Organization in accordance with the provisions of Article 94 or 95 [i.e., GATT Article XXIII], it shall consult and cooperate with the International Labour Organization.[15]

This provision has significance for the current debate in several ways.

First, the governments recognized "the rights of workers" within a trade agreement. Second, the governments agreed that fair labor standards were in the common interest, and thus not exclusively a domestic issue. Third, the governments agreed unfair labor conditions in export industries could present a trade problem. Fourth, the governments agreed that unfair labor conditions could be the subject of a nullification and impairment complaint in ITO dispute settlement (i.e., articles 94 and 95).

Unfortunately, President Harry S. Truman was unable to get Congress to approve U.S. membership in the ITO, which died after other countries decided not to go ahead without the United States. It bears noting that the fair labor standards provision was not a significant factor in making the ITO unpopular in Congress. Indeed, the National Association of Manufacturers and the U.S. Chamber of Commerce had supported the negotiation of this commitment.[16]

Some commentators have suggested that the ITO charter reflected only the views of Western or high-income countries. That is not the case. The nations that wrote the ITO were geographically and economically diverse.[17]

The ITO provision on fair labor standards was not included in GATT. Except for the provision in article XX(e) that permits governments to ban trade in goods produced using prison labor, GATT says nothing about labor standards. Several efforts have been made to remedy this omission. The Eisenhower administration sought to amend GATT with a social clause. The Carter administration sought to add labor standards to GATT's post–Tokyo Round work program. The Reagan administration sought to add "worker rights" to the negotiating topics for the Uruguay Round. The Bush administration sought to convene a GATT working party to discuss the topic. The Clinton administration sought to add labor standards to the WTO's work program. None of these efforts was successful.

Because all members of GATT are also members of the ILO, the current opposition to discussing international labor standards in GATT does not seem to stem from a denial of the legitimacy of such standards. Rather, the main concern seems to be that higher labor standards should be directly pursued only in the ILO, not in GATT. This notion of institutional specialization is a repudiation of the linkage between commerce and labor standards that the architects of the trading system saw five decades ago.

The recent effort by the Clinton administration was widely perceived to be inspired by protectionism.[18] There were several reasons for this. First, the administration did not articulate its goal on worker rights, or its proposed program, before asking GATT to put it on the agenda. Second, the administration had already pursued policies linking labor enforcement to trade sanctions in the NAFTA side agreement, and therefore it was assumed that the administration might be seeking the same remedy for the rest of the world. Advocacy of a "Blue 301" by Richard Gephardt (D–Mo.), then House majority leader, further clouded the issue, because many foreign governments may have thought that this was part of the administration's strategy. (Section 301 is the provision in U.S. trade law that permits the U.S. Trade Representative [USTR] to impose trade countermeasures against other countries; "Blue" 301 was a proposal to allow this for blue collar issues.) Third, although the administration denied that its GATT initiative was designed to push up foreign

407

wages, President Bill Clinton praised the NAFTA for raising labor costs in Mexico.[19] He also lauded the "unprecedented commitment by the Government of Mexico to tie their minimum wage structure to increases in productivity and growth in the Mexican economy and to make that a part of the trade agreement."[20] In addition, Labor Secretary Robert Reich made a widely publicized speech discussing criteria for "decisions to restrict economic relations with low-wage countries in the name of workers' rights."[21] Given the confusing signals, it was not surprising that many observers thought the United States was more interested in jacking up foreign wage levels than in promoting respect for worker rights.

Coming in a critical period before the signing of the WTO agreement, the Clinton administration's worker rights initiative caught many close observers by surprise and led to a vociferous reaction from the U.S. business community, congressional Republicans, the GATT Secretariat, and other countries. Until 1993, the pursuit of worker rights in trade policy had been a bipartisan objective. Unfortunately, the rash statements and actions by the administration have polarized the issue in the United States and may have set the cause back. The administration has little to show for its efforts so far except new attention to the issue in the OECD.

U.S. Trade Representative Mickey Kantor characterizes his initiative as a success because the WTO preparatory committee agreed to allow the United States to reintroduce the issue of labor standards. According to Kantor, "this is the first time that we have achieved a breakthrough of this kind in the GATT framework."[22] This boast is unjustified, however. The issue of labor standards was raised by the United States at GATT during the Eisenhower, Carter, Reagan, and Bush administrations. In actuality, the Clinton administration's labor rights initiative of early 1994 was more of a breakdown than a breakthrough. Not only did it instigate domestic Republican opposition to worker rights, but it also decreased the likelihood of the issue returning to the GATT or WTO agenda in the near future. So far, Kantor has not followed up on his "breakthrough."

The inability of the Clinton administration to articulate a coherent position on labor rights is perhaps most apparent in the ease with which Malaysian prime minister Mahathir Mohamad has cast the U.S. government as the villain. Mahathir has excoriated the U.S. position on labor standards as protectionist. Despite the fact that Mahathir's government is a very serious violator of such rights, the Clinton administration was unable to respond successfully.

The U.S. business community gave no support to the worker rights initiatives of the Reagan, Bush, and Clinton administrations.[23] That community has three main concerns. First, it fears that new international agreements on labor standards could be a backdoor way to push up labor standards in the United States. Second, it fears that any labor enforcement mechanism in GATT could make trading rights less predictable. Third, it fears that boosting foreign labor standards could raise the costs of overseas production and make it less profitable. It is interesting to note that this third view is echoed in other countries. For example, Singapore's foreign minister has complained that creating labor rules in the WTO would be "equivalent to removing our competitiveness."[24]

With the Republican ascent to power in Congress, the Clinton administration needs to rebuild a bipartisan consensus on this issue. That will not be easy. Instead of the lone ranger approach, the USTR should try to develop a coalition with other governments, such as Australia, that are seeking new ways to promote worker rights.[25] The European Parliament also supports giving the WTO a role in labor standards.[26]

The International Labour Organization and Its Need for Reform

The ILO is probably the most idealistic and forward-looking international institution ever created. It was highly successful in its early decades as it promulgated basic labor conventions. On its fiftieth anniversary in 1969, the ILO won the Nobel Peace Prize for its "lasting influence on the legislation of all countries." In the 1970s, the ILO began to go downhill as it got whipsawed in both East–West and North–South tensions.

The collapse of communism should have reenergized the ILO, but it has not. The ILO has continued to produce at least one new labor convention each year, but it is just now starting to weed out those that are obsolete. The present level of 175 conventions is far too high.[27] The ILO's annual budget is rather small—about $233 million—and has seen little increase in recent years. It does not have sufficient resources to provide technical assistance or to fund innovative programs aimed at raising labor standards. Its research program is also underfunded.

Unlike the new WTO treaty, which contains a specific set of obligations, the ILO treaty is fairly general. The specific labor obligations are contained in ILO conventions that must be approved separately by each country on an à la carte basis. (In this regard, the ILO resembles the GATT Tokyo Round agreements.) The ILO has an elaborate supervisory machinery for ratified conventions, but a country that fails to ratify a convention can avoid that supervision. The two exceptions to this are the Conventions on Freedom of Association (no. 87) and the Right to Organize and Bargain Collectively (no. 98), which can be reviewed by the ILO regardless of whether a member government has ratified them.

In contrast to the WTO, there are no significant legal benefits to joining the ILO. Countries join to get help in raising their own standards and to improve the international regime. The great achievement of the Uruguay Round, that is, to link together various agreements under the single WTO umbrella, could not be repeated in the ILO because there is no commercial carrot for ratification of ILO conventions. Even the ILO's technical assistance is not preconditioned on the ratification records or enforcement performance of member countries.

It is often suggested that the ILO should use trade controls to secure adherence to its conventions. (For example, the Eisenhower administration proposed this for the Convention on the Abolition of Forced Labor.) Although the ILO may have legal competence to pursue such enforcement, it has studiously avoided doing so in favor of convincing countries that to follow conventions is in their own interest because the social benefits exceed the costs. Because ILO standards are drawn up in a consensual, tripartite process, it was reasonable to hope that voluntary adherence would work.

In recent years, some analysts have questioned the usefulness of ILO conventions. It is suggested that legal standards may be ineffective in raising working conditions because the market determines the conditions that employers can afford and employees really value. Seen in this way, governments are impotent to push labor standards up in a sustainable way.[28]

This view defies both logic and economic history. Individual workers face too many impediments to bargain successfully with employers, particularly on issues such as occupational health. Just as governments must enforce certain rules for commercial markets to work well (e.g., property rights), rules are also needed for labor markets to work well (e.g., union recognition). Moreover, as the International Labour Office has noted, there is a symmetry between the freedom of trade and the freedom of workers to bargain collectively.[29] In addition, there are many key labor issues, such as child labor, in which governmental paternalism is desirable to override decisions by individuals.

Some who are skeptical of labor standards argue that better conditions will eventuate automatically through economic growth. A similar claim is often made with regard to environmental standards. It is possible that growth may have that salutary effect, but it does not necessarily follow. As Michel Camdessus, managing director of the International Monetary Fund (IMF), explains:

> The building of consensus within and among nations regarding the nature of the economic and social problems they face and the requisite remedies is a *sine qua non* if the latter are to be successful. Economic growth, by itself cannot solve these problems.[30]

Skeptics also suggest that international workplace standards may be too rigid for the diversity in national conditions. This could be true in particular instances, but the ILO has tried to avoid the "one size fits all" approach. Indeed the ILO was providing special treatment for developing countries many decades before the trading system did so. It is interesting to note that when the United States joined the ILO in 1934, there were about 14 developing country members out of a total membership of 48.[31]

Making the ILO More Effective

In its recent report, the Commission on Global Governance pointed out that greater openness of world markets and greater labor mobility are likely to increase the ILO's relevance.[32] The current ILO is unprepared for these new challenges. There are a number of steps that the ILO could take to improve its effectiveness:

1. Address Overregulation. When the ILO constitution was written in 1919, it was presumed that ever higher national labor standards were better. The drafters had not experienced the modern welfare state, and therefore did not anticipate that governments might impose regulations whose social benefits did not exceed their costs. In some instances, current ILO rules may prevent government reform. For example, one convention from 1949 would prohibit replacing bureaucratic public employment agencies with for-profit providers.

The world economy today is different, but the ILO has not changed in response. Its current approach to labor standards is unbalanced because it looks only at where countries should raise their standards. Because the goal of the ILO is to reduce unemployment and to increase national welfare, these blinders reduce its potential effectiveness. When countries require lengthy advance notice before layoffs, or provide excessive unemployment benefits, or impose high taxes on employment, these matters should draw the attention of the ILO. France has the right to complain about sweatshops in India. But India should have the right to complain about government-induced unemployment in France that reduces French demand for imported goods.

The reason why international organizations like the IMF, the WTO, or the ILO get involved in domestic policymaking is to help governments effectuate better policies. It has been found that international standards and international surveillance can facilitate governmental decisions that are politically difficult at home. If the ILO asked governments with unrealistic and inflexible labor laws why they retained such rigidities, it might be easier for reformers in those countries to get more efficient laws enacted.

Reinventing the ILO so that it deals with overregulation, in addition to underregulation, could also have the salutary effect of getting the employer members more interested in the process. For years, employers have pursued very limited agendas in the ILO, focusing mainly on "damage control." A better-functioning ILO would be of great interest to employers and, in the long run, would help workers too. As Robert J. Morris, senior vice president of the U.S. Council for International Business, has noted:

> American business has long supported efforts to redirect the focus of the ILO's work . . . toward engaging the governments and unions in a genuinely common effort to deal with issues which really matter to working people: unemployment and the low standards of living and working conditions that are the inevitable accompaniment to low levels of economic performance and growth.[33]

Frank P. Doyle, executive vice president of General Electric, expresses a similar view in stating that a new ILO agenda "will have to recognize the fact that worker rights that don't promote employment growth and economic development are not in the best long term interest of workers."[34] The ILO needs to make its standards more relevant to the high unemployment and low productivity growth that many countries suffer.

The thesis of this article differs considerably from that of many analysts who suggest that the ILO's defect is that it has no means of enforcing its conventions. Inadequate implementation of labor laws is certainly a problem in developing countries. It is a problem in many industrial countries too. But the deficiencies in the ILO would not be cured by trade sanctions. Very little of international law is in fact enforced through trade sanctions, so the ILO is not atypical in that respect.

2. Set up Committees on Forced and Child Labor. Since 1951, the ILO has had a Committee on Freedom of Association to deal with complaints submitted to it either by governments or by organizations of employers or workers. The committee will consider a complaint about a government even if that government has not ratified applicable ILO conventions. This same principle of review regardless of ratification should be applied to two other fundamental ILO principles regarding forced labor and the protection of children.

Hardly anyone defends the continued use of forced labor and prison labor by governments and the use of indentured labor and bonded labor by the private sector to produce goods for

411

commerce. Although the two ILO conventions on forced labor have a large number of ratifications, some of the most egregious violators are non-ratifiers (e.g., China). Establishing a specific committee on this topic would highlight the issue and provide greater publicity to the ILO's investigations.

In contrast to forced labor, there are many defenders of child labor who argue that although the employment of children may be bad, the unemployment of children may be worse. It is said, for example, that if an 11-year-old girl were not working in a rug factory, she might be out on the street, homeless, and working as a prostitute. This defense of the increasing use of child labor is not immoral; but it is complacent.

The ILO estimates that there are 100 to 200 million child workers today. According to the U.S. Department of Labor, less than 5 percent of these children are employed in export sectors, such as in manufacturing and mining.[35] But 5 to 10 million children producing for international trade is a huge number. It is already hard enough to defend the WTO to the American public without having to explain why the WTO has rules against the exploitation of trademarks, but no rules against the exploitation of children.

Establishing an ILO Committee on Child Labor would be a signal to the world that the status quo is not acceptable. The new committee should vigorously pursue investigations of weak government rules or lax enforcement and should publicize its findings. The ILO should also work with countries to establish better incentives to avoid child labor. Children who stay in school might be given inducements such as meals.[36] The new ILO program on the Elimination of Child Labor and the UN Children's Fund (UNICEF) are pursuing some creative strategies to address child labor conditions.[37]

The employment of children, particularly in unsafe factory jobs, is a violation of human dignity and a short-sighted development strategy. It is appropriate for international organizations like the ILO, the World Bank, the IMF, and the WTO to send signals to countries to discourage such practices. As the recent letter concerning child labor from over 80 Nobel Prize laureates noted, "the exploitation of child work is at too high a cost—rendering their future worthless."[38]

3. Promote Social Labels. In addition to institutional improvements, the ILO should also try to harness market forces to deal with problems like child labor.[39] There are already a number of social labeling programs under way to identify whether products are produced in accordance with good practices.[40] Consumers who want to avoid buying a rug woven by a 12-year-old ought to be able to do so. The ILO should not institute its own labeling program, but should instead provide technical assistance. A number of socially conscious companies, like Reebok and Levi Strauss, have already taken steps to require suppliers to meet certain minimum labor standards. The ILO should look for ways to encourage such private sector "enforcement."

Because such process-related labels can turn into unfair trade barriers, the ILO should work with other international organizations to assure that social labeling is done without protectionist intent. In particular, the ILO should promote joint attention to labeling by the WTO's new Committee on Technical Barriers to Trade, the International Organization for Standardization (ISO), and the UN Conference on Trade and Development. There will be a need to balance clarity for consumers and sensitivity to differing practices in producing countries.

4. Facilitate Codes on Conduct. The success of the Sullivan Principles in South Africa has stimulated interest in promulgating new corporate codes regarding labor rights. Although the ILO could attempt to update its 1977 Declaration of Principles Concerning Multinational Enterprises and Social Policy, such an exercise would probably not be worth the effort. Instead, the ILO should serve as a clearinghouse for information about voluntary codes and their effectiveness. Unilateral governmental efforts to develop such codes are not likely to be successful.[41]

5. Link Labor Standards to Development Aid. The idea of conditioning development aid upon labor standards was first proposed during the postwar planning meetings in the early 1940s. In 1945, an international labor union conference recommended "making long-term loans for the economic and industrial development of colonial territories and backward countries conditional upon the observance of internationally agreed working conditions."[42] It is interesting to note that this same labor conference called for the creation of an international institution "capable of promoting a steady expansion of foreign trade [and] of regulating international trade and tariffs." This was the era in which labor unions supported freer trade.

It is generally viewed as more constructive to link labor standards to aid, rather than to trade. Restricting trade typically subtracts from world economic welfare. But channeling aid to the countries with the most fruitful economic policies can add to world economic welfare. The use of aid instruments may also be a better way to get the attention of foreign governments, because trade restrictions do not immediately hurt governments in the direct way that they hurt business.

The World Bank does not condition its structural adjustment lending on whether a country follows ILO standards. On the contrary, countries are sometimes urged by the Bank to undertake changes that conflict with international labor law.[43] Much closer coordination is needed between the ILO and the Bank on issues like this so that these organizations do not work at cross-purposes to each other.

The ILO also needs to provide more technical assistance on labor and employment programs, especially in regions that are eager to improve their human resources (such as Eastern Europe). The ILO should receive greater funding for this goal either from governments directly and through the UN Development Programme (UNDP). Greater attention to employment issues by international development agencies might boost the effectiveness of aid programs.

Improving U.S. Government Policies

The Clinton administration has paid little attention to the ILO. This inattention is ironic because the ILO may be more relevant to the world's economic problems in this time of rapid economic change than it has ever been. While U.S. Trade Representative Kantor has pushed hard for GATT to become more open to nongovernmental groups, the ILO is already open to such groups—indeed these groups are full members—a policy recently reflected in the observation by ILO director general Michel Hansenne that, "It is striking that all international institutions established since 1919 should have espoused the principle of the government being the sole representative of the States."[44] In an era in which the American public is growing more skeptical of government, and at a time in which the Clinton administration has been seeking to reinvent government, it would have been timely for the administration to seek better use of the ILO and the nongovernmental groups active within it.

The United States is a permanent member of the ILO Governing Body and contributes about 25 percent of the ILO's budget. The Clinton administration could therefore exert considerable influence in reforming the ILO if it tried. When President Clinton convened a summit of the Group of Seven (G-7) in March 1994 in Detroit to discuss the unemployment challenge, he did not even invite the ILO. (The summit yielded little.) The most fruitful U.S. initiative in the ILO in recent years occurred in the early 1980s, when the Reagan administration pressed for ILO support of democratic trade unions in Eastern Europe and Latin America.

There are several ways for the U.S. government to improve its policies vis-à-vis the ILO:

1. Ratify More ILO Conventions. The United States has become a party to only 12 ILO conventions, including 5 in recent years. This is the worst record of any major industrial nation. It undercuts the diplomatic effectiveness of the United States in promoting higher labor standards and in complaining about egregious practices in other countries.[45]

This disinclination to ratify ILO conventions stems mainly from two concerns. First, because U.S. treaties are the "supreme law of the land," ratifying an ILO convention could supersede federal and state labor laws if provisions of the convention can be enforced in domestic courts. Second, many Americans are reluctant to have U.S. policy reviewed by an international organization. As a consequence, the United States has not ratified the core ILO conventions on freedom of association and the right to organize, nor has it ratified any of the child labor conventions.

In all U.S. ratifications to date, the president and the Senate have declared that it was appropriate to ratify the convention because U.S. law was already in conformity with it. This is a valid argument for ratification. But it should not be the prerequisite for ratification. In many other areas of international law, the United States changes its law in order to meet a new international standard. The legislation to approve the WTO, for example, contained a number of statutory changes to bring U.S. practice into conformity (e.g., on patents). Environmental treaties also engender changes in U.S. law. But when it comes to labor conventions, the U.S. government takes a parochial and non-cooperative stance, that is, no ratification unless the United States already meets the convention.

Obtaining Senate approval of ILO conventions by a two-thirds vote is a formidable challenge. There is no requirement in the Senate for a timely vote. The ILO Convention on Freedom of Association (no. 86) has been pending on the Senate's treaty calendar since 1949. The Employment Policy Convention (no. 122) has languished in the Senate since 1966.

Although ILO conventions have traditionally been sent to the Senate as "treaties," there may be other methods of securing approval for them. One approach is to approve ILO conventions similarly to the way that trade agreements are approved.[46] That is, Congress could pass a joint resolution authorizing the president "to enter into ILO Convention #__." Such a law could also declare that (1) the convention is not to be considered a self-executing treaty; (2) the convention does not supersede federal law; and (3) the convention does not supersede state law. Of course, the United States should not ratify a convention just to become a delinquent. This legislative method should only be used when a consultation between the executive branch, Congress, the AFL–CIO, the U.S. Council for International Business, and the National Governors Association demonstrates widespread agreement in favor of the purpose and terms of a particular convention.

2. Appoint a U.S. Ambassador to the ILO. Although the United States has an ambassador at GATT and the OECD, it lacks comparable high-level representation at the ILO. There is a U.S. ambassador to the UN in Geneva, but that individual has many other responsibilities. The day-to-day coordination of U.S. policy regarding the ILO is handled by the labor attaché in the U.S. mission in Geneva.

A new U.S. initiative on the ILO should commence by appointing an ambassador. The ambassador would spend some time in Geneva, some time in Washington, and some time visiting other countries in order to develop support for needed ILO reforms. Given the tripartite nature of the ILO, the ambassador would also need to develop close ties to international business and labor organizations.

During the Reagan administration, the deputy under secretary of labor for international affairs was given the personal rank of ambassador. That is a pertinent precedent. But the ILO ambassador ought to be a full-time job. The ambassador should not be a line official at the U.S. Department of Labor or at the U.S. Department of State.

3. Convene the President's Committee on the ILO. The President's Committee on the ILO has not met during the Clinton administration (although informal consultations have occurred). This committee is chaired by the secretary of labor and includes the secretary of state, the secretary of commerce, the director of the National Security Council, the president of the AFL–CIO, and the president of the U.S. Council for International Business. President Clinton should convene this committee and ask it to develop a plan for improving the ILO.

4. Reform International Financial Institutions. In August 1994, Congress passed a law requiring the secretary of the treasury to instruct the U.S. directors to international financial institutions to "use the voice and vote of the United States" to urge these institutions to "adopt policies to encourage borrowing countries to guarantee internationally recognized worker rights" and "to include the status of such rights as an integral part of the institution's policy dialogue with each borrowing country."[47] The Clinton administration should fully execute this law, which could have a favorable impact on many countries. The administration should also seek to multilateralize the initiative by getting other major donor nations to press for the same policy.

5. Improve International Development Efforts. The Clinton administration should assist the ILO in getting more funding for technical assistance to help countries meet international labor standards. The administration should also seek to get the UNDP to devote more attention to labor issues. It is noteworthy that the UNDP's recent *Human Development Report* contains almost nothing about employment policies, the ILO, job training, or workplace conditions. The only initiative in the labor area that it highlights is "job-sharing," hardly an effective response to global unemployment problems.[48] Job sharing may be appropriate in some occupations to provide time away from around-the-clock demands. But it is not a solution to involuntary underemployment.

In summary, many actions can be taken to improve the ILO. 1995 offers two windows of opportunity. First, the ILO conference in June will consider results from the new Working Party on the Social Dimensions of the Liberalization of International Trade that was created at the June 1994 conference. Second, the G–7 summit in Halifax in June will be considering the framework of international institutions. The United States should push to reinvent the ILO.

The World Trade Regime and Labor Standards

One of the important achievements of the Uruguay Round is the creation of a new institution for trade policy, the WTO. The WTO will be establishing relationships with the World Bank, the IMF, the ISO, the Codex Alimentarius, and the World Intellectual Property Organization. Although the charter of the International Trade Organization (of 1948) provided for a direct link to the ILO, the new WTO agreement does not even mention it. Moreover, the GATT ministerial declaration on the "Contribution of the World Trade Organization to Achieving Greater Coherence in Global Economic Policymaking" does not mention workers or the ILO. The WTO should rise above GATT's parochialism.

The expansion of the trade regime in the Uruguay Round to include intellectual property makes it harder for the WTO to avoid other collateral issues like labor standards. If the WTO can make trade relations contingent upon respect for intellectual property conventions, there is no reason in principle why it cannot do the same for labor rights conventions.[49] Although some commentators object to the use of trade measures to enforce international labor standards by saying that publicizing violations is the best solution, the same solution is not perceived as adequate for the enforcement of intellectual property standards.

Of course, intellectual property is a private right and ILO conventions largely address public policy. But one anticipated "new" trade issue, antitrust, is also a public policy. Although there is a good reason for harmonization of antitrust policy because of national regulations that can overlap on a company doing business in more than one country, competition policy is no more intrinsic to trade policy than labor standards would be. It is interesting to note that the ITO charter of 1948 included provisions on both competition policy and labor standards.

U.S. efforts since 1986 to raise the issue of "worker rights" in GATT have provoked strong opposition from many countries. The topic is often branded as "protectionist," but that is an ironic charge coming from countries like Brazil or India. The real reason why some GATT countries oppose consideration of worker rights is that their governments suppress democracy.⁵⁰ Free trade unions cannot exist without a democratic government. Thus, any examination of worker rights in such countries by an international organization may be viewed as a threat to the regimes in power.

The negotiation of regional free trade agreements raises the issue of whether labor law should be included. It is not the tariff-cutting itself that leads to this question; unilateral liberalization can be done without regard to labor standards. It is the other components of an integration agreement, such as harmonization of standards and the provisions for managing liberalization, that inevitably lead to a question of what the scope of the integration should be. As trade agreements broaden into economic agreements, it will be hard to keep labor issues off the table.

The Uruguay Round strengthens dispute resolution. The new WTO agreement provides for the automatic right to impose trade sanctions against a country that does not implement a WTO panel report. Furthermore, this retaliation can be cross-sectoral and cross-agreement. By contrast, the ILO dispute system has not been strengthened in recent years. There is no right of retaliation against a country that does not ameliorate deficiencies cited in ILO reports. When labor unions suggest the use of trade to enforce labor standards, they are told that trade sanctions do not solve economic problems. The eagerness of the trading system to legitimize such sanctions under the WTO has buttressed the belief among many worker groups that the trade regime is hypocritical.⁵¹ Indeed, one might argue that of all international economic regimes, the trade regime should have been the most resistant to granting legitimacy to new trade sanctions.

The WTO and Labor Standards

As the previous section explained, the ILO is the appropriate international institution to focus on labor standards. The WTO has many other important responsibilities. Nevertheless, given the trade-related aspects of the labor standards issue, it would be appropriate for the WTO to cooperate with the ILO, as the interim ITO started to do in the late 1940s.⁵² There are also a few areas in which the WTO could appropriately take action of its own.

1. Address Labor Standards in the WTO. Some of those opposing the Clinton administration's initiative on labor standards have argued that the only reason to incorporate rules on labor standards into the WTO would be to permit trade sanctions, but that because sanctions are a bad idea, there is no reason to involve the WTO. This view is too quickly dismissive. There are good reasons to add a labor standards provision to the WTO without any intention of justifying trade penalties.

The WTO may not be able to succeed in governing trade relations and in promoting continued liberalization if it neglects issues that the public thinks are important. In view of the serious problems with forced labor, child labor, union bashing, and so forth, it would seem reasonable for the WTO to have a rule on labor rights. In drafting such a rule, the WTO might try to blend together the provisions that were in the Treaty of Versailles and the charter of the International Trade Organization. One possibility would be:

The Members recognize that inhumane conditions of labor, particularly in production for export, create difficulties in international

417

trade. Accordingly, each Member should take all feasible action to eliminate such conditions within its territory. Members should also cooperate with any investigation of their labor practices by the WTO.

2. Undertake Surveillance. In arguing for a social clause in GATT, labor unions have consistently sought to enforce it with trade restrictions. Similarly, U.S. Trade Representative Kantor has resisted suggestions that the United States drop the matter of enforcement in the interest of gaining agreement on the principle of WTO consideration of worker rights. Because enforcement of worker rights in the WTO is a nonstarter, any policy initiative predicated on trade enforcement is going to fail.

If a general obligation on humane labor conditions can be agreed to, then the WTO should undertake surveillance, not enforcement. Using the Trade Policy Review Mechanism, the WTO (in conjunction with the ILO) might examine respect for fundamental ILO principles in each country. Major problems could be reviewed in the WTO General Council. Although the Trade Policy Review Mechanism is generally focused on trade policies, it also looks at policies that have an indirect effect on international trade.[53] Another model is the IMF, which has a provision for surveillance of national financial policies.

3. Investigate Export Processing Zones. The one area in which the WTO might reasonably take a more active stance regards labor abuses in export processing zones. When governments impose tighter restrictions on unions in such zones than they do elsewhere in their countries, such manipulation can be viewed as a trade and investment distortion. The WTO should establish a working party to investigate this problem.

4. Cooperate with the ILO. Despite their close physical proximity in Geneva, GATT has resisted any interaction with the ILO.[54] Because the two organizations share a similar mission— raising standards of living by improving the utilization of resources—they ought to coordinate their efforts. The GATT treaty itself notes the "need for appropriate collaboration" between it and agencies of the UN system "whose activities relate to the trade and economic development of less developed countries."[55] Nonetheless, GATT was very insular. One way to effect such links would be to establish a WTO working party to explore cooperative initiatives with the ILO. If the WTO showed more sensitivity to the adverse effects of trade on some workers, it might provoke less public hostility. Cooperation with the ILO would also provide a mechanism for the WTO to secure input from nongovernmental organizations.

The WTO and the Public

Increasingly, international organizations are seeking to engage public opinion in support of their objectives. The GATT Secretariat, under Director General Peter Sutherland, is doing more of this than in the past through reports, studies, newsletters, and speeches. This is a useful development.

As a new international organization with a fairly high profile, the WTO has an opportunity to shape the future debate on trade liberalization. Instead of viewing labor standards in the negative manner that it now does, the WTO should look for opportunities to promote higher labor standards as a way of generating needed public support for free trade. This potential for a fruitful connection has been noted in numerous studies. For example, in 1956, the Group of Experts examining the social aspects of European economic integration (chaired by Bertil Ohlin) suggested that preventing labor standards "from falling below an internationally accepted level might eliminate abnormal competition and thus facilitate the establishment and preservation of a regime of freer international trade."[56] In 1980, the Brandt Commission endorsed international action on "fair labor standards" for the same reason.

Fairness in Trade

Some policymakers have suggested that the harmonization of labor standards is needed to assure fairness in international trade. For example, South African president Nelson Mandela argues that: "Trade must be based on a minimum floor of standards and rights. . . . The ILO's principle of tripartism and international labour standards ought to constitute the floor upon which the nations of the world engage in trade."[57] It is beyond the scope of this article to deal with the question of which issues are appropriate for international harmonization and which are not. But there are a few issues, such as trade in prison-made goods and derogations of standards in export processing zones, that can unquestionably lead to trade "unfairness." Otherwise, fairness is somewhat subjective.

Advocates of raising labor standards should be careful in unfurling the unfairness argument. Perceiving unfairness in foreign labor standards might imply a need for antidumping or countervailing duties, but that would not be constructive. A better argument for raising labor standards is that to do so constitutes sound economic policy.

Improving U.S. Government Policies

The United States has two laws that provide for unilateral trade restrictions in response to foreign labor practices. The Tariff Act of 1930 prohibits the importation of products made by convict or forced labor. Restrictions of this type are permitted by GATT article XX(e). Even with this law, there continue to be allegations of imports of convict-made goods, especially from China.[58] The second U.S. law is section 301 of the Trade Act of 1974, which permits the USTR to take action against nations that do not accord internationally recognized worker rights. This provision has never been used; doing so would very likely not be legal under GATT.

The United States has three laws that condition trade preferences for developing nations on whether those nations are taking steps to adjust their practices to accord with internationally recognized worker rights. They are the Caribbean Basin Initiative (CBI), the Generalized System of Preferences (GSP), and the Andean Trade Preferences Program. Whether these programs are viewed as unilateral or bilateral, conditioning trade preferences on actions by foreign governments does not violate GATT. Nevertheless, the United States is the only one of 16 GSP donor countries that maintains such conditions.

The first of these trade–labor linkages, in the CBI, was initiated by the Reagan administration in 1983. The ensuing negotiations led to significant labor commitments by several governments such as Honduras, El Salvador, the Dominican Republic, and Haiti. For example, El Salvador agreed to permit union organizers to enter its free trade zone.

The GSP linkage has led the United States to withdraw trade benefits from other countries. Four countries were removed during the Reagan administration; five during the Bush administration; and one during the Clinton administration. In addition, many countries took sufficient steps to improve worker rights to avoid losing their GSP benefits.

Administering the GSP labor condition is difficult because it is a two-edged sword, as the ongoing dispute with Indonesia demonstrates. On the one hand, countries like Indonesia may be willing to make minor reforms to retain the GSP, but they do not want to appear to be yielding to U.S. "imperialism." On the other hand, the U.S. government can threaten to withdraw GSP treatment from Indonesia, but considerable opprobrium from the U.S. business community would attach to doing so. In other words, the USTR has some leverage over Indonesia but Indonesia, and its business supporters, have some leverage over the USTR.[59] This dispute may continue to exacerbate trade relations between the two countries for the foreseeable future.

The U.S. government could improve its trade policy regarding labor standards by taking the following steps:

1. Stop Trade in Goods Made Using Forced Labor. When there are credible allegations that imported products are being made by prison or forced labor, the Customs Service should demand foreign government certifications as to the "prison-free" content of suspect goods. The Clinton administration might also propose a declaration in the WTO that all countries should ban prison-made trade. In line with that goal, Congress should ban the export of prison-made goods from the United States, which is now legal.

2. Improve the GSP Program. The GSP law requires that countries not taking steps to provide worker rights be excluded from the program, but the USTR has adopted a passive stance, waiting for petitions rather than acting first. When petitions about infractions are lodged, the USTR handles them in an arbitrary fashion as it "rejects" them, "defers" them, "pends" them, or slowly investigates them. The USTR has also developed some Kafkaesque distinctions. For example, the agency has refused to consider the assassination of a trade union leader as a worker rights violation, pretending instead that it is a "human rights" violation, not susceptible to discipline under the GSP program. Even Haiti, with all its labor and human rights violations, maintained its GSP eligibility until the United States imposed a complete trade embargo.

The GSP law has both a mandatory and a discretionary worker rights condition. Paradoxically, the USTR seems to be implementing only the discretionary condition while ignoring the mandatory one. A recent report by the General Accounting Office confirms a focus by the USTR on the discretionary condition only.[60]

The USTR has a conflict of interest. The agency cannot be credible in promoting trade liberalization when at the same time it preconditions trade benefits on worker rights. The recent Indonesian episode is a case in point. How can the USTR seek Indonesia's support in the Asia–Pacific Economic Cooperation forum while at the same time threatening to withdraw its GSP? This inherent conflict suggests that the president should reassign the administration of the GSP worker rights provision to another agency, such as the U.S. Department of Labor.

Reassignment would not mean that more countries would lose GSP benefits. The GSP law allows the president to waive the worker rights condition if it is in the "national economic interest" to do so. But reassignment would allow the U.S. government to make a reasonably objective determination each year as to whether a GSP country is taking sufficient steps to improve worker rights. As of now, USTR determinations are highly subjective.

It would also be useful for Congress to modify the definition of "worker rights" in the GSP law later in 1995 (the program expires on July 31) so as to remove any reference to minimum wages. It is noteworthy that in conjunction with President Clinton's trip to Asia in November 1994, Indonesia announced that it would increase regional minimum wages and step up enforcement of minimum wage laws and occupational safety rules. This author does not know whether the USTR asked for such changes, but they send precisely the wrong signal, because many observers presume that the U.S. government used its GSP leverage to raise wages in Indonesia.[61]

A top priority for GSP reform should be to get countries other than the United States to impose labor conditions in their GSP programs. When there is only one program with such conditions, countries like Indonesia can issue counter threats. If the European Union imposed labor conditions, too, beneficiary countries would have less room for evasion. In addition, judgments as to whether the beneficiary government is taking sufficient steps could be made by a committee with many countries represented on it rather than on a unilateral basis. That would take some heat off the U.S. government's GSP decision making.

The European Commission has expressed interest in an initiative to reduce GSP benefits for countries that permit slavery or the exportation of prison-made goods. The commission would also condition supplementary GSP benefits on whether countries meet labor and other standards. In early 1994, Abraham Katz, president of the U.S. Council for International Business, suggested that the USTR work with other GSP donors to establish a common labor rights condition and to seek support from developing countries by reducing the number of products excluded from the GSP.[62]

Unfortunately, the USTR showed no interest in broadening the number of countries imposing GSP conditions. One problem was that the USTR did not seem to want to expand GSP benefits. Agency officials also viewed GSP conditionality as lacking teeth and being inferior to the establishment of a GATT committee on labor standards. Clearly, this was a missed opportunity.

3. Suspend Section 301. The section 301 provision on worker rights has never been invoked by the USTR. Surprisingly, not a single petition has been filed. Still, this provision rankles other countries. To demonstrate that he favors a cooperative approach to labor rights, President Clinton should issue an Executive Order directing the USTR to suspend any activity on section 301 worker rights. As Hansenne has pointed out, multilateral progress on labor rights "would logically entail a renunciation" by industrial countries of unilaterally imposed trade barriers related to worker rights.

4. Renew Fast Track. Fast track is the parliamentary process invented 21 years ago to streamline congressional approval of trade agreements. Congress preauthorizes negotiations, and then permits the president to submit implementing legislation, which is voted on by the House and Senate without amendment. Fast track authority expired in 1993. In fall 1994, the Clinton administration tried to get this authority renewed, but the overture was spurned by Congress. The USTR had proposed new U.S. negotiating objectives for worker rights and the environment to establish that the failure to comply with internationally recognized labor or environmental standards would be viewed as an unfair advantage in world trade. This proposal was ill-timed and legally unnecessary because current law provides sufficient direction to the president on these issues.[63]

One demand made by congressional Republicans ought to be easy for the Clinton administration to fulfill. The Republicans have said that the fast track approval process should not be used to approve trade agreements that change U.S. labor or environmental laws. The administration should embrace this suggestion, because such changes are inappropriate in privileged legislation that is unamendable on the House or Senate floor.

It would be a mistake, however, for Congress to impose restrictions on new negotiating authority—by trying, for example, to forbid the president from attempting to reach mutually beneficial labor agreements with other countries. Handicapping the president will not reverse the growing relationships between trade, investment, employment, and environmental policies.

5. *Regional Trade Agreements.* In fall 1994, the Clinton administration sought to include labor issues in the trade section of the "Plan of Action" approved by the Summit of the Americas. According to press accounts, the administration "claimed victory" for obtaining desired language about labor. The exact language obtained, however, seems less significant than advertised.

The summit's "Declaration of Principles" states that "Free trade and increased economic integration are key factors for raising standards of living, [and] improving the working conditions of people in the Americas." The "Plan of Action" states that, "As economic integration in the Hemisphere proceeds, we will further secure the observance and promotion of worker rights, as defined by appropriate international conventions." Both statements are positive. But they do not add to the labor commitments that have been enshrined in the charter of the Organization of the American States (OAS) for decades. For example, the charter lists "acceptable working conditions" as one of the OAS objectives.[64] Under the charter, nations agree to "dedicate every effort to the application" of principles such that workers "have the right to associate themselves freely for the defense and promotion of their interests, including the right to collective bargaining and the workers' right to strike." In addition, and most significant, the charter declares that

> The Member States recognize that, in order to facilitate the process of Latin American regional integration, it is necessary to harmonize the social legislation of the developing countries . . . so that the rights of the workers shall be equally protected, and they agree to make the greatest efforts possible to achieve this goal.[65]

When viewed against the backdrop of these long-agreed commitments, it is hard to view the general language obtained by the Clinton administration at the Miami Summit as exemplifying progress.

The Clinton administration has suggested that NAFTA and its side agreements will be the "floor in all respects" for the Free Trade Area of the Americas. At the very least, the administration wants to extend the NAFTA labor and environmental side agreements to Chile. The administration should rethink this idea. The NAFTA side agreements aim at the wrong target—enforcement of a nation's own laws—rather than at the attainment of better laws and adherence to international standards. In addition, the NAFTA labor commission is barely operational. It took 14 months just to name an executive director. Expanding the commission now would likely grind all activity to a halt.

In summary, although the most important initiatives on labor standards need to be accomplished in the ILO, there are also some things that can be done in multilateral and regional trade agreements. Such trade initiatives must be part of an overall program. The Clinton administration erred in beginning its efforts at reform by pushing only within GATT.

Conclusion

Promoting higher labor standards is an appropriate goal for multilateral policy and an appropriate goal for the United States. The Clinton administration's efforts so far have proved disappointing. The advent of a new Congress may complicate this policy but does not doom it to failure. The administration should develop new bipartisan initiatives that draw the support of other countries, the business community, and U.S. labor unions.

The ILO is an underutilized institution of global governance. Its mandate to reduce unemployment and raise labor standards is highly relevant to contemporary economic challenges. Its membership structure—which includes workers and employers—shows that nongovernmental organizations can play a very useful role in international agencies. Yet after 76 years of activity, the ILO needs an overhaul.

The USTR is not at fault for the administration's unimaginative policies toward the ILO. That is not the USTR's job. The responsibility lies with the members of the President's Committee on the ILO. President Clinton should convene the committee quickly and ask how U.S. leadership can be exerted to improve the ILO. Support by the business community will be critical for this. The ILO has always been concerned about equity. Now it needs to get equally concerned about efficiency.

The USTR should work with governments in other countries to develop a joint proposal for cooperation between the WTO and the ILO. The first topic could be the inclusion of core labor standards in the WTO's Trade Policy Review Mechanism. The USTR should also pursue a few concrete initiatives such as encouraging other countries to apply a GSP labor condition.

National labor standards are an important international concern and have a significant linkage to trade policy. But that does not legitimize trade sanctions as the right remedy. Although the WTO should play a supportive role, the lead agency should be a newly reinvigorated ILO that will champion worker rights as a key component of emerging international law.

The views expressed are those of the author only.

Notes

1. By *labor standards*, I mean the legal regulations imposed by governments for the employment of child labor, the formation of trade unions, etc., and the effectiveness of the enforcement of these standards. This contrasts with *labor conditions*, which are market outcomes, such as wage levels. This article excludes minimum wages from labor standards because the Interna-

tional Labour Organization (ILO) has no convention regarding the adequacy of wages. (The one exception is the ILO's convention no. 109 on maritime wages, which applies to vessels engaged in trade by sea.)

2. In calling on the president to pursue this issue in GATT, the Omnibus Trade and Competitiveness Act of 1988 uses the term "worker rights." The previous U.S. law on GATT reform goals used the term "fair labor standards." The terms are synonymous, but have different connotations. Some countries may be willing to improve labor standards without conceding that they are preexisting rights.

3. The Convention on Freedom of Association (no. 87) has been ratified by 108 countries. The Convention on Collective Bargaining (no. 98) has been ratified by 121 countries. The Convention on the Abolition of Forced Labor (no. 105) has been ratified by 112 countries, including the United States. The Convention on Labor Inspection (no. 81) has been ratified by 111 countries.

4. U.S. Council of Economic Advisers, *Economic Report of the President* (Washington, D.C.: GPO, 1995), p. 250.

5. See Guy Caire, *Freedom of Association and Economic Development* (Geneva: ILO, 1977), and Steve Charnovitz, "Fair Labor Standards and International Trade," *Journal of World Trade Law* 20 (January–February 1986), pp. 61, 70–72. See also "Democracy and Growth," *Economist*, August 27, 1994, p. 15.

6. World Bank, *The East Asian Miracle* (Washington, D.C.: World Bank, 1993), pp. 270–273.

7. Some analysts list the humanitarian motive as a third reason. See, for example, Joseph Chamberlain, "Legislation in a Changing Economic World," *Annals of the American Academy of Political and Social Science* 166 (March 1933), pp. 30–31.

8. Treaty of Peace (Treaty of Versailles), 1919, part XIII.

9. Treaty of Versailles, article 23(a). Article 23(e) called for the "equitable treatment" of commerce.

10. U.S. War Labor Policies Board, *Report on International Labor Standards* (Washington, D.C.: GPO, 1919), p. 7.

11. See ILO, *World Employment 1995* (Geneva: ILO, 1995), pp. 72–74. This new report states that "International action is clearly required to safeguard against a competitive debasement of labour standards in the drive to improve shares in world trade and attract foreign investment" (p. 74).

12. For background, see Robert W. Cox, "Labor and the Multinationals," *Foreign Affairs* 54 (January 1976).

13. For a discussion of the original provision, see Steve Charnovitz, "The Influence of International Labour Standards on the World Trading Regime," *International Labour Review* 126 (September–October 1987), pp. 575–576.

14. See Federal Trade Commission, *Antidumping Legislation and Other Import Regulations in the United States and Foreign Countries* (Washington, D.C.: Federal Trade Commission, 1934), p. 13. The Austria measure was enacted in 1924.

15. Charter of the International Trade Organization, article 7.

16. See testimony by Clair Wilcox in hearings before the Senate Committee on Finance on the International Trade Organization, March 20, 1947, p. 119. Wilcox was the director of the Office of International Trade Policy, U.S. Department of State.

17. Of the 53 national representatives that signed the ITO, only 17 were from Europe, Canada, or the United States. Another 17 were from Latin America and 10 were from Asia. The 9 remaining signatories represented countries in the Middle East or Africa.

18. For example, see George Melloan, "Even Before Birth, the WTO is a Troublemaker," *Wall Street Journal*, August 8, 1994, p. A–13. See also "Standard Deviation," *Economist*, October 1, 1994, Survey, p. 32, and "Labor Standards and Trade," *Journal of Commerce*, February 6, 1995, p. 8A.

19. See *Weekly Compilation of Presidential Documents*, 1993, pp. 2288 and 2305.

20. See *Weekly Compilation of Presidential Documents*, 1993, p. 1640.

21. See U.S. Department of Labor, *International Labor Standards and Global Economic Integration: Proceedings of a Symposium* (Washington, D.C.: U.S. Department of Labor, 1994), p. 4.

22. See "Kantor Letter to Metzenbaum," *Inside U.S. Trade*, December 2, 1994, p. 10.
23. "USCIB Paper on Trade and Labor," *Inside U.S. Trade*, March 10, 1995, p. 9.
24. See "ASEAN Members Oppose Linkage of Labor and Trade," *International Trade Reporter*, August 3, 1994, p. 1214.
25. In December 1994, Australia's minister for trade established a high-level working party to explore ways to promote labor standards. See also Guy de Jonquières and Robert Taylor, "France to Push Workers' Rights in WTO," *Financial Times*, February 2, 1995, p. 5.
26. European Parliament, "Resolution on the Introduction of a Social Clause in the Unilateral and Multilateral Trading System," Strasbourg, February 9, 1994.
27. ILO conventions are numbered sequentially. The founders of the ILO hoped to build international law as new conventions were added each year.
28. For a discussion of this view, see OECD, *Employment Outlook* (Paris, July 1994), pp. 155, 161.
29. See ILO staff report, "The Social Dimensions of the Liberalization of World Trade" (Geneva, November 1994), para. 26.
30. Michel Camdessus, "The ILO and the IMF at Major Milestones," *Visions of the Future of Social Justice* (Geneva: ILO, 1994), p. 60.
31. The following countries (using current names) were members: Argentina, Bolivia, Brazil, Chile, China, Colombia, India, Guatemala, Iraq, Liberia, Mexico, Peru, Thailand, and Turkey. This broad membership belies the suggestion that developing countries had no role in the writing of older ILO conventions.
32. See *Our Global Neighborhood*, Report of the Commission on Global Governance (Oxford: Oxford University Press, 1995), p. 269. For discussion of trade and labor standards, see pp. 169–170.
33. Robert J. Morris, "Labor Standards and International Trade," October 1994 (unpublished paper).
34. Frank P. Doyle, "International Labor Standards: The Perspective of Business," in U.S. Department of Labor, *International Labor Standards*, p. 45.
35. See U.S. Department of Labor, *By the Sweat and Toil of Children: The Use of Child Labor in American Imports* (Washington, D.C.: U.S. Department of Labor, 1994).
36. Kaushik Basu, "The Poor Need Child Labor," *New York Times*, November 29, 1994, p. A–25.
37. See Australia, Department of Foreign Affairs and Trade, *Report on Matters Relating to the Exploitation of Children* (Canberra, November 1994), pp. 7–8.
38. Open Letter from Jan Tinbergen et al., Amsterdam, January 1, 1994 (unpublished).
39. See Anna Quindlen, "Out of Hands of Babes," *New York Times*, November 23, 1994, p. A–23.
40. For example, see Mitchell Zuckoff, "'Rugmark' Certifies No Child Labor Was Used," *Chicago Tribune*, February 4, 1995, p. 16.
41. See John Maggs, "Clinton's Plan for Rights Code Breaks Down," *Journal of Commerce*, November 18, 1994, p. 1A. See also Bruce W. Nelan, "Business First, Freedom Second," *Time*, November 21, 1994, p. 78.
42. See *Declarations of the World Trade Union Conference* (London, February 1945), para. 18.
43. See Roger Plant, *Labour Standards and Structural Adjustment* (Geneva: ILO, 1994).
44. See ILO, *Defending Values, Promoting Change*, Report of the Director General (Geneva: ILO, 1994), p. 37.
45. For a discussion, see Philip Alston, "Labor Rights Provisions in U.S. Trade Law: 'Aggressive Unilateralism'?" *Human Rights Quarterly* 15 (February 1993), pp. 29–33.
46. For a discussion of the constitutional issues, see Bruce Ackerman and David Golove, "Is NAFTA Constitutional? The Rise of the Congressional–Executive Agreement in American Diplomacy," *Harvard Law Review* 108 (February 1995). See also Steve Charnovitz, "The NAAEC and Its Implications for Environmental Cooperation, Trade Policy, and American Treatymaking," *Temple International and Comparative Law Review* 8 (Fall 1994). In proposing a method similar to the trade agreement approval process, I am *not* sug-

47. 108 Stat. 1634, 22 U.S.C. 1621. The one flaw in the law is that it includes minimum wages in the list of rights.
48. See UNDP, *Human Development Report 1994* (Oxford: Oxford University Press, 1994).
49. For a good analysis of how trade enforcement of worker rights in GATT could benefit the ILO, see Clayton Yeutter, "Policy Perspective and Future Directions: A View From a Former U.S. Trade Representative," in U.S. Department of Labor, *International Labor Standards*, p. 55.
50. For example, based on the Freedom House survey, several WTO members such as Burundi, Cameroon, Chad, Cuba, Egypt, The Gambia, Indonesia, Maldives, Mauritania, Nigeria, Sierra Leone, Swaziland, Tanzania, Togo, Tunisia, and the former Yugoslavia are "not free." *Freedom in the World Yearbook, 1994–95* (New York, N.Y.: Freedom House, December 1994).
51. One response from the trade perspective is that the WTO is not authorizing trade sanctions, but rather countermeasures to reequilibrate the balance of negotiated trade concessions. This just begs the question, however: Why should the trade regime be able to reequilibrate when the international labor regime cannot?
52. The draft agreement between the ILO and the ITO of October 1948 provided that the two organizations "will act in close co-operation with each other and will consult each other regularly in regard to matters of common interest." In addition, it permitted ILO representatives to participate in ITO meetings. See GATT Doc. ICITO EC.2/21, articles I and IV.
53. For example, the recent review of Canada criticized the barriers by provinces to trade *within* Canada. See "GATT Report Criticizes Inter-Provincial Trade Barriers in Canada," *Inside U.S. Trade*, December 2, 1994, p. 28.
54. The only joint project this author is aware of was the study begun in 1960 of the relevance to international trade of differences in labor costs, and other costs of production, of textiles and clothing. GATT dropped out of the study, but the ILO later published its conclusions that the problem of textile industries in advanced countries cannot be primarily attributed to the alleged unfairness of competition with low-wage countries. Perhaps dissatisfied with these conclusions, GATT embarked upon a series of protectionist textile arrangements that continue to this day. See Gardner Patterson, *Discrimination in International Trade: The Policy Issues* (Princeton, N.J.: Princeton University Press, 1966), pp. 306–307.
55. GATT article XXXVI:7.
56. ILO, *Social Aspects of European Economic Co-operation* (Geneva: ILO, 1956), para. 180.
57. Nelson Mandela, "The Continuing Struggle for Social Justice," in *Visions of the Future of Social Justice* (Geneva: ILO, 1994), p. 184.
58. See "New Evidence of Chinese Forced-Labor Imports to the U.S.," *Human Rights Watch Asia*, May 24, 1994.
59. See Manuela Saragosa, "Indonesia Spurns U.S. Pressure over Workers Rights," *Financial Times*, August 15, 1994, p. 4.
60. See U.S. General Accounting Office, *International Trade: Assessment of the Generalized System of Preferences Program*, GAO/GGD-95-9 (Washington, D.C.: GAO, November 1994), pp. 98–100. A letter from the USTR to the GAO reprinted in the report mentions only the discretionary provision (pp. 148, 150).
61. See "Indonesia Responds to U.S. GSP Pressure with Plan on Labor Rights," *Inside U.S. Trade*, November 18, 1994, p. 13.
62. Abraham Katz, "Trade and Workers' Rights: A Proposal." This was a personal proposal in the form of a paper circulated to policymakers.
63. See 19 U.S.C. §2901(b)(14) and 104 Stat. 4905.
64. Charter of the Organization of American States, article 31(f). An earlier Central American treaty was even more specific about forced labor and child labor. See Convention on the Unification of Protective Laws for Workmen and Labourers, which was signed at the Conference on Central American Affairs in Washington, D.C., in 1923.
65. Charter of the Organization of American States, article 44.

International Firms and National Governments: Some Dilemmas

Joseph LaPalombara

HUMAN HISTORY TENDS to be sardonic. It produces surprises. Often as not, it defies our most fervent hopes; it mocks our theories; it seems unreasonable, even perverse. Thus, contrary to the predictions of those who have heralded the end of history and the universal triumph of liberalism, the market, and democracy, world developments now place all such predictions in doubt.

The unexpected historical twist is the reemergence of rampant nationalism. Not necessarily the nationalism of the last century, to be sure, but nationalism nevertheless—and of striking potency. We have seen it erupt in the Balkans and in areas of the former Soviet Union. It is also present, in less virulent forms, within the European Community (EC), as well as in every other part of the world. It is this persistent nationalism that continues to render international

---

Joseph LaPalombara is Wolfers Professor of Political Science at Yale University and consultant to European and American industries. He is also a member of the International Research Council of CSIS.

Copyright © 1994 by The Center for Strategic and International Studies and the Massachusetts Institute of Technology
The Washington Quarterly • 17:2

economic and diplomatic relationships difficult, even among peoples who share much in common.[1]

Far from marching forward toward a brave new world in which basic values are shared by everyone, we seem to be moving backward toward the reassertion of "primitive" values and loyalties. Somewhat to our surprise, neither economic nor technological imperatives turn out to be as powerful or as impelling as many of us imagined—at least not when it comes to politics. The splendid image of a single world market dominated by global enterprises that produce a cornucopia of well-being for mankind has been quickly shattered by the political realities that surround and beset us.

The symbol of this existential condition is the nation-state, whose remarkable staying power appears all the more so in a context of extensive and accelerated economic interdependence. The internationalization of finance and the globalization of enterprise have not triggered the so-called spillover effects that so many claimed would one day render the nation-state obsolete and relegate it to the dustbins of history.[2]

How could we have been so wrong? And if, as now seems certain, the imperatives of economics and politics continue to follow quite different historical trajectories, what, if anything, can be done about the more undesirable aspects of this failure of economics and politics to converge?

We fell into error, to begin with, because many of us harbor highly deterministic theories about history. For example, like Marx, we believe that capitalism will inevitably bring about certain consequences—not class conflict to be sure, but harmony and well-being. Today, even the people of the former Soviet Union, or who once lived within the Soviet orbit, believe the same things.

The spread of capitalism, however, even if inexorable, does not imply that it will evolve in an undifferentiated way, and even less that its effects will be only or even largely benign. Even more important, the advent of capitalism should not be misconstrued to presage, as so many now believe, that democracy will follow in its wake.[3] From this dubious assumption it is a short leap to the conclusion that older values and institutions that are incompatible with this type of evolution will become obsolete and give way to new ones.

Any such conclusion, needless to add, greatly underestimates the enduring force of deep culture. It fails to assign proper weight to narrow particularistic identities, to religious and ethnic drives, to deep-seated attitudes and strong predispositions about self and others, and to the institutional arrangements through which such human impulses find expression. Among such institutions, those associated with the national state remain paramount.

Another, equally deterministic, reason why we erred is the widespread belief in the West that, as certain aspects of everyday living are diffused among many nations, the people involved will also become more favorably disposed toward *internationalism in a political sense*. That is, the *internationality* of particular dimensions of social organization and behavior is mistakenly taken to imply that people are ready to give up national identity and citizenship in favor of supernational or international organizations.

This homogenization of cultures would presumably be quickened by the revolutionary advances in communications and transportation of recent decades. It was assumed that, in the face of a convergence in canons of taste, conceptions of work, recreation, and consumption, people would also take on a more international identity and thus render the nation-state less salient than in the past. That is, insofar as the nation-state might become an obstacle to these new identities and desires, it would wither away and be replaced by something else.

This argument is fundamentally untenable, and it will not do, therefore, to misname the reemergence of nationalism as "tribalism," as if to score it as such will help solve the problem. If the spread of capitalism has served to redefine the limits of national power and to compel a redistribution and sharing of national sovereignty, it is probable that this effect has now reached its peak and is not going to proceed much further, at least not for many decades.

Three major developments after World War II seemed to provide strong support for the idea that the nation-state was on the way out, or at least that it would be greatly reduced in importance. These were the emergence of the European Community (EC), the devolution of some powers held by national governments to regions located within their own borders, and the globalization of manufacturing and service enterprises.

The European Community

The EC was particularly important in this regard. Europe, after all, is the place where, during the last 130 years, nationalism has produced the most violent confrontations, the most devastating human and material annihilation—in the name of national sovereignty. In the decades following the Treaty of Rome, billions of words were written to show that national barriers had weakened; that Europeans dressed, lived, and thought alike as never before; and, indeed, that they shared similar levels of commitment to the Community itself. These common and favorable attitudes toward the EC were misunderstood to be strong indicators that commitment to the nation-state, to national sovereignty, and to national political institutions had, because of these new values, actually diminished.

The hope of many that the EC would evolve into the first exemplar of the supranational state has been rudely set back by events of recent years. Among these one need only mention:

- the total failure of the EC to develop anything like a common foreign policy—as witnessed by its responses to the Persian Gulf War, the process through which official recognition was extended to the republics of Croatia and Slovenia, and European reactions to the severe crises in Bosnia-Herzegovina and Somalia;
- the failure of the EC to develop a coherent approach to the problems created by the reunification of Germany and the attendant macroeconomic policies pursued by the Bundesbank at the expense of other members of the Community;
- the differences among Community members regarding the difficult and protracted negotiations of the Uruguay Round of the General Agreement on Tariffs and Trade; and,
- the events that followed the signing of the Maastricht agreement of December 1991.

Those who anticipated the further economic unification of Europe, and, indeed, its political integration as well, have had to confront a painful moment of truth.[4]

Subnational Governments

As for the regional devolution of national powers, the EC's leaders erred in predicting, and indeed promoting, the emergence of a "Europe of Regions," consisting of a central power in Brussels and local powers exercised by subnational regions, presumably at the expense of the EC's individual members. It is not only Lady Thatcher, after all, who maintains that nations must remain wary of giving up *political* sovereignty. When push comes to shove, the leaders of the Community's other principal members feel and behave exactly as did Lady Thatcher—if not in style, then certainly in substance. Not even the Germans, who now enjoy considerable economic hegemony in Europe, are prepared to take the steps outlined in the ill-fated Treaty of Maastricht.

In any event, the principal underlying error here is the mistaken belief that such distributions of power are essentially zero-sum in nature. A much better formulation is to note that, even as national governments decide to share some of their sovereignty with their internal regions, their own scope of power can actually grow and not decrease. In fact, the most striking aspect of the powers of nations in this century is that they have continued to grow, notwithstanding such regional devolutions or, for that matter, notwithstanding the relinquishment of some economic powers to international organizations like the EC.[5] To verify this assertion, it will suffice to compare the scope and depth of national authority today with what it was as recently as two or three decades ago. There is simply no reason to assume that this situation will change in the years immediately ahead, a point to which I will return below.

Global Enterprise

The globalization of manufacturing and service industries is also a palpable reality, and it continues apace. This implies, of course, that the organizations involved in the production and distribution of goods and services increasingly engage in cross-border transactions. It is no longer only capital that moves with unprecedented frequency and facility all over the globe; the other factors of production do so as well. This process appears inexorable, and it creates a degree of economic interdependence the world has not previously known.[6]

In one sense, therefore, it does seem fair to say that the organizations involved in this historical process, and the persons who manage them, recognize no national boundaries or national loyalties, at least not when it comes to the creation of new equity and welfare or, more crudely put, when it is a matter of increased profits.

But is it equally reasonable to infer from all of this, as so many have, that these organizations and persons are "without nationality"? If there is an impelling logic that leads the firm to behave as if there exists only a single world economy, does this necessarily imply that there must be, or will be, a single world polity as well? Indeed, is there any basis for the claim that the senior managers of world-scale industry and finance will themselves become major protagonists in any campaign to diminish the salience of the nation-state in world affairs in favor of the creation of effective supranational authorities?[7]

The answer to all of these questions is no. Indeed the evidence of recent decades will show that these organizations have made a large number of strategic adaptations to a world economy in which the nation-state deeply conditions the well-being and even the survival of enterprise. Some managers lament this; and they pay lip service to the need to accelerate the further integration of the EC. But it also turns out that a political world, consisting of many national jurisdictions, creates attractive advantages for financial and industrial operators. This being so, they will favor the aggrandizement of supranational authorities, if at all, only on a piecemeal and ad hoc basis. That is, they will be guided by careful attention to the trade-offs that might be involved, and the impact that each trade-off may have on each enterprise's generation of profits.[8]

There is nothing surprising, cynical, or morally wrong about such a posture. Industrial and financial managers, who husband the capital assets of others as well as their own, are typically in positions of stewardship that make them primarily responsible to their stockholders. Their mission is economic, not political; and they are expected to worry about the economic aspects of enterprise. We may want them to be ethical and socially responsible in their operations; and we may expect them to obey the laws.[9] But it is the managers of the policy—those who make public policy, and who pass and enforce the laws—who must worry about the negative externalities of business and financial enterprise.

The Firm and the State System

Industrial and financial managers are, above all, realists and pragmatists. They interpret with great care the environments in which enterprises are located, and they make strategic decisions based on their analyses and evaluations. Thus, during the last several decades, international firms have responded to pressures exerted by national governments in ways such as the following:

(1) *Indigenization of managers,* such that corporate affiliates everywhere are increasingly in the hands not of expatriate managers but, rather, of citizens of each respective host country. As this transformation proceeds, companies have had to modify earlier concepts of a single "corporate culture," or of a single, undifferentiated sense of "corporate citizenship."

(2) *Conformance to national regulations* that reduce the proportion of equity shares in local affiliates that the parent company may hold. In some instances, these proportions actually fall under 50 percent. The era of the wholly owned subsidiary is a thing of the past; and even U.S. multinational companies, which tended to be highly resistant to equity sharing, have adapted to this newer climate.[10] This change has in turn led to modified forms of corporate organization; revised systems of communications; as well as radically revised formats for personnel training and human resources management.

(3) *Greater propensity to enter into joint ventures* with local firms or financial institutions. This change is in part a logical consequence of the new regulations as to equity sharing. International firms have now, however, discovered the utilities that derive from the direct involvement of local partners in overseas operations.[11]

(4) *Willingness to enter into joint-venture relations with state-owned industries.* International firms, once highly suspicious of and antagonistic toward state-owned industries, have recast many of these views as well. Not only have they discovered that the ownership of an enterprise is immensely less important than the quality of its managers; they have found that the managers of indigenous state-owned firms can be very effective partners when it comes to having to confront a wide range of regulations—and other business matters—that bring local and national governments into the picture.[12]

(5) *Acceptance of host country laws* as the basis for adjudicating disputes that may arise regarding the local operations of foreign companies—even in those instances where international arbitration may be an option. This transformation is most apparent regarding the so-called NICs (newly industrializing countries), which are highly attractive sites for foreign direct investments and are increasingly present in international markets with multinational corporations of their own nationality.[13]

(6) *Willingness to accept local content and export quotas* as conditions for doing business in a given country. These particular changes are strongly induced wherever a developing country, for example, shifts its economic policies from the import-substitution to the export-driven model. Although negotiations as to local content requirements are often complex, and sometimes acrimonious, it is noteworthy that they are now widely accepted (as they were not earlier) as a normal aspect of doing business in today's international economy.

(7) *Acceptance of the inevitability of the "obsolescent bargain,"* wherein, when it

suits the needs, or interests, or even the whim, of the national authorities of host countries, the terms of the original contracts, under which the foreign investor entered a country in the first place, can be renegotiated. Today's newspapers carry daily stories of confrontations of this kind between foreign investors and local authorities in Asia and eastern Europe. Beyond the acrimony and legal and diplomatic fencing, however, lies a more basic reality: the relationship between the international firm and host country governments is not as unbalanced as in decades past; and, in any case, whatever excessive advantage may be squeezed out today may carry a higher price tomorrow, when circumstances change.

This list might easily be expanded. Perhaps the most significant indicator of the basic point I am making is the organizational changes that now come increasingly to characterize the international firm. The global firm is no longer a single pyramid, managed from a single apex in its worldwide operations. Increasingly—and not merely for reasons of internal efficiency—decision-making authority has been delegated to the firm's affiliates located abroad.

With the possible exceptions of strategic planning, capital budgeting, and particularly corporate finance, the structure of the international enterprise comes to look less like a pyramidal or monolithic structure and more like a confederal system, in which affiliates located abroad enjoy considerable autonomy.[14]

These structural changes are dictated not only by the kinds of national regulations regarding foreign investors summarized above; they also grow out of the corporate community's recognition that national cultural differences demand that enterprise, if it wishes to succeed, must adapt to these local cultural nuances. For all of these reasons, the recent history of the global enterprise reflects a near-universal understanding on the part of managers that the nation-state will for many decades remain a major factor to be reckoned with by business.

This being so, the question then arises as to how best to deal with aspects of international business and finance that are less than salutary and even inimical to the health and wealth of nations and of their inhabitants. The solution does not lie in supranational organizations like the EC. It will be time enough to turn to them if and when they actually emerge as real wielders of effective powers. In the meantime, it will remain for individual nation-states to bring the more unacceptable business and financial practices under better control.

It will not be easy to achieve this end. But bilateral and multilateral negotiations on specific problems will turn out to be much more rational than, for example, waiting around for a company law to materialize within the EC or for the United Nations or the Organization for Economic Cooperation and Development to provide effective policing of business or financial practices. The so-called codes of conduct of business practices abroad produced by such bodies have been, at best, very weak instruments.[15]

Even less efficacious is the form of "self-policing" that businesses engage in when they produce their own internal codes of conduct. Such steps should not be discouraged; but, for many years to come, the only effective way to deal with the unwanted aspects of international financial and business operations will be through parallel national legislation and ad hoc agreements among nation-states.[16]

Some progress along these lines has already been achieved. One might cite the areas of taxation, capitalization and local content requirements, royalty payments, and the like. It is probable that more parallel regulations will begin to emerge that address aspects of enterprise that have negative environmental effects or that subject consumers to dangerous products and workers to unacceptable levels of risk.

But there remains much to be done. Transfer pricing, for example, is a universal practice that not even the most developed and experienced authorities in advanced industrial countries have been able to bring reasonably under control. Consolidated balance sheets may have their utility, but they do not begin to reflect the extent to which the transfer-pricing mechanism is utilized by international enterprises. More nation-by-nation attention to this problem is required.[17]

The matter of antitrust remains, at best, in a somewhat chaotic state, and steps might be taken to ensure, for example, that the European Commission's directives and regulations in this important area are formally incorporated into the national legislation of the EC's member states. What I have said above about the unlikelihood that a supranational state will emerge in Europe should not be misunderstood to mean that, in the economic regulatory sphere, the Commission at Brussels is without teeth. Were this the case, fewer international firms would have established contacts or opened up offices there! But the Commission's decisions regarding competition would be immensely more effective if members of the EC established their own internal, and parallel, antitrust norms.

In this same regard, the European Commission should be pressed to abandon its efforts to come up with a comprehensive "company law" in favor of getting agreement among its members regarding such specific and fundamental issues as information disclosure by industrial enterprises and financial institutions. At the national level, the need for parallel regulations regarding the operation of stock exchanges should by now be painfully apparent.

It is also essential that national governments recognize and come to grips with another reality, namely, that some of their own institutions, including those with specific public responsibilities, do not always act in the national interest or for that matter, in conformance with national economic policies.

We witnessed a dramatic example of this, the full story of which remains to be told, in fall 1992, when the European Monetary System (EMS) began to fall apart. As the run against sterling and the Italian lira got under way in September of that year, the world press reported that speculators were responsible for this maneuver, which drove Britain out of the EMS and forced Italy first to devalue its currency and then to leave the EMS as well. The reading public was left with the impression that this crushing defeat of the EMS, and concomitantly of the Maastricht agreement, was engineered by the cynical barons of international finance.

But the key players in this gigantic multi-billion dollar maneuver were not the speculators per se, but rather the so-called corporates, the major banks and the largest international firms in Germany, Italy, France, Britain, and elsewhere, which made the correct judgment that neither Britain nor Italy could continue to support its own overvalued currency, even with outside help, against a massive sell-off in favor of the deutsche mark.[18]

These hardheaded managers of international business—and of major banks—correctly assumed that the EMS-dictated parity levels of these currencies simply did not reflect the underlying economic realities of Britain, Italy, and (a few months later) France. And so they made their fateful decisions. The speculators, however, did not lead this rout; they jumped on the bandwagon (as they usually do) only after they learned, privately, what the big banks and the big industries would do.

It goes without saying that central banks were also intimately involved in this process, and that some of them at least were not at all interested in following, or shoring up, the policies pursued by their own prime ministers or finance ministers. Such a problem is compounded by the fact that, when governments act (as in setting monetary targets, interest rates, and currency parities), these acts are quintessentially transparent, whereas the intentions and decisions of those who manage the immense pool of international capital are not. And even when these investors and speculators act, they can change course instantly, unlike governments—and just as instantly have their buy and sell orders implemented through a worldwide network of computerized and telecommunicated financial transactions.

To conclude on a somewhat despondent note, we live in a world in which those who manage international business will, for hardheaded economic reasons and without any compunction, "bet" against their own national governments. When national governments and the financial markets clash with each other, the latter are likely to win. Not because these money managers are "without nationality" or lack patriotism, but, rather, because they lack the conviction that political managers can manage economies.

One correct way to deal with this dilemma was well understood by those who drafted the economic integration sections of the Maastricht agreement. They calculated that the monetary unification of the EC would bring to heel at least some of the devastating effects of the 1992 EMS maneuvers. But if Germany itself, as now seems apparent, is no longer interested in the monetary unification aspects of Maastricht, the internationalization of monetary policy must remain a pyrrhic hope.

Looking to the Future

The globalization of business and finance will permit these organizations to remain outside the effective control of any single national government.[19] The question is whether nationalism will continue to stand in the way of even modest efforts, at least by the national governments whose industries and banks control most of the massive international capital pool, to bring this system under better control. The answer to this question will not be found in Brussels. It will be provided by the postures assumed by political leaders in Washington and Tokyo, in Berlin, London, Paris, and Rome. If the post-Maastricht events are an indication of the narrow, erosive, and self-defeating forms that economic nationalism can take, the prospects for the future are anything but reassuring.

The views expressed in this article are strictly and entirely those of the author. They should therefore not be attributed to either Yale University or any other organization with which he is affiliated. An earlier version of the article was presented to the 19th International Conference of the Pio Manzu'

Research Center on "The Third Round: The Global Enterprise in a World Torn between Neo-Tribalism and the Challenge of Trans-National Solidarity," Rimini, Italy, October 16–19, 1993.

Notes

1. On the complex matter of nationalisms, old and new, see Benedict R. Anderson, *Imagined Communities: Reflections on the Origin and Spread of Nationalism* (New York, N.Y.: Verso, 1991); Eric J. Hobsbawm, *Nations and Nationalism Since 1778* (Cambridge: Cambridge University Press, 1990); Eric J. Hobsbawm and Terence Ranger, eds., *The Invention of Tradition* (New York, N.Y.: Cambridge University Press, 1984); Ernest Gellner, *Nations and Nationalism* (Ithaca, N.Y.: Cornell University Press, 1983); William Pfaff, *The Wrath of Nations: Civilization and the Furies of Nationalism* (New York, N.Y.: Simon and Schuster, 1993); and Hans Kohn, *The Age of Nationalism: The First Era of Global History* (Westport, Conn.: Greenwood Press, 1976).

2. The intellectual community of the West easily developed the credo that the follies and tragedies of nationalism would be overcome once and for all by the emergence of the supranational state, first in Europe and perhaps later elsewhere. For a sampling of this earlier writing, see Ernst Haas, *The Uniting of Europe* (London: Stevens and Sons, 1958); Leon Lindberg and Stuart Sheingold, eds., *Regional Integration: Theory and Research* (Cambridge, Mass.: Harvard University Press, 1971); and James A. Caporaso, *The Structure and Function of European Integration* (Pacific Palisades, Calif.: Goodyear, 1974).

3. This is, alas, exactly the view of things that has been diffused after the termination of the Cold War, the disintegration of the Soviet sphere of influence, and the breakup of the Soviet Union itself. Leading newspapers, diplomats, political leaders, distinguished economists, and others who should know better beat the drums for the mistaken idea that economics drives politics. Events of recent months have given some of these reason for pause and reflection.

4. It must be said that enthusiasms die hard, particularly when they involve one's ideological and intellectual proclivities. Thus, books published before the Maastricht ratification included such items as Clifford Hackett, *Cautious Revolution: The European Community Arrives* (Westport, Conn.: Greenwood Press, 1990); Nicholas Colchester and David Buchan, *Europower: The Essential Guide to Europe's Transformation in 1992* (New York, N.Y.: Random House, 1990); and David Burstein, *Euroquake: Europe's Explosive Economic Challenge Will Change the World* (New York, N.Y.: Simon and Schuster, 1991). Cf. Nicholas Colchester and David Buchan, *Europe Relaunched: Truth and Illusions on the Way to 1992* (London: Hutchinson, 1992).

5. See Jeffrey Anderson, "Skeptical Reflections on a 'Europe of Regions: Britain, Germany and the European Regional Development Fund,'" *Journal of Public Policy* 10 (October-December 1990), pp. 414–447.

6. Foreign direct investment in manufacturing, mining, and service industries now approaches $1.5 trillion in book value. Internationalization of enterprise, in one form or another, is the single most important organizational aspect of the modern industrial world. See Mark Casson, ed., *The Growth of International Business* (London: Allen and Unwin, 1983). Cf. Norman J. Glickman and Douglas P. Woodward, *The New Competitors* (New York, N.Y.: Basic Books, 1989).

7. See Richard J. Barnet and Ronald Muller, *Global Reach* (New York, N.Y.: Simon and Schuster, 1974), for the most sweeping claims about the implications of the internationalization of business. See also Raymond Vernon, *Sovereignty at Bay: The Multinational Spread of U.S. Enterprises* (New York, N.Y.: Basic Books, 1971). Cf. Raymond Vernon, "Sovereignty at Bay: Ten Years After," in Theodore H. Moran, ed., *Multinational Corporations: The Political Economy of Foreign Direct Investment* (Lexington, Mass.: D. C. Heath and Co., 1985), pp. 247–259.

8. On the adaptive capacities of the multinational corporation, see Robert Gilpin, *The Political Economy of International Relations* (Princeton, N.J.: Princeton University Press, 1987), pp. 231–262. Cf. J. S. Lizondo, "Foreign Direct Investment," Working Paper WP/90/63 (Washington, D.C.: International Monetary Fund,

1990); F. C. Schuller, *Venturing Abroad: Innovation by U.S. Multinationals* (New York, N.Y.: Quorum, 1988); and Allen J. Morrison, *Strategies in Global Industries* (New York, N.Y.: Quorum, 1990).

9. It is, of course, not always the case that a keen sense of ethics and/or law-abidingness characterize the behavior of managers. See, for example, Thomas Donaldson, *The Ethics of International Business* (New York, N.Y.: Oxford University Press, 1989); and Irwin Ross, *Shady Business: Confronting Corporate Corruption* (New York, N.Y.: Twentieth Century Fund, 1992).

10. See Joseph LaPalombara and Steven Blank, *Multinational Corporations in Developing Countries* (New York, N.Y.: Conference Board, 1979); Denis Encarnation, *Dislodging Multinationals: India's Strategy in Comparative Perspective* (Ithaca, N.Y.: Cornell University Press, 1989); and Thomas Biersteker, *Multinationals: The State and Control of the Nigerian Economy* (Princeton, N.J.: Princeton University Press, 1987).

11. For a succinct, insightful commentary on new approaches to business ventures abroad, see Harvey S. James, Jr., and Murray Weidenbaum, *When Businesses Cross International Borders: Strategic Alliances and Their Alternatives* (Westport, Conn.: Praeger, 1993). Cf. Paul Beamish, *Multinational Joint Ventures in Developing Countries* (London: Routledge, 1988).

12. See Raymond Vernon, *Exploring the Global Economy: Emerging Issues in Trade and Investment* (Boston, Mass.: University Press of America, 1985), pt. 3, "The State-Owned Enterprise."

13. See Graeme C. Hughes, *Foreign Investment Law in Canada* (Toronto: Carswell, 1983); L. R. Kumor and K. V. Iyer, *Foreign Investment and Collaboration: Legal Parameters* (New Delhi: L. R. Kumor Associates, 1986); A. K. Ho, *Joint Ventures in the People's Republic of China* (New York, N.Y.: Praeger, 1990); Attila Andrade Junior, *Guidelines on Brazil's Foreign Investment Law* (Rio de Janiero: Interinvest Editora, 1980); Jack Behrman, *International Business and Governments: Issues and Institutions* (Columbia, S.C.: University of South Carolina Press, 1990); and P. E. Bondzi-Simpson, *Legal Relationships between Transnational Corporations and Host States* (New York, N.Y.: Quorum, 1990).

14. The pressures driving international firms to effect organizational changes are multifarious, and they obviously include considerations that have less to do with the social or political environment than with the existential conditions of doing business in a competitive world. See, for example, Michael Best, *The New Competition: Institutions of Industrial Restructuring* (Cambridge, Mass.: Harvard University Press, 1990); Kenichi Ohmae, *Triad Power: The Coming Shape of Global Competition* (New York, N.Y.: Free Press, 1985); and Michael Porter, *The Competitive Advantage of Nations* (New York, N.Y.: Free Press, 1990).

15. See Kwamena Acquaah, *International Regulation of Transnational Corporations: The New Reality* (New York, N.Y.: Praeger, 1986).

16. See Bart S. Fisher and Jeff Turner, eds., *Regulating the Multi-National Enterprise: National and International Challenges* (New York, N.Y.: Praeger, 1983).

17. On transfer pricing, see G. F. Mathewson and G. D. Quirin, *Fiscal Transfer Pricing in Multinational Corporations* (Toronto: University of Toronto Press, 1979); Robert Tang, *Transfer Pricing in the United States and Japan* (New York, N.Y.: Praeger, 1979); Sylvain Plasschaert, *Transfer Pricing and Multinational Corporations* (Farnsborough, U.K.: Saxon House, 1979); and Organization for Economic Cooperation and Development, *Transfer Pricing and Multinational Enterprises* (Paris: OECD, 1984).

18. I am indebted to Richard Medley for a number of acute insights regarding this crisis. Medley is at work on a study that will provide sobering confirmation regarding the intractability of problems of the kind described here.

19. Raymond Vernon asserts that the international firm, by its very nature, develops global interests of its multinational network as a whole, and "hence *can never respond single-mindedly to the requirements of any one national jurisdiction*" (emphasis supplied) (*Exploring the Global Economy*, pp. 51–52). He also observes: "Nations are no longer very manageable as economic units. Their external economic links have become vital to their national existence; and these economic links are beyond their control to manage, except jointly with other nations. The problem is seen just as

vividly in monetary and countercyclical economic policies as in trade" (p. 25).

Cf. John Robinson, *Multinationals and Political Control* (New York, N.Y.: St. Martin's Press, 1983). For a broad overview of trends in the relationships between multinationals and public authorities in both developing and developed countries, see Theodore Moran, "Introduction," in Moran, ed., *Governments and Transnational Corporations* (London and New York, N.Y.: Routledge, 1993), pp. 1–26.